The Poetics of Late Latin Literature

OXFORD STUDIES IN LATE ANTIQUITY

Series Editor
Ralph Mathisen

Late Antiquity has unified what in the past were disparate disciplinary, chronological, and geographical areas of study. Welcoming a wide array of methodological approaches, this book series provides a venue for the finest new scholarship on the period, ranging from the later Roman Empire to the Byzantine, Sasanid, early Islamic, and early Carolingian worlds.

The Arabic Hermes
From Pagan Sage to Prophet of Science
Kevin van Bladel

Two Romes
Rome and Constantinople in Late Antiquity
Edited by Lucy Grig and Gavin Kelly

Disciplining Christians
Correction and Community in Augustine's Letters
Jennifer V. Ebbeler

History and Identity in the Late Antique Near East
Edited by Philip Wood

Explaining the Cosmos
Creation and Cultural Interaction in Late-Antique Gaza
Michael W. Champion

Universal Salvation in Late Antiquity
Porphyry of Tyre and the Pagan-Christian Debate in Late Antiquity
Michael Bland Simmons

The Poetics of Late Latin Literature
Edited by Jaś Elsner and Jesús Hernández Lobato

The Poetics of Late Latin Literature

Edited by
Jaś Elsner and Jesús Hernández Lobato

Oxford University Press is a department of the University of Oxford. It furthers
the University's objective of excellence in research, scholarship, and education
by publishing worldwide. Oxford is a registered trade mark of Oxford University
Press in the UK and certain other countries.

Published in the United States of America by Oxford University Press
198 Madison Avenue, New York, NY 10016, United States of America.

© Oxford University Press 2017

All rights reserved. No part of this publication may be reproduced, stored in
a retrieval system, or transmitted, in any form or by any means, without the
prior permission in writing of Oxford University Press, or as expressly permitted
by law, by license, or under terms agreed with the appropriate reproduction
rights organization. Inquiries concerning reproduction outside the scope of the
above should be sent to the Rights Department, Oxford University Press, at the
address above.

You must not circulate this work in any other form
and you must impose this same condition on any acquirer.

CIP data is on file at the Library of Congress

ISBN 978-0-19-935563-1

Contents

List of Contributors vii

Introduction: Notes towards a Poetics of Late Antique Literature 1
Jaś Elsner and Jesús Hernández Lobato

Part I The Explosion of Form: Late Antique Experimentalism

1. POP Art: The Optical Poetics of Publilius Optatianus Porfyrius 25
   Michael Squire

2. Polymetry in Late Latin Poems: Some Observations on Its Meaning and Functions 100
   Franca Ela Consolino

3. Words Pregnant with Meaning: The Power of Single Words in Late Latin Literature 125
   Isabella Gualandri

Part II Late Antique Intertextuality

4. Intertextuality in Late Latin Poetry 149
   Helen Kaufmann

5. Late Narcissus: Classicism and Culture in a Late Roman Cento 176
   Jaś Elsner

Part III Programmatic Reflections: A Metaliterary Twist

6. Displacing Tradition: A New-Allegorical Reading of Ausonius, Claudian, and Rutilius Namatianus 207
   Marco Formisano

vi   Contents

7. Metapoetics in the Prefaces of Claudian's *De raptu Proserpinae*   236
   Stephen Harrison

8. Rewriting Ausonius   252
   Scott McGill

9. To Speak or Not to Speak: The Birth of a "Poetics of Silence"
   in Late Antique Literature   278
   Jesús Hernández Lobato

Part IV   Literature and Power

10. The Poetics of Latin Prose Praise and the Fourth-Century Curve   313
    Roger Rees

11. The Lies the Poets Tell: Poetry in Prose Panegyrics   345
    Catherine Ware

Part V   A New Literary Space: The Challenges of Christian Poetry

12. Lactantius's *Phoenix* and Late Latin Poetics   373
    Michael Roberts

13. The Early Christian Response to Platonist Poetics: Boethius, Prudentius, and
    the *Poeta Theologus*   391
    Marc Mastrangelo

14. In Praise of the Wax Candle: Augustine the Poet and Late Latin Literature   424
    Gillian Clark

Bibliography   447
Index Locorum   491
General Index   525

List of Contributors

Gillian Clark is Professor Emerita of Ancient History, University of Bristol.

Franca Ela Consolino is Professor of Latin Language and Literature at L'Aquila University, Abruzzo.

Jaś Elsner is Humfrey Payne Senior Research Fellow at Corpus Christi College, Oxford, Visiting Professor of Art and Religion at the University of Chicago, and Leverhulme Senior Research Keeper in the Empires of Faith project at the British Museum.

Marco Formisano is Professor (docent) of Latin Literature, Ghent University.

Isabella Gualandri is Retired Professor of Latin Literature at Milan State University.

Stephen Harrison is Fellow and Tutor in Classics, Corpus Christi College, Oxford, and Professor of Latin Literature, University of Oxford.

Jesús Hernández Lobato is a Lecturer in Latin Language and Literature at the University of Salamanca.

Helen Kaufmann is a College Lecturer in Classics at Lady Margaret Hall, Oxford.

Marc Mastrangelo is Professor and Chair of Classical Studies at Dickinson College in Carlisle, Pennsylvania.

Scott McGill is Professor of Classical Studies at Rice University, at Houston, Texas.

Roger Rees is Reader in Latin at the School of Classics, St Andrews University.

Michael Roberts is Robert Rich Professor of Latin and Professor of Classical Studies at Wesleyan University, Connecticut.

Michael Squire is Reader in Classical Art at King's College London.

Catherine Ware is a Lecturer in Classics at University College Cork.

Introduction

Notes towards a Poetics of Late Antique Literature

JAŚ ELSNER and JESÚS HERNÁNDEZ LOBATO

THE AESTHETIC CHANGES IN LATE ROMAN LITERATURE SPEAK TO the foundations of modern Western culture. The dawn of a new way of being in the world and of experiencing reality, one that most Europeans and Americans still consider their own, is to be found, not in the distant Antiquity of Greece nor in the golden age of a Roman Empire that spanned the Mediterranean, but more fundamentally in the original and problematic fusion of Graeco-Roman culture with a new and unexpected foreign element—the arrival of Christianity as (soon to be) an exclusive state religion.[1] This fusion of cultural continuity with religious transformation creates the enduring excitement of one of the more turbulent periods of human history. This is not to question the relevance of Homer and Vergil, Plato and Seneca, Demosthenes and Cicero, Thucydides and Tacitus, for forging many of our most cherished humane values and cultural assumptions. Nevertheless, there is an inescapable pre-Christian otherness in all these classical texts which stands between us and any simple claim to being their direct descendants.[2] Antiquity, in other words, is not wholly ours. European culture in the Christian era is something radically different from its illustrious

---

1. By the end of the fourth century, anti-pagan legislation had established the exclusivity of Christianity—at least as a public official religion.
2. Cf. Marías 2000: 8–9: "This is quite different from the case of those ways of life which bear a considerable resemblance to our own but which are separable from Christianity. Here differences are perceived that in a certain way are 'unexpected' for they appear against a backdrop of similarity or commonality. It is not a question of 'remote' ways of life such as the African, Chinese, Indian, or pre-Columbian American, but of those in 'proximity' such as the Greek or the Roman, those which belong to us insofar as they are included in our own reality. In such cases we come to see that we are in the presence of another *configuration* of life, that we are dealing with a different perspective, but yet one that is not foreign to us because it is included in our own. Thus it appears to us as somehow incomplete because it lacks something we ourselves possess and which we count on spontaneously and almost without thinking. These different perspectives surprise and disturb us, not for what they possess but for what they lack from our standpoint. They seem to be missing essential elements that are a part of our reality. [...] In reading a text that is foreign to Christianity, either because it was written before the Christian era or because it belongs to a society that has not known or received the Christian faith, it may be obvious that the writing is admirable, perhaps even essential to our own condition. Yet at the same time one discovers in it a *strangeness* arising from the absence of something we bear within us which determines our vision of reality and our manner of perceiving, projecting and hoping."

pre-Christian precursors and something radically new. It was the Christian appropriation and sometimes violent reformulation of the centuries-old legacy of Antiquity that made it ours, by creating a powerful cultural construct—a vortex of conflictive creativity—which is still largely in force today.

Despite the weight of a rhetorical tradition of modern continuity with Antiquity that has been in place since the Renaissance, one may argue that Western civilization emerged from a crisis of identity rather than from an affirmation of cultural hegemony. In literary terms, we might see this as the result of a self-conscious yet questioning sense of the burden of the past (a kind of "baroque")[3] rather than as emerging from any monolithic metanarrative inherent in classicism. In part, late antique sensibility is rooted in a clash of conflicting civilizations, intensified by the increasing and always menacing presence of certain unwanted guests (such as the Huns or the ubiquitous Germanic invaders—Vandals, Goths, Visigoths) who were ultimately welcomed into the mix of post-Roman cultures across Europe and North Africa. The fraught cultural atmosphere produced some of the most remarkable works of literature of the ancient world, from Augustine's *Confessions* to Ausonius's *Mosella*. As Ernst Robert Curtius wisely remarked, all Western literature, from Shakespeare to Cervantes, from Dante to Goethe, from the *chansons de geste* to T. S. Eliot, depends on and cannot be understood without the Latin writing of this period[4]—which was anti-classical, challenging, and unconventional. In too much modern scholarship, that challenging anti-classicism has led to late Roman literature being mistreated or simply ignored by critical prejudice. The principal goal of this volume, comprising fourteen newly written essays by a series of experts in the field, is to offer a way into this foundational literature and to prise open the vibrant, complex and too often misunderstood poetics that underlay and made possible the cultural revolution of the later Roman world.

---

3. Late antique literature has been intriguingly described as "a late Latin Baroque" (Fontaine 1998b: 49) and as the final and most radical stage of "the ancient Roman Baroque" (Fontaine 1998a: esp. 34–41).

4. Cf. Curtius 1953: viii and 13: "[My book] seeks to serve an understanding of the Western cultural tradition in so far as it is manifested in literature. It attempts to illuminate the unity of that tradition in space and time by the application of new methods. In the intellectual chaos of the present it has become necessary, and happily not impossible, to demonstrate that unity. But the demonstration can only be made from a universal standpoint. Such a standpoint is afforded by Latinity. Latin was the language of the educated during the thirteen centuries which lie between Virgil and Dante. Without this Latin background, the vernacular literatures of the Middle Ages are incomprehensible. [...] No stretch of European literary history is so little known and frequented as the Latin literature of the early and high Middle Ages. And yet the historical view of Europe makes it clear that precisely this stretch occupies a key situation as the connecting link between declining Antiquity and the Western world which was so very slowly taking shape."

There is no doubt that, without a real insight into the intricacies of late antique literature, we cannot comprehend the nature of an age that forged—and ultimately *invented*—what we are.

1.1. LATE ANTIQUE LITERATURE, CHRISTIANITY AND CLASSICAL SCHOLARSHIP

In the surge of scholarship on Late Antiquity in the last couple of generations, stimulating new approaches and developments have changed our understandings of the period's history, archaeology, art history, philosophical and theological creativity, religious history, and cultural complexity—not least extending the scope of the period as a meaningful historical nexus to as late as 1000 AD.[5] Late Antiquity has been, alongside the study of the reception of classics in later eras, one of the two great flowerings of the field of classical studies in the last twenty years or so, with the rise of new journals and a plethora of innovative scholarly approaches.[6]

In this resurgence, the literary study of late Roman poetry has been the poor relation—less developed as a specific field within the bigger picture of Greek and Latin literature and much less integrated within the larger narrative of continuity and change that has intertwined material-cultural with historical research, than any other field within late antique studies. In substantial part, this has been due to an old prejudice among traditional classical philologists against the supposed second-rate-ness of Latin and Greek poetry in the Christian era, a prejudice not shared by those historians who work on Ammianus, Cassius Dio, and Procopius (for instance) or those literary critics who have made the study of the ancient prose romance one of the most vibrant fields in classical studies in the last couple of decades.[7] The resistance to many aspects of late poetry is exemplified by D. R. Shackleton Bailey's remarkable decision to exclude the Latin centos from his edition of the Latin Anthology, as if these poems were so bad and so derivative as not to merit edition or even presence in the new Teubner of the major Latin collection of shorter poems, despite their place at

---

5. The case for a Late Antiquity that extends to the end of the first millennium AD has recently been made by Fowden (2014: esp. 49–91), with a discussion of earlier models at 18–48. The apostle of the long Late Antiquity is Brown 1971. For what is currently the more usual c. AD 250–800 model, see, e.g., Bowersock, Brown, and Grabar 1999.

6. One thinks for instance of *Antiquité tardive* (from 1993) and the *Journal of Late Antiquity* (from 2008). On reception studies, see, e.g., Kallendorf 2007, and Hardwick and Stray 2008; new journals: the *International Journal of the Classical Tradition* (from 1994) and the *Classical Receptions Journal* (from 2009).

7. For instance, Whitmarsh 2008, for a recent summary, and the many papers in the journal *Ancient Narrative*.

the front of the key codex Salmasianus as well as in several other manuscripts.[8] The distaste for late Latin has extended to a distrust of pseudepigrapha, pastiche, and forgery (an interesting field in fact, recently revalorized by Peirano 2012) and the creative extension of poems by later hands, as in the case of the poem *de anima* (*Anth. Lat.* ed. Reise (1906) 1.2 no. 489), whose first three lines were composed by Augustine and published in his *City of God* 15.22, as discussed in this volume by Gillian Clark.

It is as if modern classicists have collectively and over perhaps a century reacted against a series of very specific qualities which mark out the literature of the later Roman empires, both Greek and Latin, as distinctive and remarkable. These qualities include the conscious awareness of rhetorical performance, extending (as discussed in the chapters by Roger Rees and Catherine Ware) to a real interrelationship of poetry and panegyric (the latter being hardly a popular genre in the modern era); this is a feature scarcely absent from late Republican and Imperial poetics, but it has a greater explicit self-consciousness in the fourth and fifth centuries, perhaps in part dependent on the awareness of and play with earlier tradition. Still more significant for the distaste of a discipline—classics—founded to foster the love of, and to affirm continuity with, Graeco-Roman literary tradition is the particular self-reflexive sense of late Roman writing as being both within that tradition and yet outside of it. Late Latin literature is an extraordinary composite of two qualities—*homage* to a glorious literary culture, deeply appreciated, and *resistance* to its fundamental pagan underpinnings. This conflict of homage and resistance to the past comprises the Catch-22 of the late antique poet as educated classicist but also as Christian. Late antique poetics, in other words, possessed a very particular and distinctive set of responses to the burdens and anxieties of antique influence.[9] It not only bore the weight of a great tradition whose original masters (Homer, Ennius, Vergil) were deemed better poets than their modern successors, but it was also beset by a deep ambivalence about that tradition. For the essential paganism of classical literature and its distinctive position as articulating the essence of paganism through literate education were in deep conflict with the Christianity espoused by almost all the major writers from the fourth century and after. Of course, the range of responses to this underlying conflict was varied—from the mild and *apparently* unproblematic fusion of Christian and pagan elements, fostered by an overwhelmingly classical school curriculum,[10] to the flat refusal to invoke the inspiration of the

---

8. See Shackleton Bailey 1982, with some discussion in Elsner's chapter in this volume.
9. On the seminal notion of the "anxiety of influence," see Bloom 1975.
10. On the essential unity of Christian and pagan literature, see, e.g., Fontaine 1998c (who states that Christianity and Classical Antiquity are one and the same thing), and Alan Cameron 2004b: esp. 339–44. According to Cameron 2004b: 342–3: "Classical mythology was one of the indispensable components

Muses,[11] which were by no means to be regarded as harmless or strictly literary.[12] Yet Christian faith might be confronted, on the part of many a well-educated Christian, with distaste—even aversion—for the dullness and poverty of the biblical style,[13] whose new cultural significance undermined the foundations of classical literature.[14] This diversity of responses confirms the pervasiveness of the identity crisis shaping late antique culture as a whole.

Modern classics, developed in the Enlightenment as an alternative educational system to the theological curriculum (which was itself founded in Late Antiquity), has always been in profound discomfort with the kind of Christian

---

of a liberal education. It always had been, and in this area at least the Christianization of the Roman state made no difference. It was indispensable for any reader of the poets, and of much other classical literature; also most contemporary poetry and oratory as well. [...] Most recent studies have accepted that it was possible, then as now, to be a sincere Christian and yet write on secular rather than Christian subjects. For most lay Christians, classical culture, culture based on the poets and ancient mythology, was the only culture there was." On the weight of classical education, see, e.g., Marrou 1982: 299–329, and Brown 1992: 35–70.

11. See esp. PAUL. NOL. carm. 10.19–46. This explicit rejection of the Muses, driven by a wish to refound poetry on Christian grounds, is reiterated by other late antique authors: IVVENC. 1.25–7, PRVD. cath. 3.26–30, SIDON. carm. 16.1–5, PAVL. PETRIC. Mart. 4.245–50, VEN FORT. Mart. praef. II 37–40, CORIPP. Iust. 1.7–13, BOETH. cons. 1.1.26–41. Shorrock 2011: 13–48, provides an analysis of the phenomenon by introducing the notions of the "poet of Christ" and the "poet of the Muses," two different literary personae available to late antique authors: "The first [poetic 'personality'], as exemplified by Paulinus of Nola, presents a new poet of Christ who declares a noisy and absolute breach with the traditions of the Classical world (poetic dissent); the second, exemplified by Ausonius, is the poet of Muses who is consciously positioned within a tradition that stretches back to Virgil and Homer (poetic descent). [...] In both cases [...] the positions adopted cannot be taken at face value: for the poet of Christ, the rhetoric of difference and rupture masks a significant degree of similarity and continuity with the Classical tradition; for the poet of the Muses the rhetoric of similarity masks a significant degree of difference and rupture" (Shorrock 2011: 45–6).

12. Cf. the comments of François Paschoud on Alan Cameron 1977 (at Cameron 1977: 40): "Je ne crois pas que la culture et la littérature profanes fussent totalement innocents aux jeux des chrétiens. Si Jérôme a mauvaise conscience d'être 'cicéronien', c'est que les auteurs profanes sont les porte-drapeaux d'un système de valeurs, d'une vision de l'histoire et du monde qu'un chrétien ne pouvait que condamner à maints égards." See also Shorrock 2011: 36: "That writers felt it necessary to emphasise time and again the silence of the oracles suggests that the theme of prophecy and inspiration continued to exert a powerful influence, that the traditional routes to divine knowledge still presented a challenge and threat to a newly emerging Christian age. After all, why make an issue over something that is no longer an issue?"

13. HIER. epist. 22.30: *Post noctium crebras uigilias, post lacrimas, quas mihi praeteritorum recordatio peccatorum ex imis uisceribus eruebat, Plautus sumebatur in manibus. Si quando in memet reuersus prophetam legere coepissem*, sermo horrebat incultus *et, quia lumen caecis oculis non uidebam, non oculorum putabam culpam esse, sed solis.*

14. See on this Auerbach 2003: 154: "But the question of style became really acute when the spread of Christianity exposed Holy Scripture, and Christian literature in general, to the aesthetic criticism of highly educated pagans. They were horrified at the claim that the highest truths were contained in writings composed in a language to their minds impossibly uncivilized and in total ignorance of stylistic categories. [...] It [i.e., Holy Scripture] had created an entirely new kind of sublimity, in which the everyday and the low were included, not excluded, so that, in style as in content, it directly connected the lowest with the highest."

hegemony that late Roman literature was trying to establish within the classical tradition.¹⁵ So modern resistance to the literature of the period is not surprising: it is in the end a kind of self-hatred of the Christian intellectual heritage that so many classical philologists, brought up with the Christian culture of nineteenth- and twentieth-century Europe and America, have turned to Antiquity in order to wish away.

1.2. The Poetics and Aesthetics of Late Antiquity

As is discussed in a number of chapters in this volume, one of the striking aspects of late Latin literature is the ways exegesis is intimately interconnected with poetics.¹⁶ Introductions and commentaries—both verse prefaces (such as those discussed by Stephen Harrison) and prose frames (as in Scott McGill's account of the works of Ausonius)—specifically address the issues at stake in the writing of poetry; textual exegesis becomes a dominant genre that shapes both the production and the reception of literature; panegyric exploits poetry; all forms of writing are highly indebted to rhetorical training (with many of the classiest poets, such as Ausonius or Pacatus, also being among the major orators and rhetorical teachers, and others, such as Augustine, Ambrose, and Lactantius, being major writers, preachers, and theological intellects). Discourse and dialogue (and especially the emergence of a specifically Christian way of doing both), in other words, were not only central to the late antique reinvention of culture but became the object of self-conscious attention.¹⁷ Late Antiquity, in its extremely creative revision and audacious revaluation of its Graeco-Roman and Jewish roots, can rightly be described as an "era of interpretation"¹⁸ or as an "age of the preface" (as suggested in this book by Scott McGill).¹⁹ In short, the late Roman world was a time when literature itself became one of literature's main concerns.

This striking metaliterary twist stemmed in part from an unprecedented *mise en crise* of the very notions of language and representation (as proposed by Hernández Lobato in this volume), a problem which seems to underlie and determine almost every aspect of the culture of its era and thus constitutes one of its most genuine expressions. Language, which had been taken for granted as a given beyond question, became an obsession in the late Roman world as the whole rhetorical edifice of pagan Antiquity was recalibrated to articulate

---

15. Cf. Formisano 2014: esp. 9.
16. A reflection on this phenomenon can be found in Gualandri 1995, and now Pelttari 2014: 12–44.
17. On discourse, see esp. Averil Cameron 1991; on dialogue, Averil Cameron 2014, contra Goldhill 2009: 1–11.
18. Hernández Lobato 2012: 91–107.
19. On the cardinal role of prefaces in late Latin poetry, see Pelttari 2014: 45–72.

Christian truths. To see this in terms of elite Christians and pagans—their invectives and apologetics and the absence of a pagan revival in response to Christian hegemony—which has been the thrust of the most recent major monograph on late antique literature (Alan Cameron 2011), is perhaps correct in relation to the narrow religious politics of the time; but this is reductive and limited as a thesis of cultural transformation. The last centuries of the Western Roman Empire witnessed not only the birth of a fully fledged semiotics (one of Augustine's major contributions to Western thought) and a far-reaching apophatic theology (which boldly and controversially denied the ultimate capacity of human language to access or convey reality) but also the progressive emergence of a radically questioning literature which was set to become an ideal vehicle for the challenges and anxieties of an era in continuous reformulation. Therefore, the self-reflexive commentarial qualities of the poetic developments of late antique Latin—the move to allegory,[20] for instance—supply a deep and empathetic, if in certain respects distanced, review of the classical tradition from a series of great writers utterly committed to its canonical status. But they also offer a penetrating cultural commentary on the time, which needs to be integrated into the bigger historical picture by scholarship that is not primarily literary in its focus.

While earlier eras of literary revival—the Hellenistic period in ancient Greek, the flowering of Latin literature in the late Republic and early Empire, or the "Second Sophistic" efflorescence of Greek letters in the Imperial Roman world—are important stages in the development of classicism and the reception of Antiquity, arguably Late Antiquity is the cardinal point at which modern models of classicism and reception were forged. For it was in the post-Constantinian period that an active and deeply learned commitment to the literary past was juxtaposed with the fundamental distancing born of Christianity: reception is always as much the mark of distance as it is of the desire for emulation and continuity. It is precisely in the newly defined Christian context, which enacted a fundamental fissure with the Graeco-Roman past in terms of religious, social, cultural, and sexual mores, that the nature of the cultural assimilation of the ancient tradition (as continuity with the past) was transformed radically from previous forms of reception. For in Late Antiquity, for all the urge to continuity with previous culture, the frame of the enactment of continuity was profoundly transformed by Christianity, a faith always eager to assert its radical novelty and the new world order brought about by the coming of Jesus.[21] The classical tradition as we know it—from the Middle Ages, via the Renaissance and neoclassicism

---

20. E.g. Herzog 2002: 115–77, on varieties of exegesis and metaphor in late Latin literature.
21. Cf. Rev. 21:5: "Then he who sat on the throne said, 'Behold! I am making all things new!'" (translation: *The New English Bible*, New York, Oxford University Press, 1976).

to modernity, in all forms of cultural epiphenomena from prose and verse to art and architecture, from law and government to urban planning and decoration—began when pagan Antiquity ended, at the point of Christian hegemony in the very period and in the very literature with which this book deals. In its often problematic relationship to its two cultures of origin (the Graeco-Roman and the Jewish), early Christianity developed an original and highly characteristic cultural dynamics based on the ideas of alterity, "otherization," and appropriation.[22] This novel attitude, sustained and justified by a twofold interpretation of Moses's plundering of the treasures of the Egyptians (alternately identified either with the pagans, whose philosophy and rhetoric had to be used in support of the new faith, or with the Jews, whose Bible had been conveniently purloined as the "Old Testament"),[23] set the foundations of one of the most outstanding features of late antique culture as a whole: appropriationism.

The self-consciousness of late Roman literary production and its irrepressible drive for appropriation are not only important in their own right, but they mirror other forms of cultural self-reflection in the period, especially in art and architecture. The use of architectural and sculptural *spolia* borrowed from objects made in the past and recycled wholesale in monuments (from large-scale buildings like the church of Saint Sabina in Rome or the arch of Constantine [figure I.1] to much smaller artefacts like the eighth-century cross of Desiderius in Brescia) has similarities to the use of literary *spolia*,[24] such as the segments of Vergilian lines employed in centos or the many quotations from famous earlier texts scattered in speeches and poems.[25] Such *spolia* (both literary and material-cultural) both are an intrinsic part of the new late antique text or monument and stand out in their own right as quotations of, or items from, the hallowed past.[26] Nevertheless, the idea of paying homage to Rome's golden days did not always dominate these curious patchworks. They could be used as ironic devices aimed at appropriating the literary past in a playful and even irreverent manner (as in Ausonius's vivid description of defloration on a wedding night made up of a series of rearranged lines from the chaste Vergil)[27] or as ideological tools to

---

22. See Hernández Lobato 2010a (revised and expanded in Hernández Lobato 2012: 76–126).

23. On this multipurpose exegesis of Exod. 12:35–6 and its impact on the early Christian cultural praxis, see Hernández Lobato 2012: 120–6. For some of the ways this worked in early Christian visual culture, see Elsner 2011.

24. See Elsner 2000: 175–8.

25. On late antique centos, see the extensive bibliography provided in J. Elsner's contribution to this volume.

26. The literature on *spolia* is vast. One might begin with Settis (1986), Pensabene and Panella (1993–4), de Lachenal (1995), Kinney (1995 and 1997), Poeschke (1996), Hansen (2003), Bernard, Bernardi, and Esposito (2008), Brilliant and Kinney (2011).

27. Avson. *cento* (Green 18).

Notes towards a Poetics of Late Antique Literature 9

Figure I.1. The arch of Constantine, north side, 312–15 AD, Rome. Sculptural *spolia* on this side include the four oblong panels from an arch of Marcus Aurelius, as well as the four statues of Dacians from a monument of Trajan in the Attic, and the four roundels from a hunting monument of Hadrian on the two sides of the central passageway (cf. figure 1.31). Architectural *spolia* include the columns and much of the decorative cornice. Photograph: J. Elsner.

reverse or to cap pagan values (as in the case of Christian centos). But centos and *spolia* are only the most evident exponents of a much broader phenomenon: an incipient "aesthetics of the fragment" (Hernández Lobato 2012: 257–317) that covered a wide range of cultural manifestations, from the antiquarian dismemberment of the past in the form of anthologies, verse-by-verse commentaries, or all kinds of heterogeneous compilations to the emergence of a well-established cult of relics (Cox Miller 1998 and 2009: 42–61; Elsner 2000).

The imitation of *spolia*, objects made in Late Antiquity but emulating the forms and styles of earlier work (such as the roundels of the rising and the setting sun on the arch of Constantine, figure I.2, or many a gem cut in imitation of classical intaglios), resembles the rich texture of pastiche, "forgery," and emulation of late Latin verse.[28] Again in both poetry and art, antiquarian forms are

---

28. On late Latin *pseudoepigrapha*, see Peirano 2012.

Figure I.2. The arch of Constantine, east side. The large landscape relief panel at the top, as well as the statues beside it, are *spolia* from the period of Trajan. The central roundel is Constantinian but imitates the shape, size, and embedded placement of the Hadrianic roundels on the north and south of the arch (cf. figure 1.31). Photograph: J. Elsner.

an essential element of the text or object that has been newly constructed, and deliberate antiquarian gestures signalled not only a knowing acknowledgment of the past but also the panache to create something that could pass for a literary or artistic relic. Most interestingly, all these cultural practices entail a self-conscious blurring of the classical boundary between copy and original and a considerable weakening of the notion of authorship.[29]

The emerging taste for all kinds of "exquisite miniatures" represents another meeting point of late antique literature and art.[30] While the literary arena was increasingly dominated by a plethora of old and new microgenres (such as epigrams, dedicatory inscriptions, *ekphraseis, propemptica*, epitaphs, *genethliaca*, thanksgivings, riddles, erotic poems, sermons, *passiones*, church dedications, *acta martyrum*, hagiography, prefatory epistles, and so on), a wide range of tiny, beautifully crafted objects was gradually shaping a new way of conceiving material culture: finely carved ivory diptychs, intricate silverware, delicate cameos, convoluted glassware, decorated gowns enacting a real "revolution of dress" (Marrou 1977: 14), lavishly illuminated manuscripts. The "cumulative aesthetics" (Elsner 2004: 304–9) underlying all these kinds of art works can be easily recognized in many well-known features of the late antique literary praxis: its so called jeweled style (Roberts 1989a), its unrestrained "cataloguing passion" (Wedeck 1960: 6), the "aesthetic atomization" (Hernández Lobato 2012: 381–3) leading to an emancipation of the isolated word as the new basic unit of literary creation (a phenomenon studied in depth by Isabella Gualandri in this volume) and composition by a series of semi-autonomous medallions (Fontaine 1977: 428–9). All these phenomena, resulting in an unprecedented miniaturization of taste, ultimately stem from a pervasive "aesthetics of detail" that privileges the part over the whole and breaks up the literary/artistic experience into a kaleidoscope of sharp close-ups.[31]

The network of allusion and intertextuality of late Roman literature and its formal as opposed to substantive or content-related use (as argued by Helen Kaufmann) has numerous parallels in the mythology-related, classicizing works of late antique silver plate and ivory, whose meanings might be actively pagan in senses somewhat removed from those of earlier Antiquity but are more likely to be forms of Hellenizing antiquarianism—one thinks for instance of the Parabiago plate, the Corbridge Lanx (figure I.3) or the Symmachorum ivory panel (figure I.4) now in the Victoria and Albert Museum (V&A).[32] These

---

29. The cultural phenomenon is redolent of, indeed ancestral to, Roland Barthes's "death of the author": Barthes 1977.
30. See Elsner 2004: 287, and 293–303.
31. See Hernández Lobato 2012: 318–401.
32. See Elsner 1998: 186–97.

Figure I.3. The Corbridge Lanx, silver, second half of the fourth century AD. Found in Britain. The iconography, including Apollo and Artemis, is paganizing but obscure. It may have strong pagan intimations but is more likely to be antiquarian. Photograph: British Museum.

traditions of allusion operate both in relation to the *forms* of ancient art, including naturalism, and to its non-Christian mythological *subject matter*—for instance, in the Projecta casket from the Esquiline Treasure, with its sexy nude Venus in naturalistic style, juxtaposed against a Christian inscription. They run rich and late into Byzantium (beyond the tenth century certainly) via the magnificent surviving traditions of woven textiles from Egypt to ivory boxes like the Veroli casket in the V&A (figure I.5) and rare decorated glassware like the Hercules cup from Byzantium now in the Treasury of San Marco in Venice.[33] In both text and image, this late antique tradition has been dubbed Hellenism on the Greek side of the late Roman world, but it is equally strong in Latin literature and visual culture, at least until the sixth century.

Christian (mis)readings, sometimes allegorical,[34] of pre-Christian *texts* (famously the late antique readings of Vergil's Fourth Eclogue to signal the

---

33. See Chatterjee 2013, on the Veroli Casket; Cutler 1974, on the San Marco cup.
34. On the notion of "misreading," see Bloom 1975: esp. 95: "There are no interpretations but only misinterpretations, and so all criticism is prose poetry."

Figure I.4. The Symmachorum ivory panel, about 390 AD. Both in style and subject matter this is a highly classicizing object showing a priestess sprinkling incense on an altar. Photograph: Victoria and Albert Museum.

Figure I.5. The Veroli Casket, ivory box of the tenth century AD, probably from Constantinople. Highly classicizing style and iconography is used here for a mythological subject with Dionysiac figures in an antiquarian context. Photograph: Victoria and Albert Museum.

coming of Christ[35] or Fulgentius's interpretation of the *Aeneid* as an allegory of the ages of man)[36] are no less potent for the interpretation of earlier *objects*. We have evidence of a statue of Asclepius in Constantinople interpreted as a Christian bishop, for instance.[37] The juxtaposition of an image of Christ with the mythological theme of Bellerophon killing the Chimaera on the mosaic floor of the late Roman villa at Hinton St Mary in Britain (figure I.6) offers the potential for allegorical interpretation of the pagan theme in Christian terms or of syncretism between pagan and Christian in a form that is hardly orthodox by the standards of the church. The creation of visual designs in words in the poetry of Optatian Porfyry (discussed here briefly by Gualandri and at length by Michael Squire) can be seen as an artistic instantiation in verbal form of the potential for allegory and hidden meanings both within the created world and within the formal poetics of the classical tradition.[38]

But Optatian's visual poems can also be seen as an example of a characteristically late antique trend: the taste for formal experiment and a mistrust of

---

35. It is worth mentioning that the emperor Constantine himself subscribed so enthusiastically to this reading that he even used part of it in his speech to the "Assembly of the Saints" (now appended to the Eusebian *Vita Constantini*), thus acting as a fully fledged Christian exegete. Cf. Courcelle (1957), Nisbet (1978), Benko (1980), Bernardi Perini (1999–2000 and 2001), and Barnes (2001).

36. Fvlg. *Virg. cont.*, briefly discussed by Hernández Lobato in this volume.

37. The relevant texts are Leo Grammaticus 257 and Symeon Magister 692, with Mango (1963: 63) and Bassett (2004: 148 n. 16).

38. On the "openness" and "layered meanings" of many late antique poems, see Pelttari 2014: 73–114.

Figure I.6. Large mosaic floor from a late Roman villa at Hinton St Mary, in Dorset (cf. also figure 1.26). The main room has Christ in the central roundel, with images of vegetation or hunting with dogs in the lunettes and of the four seasons or the four winds in the corners. The smaller room has more hunting scenes, with Bellerophon and the Chimaera in the main medallion. Photograph: British Museum.

the classical compartmentalization of art and literature. This sensibility brought about what might be called an "aesthetics of hybridization"[39] that operates simultaneously on two levels: as an "*intra*systemic hybridization" (i.e. working within the limits of literature),[40] it eroded or even abolished the traditional boundaries between literary genres, styles, registers, and conventions, thus producing unclassifiable masterpieces such as Ausonius's *Mosella* or Rutilius Namatianus's *De reditu suo* (discussed by Marco Formisano); as an "*intersys*temic hybridization" (i.e. combining materials from different artistic realms),[41]

39. Hernández Lobato 2012: 466–518.
40. Hernández Lobato 2012: 468–70. This terminology is based on Even-Zohar's polysystem theory, on which see Even-Zohar 1990.
41. Hernández Lobato 2012: 468 and 470–518.

it was prone to merge image and text under the form of visual poems, *ekphraseis*, illuminated manuscripts, highly textualized images,[42] objectualized texts,[43] and so forth. All these practices—profoundly challenging and innovative in relation to earlier Latin poetics yet deeply genuflective to the tradition at the same time—ultimately derive from the burden and anxieties of the canon. They are a creative response to the sense that the major paths of literature had proved exhausted and the masterworks of the past were discouragingly unbeatable. As a consequence of what might be called this "epigonal" awareness, late antique poets embarked on a "poetics of the uncommon" (Gualandri 1979: 83), aimed at dazzling their discerning—and often overcritical—audiences by means of a lavish display of rhetorical fireworks. After all, literature should not be taken too seriously, as poets like Ausonius and Sidonius never tire of repeating in their witty and often ironic prefaces, distancing themselves from the highbrow poetic statements of their classical predecessors yet at the same time indulging the playful character of their own flamboyant trifles. This self-ironic twist, widespread in literature and brought to its peak in Ausonius's dry wit, is conspicuously absent—with rare exceptions—from the visual arts, something probably due to the constraints imposed by the employment of visual culture in the service of aristocratic, imperial, or ecclesiastical propaganda.[44]

What a careful grasp of the literary material adds to the range of artistic productions of Late Antiquity is a careful working out of the issues and contradictions of change and continuity on the level of a deeply antiquarian and well-educated elite. That evidence is essential to any cultural history fully committed to extrapolating the dynamics of social change in Late Antiquity as its actors and participants perceived and experienced it. What the poetics of Late Antiquity offers the historian is a sophisticated commentary from within the culture on the formal and thematic complexities of cultural change that is simultaneously affectionate and antiquarian in relation to the past and sufficiently distanced from the past to be able to see it with an unusually sceptical clarity.

---

42. That is the case of the newborn Christian iconography, often conceived as a kind of textless illustration. In J. Elsner's words (2004: 284): "Christian images illustrated, commented upon, reformulated a textual canon, while pagan images were contributions in their own right to an undogmatic culture of relatively unfixed mythical narratives. The viewer's relation to a prior text (always posited by Christian art) and to the initiations and dogmas implied by Christian belief was a remarkable and radical innovation in Roman visual culture. It created of every viewer a potential exegete." Cf. Hernández Lobato 2012: 481–4.

43. Hernández Lobato 2012: 485–9.

44. Of course, irony and propaganda do not usually belong together, regardless of the artistic discipline selected towards goal. Late antique panegyrics (including those written by an author as playful and self-ironic as Sidonius Apollinaris) provide a good example of this golden rule in the literary realm. An in-depth discussion of this problem can be found in Hernández Lobato 2012: 239–45. On the gradual loss of irony in late antique visual arts, see Elsner 1995: 10 and passim.

1.3. THE CULTURAL FRAME

In the great book where the notion of Late Antiquity was first convincingly flagged over a century ago,[45] Alois Riegl argued that all the epiphenomena of the period (not only the painting, sculpture, architecture, and arts and crafts on which his main chapters focused but also law, philosophy, theology, and poetry) were the product of a single cultural drive—psychological, social, shared by both producers and viewers—what he called *Kulturwollen* or, in relation to material art, *Kunstwollen*.[46] The concept has proven both controversial and fundamental in the discipline of art history, dominating the development of that field in the 1920s and 1930s particularly and giving rise to fundamental contributions from some of the greatest of all art historians.[47] The still current scholarly model of art as reflecting cultural mentalities or expressing the energy of its time is effectively a form of *Kunstwollen*, without the concept being named explicitly. Notably many of the principal discussions of late antique art in the second half of the twentieth century have been profoundly under the spell of the model of a period-related drive to art and other epiphenomena,[48] and the classic book on late antique poetry of the last generation—Michael Roberts's *The Jeweled Style*—certainly saw poetic production as operating in a fundamental homology with visual and artistic production. Likewise, the sense of an all-encompassing psychological problematic, embedded in the culture itself as a drive to its transformation, has informed such important and influential historical accounts of the shift to Christianity as E. R. Dodds's *Pagan and Christian in an Age of Anxiety* (1965).

We do not, however, need to resort to collective psychology or cultural drives or the urgency of a historically situated generative impulse to explain what is undoubtedly a remarkably wide cultural phenomenon of transformation both within the classical tradition and looking beyond it into medieval culture. Rather, it is the transformed frame within which the Roman Empire (and culture itself) now operated that is the key factor in generating transformed literary and artistic responses to the world. That changed frame is the demand of the late empire both to be traditionally classical and to be Christian. The typical late

---

45. See Giardina 1999: 157–9; Ghilardi 2002: 119–20, 126; Elsner 2002b; Liebeschuetz 2004: 254–5; James 2008: 20–1; Inglebert 2012: 1; Fowden 2014: 26–7 and 42–4.

46. Riegl 1901: 209–17, translated as Riegl 1985: 223–34. On Kunstwollen, see, for instance, Olin 1992: 71–2, 129–53; Neher 2004; Elsner 2006b.

47. Key interventions include Panofsky 1981 (published in 1920); Panofsky 2008 (published in 1925); Wind 2009 (published in 1925); Sedlmayr 2001 (published in 1929); Panofsky 2012 (published in 1932); Kaschnitz-Weinberg 2016 (published in 1929).

48. For instance, L'Orange 1965; Bianchi Bandinelli 1971; Kitzinger 1977.

antique writer (not only the poets but also the theologians, orators, and historians) and the typical late Roman patron of the visual arts were educated in the great heritage of *paideia*, with its complex of rhetorical training, its immensely rich literary and artistic offerings, reaching back as far as the Homeric past on the Greek side and the Republic on the Roman and including the wealth of mythological subjects and stories that make up that tradition.[49] But they were also Christian—with some exceptions and many fewer after the fourth century (one thinks particularly of Julian, Libanius, and Symmachus as key pagan voices). Many of the Christian writers (especially those who became bishops, like Ambrose, Paulinus of Nola, and Augustine on the Latin side or like Basil, John Chrysostom, and Gregory of Nazianzus on the Greek) were themselves part of that extraordinarily energetic and brilliant group of Christian intellectuals who drove the transformation of Imperial culture in such a short time towards an exclusively Christian state.

The cultural frame—simultaneously Roman, reaching back in seamless tradition for over a thousand years (Philip the Arab had celebrated the millennium of the Roman Empire in 248 AD), and Christian—meant that there was an inevitable and fundamental conflict of identities and a profound challenge to individuals to find a comfortable place in determining their own identity within this context.[50] The options were many, from the kinds of syncretistic accommodations preached by Mani in the third century (which were condemned and ruthlessly persecuted by the church), via the attempt to preserve a pagan identity in the philosophical schools and among some of the aristocracy, to all forms of Christianity, from the broadly tolerant and inclusive to the vituperatively exclusivist and persecutory. The poetics of the period shows the working out of this cultural conundrum from different angles and among writers effectively in dialogue with each other and with the past. Such a poetics is inevitably inconsistent—or, we may say, multifarious—since it exhibits the multiplicity and range of options in a highly rhetorical context where polemic and apologetics were normal forms of communication and cultural discourse. We have, as moderns, to be particularly sensitive to our own broad resistance to many of the issues fundamental to intellectuals in the period of Late Antiquity—especially the centrality of religion (where most modern scholarship is resolutely secularist) and the centrality of a deeply antiquarian commitment to earlier culture (where so much of modern artistic experience is about the rejection of old forms).

---

49. For *paideia* as an explanatory model for late antique culture, see, e.g., Brown 1992: 35–70; Kaldellis 2007: 31–7, 56–8, 127–34, 144–51, 321–5; van Hoof 2013. For a critique, see Elsner 2013.

50. Famously, Jerome became feverish over his guilt complex about disliking the dullness of biblical style and admiring the pagan classics and saw God himself reproaching him for being a Ciceronian instead of a real Christian (HIER. *epist.* 22.30).

1.4. POSTMODERN LATE ANTIQUITY/
LATE ANTIQUE POSTMODERNITY

Given the problematic nature of late Roman classicism—always performing an act of homage but at the same time in conflict (both formally and substantively) with pre-Christian models of thought and expression—it is no surprise that the advocates of late antique culture have often looked to the contemporary avant-garde as their model and justification for Late Antiquity. At the end of the nineteenth century, Riegl explicitly cited a positive assessment of modern aesthetics against classicizing academicism in art as a justification for late antique styles.[51] A century later, Jacques Fontaine described late antique literature as a baroque *avant la lettre*.[52] Likewise, one may draw attention to some aspects of postmodernity (which has been provocatively described as Europe's most recent form of mannerism)[53] as a helpful prism through which to see late antique literature. Many of the bold and sometimes even bizarre features of late antique art and literature have striking correlations in our own time. For example, the (often ironic) cataloguing passion of late antique literature—as expressed in Ausonius's caustic catalogues of fish,[54] monosyllables,[55] or dead Trojans;[56] in Sidonius's disconcerting catalogue of negations (explored by Hernández Lobato's contribution); or in the lively enumerations of single words discussed in Gualandri's chapter—has had its twentieth-century counterpart in works like Gerhard Richter's *Atlas*, Bern and Hilla Becher's mock-archival photographs (1965–91), Christian Boltanski's *Reserve of Dead Swiss* (1991) or Borges's famous encyclopaedic list, which was the inspiration for Foucault's *Les mots et les choses* (1966). The blatant appropiationism inherent in late antique centos (such as that discussed by Elsner) compares with works like Walter Benjamin's unfinished *Passagenwerk* (1927–40),[57] Roland Barthes's *Fragments d'un discours*

---

51. Riegl 1985: 55–6: "what is most startling is to recall that our most recent art is essentially based on optical perception and particularly on momentary coloured impression, as with late Roman art. The Constantinian *Kunstwollen* accordingly appears virtually identical with our own very modern *Kunstwollen*." Cf. Wickhoff 1900: 54–60.

52. Fontaine 1998a and 1998b, discussed in note 3.

53. Eco, 1984: 66: "I believe that postmodernism is not a trend to be chronologically defined, but, rather, an ideal category—or better still, a *Kunstwollen*, a way of operating. We could say that every period has its own postmodernism, just as every period would have its own mannerism (and, in fact, I wonder if postmodernism is not the modern name for mannerism as a metahistorical category)." On postmodernity as a "neo-baroque," see Calabrese 1992.

54. Avson. *Mos.* 85–149. On the ironic and deconstructive character of this catalogue, see Hernández Lobato 2012: 391–4.

55. Avson. *technop.* (Green 25).

56. Avson. *epit.* (Green 12).

57. For an English translation see Benjamin 2002.

amoureux (1977),[58] Umberto Eco's *The Name of the Rose* (1980),[59] or even the popular pastiche-jukebox of a film like *Moulin Rouge!* (2001). The deliberate choice to make light of literary subject matter, which was to inspire ironic odes on a hand towel[60] or the best day for nail-cutting[61] or the alleged subtleties of the words "yes" and "no"[62] shares with pop art, "ready-mades," and Dada an interest in raising awkward questions about the limits of art and the conventionalities of what is traditionally assumed to be artistic. The twentieth-century linguistic turn has its late antique counterpart in the problematization of language and representation, as expressed in Augustine's semiotics, in the apophatic theology of Gregory of Nyssa and Pseudo-Dionysius the Areopagite, or in the pervasive "poetics of silence" discussed in Hernández Lobato's chapter.[63] This book is an invitation to discover the inspiring topicality of late antique literature and the ways it might become an unsuspected ally for a deeper and richer understanding of the writing of today's world.

1.5. Summary of the Essays

This volume of collected papers attempts, for the first time in English-language scholarship, to tackle the specificity and complexity of late antique Latin literary aesthetics; its aim is to redefine a territory which has been largely ignored in the overwhelmingly historical and archaeological emphasis of late antique studies. Contributors have been encouraged to deal with general aesthetic phenomena and literary trends within the period, as well as focusing on given texts or authors, and to relate their conclusions to new methodological frameworks or unexplored connections between different expressions of late antique creativity.

This journey through the cultural foundations of Western civilization begins with three contributions on some of the most innovative and surprising formal features of late antique literature (characterized as a whole by an unprecedented experimentalist drive): the undermining of the boundary between image and language in Optatian Porfyry's visual poetry (Michael Squire), the combination of different meters in a single poem (Franca Ela Consolino) and

---

58. For an English translation see Barthes 1978.
59. This global best-seller was translated into English in 1983.
60. Sidon. *epist.* 5.17.10. On this poem see La Penna 1995, and Hernández Lobato 2012: 233–8.
61. Avson. *ecl.* 18 (Green). To make it even more caustic, the second part of this twofold poem refutes the first one.
62. Avson. *ecl.* 21 (Green).
63. For a postmodern approach to late antique poetics, see Nugent 1990 (restricted to Ausonius), and Hernández Lobato 2012 (with more examples).

the emphasis on the single, isolated word as a new unit of aesthetics (Isabella Gualandri). The second section focuses on the way late antique literature related to its past through novel forms of that most traditional of Roman literary tropes, intertextuality.[64] Helen Kaufmann proposes a new theoretical frame aimed at distinguishing the different modes of intertextuality operating within late antique literature (from the traditional content-related model to a new form-related one), while Jaś Elsner explores the peculiarities of the cento as Late Antiquity's quintessential expression of unbridled intertextuality. The central section of the volume, acting as a kind of thematic hinge, examines the unprecedented metaliterary and self-referential twist which characterized late antique letters as a whole. Marco Formisano revisits three of the best known late Latin poems (Ausonius's *Mosella*, Claudian's *De raptu Proserpinae*, and Rutilius Namatianus's *De reditu suo*) to explore their shared quasi-allegorical reflection on their displacement from tradition. Scott McGill and Stephen Harrison discuss the programmatic considerations of two of the most influential late antique authors (Ausonius and Claudian) as performed by their prefaces. Jesús Hernández Lobato detects a pervasive "poetics of silence" that questions the pertinence of language and literature in the works of Sidonius, Fulgentius, Augustine, Ausonius, Rutilus Namatianus, and the anonymous writer of the *Peruigilium Veneris*. The volume's fourth part explores how this new literature relates to the outer world, in particular to the very centre of Imperial power. Roger Rees and Catherine Ware focus on the study of prose panegyric, showing, on the one hand, the progressive fusion of the traditional conventions of prose and verse and, on the other, the quasi-encyclopaedic character of a genre which seemed set to become the sum of all. The last section deals with the most crucial sociocultural transformation of the era—the irruption of Christianity. It offers three different but complementary approaches to the complex issue of the emergence of a specifically Christian literature, from the underground symbolism of Lactantius's hymn to the phoenix (Michael Roberts) via the enlightening responses of Boethius and Prudentius to the traditional quarrel between philosophy and literature (Marc Mastrangelo) to Augustine's hugely influential reflections on the viability a fully fledged Christian poetry (Gillian Clark).

The book's challenge, within a picture of continuity and change, classical traditionalism and Christian innovation, is both to literary critics of Antiquity and to students of Late Antiquity more broadly to take on board the insights

---

64. On intertextuality, see, e.g., Conte and Barchiesi 1989; Edmunds 1995 and 2001; Barchiesi 1997; Wills 1996; Fowler 1997; Hinds 1998; Bécares et al. 2000; Hutchinson 2013. For an exhaustive intertextual analysis conducted on a late antique author (Ammianus), see Kelly 2008.

and self-reflexive critiques of late Roman writing as a model for helping us think through late antique culture in a wider interdisciplinary perspective. The key point is that late Roman literature's own obsessions with and intense commentaries on the cultural fissures and discursive conflicts of its own epoch not only are among our surest historical guides to the interpretation of the period from within its own resources but are also fundamental to the attitudes developed towards Late Antiquity by its inheritance, even if they have been underacknowledged.

PART I

The Explosion of Form

Late Antique Experimentalism

POP Art

The Optical Poetics of Publilius Optatianus Porfyrius

MICHAEL SQUIRE (KING'S COLLEGE LONDON)

Of all late antique Latin poets, few have been so readily dismissed as Publilius Optatianus Porfyrius (the "POP" of my title—better known in English as "Optatian").[1] As the introduction to this volume explains, the "late" of "late Latin literature" still all too often serves as a badge of ageist prejudice—to delineate works that are deemed both chronologically and qualitatively peripheral to an established classical canon. Yet even among his late antique contemporaries, Optatian, active in the first decades of the fourth century, has come in for more than his fair share of bigotry. Most classicists have not heard of—never mind read—Optatian.[2] Those who have spent time with his literary creations, moreover, have not generally held back in their rebuke. "The corruption of triviality had eaten deeply into poetry," declares one mid-twentieth-century scholar, concluding that "Optatian's ridiculous verses" champion "the poet's futility."[3] Deprived of all interest save its curiosity, in the words of another, Optatian's oeuvre "bears witness to the decadence of an art and of a culture."[4] With the works of "unspeakable" Optatian,[5] riddled with an "unending

---

1. Throughout this chapter, I refer to the Latin text of Polara 1973 in preference to Müller 1877 and Kluge 1926; my numbering of individual poems—as indeed of Optatian's *uersus intexti* (with verses delineated by Roman numerals)—likewise follows Polara's edition. There is still no English translation of Optatian's poems, but Polara 2004a offers an accessible Latin and Italian text (first published in 1976), while an unpublished French doctoral dissertation provides an appendix of French translations (Bruhat 1999: 462–93); Ernst 2012: 21–63 provides a text, German translation, and commentary on six poems (1, 6, 10, 15, 21, and 25). A German critical edition is being prepared by Johannes Wienand and John Noël Dillon for Mohr Siebeck's "Studien und Texte zu Antike und Christentum" series—and is eagerly awaited.

2. Even amid specialist "classicist" handbooks to Late Antiquity, Optatian seems more or less invisible: for all the references to his more famous "Porphyrian" philosophical namesake in the third and early fourth centuries AD, for example, there is no mention of Optatian in Swain and Edwards 2007; likewise one finds only a passing mention in Fuhrmann 1994: 47–8. The major exception to this scholarly situation has been Giovanni Polara, applying a rigorous philological acumen to the textual transmission of the manuscripts (Polara 1971): as well as his edition and Latin commentary (Polara 1973), Polara has published numerous more discursive analyses (e.g., Flores and Polara 1969; Polara 1987, 1987–8, 1991).

3. Raby 1957: 1.45.

4. Bardon 1975: 453 ("Le texte même est dépourvu de tout intérêt qui ne soit de curiosité: il témoigne de la décadence d'un art et d'une culture"); cf. González Iglesias 2000, which, while offering a hugely sensitive series of readings, nonetheless associates Optatian's oeuvre with "una especie de autoerotismo masturbatorio" (362).

5. Alan Cameron 1980: 134.

flow of tasteless platitudes and trifles,"[6] we seem to be dealing with poems that "have lost all contact with reality and do not merit discussion."[7]

But the critical tide seems slowly to be turning. Like so many "late antique" Latin poets,[8] Optatian has piqued a new (post-)postmodern interest over the last twenty years or so, not only for his games of words and images but also for his testimony to a "pagan" world turning "Christian."[9] Already in 1979 (in a book little known among classicists), Charles Doria pointed to the historical importance of Optatian's work for approaching "visual literature criticism";[10] a little later, in 1985, William Levitan likewise championed his poetry as "linguistic artifact," in which "each poem also contains a number of inherent permutations of itself, a number of potential dispositions."[11] During the last decade in particular, a flurry of articles have followed (albeit mostly outside the field of anglophone scholarship)—from Meike Rühl's discussion of the "intermedial tendencies" of later Latin panegyric, through Martin Hose's analysis of "Constantinian literature" (comparing Optatian, Proba, and Iuvencus), to Marie-Odile Bruhat's

---

6. Cf. Schanz 1914: 13: "Verwunderlich ist es nur, dass ein Mann so unendlichen Fleiss auf solche Abgeschmacktheiten und Nichtigkeiten verwenden wollte; noch verwunderlicher aber ist, dass solche Torheiten am Hofe beifällige Aufnahmen fanden." Still more dismissive of Optatian's "hare-brained frivolities of verse" is the entry in *Paulys Realencyclopädie*, which mirrors at once Schanz's phrasing and sentiment (R. Helm 1959: 1928): "Publilius Optatianus Porfyrius ... ist der Verfasser hirnverbrannter Versspielereien, bei denen man ebenso staunen muß, dass ein Mensch auf derartige mühselig ausgetüftelte Künsteleien seine Zeit vergeuden und sie für Poesie halten konnte, wie daß er damit bei einem Kaiser Beifall zu finden vermochte."

7. Courtney 1990: 5; cf. Green 2010: 65: "Optatian ... is not a household name. He has low visibility, and perhaps, even in today's inclusive age, a high degree of risibility in the eyes of some scholars, depending on their viewpoint." Smolak 1989 offers a useful review of bibliography on Optatian up to and including the late 1980s; cf. Polara 1974a, 1974b, 1975.

8. For a review of recent re-evaluations, see this volume's introduction: other helpful overviews include Alan Cameron 2004b; Formisano 2007 (likewise attempting to reach "toward an aesthetic paradigm of Late Antiquity"); McGill 2012a (discussing Optatian briefly at 336–7); Hernández Lobato 2012 (esp. 307–11, 471–9, on Optatian); and Pelttari 2014: esp. 1–11 (with analysis of Optatian at 75–84). Earlier—but still fundamental—are Malamud 1989 (with fleeting mention of Optatian on 39–41) and Nugent 1990 (arguing that "our time may be peculiarly well-suited to understand the poetics of Ausonius," 27).

9. Since the original submission of this chapter in early 2014, the "morphogrammatic" nature of Optatian's poetry—and in particular its testimony to the "cultural transformations in the age of Constantine"—has been made the subject of an interdisciplinary workshop, co-organized with Johannes Wienand at Cologne's Internationales Kolleg Morphomata (in July 2015): for a preliminary overview of that project, see Wienand and Squire 2015; an edited book, based in part on workshop presentations, will be published as Squire and Wienand, forthcoming.

10. Doria 1979.

11. Levitan 1985: 249. Levitan was nonetheless rather ambivalent about Optatian's project, associating it with a cultural and literary "impasse" in the early fourth century (269): "Frankly, the poems make unremarkable, even banal reading—competent verse for the most part but repetitive and very tired ... Optatian is not a good poet; he is not even a bad poet. His poems are prodigies, monsters in the literal sense" (246).

discussion of Optatian's "spectacle du pouvoir" and "écriture 'à contraintes.'"[12] Beyond the disciplinary realm of (Anglo-Saxon) classics, and within the wake of Ulrich Ernst's landmark 1991 study of *carmina figurata*, scholars have also turned to Optatian's Western medieval reception:[13] we can be sure that Middle Age readers held Optatian in considerably higher esteem than their nineteenth- and twentieth-century counterparts, composing erudite commentaries,[14] as well as revivalist imitations.[15] All this suggests a more complex picture than the one so often assumed. Optatian, I suggest, *does* merit discussion—not only on account of his posthumous influence, but also because of his unique and multifaceted contribution to the literature of the fourth century.

Such revisionist scholarship provides the scholarly backdrop for my own reappraisal in this chapter. Through his combined visual and verbal modes, as we shall see, Optatian gives figurative form to the dynamics of cultural transformation in Constantinian Rome. Like Optatian's kaleidoscopic *carmina* themselves, perpetually poised between different modes of signification, Optatian's hybrid poetics display a Janus-face, at once looking forward and back. Wherever we turn, we find Optatian painting an extraordinarily graphic picture of a world in cultural, intellectual, and theological flux.

---

12. Cf. Rühl 2006 ("Die Materialität der Zeichen, die normalerweise beim Lesen zurückgedrängt wird, ist hier gerade Verständnisprinzip und tritt gleichberechtigt neben die Signifikatsfunktion," 84); Hose 2007: esp. 548–51 ("eine exegetische Operation [wird] durch den Leser verlangt, der einen neuen 'Sinn' aus dem Text ermitteln kann," 551); Bruhat 2009 ("En inventant un langage poétique visuel dans lequel les contraintes formelles reflètent au plus près la contrainte de l'idéologie constantinienne, la poésie porfyrienne à la fois produit son propre spectacle et reproduit le spectacle de pouvoir," 125). Numerous other studies could be cited here: e.g., Cox Miller 1998: 122–6 (rearticulated in 2009: 48–52); Bruhat 1999: esp. 439–51, 2008; González Iglesias 2000; Okáčová 2006, 2007; Scanzo 2006; Letrouit 2007; Green 2010; Pipitone 2012b: esp. 95–146; Pelttari 2014: 75–84 ("Optatian's poems are more than poetic puzzles, and they are not mindless games or angst-ridden exercises," 84); cf. also Squire 2015a.

13. Ernst 1991: esp. 95–142 (with further comments in Ernst 2012: 58–61); cf. Smolak 1989: 242–3. On Optatian's place within a longer Western tradition of "optical poetry," Ernst 2012 now provides the best anthology (with a second volume eagerly awaited: Ernst, forthcoming); cf. d'Ors 1977; Adler and Ernst 1987; Higgins 1987 (discussing Greek and Latin examples on 19–24 and 25–53, respectively, with reference to Optatian on 25–8); Grimm 1989; Ernst 1992, Ernst 2002: esp. 8–10, 28–32; Pozzi 2002; Dencker 2011; Hamburger 2011; Milewska-Waźbińska 2013.

14. See Polara 2004b and above all Pipitone 2012b (classifying the extant scholia into three dominant chronological groups: 25–94), with detailed review of earlier scholarship. On Optatian's manuscript transmission, see below, n. 26.

15. The most important discussion remains Ernst 1991: esp. 143–842 (with overview on 838–41); cf., e.g., Kluge 1924: 328–36; Düchting 1968 (on Sedulius Scottus in ninth-century Ireland); Ernst 1984; Higgins 1987: 25–53; Polara 1987, 1987–8, 1991, 2004a: 19–24; Dachowski 2008: 198–9, 226–31 (on Abbo of Fleury's tenth-century imitations); Pipitone 2011; Ganz 2013 (on Hrabanus Maurus's ninth-century *In honorem sanctae crucis*); Squire, forthcoming b (with figures 1.8–11 and plates 8–12). The poems were evidently familiar to such authorities as Saint Bede—even if he ultimately judged Optatian's poems unsuitable monastic reading "because they were pagan" (*quia pagana erant, nos tangere non libuit: de arte metr.* = Keil 1857–70: 7.258).

But the cultural poetics of "POP art" take on a still broader significance. If Optatian's concerns are inherently metapoetic and metaliterary, always turning in on the stakes of writing, they are also "meta-artistic," formed from an interpretive homology between pictorial and poetic composition. Optatian might epitomize what Michael Roberts has characterized as the "jeweled style" of late antique poetry.[16] But his poems also parallel what Jaś Elsner has called the "exquisite miniatures" of contemporary fourth-century art:[17] by interrogating the interface between visual and verbal signs, Optatian's works make sense only in the context of late antique visual culture—the shifting trajectory of what Alois Riegl famously (and in deeply Hegelian terms) deemed "art's will to itself," or *Kunstwollen*.[18] Such intermedial complexity makes Optatian a particularly rich case study for approaching late Latin poetics. And yet, in practical terms, it only adds to the challenge of finding a place for "POP art" within the disciplinary field of classics. Indeed one of the reasons why Optatian is less known than he should be, I think, is that he breaks free of modern (sub)disciplinary classifications: his works defy our strict categorizations between "art" and "literature"—the strict segregation of German "Klassische Philologie" on the one hand from "Klassische Archäologie" on the other.[19]

It is the intertwined visual and literary dimensions of "POP art" that the present chapter sets out to explore. Now, there is much to say about Optatian, both in terms of the political and historical backdrop of Constantinian Rome and in literary relation to other fourth-century Latin (one might also add *Greek*) poets.[20] Because Optatian's poems amount to miniature creations in their own right, moreover, each and every poem calls for individual attention: turning poetry into a self-standing concern of poetic composition, all the while giving rise to further exegetic commentary (hence the various scholiast embellishments, in some cases perhaps even as early as during the fourth

---

16. See Roberts 1989a (with brief mention of Optatian on 58).

17. For the phrase, see Elsner 2004: 283–4, on the "move from large-scale work in sculpture to the making of exquisite miniatures (in ivory, silver, glass, and precious stone, as well as in painted manuscripts"), along with 293–303; cf. Elsner and Hernández Lobato's introduction to this volume.

18. See Riegl 1901: esp. 209–17 (translated as Riegl 1985: 223–34): for discussion, cf. Elsner and Hernández Lobato (in the introduction to this volume, 25, with n. 46), along with Squire 2009: 74–7 for bibliography on the broader "Vienna School" context.

19. On the scholarly stakes and history of that disciplinary split, see Squire 2011: 372–81, esp. 377–81 (with further bibliography), arguing against the model of "classical art and text" championed by, e.g., Small 2003. Specifically on the "intersystemic hybridization" of late antique art and literature, see Hernández Lobato 2012: 468, 470–518.

20. The most important historical reading of Optatian's poems—as a commentary on Constantine's political exploits—is now Wienand 2012a: 355–420; cf. also Wienand 2012b and 2012c, along with Van Dam 2011: 158–70.

century itself),²¹ the Optatianic corpus knowingly defies hermeneutic finality. This short chapter cannot therefore survey all thirty-one extant poems attributed to Optatian, nor does it tackle issues of sequence and evolution—the contested (but important) philological attempt to put his works in temporal order.²² Instead, I restrict myself to "aesthetics" in the broadest sense, exploring the shared poetic and artistic dynamics that stretch between Optatian's poetry and contemporary visual culture.

Three overlapping themes provide us with our structural framework. First, I draw attention to Optatian's "materialist aesthetics,"²³ exploring the poet's celebration of the physical artefactuality of his works, while also situating that concern against a longer classical literary, artistic, and critical backdrop. The second section then homes in on the "dynamic signs" that make up the Optatianic corpus: on the one hand, I argue, Optatian's obsession with oscillating visual-verbal forms—with signs that change before the very eyes of his reading/viewing

---

21. For the earliest scholia, see Pipitone 2012b: 28–30, 91–3, endorsed by Wienand 2012a: 371, n. 44: regarding the scholia of poems 2–3, 5–8, 10, 12–16, 20–1 and 25, Wienand argues, we might recognize "einen gemeinsamen Autor ... , der seine Lektüreanweisungen möglicherweise bereits in constantinischer Zeit verfasst hat." Perhaps still more significantly, that idea of commentary is itself inscribed within the Optatianic corpus: so it is, for example, that poem 4 offers a clear introduction to poem 5 (Polara 1973: 2.39–41), commenting on both its context and *uersus intexti*; likewise poem 17 functions as a preface to poem 18 (cf. Polara 1973: 2.100–1), citing in full the seven verses hidden in the following poem, which are readable in so many different directions (17.14–20). While poem 17 is usually deemed a posthumous insertion, other poems likewise offer elaborate instructive glosses on how to proceed, as best demonstrated by 2.12–18.

22. Of the 31 *carmina*, poems 21–8 are frequently considered later than the others (whether written by Optatian or by some subsequent imitator); poems 29–30 derive from Fulgentius, and poem 31 was associated with the corpus in the nineteenth century. This tradition is already enshrined in the edition of Müller 1877 (which prints poems 1–20 as the *Panegyricus Constantini* and poems 21–8 as *carmina reliqua*). Much has been written about the respective chronology of Optatian's poems (cf., e.g., Barnes 1975: 177–83; Bruhat 1999: 273–4, 493–501; J. S. Edwards 2005; and Wienand 2012a: esp. 371–3): many of poems 1–20 refer to victorious military campaigns led by Constantine, and the first poem is clearly written from exile (with multiple allusions to Ovid's own exile poetry). Rejecting poem 17 as a later imitation ("a metrical explanation of [poem] XVIII composed by a much later hand": Barnes 1975: 178), Barnes consequently proposed that the remaining first twenty poems of Polara's edition were sent to Constantine in the autumn of AD 324, and that Optatian returned from exile to Rome soon thereafter (ibid. 184; cf. below, 31–2). But there are good reasons for rejecting this hypothesis (and above all the supposed connection between Optatian's exile and that of Ceionius Rufius Volusianus in AD ca. 315): on the one hand, Bruhat 1999: 9–16 has convincingly given Optatian's exile a *terminus post quem* of AD 322–3; on the other, there are substantial grounds for situating Optatian's return from exile at some time after the summer of AD 326 (cf. Wienand 2012a: 355–6, n. 1, Squire 2015a: 111, n. 50, and below, 73). I am evidently more sceptical than others about the precise chronology of the poems, as indeed about the reconstruction of their specific historic contexts and audiences: Johannes Wienand will return to these issues – and to Optatian's biography – in his contribution to Squire and Wienand, forthcoming.

23. I take the phrase from Porter 2010, who uses it in relation to broader Graeco-Roman ideas about "matter, sensation and experience" (cf. esp. 7–14). While I do not mean to suggest this to be something wholly "new" in Late Antiquity (cf. Squire 2011: 247–302 and Porter 2011 on the shared literary and

audience—aligns with a broader cultural preoccupation with multilayered levels of poetic meaning; on the other, I suggest that this new-found interest also responds to the syncretic melting pot of fourth-century visual culture, whereby single images could perform multiple sorts of hermeneutic duty. Just as Optatian probes the dynamic role of the reader, he also interrogates the active contribution of the viewing subject: reading and viewing are figured as parallel (if mutually implicated) acts of subjective volition. The point goes hand in hand with my third and final theme, dealing as it does with "poetry in pieces."[24] Perhaps more than any of his contemporaries, Optatian constructs his literary creations as fragmented (and fragmentable) *spolia*: from the collective level of the anthologized "book" to the tessellated unit of the individual letter (each woven into multiple constructive and deconstructive patterns—and hence pregnant with multiple registers of visual-verbal meaning), Optatian's dynamic artefacts prove simultaneously old and new. While forged from the past, these are poems that are defiantly—and self-consciously—innovative, always lending themselves to further feats of subjective *re*-creation.

Taken together, these three aesthetic themes prefigure many of the concerns that subsequent contributors will chart in relation to other late antique Latin authors. When it comes to "POP art," however, my suggestion is that such preoccupations take on a knowingly optical dimension, at once poetically *and* visually attuned, and thus as relevant to the historian of fourth-century art as to the classical philologist. If Optatian encapsulates some of the shifting perspectives of late antique Latin literature, he also figures a prototypically late antique recalibration of the image: Optatian's iconotextual creations probe not just what it is to *read* but also (and very much by extension) what it means to *view*.[25]

1. A Materialist Aesthetics

Let us begin, then, with Optatian's carefully crafted calibration of poetry as physically manufactured entity. I restrict myself here to three observations, relating first to Optatian's concern with the material presentation of his poetic

---

materialist concerns of Hellenistic poetry and visual culture), I do think that Late Antiquity sees an intensification of that earlier materialist literary concern: cf. M. Roberts 1989a, along with, e.g., E. James 1996, 2004, and 2007 (on later Byzantine materials).

24. More generally on the "aesthetics of fragmentation," see Hernández Lobato 2012: 257–317; cf. ibid. 381–3 on "atomización estética"; also, see Elsner and Hernández Lobato in their introduction to this volume (8–11).

25. For the language of the "iconotext," see Wagner 1995: 12, with discussion in, e.g., Squire 2009: 300–1.

oeuvre; second, to the associated "pictorial" poetics that governs his work; and third, to the cultural parameters shaping that particular outlook (the way in which the very form of Optatian's poetry constructs and reflects a larger view of the world, or *Weltanschauung*). "POP art," I argue, literalizes a long-standing literary critical parallel between "painting" and "poetry." But it also expresses a new preoccupation with the interface between seeing and reading—a theme that would in turn be instantiated in the theological disputes of late antique Christian thinkers.

So what sorts of material form did Optatian's work take? Despite the best efforts of classical scholarship, we cannot be sure about the "original" anthological form(s) in which Optatian's poems were collected. The thirty-one extant *carmina* attributed to Optatian are preserved in over twenty extant codices dating from between the eighth and seventeenth centuries; most of those manuscripts, moreover, differ in both the number of anthologized poems and in their sequence. While traditional philology has attempted to trace the textual transmission of different *stemmata*, there is in fact very little evidence about what—in concrete terms—any fourth-century edition(s) looked like.[26] We can nonetheless be confident that Optatian envisaged at least some of his poems as making up a single, physical "book." It is also clear that Optatian put particular emphasis on the physical appearances of that collection. The first poem, which leads the sequence in six manuscripts (and which was clearly intended as an opening preface to a larger collection), champions the point: not only does the poem refer to Optatian's "beautiful little book" (*pulchro ... libello*, 1.1), its elegiac couplets are also carefully modelled after (inter alia) the opening lines of Ovid's first book of *Tristia* (*trist.* 1.1.1–14).[27]

The allusion to Latin literature's most famous exile poet is important. In this chapter, I resist the temptation to get sidetracked into details about Optatian's biography and political career (something that scholars have tried to reconstruct not only from his poems but also from tantalizing inscriptions and later literary

---

26. Poems 1–3, 5–16, and 20 recur most frequently and in the most important manuscripts. On the manuscript tradition, see Polara 1971, summarized in 1973: 1.vii–xxxiv, and 2004a: 33–8; cf. Gualandri 1977: esp. 179–84, Ernst 1991: 209–21, and Wienand 2012a: 371–3. "All we can say for certain is that Optatianus created an unknown total number of poems over an unknown span of time," concludes J. S. Edwards 2005: 449, "and that some lesser portion of those poems were composed specifically for presentation to Constantine." But I am not convinced by Edwards's associated a priori argument that "a sequential chronology for the poems can be established when evidence of relative complexity is considered" (448).

27. For a hugely stimulating discussion of the late antique "preface"—and its relation to "a late antique turn towards an aesthetics focused upon the reader's work of interpretation" (72)—see now Pelttari 2014: 45–72; compare also the chapters by Harrison and McGill in this volume.

references).²⁸ But the fact that our poet modelled his anthology on Ovid's—that Optatian too was banished from Rome, compiling a collection of poems from exile—is fundamental to understanding his materialist concerns. We do not know the precise reason for Optatian's exile, nor indeed can we be certain about its date (most likely sometime between the years AD 322 and 326): an "unjust lot" (*sors iniqua*, 20a.22) and "sad destiny" (*fata | tristia*, 2.11–12) are said to have befallen the poet, derived from a "false accusation" (*falso ... crimine*, 2.31; cf. 2.5–6).²⁹ Crucially, though, Optatian's exile seems to have spurred a particular collection of poems addressed to the emperor. According to the *Chronicle* of Eusebius (in the version of Saint Jerome), "[Optatian] Porfyrius was released from exile after a remarkable volume was sent to Constantine" (*Porphyrius misso ad Constantinum insigni uolumine exilio liberatur*) in the year AD 329: it was thanks to an *insigne uolumen* that Optatian was able to ingratiate himself with the emperor's inner circle—and resume his political career in Rome.³⁰

This "panegyric" context helps to explain Optatian's particular attention to the physical presentation of his work.³¹ Consider, for example, the elegiac *sphragis* poem that we have already mentioned: Optatian paints a vivid picture of a former mode of presenting his poems, "all shining in purple, written with letters that glitter in silver and gold ... well adorned by the hand of the writer" (*ostro tota nitens, argento auroque coruscis | scripta notis ... | scriptoris bene compta manu*, 1.3–5); at the same time (and in deeply Ovidian terms), Optatian contrasts that poetic artefact with his present gift from exile—where the page is "now pale, tinted with each leaf in a black colour, scarcely distinguishing

---

28. For a brief overview (with bibliography), see Squire 2015a: 90–1. The 21 most relevant *testimonia* are catalogued in Polara 1973: 2.1–6, and the author offers an additional summary in the "nota biografica" of Polara 2004a: 25–6; cf. Seeck 1908, Barnes 1975, Smolak 1989: 237–9, Bruhat 1999: 2–31, and Wienand 2012a: 355–61. Note also the recent contribution of Davenport 2013: esp. 232–3 (a discussion of an important inscription from Sparta, which confirms that Optatian served as proconsul of the province of Achaea between AD 326 and 329: *SEG* 11.810 = *AE* 1931.6).

29. The best discussion of this exile motif is Bruhat 1999: 16–20. On the dating of Optatian's exile, cf. above n. 22.

30. *Chron.* on 329 [= R. Helm (ed.) 1956: 232]. This historical context (and Optatian's exile in particular) might perhaps be seen as reflected in the generic heading for his poems in extant manuscripts. Despite their wide variations in the number and arrangement of poems, most extant codices preserve a single title for their anthologies: Optatian's collective work amounts to a *Panegyricus*. On the significance of that title, see Polara 1973: 1.viii–xvi, along with Bruhat 1999: 31–43, and Wienand 2012a: 365–73 (albeit supposing that the "panegyric" title "möglicherweise nicht aus constantinischer Zeit stammt," 371); like Pelttari 2014: 75, n. 5, I see no reason to doubt the title's authenticity. More generally on the "panegyric" stakes of Optatian's poetry, see Rühl 2006.

31. I know of no evidence to support the conjecture of J. S. Edwards 2005: 452, n. 15 (mistakenly attributed to Higgins 1987: 26), that "the poems may have been presented as engravings on colored stone tablets with the lettering filled in by varicolored precious metals." Higgins instead suggests that the poems "were probably realized in a large format in gold or silver on blue, purple, or black background."

its poems with impoverished cinnabar" (*pallida nunc, atro chartam suffusa colore, | paupere uix minio carmina dissocians*, 1.7–8).³² In the poems that follow, we find numerous references to the painterly qualities of the collection.³³ With their varying shades of (for example) purple, cinnabar, gold, and silver, these graphic works are even said to outstrip the palette of Greek Antiquity's most famous painter ("the painted page will dare surpass the waxes of Apelles": *picta ... | uincere Apelleas audebit pagina ceras*, 3.iii–iv).³⁴ Despite their much later date, extant presentations play out Optatian's thinking, adorning the page with not only black letters but also lines, letters, and grids of (for example) red, orange, and golden yellow (e.g., figure 1.1).³⁵ Although beyond

32. Cf. Polara 1973: 2.27–8, along with Garzya 1984: esp. 36–40, Rühl 2006: 90–1, and Pipitone 2012b: 100–3.
33. For the self-declared "painterly" and "colourful" qualities of Optatian's work, cf., e.g., 3.15, 3.35, 3.iii–iv, 4.7, 5.7–8, 5.25, 5.26, 5.iii, 6.34, 7.7, 8.1–2, 10.9, 18.21, 19.20, 22.9, 22.viii, 22.xiii–xiv, with discussion in Bruhat 1999: 114–15 and Bruhat 2009: 116 (with 115, n. 36). As Rühl 2006 argues, the physical—and deeply "epigraphic"—qualities of "POP art" materialize its "panegyric" role: if the texts double up as elaborately inscribed monuments to Constantine ("Der Einsatz dieser Schrift [*capitalis quadrata* resp. *monumentalis*] stellt Optatians Gedichte in eine Reihe mit Ehreninschriften und läßt das Pergament gleichsam zum steinernen Monument werden," 91), their use of multiple gold, silver, and purple colours relate to "der 'klassischen' Farbe erhabener Majestät" (97; cf. Bruhat 2009: 103–4). But a number of further puns operate behind these polychrome references, I think. For one thing, Optatian's talk of the colour "purple" (1.17, 20.13, 28.9 = 28.12) might be thought to play upon his own "porfyrian" name: the colour suits not only the imperial honorand but also Optatian Porfyry himself (and nowhere more so than in the final couple of the *sphragis* poem, with its reference to something "sparkling in its purple condition," *purpureo fulgens habitu*: 1.17); likewise, when Optatian embroiders another poem with the boast that "I, Publilius Optatianus Porfyrius, have played these [games]" (*Publilius Optatianus Porfyrius haec lusi*, 21.i), did part of the "play" lie in the use of colour to visualize the hand of "Mr Purple"? For another thing, the references to "gold" nicely pun on Constantine's own "golden age"—on the *aurea saecula* to which Optatian refers throughout the corpus (3.12, 3.18, 5.28, 7.24, 14.19, 15.6, 19.2, 19.32), not least in the hidden verses adorning his pages (*aurea sic mundo disponas saecula toto*, 2.ii; *uersu consignans aurea saecla*, 3.v; *aurei saeculi*, 10.v; *aurea ... insignia*, 12.iii; *aurea uictorem pietas sonat ubere lingua*, 18.iv): in these cases, the very presentation of Optatian's poems likely instantiated their message about the "golden" emperor whom they celebrate.
34. For the significance of 3.iii–iv, see Ernst 1991: 109, rightly emphasizing the intermedial nods not only to the "Vorbild" of Apelles's painting but also to music. Rather more puzzling about this declaration is the figurative form revealing it (figure 1.1) (cf. Bruhat 1999: 141–6; 2009: 119–20). For what are we to make of this image that purports "in such song to forge the countenance of Augustus" (*fingere ... tali ... carmine uultus | Augusti*, 3.i–ii)? Is this a knowing joke? Or does the claim to outstrip Apelles depend upon a different (and superior?) configuration of what images are/ might be? Since preparing this chapter, I have returned to those questions in a separate article dedicated to "reading" the portrait of the third poem (Squire, forthcoming a).
35. For a presentation of the manuscripts (albeit without illustrations), see Polara 1971: 7–35; cf. Squire and Wienand, forthcoming: plates 1–7. Figure 1.1 illustrates folio 5r (poem 3) from a sixteenth-century manuscript held in the Herzog-August Bibliothek at Wolfenbüttel (Codex Augustaneus 9 Guelferbytanus: cf. Polara 1971: 18–19, labelling the codex "W"): the letters of the *uersus intexti* are here written in red ink, and the gridded boxes containing them are likewise marked out in a golden yellow tint. But other extant manuscripts play with different presentations. Sometimes the patterns are marked using lines of precious gold (e.g., the sixteenth-century Codex Monacensis Latinus 706ᵃ: cf. Polara 1971: 19, on manuscript "M"). At other times multiple colours are used (e.g., Codex Parisinus 8916, dating to

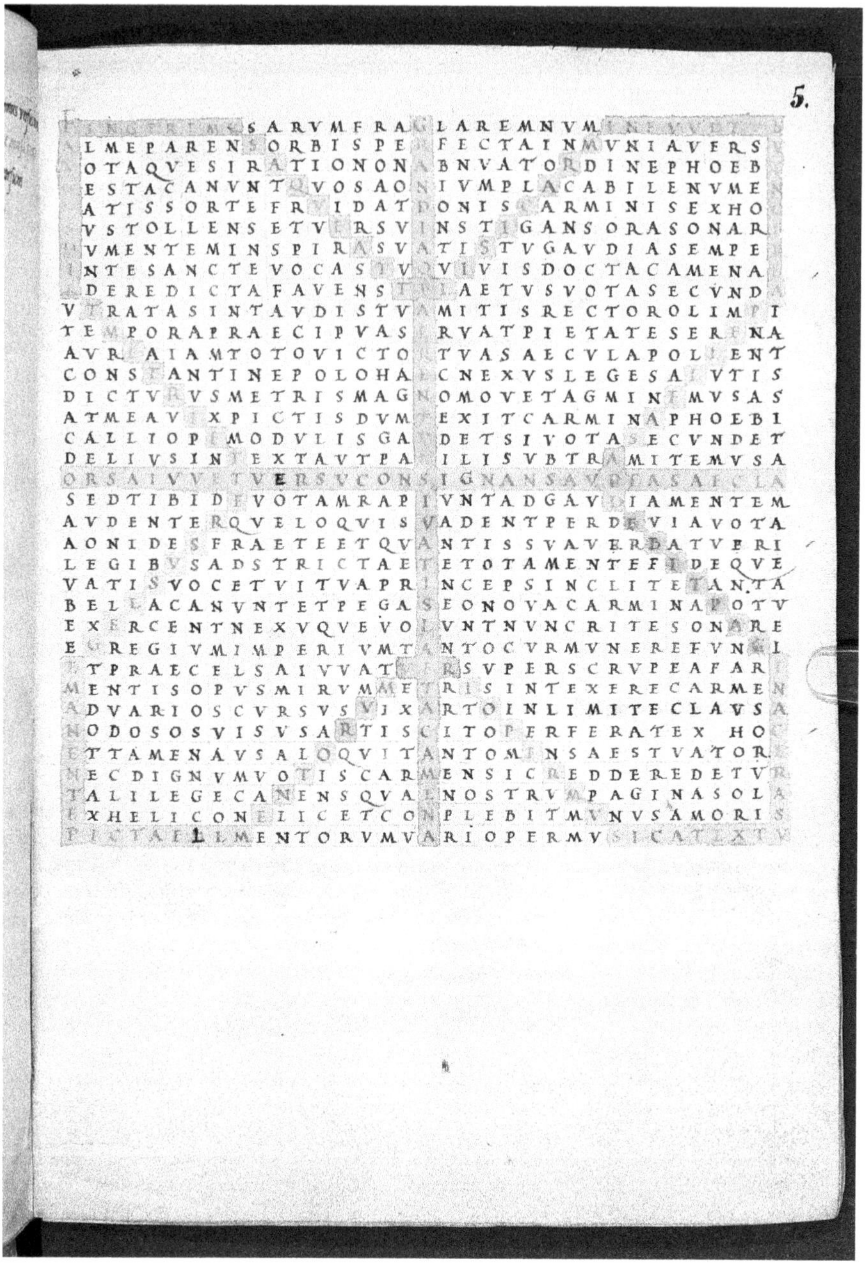

Figure 1.1. Folio 5r, from the sixteenth-century Codex Augustaneus 9 Guelferbytanus, showing a posthumous manuscript presentation of Optatian, poem 3. Reproduced by kind permission of the Herzog August Bibliothek, Wolfenbüttel.

empirical proof, Optatian's talk of the individual "leaf" (*charta*) and "page" (*pagina*) perhaps also suggests a particular physical conception of the material manuscript:[36] we are dealing here not with an unfolding scroll, I think, but with a bound codex, with each luxurious page carefully delineated from the one before and after.[37] The result is a physical book that literalizes the "floral" metaphor of the poetic "anthology": with its "varied flower" (*flore uario*, 19.35), each folio materializes the "blossoming" achievements (*florentia*, 19.12) of the Constantinian "golden age."[38]

At the heart of Optatian's poetry, then, is an idea of the work as a simultaneously material and literary entity—as something designed to be read with the *eyes*.[39] But the concern with the physical form of the text is not just an issue of material presentation. For Optatian, the artefactual aesthetics of his poetry is itself intrinsic to a new "calligrammatic" art of written composition.

the late fifteenth century, and omitted from Polara's survey: Optatian's poems are here set within colourful frames, sometimes of more than one colour; not only are the red cursive letters of the *uersus intexti* set apart from the black letters of the ground text, they are also marked out through additional lines painted in green, yellow, blue, red, and mauve colours—and indeed at times multiple polychrome combinations).

36. For references to the *pagina*, see 3.33, 3.iv, 4.2, 4.9, 7.11, 8.i, 9.13, 19.4, 19.35; for *charta*, see 1.7. Cf. Ernst 1991: 141, 2012: 59–60; Wienand 2012a: 364 ("Denkbar ist, dass damit lose Seiten gemeint sind, möglich—und wohl insgesamt wahrscheinlicher—ist aber auch, dass die einzelnen *paginae* zu einem Codex gebunden waren").

37. On the rise of the codex form, see especially C. H. Roberts and Skeat 1983, Blanck 1992: 75–101, Mazal 1999: 125–51, Stanton 2004, and Schipke 2013: esp. 143–52; cf. Engels and Hofman 1997: 67–76. On the luxury codices of Late Antiquity, see Mazal 1999: 95–8 (mentioning Optatian on 96), Mratschek 2000, and Zimmerman 2001. Schipke 2013 now provides the most detailed overview of 'das Buch in der Spätantike'—albeit without reference to Optatian.

38. For the image of "flowering," see, e.g., 7.28, 7.35, 10.32, 14.35, 17.19 (= 18.vi), 20a.9, 26.5, 28.9–12; for Constantine's "flowering leadership" (*florenti . . . ductu*), cf. also 18.11. The image, of course, takes on a metaliterary hue, referring back to the epigrammatic "Garlands" of Meleager and Philip (Argentieri 2007 provides a solid introduction, but the most important recent work is that of Kathryn Gutzwiller—e.g., K. J. Gutzwiller 1997, 1998: esp. 227–322, 2003). With Optatian, though, the image is itself literalized through poetic form: one way of making mimetic sense of the interwoven figure of poem 7 (figure 1.8), for example, is as itself a "flower," materializing the verbal image of the text (*florent*, 7.28; *floret*, 7.35).

39. One of the most revealing articulations of such thinking is to be found in the purported exchange of letters between Optatian and Constantine (for the text, see Polara 1973: 1.1–6, with commentary in ibid. 2.19–27; cf. Ernst 2012: 22–9): his work, Optatian writes, is to "be read by your serene eyes" (*legendum serenis oculis tuis, epist. Porf.* 2), just as Constantine purportedly responds by stating that "the variegated pigments of colours may delight the sensations of the eyes" (*oculorum sensus interstincta colorum pigmenta delectent, epist. Const.* 11). These letters—preserved in eight extant manuscripts—have long been declared by some as later medieval forgeries (cf. Polara 1973: 1.xxxi–xxxii, 2.19–20). But there are good linguistic and contextual reasons for thinking them authentic: the fullest recent discussion is Bruhat 1999: 23–31 (concluding that, despite problems of style and content, "en somme, il ne semble pas possible de prouver que ces lettres sont des faux," 31); cf. Müller 1877: viii; Dörries 1954: 127–8; Barnes 1975: 174, n. 4, 185–6 (suggesting a date in the winter of AD 312–13, as restated in 2011: 84, 209–10, n. 34); Millar 1977: 472 n. 46; Bruhat 2009: 106–7, n. 12; Green 2010: esp. 69–71; Van Dam 2011: 159–62; Pipitone 2012a; Wienand 2012a: 358, n. 6. Whether or not these letters amount to a genuine correspondence between poet and emperor, they certainly do give an excellent insight into Optatian's early critical reception.

Optatian's three surviving "picture-poems" provide the neatest introduction to that thinking. Dealing respectively with an altar (poem 26 [figure 1.2]), a set of panpipes (poem 27 [figure 1.3]), and a "pneumatic organ" (poem 20, [figure 1.4]), these poems exploit their external material form to convey a mimetic impression of the objects that they verbally evoke.[40] In each of these so-called *imagines metrorum* (literally "images of verses": 26.23), the feat lies in using alphabetic letters as figurative building blocks. Optatian's talking altar (figure 1.2), for example, is made not from any three-dimensional material medium ("not from hard stone has the artist smoothed me," *non caute dura me poliuit artifex*, 26.7), but rather from acatalectic iambic trimeters ("the metrical measures fashion me from the models of the Muses," *me metra pangunt de Camenarum modis*, 26.19): as a result, readers can actually *view* our altar as it speaks ("you see how I stand as an altar dedicated to the Pythian Apollo," *uides ut ara stem dicata Pythio*, 26.1).[41] Optatian's sounding *Fistula* (figure 1.3) exploits its fifteen hexameters to accomplish something similar: by consecutively decreasing the number of letters in each of the poem's fifteen verses—by starting out with forty-two alphabetic units in the first line but ending with twenty-eight letters in the last—the poem gives a schematic impression of the stepped musical instrument to which it refers. The same feat—albeit now reversed—also gives shape to Optatian's *Organ* (figure 1.4). This time, the poetic artefact is composed of two sets of twenty-six verses sandwiched either side of an additional hexameter (which substitutes the organ's "valves": "it is pleasing to pay certain vows with Augustus as victor," *Augusto uictore iuuat rata reddere uota*): where the left-hand poem (20a) is written in catalectic iambic dimeters, with eighteen letters in each line, the right-hand hexameter poem (20b) ascends from twenty-five letters in verse 1 to fifty letters in verse 26.[42]

Of course, such picture-poems were not a new feat in the early fourth century. If Optatian's altar, panpipes, and organ remind modern audiences of much later Western literary parallels (above all, works from the late nineteenth and twentieth centuries associated with Stéphane Mallarmé and Guillaume Apollinaire in particular [e.g., figure 1.5]),[43] they also knowingly respond to an

---

40. On these poems, see, e.g., N. W. Helm 1902: 43–4; Levitan 1985: 255; Polara 1987: 163–5, 1991: 295–301; Ernst 1991: 98–108; Rühl 2006: 76–7; Bruhat 2009: 102–3; Wienand 2012a: 361–2; Pelttari 2014: 76–7.
41. For the allusion here to *AP* 15.25.7, see below, n. 47.
42. On the imperial connotations of the visualized object in poem 20 (and its knowing response to the bucolic *syrinx* of Alexandrian precedent), see the important discussion of Bruhat 2009: 120–2: "la virtuosité de cette poésie, elle aussi savante, égale celle de l'instrument impérial" (122).
43. On the history of Western "calligrams," see now Dencker 2011 (with brief mention of Optatian on 181, 620–3), along with the bibliography cited above, n. 13. For a bilingual edition (with critical notes) of Apollinaire's *Calligrammes* (*Poems of War and Peace*, 1913–16), see Apollinaire 2004.

XXVI

```
          V I D E S V T A R A S T E M D I C A T A P Y T H I O
          F A B R E P O L I T A V A T I S A R T E M V S I C A
     S I C P V L C H R A S A C R I S S I M A G E N S P H O E B O D E C E N S
          H I S A P T A T E M P L I S Q V I S L I T A N T V A T V M C H O R I
 5        T O T C O M P T A S E R T I S E T C A M E N A E F L O R I B V S
          H E L I C O N I I S L O C A N D A L V C I S C A R M I N V M
          N O N C A V T E D V R A M E P O L I V I T A R T I F E X
          E X C I S A N O N S V M R V P E M O N T I S A L B I D I
          L V N A E N I T E N T E N E C P A R I D E V E R T I C E
10        N O N C A E S A D V R O N E C C O A C T A S P I C V L O
          A R T A R E P R I M O S E M I N E N T E S A N G V L O S
          E T M O X S E C V N D O S P R O P A G A R E L A T I V S
          E O S Q V E C A V T E S I N G V L O S S V B D V C E R E
          G R A D V M I N V T O P E R R E C V R V A S L I N E A S
15        N O R M A T A V B I Q V E S I C D E I N D E R E G V L A
          V T O R A Q V A D R A E S I T R I G E N T E L I M I T E
          V E L I N D E A D I M V M F V S A R V R S V M L I N E A
          T E N D A T V R A R T E L A T I O R P E R O R D I N E M
          M E M E T R A P A N G V N T D E C A M E N A R V M M O D I S
20        M V T A T O N V M Q V A M N V M E R O D V M T A X A T P E D V M
          Q V A E D O C T A S E R V A T D V M P R A E C E P T I S R E G V L A
          E L E M E N T A C R E S C V N T E T D E C R E S C V N T C A R M I N V M
          H A S P H O E B E S V P P L E X D A N S M E T R O R V M I M A G I N E S
          T E M P L I S C H O R I S Q V E L A E T V S I N T E R S I T S A C R I S
               5        10       15       20       25       30       35
```

Figure 1.2. Optatian, poem 26 (after the typographic presentation of Polara 1973). Reproduced by kind permission of Giovanni Polara.

XXVII

```
          P R A E C E L S A E Q V E R C V S F R O N D E N T I I N V E R T I C E P E N D E N S
          T E S T O R T E M P L A L O C I F A V N O S C E L E B R A R E F R E Q V E N T E S
          D I S P A R I B V S C O M P A C T A M O D I S T O T I D E M Q V E C I C V T I S
          D V L C I S O N O P A N V M O B L E C T A N S M O D V L A M I N E S I L V A S
 5        N A I A D V M D R Y A D V M Q V E C H O R O S A R C A N A Q V E B A C C H I
          O R G I A E T H E V V A N T I S S A T Y R O S P E R M V S I C A T E M P E
          M E P A N A D T H I A S O S D O C V I T M O D V L A M I N A C A N T V S
          E T V A R I A T A S O N I S V I N X I T C O N S O R T I A P R I M V S
          A T T I S A L M V S A M A N S T V A M A X I M A C V R A C Y B E L E
10        E R O S E O T E R I T O R E D E V S M O L L I Q V E L A B E L L O
          A C C E N D I T Q V E T V O S I D A E O S M A T E R A M O R E S
          I N M E F E L I C E S A N I M A V I T C A R M I N E M V S A S
          M E I V D E X F O R M A E A L T A G E S T A V I T I N I D A
          M E L A E T I S O C I A M V O T I V I C I N A M A R I T O
15 E O O L V C I S C A N I T I N V I T A T A S V B O R T V
               5        10       15       20       25       30       35       40
```

Figure 1.3. Optatian, poem 27 (after the typographic presentation of Polara 1973). Reproduced by kind permission of Giovanni Polara.

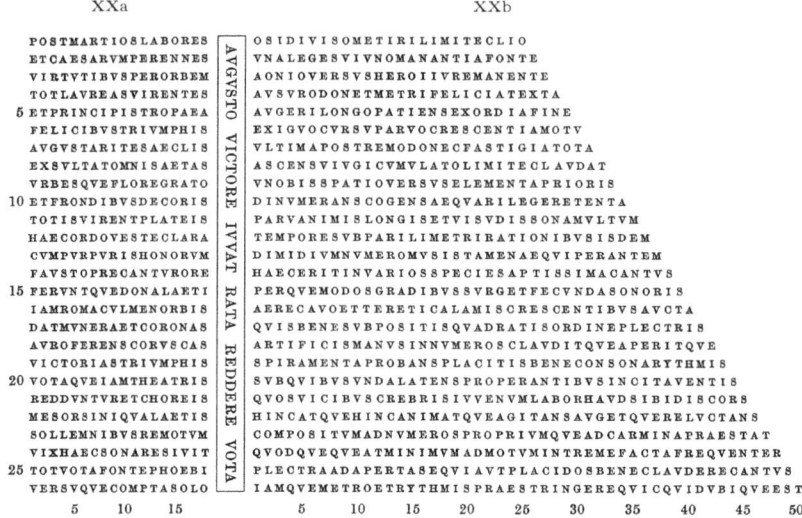

Figure 1.4. Optatian, poem 20 (after the typographic presentation of Polara 1973). Reproduced by kind permission of Giovanni Polara.

earlier Alexandrian tradition of so-called *technopaegnia*. Six Greek picture-poems are preserved in the Palatine Anthology (*AP* 15.21-2, 24-7), ascribed respectively to Simmias (probably in the early third century BC: an "egg," "axe," and "wings of Eros," *AP* 15.22, 24, 27 [figure 1.6]), "Theocritus" ("panpipes": *AP* 15.21), Dosiadas (an "altar": *AP* 15.26), and Besantinus (an "altar," complete with acrostic: *AP* 15.25 [figure 1.7]);[44] we also know of a neoteric first-century BC Latin imitation (Laevius's poem on a *Pterygium Phoenicis*).[45] Our poet seems to have had this genre very much in view:[46] for Optatian, as for earlier writers, the game lay in literalizing epideictic epigram's invocations to "look!"—offering physical images of the objects described.[47] No less revealingly, Optatian also changes the working

---

44. For a detailed commentary on the six extant Greek picture-poems, see Kwapisz 2013: 59–190, along with the earlier work of Strodel 2002. There has been a surge of scholarly attention over the last five years: for my own views (and further bibliography), see Squire 2011: esp. 231–5, and 2013c: 98–107; cf. Ernst 1991: 54–94; Guichard 2006; Männlein-Robert 2007: 140–54; Luz 2008, 2010: 327–53; Kwapisz 2013: 3–56; Pappas 2013.

45. Cf. Ernst 1991: 95–6, along with Courtney 1993: 119, 136–7.

46. On Optatian's debt to his Alexandrian predecessors here, see Bruhat 1999: 45–75 and Squire 2015a: 93–8, as well as the earlier discussion of N. W. Helm 1902: esp. 43–4. More generally on the supposed "neo-Alexandrianism" of late antique poetics, see Charlet 1988, with sanguine response by Pelttari 2014: 4–5.

47. Note, for example, the opening call to "look upon me" in Simmias's poem on "Eros" (λεῦσσέ με, *AP* 15.24.1), as well as Besantinus's declaration that the reader "look upon me as an altar" (ἐς γὰρ βωμὸν ὁρῇς με, *AP* 15.25.7)—a phrase directly translated in poem 26.1 (*uides ut ara stem dicata Pythio*). On Greek epigram's trope of "looking," see, e.g., Rossi 2001: 17, n. 13, along with Squire 2010a: esp. 613, and 2010b. The classic analysis is Goldhill 1994, but cf. also D. Meyer 2005, 2007; Petrovic 2005; Männlein-Robert 2007; Prioux 2007; Tueller 2008.

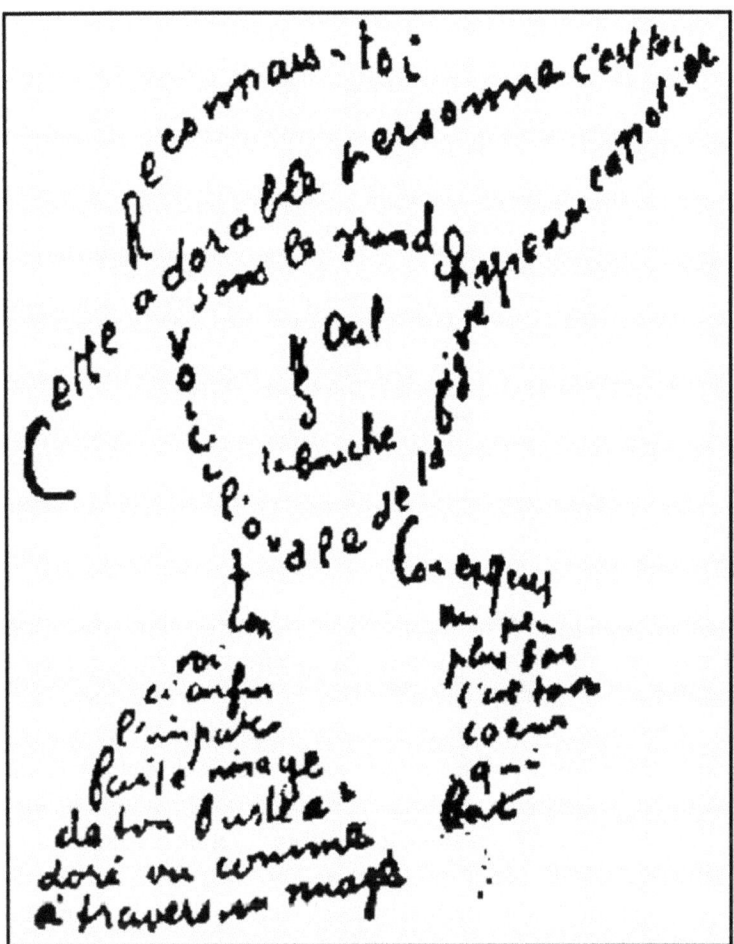

Figure 1.5. Line drawing after Guillaume Apollinaire, "Reconnais-toi" ("Recognize yourself"), 1915. Although the order of the text can be read in multiple ways, the lines that make up this female portrait read: "Reconnais-toi / Cette adorable personne c'est toi / Sous le grand chapeau Canotier / Oeil / Nez / La bouche / Voici l'ovale de ta figure / Ton cou exquis / Voici enfin l'imparfaite image de ton buste adoré / Vu comme à travers un nuage / Un peu plus bas c'est ton coeur qui bat." Photograph by the author.

principle. Where Greek poets had constructed their poetic pictures through metrical means—by lengthening and shortening the number of metrical units in each verse—Optatian instead varies the number of alphabetical letters in his lines. The number of metrical feet consequently stands on a steady isometrical footing, even while "the elements of their poems increase and decrease" (*elementa crescunt et decrescunt carminum*, 26.22).[48]

---

48. For the difference, cf. Luz 2010: 329–30 (with 330, n. 13). As Okáčová 2007: 62–3 rightly emphasizes (comparing 20b.14–19 and 27.3), the innovation in these three picture-poems is therefore not just of form

40 *The Poetics of Late Latin Literature*

```
1                           κωτίλας
3                         τῇ τόδ' ἄτριον νέον
5                    πρόφρων δὲ θυμῶι δέξο·δὴ γὰρ ἁγνᾶς
7                   τὸ μὲν θεῶν ἐριβόας Ἑρμᾶς ἔκιξε κᾶρυξ
9              ἄνωγε δ' ἐκ μέτρου μονοβάμονος μέγαν πάροιθ' ἀέξειν
11         θοῶς δ' ὕπερθεν ὠκυλέχριον φέρων νεῦμα ποδῶν σποράδων πίφαυσκεν
13          θοαῖς ἴσ' αἰόλαις νεβροῖς κῶλ' ἀλλάσσων, ὀρσιπόδων ἐλάφων τέκεσσι·
15        πᾶσαι κραιπνοῖς ὑπὲρ ἄκρων ἱέμεναι ποσὶ λόφων κατ' ἀρθμίας ἴχνος τιθήνας·
17      καί τις ὠμόθυμος ἀμφίπαλτον αἶψ' αὐδὰν θὴρ ἐν κόλπωι δεξάμενος θαλαμᾶν μυχοιτάτωι
19      κἆιτ' ὦκα βοᾶς ἀκοᾶν μεθέπων ὅ γ' ἄφαρ λάσιον νιφοβόλων ἀν' ὀρέων ἔσσυται ἄγκος·
20       ταῖς δὴ δαίμων κλυτὸς ἴσα θοοῖσι ποσὶν δονέων ἅμα πολύπλοκα μεθίει μέτρα μολπᾶς.⁴⁰
18       ῥίμφα πετρόκοιτον ἐκλιπὼν δροῦς· εὐνὰν ματρὸς πλαγκτὸν μαιόμενος βαλιᾶς ἑλεῖν τέκος·
16         βλαχαὶ δ' οἰῶν πολυβότων ἀν' ὀρέων νομὸν ἔβαν τανυσφύρων τ' εἰς ἄντρα Νυμφᾶν·
14            ταὶ δ' ἀμβρότωι πόθωι φίλας ματρὸς ῥώοντ' αἶψα μεθ' ἱμερόεντα μαζόν,
12               ἴχνει θενὼν (     )ταν παναίολον Πιερίδων μονόδουπον αὐδάν,
10                  ἀριθμὸν εἰς ἄκραν δεκάδ' ἰχνίων, κόσμον νέμοντα ῥυθμῶν,
8                         φῦλ' ἐς βροτῶν ὑπὸ φίλας ἑλὼν πτεροῖσι ματρός.
6                            λίγειά μιν †καμφι ματρὸς ᾠδίς·
4                                 Δωρίας       ἀηδόνος·
2                                        ματέρος
```

Figure 1.6. Egg of Simmias (*AP* 15.27). Text and typesetting reproduced by kind permission of Christine Luz.

It is this principle of gridded letters, laid out symmetrically in space, that seems to have inspired Optatian's "trademark" compositional form: the so-called *carmen cancellatum*, or "gridded poem."[49] With the three picture-poems discussed above, we remember, the materialist conceit depends upon the number of verses and letters in each line: words are broken down into single alphabetic units; the overarching effect resembles an elaborate *stoichêdon* inscription—a network of boxed letters transferred from stone to the page.[50] Yet by marking out individual gridded letters with additional patterns—by using either lines or different colours to "embroider" the selected squares within the poem—Optatian saw

---

alone but also one of metapoetic commentary ("the description of the imitated objects goes hand in hand with the explanation of the designs of the poems": 63, n. 35). The most striking example comes in Optatian's *Organ* (figure 1.4), where the isometric variation in the number of letters is explicitly compared with the instrument's capacity to vary musical pitch: although the poetic game here depends upon a visual response to the "organ" evoked, to declaim the poem aloud would be to occlude its visual form—so that its literal lengthenings (are said to) imitate this instrument of aural music. Here, as throughout the corpus, Optatian is responding to a much longer tradition of theorizing "voice, writing and image," ultimately rooted in the conceits of Hellenistic Greek poetry, and of epigram in particular (on which, see Männlein-Robert 2007, Tueller 2008, Floridi 2013, and Christian 2015: esp. 28–107): "What the poet basically presents us with in his creations is a 'voiceless text', impossible to be read aloud, but at the same time open to a variety of readings (e.g., backward, forward, horizontal or vertical)—that is, he makes us concentrate on the linguistic structure instead of the meaning it communicates" (Okáčová 2006: 44; cf. Bruhat 2009: 110–13, arguing for a much more complex "complémentarité parfaite, organique, de l'écrit—ou de l'inscrit—et de l'oral," 113).

49. Although not directly attested, the name is taken from poem 21.i–ii: "the Muses disperse verses that are intermingled either with circuitous windings or else with gridded bends that proceed in the opposite track" (*mixta per amfractus diducunt carmina Musae, | seu cancellatos spatia in contraria flexus*).

50. On the history of Greek *stoichêdon* inscriptions, see Austin 1938, along with, e.g., M. J. Osborne 1973, McLean 2002: 45–8, and Butz 2010.

Ὀλὸς οὔ με λιβρὸς ἰρῶν
Λιβάδεσσιν οἷα κάλχη
Ὑποφοινίηισι τέγγει·
Μαύλιες δ' ὕπερθε πέτρης Ναξίης θοούμεναι
Παμάτων φείδοντο Πανός· οὐ στροβίλωι λιγνύι
Ἰξὸς εὐώδης μελαίνει τρεχνέων με Νυσίων.
Ἐς γὰρ βωμὸν ὁρῆις με μήτε γλούρου
Πλίνθοις μήτ' Ἀλύβης παγέντα βώλοις,
Οὐδ' ὃν Κυνθογενὴς ἔτευξε φύτλη
Λαβόντε μηκάδων κέρα,
Λισσαῖσιν ἀμφὶ δειράσιν
Ὅσσαι νέμονται Κυνθίαις,
Ἰσόρροπος πέλοιτό μοι·
Σὺν οὐρανοῦ γὰρ ἐκγόνοις
Εἰνάς μ' ἔτευξε γηγενής,
Τάων ἀείζωιον τέχνην
Ἔνευσε πάλμυς ἀφθίτων.
Σὺ δ', ὦ πιὼν κρήνηθεν, ἥν
Ἲνις κόλαψε Γοργόνος,
Θύοις τ' ἐπισπένδοις τ'ἐμοὶ
Ὑμηττιάδων πολὺ λαροτέρην
Σπονδὴν ἄδην. ἴθι δὴ θαρσέων
Ἐς ἐμὴν τεῦξιν· καθαρὸς γὰρ ἐγώ
Ἰὸν ἰέντων τεράων, οἷα κέκευθ' ἐκεῖνος,
Ἀμφὶ Νέαις Θρηικίαις ὃν σχεδόθεν Μυρίνης
Σοί, Τριπάτωρ, πορφυρέου φὼρ ἀνέθηκε κριοῦ.

Figure 1.7. Altar of Besantinus (*AP* 15.25). Text and typesetting reproduced by kind permission of Christine Luz.

that new material forms could be teased out of each miniature poetic composition. Still more significantly, those graphic forms, spun from the written fabric of the text, could themselves be read in metrical terms.

Throughout the corpus, Optatian plays with the figurative capacity of writing (no less than the "readable" capacity of images) in hugely innovative ways. The genre evidently grew from the poet's penchant for acrostics, mesostics, and telestics (as reflected in the thirty-first, thirteenth, eleventh, and sixteenth [figure 1.19] poems, which respectively feature one, two, three, and four such vertically readable lines, each tumbling down the horizontal march of the verses).[51] But Optatian soon exploited such multilinear logic to weave designs that shuttle in horizontal, vertical, and diagonal directions. Sometimes, his grids are arranged in nonsymmetrical or uneven designs (poems 9 [36 letters down: 37 letters across], 12 [18: 35], 19 [38: up to 38], 21 [16: up to 43], 22 [10: 36]); at other times, Optatian returned to his most common mode of presentation, with grids consisting of a symmetrical square of thirty-five letters both across and along

---

51. Compare also poem 12, which binds an acrostic and telestic with a central double lattice pattern (cf. Hose 2007: 549–51). On the history of Greek and Roman acrostics, the two most important overviews are Vogt 1966 and Courtney 1990; cf. Luz 2010: 1–77 and Squire 2011: 224–6 (with references to other more recent discussions).

VII

Figure 1.8. Optatian, poem 7 (after the typographic presentation of Polara 1973). Reproduced by kind permission of Giovanni Polara.

the horizontal/ vertical axis (poems 2, 3 [figure 1.1], 5, 6, 7 [figure 1.8], 8, 10, 14, 18, 24). In each case, the individual verses proceed in linear fashion from left to right. At the same time, though, the gridded poems also operate spatially: they contain within them patterns that can themselves be read as additional poems—"interwoven verses" (*uersus intexti*) spun from the fabric of the text.[52]

One of the most remarkable aspects of these *carmina cancella* is their variety. Optatian's visual-verbal patterns take on different representational rationales,

---

52. The term *intextus uersus* is itself embroidered into the final "interwoven verse" of the ninth poem (9.v): cf. 21.16 (*texti . . . uersus*). On Optatian's metapoetic language of "weaving" here, cf. below, 84–5.

ranging from the mimetic through the alphabetic to the more abstract and ornamental.⁵³ Sometimes, the *uersus intexti* add up to geometric patterned or floral adornments (poems 2, 3, 7, 12, 18, 21, 22 and 23); at other times, they comprise recognizable schematic forms—perhaps a shield in poem 7 (figure 1.8), a palm frond in poem 9, and a military operation in poem 6 (the schematic outline of an army in quincunx formation). Alternatively, the cryptic outlines take on the cumulative shape of giant alphabetic (and by extension also numerical) forms: so it is, for example, that we find *uersus intexti* in the shape of the letters *AVG. XX CAES. X* in poem 5 (celebrating the anniversaries of Constantine and his two sons in AD 326) or else the name *IESVS* spelled out in poem 8 (figure 1.20). Optatian characteristically blurs any straightforward distinction between the alphabetical and the ornamental, always delighting in the combined material and symbolic qualities of his figurative writing: the dizzying designs of poem 10, for example, are simultaneously structured around a figurative letter *X* at the centre, chiastically criss-crossing the poem (figure 1.9); likewise the monogrammatic *chi-rho* "chrismons" of poems 8, 14, 19, and 24 (figures 1.20–1.23) add up to symbolic *and* alphabetic designs, combining at one and the same time both verbal and visual patterns of significance.⁵⁴ In arguably the most complex of all such examples, the nineteenth poem combines multiple visual and verbal rationales on a single "page"—a ship (complete with tiller, rudder, oars, and ramming spike) is topped with a mast and sail (emblazoned with a *chi-rho*), with other letters set around it (both the *VOT*, above, and the numerical *XX* that comprises the ship's hull) [figure 1.23].⁵⁵

What, then, should we make of Optatian's concern with the graphic qualities of writing?⁵⁶ In one sense, Optatian could of course look back to a much longer tradition of thinking about words, images, and the interplay between the two. The idea of "writing" as "drawing"—literalized in Hellenistic and Imperial calligrams—is inscribed into the very language of ancient Greek, in which *graphein* (likes its cognates *graphê* and *gramma*) figures both activities

---

53. For the categories ("geometrische Gittergedichte," "literale *carmina cancellata*," and "gegenstandsmimetische Gittergedichte"), see Ernst 1991: 108–35; cf. Bruhat 1999: 134–70 and Rühl 2006: 81–2 ("graphische Muster," "'Bilder,'" and "neue Buchstaben").

54. Cf. below, 64–74.

55. Cf. below, 72–4.

56. The classic discussion of "script" as a language in its own right—as a mode of textual organization revealing patterns of significance that are at once distinct *and* indistinguishable from the structures of linguistic convention—is Kristeva 1989: esp. 18–40; cf. more recently Hamburger 2011. Needless to say, Optatian's graphic creations also resonate with Jacques Derrida's diagnosis of writing's "aphoristic energy" (Derrida 1976: 18)—its intrinsic mode of not just "communicating" meaning, but also "supplementing" it.

44   *The Poetics of Late Latin Literature*

Figure 1.9. Optatian, poem 10 (after the typographic presentation of Polara 1973). Reproduced by kind permission of Giovanni Polara.

alike;[57] later in the fourth century AD, Servius commented on that homology explicitly, noting a conceptual parallel between "reading" and "seeing."[58] This was an idea enshrined in ancient literary and artistic criticism, too. As early as the fifth century BC, Simonides had likened painting to "silent poetry" and poetry to "talking

---

57. For the pun, see Lissarrague 1992; cf., e.g., R. Osborne and Pappas 2007 (on the earliest inscriptions of Greek vases) and Squire 2011: 235–42 (in relation to the *grammata* on the back of seven *Tabulae Iliacae*). On the consequent "graphic" games of Hellenistic ekphrastic epigram, see especially Männlein-Robert 2007: 123–7 and Tueller 2008: esp. 141–54. No extant ancient writer delighted in the pun more than the Elder Philostratus, exploiting the verb and noun some 130 times to refer to the collaborative "writings/paintings" in his third-century AD *Imagines* (cf., e.g., Squire 2013b: esp. 106–7, 109–10, 114–16; cf. Squire and Grethlein 2014: esp. 316–19; Squire and Elsner, forthcoming: 80).

58. Cf. SERV. ad *Aen.* 6.34 (= Thilo and Hagen 1923–7: 2.11): glossing Vergil's choice of the verb *perlegere* to refer to the act of looking (*perspectare*), Servius notes how, in Greek, the aorist infinitive γράψαι

painting."[59] By giving material form to the subsequent Horatian notion of *ut pictura poesis* ("as is painting, so is poetry": *ars p.* 361), Optatian crafts pictures which quite literally speak:[60] in these creations, we remember, self-declared *signa* are made to talk in the first person (as with his *Altar*), their pictorial form mimicking the musical instruments evoked (it is by *speaking* that the reader makes Optatian's pictorial *Organ* and *Fistula* sound).[61] All this knowingly develops a standard topos of Roman rhetoric, in which the gesture of summoning up a silent image was judged so powerful as "to seem sometimes to trump the force of speech itself" (*pictura . . . ut ipsam uim dicendi nonnumquam superare uideatur*, QUINT. *inst. or.* 11.3.67).[62] No less importantly, Optatian's poetry also works against the critical backdrop of what Greek rhetoricians came to label a "speaking out," or *ekphrasis* (both in the *Progymnasmata* and in elaborate scholiastic commentaries on canonical Greek texts). "Ekphrasis is a descriptive speech which vividly [*enargôs*] brings the thing shown before the eyes," as Theon's standard definition puts it (ἔκφρασίς ἐστι λόγος περιηγηματικὸς ἐναργῶς ὑπ' ὄψιν ἄγων τὸ δηλούμενον).[63] In Optatian's poems, the associated idea of oratorical *enargeia* ("vividness") is given material form on the page: verbal discourse metamorphoses into actual visual spectacle.[64]

---

may be said to mean both "to paint" and "to write" (*cum graece* γράψαι *et pingere dicatur et scribere*); cf. Squire 2009: 146–50 (esp. 147–8, n. 221, on a parallel use of the verb form *legis* on a mosaic from Pèbre, near Vinon in Roman Gaul).

59. PLUT. *mor.* (*de glor. Ath.*) 346F (= SIMON. frg. 190b Bergk): "Simonides relates that a picture is a silent poem, and a poem a speaking picture" (. . . ὁ Σιμωνίδης τὴν μὲν ζωγραφίαν ποίησιν σιωπῶσαν προσαγορεύει, τὴν δὲ ποίησιν ζωγραφίαν λαλοῦσαν); the bon mot was "bandied around" (θρυλούμενον), as Plutarch elsewhere puts it (*mor.* [*quomodo adul.*] 17F); cf. Carson 1992, Franz 1999: 61–83, and Sprigath 2004. On Simonides's debt to Homeric ekphrasis, see Squire 2013a; for the Platonic development of the topos (above all in *Phdr.* 275d, where the silence of painting is pitched against the destiny of words perpetually to repeat the same sentiment), see Männlein-Robert 2007: 31.

60. On the Horatian maxim, see esp. Hardie 1993, cf. Brink 1971: 368–72, Trimpi 1973: 1–34, Benediktson 2000: 127–39. For its rich subsequent reception, see, e.g., Hagstrum 1955, Praz 1970, and (more generally) Barkan 2013.

61. For the thematic of the sonorous and the visual in Optatian, see Bruhat 1999: esp. 66–7. More generally on ancient traditions of "ventriloquist" epigram, see Burzachechi 1962, with further comments in Tueller 2008: 16–27.

62. For the underlying Simonidean framework, cf., e.g., *rhet. Her.* 4.39: *poema loquens pictura, pictura tacitum poema debet esse*. More generally on Quintilian's advice about "summoning up" *uisiones* (translated from the Greek *phantasiae*), see Webb 2009: 93–6 on *inst. or.* 6.2.29–32, along with I. Henderson 1991, Vasaly 1993, Scholz 1998, Chinn 2007, Sheppard 2014: esp. 19–46; for associated Roman rhetorical discussions of *euidentia*, cf. Lausberg 1990: 359–66 (nos. 810–21).

63. Theon, *prog.* 118.7 (= Patillon and Bolognesi 1997: 66). The most insightful recent discussion of ancient ekphrasis is Webb 2009 (complete with appendix of the most important passages on 197–211); somewhat problematically, though, Webb treats the evidence of the *Progymnasmata* in isolation from broader traditions of ancient literary and rhetorical criticism (for some correctives, see, e.g., Rispoli 1984, Meijering 1987: esp. 29–52, Manieri 1998: esp. 179–92, and Nünlist 2009: 153–5, 194–8; cf. also Squire 2015b). More generally on late antique ideas of voice and vision, the best overview remains Boeder 1996.

64. Antiquity's most sophisticated dramatization of associated themes of "seeing" through "hearing" comes in Philostratus's third-century *Imagines* (a text already known and imitated by the time Optatian was writing: cf. Squire 2013b and Braginskaya 1985: esp. 26–7 on the ancient reception). Importantly,

46   *The Poetics of Late Latin Literature*

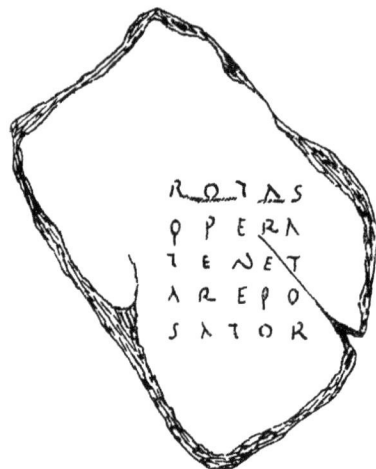

Figure 1.10. "Sator" palindrome square graffito from Watermore (near Cirencester), date uncertain. After Collingwood 1930: 174, fig. 49e.

If Optatian's pictorial-poetic feats resonate with traditions of literary criticism and rhetoric, they also find material parallels.⁶⁵ The fundamental concern with breaking the linearity of language—with spinning the logic of words into multiple semantic directions—recalls, for example, the rationale of so-called palindrome squares, in which short symmetrical Latin words could be read along both a horizontal and vertical axis (e.g., figure 1.10);⁶⁶ likewise, Optatian's

though, Optatian's text reaches poignantly beyond the limits of ekphrastic *enargeia* ("visual vividness"). Ekphrasis, as the *Progymnasmata* make clear, is always an art of "as if"—one that (as Philostratus acts out with phenomenal self-referentiality) *almost* brings about "seeing" through "hearing" and *all but* renders the audience as spectators (σχεδόν/ μονονού: Ps.-Hermog., *prog.* 10.48 [= Rabe 1913: 23]; Theon, *prog.* 119 [= Patillon and Bolognesi 1997: 69]; Nikolaus, *prog.* [= Felten 1913: 70]; "even if the speech were ten thousand times vivid (*enargês*)," as John of Sardis later remarked on a passage of Aphthonius's *Progymnasmata*, "it would be impossible to bring "the thing shown" or ekphrasized itself "before the eyes" (κἂν γὰρ μυριάκις ἐναργὴς εἴη ὁ λόγος, ἀδύνατον αὐτὸ κατ' ὄψιν ἀγαγεῖν τὸ δηλούμενον ἤτοι ἐκφραζόμενον = Rabe 1928: 216). By forging literal images out of his readable letters, Optatian's work rises to the ekphrastic challenges of the rhetoricians: the very fabric of his texts endows them with an *actual* iconicity.

65. See Squire 2011: 197–245 (with detailed bibliography), along with Habinek 2009.
66. The best discussion remains Ernst 1991: 429–59. On the numerous *Roma-olim-Milo-amor* inscriptions, see Guarducci 1965: 262–6, with further comments in 1967 and Veyne 1968; on related *Sator-Arepo-tenet-opera-rotas* "palindrome squares," see also Guarducci 1965: 266–70, along with 1978: 1743, n. 26 (with detailed bibliography, discussing numerous other such "giochi letterali"), and Dencker 2011: 577–82; I have not been able to consult Varone 1979: 53–71, 97–113. For a parallel Greek "palindrome square"—a (?) third-century AD example from under the Church of Santa Maria Maggiore in Rome, set alongside Latin word games (including Sator and Milo palindrome squares: nos. 18, 40)—see Castrén 1972: 71–2 (with ibid. 79, no. 24: σῦκα | ὕδωρ | κώπη | Ἄρης); cf. also Bua 1971: 16–17 on a Latin mosaic from a villa in Négrine el Kdima. As Habinek 2009: 133 concludes, "it is hard to see what function the palindromes have other than that of calling attention to writing's insistence on arbitrary patterns of visual perception."

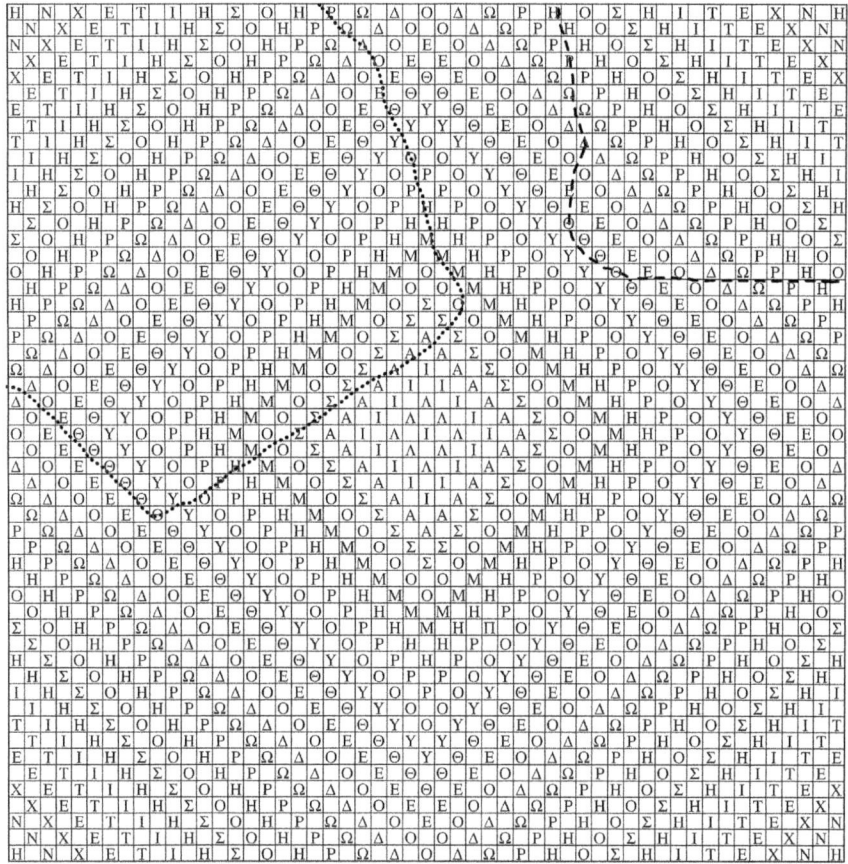

Figure 1.11. Reconstruction of the "magic square" on the reverse of two *Tabulae Iliacae* ("Iliac tablets"), late first century BC / early first century AD. The reconstruction incorporates the surviving portions of tablets 2NY (top left: New York, Metropolitan Museum of Art, inv. 24.97.11) and 3C (top right: Paris, Cabinet des Médailles, inv. 3318). Reconstruction by the author, after Squire 2011: 204, fig. 103.

gridded forms might remind us of the "magic squares" on the back of seven early Imperial *Tabulae Iliacae*, with their titular texts readable along multiple paths (and in two cases complete with the additional instruction to "seize the middle letter and glide wherever you choose," γράμμα μέσον καθ[ορῶν παραλαμβα]νε οὗ ποτε βούλει) [figure 1.11]).[67] The interest in making pictures out of alphabetic letter forms also finds earlier epigraphic precedent—from graffiti names laid

---

67. For the hexameter text (evidently repeated on tablets 2NY and 3C), and two different attempts to restore its missing middle feet, see Squire 2011: 204–5 and Petrain 2014: 67–8: the Greek word *gramma* underscores the visual-verbal point, referring simultaneously to the "strokes" of both alphabetical letters and pictures (cf. above, n. 57).

48 *The Poetics of Late Latin Literature*

out in iconic form[68] to inscribed couplets where the very subject is mimicked in the text's visual appearance.[69] But for all their conceptual archaeology in earlier traditions, Optatian's poems go much further. By self-consciously turning the poetic page into material artefact, Optatian emerges as a supreme *artifex*: with his "art painted in letters" (*arte notis picta*, 19.20; cf. *accipe picta nouis elegis*, 8.1), the poet spins a self-consciously "new art" (*ars noua*, 22.11)—and an art that proves to be both material and metric at once.[70]

In this sense, Optatian's feat is premised upon turning texts into material images, no less than transforming images into texts. In the fourth century, at the time when Optatian was working, we find numerous scenarios where language is used to comment upon (and indeed undermine) the picture. In line with a longer Greek and Latin tradition of pairing images with epigrams,[71] for example, a mosaic from the *triclinium* of a Romano-British villa at Lullingstone juxtaposes an elegiac couplet with its image of Europa and the bull, reframing the subject in literary terms (figure 1.12): while audiences are called upon to recognize the mythological story, the inscription invites them to read the image in terms of a distinctly Ovidian take on Vergil's *Aeneid*.[72] The later fourth century seems also to have witnessed the rise of a new form of presenting the canonical greats of classical literature, whereby codices of Homer, Vergil, and others were—for the first time, I think—adorned with painted miniatures.[73] Where a manuscript like the "Vatican Vergil" offsets its miniature vistas in elaborate frames of gold,

---

68. See esp. Langner 2001: 27–9 (on "Buchstabenspiele"), along with, e.g., J. R. Clarke 2007: 44–9.

69. Cf., e.g., Wojaczek 1988: 248–52, Courtney 1995: 328–9, no. 120, and Ernst 2002: 232–3 on CIL 4.1595 (= CLE 927: two snaking couplets on snake charming).

70. For the image of the *artifex*, cf. 26.7 and 20b.18. For Optatian's talk of *ars*, cf. 3.30, 6.14, 7.19, 19.20, 21.6, 21.9, 26.2, and 26.18 (and cf. also *epist. Con.* 10).

71. Cf., e.g., Prioux 2008 and Squire 2009: 239–93 on the "Casa di Properzio" at Assisi (evidently known in the fourth century—and labelled as a *Domus Musae*) and Squire 2013d on the "Casa degli Epigrammi" in Pompeii (V.1.18).

72. The inscription (= RIB 2447.9) reads *Inuida si t[auri] uidisset Iuno natatus | iustius Aeolias isset adusque domos* ("If jealous Juno had seen the swimming bull, more justly would she have approached the house of Aeolus"). For review of bibliography, see Squire 2009: 168–71; on the Ovidian allusions, see esp. Barrett 1978: 309–13; on the architectural context and iconography, see Scott 2000: 123–4. One modern (but I think unconvincing) interpretation has read the inscription in deeply cryptographic terms—as hiding within it a series of elaborate Christianizing messages: Henig 1997, 2000; cf. Thomas 1998: 47–54. More generally on Western Roman "literary" mosaics, including 26 with inscriptions, see Lancha 1997, along with Leader-Newby 2007.

73. Buonocore 1996: 142–58, nos. 1–3, provides a good overview with colour plates; for my own views about the emergence of narrative "illustration" in the fourth century, see Squire 2011: 129–39 (arguing against the still-canonical thesis of Weitzmann 1947 and 1959); cf. the essays in J. Williams 1999 (esp. Lowden 1999) and Mazal 1999: 293–377, along with Zimmermann 1998 and Schipke 2013: 152–62. Specifically on the "Vatican Vergil" (Codex Latinus 3225), presenting the *Georgics* and *Aeneid* along with 50 miniatures, de Wit 1959 is still key, but see too T. B. Stevenson 1983, Geyer 1989: 205–32, and Wright

Figure 1.12. Europa mosaic from the dining room of a Roman villa at Lullingtone in Kent, fourth century AD. Photograph by the author.

red, and black paint (e.g., figure 1.13), however, Optatian's ruse lies in a mutual layering of media: the text itself becomes the frame for the picture, just as the material text serves as frame for the multiple iconic poems contained within.[74]

Part of the explanation for this "materialist aesthetics" lies of course in the (explicit and deeply self-referential) quest for innovation.[75] A pragmatist interpretation might point to Optatian's need to attract the attention of the emperor— to wow Constantine with that alleged *uolumen insigne* so as to secure return

---

1993. More generally on the associations of these developments with the rise of the codex form, as well as the proliferation of monogrammatic emblems and alphabetic adornments in fourth-century manuscripts, the classic analysis remains Nordenfalk 1970: esp. 181.

74. On related issues of framing words and pictures here, see the essays in Platt and Squire, forthcoming—especially the contributions by Courtney Roby (on illustrated manuscripts) and Sean Leatherbury (on late antique mosaic inscriptions).

75. This idea of "novelty" emerges particularly clearly in Constantine's letter to Optatian (e.g., *noua iura, epist. Const.* 9), but it in fact recurs throughout the corpus (cf. below, 84–6): e.g., *noua carmina*, 3.24; *picta nouis elegis . . . | clementis pia signa dei*, 8.1–2; *nouas metris leges*, 9.iii; *noua uincula mentis*, 10.18; *nouare*, 16.3; *nouis . . . curis*, 21.4; *nouis mea pagina uotis*, 19.4; *nouum numen*, 19.8; *nouo . . . plectro*, 19.19; *ars noua*, 22.11; *noua gaudia*, 22.27, etc.

Figure 1.13. Folio 41r of the "Vatican Vergil" (Codex Vaticanus Latinus 3225), with a painted miniature of Dido's death and the text of VERG. *Aen.* 4.663–7. © HIP / Art Resource, NY.

from banishment. In literary terms, the ultimate aesthetic is likewise one of neoteric (and we might add deeply Alexandrian) "play." Within the rubric of what Ausonius would later in the fourth century label *technopaegnia*, Optatian paints his project in expressly ludic brushstrokes:[76] as the *uersus intexti* of poem 21 put it, boasting of their multicolour differentiations (*uario colore dispar*, 21.iii), "I, Publilius Optatianus Porfyrius, have played these [games], composing every

---

76. For the "ludic" terminology—and in a closely related context—cf. the introductory letter to Ausonius's *Technopaegnia*, where the book is expressly related to the activity of play (*lusi*): "I have given the little book the name *Technopaegnia* in order that you do not think it has been all work without play, or all play without art" (*libello Technopaegnii nomen dedi, ne aut ludum laboranti, aut artem crederes defuisse ludenti*, = Green 1991: 175, with ibid. 583–5). For discussion, see Flores and Polara 1969; M. Roberts 1989a: 38–65, esp. 58–9; McGill 2005: 4–10 (with further bibliography at 164, n. 19); Luz 2010: esp. xiii–xvii.

type of metre" (*Publilius Optatianus Porfyrius haec lusi* | *omne genus metri . . . pangens*, 21.i–ii).[77]

But I think something more is at stake. Optatian's concern with the iconicity of language certainly looks back to earlier literary and material traditions. At the same time, his materialist aesthetics also reflects a peculiarly new, late antique interest in the interrelated mechanics of visual and verbal representational modes.

To label that interest "Christian" would be too simple. For Optatian, as will become clear in the following section, "Christianity" seems to have preserved all the mystique of a new (and perhaps somewhat bemused) onlooker. One of the most kaleidoscopic aspects of Optatian's poems is in fact their slippage between different semantic frames of reference—their defiance of our shorthand scholarly dichotomy between "pagan" and "Christian": Christianity provided just one significatory system out of which to craft, shape, and mould panegyric.[78]

Optatian's "materialist aesthetic" is by no means exclusively (or straightforwardly) "Christian." Yet it does give figurative form to a thematic that would define the course of Christian thinking about images, no less than Western attitudes to writing. As at once "the Word made flesh" (ὁ λόγος σάρξ ἐγένετο: John 1:14) and the "image of the invisible God" (εἰκὼν τοῦ θεοῦ τοῦ ἀοράτου: Colossians 1:15), Christ might be described as be the ultimate "iconotext," His Incarnation fathomable only by pondering the relationships between what can be visually and verbally expressed.[79] Christology would subsequently come to be theorized in expressly visual-verbal terms, while giving rise to new ways

---

77. The same language recurs throughout the corpus: e.g., 5.16 (*ludent*), 10.10 (*ludere*). On earlier Greek and Latin traditions of spelling the poet's name through autographic acrostics (e.g., Nic. *Ther.* 345–53; Nic. *Alex.* 266–74; *Ilias Latina* 1–8, 1063–70; *P. Par.* 1; cf., e.g., Cic. *div.* 2.111–12), see Squire 2011: 224–6 (with more detailed bibliography).

78. The eighth poem is in fact the only one to spell out "Jesus" by name—and even then it does so figuratively (within the *uersus intextus* rather than in the hexameter fabric of the poem: see below, 64–70). Something similar can be said about the name "Christ," which is figured in the *chi-rho* chrismons of *chi-rho* of poems 8, 14, 19, and 24 but which (with the exception of 31.1, 3, 7, 12, falsely attributed to Optatian) only rarely occurs in the corpus: in poem 16, the name Χριστός is hidden in a Greek *uersus intextus* (16.ii; cf. below, 62–4); likewise, even in poem 24—the most explicitly "Christian" in outlook (but of doubted authenticity: see below, 71–2)—Christ's name occurs only twice (24.4, 18). On Optatian's "Christianity" and its Constantinian associations, see most recently Van Dam 2011: 168–70, Green 2010: 66–7, and above all Wienand 2012a: 396–420 ("Constantins Gott bleibt bei Optatian also primär ein Gott, der die Siege des Kaisers verbürgt," 397).

79. On the Christian theological word-image dichotomy and its intellectual roots in the writings of Saint Paul, see now Heath 2013: esp. 21–7; cf. Heath 2016 (the best introduction to "Christian" thinking about sensory sight more generally). On the development of new modes and forms of "graphicacy" in the fourth century ("a hybrid graphic formation that, properly speaking, is neither a text nor image," 9), cf. Garipzanov 2015.

of conceptualizing both visual and verbal signs in turn. On the one hand, the Incarnation sparked fierce debates about the (il)legitimacy of visually figuring Christian truths by pictorial means: Christian art, as is well known, was forged out of the impasse between Judaic strictures against the image and Graeco-Roman traditions of materializing the divine; as ever, moreover, such debates about pictorial representation were themselves waged in relation to the sanctified revelations of scripture (not least in Saint Gregory's later sixth-century defence of pictures as "the poor men's bibles," or *biblia pauperum*—a sentiment anticipated already in the fourth century AD).[80] On the other hand, Christianity would bring with it as a set a new and distinctive culture of reading, one focused around the "Gospel truth" of the Bible:[81] while championing the supremacy of the text, fourth-century Christianity would put great store in the material qualities of writing—and nowhere more so than when it came to so-called *nomina sacra* (pictographic figurations of holy names that facilitated a new, internalized mode of spiritual engagement with the names represented).[82]

Now, I do not mean to suggest that Optatian's concern with the materiality of poetry map straightforwardly onto these emerging "Christian" currents. But I do think that his layerings of different levels of meaning—his probing of the relationship between the immaterial and material, figurative and literal, alphabetic and iconic—is shaped by (and in turn gives shape to) a larger set of cultural ideas, ideas that would come to take on an expressly theological hue.

---

80. While the likes of Irenaeus argued in the second century that the Incarnation legitimated the image, others—among them, Justin Maryr, Origen, and (a little later) Eusebius—famously condemned images as idolatrous. Finney 1994 provides a good introduction, but see also Finney 1977, Barasch 1992: 95–182, Jensen 2000, and above all (the Hegelian retelling of) Besançon 2000: 81–108; there are also relevant discussions in Nasrallah 2010 and Kristensen 2013. On the Christological stakes of the argument, see especially von Schönborn 1976: 54–141, together with Elsner 1995: 97–124 (from the perspective of visual evidence itself). Saint Gregory's comments come in his thirteenth letter to Serenus (conveniently translated in Chazelle 1990: 139–40): see, e.g., Camille 1985: 26–7, Duggan 1989, Markus 1997: 34–50, and Gilbert 2001. Thomas of Aquinas would famously take up such thinking (cf. Besançon 2000: 148–64). But the Christian biblical justification for images already finds expression at the end of the fourth century: see Mratschek 2002: 404–6 and 595–6 on Paulinus of Nola, *carm.* 27.

81. On the "textual turn" of the fourth century, see in particular Elsner 2004: 284: "Christian art, with its explicit reference to scripture and other texts (commentarial, apocryphal, exegetic), stood in a fundamentally different relation to its subject-matter from pagan art. Christian images illustrated, commented upon, reformulated a pre-existing textual canon, while pagan images were contributions on their own right to an undogmatic culture of relatively unfixed mythological narratives."

82. On the *nomina sacra*, see the excellent analysis of Heath 2010 (with full review of historiography): "the *nomina sacra* provide a *visual* counterpart to the creeds, expressing the *intention* of the whole at the visual level of the page," Heath 2010: 537 concludes; "like a picture they highlight all at once the significance of the whole, though they are unable on their own to organize it semantically . . . it is plausible that seeing the page marked with the *nomina sacra* could have an immediate and vivid emotional power that was not fully transposable into creedal statement." More generally on the Christian, late antique cult of the material book, see especially Nicklas 2008.

The materialist experiments of Optatian's poetic-pictorial forms play upon the Christian inheritance of Graeco-Roman Antiquity, we might say, no less than upon the Graeco-Roman inheritance of Christianity.

2. Dynamic Signs

My comments about the "Christian" undercurrents surging beneath the Optatianic surface lead directly to my second frame for approaching his corpus: namely, as signs that metamorphose before the reader's eyes. Like the infamous "duck-rabbit" image discussed by Ludwig Wittgenstein (figure 1.14), Optatian's forms slip and slide between not just different registers of significance but also divergent worlds of meaning.[83] As such, his creations raise questions about how exactly to understand the boundaries not only between word and image but also between the symbolic and the literal—indeed, between the apparent, the figurative, and the *true*.[84]

Optatian, I suggest, was fully aware of that instability. Again and again—in the linear lines of his poems as well as (revealingly) in their revelatory hidden verses—Optatian talks of his poems as "signs," or *signa*.[85] When Saint Jerome mentions Optatian's *insigne uolumen* (that is, of a volume that is "notable" or "distinguished" for its *signa* within), he likewise responds to a critical tradition already written into the fabric of the extant corpus: not only does Optatian explicitly bill his work as something *insignis*, he also aligns it with his *insignis* imperial honorand.[86] But for the reader responding to these "heavenly signs" (*caelestia signa legenti*, 19.1), the objects of Optatian's stylus resist any uniform

---

83. See Wittgenstein 1972: 193–229 (first published in 1953), with the pertinent discussion of "multistable" images in Mitchell 1994: 45–57. On the "openness" and "layered meanings" of Optatian's poems, see now Pelttari 2014: 75–84: Pelttari draws a stimulating comparison with Umberto Eco's talk of *opera aperta* (first published in 1961, and translated into English—albeit in somewhat different form—as Eco 1989): "by creating a poem that can be read in more than one way (i.e., on various levels), a poet [like Optatian] allows the reader to inhabit the space between each layer" (Pelttari 2014: 74).

84. On Late Antiquity as an "era of interpretation," see this volume's introduction by Elsner and Hernández Lobato, 6–7.

85. Consider the following examples: *uicennia signa* (4.1); *signare* (5.2); *signare* (6.34); *signatur* (7.12); *pia signa* (8.2); *insignia magna* (8.27); *salutari nunc haec tibi pagina signo | scripta micat* (8.i–ii); *insignit* (11.8); *aurea . . . insignia* (13.iii); *signa* (16.29); *suis signis* (18.23); *caelestia signa* (19.1); *signis . . . notare* (19.17); *signa . . . laetissima* (19.29); *aeturnum . . . signum* (24.35).

86. One might compare here Optatian's purported letter to Constantine (on which, see above, n. 39), which frames the poet's works in relation to the many distinguishing honorific "signs" of Constantine's divine majesty (*tot diuinae maiestatis insignia*, epist. Porf. 6). For the trope of the "marked out," cf., e.g., *insigne . . . imperium* (7.5–6); *resonans insignia ramis* (9.19); *armis insignibus ardens* (9.23); *insignia fata* (19.36—referring to the "remarkable destinies" that the "blessed page" celebrates in its figured numerical characters of "floral polychrome," *flore notans uotum uario dat pagina felix*).

Figure 1.14. Optical illusion diagram of "Kaninchen und Ente" ("rabbit and duck") from the October 23, 1892, issue of *Fliegende Blätter*. Photograph by the author.

mode of "decoding." Taking shape against an incipient tradition of Christian semiotics, Optatian's creations give form to a world in cultural and religious flux. While in one sense prefiguring (as indeed destabilizing) the central concerns of Christian hermeneutics in the later fourth and fifth centuries, the dynamic "flips" of these signs figure the dynamics of a more substantive set of cultural transitions.

So what kind of *signa* do we find in Optatian's oeuvre, and what is at stake in their movement between different significatory systems? First and foremost, as we have said, Optatian's works fluctuate between verbal and visual modes. As with his so-called *carmina cancellata*, laid out in multidimensional grids, Optatian delights in *signa* that are poetic and pictorial at once—in an *ars* of visual and verbal craftsmanship that is quite literally squared on the page.[87] Many of the examples introduced in the first part of this chapter demonstrate

---

[87]. "The reader is pushed over the threshold of one order of experience—reading a text—into another—seeing a picture," as Malamud 1989: 39 concludes. Crucially, however, such "thresholds" remain perpetually open: audiences can always cross from one liminal mode of experience back to another.

the thinking. But few prove more revealing—or indeed more dynamic—than Optatian's eighteenth poem, comprising 1225 "boxed" alphabetical units within a grid of thirty-five by thirty-five letters (figure 1.15).

Despite its concrete appearance, the eighteenth poem self-consciously resists any unilinear reading. A single verse is inscribed around all four sides of the gridded square, so that its opening hexameter is not only repeated in its final

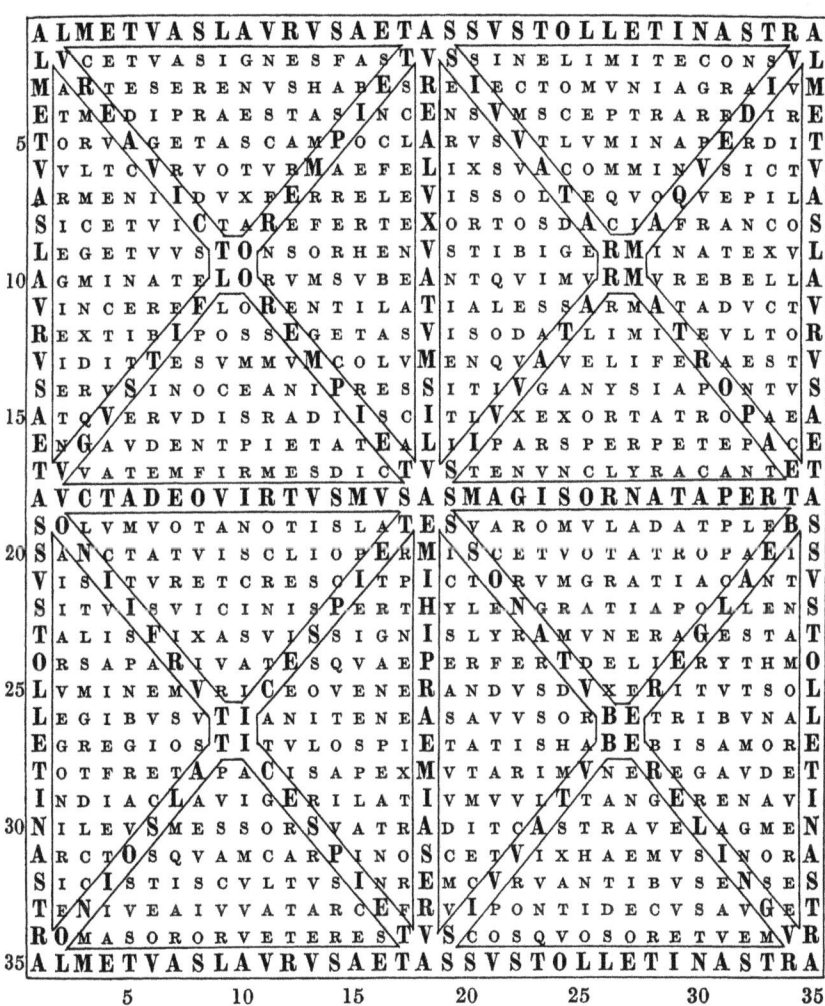

Figure 1.15. Optatian, poem 18 (after the typographic presentation of Polara 1973). Reproduced by kind permission of Giovanni Polara.

verse but also woven as an acrostic and telestic along the poem's left- and right-hand vertical lengths: *alme, tuas laurus aetas sustollet in astra* ("o propitious one, the age will lift up your laurels to the stars"). An additional mesostic runs down the symmetrical horizontal midpoint, itself perhaps once highlighted in gold (*aurea lux uatum, siluae mihi praemia serua*, literally "golden light of the poets, supply me with the rewards of the forest"). The overarching effect, when seen against the poem's symmetrical middle verse (v. 18), is to divide the poem into four quarters: in visual terms, our square is derived from (and in turn generates) yet more squares, giving shape to a quadruple field within.

While bound with a single verse on each of its four sides, the eighteenth poem also invites its audiences to think "outside" the box. Look more carefully, after all, and we find yet more squares squared within this gridded space: additional lattice patterns, rotated at a forty-five-degree diagonal angle, cut across both the poetic whole and its internal parts. For one thing, audiences are able to read along the thirty-five-letter lengths of its diagonals: if we proceed from left to right along the two criss-crossing diagonals—both from the first letter of the first verse to the last letter of the final line, and from the first letter of the final line to the last letter of the first verse—two further verses emerge (*aurea uictorem pietas sonat ubere lingua*, "A golden piety sounds the victor with copious tongue"; *Aonios latices pietas iuuat armaque diua*, "A piety delights the Aonian springs and the divine arms"). For another, additional diagonal patterns can be found within each of the four internal squares, metaphorically spinning the poem on its central axis, all the while furnishing yet more squares within the squared field of verse. As long as we read from left to right, each of these lattice patterns makes up a partial metrical unit. But to turn those units into self-standing hexameters, readers must choose between a multitude of different paths (each at once beginning and ending with the first letter of the alphabet).[88] If audiences start with the opening letter of v. 18 and move diagonally upwards, for example, they find *Augusti fl-*: depending on their subsequent exploratory direction, all manner of verses come into bud (*Augusti florem pietas sustollet in astra; Augusti florem pietas magis ornat aperta; Augusti florem pietas sonat ubere lingua; Augusti florem pietas iuuat armaque diua; Augusti florem pietas iuuat arma tropaea; Augusti florem pietas sonat ubere glaeba*).[89] Proceed from the same letter and along a lower diagonal (*Aonii fruti-*), and the poetic crop is no less fruitful or for that

---

88. On Optatian's "protean" poetry, see below, 86–90.
89. "Piety raises the splendour of Augustus to the stars"; "The disclosed piety adorns the splendour of Augustus all the more"; "Piety sounds the splendour of Augustus with a fertile tongue"; "Piety benefits the splendour of Augustus and his divine weapons"; "Piety benefits the splendour of Augustus, his arms and his trophies"; "Piety benefits the splendour of Augustus with fertile earth."

matter metrical: *Aonii frutices pietas sustollet in astra; Aonii frutices pietas magis ornata aperta; Aonii frutices pietas sonat ubere lingua; Aonii frutices pietas iuuat armaque diua; Aonii frutices pietas iuuat arma tropaea; Aonii frutices pietas sonat ubere glaeba*.[90] The preceding poem—which is sometimes deemed a later, non-Optatianic gloss on the poem at hand—comments on the dynamic spin, spelling out seven different available verses ("equal in their number of letters and analogous in their metrical law," *sunt septem numeros pares ac lege metrorum | consimilis uersus*, 17.1–2): "if you were thoroughly to explore the intricate word [*uerbum textum*] with a Latin mouth, connecting the verses in an order that is other than their own, you will be able to fill a long volume sounding out its vows" (*si uerbum textum pertemptes ore Latino | in sese alterno conectens ordine uersus, | uota sonans longum poteris implere uolumen*, 17.8–10).[91]

What fascinates me about the eighteenth poem is its simultaneously stable and unstable presentational mode. On the one hand, we are dealing with a "closed", single form—a solitary *uerbum textum*, bounded on all four sides with the same delineating verse. On the other hand, the individual constituent letters defy any single response, "opening up" multiple paths of interpretation: in the words of the preceding poem (whether a later, interpolative response or not), our explorations must necessarily stretch beyond the material *uolumen* before us. The poet ultimately leaves it to the reader to work out the verbal limits of this material form. But he also leaves the precise rules unstated. Of course, there *are* semantic limits at work here (one need only attempt to track the diagonals from right to left, for example, or else try marshalling one's verses through the centre, which would contravene both grammar and meter: e.g., *Augusti florem pietae mihi praemia serua*).[92] Crucially, though, readers are invited to determine those

---

90. "Piety raises the Aonian bushes to the stars"; "The disclosed piety adorns the Aonian bushes all the more"; "Piety sounds the Aonian bushes with a fertile tongue"; "Piety benefits the Aonian bushes and divine weapons"; "Piety benefits the Aonian bushes its arms and its trophies"; "Piety benefits the Aonian bushes with fertile earth." Cf. Levitan 1985: 261–3 (counting "through this field of thirty-five lines . . . over fifty paths and more than forty additional and unique hexameters"): ". . . the figure is so constructed that, in fact, *every* path of hierarchically distinguished letters a reader chooses to follow, beginning with the opening of *any* hexameter and ending with the close of *any* other, yields a sensible and metrically competent hexameter line" (263); see also Bruhat 2009: 109–10.

91. Such a sentiment, of course, poignantly foreshadows Barthes's famous analysis of the *lisible* in relation to the *scriptible* in the late twentieth century (Barthes 1974): "the goal of literary work (of literature as work) is to make the reader no longer a consumer, but a producer of the text" (4). For Optatian's own play with such thinking—in the context of poem 25—see below, 88–91.

92. The point strikes me as important. Every act of finding "sense" in Optatian's *signa* means trekking across all manner of nonsensical alternatives. For Optatian, as for Susan Stewart, "nonsense" consequently plays a key role interrogating how meanings are constructed: it "not only exaggerates features of common-sense reasoning to make them problematic, it also exaggerates aspects of the language in which that common sense is constructed, pointing to the arbitrary and potentially 'treacherous' nature of language as pure form" (S. Stewart 1978: 201).

semantic constraints for themselves: audiences must experiment with different modes of "delimiting" a poem in honour of Constantine, in turn declared "a consul without limit" (*sine limite consul*, 18.2). It is a game of experimentation—of trying out different modes of containing meaning—that is played out no less self-consciously in other scenarios. In poem 22 (figure 1.16), for instance, readers likewise have to reach beyond their initial wonder at this self-declared

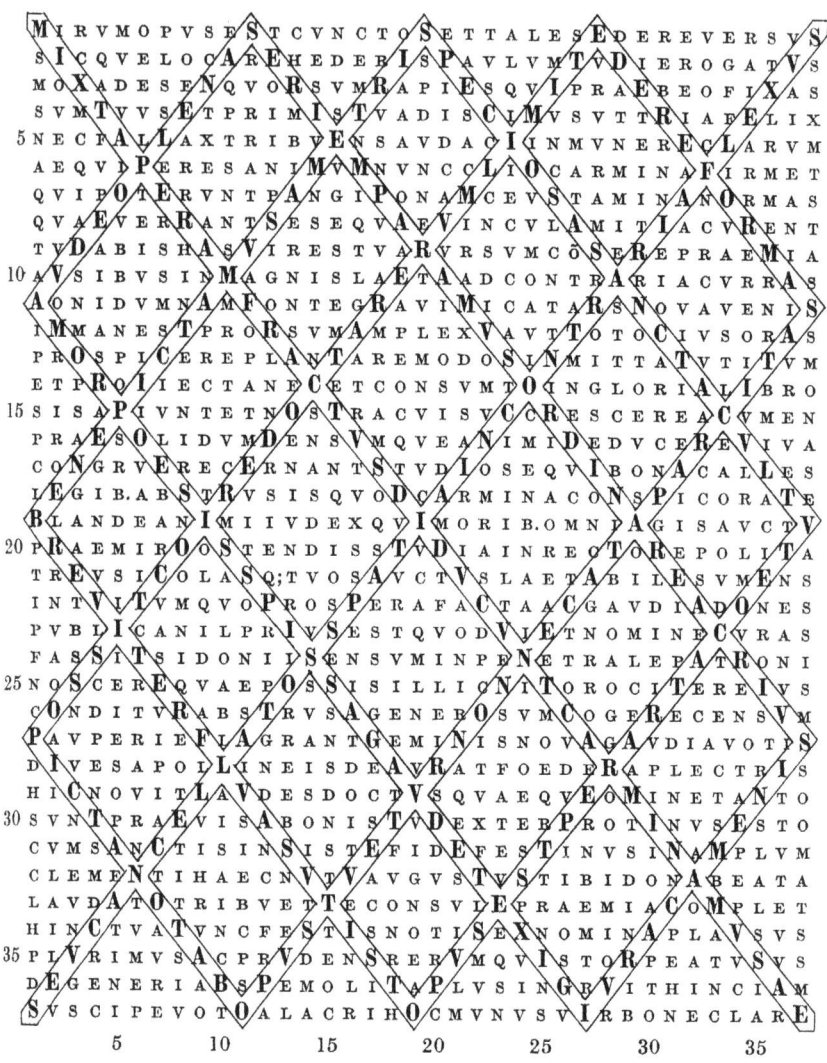

Figure 1.16. Optatian, poem 22 (after the typographic presentation of Polara 1973). Reproduced by kind permission of Giovanni Polara.

```
                                XXII

      MIXTAPERAMFRACTVSDIDVCVNTCARMINAMVSAE
      SEVCANCELLATOSSPATIAINCONTRARIAFLEXVS
           SERIEMPARAMVSORDINAREACRIVS
           AMORPOESISSPISSAGAVDETEXIGI
   5       POSSITCOIREDOCTARERVMLIMITE
           OPVSTVETVRNONNECATAPARCITAS
                SPECIOSASANCTACVLTV
                BENEPICTAMVSAMETRIS
                BREVITERFLVASVTISTO
   10           OPVSESTPERARTACOETV
                     AVDEOPLENAS
                     EDEREFORMAS
                     PICTANOTABO
                     IVRACAMENIS
           5      10     15    20    25    30    35
```

Figure 1.17. Rearranged *uersus intexti* of Optatian, poem 22 (after the typographic presentation of Polara 1973). Reproduced by kind permission of Giovanni Polara.

"marvellous work" (*mirum opus*, 22.1): in this case, it is only by reordering the latticed lines according to length—and then rejumbling those metrical constituent units—that audiences can arrive at an additional stepped figure-poem, one that otherwise goes unspoken within the linear lattice of the text (figure 1.17).[93]

But it is not just between visual and verbal *signa* that Optatian's works oscillate. In three poems (16, 19, and 23 [figures 1.19, 1.23, and 1.18]), we find Latin letters doing double duty as Greek signs: the single alphabetical units of each Latin hexameter are made to bear Greek registers of meaning, fluctuating between different lexigraphic systems.[94] With each example, the poems demand a change in readerly perspective (not to mention a degree of semantic judgment): where the Latin "C"

---

[93]. It should be noted here that the poem's authenticity has been questioned. According to Polara 1973: 1.xxix–xxxi, 2.140–1, there are sound reasons for thinking the poem a later addition to the corpus (cf. also Bruhat 1999: 36–9): quite apart from the abbreviations found only here and in poem 24 (*legib.* for *legibus*, 22.18; *morib.* for *moribus*, 22.19; *treuiscolasq.* for *treuiscolasque* 22.21), Polara points to, e.g., *proiiecta* (22.14), and *gaudia* (22.27—six letters squeezed into the space of five letters); he also notes the form *treuiscolas* (22.21), which he deems to have been derived from the German word 'Treue' (Polara 1973: 2.145–6). But however *difficillima* and *obscurissima*, the poem's more puzzling aspects can nonetheless, I think, be considered *antiquissima* (Müller 1877: xlii; cf. also Barnes 1975: 174, n. 4). "It is true ... that in this poem there are some uncharacteristic turns of phrase," concludes Levitan 1985: 260, "but on the whole its language is not so idiosyncratic as to warrant suspicion; and, considering the extreme difficulty of this type of writing and the individuality of the problems posed by each composition, we would do best to suspend judgment ..." (260). Something similar can be said, in my view, of poem 24, which Polara likewise deems a posthumous imitation (see below, 71–2, along with Squire and Whitton, forthcoming).

[94]. Optatian's intermingling of Greek with Latin finds intriguing contemporary parallels: among the most spectacular is Ausonius's "macaronic" 45-verse epistle to Paulus, written a little later in the fourth century and playfully mixing Latin and Greek words in its "two-tongued conversation" (*sermone ... bilingui: epist.* 6.2; cf. Green 1991: 614).

XXIII

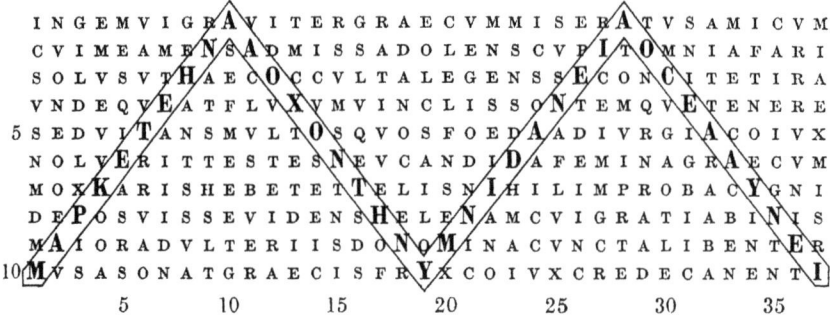

Figure 1.18. Optatian, poem 23 (after the typographic presentation of Polara 1973). Reproduced by kind permission of Giovanni Polara.

performs the duty of a Greek *sigma* (and likewise "H" as *eta*, "P" as *rho*, and "X" as *chi*), other letters depend on context for their appropriate Greek conversion ("T" serves as both *theta* and *tau*, just as "A" can signal the letters *alpha, delta*, and *lambda*). Proceed from this Greek linguistic viewpoint, and the Latin texts metamorphose before our eyes.

Poem 23 nicely demonstrates the "morphogrammatic" conceit (figure 1.18). In this example, Optatian claims to convey "hidden things" to the reader (*haec occulta legens*, 23.3)—to reveal something that is only obliquely implied in the poem's ground-text (with its talk of a "Phrygian husband," "Helen," and "two adulterers"). Heeding the explicit declaration that the "Muse sounds to the Greeks" (*Musa sonat Graecis*, 23.10), as well as the promise that the poet "gladly gives all the names" (*do nomina cuncta libenter*, 23.9), we duly find a new sort of significance. Not only does a zigzagging "M"-pattern spell out a shared Latin and Greek initial of a name (the "Marcus" addressed in the *uersus intextus*), its individual letters also yield a Greek hexameter:

Μάρκε, τεὴν ἄλοχον τὴν Ὑμνίδα Νεῖλος ἐλαύνει.
Marcus, Neilos is banging your wife Hymnis.

Optatian's Latin poem here conceals a literal Greek subtext: forms which might look like Latin nonsense ("M-A-R-K-E-T-E-H-N-A-A-O-X-O-N-T-H-N-Y-M-N-I-D-A-N-E-I-A-O-C-E-A-A-Y-N-E-I") spell out the otherwise unspoken *praenomen*, while also revealing the truth about Marcus's wife ("Hymnis") and her adulterer ("Neilos"). The movement from verbal units to zigzagging graphic pattern—that is, to a visual arrangement which, as an "M"-shape, can also be read in its own written right—acts out a literal transfiguration: the poem morphs between divergent sorts of *signa*.

In the case of Optatian's "Marcus" poem, the text presents signs that are literally dynamic—letters which not only break free from the linearity of language but which also fluctuate between different linguistic rules (*paroles*, we might say, that lend themselves to multiple *langues*).[95] With other poems, however, the dynamics prove in and of themselves figurative. For the switching between Latin and Greek, like that between visual and verbal forms, itself gives form to a pendulation between (as indeed a synthetic coadunation of) different modes of exegetic response.

Intrinsic to this "switching," as we shall see, is an ambiguity of cultic reference, and in particular an instability between the "pagan" and the "Christian". We have already mentioned "Christianity" in the context of Optatian's "materialist aesthetics." Historically speaking, of course, Licinius and Constantine's combined Edict of Milan decriminalized Christian worship in AD 313; through a slow (and still rather opaque) process, Christianity would subsequently emerge as a unifying cult of Constantine's empire. But the point to stress here is the pliability, throughout the period when Optatian was writing, of what would subsequently be pulled apart into "pagan" and "Christian" poles. R. P. H. Green nicely expresses the point:[96]

> It would be rash to label him [Optatian] as essentially a pagan, or a non-Christian, or a time-serving Christian; not only because, as scholars have learnt long ago, it may be unwarranted to reject as pagan traditional authors who make sparse references to Christian issues and frequent ones to traditional deities or related matters, but because in this period there was surely a high degree of fluidity, of uncertainty, and of intermediate positioning between the poles, which makes a simple division into sheep and goats quite unhelpful.

Where it is all too easy to project a later, binary "Christian"/ "pagan" dichotomy back onto the fourth century, Green rightly reminds us of the need to

---

95. For the terms, see Saussure 2011 (first published in French in 1916): for Saussure, the difference between *langue* and *parole* could famously be likened to the differences in chess between the overarching rules of the game and the individual moves of the player (88–9); for Optatian's "anticipation" of such thinking, and relation in particular to Derridean deconstructionism, see the stimulating discussion of Okáčová 2006: esp. 45–7.

96. Green 2010: 67. More generally on the historiographic shifts over the last half-century in approaching late antique "paganism" and "Christianity," see Brown 2011. Two important recent interventions are Alan Cameron 2011 (puzzlingly declaring in its single reference to the poet that "Publilius Optatianus Porphyrius undoubtedly became a Christian," 181) and Jones 2014 (arguing "not only that Christianity and paganism had much in common, with Christianity drawing heavily on the beliefs and practices of paganism", but also that "Christians such as St. Paul could use the traditional culture of Greeks and Romans to build a bridge from their own side to the other," xiv).

approach these categories in much less monolithic—or for that matter mutually exclusive—terms. But I think we can go still further. For if, in cultural-religious terms, Optatian's world is one of "fluidity," "uncertainty," and "indeterminacy," "POP art" itself gives form to such interbleeding: what we find here are words, images, and ideas that move across hermeneutic frames.

Poem 16 provides a rich preliminary example of what I mean here (figure 1.19). On reading the thirty-eight hexameters comprising this poem, audiences can make sense of the text as a fairly standard panegyric to its imperial addressee: Constantine is invoked as (amongst other things) "lord," "Roman father," "splendour of the world," "celebrated light," and "saviour" (*dominum*, 16.10; *parentem | Romanum*, 16.10–11; *decus orbis*, 16.15; *lux inclyta*, 16.21; *saluator*, 16.33).[97] While surveying the terrestrial limits of the world under Constantine's sway, the page nonetheless hints at another world of significance—one that, like the vertically flowing messages woven out of the poem, sings a different tune. The left-hand Latin acrostic reads as a formulaic dedication (*domino nostro Constantino perpetuo Augusto*, "to our Lord Constantine, the perpetually August"). Decode the following three mesostics, however, and we find a trio of Greek hexameters working along altered semantic lines:

νεῖμέν σοι, βασιλεῦ, Χριστὸς καὶ σοῖς τεκέεσσι
τίμιον εὐσεβίης κρατέειν ἀρετῆς τε βραβεῖον
εὐνομίης ἄρχειν τε καὶ Αὐσονίοισιν ἀνάσσειν.

To you and your sons, o king, has Christ conceded—in honour of your piety and as a gift for your virtue—the power of command: to rule over good governance, and to be sovereign over the Ausonians.

Where the Latin poem constructs its praise of Constantine out of the fabric of traditional Latin panegyric (complete with references to the Muses and Apollo: vv. 3, 7, 8), these hidden verses operate in a landscape where Christ presides supreme: Constantine's power as "king" (βασιλεύς) is ultimately situated in relation to the divine regency of Christ (Χριστός).[98] Combined in one and the

---

97. There are numerous parallels for such language, above all in relation to the shining "light" of the emperor—an aspect that brings to mind Constantine's imperial association with *Sol Inuictus*: cf. Wienand 2011, 2012a: esp. 392–6; 2012b: 438–40 (with parallels in 439, n. 64); more generally on Constantine as the "Sun," see now Girardet 2010: 34–43 and Wallraff 2013 (with reference to Optatian on 173).

98. For discussion of related passages, cf. Wienand 2012a: 400–2 on these verses in connection with 7.23–6 and 8.3–5 ("In allen drei Textstellen wird die Gerechtigkeit des Herrschers explizit an das Gesetz Christi bzw. Gottes zurückgebunden und von diesem abgeleitet," 400–1).

XVI

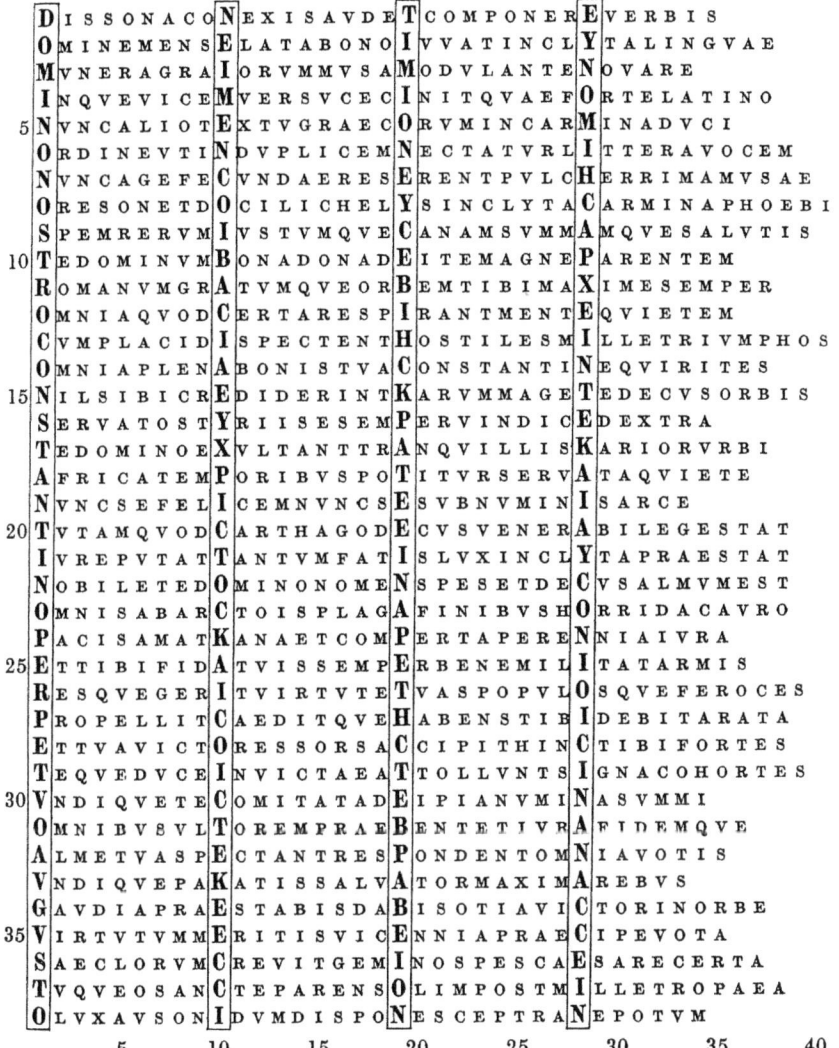

Figure 1.19. Optatian, poem 16 (after the typographic presentation of Polara 1973). Reproduced by kind permission of Giovanni Polara.

same field are multiple frames of reference, themselves premised upon different modes of literal readerly response—a switch from horizontal verses to vertical lines, on the one hand, and from Latin to Greek *signa* on the other. As so often, Optatian flags the resultant "double voice" explicitly (*duplicem* ... *uocem*, 16.6). Indeed, the very first verses of the poem tease out the semantic "dissonance" involved: "exalted by a good omen," as Optatian puts it, "the mind dares to compose dissonant things out of words that are entwined together" (*dissona conexis audet componere uerbis | omine mens elata bono*, 16.1–2).

This idea of shifting *signa*, bound together in *conexis uerbis*, resurfaces elsewhere in the corpus. In numerous cases, Optatian composes texts that totter not only between visual and verbal modes—or indeed between Greek and Latin alphabetic forms—but also between the frames of imperial panegyric and Christian hymn. It is a tripartite instability brilliantly encapsulated in the image of the chrismon *chi-rho*.[99] In four *carmina cancellata* (poems 8, 14, 19, and 24 [figures 1.20–3]), we find this monogrammatic form emblazoned towards the centre of the page, with the *chi* either stretched along its full diagonal span (poems 8, 14, and 24) or else incorporated within a larger graphic design (poem 19). But how is the *signum* to be understood? With each poem, as indeed within the corpus as a collection, the pictographic form of the *chi-rho* is made to perform different sorts of significatory work: it can refer to a politically charged Constantinian emblem (the *signum* that, already in the mid-310s, Constantine transformed into a personal logo of imperial power [e.g., figure 1.24]), or offer an epiphanic apparition of a revealed Christian truth (a pictorial *signum* pregnant with the name of "Christ"), as indeed both.[100] As a Greek form incorporated into Latin poems—one that exists between the realms of image and text, as indeed between the figurative and the literal—the emblazoned chrismon draws out much larger semantic questions about the crafting of semantic meaning.

The point can best be demonstrated by comparing the parallel appropriations of the chrismon monogram in poems 8 and 24. As a pictogram derived from the visual amalgamation of the first two letters of Christ's name, the Greek

---

99. There is a substantial bibliography on the history of the *chi-rho* monogram as Christian sign (and not least its relationship to the image of Constantine's vision before the Battle of the Milvian Bridge in October AD 312). But scholars have made minimal reference to the hugely important evidence of Optatian's poems, which unlike so many other materials, can be dated in fairly precise terms: cf., e.g., Sulzberger 1925, Bruun 1963, Black 1970, Burzachechi 1955–6, Jensen 2000: 130–55, and Girardet 2010: esp. 52–62; for inscribed *chi-rho* symbols on gems and intaglios, cf. also Spier 2007: 20–39, nos. 26–189, and 30–34, nos. 112–48. A separate article returns to Optatian's *chi-rho* monograms in more detail (Squire and Whitton, forthcoming, concentrating on poem 24).

100. For figure 1.24, see *RIC* 7.63, Ticinum no. 36, with detailed discussion in Overbeck 2005: the *chi-rho* would become a standard *signum* in Constantinian coinage from AD 327 onwards. On Constantine's use of the chrismon as a political emblem, see, e.g., Leeb 1992: esp. 39–42; Brunn 1997; Girardet 2010; Bardill 2012: esp. 159–202 (discussing this medallion on 177–8), 220–7; and, above all, Wienand 2012a: 254–74 (with references to earlier bibliography). As Wienand argues (2012a: 398), "das Christogramm [wurde] auf eine wohl kaum jemals genau bestimmbare Weise im Zusammenhang mit dem Krieg Constantins gegen Maxentius als Zeichen der himmlischen Unterstützung des Feldzuges eingeführt und taucht in den Zeugnissen zur konstantinischen Selbstdarstellung fast ausschließlich im militärischen Kontext auf—auf der Rüstung, auf Waffen und auf Standarten."

VIII

Figure 1.20. Optatian, poem 8 (after the typographic presentation of Polara 1973). Reproduced by kind permission of Giovanni Polara.

chi and *rho* stand at the literal midpoint of both these Latin hexameter poems. Significantly, I think, both poems also have the ligaments of the *chi* stretching from the first to the last letters of the Greek alphabet, marking the literal and figurative limits of the poem's world of letters on the one hand, and the figurative limits of Christ on the other (as all-encompassing divine being, Christ is at

66 *The Poetics of Late Latin Literature*

XIV

Figure 1.21. Optatian, poem 14 (after the typographic presentation of Polara 1973). Reproduced by kind permission of Giovanni Polara.

once the beginning and the end—*alpha* and *omega* in one).[101] With these two poems, we are dealing with the same figurative apparition. But in each case, the significance of the emblem functions in markedly different ways: in poem 8, the chrismon might be seen as an expedient political metaphor for figuring the

---

101. Is it coincidence that one of the *uersus intexti* stretches from the "A" of *alme* to the "O" of *signo* in poem 8—and that we find the same configuration stretching between the "O" of *omnipotens* to the "A" of *mixta* in both the diagonal ligaments of poem 24? One might also note the pivotal position of the letter "T" in poems 14 and 24—a cruciform shape that stands at the crux of each *chi-rho* (for the letter's symbolic associations, cf. Isidore, *Etym.* 1.3.9).

XXIV

Figure 1.22. Optatian, poem 24 (after the typographic presentation of Polara 1973). Reproduced by kind permission of Giovanni Polara.

emperor Constantine, whereas in poem 24 it is loaded with the divine significance of a Christian revelation.

Poem 8 offers a particularly rich reflection on the dynamic shifts involved (figure 1.20). In this case, the "pious signs of the mercy of god/God" (*clementis pia signa dei*, 8.2) make up not only the Greek name of Christ (in the central *chi-rho* monogram) but also the literal alphabetical letters of the Latin "I-E-S-V-S."

68 *The Poetics of Late Latin Literature*

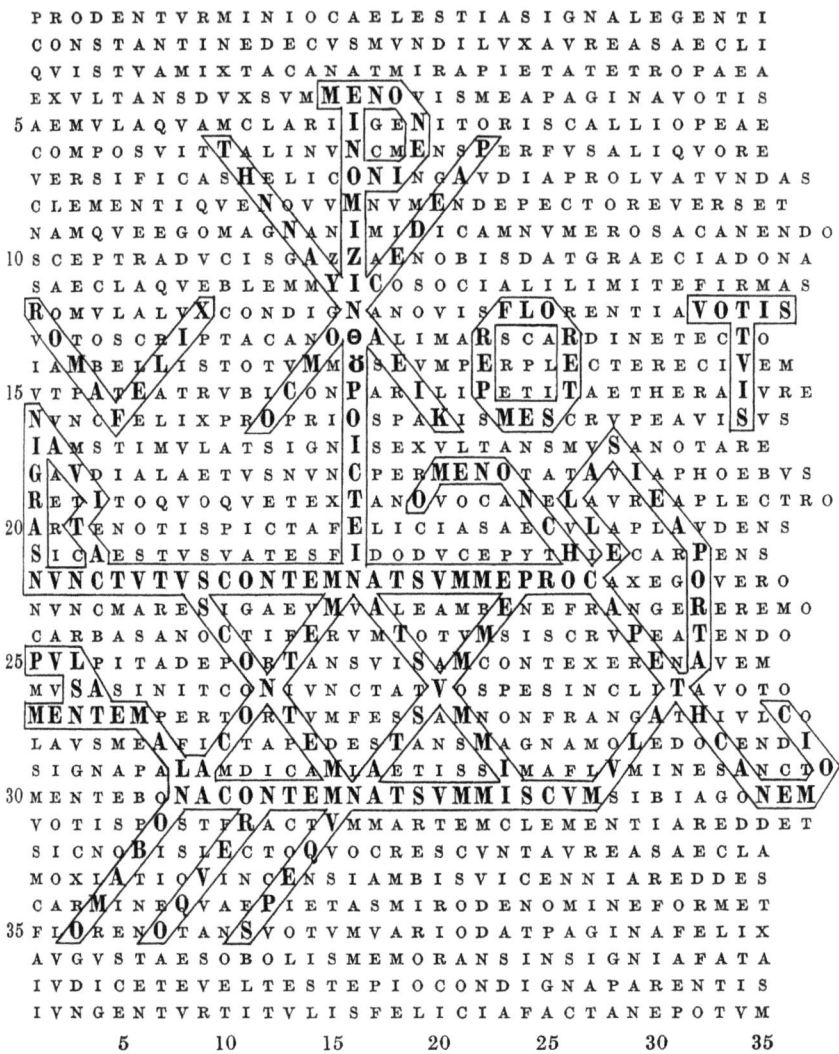

Figure 1.23. Optatian, poem 19 (after the typographic presentation of Polara 1973). Reproduced by kind permission of Giovanni Polara.

Significantly, however, the poem stitches an apparition of "Jesus Christ" from the looming presence of its imperial addressee. Although the name of "Christ" does appear in one of the poem's verses (*Christi sub lege probata*, 8.4), it is Constantine, not Jesus, who is here presented as the "golden light of the world" (*lux aurea*

Figure 1.24. Obverse of a silver medallion struck in Ticinum (modern-day Pavia), AD ca. 315: Constantine is portrayed carrying a sceptre or standard over the left shoulder and wearing a helmet complete with *chi-rho* monogram on its crest. Munich, Staatliche Münzsammlung. Photograph reproduced by kind permission of the Archiv, Institut für Klassische Archäologie und Museum Klassischer Abgüsse, Ludwig-Maximilians-Universität, Munich.

mundi, 8.1).[102] The merging of Constantine into Jesus and Jesus into Constantine is nowhere more evident than in the *uersus intexti* of the graphic monogram:

Alme, salutari nunc haec tibi pagina signo
  scripta micat, resonans nominibus domini;
nate deo, solus saluator, sancte, bonorum,
  tu deus es iusti, gratia tu fidei.
      sit Victoria comes Aug. et natis eius.

Gracious one, this page now glitters for you, written with the sign of salvation, resonating with the names of the lord: holy son of God, you are the sole saviour of good people, god of the righteous, the grace of our faith.
  May victory be the companion of Augustus Caesar and his sons.

These lines yield two elegiac couplets, complete with a final prose *laudatio* (in the inner *rho* of the chrismon). But their addressee—as "lord," "son of God," "sole saviour," "holy one," indeed "god" himself (*dominus, nate deo, solus saluator,*

---

102. On Optatian's "religiös-kosmische Überhöhung des Herrschers," the key discussion is now Wienand 2012a: 390–6: "Die quasi-göttliche Stellung des Kaisers bringt Optatian durch unterschiedliche Sinnbezüge zum Ausdruck" (390).

sancte, deus)—is left ambiguous. The very letters of the ground-text that make up this pictographic reference to "Jesus Christ," we remember, are filled not with a Christian hymn but rather with an imperial panegyric: despite standing so prominently on the page, the Christian name is in one sense empty—it functions as a cipher, a symbolic means of praising Constantine *through* the Christian monogram. The page might spell out the name of Jesus Christ, then. Yet Optatian leaves the relationship between the Christian *dominus* and the Constantinian lord of Rome unspoken: for just what kind of imperial figure is Christ, and what kind of Christian figure is Constantine?[103] Like the oscillating resplendent page on which it is written (*pagina ... micat*), this poem wavers knowingly between different modes of "salvific sign" (*salutari ... signo*)[104]— between divergent "lords," "gods," and "saviours," no less than between the "son of God" (*nate deo*) and the "sons" (*natis*) of "august" Constantine. Resonating with the pluralistic "names of the lord" (*resonans nominibus domini*), the poem's lines run in multiple directions, pertaining at once to Christ *and* to Constantine.[105]

---

103. Such ambiguities—themselves figured in the shift from poetic grid to *uersus intexti* within— have been somewhat downplayed, in my view (e.g., Wienand 2012a: 397, n. 129: "Dass hier Christus gemeint ist, geht aus der vorausgehenden Wendung hervor, das 'heilbringende Zeichen' (gemeint ist das Christogramm) gebe den Name des Herrn wieder"). More sensitive to the dynamic semantic shifts involved is Ernst 1991: 122–4, emphasizing, on the one hand, how "Christliches und Paganes, Gottesliebe und Kaiserlob, hier eine enge Verbindung eingegangen sind" (124) and, on the other, how (in the context of poem 14) "Prosa und Vers, lateinische und griechische Sprachzeichen ... in der Textkonstellation artistisch kombiniert [werden]."

104. Optatian's talk of a *salutare signum* here has a particular resonance, echoing accounts of Constantine's Christian vision before the Battle of the Milvian Bridge. The closest parallels come in the context of Eusebius's discussions of the *chi-rho* as "saving sign" (σωτήριον σημεῖον), not only in his biography of Constantine (e.g., Euseb. *vit. Con.* 1.28–32) but also in the ninth and tenth chapters of his AD 335 *Tricennial Oration* extolling the emperor (= Heikel 1902: 217–23); cf., e.g., Drake 1976: 72–4, Leeb 1992: 112 (with detailed references in n. 76), and Averil Cameron and Hall 1999: 204–13. Optatian, in other words, uses a terminology that—at least for a writer like Eusebius—was wholly pregnant with Christian registers of meaning. At the same time, he taps into an "official" Constantinian language for referring to the symbol: according to Eusebius (*hist. eccl.* 9.9.10–11), a statue erected in the Forum to commemorate the Battle of the Milvian Bridge portrayed the emperor holding in his right hand a "saving sign" (σωτήριον σημεῖον), itself referring to the "saviour's passion" (τοῦ σωτηρίου πάθους); moreover, Constantine ordered that the statue be inscribed—in Latin (τῇ Ῥωμαίων... φωνῇ)—with a reference to how he conquered through "this sign of salvation" (τούτῳ τῷ σωτηριώδει σημείῳ). In both its language and its inflection, in other words, Optatian's graphic reference to this *salutari signo* most likely also had an *epigraphic* model in sight.

105. Something similar can be said of poem 14 (figure 1.21), written in honour of Constantine's defeat of Licinius (on the language, cf. Wienand 2012a: 373–5, 401–2, and 2012b: esp. 440–1). Throughout the hexameter verses, it is Constantine who is addressed as "the holy one, glory of the world and exalted salvation of the state, the pious light of the lands" (*Sancte, decus mundi ac rerum summa salutis, | lux pia terrarum* 14.1–2). But the precise relationship between Constantine and "God" is unclear—and nowhere more so than in the lettered text of the *chi-rho* monogram ("Safe through the help and constant assent of God on high, Constantine, the pious and eternal emperor, restorer of the world, has pacified the whole world through his slaughter of the tyrants," *Summi dei auxilio nutuque perpetuo tutus | orbem totum pacauit trucidatis tyrannis | Constantinus pius et aeternus imperator | reparator orbis*).

Contrast the situation in poem 8 with the Christian monogram of poem 24 (figure 1.22). Once again, this hexameter text is composed out of 1,225 alphabetical units, arranged in a grid of thirty-five letters across both its horizontal and vertical axes. This time, however, our chrismon stands alone, occupying the full poetic frame. Still more significantly, the poem is addressed to Christ rather than to the emperor (*Christe*: 24.4, 18); indeed, there is no mention here of Constantine or of his imperial feats. That lack of Constantinian reference (taken together with certain other anomalies) has led some scholars to doubt the poem's attribution to Optatian, deeming it a posthumous medieval imitation.[106] But I do not think the poem can be so easily dismissed.[107] In offering a carefully worded Christological celebration, the poem actually fits rather neatly against a specific historical backdrop: it offers a figurative encapsulation of the Nicaean Creed, sanctioned by the council over which Constantine himself presided in AD 325.[108] That Nicaean view of Christ—as of one Being with God the Father and the Holy Spirit—is duly enshrined in the *uersus intexti* of the poem's *chi-rho*:

Omnipotens genitor tuque o diuisio mixta,
filius atque pater et sanctus spiritus unum,
faueas uotis.

O omnipotent father and you, o intermingled division—Son and Father and Holy Spirit in one—may you favour my prayers.

Although these visual *signa* may look very similar to those of poem 8, poem 24 is premised upon a shift in semantic perspective. If the embroidered name of

---

106. Doubts were first raised by Giovanni Polara: Polara 1973: 1.xxix–xxxi, 2.153, 2.157–8; cf. Polara 1974b: 298; 1983: esp. 115, n. 13; 2004a: 20, 43. Polara's rejection of poem 24 is bound up with his arguments about poem 22 (cf. above, n. 93) and has been followed by numerous others (e.g., Bruhat 1999: 38–9 and most recently Moreschini 2013: 612–14). Polara notes not only the poem's "Christian" logic (declaring *Optatianum paganum fuisse sine controversia*: Polara 1973: 1.xxx) but also, e.g., its high frequency of *adiunctae propositiones*, the different form of the *rho*, the use of a right-to-left diagonal, the abbreviated word forms (e.g., *positoq.*, 24.6; *prudensq.*, 24.9; *natalib.*, 24.13; *quaeq.*, 24.20; *hominiq.*, 24.27; *teq.*, 24.30; *uehitq.*, 24.34), and the spelling of *sobolem* (24.10); one might also note the absence of scholia on both this poem and poem 22 (cf. Pipitone 2012b: 22). For a more detailed response to Polara's arguments, and a translation and analysis of the poem, see Squire and Whitton, forthcoming.

107. See Squire and Whitton, forthcoming, following Kluge 1926: xxiii. For other related sentiments—albeit without engaging in any detail with Polara's philological points—cf., e.g., Barnes 1975: 174, n. 4 (declaring Polara's argument "far from persuasive"); Ernst 1991: 98, 138, n. 80; Green 2010: 67 (suggesting that the poem "should not be dismissed as an interpolation, for the manuscript tradition ... is not significantly different from that of the others, and it has not been shown to be otherwise anomalous").

108. On Constantine's active role in the proceedings—and the "Verschränkung des Konzils mit der Symbolik und Semantik des constantinischen Herrschaft" (416)—see especially Wienand 2012a: 415–8 (with further bibliography); cf. Girardet 2010: 140–9 (with more detailed bibliographic overview).

"Jesus Christ" could in other examples serve an essentially decorative function—as literal ornament framing imperial encomium—the monogram is here loaded with the full force of Christian symbolism. More than that, the very form of the poem is made to reflect the mysterious workings of Christ's Incarnation. For what better expression of the Trinity's "intermingled division" (*diuisio mixta*) than the epiphany of this Greek monogram within the letters of our Latin text? As divine outward embodiment of an "inner God" (*dei deus interioris*, 24.9), Christ himself provides the model for the poem's own iconotextual synthesis. Like the Son of God, "derived from the sumptuous Word" (*opulento exertus uerbo*, 24.18–19), the very form of the poem's monogram materializes a divine force: "the sacred contrivance gives an eternal sign [*aeternum signum*] to those who are saved" (*aeternum saluis signum dat machina sacra*, 24.35).[109]

Whatever we decide about the attribution of poem 24, related themes resurface elsewhere in the extant corpus. To demonstrate the point, we need only turn to a fourth poem to incorporate a chrismon in its design: poem 19 (figure 1.23). I have written about this poem at greater length elsewhere.[110] What concerns me here, though, is the dynamic nature of its professed *signa* (*caelestia signa*, 19.1; *signis ... notare*, 19.17; *signa ... laetissima*, 19.29).[111] This is a creation that brings together a dizzying array of different signs, all united

---

Wienand nonetheless deems poem 24 "evtl. unauthentisch" (2012a: 397). An important comparandum for poem 24 comes in a Greek picture-poem (preserved in a ninth-century codex in Saint Petersburg: Codex Petropolitanus Gr. 216, folio 345v = Squire and Wienand, forthcoming: plate 8), complete with *chi-rho*, perhaps composed as early as during the fourth century: for the parallels, see Follieri 1974: esp. 152–4 and Ernst 1991: 756.

109. The only scholar, so far as I know, to have appreciated the point (likewise apparently assuming that the poem is genuine: 98, 138, n. 80) is Ernst 1991: 138: "Der Vorstellung des Christentums von einem mehrfachen Schriftsinn korreliert die Hierarchisierung mehrerer Sinnebenen im Gedicht, die christliche Idee eines unendlichen Gottes und einer transzendenten *aeternitas* spiegelt sich im Konzept eines durch Permutation angestrebten infiniten Sprachkunstwerks und die Einbindung des Bildes in den Text ist gewiß auch ein Reflex auf bilderfeindliche Tendenzen im frühen Christentum." For the Incarnation as a paradoxical apparition already by the late second century—"the invisible made visible, the incomprehensible made comprehensible, the passionless made capable of passion and the Word made man, gathering together all things in Itself" (*inuisibilis uisibilis factus et incomprehensibilis factus comprehensibilis, et impassibilis passibilis, et Verbum homo, uniuersa in semetipsum recapitulans*)—see, e.g., Iren. *adv. haer.* 3.16.6: I owe the reference to Jesús Hernández Lobato.

110. See Squire 2015a: 104–21. Other discussions include Simonini and Gualdoni 1978: 58–62; Levitan 1985: 257–8; Ernst 1991: 129–31; Polara 1991: 309–10; Bruhat 1999: 261–7, 2008; Rühl 2006: 88–90; Pipitone 2012b: 86–91, 119–24; Hernández Lobato 2012: 475–7 (on the "hibridación estética" and "doble decodificación"); Wienand 2012a: 363–4.

111. Just as Optatian's reference to the *chi-rho* as a *salutari signo* in the eighth poem seems to have been highly charged (cf. above, n. 104), so too does poem 19's talk of *caelestia signa* resonate with a particular Constantinian significance. In his account of Constantine's vision before the Battle of the Milvian Bridge, Lactantius tells how Constantine was directed "to mark the heavenly sign [*caeleste signum*] of God on the shields of his soldiers" (*ut caeleste signum dei notaret in scutis: de mort. pers.* 44.5): for discussion of the passage—and the lettered form inscribed onto the shields ("he marked Christ on their shields by means of a rotated letter X with its upper tip curved around," *transuersa X littera, summo capite circumflexo, Christum in scutis notat*), see, e.g., Girardet 2010: esp. 72–6, albeit without reference to Optatian.

in a single graphic form (consisting of 38 verses, each of between 35 and 38 letters): in the upper register, we find the letters *VOT* (an abbreviated form of the *uota* mentioned in vv. 4, 12, 13, 26, 31, and 35);[112] below those letters comes the mimetic image of a ship (complete with rudder and tiller to the right, ramming spike to the left, and three oars down below). The ship in turn provides the rationale for the Greek chrismon, sandwiched between the Latin letters *V* and *O*. In this case, the emblem is incorporated within an iconic frame, doubling up as the combined mast and sail for our depicted trireme. It is also worth noting that the poem furnishes a secure chronological context. Just as the ship draws out the number "20" (*XX*) in its hull, so too do vv. 32–4 make reference to Constantine's twenty-year *uicennalia*: the poem can be confidently dated to the years AD 325 and 326 (and was most likely written in the summer of 326).[113]

If the nineteenth poem brings together multiple signs, it simultaneously floats questions about how those *signa* might be deciphered. In line with its depicted naval subject, the poem is in fact navigable in a multitude of different ways: depending on our point of departure, the visual fabric of the ship yields no less than five different hexameters, many of them (like the verses in poem 18 [figure 1.15]) running in multiple itinerant directions across the page.[114] Most intriguing of all are the lettered *signa* that comprise the chrismon sail and mast (along with the rudder and tiller to the right). Once again, our Latin hexameter poem steers a Greek text—this time, a self-contained elegiac couplet:

τὴν ναῦν δεῖ κόσμον, σὲ δὲ ἄρμενον εἰνὶ νομίζιν
  θούροις τεινόμενον σῆς ἀρετῆς ἀνέμοις.

One must think that the ship is the world and that you are the hoisted rigging within, tautened by the raging winds of your virtue.

---

112. J. S. Edwards 2005: 459 speculates that the letters might better be read as an acronym for Constantine as *Victor Orbis Terraeque* or *Victor Orbis Terrarum* ("This same hyperbolic sentiment would be consistent with the panegyric form and is supported by the usage in line 2 of 'decus mundi' to describe Constantine"); cf. also Pipitone 2012b: 91. As ever, Optatian allows his *signa* to be read in multiple ways—the letters inscribed within the verbal fabric of the poem, themselves pregnant with words within ("Blessed Rome always flourishes under your vows," *Roma felix floret semper tuis uotis*), can be read both as an acronym *and* in relation to their written "vows" (*uota scripta cano*, 19.13).

113. There are numerous parallels for Optatian poems that celebrate both Constantine's *uicennalia* and the *decennalia* of his sons: a related set of *uersus intexti* can be found in poem 5 (which collectively spell out the abbreviation *AVG. XX CAES. X*); other references include 4.1, 4.7, 5.8, 9.35–6, 16.35, and 20a.12–26. On the dating of poem 19 (most likely in the summer of AD 326)—and its significance as a *terminus post quem* for Optatian's return from exile—see Wienand 2012a: 355–6, n. 1; cf. above, n. 22. In this case, of course, the double-X formation of the ship's hull, complete with its cryptic numerical significance (referring to the number 20), also echoes the graphic shape of the figured *chi-rho* above.

114. Cf. Squire 2015a: 112–13.

Tottering between the verbal and the iconic, this Greek couplet offers a distinctive commentary on the picture-poem's signs. What matters, we are told, is a particular mode of allegorical intellectualization, one premised around the cerebral act of "considering" (νομίζ<ε>ιν). Like the *cosmos* itself (which is here said to take on the likeness of a ship), the world of Optatian's picture-poem sails between different states of "being" (εἰνί). In all this, I think, the perspectives of Christianity have the potential to form an integral part of that picture. Of course, Christ himself goes unmentioned in the poem, with its nods to Mars, Apollo, and the Muses; in Optatian's hymn to the emperor, it is once again Constantine, not Christ, who is addressed as "the glory of the world and golden light of the age" (*Constantine, decus mundi, lux aurea saecli*, 19.2). And yet the "you" of our Greek couplet—figured out of the Christian chrismon—is poignantly polyvalent: depending on the reader's frame of seeing and reading, these *signa* could be understood to refer either to Constantine or else to a Christian God made present through the *chi-rho* apparition.[115] Ultimately, the poem leaves its figurations undulating between different frames of reference, as indeed between physical entities and immaterial abstractions. It is left to the audience to pilot both the words and imagery through the seas of potential literal and figurative meaning: the games of word and image at once present things to *see* (an iconic sail, a mast, an emblematized emblem) and indeed things to *un*-see (a text that knowingly renders the picture an allegorical symbol).

How, then, should we make historical sense of such dynamic signs, and how might they correspond with some of the broader aesthetic concerns of later Latin poetics? Of course, Optatian's active engagement of his reading and viewing audience finds earlier parallels:[116] we might remember the *Tabulae Iliacae*'s

---

115. Something similar can be said of the poem's ship imagery itself. Like the *chi-rho*, this *signum* can be understood as a political emblem of Constantine (one with numerous parallels, above all in Constantinian coinage (cf. Bruhat 1999: 297–324; 2008). But the ship also bears within it a potential *Christian* cryptographic reference. As Ernst 1991: 130–1 points out, the image of the ship—specifically, with the Christian cross as its mast—"hat eine lange Bildtradition im Christentum" (130, with references to Minucius Felix, Tertullian, and Justin in n. 64; cf., e.g., Bruun 1963: 129–30); writing in the second century, Justin had noted a parallel between the cross and the mast of a ship (*apol*. 1.55), and we find Clement of Alexandria specifying the ship as an appropriate symbol for Christian seal rings (*paed*. 3.11.59.2; cf., e.g., Spier 2007: 52, nos. 310–15). One might also compare the recent analysis of Mratschek 2015: 139–44, discussing the figurative "sacred ship" of the Church" (144)—and Christ as its imagined helmsman—in Paulinus, *epist*. 49 (with numerous parallels listed at 143, n. 43). No less intriguing is the manuscript transmission of verse 13: the Codex Augustaneus 9 Guelferbytanus presents the relevant letter—the first letter of the Latin word *tali* in the ground text—as a Greek Θ (whereas the Codex Parisinus 7806 presents it as a Latin O: cf. Polara 1973: 2.120–1; Pipitone 2012b: 88–90): is it mere coincidence that, at the crux of our chrismon, the monogram yields the sign "of God" (Θ-Υ, or Θεοῦ)?

116. Cf. Ernst 1991: 141–2, also comparing extant palindrome square inscriptions (e.g., figure 1.10).

instruction to "go wherever you choose" across the field of their "magic square" inscriptions (figure 1.11), for example; likewise, two of Simmias's Alexandrian picture-poems seem in fact to have demanded audiences to operate between visual and verbal modes (the "figurative" forms of Simmias's "Axe" and "Egg" [figure 1.6] make semantic sense only when the reader deconstructs their visual appearances, reading first the opening lines, then the last, and continuing the process until the verses meet in the middle).[117] "POP art" certainly has an archaeology in earlier classical precedent. But Optatian, I think, goes markedly further in his significatory play. However one proceeds with the *Tabulae Iliacae* or Greek picture-poems, the words themselves hold fast: they offer a single text. With Optatian, by contrast, the very pictures and texts fluctuate between different sorts of figurations, yielding within them multiple *signa* (not to mention multiple—and sometimes divergent—paratextual commentaries on how to approach them). As a result, there are always numerous modes of response: it is a "wondrous work of the mind," as Optatian characteristically puts it in his third poem, to "weave a poem into metre along various paths" (*mentis opus mirum metris intexere carmen | ad uarios cursus*, 3.28–9).

Optatian's talk of the "mind" (*mens*) hints at an additional framework for situating his concern with dynamic *signa*. Throughout the corpus, we find Optatian anticipating the concerns of later Neoplatonic philosophers, emphasizing the audience's active share in making sense of the world on the page.[118] This is an interest that Optatian also shared with other contemporaries, anticipating later Christian writings about visual and verbal signs. As Isabella Gualandri explores in her contribution to this volume, Augustine provides a particularly important parallel here, writing less than a century after Optatian in the later fourth and early fifth centuries. In Augustine's commentary on the opening of John's Gospel, we find Augustine not only delineating between the written word and the visual image but also exploiting that distinction to develop an incipient tradition of Christian semiotics, premised on the relationship between *res* ("things") and *signa* ("signs"). "A picture is looked at in one way," as Augustine puts it, "and letters are looked at in another" (*aliter enim uidetur pictura, aliter uidentur litterae: In Evang. Iohan.* 2): if the activity of seeing a picture is completed through the act of viewing, looking at letters—however beautifully crafted they might be—can only ever preface a deeper mode of internal intellectual engagement ("when you have seen the letters, the thing is not complete, for you are

---

117. Cf. esp. Luz 2008, along with Squire 2011: 231–5 and Kwapisz 2013: esp. 34–7 (concluding that the "decision whether the *Egg* was originally a figure poem should belong to the reader of this book, not to its author").

118. Cf., e.g., Levitan 1985: esp. 263–6, along now with Moreschini 2013: 597–617.

reminded also to read," *litteras cum uideris, non hoc est totum; quoniam commoneris et legere*). Optatian's poetry takes shape against a related critical tradition. Importantly, however, Optatian ultimately leaves the relationship between *res* and *signa* open: the ultimate significance of Optatian's creations, we might say, lies in their oscillation between different significatory modes.[119]

The point leads us directly back to the cultural milieu in which Optatian was writing during the early fourth century and, above all, to the world of its visual imagery. Optatian's immediate successors would come up with elaborate Christian defences of visual *signa*, not least in the context of Christian worship. What matters, as Paulinus of Nola would put it a little later in the fourth century, was the beholder's active spiritual involvement in the act of looking, exploiting "empty" images as vessels to upload the inner visions of the subjective imagination (*carm.* 27.514–15):[120]

> *Qui uidet haec uacuis agnoscens uera figuris*
> *non uacua fidam sibi pascit imagine mentem.*

> The man who looks at these things and acknowledges the truth within the empty pictures nurtures his believing mind with an image which for him is not empty.

Paulinus's talk of "empty" and "non-empty" imagery might be associated with larger stylistic shifts in fourth-century visual culture. In the words of John Onians,

---

119. In this sense, my interpretation departs from that of Martin Hose (Hose 2007). For Hose, Optatian's exegetic concerns can be related to a broader trend in "Constantinian literature" (comparable with the works of Proba and Iuvencus above all): "Sowohl in den Technopaignien des Porfyrius als auch in den Bibelepen der Proba und des Iuvencus wird eine hohe exegetische Leistung des Lesers verlangt, der im Text einen zweiten Text, eine höhere Wahrheit erkennen muß." Like Pelttari 2014: 73–114, I think we are dealing with more "open" texts, less oriented around "solutions" than divergent sorts of readerly "opportunities": "The verbal surface of the poetry conceals a variety of meanings that must be encountered and either accepted or rejected . . . the textual layers draw the reader into the text so that she may participate in making the poem's words and lines mean in some way. . . . More than creating ingenious patterns, the late antique poet creates a series of meanings that are purposefully and intentionally fluid" (Pelttari 2014: 113). The poems, in other words, leave it to the reader to navigate through a variety of literal and hermeneutic paths.

120. For Paulinus's ideology of the visual here, see esp. Thümmel 1978; Lowden 1999: 56–7; Mratschek 2002: 404–6, 595–6. Cf. also Elsner 1995: 249–87: "Perhaps more than any other ancient writing on art," as Elsner writes (249), "these comments by Paulinus indicate an awareness of the arbitrariness of meaning and of the fact that meaning depends as much on what the viewer brings to interpretation as it does on the actual object he or she interprets"; cf. most recently Goldhill 2012: 89–98, noting how "the Christian viewer is asked to look beyond the particularities to an eternal truth" (98). For some introductions to Paulinus's thinking, see especially Mratschek 2002: esp. 250–66, along with Trout 1999 and Conybeare 2000.

we can witness during this period—above all over the course of Optatian's own lifetime—the gradual emergence of a "visual sensibility which enabled the late antique spectator to make more and more out of the same or less information": "not only was it inherent in this visual imagination that it did not need to be limited by the reality of what was presented to the eyes, it was actually desirable for one to be able to imagine the exaggerated and the false."[121] For Onians, the result is a sort of proto-"linguistification" of the image, in which the inflation of verbal *signa* (ultimately premised on the sanctity of biblical scripture) went hand in hand with a denigration of the visual. Whether or not we agree with Onians's assessment, there can be no doubting that this was a period when images (and modes of critiquing them) underwent a radical transformation. With the rise of so many new cults—of which Christianity was just one—the same visual schemes had come to serve multiple hermeneutic ends: it was ultimately left to the viewer to "fill" the image with requisite registers of significance.[122]

Such visual syncretism seems central to Optatian's own significatory games. "POP art" materializes—indeed, through its lettered forms, it quite literally literalizes—a broader cultural concern with how *signa* could oscillate between "multiple, flexible, and not always mutually exclusive interpretation and combination."[123] The first decades of the fourth century—that is, the exact time when Optatian was active—prove fundamental here. This is the period when we can first talk about "Christian" art in any meaningful sense: consider, for example, the rise of "Christian" sarcophagi, and not least the frescoed catacombs outside Rome (of which cubiculum C of the Via Latina catacomb, painted around AD 320, provides just one reflection [figure 1.25], furnishing its space with framed images of Old and New Testament themes).[124] As is well known, such Judaeo-Christian

---

121. Quotations from Onians 1980: 12 and 1999: 261. On the whole history of ancient (and modern!) thinking about the "imagination," see now the stimulating overview of Sheppard 2014.

122. There is a large bibliography on late antique and early Christian syncretic forms. The best general introductions remain Grabar 1968, Kitzinger 1977, and Elsner 1998 (with further comments in 2004 and 2006c); other discussions include Mathews 1993, Engemann 1997, Jensen 2000, Hannestad 2001, and Suzawa 2008; Jefferson and Jensen 2015. For analysis of one particularly revealing case study, cf. Elsner 2011. More generally on the continuity of Graeco-Roman mythological themes in late antique sculptural assemblages (among "pagan" and "Christian" patrons alike), see Stirling 2005: esp. 165–232.

123. Elsner 1998: 154. As the author elsewhere puts it (Elsner 1998: 221): "There was no one interpretation, and this in itself throws light on the remarkable flux and creativity of sacred art and exegesis in the third and fourth centuries. This period was (in religious and artistic terms) a kind of melting pot where all the traditions of Antiquity—from centre to periphery, from élite to relatively plebeian—were thrown together, combined, redefined, and adapted, ultimately to produce something both wonderfully new and at the same time deeply indebted to the classical heritage. That new product would be the Christianity, and the arts, of the middle ages." Compare also Elsner and Hernández Lobato in their introduction to this volume, 8–13 (with figures I.3–I.5).

124. For a discussion of the illustrated painting—and its iconographic debts—see Hoogland Verkerk 1999: 105–8: the paintings of cubiculum C contain a number of Old Testament themes (crowned by a ceiling image of the enthroned Christ)—among them, Jonah and the whale, the sacrifice of Isaac, and the

78 *The Poetics of Late Latin Literature*

Figure 1.25. Old Testament scene of uncertain identity (perhaps Moses leading the Israelites towards Sinai after crossing the Red Sea), from cubiculum C, Via Latina catacombs, AD ca. 320–50. © Scala / Art Resource, New York.

images were themselves coined from the iconographic currency of earlier Graeco-Roman forms: depictions of Christ were drawn from images of (for example) Orpheus, Hermes Kriophoros, and Sol Inuictus, just as the schema of "mother and child" could refer simultaneously to (amongst other subjects) Isis and Horus as well as Mary and Jesus. Throughout the fourth century and across the Roman Empire, we find visual forms that combine Christian subjects with the familiar repertoire of Greek and Roman mythology. From the head of Jesus juxtaposed alongside a scene of Bellerophon and the Chimaera in the mosaic from Hinton St Mary in Dorset (figure 1.26; cf. figure I.6), to more luxurious objects like the Projecta casket (with its inscribed instruction to "live in Christ" appearing in no way contradictory to the image of Venus's toilette emblazoned on its lid [figure 1.27]), the visual field could flip

good shepherd (cf. Jefferson 2014: 126–7). On the imagery of the Via Latina catacombs and its development, see especially Ferrua 1960 and Tronzo 1986 (with discussion of cubiculum C on 51–65); for some broader illustrated guides to the early Christian catacombs outside Rome, see J. Stevenson 1978, Fink and Asamer 1997, Pergola and Barbini 1997, Pavia 1999: 67–98, and Rutgers 2000.

Figure 1.26. Reconstruction diagram of the Hinton St Mary mosaic, fourth century AD (cf. figure I.6): the central image shows either Christ or a Roman Emperor (Constantine?) surrounded by busts of the winds or seasons. The upper section has an additional scene of Bellerophon slaying the Chimaera. Photograph reproduced by kind permission of the Archiv, Institut für Klassische Archäologie und Museum Klassischer Abgüsse, Ludwig-Maximilians-Universität, Munich (after David S. Neal's watercolour reconstruction in Cosh and Neal 2002–10: 2.158, fig. 152).

Figure 1.27. Detail of Venus's toilette on the silver Projecta casket (Venus is shown seated on a cockleshell and surrounded by Nereids riding a *kêtos* and hippocamp), late fourth century AD. © The Trustees of the British Museum / Art Resource, New York.

between different hermeneutic modes.[125] Depending on context—and above all, the perspective of the beholder—the stories of ancient gods and heroes could be appropriated to bear new registers of Christian meaning: it is such formal syncretism that allowed stories of Hercules, Admetus, and Alcestis to figure the sacred truths of the Christian resurrection in Roman catacombs (figure 1.28)[126] or the motif of the sleeping Endymion to be repackaged as "Jonah," incorporated within a myriad of other biblical scenes (figure 1.29).[127]

The syncretic melting pot of fourth-century art is of course a well-trodden scholarly subject. But my suggestion is that Optatian's works—so conspicuously overlooked by archaeologists and art historians—encapsulate the underlying cultural dynamics. If "POP art" figures the fluctuations of the period, it also offers a unique sort of metavisual and metaliterary commentary: it gives form to a world in which the meanings of *signa* fluctuate knowingly between different

---

125. On the Hinton St Mary mosaic, see Cosh and Neal 2002–10: 2.156–60 (with references): the identity of the figure named "Jesus" is of course debated, since the iconography fuses the imagery of Christ with that of the Roman emperor (cf. Pearce 2008; Levine 2015). On the Projecta casket, see Elsner 2008: esp. 33–5.

126. On the paintings of cubiculum N in the Via Latina catacomb, see J. Stevenson 1978: 124–6.

127. On the sarcophagus, see especially Deichmann and Klauser 1966: 23–4, no. 2; Weitzmann 1979: 405–6, no. 361 (with further bibliography); Elsner 1998: 154–5. On the allegorical significance of such scenes in the third and fourth centuries, see Davis 2000 (along more generally with, e.g., Squire and Elsner, forthcoming: 69–72).

Figure 1.28. View of the lunette (with an image of Hercules rescuing Alcestis and returning her to Admetus) in the arcosolium (an arched recess for a sarcophagus) of cubiculum N, Via Latina catacombs, AD ca. 320–50. © Scala / Art Resource, New York.

Figure 1.29. Front of a late third-century AD limestone sarcophagus with biblical imagery (Vatican Museums, Museo Pio Christiano: inv. Lat. 119). Besides a Jonah cycle, depicted scenes also include the raising of Lazarus (top left), a shepherd shepherding his sheep (top right), and Moses striking the rock (to the top right of the ship's sail). © Alinari / Art Resource, New York.

realms of possibility, at once collaborating and competing with scripted (as indeed unscripted) regimes of verbal meaning.

3. POETRY IN PIECES?

In the third and final section of my chapter, I turn to Optatian's aesthetics both of the literary fragment and of literal fragmentation. So far in my analysis, I have examined "POP art" in terms of its combined material and poetic medium, situating the dynamic permutations of Optatian's *signa* against the cultural and, above all, religious transformations of the fourth century. But such significatory fluidity—such fluctuation between different media, forms, and semantic registers—ultimately relies on an idea of the elemental building blocks of both language and imagery. If Optatian constructs collaborating and competing fields of significance, his works are premised on an art of extractive demolition on the one hand, and of appropriative salvage on the other. These laborious compositions lend themselves to perpetual de- and reconstruction: on a variety of levels, they at once break down before our eyes and regroup into new compounds of poetic-pictorial artifice.

The point is fundamental, I think, for getting to grips with Optatian's larger world view. One way of theorizing his works might be in relation to what Gérard Genette would call "texts" and "paratexts":[128] these poems create internal spaces

---

128. For an English translation of *Seuils* (first published in 1987), see Genette 1997. On the relevance of Genette's theories for approaching Roman literary and artistic creations, see the essays in Jansen 2014; on the associated concerns of late antique Latin writers specifically, above all their use of the "paratextual preface," see Pelttari 2014: 45–73, esp. 46–8.

for the writer (no less than the reader) to step outside their containing frames; indeed, Optatian's interwoven verses themselves explicitly reflect upon the gesture, within the context of graphic designs that exist between the realms of text and picture (offering "para-images," we might say, as much as "para-texts"). But such concern with "inside" and "outside" goes hand in hand with an idea of literary and visual dismantling. The very assemblage of Optatian's verse rests upon the potential of being disassembled once more: each creation can be broken down to the individual line, word, syllable, and letter, texturing the work, piece by piece, through multiple acts of retrieval, reappropriation, and reuse.

Before explaining what I mean here, it is worth emphasizing how Optatian's works are themselves shaped from the sound bites of earlier Latin poets. The rich and allusive tapestry of Optatian's poetry has yet to receive any detailed treatment: while the operative mechanics of Latin allusion and intertextuality have come in for much discussion in recent years,[129] analysis of Optatian's own textual fabric has been essentially limited to source criticism—to noting his manifold "debts" to others. One need only examine Polara's critical edition to see just how rich and varied this literary texture proves, nodding not just to Vergil and Ovid but also to Catullus, Lucretius, Tibullus, Horace, Valerius Flaccus, Lucan, Martial, Statius, and Silius Italicus (to name but a few). In each case, we find Optatian's poems woven from the literary fabric of his predecessors, and in deeply knowing and self-referential ways. Although respun into complex self-standing creations, Optatian's poems simultaneously lead beyond the confines of the page. Individual words and phrases consequently guide audiences through a library of canonical texts: the very sights with which Optatian confronts his reader are built up from textured literary citations.

With "POP art," then, we are dealing with "poetry in pieces" in two interconnected senses. On the one hand, Optatian's works are crafted with a knowing attention to the constituent elements of language: each laboured design is built up from the individual alphabetical unit, and audiences are invited to read and view those units in multiple directions, breaking the bonds between letters and words. On the other hand, the very fabric of this poetry is constructed from the building blocks of established literary tradition: Optatian's creations appropriate the interwoven fragments of poetic precedent. To call Optatian's poems *centones*—after the manner of "patchwork" poems composed entirely of single verses or half-lines

---

129. Among numerous other contributions, one thinks of Pasquali 1951: 11–20 (first published in 1942), Conte 1986, Hinds 1998, Thomas 1999, and Pucci 1998. On the allusive workings of late antique Latin poets in particular—their use of "classical fragments" both to draw "attention to the individual unity of composition" and hence to "create an ideal of classical poetry against which ... to write their own poetry" (160)—see now Pelttari 2014: 115–60 (with wide-ranging bibliographic review); cf. also Kaufmann's chapter in this volume.

of dactylic hexameter (a literary form that came into its own in the fourth century)—would be to express the point too strongly.[130] Not only are Optatian's poems spun from a wide range of authors, they also playfully adapt the words and phrases that they cite. But there is nonetheless an important parallel between Optatian's aesthetic concerns and those of the cento. Optatian's very talk of "weaving"—as indeed of "spinning" his poems and "embroidering" them with elaborate designs—encapsulates the shared thinking, adapting the cento's intertextual cross-stitch to fabricate a new sort of poetic design.[131] Playing on the "fabric" (no less than fabrication) of his crafted artefacts, Optatian materializes an underlying idea of intertextuality, "cross-sti(t)ching" multiple texts within and between poems.

Like the authors of contemporary *centones*, Optatian also demonstrates a profound awareness about making something "new" out of something "old." For all their literary debts and derivations, his artefacts insist on being *noua carmina* ("new songs," 3.24) and *noui elegi* ("new elegies," 8.1), premised upon *nouae curae* ("new concerns," 21.4).[132] It is a theme that comes to the fore in the preserved epistolary exchange between Optatian and Constantine. Although debates continue as to whether or not these letters are genuine (as I think seems most likely), they are suffused with a sense of both literary tradition and poetic innovation. Take Constantine's alleged letter to our poet, commenting on the "later age" (*posterius aeuum*) that has given rise to Optatian's oeuvre (*epist. Const.* 2):[133]

Sed quoniam semper in propatulo usus istius fuit nec ulli negatum est id ex ea indicere, quod possit, illos etiam quos posterius aeuum tulit non penitus

---

130. On the 16 extant Latin *centones* and their history (stretching back to at least the second century but reaching a climax in the fourth and early fifth), see Elsner (this volume), along with the introduction in Charlet 1997: 533–7. Among the most important discussions are Polara 1989, Salanitro 1997, McGill 2005, Bažil 2009, Formisano and Sogno 2010, Hernández Lobato 2012: 262–317, and Pelttari 2014: 96–112. On the associated history of the Greek cento, see Salanitro 1997: 2325–34, Whitby 2007, Agosti 2009, 2010, and Prieto Domínguez 2010.

131. The punning language of "weaving" (*texere*) the manufactured "fabric" of the text (*textus*) is a mainstay throughout the corpus: 3.15 (*texit*); 3.17–18 (*intexta ... orsa*); 3.28 (*intexere*); 3.35 (*uario ... textu*); 3.iii (*uario ... textu*); 4.9 (*textu*); 6.2 (*texit*); 9.13 (*texens*); 9.v (*intextus uersus*); 16.5 (*alio textu*); 17.8 (*uerbum textum*); 19.19 (*texta*); 19.25 (*uisam contexere nauem*); 20b.4 (*texta*); 21.16 (*texti ... uersus*). On Optatian's metapoetic language of "weaving," see Bruhat 1999: 107–14, 2009: esp. 116–17, 124–5; more generally on the metaphor and its significance, see Scheid and Svenbro 1996; cf. most recently Scheidegger Lämmle 2015 (discussing Optatian at 176–83). On the Vergilian ancestry to such puns, the key discussion is Bartsch 1998: esp. 326–8 (arguing of Vergilian ekphrasis that "the epic *textum*, in both form and content, enacts the controlling role of the art-work").

132. On Optatian's self-conscious talk of "innovation," see above, n. 75. More generally on ideas of poetic "originality" in the late third and fourth century, see now Pelttari 2014: esp. 5–7 on Nemesianus, *Cyneg.* 46–7 and Claudian, *Rapt.* 1 praef.

133. On the authenticity of the letters, see above, n. 39. For their revealing rhetoric of both poetic and imperial "self-fashioning" (68), see the excellent analysis of Green 2010: esp. 67–9. Like Green, I think that "pending strong evidence to the contrary ..., the letter ascribed to Constantine, along with

a fructu fauoris exclusit, qui relictis grauioribus sonis modos ad leniora flexerunt.

But since the use of that [poetry] was always available for all, and since everyone was entitled to declare which part of it he could do, even those whom a later age produced have not been wholly excluded from the fruits of favour—those who, after leaving behind the graver tones, gave its modes a lighter turn.

The letter expressly frames Optatian's feats not only in terms of past poetic achievements but also in relation to the cultural parameters of the present (the poet, as the letter continues, "must delight in the success of the present time," *prouentu praesentis temporis exultare debebis*: *epist. Const.* 14). Perhaps most revealingly, the semantic shapes of Optatian's works are approached against the backdrop of an established literary canon: what gratifies, we are told, is Optatian's mode of "serving the ancient rules while fashioning for itself new ones" (... *ut in pangendis uersibus dum antiqua seruaret etiam noua iura sibi conderet*: *epist. Const.* 9).

Optatian's poems defiantly appropriate the literary past, weaving the piecemeal fragments of poetic expression into new forms of textured composition. And yet they are themselves designed to be broken down into ever smaller elemental units. This is true, of course, on the level of the anthology (whatever form or forms we imagine Optatian's "volume" to have taken): if, as we have said, Optatian talks of his collection as a *libellus* (1.1), that "little book" amounts to a series of even smaller units, each to be enjoyed on its own miniaturist terms;[134] not for nothing, indeed, did Optatian frequently liken his poetry to a "chain" or "fetter" (*uinculum*)—an appropriate figure for an entity in some sense "shackled" by the past but also "bound" together from multiple parts.[135] But a similar modus operandi also governs each individual poem. Optatian's *carmina cancellata* function as self-standing artefacts that can be dismantled

---

the one to which it apparently replies, may be taken as genuine": "it should be seen as a strong statement of intent, a strong commitment to the value of creative literary work made early in his [Constantine's] career" (71).

134. More generally on the "aesthetics of discontinuity" that underlies late antique literary collections, see M. Roberts 1989a: esp. 56–61; cf. Elsner and Hernández Lobato's introduction to this volume.

135. The idea informs Optatian's purported letter to Constantine (*artioribus Musarum ... uinculis, epist. Porf.* 2) and can be found throughout the corpus: 6.14 (*uinciri*); 9.6 (*uincula*); 10.18 (*noua uincula mentis*); 21.4 (*nouis ... uincula curis*); 22.8 (*uincula mitia*); 25.2 (*uincula*); cf. Bruhat 2009: 114, n. 33, on the associated language of *nectere, nexus, innectere, connectere, nodus*, and *nodosus*. The significance of the figure is discussed by Levitan 1985: 249, who likewise draws attention to Optatian's labelling of his poetic constituents as *elementa* (3.35, 3.iii, 20b.9, 26.22). Ausonius offers an associated image, within a closely associated project of self-declared *technopaegnia* (cf. Cox Miller 1998: 127–8): writing to Paulinus,

not only verse by verse but also letter by letter. Such poems work by breaking down their texts into alphabetic units that can be put back together to form pictorial and poetic compounds. In visual terms, the closest analogy is perhaps to be found in contemporary mosaics: like mosaicked designs, Optatian constructs his elaborate forms piece by piece from the tesserae of verbal expression.[136] The difference, of course, is that, for Optatian, those tesserae can be approached in different ways. Where mosaics exploit their constituent elements to offer a single framed figurative representation and ornamental field (or for that matter inscribed text), Optatian's lettered components knowingly seep beyond any single graphic form—they can form both pictures and further words, and indeed words in Greek as well as in Latin. One remembers, for example, the multiple verses emblazoned within the figurative forms of poems 18 (figure 1.15) and 19 (figure 1.23), in which individual letters yield a single graphic design but nonetheless provide the lettered elements for different literary texts: if Optatian's parts add up to an artful whole, whole poems can also be broken back down to their compositional parts, thereby offering new modes of seeing and reading them.[137]

This notion of factured fragmentation recurs throughout the corpus. Wherever we look, we find "POP art" intently aware of its potential to be unravelled: on the one hand, Optatian flags the capacity of lines to be dissected into their constituent words; on the other, he showcases how words can be unlaced into their singular letters. To explain what I mean here, let me turn to a handful of poems which, while in one sense distinct from the "picture-poems" so far explored in this chapter, nevertheless encapsulate a concern with "permutative Versartistik."[138] A first example comes in poem 15. The fifteen verses of this poem ostensibly offer an imperial panegyric. But upon closer inspection— upon examining each individual line, word, and syllable—we find all manner of pyrotechnics sparking behind these self-declared "difficult verses" (*ardua*

Ausonius prefaces the first poem of the collection by talking about "the heart-breaking business of linking up" its monosyllabic parts (*sed accessit ad miseriam concinnandi*) to forge a work that "is disjointed and intertwined/confused" (*inconexa, et implicatur* = Green 1991: 176). By extension, Ausonius opens his book of *technopaegnia* by declaring his rejection of all that cannot find expression in a single verse (*quae in uno uersu esse non possunt*): his creations, we are told, hold together like the individual links of a chain (*sed cohaerent ita ut circuli catenarum separati* = Green 1991: 175; cf. ibid. 583–5).

136. For the analogy between late antique poetry and mosaics, see especially M. Roberts 1989a: 57, 70–3. More specifically on the parallels between Optatian's poetry and contemporary fourth-century mosaics, see Bruhat 1999: 136–41 (on the analogies between mosaic patterns and the geometric shapes of poems 7, 12, 18, 21, 22, and 23).

137. Cf. Bruhat 1999: 152–70, comparing also poems 6 and 25.

138. I take the phrase from Ernst 1991: 131.

metra, 15.15).[139] The first four verses introduce the lettered labour, constructed as they are in an ascendance of disyllabic, trisyllabic, tetrasyllabic, and pentasyllabic words. If the poem begins by underlining its elemental verbal units (culminating in a fifth verse, with its five words proceeding from one syllable to five), it proceeds to offer lines for reading in multiple sequences. Because of its symmetrical arrangement of dactyl and molossus, for example, the words of verse 6 can be transposed to offer four different permutations of the same line; by extension, the ninth and tenth verses offer a hexameter and pentameter respectively, whether read forwards or backwards. This invitation to reshuffle individual verbal units reaches its culmination in the final verses. In verse 11, the hexameter metamorphoses into a pentameter if read in reverse sequence (*est placitum superis tunc haec in gaudia mundi/mundi gaudia in haec tunc superis placitum est*, 15.11). Still more significant is the conceit that brings the poem to its climax: whether one reads the individual words of verses 12–13 forwards or backwards, the elegiac couplet holds fast (with hexameter turning into pentameter and vice versa); by contrast, when approached in reverse sequence, the words of verses 14–15 deliver two sotadaeans (based on three Ionic feet and a final catalectic foot).[140]

How should we explain such verbal and metrical play? Part of the fifteenth poem's motivation lies, of course, in the self-conscious display of technical virtuosity. But no less important is the associated idea of fragmentation. To appreciate the poem's "arduousness," the reader must not only approach it as a single text but also pay attention to each individual line, metrical unit, and syllable: it is only by breaking down the textual fabric of the whole that its parts can be recomposed anew. Again and again, we find Optatian delighting in a related game. The thirty-two verses of the twenty-eighth poem, for example, comprise just eight elegiac couplets, but by reversing the word order, each individual couplet (28.1–2, 5–6, 9–10, 13–14, 17–18, 21–2, 25–6, 29–30) yields its mirror inversion while nonetheless maintaining the metrical measure (28.3–4, 7–8, 11–12, 15–16, 19–20, 23–4, 27–8, 31–2).[141] No less revealing is poem 13 (figure 1.30).[142] As text laid out on the page, the poem's twelve verses yield an acrostic and telestic

---

139. For discussion, see Ernst 2012: 46–8 (also providing a German translation), along with, e.g., Polara 1973: 2.92–4, Levitan 1985: 246–50, Consolino 1997, Okáčová 2006: 60–1, and Bruhat 2009: 104–6. On the poem's scholia, see Pipitone 2012b: 59–63.

140. 15.11–15: *Est placitum superis tunc haec in gaudia mundi | perpetuis bene sic partiri munera saeclis; | sidera dant patri, et patris imperium, | sancte, tibi. magnae data tu lux aurea Romae. | ista canit ruris tibi uates ardua metra.* On the longer history of such palindromes, see esp. Luz 2010: 179–211, with the catalogue of 49 Greek examples at 387–90.

141. For the rationale, see esp. Polara 1973: 2.165–7 and Levitan 1985: 252–3.

142. Cf. Polara 1973: 2.86–7; Levitan 1985: 253–5.

XIII

```
 P R I N C E P S B E A T E P L A C I D O S V B A X E I A M N V N C
 I V S T I S S E R E N E P O P V L I S F A V E N T E M V N D O
 V I C T O R T R I V M P H A T R I B V E N S S A L V B R E N V M E N
 S A E C L I S A M O R E D O M I N A N S P E R E N N E F A V S T I S
5A V C T O R S A L V T I S O R I E N S Q V I E T V S I B I T
 V O T I S F A V E N T E D O M I N I S V P E R N E D E X T R A
 G A V D E T S V B I R E P L A C I D V M R E G E N T I S O M E N
 V I R T V S V I G O R E R A D I A N S S E R E N A P R A E S T A T
 S A N C T I S V I D E R E S V P E R I S R E M O T A M V N D I
10T O T V M S V B O R B E M O D E R A N S S A L V B R E N V M E N
 V I N C E N S V B I Q V E S V P E R O F A V E N T E N V T V
 S A E C L V M P E R O M N E D O M I N A N S B E A T E S O L V S
          5       10      15      20      25      30
```

Figure 1.30. Optatian, poem 13 (after the typographic presentation of Polara 1973). Reproduced by kind permission of Giovanni Polara.

in honour of the emperor (*Pius Augustus Constantinus*). But just as the poem's individual letters operate across two verbal fields—along its horizontal and vertical axis alike—so too can the poem's individual words be read from right to left, as well as from left to right, within each verse. The central anapaest allows for interchangeable metrical configurations: in the words of the scholiast, "the verse consists half of iambic and half of trochaic forms"; as such, it "turns its trochaic part into iambic, and its iambic part into trochaic."[143]

The supreme example of such "poetry in pieces" comes in poem 25.[144] At first sight, the poem looks somewhat unpromising: it consists of just twenty words—four verses of five words apiece. Once written, though, the text takes on a life of its own:

Ardua componunt felices carmina Musae
dissona conectunt diuersis uincula metris
scrupea pangentes torquentes pectora uatis
undique confusis constabunt singula uerbis.

The blessed Muses put together difficult poems:
they bind together dissonant chains from diverse measures,

---

143. For text and discussion, see Pipitone 2012b: 55–7: *In hac pagina uersus est ex dimidio iambico et dimidio trochaico constans, qui dum fit reciprocus trochaicam partem in iambicam uertit et iambicam in trochaicam*. For an associated but distinct tradition of *uersus recurrentes* that operate on the level of the individual letter rather than word, see Squire 2011: 222–4 (with bibliography at 223, n. 61).

144. For discussion, see especially Polara 1973: 2.158. Cf. Flores and Polara 1969; Levitan 1985: 250–2; Ernst 1991: 133–5, 2012: 1.50–2; Bruhat 1999: 152–70 (comparing the *uersus intexti* of poems 6, 18, and 19); González Iglesias 2000; Buisset 2006; Okáčová 2007: 61; Letrouit 2007; Pelttari 2014: 77–9.

setting their challenges, twisting the hearts of the poet;
though the words be shuffled in every way, they will still stand
      individually.

As Optatian makes clear, the poem's individual words can themselves be shuffled at whim (*confusis . . . uerbis*, 25.4): its constituent verbal and metrical units once again operate as "chains" (*uincula*, 25.2), each of them bound together one by one (*singula*, 25.4). Jumble the words within the poem, then, and the quatrain generates more variant quatrains, all the while maintaining its metrical structure.[145] Some extant manuscripts play out the conceit, lengthening the poem from the four hexameters cited above to seventy-two (in the longest manuscript version), whether by shuffling words within the same line (e.g. *carmina felices componunt ardua Musae*, 25.5) or else by rearranging words and hence metrical units between verses (e.g., *ardua constabunt torquentes carmina Musae*, 25.9, stealing a participle and verb from the third and fourth verses, respectively). The exact rules of the game have been much debated.[146] According to the extant scholia, there are "eighty-four" available versions, so long as we keep the final word in place.[147] If one sticks to the rules of the surviving manuscript versions and commentary, as William Levitan has argued, one can in fact count a total number of 1,792 potential verses; abandoning the scholiast's compositional rule about the position of the final word, Levitan himself arrived at 12,544 variants.[148] More recent counts put the figure considerably higher, at least if one considers the total number of possible quatrains rather than the number of single lines: "even if one does not change in any way the metrical shape of the quatrain, it is possible to compose 39,016,857,600 different quatrains from Optatian's

---

145. The composition "virtually explodes under the reader's eye," as Levitan 1985: 250 puts it. Fourth-century readers would surely have understood such a "proteus" composition within the rubric of Ausonius's *technopaegnia*: cf. Flores and Polara 1969, along with, e.g., Alan Cameron 1980: 133–5, Pozzi 1984: 147–51, M. Roberts 1989a: esp. 58–9, and Rühl 2006: 77–8.

146. For a review, see most recently Letrouit 2007 and Pelttari 2014: 77. As Pelttari summarizes, "Each of these variants (1) retains *Musae, metris, uatis, uerbis* in that order at the end of each line of the quatrain; (2) does not exchange words from the first and fourth feet with words from the second and third feet; and (3) does not use in any single line two dactyls that are both from the same metrical position in the original lines."

147. For the text and commentary, see Polara 1973: 1.98, 2.158–9, and Pipitone 2012b: 72–5: *ita dumtaxat, ut primae partes cum primis uel quartis uersuum uices mutent, secundae cum secundis uel tertiis, et possis, si uelis, nulla parte orationis addita ex his quattuor uersibus mixtis octoginta quattuor facere ita, ut nullus sui similis sit*. Pipitone 2012b: 28–30, 91–3 sees the commentary on this poem as belonging to a first group of scholia—perhaps stretching all the way back to the fourth century (cf. above, nn. 14, 21).

148. See Levitan 1985: 251, n. 17 (responding to Flores and Polara 1969, who count 3,136 potential verses).

original," concludes Aaron Pelttari; "if one retains the original order of the final word of each line, the number of total quatrains is reduced to 1,625,702,400."[149]

The sheer number of yielded readerly options returns us to the issue of "dynamic signs." Teasing out the different variants, swapping the individual words within and across the poem's four lines, readers are invited to explore the rules and limits that give rise to the authorial game. In doing so, audiences also take over the project of literary composition that the poem has begun: the text provides the elemental resources for a sort of "do-it-yourself" poetry kit; it prompts the reader to take up the present words and generate absent variants.[150] Despite the attempts of some manuscripts to give examples, the total number of possibilities lies beyond graphic expression.[151] In its perpetual self-regeneration, the poem stretches beyond the confines of the page: by spurring readers to turn over the different possibilities in their minds, it materializes an idea of the poetically immaterial.[152]

But it is the poem's capacity to break down before our eyes—to self-fragment and be put together anew—that I want to emphasize here. More than with any other extant example in the corpus, the integrity of poem 25 depends upon a form that can be dismantled. In this case, it is the individual words (rather than their single letters, as in Optatian's *carmina cancellata*) that provide the poetic building blocks. And yet the poem configures its literal deconstruction as a constructive process: what ultimately matters is the reader's extraction of individual verbal units to create something new. In that connection, it is worth emphasizing how the poem is itself stitched together from the textured fabric of earlier Latin texts. Commenting on the four verses of the "original" text, Polara has noted some twenty parallels in verses by (among others) Catullus, Ovid, Vergil, Martial, and Statius.[153] To label those parallels "allusions" would be

---

149. Pelttari 2014: 78: cf. Letrouit 2007; Pipitone 2012b: 73–5.

150. Cf. Rühl 2006: 93: "Je intensiver der Leser sich mit dem Gedicht auseinandersetzt, desto mehr Sinngehalt wird er ihm entlocken. Der Reiz des Gedichtes liegt damit in der jeweils individuellen Interaktion zwischen dem Text und seinem Leser." For a closely related reading, cf. Pelttari 2014: 79, on how the poem "allows the reader to share in the work of composition."

151. For the sentiment, cf. above, 57 on 17.8–10: "if you were thoroughly to explore the intricate word [*uerbum textum*] with a Latin mouth, connecting the verses in an order that is other than their own, you will be able to fill a long volume sounding out its vows" (*si uerbum textum pertemptes ore Latino | in sese alterno conectens ordine uersus, | uota sonans longum poteris implere uolumen*).

152. On the underlying trope of "le poème inexistant," see Buisset 2006; cf. Levitan 1985: 249–50: "there are ... more verses in Optatian's poetry than a mere line-count will reveal: each poem also contains a number of inherent permutations of itself, a number of potential dispositions. And there are more grand designs than there are poems ... they require contemplation as if worlds."

153. See Polara 1973: 99; on the poem's richly allusive fabric, see above all González Iglesias 2000 and Buisset 2006: 196–209.

overly simplistic: the capacity to see this poem in relation to others is contingent upon the individual subjective connections that we draw; inevitably, they must also depend upon the "text" that we construct from the poem—that is, the precise arrangement of its words. Crucially, though, the poem's very units take us back to the "diverse verse-measures" (*diuersis . . . metris*) of past literary paradigms. One particularly revealing parallel, as Juan Antonio González Iglesias has observed, comes in Ovid's *Amores* (1.8.57–8):[154]

> *Ecce, quid iste tuus praeter noua carmina uates*
> *donat? amatoris milia multa leges.*

Look, what does this poet of yours give you other than new songs? You will read many thousands from a lover.

In this passage, Ovid voices the imaginary advice given to his beloved—the idea that she should discount the amorous advances of the poet. At first, the parallel with Optatian's poem may remain hidden: perceiving any connection among the poem's "dissonant chains" (*dissona . . . uincula*) must depend on the reader's reshuffling of the words *carmina* and *uatis* from the first and third lines of Optatian's "original" text. Once seen, though, the parallel has the potential to reconfigure our view of the poem at hand. The seemingly countless permutations of Optatian's own miniature creation echo Ovid's *carmina uatis*: for all their variations, the quatrains spun from the poem lead back to the "many thousands" (*milia multa*) prefigured in Ovid's single couplet.

Needless to say, such concern with the constituent "elements" of linguistic expression was informed by a much longer critical tradition. In the first century BC, Lucretius had turned to the example of alphabetic letters to expound his theory of *elementa* (LUCR. 2.682–92; cf. 1.196–7): as the elemental units of cultivated language, letters were deemed analogous to the elements of nature.[155] Lucretius' "atomistic" view of language seems likewise to have been institutionalized in Roman pedagogic practice. According to Quintilian, young children should be offered the "ivory form of letters to play with" (*eburneas . . . litterarum formas in lusum offerre, inst. or.* 1.1.26): by shuffling around such letters, children could actively learn the literal building blocks of language.[156] A related game,

---

154. Cf. González Iglesias 2000: 356 and Pelttari 2014: 78–9.
155. For discussion (and analysis of Lucretius's earlier intellectual debts), see Dionigi 1988: 34–7. For the relevance of these Lucretian passages to Optatian, see Buisset 2006: 202–4, supposing a direct allusion in poem 25 ("L'image, très parlante, des lettres constituant les mots convient à Lucrèce pour illustrer la théorie des atomes, et il est certain que les vers d'Optatien évoquaient ce passage pour son public").
156. Cf., e.g., Baroin 2010: 79–80 and Squire 2014: 413–15.

albeit acted out on the level of syllables rather than letters, seems to lie behind the so-called *Tabulae Lusoriae* that survive from all across the Roman Empire: by rolling the die and putting together the different verbal and visual units, players of such *Tabulae* moved across the board to formulate different expressive forms.[157] As Isabella Gualandri argues in this volume, late antique grammarians developed this underlying attitude to language, analysing the compound creation of verbal discourse in terms of words, syllables, and letters. Individual letters, writes Sergius (most likely in the fifth century AD), serve as the essential units of all rhetoric: "the letter alone cannot be split (*littera sola non habet quo soluatur*)," and "it is for this reason that it is called "indivisible" by philosophers" (*ideo a philosophis atomos dicitur*).[158]

This "atomistic" or "elemental" view of language is absolutely integral to "POP art." On the one hand, Optatian exploits poetic precedent as the verbal building blocks for his craft: isolating single words and phrases, his poems are constructed from the fragments of the literary past. On the other hand, Optatian's works are steeped in a knowing sense of their own fragmentation—an awareness of how each compound poem can be broken down into its constituent verses, words, syllables, and even letters, all the while yielding the elements for new feats of creative literary composition. Optatian certainly looks back to an older critical tradition. Yet what is so innovative about Optatian's poetry is the way in which this ideological framework shapes the very form of his literary creations: Optatian's compositions are designed precisely in order to be de- and recomposed.

But there is another innovation besides. After all, Optatian's *carmina cancellata* materialize this atomistic view of language in concrete terms—as *material*

---

157. For the extant Roman "gaming tablets," see the catalogue of Ferrua 2001 (with earlier discussions in Ferrua 1946, counting 52 examples, and Ferrua 1948 and 1964); cf. Purcell 1995: 17–28 (citing earlier bibliography on 18, n. 69), Friedrich 2001: 81–100, and Habinek 2009: 125–7. "The most eloquent [tablets] historically" (Purcell 1995: 19) seem to have been made up of 6 words of 6 letters (i.e., 36 spaces in total, with 12 letters per line), usually interspersed with various images and symbols: the objective was evidently to move across the tablet with gaming pieces, "playing" with and through the letters. While Purcell suggests that the *tabulae lusoriae* grant "direct contact . . . with the snorting plebeians" (Purcell 1995: 19), their graphic games can certainly be contextualized alongside elite forms of Imperial Latin literary production; indeed, as Purcell himself acknowledges, "such playful writing games were as much a game for the rich as for the poor" (Purcell 1995: 28–37). "The playfulness of the script on the game boards," as Habinek 2009: 125 concludes, mirror "certain kinds of play in literary texts": "they are manifestations of the same underlying attitude to writing, which treats it not just as an expression of speech but also as a distinctive means of graphic communication that entails strictures and constraints not characteristic of spoken language"; they therefore demonstrate "a certain self-consciousness with respect to the interrelated processes of reading, writing, and playing" (126).

158. = Keil 1857–70: 4.475; for discussion, see also Gualandri (this volume, 143).

form on the page. The point strikes me as important, premised as it is not only on the fragmentary elements of language but also on the elemental units that comprise a pictorial design: rather like the pointillist painters of the late nineteenth century (albeit in a rather different cultural context), Optatian underscores the fact that images too are made up from individual constituents marks, dots, and strokes. Already in the late second century AD and concerned with Christian modes of biblical exegesis, Irenaeus had compared Gnostics who have "stitched together" (συγκαττύσαντες) scriptural passages to people who rearrange the pieces of a "beautiful image that some skilful artist has carefully constructed out of precious stones" (εἰκόνος καλῆς κατασκευασμένης ἐπιμελῶς ἐκ ψηφίδων ἐπισήμων ὑπὸ σοφοῦ τεχνίτου, adv. haer. 1.8.1). For Irenaeus, the Valentinian Gnostics resemble those who "strive to weave together ropes made of sand" (ἐξ ἄμμου σχοινία πλέκειν ἐπιτηδέοντες). But their verbal artifice is expressly likened to a botched attempt to de- and reconstruct the pieces of a mosaic. In weaving their heresy from individual verbal units of scripture, the Gnostics bring to mind someone who, deconstructing the tessellated pieces of a depicted "king," reformulates those precious stones into the shape of a poorly executed "dog" or "fox." Just as the Gnostics attempt to dupe their audiences by citing piecemeal extracts from the Bible, the dishonest artist might point to the jewelled form of his creation, attempting to persuade his ignorant viewers that his image still represented its original royal likeness.[159]

Subsequent writers duly developed this artistic metaphor for literary "patchworks." Returning to the image of his king-fox mosaic in the following chapter of his *Adversus Haereses*, Irenaeus himself compared the Gnostics' scriptural "stitchings" to poems woven together from individual lines of Homeric epic: among the simple-minded (τῶν ἀπανούργων), Irenaeus writes, a reader "will not receive the fox instead of the likeness of the king," even if he acknowledges the underlying gems of Homer (καὶ γὰρ εἰ τὰς ψηφίδας γνωρίσει, ἀλλὰ τὴν ἀλώπετα ἀντὶ τῆς βασιλικῆς εἰκόνος οὐ παραδέξεται, adv. haer. 1.9.4). We find the same image in the preface to Ausonius's *Cento Nuptialis*—a letter addressed to Axius Paulus. Writing in Optatian's immediate aftermath, Ausonius explains how the cento is structured "out of various passages and diverse meanings" (*uariis de locis sensibusque diuersis*). As such, Ausonius continues, this literary

---

159. For discussion, see most recently Heath 2010: esp. 534–7, Sandnes 2011: 132–9, and Blaising 2013: 377–8; on the larger context of Irenaeus's comments, see Perkins 1976; for a commentary, see the notes accompanying Unger and Dillon 1992: 41. Irenaeus's comments here may be compared with Optatian's third poem, which really does claim to portray the *uultus Augusti* (cf. Squire, forthcoming a).

project is "like the game that the Greeks have called *stomachion*" (*simile ... ludicro, quod Graeci stomachion uocauere*):[160]

> *Ossicula ea sunt: ad summam quattuordecim figuras geometricas habent. sunt enim aequaliter triquetra uel extentis lineis uel frontis angulis uel obliquis ... harum uerticularum uariis coagmentis simulantur species mille formarum: helephantus belua aut aper bestia, anser uolans et mirmillo in armis, subsidens uenator et latrans canis, quin et turris et cantharus et alia huiusmodi innumerabilium figurarum, quae alius alio scientius uariegant. sed peritorum concinnatio miraculum est, imperitorum iunctura ridiculum. quo praedicto scies, quod ego posteriores imitatus sum. hoc ergo centonis opusculum ut ille ludus tractatur, pari modo sensus diuersi ut congruant, adoptiua quae sunt ut cognata uideantur, aliena ne interluceant, arcessita ne uim redarguant, densa ne supra modum protuberent, hiulca ne pateant.*

There you have little pieces of bone, fourteen in number and having the form of geometric figures. For there are triangles with lengths of equal sides or else with extended lines; some are symmetrical in angle, others are oblique. ... Through the various connections of these joining pieces, the visual appearance of countless forms are imitated: a monstrous elephant or a brutal boar, a flying goose and a gladiator in his armour, a crouching huntsman and a barking dog—even a tower and a tankard, and countless other figures of this sort, which different artists vary with different skill. But while the harmonious arrangement of experts is marvellous, the jumble made by non-experts lends itself to ridicule (you will know from this preface, that I have imitated the latter sort!). And so this little work of my cento is handled in the same way as that game: the purpose is to bring together different meanings in a harmonious manner and to make the adopted pieces seem like they are naturally related; the purpose is to prevent things that are foreign from showing any light between them and to prevent the far-fetched from proclaiming the force which has untied them—to prevent the closely packed from bulging unduly, and the loosely knit from gaping open.

---

160. There are various textual problems with the passage (see Green 1991: 521–2, on ibid. 133–4): both my text and translation are adapted from H. G. E. White 1919: 374–5. On the passage, see McGill 2005: 1–11, 18–21, Prieto Domínguez 2010: 31–4, and Pelttari 2014: 104–7. More generally on Ausonius's "kaleidoscopic" turns, see Nugent 1990: 37–41, along with Elsner 2002a: 9–13, on Ausonius's knowing Latin appropriations of Greek epigram. For Archimedes's associated description of the game of *stomachion*, cf. Netz and Noel 2007: 255 and Morelli 2009 on Heiberg 1910–15: 2.416–24.

Where Irenaeus (like Tertullian and Jerome)[161] chastises the cento—or rather "patchwork" texts drawn from passages of scripture—Ausonius tenders a playful celebration of it. But what interests me about Ausonius's particular defence is his analogy between the cento and the visual games of pictorial representation. For Ausonius, the art of weaving together the fragmented metrical units of Vergil resembles the skill of forging make-believe pictures out of geometric shapes—of using abstract patterns to "imitate the visual appearance of countless forms" (*simulantur species mille formarum*).

Optatian's poems can be seen in closely related terms, offering a counterpart to the "various connections of joining pieces" that Ausonius describes (*harum uerticularum uariis coagmentis*). Crucially, however, the units of his works operate on the combined level of words *and* pictures: Optatian's *carmina cancellata* offer piecemeal constructions that lend themselves to *both* seeing and reading alike. In this sense, Optatian gives material form to Ausonius's analogy between visual and verbal "play." Operating piece by piece and line by metrical/geometrical line, the lettered creations of "POP art" at once figure and literalize Ausonius's figurative literary metaphor. These pictorial-poetic forms, we might say, play out Ausonius's comparison not only between poems and pictures but also between poems and pictures *in pieces*.

Such analogies between the acts of piecemeal literary and artistic creation return us squarely to the visual cultural context in which Optatian was writing. In both their appropriation of past poetic sound bites and their concern with the elemental properties of language, Optatian's works parallel the assemblages of contemporary fourth-century art: they give combined literary and visual form to an aesthetic of appropriative spoliation.[162] Now, the recourse to *spolia*—that is, to the architectural or sculptural elements drawn from one complex that were deliberately selected, removed, and redeployed in another—had a longer history in Roman art. Already in the late third century (and quite possibly before), we know of monuments that functioned as eclectic assemblages, drawn together from multiple sources: the much debated Arcus Novus and Arco di Portogallo in Rome, for example, attest to a pre-Constantinian idea of constructing, adorning, and reframing architectural forms out of the dismembered units of earlier

---

161. On Christian attitudes towards the cento, see McGill 2005: esp. xvi–xvii, 2007b; Sandnes 2011; Pelttari 2014: 107–12 (on Tert. *de praescr. haer.* 38–9 and Jer. 53.7).

162. There is now a vast literature on spoliation, both in Roman Late Antiquity and beyond. For some introductory guides, see Settis 1986; Kinney 1995; de Lachenal 1995; Hansen 2003; Liverani 2009; Brilliant and Kinney 2011; Hernández Lobato 2012: 271–317, esp. 276–81; Varner 2014; cf. the bibliography cited in the introduction to this volume (8–11). On the appropriative "spoliatory" practices of early Christianity more generally, see the excellent discussion in Hernández Lobato 2012: 76–126.

prototypes.[163] But it is no coincidence, I think, that such a syncretic attitude to the formal remains of the past reached its zenith in the early fourth century. Patricia Cox Miller has suggested that this "aesthetic of discontinuity ... rooted in the production of fragmentation" is reflected in the changes in the narratological rationale of fourth-century Christian sarcophagi: objects like the "Dogmatic sarcophagus" (and a little later, column sarcophagi, such as that of "Junius Bassus"), Cox Miller argues, break the integrity of "scenic coherence," "thereby creating self-contained compositional units and drawing attention to the episodic quality of the work as a whole."[164] Whether or not we agree with this assessment, it is clear that Constantine ruled over a Rome well aware of its cultural spoliation of the monuments, texts, and indeed cultic practices of its Imperial past. Constantine's newly sanctioned cult of Christianity, as Jaś Elsner puts it, was the ultimate *spolium*, a compound creation refashioned out of Judaic and pagan practice.[165] The city of Constantinople, consecrated in AD 330, gave concrete urban form to a similar aesthetic: such were the number of statues and monuments appropriated from across the Mediterranean to adorn Constantinople, as

---

163. For reviews of the evidence and bibliography, see Kinney 1997: 129–34. "Like the translation of statues and the use of 'renovated stones' in architecture," as Kinney 1997: 142 concludes, "the display of secondhand reliefs on the Arch of Constantine could not have struck the fourth-century viewer as unprecedented or unique." On the Arcus Novus (erected by Diocletian in AD 293–4), which incorporated Claudian or Antonine reliefs alongside tetrarchic sculptures, see Laubscher 1976, Buttrey 1983, Kleiner 1992: 409–13 (with further bibliography on 428), Torelli 1993b. On the Arco di Portogallo—of contested date, but perhaps constructed in the third century (Bertoletti and La Rocca 1986: 21–32, Torelli 1992: 122–3)—see Kleiner 1992: 253–4 (with further bibliography on 265) and Torelli 1993a.

164. Cox Miller 1998: 118, 119 (the second citation is a direct quotation of M. Roberts 1989a: 95); cf. M. Roberts 1989a: 66–121; Cox Miller 2009: 42–61. Cox Miller associates this aesthetic fragmentation with the rise of new, Christian ideas about the relic, "which remained miraculously whole despite being constantly broken up into fragments, themselves considered to be 'whole'" (Cox Miller 1998: 123): analysing Optatian specifically, she concludes that the fragmentary and sensory "aesthetics of late Latin poetry has an exact analogy in the cult of relics, where a dead body (like language) no longer functioned primarily as a record of human living (like speech) but rather as a material artefact whose referent lay outside itself in a spirituality that demanded sensory expression for its abstract belief in conduits of divine presence" (126). Cox Miller draws an important—and stimulating—link between literary and artistic forms, on the one hand, and Christian cultic practice on the other. The difficulty, though, is that her interpretation imposes back onto the earlier fourth century theological ideas and writings that are somewhat (and sometimes very much) later in date: Gregory of Nyssa, Victricus of Rouen, and Theodoret of Cyrrhus risk providing a misleadingly anachronistic lens for viewing the cultural history of the earlier fourth century. From the huge bibliography on early Christian sarcophagi, I have particularly benefited from Deichmann and Klauser 1966, Kaiser-Minn 1983, and Koch 2000.

165. Elsner 2004: 293. Cf. ibid. 304: "The cumulative aesthetic of late-antique art allowed these pieces both to be themselves and to become parts of a new whole. This enabled the new work to make a delicate gesture of continuity with earlier eras whereby the past could be respected in the integrity of its original pieces but transformed through a new framing." See also this volume's introduction by Elsner and Hernández Lobato, comparing literary *spolia* to iconic artworks like the eighth-century cross of Desiderius in Brescia (8).

Eusebius's *Chronicle* (in the version of Saint Jerome) famously complained, that the city was "dedicated with the nudity of almost all other cities."[166]

Perhaps the most tangible artistic parallel for Optatian's "poetry in pieces," though, comes in the eponymous arch that Constantine dedicated on Rome's *Via Triumphalis* in AD 315.[167] The poet's recourse to past precedent finds its material analogy in the arch's selection, appropriation, and juxtaposition of different visual forms: Constantine's own fourth-century figurative *elementa* are set alongside the upper Trajanic sculptures of prisoners (as well as side reliefs of Trajan's Dacian campaign), Hadrianic roundels, and Aurelian reliefs (figure 1.31; cf. figures I.1–I.2). Like Optatian's poems, the monument unites various compositional elements drawn from different moments of the Roman Imperial past. But such factured juxtapositions are themselves predicated on a sense of piecemeal fragmentation. If the arch unites its diverse *spolia*, those individual elements can be viewed alongside and against each other. The resulting stylistic discrepancy—the eclectic mix of visual forms—underscores the disconnections of the whole: while of course standing as a single coherent unity, the monument invites audiences to view its parts in isolation, comparing and contrasting its visions of Constantinian Rome in relation to the differently stylized achievements of former emperors.[168]

With the arch of Constantine, installed at the heart of Rome, Optatian's "poetry in pieces" finds its most monumental Imperial counterpart. While the building's individual elements construct a totalizing vision, they simultaneously insist upon a more piecemeal mode of exegetic response, relying upon the active engagement of the viewer. Optatian's triumphs of poetic form work in related ways to construct an analogous image of the Constantinian achievement: if they are premised on fragmentation, they are also founded on an idea of concordance, consonance, and cohesion.

---

166. *Chron.* on 330 [= R. Helm 1956: 232]. "Nudity" (*nuditas*) is used here literally and metaphorically: not only are these statues undressed, but their concentration has stripped other cities of their sculpture; cf. Elsner 2000: 154–6, Bassett 2004: 16. On Constantinople's sculptural collections, see esp. Bassett 1991, along with Bassett 2004: 224–8, surveying the "self-conscious creation of . . . this collection, composed largely of antiquities of pre-fourth-century manufacture" (1). More generally on Constantinople as a "ciudad-centón," see the sparkling analysis of Hernández Lobato 2012: 282–9.

167. The monument has attracted a suitably monumental (if indeed itself somewhat piecemeal) secondary literature: among the fullest discussions is Pensabene and Panella 1999; but the best analyses of the arch's spoliatory aesthetics—combined with a masterful overview of the literature and historiography—are Brandenburg 1979: 439–50 and Elsner 2000; cf. most recently Hughes 2014 and Varner 2014: esp. 64–70. For the comparison with Optatian's creations, see esp. Elsner 2000: 175, along with Doria 1979: 67, Levitan 1985: 269, and Rühl 2006: 91–2.

168. Cf. Elsner 2000: 163–75.

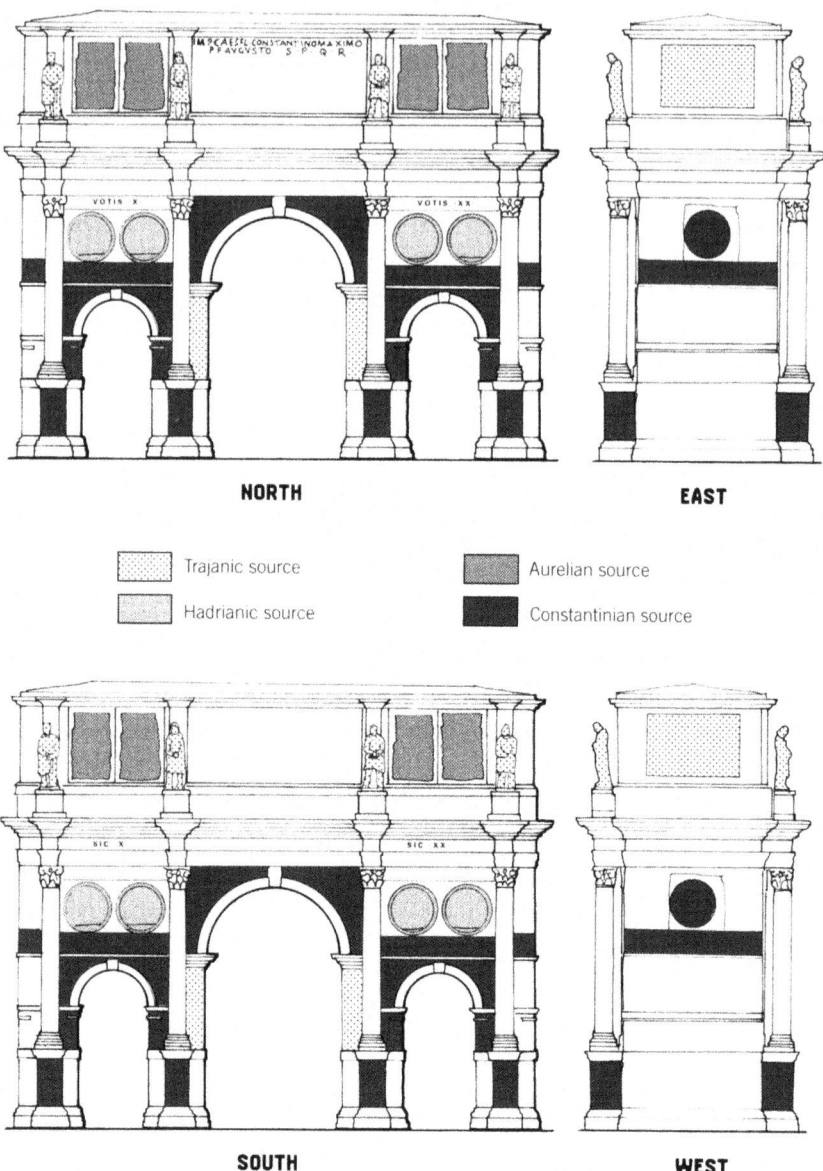

Figure 1.31. Diagram of the arch of Constantine (dedicated in AD 315), showing the Imperial derivation of its different sculptural spolia (cf. figures I.1–I.2). Photograph reproduced by kind permission of Jaś Elsner (after Elsner 1998: 188, fig. 126).

*****

"POP art" is certainly a less celebrated icon of Constantinian Rome than the arch of Constantine. As this chapter has argued, however, Optatian's complex view of past and present proves no less varied, rich, and self-conscious. For many readers (above all in the nineteenth and twentieth centuries), what has disappointed about Optatian is his seeming reduction of poetry to pure form: meaning, it is said, has become, if not quite arbitrary, at least secondary to the display of surface artistry (played out on the level of the poetic line, word, and letter). Within an edited collection on the poetics of late Latin literature, the important point strikes me as rather different. Working across the bounds of visual and verbal media, the ultimate significance of Optatian's poetry lies in its playful questioning of *how* we make sense of what we read—no less than of what we see.

Allow me to end with a final word about my title. "POP art" may seem a rather odd way of labelling Optatian's optical poetic concerns. These works are a far cry from the "mass cultural" appropriations of (for example) Andy Warhol, Roy Lichtenstein, and Jasper Johns; needless to say, there is likewise nothing "pop" about Optatian's erudite games with the philosophy of language and his highbrow recourse to Latin literary precedent. For all those differences, however, I suggest that "POP art" does find a resonance in more (post)modern artistic movements.[169] The themes of authorship, medium, originality, and reception—so self-consciously played out in Optatian's corpus—certainly have their own historical context. But they also seep beyond that cultural frame. If Optatian's works can still entrance, enrapture, and enthral, they also resonate with our own intellectual concerns—and at no time more so, perhaps, than in the uncertain world of the twenty-first century itself.[170]

---

169. For postmodernism as "not a trend to be chronologically defined," see Eco 1994. 66. "every period has its own postmodernism, just as every period would have its own mannerism"; cf. Squire 2011: 377, n. 21. More generally on Late Antiquity's prefigurations of "modernist" and "postmodernist" concerns, see the introduction to this volume by Elsner and Hernández Lobato.

170. The present chapter derives from research undertaken during two generous fellowships—first, at the Wissenschaftskolleg zu Berlin in 2012 (originally oriented towards another project: Squire 2015a), and second, at the Internationales Kolleg Morphomata at the Universität zu Köln in 2014; it is also a pleasure to acknowledge the support of the Leverhulme Trust, who facilitated this work through the award of a 2012 Philip Leverhulme Prize. Parts of what follows have been given as seminars and lectures at the University of Oslo, Albert-Ludwigs-Universität in Freiburg, Internationales Kolleg Morphomata, and the Sterling and Francine Clark Institute in Williamstown, Massachusetts: I am hugely grateful to those various audiences for their engaged critique and suggestions. Four other brief words of thanks: first, to the editors for their invitation to participate in this volume, their stimulating responses to an earlier draft, and for assigning an extended word count to the chapter; second, to the book's anonymous reviewers and to four additional readers—John Henderson (always the most inspiring of interlocutors), Sigrid Mratschek (for numerous suggestions), Johannes Wienand (for bibliographic guidance), and Christopher Whitton (who saved me from countless errors); third, to Giovanni Polara, for allowing me to reproduce his typographic presentations of Optatian's poems; and fourth, to Mary Morton, for her help copy-editing the final text. All translations—and errors!—are my own unless otherwise stated.

Polymetry in Late Latin Poems

Some Observations on Its Meaning and Functions

FRANCA ELA CONSOLINO

From a metrical point of view, Latin poetry from the fourth to sixth century CE is a complex and partially contradictory reality: on the one hand there is an increasing dominance of the hexameter; on the other hand we find a remarkable tendency to use a wide range of different metres that had been more or less practised in the classical period, even to experiment with some new metres or strophes, as in the case of Boethius. This runs in parallel with another feature of late Latin poetry: the tendency of proposing new kinds of poems or collections. Consequently, the choice of the metres was no longer necessarily connected with the Greek and Latin conventions, heavily depending on literary genres. A good example is offered by the Phalaecean hendecasyllable, whose use, while following in the footsteps of Catullus and Martial, was extended to quite long poems; equally unprecedented were the sequences of Adonics kata stichon.

Late Latin poetry is therefore characterized by an increasing use of polymetry: epigrams such as those of Ausonius, whose main themes are inspired by those of the Greek Anthology, have a percentage of elegiac couplets much lower than Martial,[1] while an amazing variety of metres characterizes Ausonius's two works, *Parentalia* and *Professores*, where elegiac couplets still dominate, just to indicate that these two collections of poems are very close to the epigram as a literary genre but do not perfectly coincide with it. There are also many different metres in two collections of small poems by Ausonius whose exact genre is problematic, for in conception and form they are unprecedented in Latin literature: the *Ephemeris totius diei* and the *Bissula*. Taste of variety and aim to originality are also testified by Prudentius, who for his *Prologus* constructs strophes made of an unprecedented combination of metres, while purposefully alternating different metres in his lyrical collections. Even Claudian, who is normally content with hexameters and elegiac distichs, wrote his four *fescennini* in four different metres.

Polymetry is also a main feature of the two *prosimetra* by Martianus Capella and Boethius, both of them deserving attention, the latter in particular, due to poetry regularly alternating with prose and to the rich variety of metres chosen

---

1. Consolino 2003: 157–8.

and sometimes occurring for the first time in the *Consolatio*. Yet what I discuss in this chapter is not polymetry in the wider meaning, which applies to collections of poems and affects their inner organization, or to prosimetra, where the treatment of polymetry involves the relationship between prose and verses and their possibly different functions. Such a discussion would involve much more extended analysis, requiring a book rather than an article. Among the Latin poetic output of Late Antiquity, in addition to polymetric collections, there are also some single polymetric poems; my contribution focuses on them.

Not all Latin poets of Late Antiquity are interested in polymetry, nor are they equally practised in polymetric compositions. The authors who actually are neither practice polymetry to the same extent nor adopt the same patterns: two or more metres can be employed, and these metres are not always the same. I therefore analyse every single poem with its peculiar characteristics, inquiring into the possible meaning of the recourse to polymetry. In this way, I should be able to verify case by case if the use of more than one metre and the particular choice of some metres instead of others goes beyond a virtuoso performance and conveys a special message or gives particular connotations to the piece being examined. This is a question that may sometimes prove difficult, if not impossible, to answer, but intertextuality can certainly help us to a better understanding of what at first glance could seem arbitrary choices. For this reason, I pay special attention to any element that hints at an interpretation of metrical choices which can cast some new light on the suggestions transmitted to the reader, as well as on the individual attitude of each author and the actual extent of his experimentalism. Individual analyses of single poems have already been made by some scholars, including myself, and answers attempted. What I would like to reach is an overall view on polymetric poems, considered in their totality as a specific feature of late Latin poetry.

To fix our field of investigation, we start by drawing a map of the poems and poets we are dealing with[2]:

- Ausonius
    1. *epigr.* 42: 2 hexameters + 1 elegiac distich;
    2. *par.* 17: 1 iambic trimeter + 18 anapaestic dimeters catalectic (paroemiacs)

---

2. The list does not include CLAUD. *c.m.* 25 (4 elegiacs + 145 hexameters) and VEN. FORT. *carm.* 6.1 (12 elegiacs + 119 hexameters) because each of them contains a preface in elegiac distichs and an epithalamium in hexameters, which have been transmitted by the manuscript tradition as if they belonged to a single poem. For the same reason I do not consider as polymetric the *carm. de prou.*, whose preface in elegiacs has been transmitted continuously, along with the quite long hexameter text it precedes. As far as possible the poems are listed in chronological order.

3. *prof.* 19: 3 distichs of pythiambic strophe 2 (dactylic hexameter and iambic trimeter) + 4 elegiac couplets

4. *prof.* 21: 8 strophes of 2 anapaestic dimeters followed by an Adonic + 2 elegiac couplets³

5. *ep.* 6: 46 hexameters + the last two verses (the second in Greek) of an alcaic strophe

6. *ep.* 8: 17 elegiacs + 1 pythiambic strophe 2

7. *ep.* 13: 70 hexameters + 11 iambic dimeters + 23 Phalaecean hendecasyllables

8. *ep.* 14b: 18 hexameters + 1 choliambus + 4 iambic trimeters + 12 Phalaecean hendecasyllables + 21 lesser asclepiads

9. *ep.* 16: 2 elegiacs + 2 iambic trimeters

- *epigr. Bob.* 70: 1 elegiac distich + 2 hexameters
- Paulinus of Nola
  1. *carm.* 10: 9 elegiac distichs + 42 iambic distichs + 229 hexameters
  2. *carm.* 11: 48 hexameters + 10 iambic distichs
  3. *carm.* 21: 104 hexameters + 167 iambic trimeters + 36 elegiac couplets + 515 hexameters
  4. *carm.* 25: 119 elegiac distichs + 3 pentameters
- *poema coniugis ad uxorem*: 16 anacreontean verses + 53 elegiac couplets
- *de obitu Baebiani*: 20 iambic trimeters + 20 hexameters + 20 lesser asclepiads kata stichon + 40 hexameters (ll. 61–100) + 16 elegiac distichs (ll. 101–32)
- Cyprianus Gallus, *heptateuchos*: amid the hexameters of this epic paraphrase, there are three lyrical passages in Phalaecean hendecasyllables
- Hilary of Arles, *AL* 487 R: 2 hexameters + 1 elegiac distich
- Sidonius Apollinaris, *carm.* 13: 10 elegiac distichs + 20 Phalaecean hendecasyllables
- Ennodius
  1. *epist.* 5.8 = 224 V: 6 elegiac couplets + 2 hexameters
  2. *epist.* 7.29 = 362 V: 2 elegiac couplets + 3 Phalaecean hendecasyllables
  3. *carm.* 1.7 = 26 V: 16 elegiac distichs (ll. 1–32) + 12 hexameters (ll. 33–44) + 2 elegiac distichs again (ll. 45–8) + 5 lesser Sapphic strophes (ll. 49–68) + 12 Adonics kata stichon (ll. 69–80)

---

3. The Adonics of the eight strophes can also be interpreted as anapaestic monometers, as does Pighi 1968: 529 and as the 1548 Lyon edition should have done, which printed these verses together with the preceding line, to form an anapaestic trimeter: see Green 1991: 358.

4. *carm.* 1.4 = 388 V: 12 elegiac distichs (ll. 1–24) + 4 catalectic trochaic tetrameters (ll. 25–8) + 6 lesser Sapphic strophes (ll. 29–52) + 70 hexameters (ll. 53–122) + 6 Phalaecean hendecasyllables

In these poems, almost completely the work of poets certainly or very probably (the uncertain authors of the *poema coniugis* and the *de obitu Baebiani*) originating in Gallia,[4] there is only one very extended epic poem in more books, the *heptateuchos*, which is in a way an easier case to answer, as we shall see. The remnant evidence is represented by shorter (sometimes very short) single poems, and the grammarian and rhetorician Ausonius turns out to be the oldest to practise this kind of polymetry (at least after the Poetae Novelli),[5] opening the way to the others.

2.1. Ausonius

Epigr. 42 (2 hexameters + 1 elegiac distich) plays on the names of the two brothers Chrestos ("good") and Acindynos ("without danger"), who are the opposite of what their names mean. So the poet suggests moving the privative alpha from the latter to the former, in order to establish an exact correspondence between the two men and their names. According to Green (1991: 397) the pentameter following three hexameters is an "oddity" to which parallels are not uncommon both in Greek and Latin epigrams, "but one does not expect it in Ausonius," and he wonders if Scaliger was right in rejecting the first couplet. As a matter of fact, Ausonius himself presents other cases of changes of metre in the last verse[6], and the occurrences elsewhere of this same feature, mentioned by Green (1991: 397) and Kay (2001:164), point to its epigrammatic origin.[7]

As for this epigram, a specific explanation could perhaps be advanced for the final pentameter. This epigram is the second on Chrestos and Acindynos, the first one (*epigr.* 41) being in three bilingual elegiac couplets, whose hexameters are in Greek, while the pentameters are in Latin, with the exception of the two Greek names in the third distich. It is not impossible that in the

---

4. The only exception could be *epigr. Bob.* 70, on which see below, 108.

5. We have no surviving polymetric poems by the Poetae Novelli, but we cannot exclude the possibility that they composed some of them: cf. Mattiacci 1982: 39–40.

6. Green himself (1991: 397) records the similar cases of *par.* 17.1–2, *prof.* 6.52–3 and *ep.* 14b.19.

7. Some inscriptions from the second and the third century present this same feature (cf. Pighi 1968: 509), probably due to the fact that they were composed by amateur poets, and this could be confirmed by the epigram recited by Trimalchio during his *cena* (PETRON. 34.10) consisting of two hexameters followed by one pentameter.

second epigram on the same theme, as well as coming back to Latin, Ausonius looked for another variation: after the opening hexameters, the final pentameter unexpectedly transforms the metre, which becomes an elegiac, underlining the *pointe* present in the last two verses.

However, I must confess to being unable to detect any reason either for changing the metre after the first line or for the choice of the metres used in *par.* 17 (1 iambic trimeter + 18 paroemiacs). It is also difficult to find an explanation for the two very similar cases of *prof.* 19 and *prof.* 21. In the first poem, dedicated to the rhetorician Sedatus, three distichs of pythiambic strophe 2 (dactylic hexameter and iambic trimeter) are followed by four elegiac couplets, the only (somewhat weak) possible justification being that l. 7 introduces a posthumous balance of his activity and importance. The second composition commemorates together the Latin and Greek grammarians Crispus and Urbicus; the two elegiac couplets, which close the composition after eight strophes made of two anapaestic dimeters followed by an Adonic (or an anapaestic monometer), contain the final appreciation of their skills and their worth. Less rich than *Parentalia* in literary echoes, the *Professores* are also written in a poorer style: the variety of metre and the presence of two polymetra could enhance the originality of this collection of short poems, which do not properly correspond either to epigrams or to poetical *laudationes*.

Ep. 6 is a bilingual letter of invitation the poet addresses to his friend Axius Paulus, where forty-three hexameters are followed by the last two verses—the second in Greek translation—of one alcaic strophe coming from Horace's ode to Dellius.[8] In this case, the reader's attention is drawn to the alphabetical, lexical, and morphological aspects of the author's Graeco-Latin pastiche, returning to a tradition that goes back at least to Lucilius.[9] Yet as I suggested elsewhere (2003:164), the final change of metre is not devoid of significance, for its allusion to Horace conveys a clear message to the reader. In *sat.* 1.10 Horace speaks against mixing (l. 29: *intermiscere*) Latin and Greeks words and also against Latin poets composing in Greek (ll. 31–5). Written, of course, in hexameters, as well as the main body of our letter, *sat.* 1.10 was well known because it is the last one in the book and contains the famous harsh judgment on Lucilius. To help the reader to remember it, Ausonius recalls Horace by quoting two verses belonging to another of his poems and marks his disobedience of Horace's precept by the Greek translation of the second verse he

---

8. *Ep.* 6 (= 12 Mondin 1995), 44–5 corresponds to Hor. *carm.* 2.3.15–6: *dum res et aetas et sororum / fila trium patiuntur atra*: l. 16, translated into Greek, becomes νήματα πορφύρεα πλέκηται.

9. Cf. Mondin 1995: 168.

cites. The choice of Hor. *carm.* 2.3, a poem alluded to already at ll. 35–6,[10] is also significant, because it treats seriously and thoughtfully the same themes (the invitation to appreciate the convivial moments of life and the awareness of approaching death) that Ausonius develops playfully. As Luca Mondin (1995: 171) observes, "è come se il poeta stesso ironizzasse sull'insolita serietà dei contenuti divertendosi a sliricarli in una veste formale bizzarra e dichiaratamente ludicra."

Ep. 8 is a bilingual invitation to a friend, possibly Axius Paulus.[11] The metre adopted is the elegiac, which is normal in letters, as well as the hexameter, but in the final couplet instead of the pentameter we find an iambic trimeter; thanks to this metrical *aprosdoketon* the poem ends with one pythiambic strophe 2. To encourage his friend to visit him, Ausonius tells him that he does not need to bring his own books, for in the poet's house he will have at his disposal a well-furnished library, with plenty of poems, which are evoked through their more or less common metres. The iambic trimeter is the last to be mentioned, five verses before the end of the letter, and is also the metre of its last verse.[12] In this way, after enumerating the metres used by the poets whose works are collected in his library, Ausonius suggests that his ability in versification is not inferior to that of the *auctores* collected in his library.

In the collection of epistles transmitted by the manuscript family Z, our letter occupies the last position; we do not know if this was the poet's intention. If so, *ep.* 8 closed that collection with its final pythiambic strophe functioning as a *sphragis*, witnessing the unusual character of the collection itself, all the more so as—instead of publishing his prose letters—the author preferred to collect and transmit to posterity a collection of metric or prosimetric epistles[13].

The three remaining polymetric letters (*epp.* 13, 14, and 16) are all addressed to the otherwise unknown Theon, a friend of the poet and a (bad) poet himself, who lived in the country of Médoc. *Ep.* 13, very probably composed after Ausonius's appointment as the tutor of Gratian,[14] is made up of seventy hexameters plus eleven iambic dimeters plus twenty-three Phalaecean hendecasyllables. The hexameter section contains a heavily ironic, not to say sarcastic, portrait of

---

10. HOR. *carm.* II, 3,1–2: *aequam memento rebus in arduis / seruare mentem* is echoed by AUSON. *ep.* 6, 35 *aequanimus quod si fueris*; see Mondin 1995: 178.

11. According to the extant manuscripts, Green 1991 publishes separately a Greek invitation of one elegiac to Assius Paulus (*ep.* 7) and the following letter (*ep.* 8) to an unnamed friend, while Mondin 1995 is probably right in joining the two compositions (*ep.* 13); see Mondin 1995: 179–180.

12. Which are respectively ll. 31 and 36, corresponding to Mondin 1995, *ep.* 13.33 and 38.

13. Cf. Mondin 1995 XXXII–XXXIV.

14. Cf. l. 1 *Ausonius, cuius ferulam nunc sceptra uerentur*: "Ausonius, whose rod now overawes a sceptre." Excepted l. 4 of *ep.* 16, the English translations of Ausonius are those of Evelyn White 1919–21.

the *paganus* Theon (l. 2), *cultor harenarum uates* (l. 4),[15] who is described in his imagined activities, including literary plagiarism.

After offering Theon the gift of some *nugae* that will prove too difficult for him to understand (ll. 67–70), Ausonius moves to the iambic trimeters, with which he invites his correspondent to ask the help of an interpreter able to explain the *aenigmata* the poet sent to him. The Phalaecean hendecasyllables that close the poem can be traced back to Phalaecos, the originator of this metre, and conclude by promising to free Theon of the accusation of plagiarism if he solves the proposed riddles. The choice of the hexameter could have been inspired by some letters of Horace.[16] The only justification for the change of metre is the desire to underline the transition to another subject, while the Phalaecean hendecasyllables seem to be employed to give Ausonius the opportunity of evoking the story of their invention.

Introduced by a short prose passage (*ep.* 14a), *ep.* 14b is Ausonius's most metrically varied text, for it contains five different metres (18 hexameters + 1 choliambus + 4 iambic trimeters + 12 Phalaecean hendecasyllables + 21 lesser asclepiads). It is presented as the reworking of an old poem Ausonius had composed in his youth, probably for Theon, who had recently sent thirty oysters to the poet without accompanying his gift with some verses. Each metrical section indicates the number of the oysters in many different ways: the hexameters mostly allude to mythical stories, while the iambic trimeters, preceded by a scazon, announce for the following section the transition to suggestions of a different kind based on mathematical calculations (ll. 24–35).

The last section, in lesser asclepiads, describes where and how oysters can be found and ends on the need to end the poem in order to prevent the paper costing the poet more than the oysters he received. We can agree with Green (1991: 634) in defining this brilliant conclusion as "a most grandiose coda, displaying rare or unique adjectives (*fissipedis* 49, *atricolor* 52, *lacticolor* 54), untypical diminutives (*aridulae* 51, *filiolis* 52), and a general luxuriance of expression." Yet it is impossible (at least for me) to find an explanation for the use of different metres that goes beyond the intention of marking the transitions from one motif to another and of confusing poor Theon with this outburst of virtuosity.

Ep. 16 consists of two elegiacs plus two iambic trimeters and is very interesting in construction. First, its heading is a hexameter greeting the addressee: *Ausonius consul uatem resaluto Theonem* ("I, Ausonius the consul, return greeting to Theon the Bard"). The metrical form of the heading, attracting the reader's

---

15. On this definition of Theon and the possible influence of Persius, cf. Smolak 1980.
16. Particularly by HOR. *ep.* 1.3; further indications are given by Mondin 1995: 86.

attention, indicates the nature of the composition, which is a short letter of greetings. Secondly, its six verses are grouped two by two in quite loose succession. The first elegiac couplet contrasts with each other the two gifts Theon sent to him, golden apples with verses of lead:

Aurea mala, Theon, sed plumbea carmina mittis;
  unius massae quis putet has species?

Apples of gold thou sendest, Theon, but verse of lead: who would think these species were of the same substance?

The second distich is a variation on the theme of the first couplet and plays on the difference between *mālum* ("apple") and *mălum* ("bad"):

Vnum nomen utrisque, set est discrimen utrisque:
  poma ut mala uoces, carmina uero mala.

Both have one name, but both have differences: one calls *māla* ("apples") your apples, but *măla* ("bad") your verses .

The two final iambic trimeters are on the possible Greek etymologies of the name Theon:

Vale, beatus nomen a diuis Theon,
Metoche sed ista saepe currentem indicat.

Farewell, Theon, whose blessed name comes from the gods, but often as a participle it means one running.

In this letter, which resembles the sequence of three different epigrams, the use of the same metre in the first two couplets seems to suggest their thematic affinity, whereas the recourse to a different metre for the last two verses signals the transition to a new theme.

All in all, Ausonius's taste for polymetry perfectly fits his tendency to experiment and create works that have no parallel in previous poetry. In examining his polymetric pieces, however, we are sometimes faced with a use of different metres that is more than a search for originality and a dazzling exhibition of virtuosity. Polymetry seems to be primarily a poetic *lusus*, neither conveying really important messages nor dealing with serious questions, as is proved by the choice of the hexameter for the letters he sent to Paulinus after his conversion.

2.2. Epigr. Bob. 70

Particularly interesting is the parallel with AUSON. *epigr.* 42 provided by *epigr. Bob.* 70, a play on the result of changing the letters in the Latin name *Romulus*, which becomes *Morulus*, the Latin diminutive of the Greek adjective μωρός ("stupid"). The *Wortspiel* of this epigram proves that, unlike many *epigrammata Bobiensia*, it cannot be the translation of a Greek model but presupposes a Latin author who knows the Greek. In comparison with the epigram of Ausonius, the change of metres is inverted, the two hexameters following the elegiac couplet.[17] The epigram is anonymous, and so it is possible that its author did not come from Gallia.[18] If so, it would be the only case of a late Latin polymetric epigram not belonging to the Gallic area.

2.3. Paulinus of Nola

Paulinus of Nola is the author of four polymetric compositions. The first two (*carm.* 10 and 21) are the letters in which he answers Ausonius, who had solicited him to return to his old way of life and his previous literary interests. *Carm.* 10 begins with nine elegiac distichs, in which Paulinus greets Ausonius and affirms that the joy he felt in receiving three letters from him is absolutely superior to the grief provoked by the criticisms of his old master and friend. The author closes this section by announcing to his addressee which metres he will use in his answer and in which order (ll. 13–18):

> *ista suo regerenda loco tamen et grauiore*
>   *uindicis heroi sunt agitanda sono.*
> *interea leuior paucis praecurret iambus*
>   *discreto referens mutua uerba pede.*
> *nunc elegi saluere iubent dictaque salute,*
>   *ut fecere aliis orsa gradumque, silent.*

Even so, those charges must be rebutted in due course, and treated in the sterner voice of the avenging heroic measure. Meanwhile, the

---

17. According to Canali and Nocchi 2011: 131, n. 266, "l'uso del metro epico, congiunto con l'impiego di un linguaggio intessuto di reminiscenze virgiliane (per il v. 2 cfr. VERG. *Aen.* I.7) e ovidiane (*fast.* IV, 355) potrebbe essere funzionale all'intento parodico." Yet these two reminiscences are in the elegiac distich, not in the following hexameters, which have a more technical character.

18. In his commentary, Speyer 1959: 116–19 proposes as the author of this piece Anicius Probinus, the consul of 395 who is the dedicatee of Claudian's *Panegyrik* and the addressee of his *carm.min.* 41. This proposal cannot be accepted in the absence of any sound evidence; cf. Zicàri 1959: 331–2 and Schmid 1960: 349.

lighter iambic will briefly take the field first, to repay my debt of words in a different metre. The elegiacs now give their greeting, and having performed this and made a beginning, a first step for others, they say no more.[19]

In the forty-two iambic distichs that follow, Paulinus declares he has forever rejected Apollo and the Muses in favour of Christ and explains how important it is for him to put his life in the hands of God. At any rate, whatever Paulinus's reason for doing so, if Ausonius really loves him, he should be indulgent towards his conversion and congratulate him on living as he likes. The same considerations are more extensively developed in the two hundred twenty-nine hexameters of the third and last section. The introductory function of the elegiac couplets is evident, and Filosini (2008: 40) is right in observing that their use could have been suggested by Ausonius's preference for them in his *praefationes*. It is, however, difficult to perceive a real difference in content between the two other sections of this poem, while—as Filosini (2008: 41) remarks—there is a difference in the tone, which is calm in the iambic distichs, resentful and occasionally aggressive in the hexameters.

Two of the three metres of *carm.* 10, the hexameters and the iambic distichs, are also employed in *carm.* 11, Paulinus's second and last answer to Ausonius. Here the metres run in reverse order: forty-eight hexameters are followed by ten iambic distichs (ll. 49–68), the former refuting Ausonius's arguments and confirming Paulinus's love for him, the latter setting this love in a transcendent Christian perspective.

Paulinus's third polymetric poem, *carm.* 21, was composed about thirteen years later for a *natalicium* in which the poet celebrates two events at once: the feast of the saint and the arrival in Nola of his saintly relatives Apronianus, Pinianus, and their families, who have all embraced a life dedicated to Christ. The first 104 verses are hexameters, as well as the last 515 (ll. 344–858), which are preceded by 167 iambic trimeters (ll. 105–271) and 36 elegiac couplets (ll. 272–343). The poem opens exulting in the escape from the danger represented by the Ostrogoths of Radagaisus, and Paulinus gives thanks to Saints Peter and Paul and to all the martyrs with Felix, whose prayers have dispelled the Gothic menace and saved the Roman empire (ll. 1–36).

Paulinus then declares his intention to pass from the merits Felix shares with the other saints to the gifts his heavenly *patronus* has showered on him. To

---

19. Here and elsewhere I adopt Paulinus's English translation by Walsh 1975.

better express his own gratitude, and in accordance with the exceptionality of the day, he will dispense with his customary practice and modulate his song by recourse to many metres (ll. 56–9):

et contra solitum uario modulamine morem,
sicut et ipse mihi uarias parit omnibus annis
materias, mutabo modos serieque sub una,
non una sub lege dati pede carminis ibo.

I shall dispense with my usual habit; just as Felix every year procures for me material things of different kinds, so I shall change my tunes and vary the metres. I shall proceed with one connected work, but regulate the rhythm on my verse to more than one pattern.

What makes this *natalicium* very special for him is the presence of his noble relatives, who consecrated their lives to God. After describing them for the first time, at the end of the hexameter section Paulinus expresses his intention to render the rich variety of the contents through the variety of metres: may they flourish in the new meadow of his song (ll. 100–4):

floreat ergo nouo mihi carminis area prato
laudibus et domini, qui conditor oris et artis
omnimodae est, uario famulans pede musica currat.
iamque intertextis elegus succedat iambis,
sit caput herous fundamentumque libello.

I pray, then, that the arena of my song may flourish in its new meadow, and that the rhythm with its differing metres may hasten to give service, singing the praises of the Lord, the Creator of both voice and every kind of art. Elegiacs must soon follow upon interwoven iambics, while the heroic hexameter must be the head and the base for my composition.

At the beginning of the following section, composed in iambic trimeters, the poet recalls once again the occasion of his song: it is the annual feast of his patron saint Felix, who this year too has brought something new to the poet, namely the visit of his relatives Turcius Apronianus and valerius Pinianus, once nobles to the world and now servants of Christ, who are in Nola as Felix's guests in his house. After lengthily praising Apronianus and Pinianus for renouncing the world, Paulinus invites all of his relatives who are present to join him in the choir singing the praise of the Lord (ll. 272–3, *magnificate deum mecum et sapienter honestis / unanimes pueri, psallite carminibus*, "Come, boys so dear, and join me in glorifying God, singing noble hymns with trained voices"), and this invitation is made in elegiac couplets.

The last and by far the longest section of the poem, again in hexameters, is occupied by Paulinus's commemoration of how Felix has guided him at all times and is introduced by the declaration that he will address his saint in a different metre (ll. 344–6, *nunc ad te, uenerande parens, aeterne patrone, / susceptor meus et Christo carissime Felix, / gratificas uerso referam sermone loquellas*, "Now I shall change my manner of address and speak words of gratitude to you, revered father and perennial patron, my guardian Felix most dear to Christ"). After evoking the most important events of his life, Paulinus closes the poem with a lengthy narrative relating the opening of Felix's sepulchre, the construction of the edifices relating to the sanctuary, and finally the restoration of the aqueduct bringing the necessary water. The first part of this section (ll. 344–582) is of the utmost importance, because nowhere does Paulinus speak so much and so openly of himself or represent so vividly his deep affection for and spiritual dependence on his saint.

Unlike the last section, which is dedicated to the personal relationship of Paulinus with his *patronus* Felix, illustrated in masterly fashion by Peter Brown (2009: 53–64), the three others share the same motifs (Felix and his feast; the mention and praise of Paulinus's saintly relatives), and the change of metre marks the transition to a different moment in the celebration rather than the introduction of a new theme. Of all the extant *natalicia* composed by Paulinus, *carm.* 21 is certainly the most complex and diversified in content; it is also the only one that is a polymetrum, and the author's insistence on this particular feature proves he sees polymetry as a suitable device for underlining the outstanding significance of the poem and the subjects he sings.

In *carm.* 25, which is the last poem by Paulinus we are concerned with, polymetry has an absolutely limited dimension, the only change of metre being in the three final pentameters following the previous 119 elegiac couplets. This conclusion, so unusual from a metrical point of view, has been interpreted by Bouma (1968: 117) as a "klein metrisch experiment" which marks the end of the poem. Moreover, as the last four verses constantly repeat the name of the bishop Memor,[20] who was the father of the dedicatee (Julian, the future bishop of Eclanum), the pentameter of the last distich is echoed by three more pentameters that draw the attention of audience and readers to the closing *Wortspiel*.

---

20. *Carm.* 25, 238–41: *et domus Aron sit tota domus Memoris / christorumque domus sit domus haec Memoris. / Esto et Paulini Therasiaeque memor, / et memor aeternum Christus erit Memoris.* "May the whole house of Memor be a house of Aaron. May this house of Memor be a house of anointed ones. Preserve the memory of Paulinus and Therasia, and Christ will preserve the memory of Memor forever."

Yet there is in my opinion a further message in this ending of the poem. *Carm.* 25 is an epithalamium, actually the only late Latin epithalamium to be Christian in content, and Paulinus often insists on the difference from the pagan ceremony. His poem differs from those of Statius and Claudian not only in the motifs it develops but also in the use of elegiac couplets instead of the hexameter adopted by Statius and Claudian. By concluding his song with three more pentameters, he brings out the very special feature of his poem, where the presence of pentameters "converts" the canonized hexameters into elegiac distichs.

Carm. 10, 11, and 21 deal with very personal issues in Paulinus's life. Thus we can state how he considers polymetry as a means to underline events and decisions that really matter to him, unlike Ausonius, who never discards the ludicrous character of his polymetric compositions.

2.4. POEMA CONIUGIS AD UXOREM

This poem, which has been attributed to both Paulinus of Nola and Prosper of Aquitania and is probably the latter's,[21] consists of sixteen anacreontean verses followed by fifty-three elegiacs. In the first sixteen verses the author urges his wife to immediately renounce the world, which is now hurrying towards its own ruin. The following elegiac couplets consist of short descriptions illustrating the many aspects of a by now desperate situation. After showing how all things hasten towards the end, the poet turns again to his wife, asking her to embrace ascetic retirement and engage with him in a pious life based on mutual help.

The exhortative and moralizing character of the second section can easily justify the recourse to the elegiac distich, for as Michele Cutino (2006: 345–8) rightly remarks, this metre is also employed in other paraenetic poems composed in the same intellectual milieu. It is not, however, clear why the author used the anacreontean metre, traditionally connected with *ioca* and *conuiuia*,[22]

---

21. The poem (once published by Hartel 1894: 344–48 and recently by Santelia 2009) was transmitted with the *liber epigrammatum*, certainly written by Prosper but without any indication of its paternity, the only old testimony on Prosper's authorship being represented by Bede, *de arte metrica* I, 22 Keil GL 7, 257 (= CChr 123A, 1, 136–7). There are in fact no major arguments against Prosper's paternity, which is now accepted by the majority of scholars, with the dissenting voice of Hwang 2009: 26–7. On the vexed question of Prosper's authorship, see Cutino 2006: 312–14, Santelia 2009: 12–13.

22. See particularly PORPH. *ad Hor. carm.* 4.9.9: *Anacreon... iocis et conuiuiis digna scripsit* (cf. Ps. ACRO) and the commentary by PORPH., *Qualia sunt Anacreontis carmina*, at Hor. *ars* 85, *Libera uina referre*. See also TER. MAUR. 2850–1, *metrum quo memorant Anacreonta / dulces composuisse cantilenas*, who quotes (l. 2852) the example of Petronius. The other cases of late Latin uses of this metre are of no use because they occur either in strophic combination (CLAUD. *Fesc.* 2) or in texts later than ours, as is the case of SIDON. *ep.* 9.13.5; LUX. *AL* 298 and 309; BOETH. *cons.* 3, m 7, and perhaps of Martianus Capella, who can have written his *de nuptiis* either in the same period of our author or after (on the question, cf. Guillaumin 2003, x–xvi).

to transmit such a dramatic message. Therefore, we cannot but agree with the conclusion reached by Michele Cutino (2006: 349): "Nell'*ad coniugem* l'impiego del metro anacreonteo, connesso di solito alla poesia leggera e ad argomernti poco seri, è portatore anch'esso di significato: infatti tale metro, essendo utilizzato all'inizio della composizione per trascrivere il rapido dileguarsi delle caduche realtà terrene, serve a rimarcare ulteriormente il fulcro del messaggio, che è costituito appunto da una radicale rinuncia ai falsi valori del mondo. Insomma Prospero attraverso la continuità, sul piano formale, con la tradizione poetica sottolinea la discontinuità dei contenuti proposti."[23]

2.5. DE OBITU BAEBIANI

We have no external information about the *de obitu Baebiani*, a poem transmitted only by a miscellaneous manuscript, the codex Parisinus 7558 IX saec., that reports it without indication of its author, immediately after Paulinus of Nola's *carm.* 22 (the poem is published as Paulinus's *carm.* 33 by Hartel). Even though its proximity to Paulinus's poem has suggested the attribution to him, there are actually no conclusive arguments in favour of this attribution.[24] The poem, consisting of 132 verses, is composed in four different metres and starts with twenty iambic trimeters that give general information on the protagonist, the affluent and noble Baebianus, who after an easy and thoughtless life is taken seriously ill and suddenly realizes he is mortal. Consequently, he changes his mind, begs God's forgiveness, and offers to him what remains of his life. The twenty hexameters that follow relate how the ailing Baebianus receives the sacraments and declares that he is now ready to die at any time (ll. 21–40). Twenty lesser asclepiads kata stichon (ll. 41–60) contain the dialogue between Baebianus, who hopes to die, and his wife, who implores him to dwell on earth some more.

At this point, the poet turns again from asclepiads to hexameters (ll. 61–100) and from the dialogue to the narrative. As soon as Baebianus stops speaking, he falls on his back and lies in bed as if he were dead. The angels transport his soul for a time to heaven, from where he comes back to his body to tell of what has happened to him and describe the heavenly world. He then dies. The sixteen

---

23. See Fontaine 1981: 232: "ce mètre de la poésie légère sert ici à dénoncer, sur le ton de l'*Ecclésiaste*, la vanité d'un monde fugace."

24. On this question, see Döpp 1995: 67, Trout 1999: 272, and Guttilla 2003, who bases his strenuous defence of Paulinus's authorship on the widespread presence of echoes from Ausonius's poems. Paulinus, however, was not the only one to read him, and Guttilla's arguments prove only the influence of Ausonius on the following poets of Aquitania. Moreover, there is no point in using (as Guttilla does) possible consonances with some passages of Paulinus's poems to give the *de obitu Baebiani* a place in the evolution of Paulinus's poetry before proving his paternity.

elegiacs (ll. 101–32) that close the poem are addressed to Baebianus's widow, Apra, and refer to the present: she has lost one of her children, but at the end of her life she will be reunited with her husband, who will greet her in paradise together with their son.

Apart from the two sections in hexameters, which are appropriate to narrative, the choice of the other metres is neither transparent nor easy to explain, and the interpretation I can propose is only tentative. The decision to begin in iambic trimeters seems to be under the double influence of Horace and Paulinus of Nola, for the incipit *o uir beatus cui remissa iniquitas*, which is the poetical paraphrase of Ps. 1:1 and 31:1, recalls Paulinus's *carm*. 7, 1: *beatus ille qui procul uitam suam*, which is the poetical paraphrase of Ps. 1:1 inspired to HOR. *epod*. 2.1 *beatus ille qui procul negotiis*. Horace could also have suggested the use of the lesser asclepiads kata stichon, because they start with Baebianus recalling his past life; Horace used them in *carm*. 1.1 to defend his own choice of life and in *carm*. 3.30, the last of the first collection of odes, to proclaim his faith in the survival of his poetry, while Baebianus ends by declaring the beauty of eternal life.

The passage from hexameters to elegiac couplets marks the end of the narrative and the shift of the focus from Baebianus to his widow, who is addressed in the second person. The use of elegiacs, which had already occurred in the *consolatio ad Liuiam*, can also be found in Paulinus of Nola's *consolatio* to the parents of Celsus (*carm*. 31) and in exhortative poems like Orientius's *Commonitorium* or Paulinus's address to Licentius (*ep*. 8, 3), as well as in his rather paraenetic epithalamium for Julian and Titia (*carm*. 25), and in the second section of the *poema coniugis ad uxorem* . Its use in the last section of our poem gives the consolatory address to Apra a moralizing and more colloquial character.[25]

2.6. HEPTATEUCHOS

This epic poem of 5550 verses, containing the Pentateuch and the books of Joshua and Judges, is in reality the extant part of a more extended poem which originally included other historical books of the Old Testament as well. It was very probably composed in Gaul in the first quarter of the fifth century and is attributed to a certain Cyprian (the so-called Cyprianus Gallus).[26] It is written in hexameters, as

---

25. Guttilla 2003: 98–9 interprets the *de obitu Baebiani* as a consolatory poem; this could be partially true for the last section (even if the poem seems to have been written some years after Baebianus's death), not so for the others, where Baebianus's story can work as an *exemplum* for any faithful Christian: see the analysis of the poem by Döpp 1995.

26. See Hamm 2000: 153.

is required by any biblical epos, but it also presents three sequences in Phalaecean hendecasyllables.[27] This unique feature can be explained, if not justified, by the character of these three passages. The first one, *Exod.* 507-42, is the paraphrase of Ex. 15:1-18, that is, the Canticle of Moses (Ex. 15:1, *cecinit Moyses ... carmen hoc*) after crossing the Red Sea; the second, in *Numbers* 557-67 is the paraphrase of Num. 21: 18, which is the song of Israel at the well (*cecinit Israel carmen istud*: Num. 21:17), and the third, which is also the longest, in *Deuter.* 152-278, corresponds to Deut. 32:1-43, the song (*carmen*: Deut. 3130) recited by Moses shortly before his death. As in the Latin translation they looked different from the narrative parts and as all of them are described as *carmen* in the Bible, the unknown author apparently tried to render their poetic character by having recourse to the unheard-of adoption of a lyric metre inside the hexameter poem.[28] We might ask why he preferred the Phalaecean. The previous use of this metre in hymns seems to be proved by *CLE* 1504, a very long inscription of the first or second century AD containing a prayer to Priapus,[29] but what matters more is the very fact that Prudentius had employed it in *Cath.* 4.

2.7. HILARY OF ARLES

Among the extant works of Hilary of Arles[30] there is an epigram on the hot springs of Grenoble (*AL* 487) transmitted by Gregory of Tours (*De cursu stellarum* 14), who quotes the first four verses. The first two hexameters ask how it is possible for the waves to survive the fire that burns everything and the fire to survive the water that normally extinguishes it (*Si uere exurunt ignes, cur uiuitis undae? / Si uere extingunt undae, cur uiuitis ignes?*). The elegiac couplet that follows attributes these phenomena to a hand from above (*Lympharum in gremiis inimicus condidit ignes: / communes ortus imperat alta manus*). After this quotation, Gregory adds *et reliqua*, which proves that the poem was longer than four verses. The very similar case we shall see in Ennodius suggests that this short poem did continue in elegiacs.[31]

---

27. Namely in *Exod.* 507-42 (cf. Ex. 15:1-17); *Numeri* 557-67 (cf. Num. 21:18), and *Deuter.* 152-278 (cf. Deut. 32:1-43).

28. It has been remarked by Kirsch (1979: 43): "Wenn nun Ps.-Cyprian an den bezeichneten Stellen vom Hexameter in ein lyrisches Versmass überwechselte, so hat der vielgescholtene Dichter doch ein rechtes Gefühl dafür bewiesen, dass sich diese hymnischen Partien auch strukturell deutlich aus dem Fluss der Erzählung herausheben."

29. On this poem, cf. Courtney 1995, n. 155 and 356-8; on its hymnical structure, see La Bua 1999: 435-6.

30. Information on Hilary of Arles in Kasper 2000.

31. Cf. below ENNOD. *ep.* 5.8 = 224 V 6.

2.8. Sidonius Apollinaris

Sidonius's output includes only one polymetric poem, *carm.* 13, addressed to Majorian, consisting of ten elegiacs followed by twenty Phalaecean hendecasyllables.[32] In the first part of the poem our author, after recalling Hercules's labours, asks the emperor to act as a second Hercules and to deem Sidonius to be an actor playing the role of the victim and the tax to be the monster: so to let him live Majorian should remove the three heads (*tria capita*) from the tax as the Greek hero took them from Geryon:

Amphitryoniaden perhibet ueneranda uetustas,
    dum releuat terras, promeruisse polos.
sed licet in nuda toruus confregerit ulna
    ille Cleonaeae guttura rauca ferae,
et quamquam ardenti gladio uix strauerit hydram,
    cum duplices pareret uulnere mors animas,
captiuumque ferens silua ex Erymanthide monstrum
    exarmata feri riserit ora suis,
collaque flammigenae disrumpens fumida furis
    tandem directas iusserit ire boues,
taurus, cerua, Gigas, hospes, luctator, Amazon,
    Thraex, canis, Hesperides sint monimenta uiri,
nulla tamen fuso prior est Geryone pugna,
    uni tergeminum cui tulit ille caput.
haec quondam Alcides; at tu Tirynthius alter,
    sed princeps, magni maxima cura dei,
quem draco, ceruus, aper paribus sensere sagittis,
    cum dens, cum uirus, cum fuga nil ualuit,
histriones nos esse puta monstrumque tributum;
    hinc capita, ut uiuam, tu mihi tolle tria.

Allowed Antiquity records that the son of Amphitryon by succouring earth earned heaven as his reward. But although with grim look he crushed within his bare arms the *hoarse* throat of the monster of Cleonae;

---

32. Notwithstanding the indication of manuscript T, which introduces the second section by the title *de eodem endecasyllabi*, the two sections are not to be divided because, as we shall see, it is impossible to understand the second part without reading the first. A commentary on this poem is now provided by Santelia 2005. For Sidonius's poem I partially accept (see below, footnote 33) the interpretation proposed by Hernández Lobato 2007b (this paper is reproduced with minor modifications in Hernández Lobato 2012: 159–221), who examines the poem from a different point of view in this book.

although with his fiery sword he just availed to lay the hydra low, as one
death ever brought forth two lives from the wound; although he carried
the captured monster from the Erymanthian forest, laughing at the wild
boar's disarmed mouth; and although, bursting open the smoking neck of
the fire-born thief, he compelled the cows at last to go frontwise; although
the bull, the deer, the giant, the host, the wrestler, the Amazon, the Cretan
beast, the dog, and the Hesperides are memorials of the hero's prowess—
yet none of his fights takes rank before the overthrow of Geryon, from
whose one body he took three heads. Thus Alcides of old; but do thou, as
a second Hercules, and our good sovereign to boot, and our great God's
greatest care—thou, whose arrows made snake, stag, and boar alike to feel
thy prowess, when tooth, poison, and flight availed them not—deem us *to
be actors* and the tax to be the monster, and favour me by taking from it
three heads, that I may be able to live.[33]

In appearance this first section is similar to an epigram. The Priamel of Hercules's labours ends with the assessment that fighting against Geryon was the worst of them. So prepared, the final *pointe* comes, comparing Majorian to Hercules and inviting him to take the three heads from the monstrous tax Sidonius has to pay.

The piece begins with *Amphitryoniaden* occupying the first *hemiepes* as *Amphitryoniades* does for the first time in Verg. *Aen.* 8.214, and immediately after in Prop. 4.9.1, both introducing the evocation of the slandering of Cacus, who had stolen from Hercules the cows that had once belonged to Geryon. The solemnity of this opening is followed by the catalogue of Hercules's labours, culminating in the victory over Geryon, and so prepares the *aprosdoketon* of the conclusion. The comparison of the Roman emperor to the Greek god is not only ironic in the proposed decapitation of the tax; it is, indeed, flattering, for it suggests the superiority of the second Hercules, who is the greatest care of the true God.[34] Finally, we can state that the first section of our poem is complete in itself and does not need the following twenty verses to be perfectly understood.[35] Composed as it is in the canonical metre of epigrams, it also ends with a *pointe*.[36]

---

33. At l. 19 I adopt the transmitted text *histriones*, brilliantly defended by Hernández Lobato 2007b, but I would rather refer *nos* only to Sidonius, who acts as the victim of a new monster, the tax with *tria capita*, that is assimilated to Geryon. Against Santelia 2005: 195, who suggests the emendation *hic triones*, see the convincing arguments of Hernández Lobato 2008 and recently of Canobbio 2013, 377–9, who supports the emendation *Geryones* with new arguments. Here as below I quote the translation of Anderson 1936, only modified in two places (my modifications are written in italics).

34. For Heracles as a model of *optimus princeps*, Santelia 2005: 201–2 and 207–8.

35. This is very probably the reason why in manuscript T l. 21 is considered the start of a new epigram (see above, n. 30).

36. On the political implications of this first section and of all the poem, see Hernández Lobato 2007b.

Let us now read the second section of the poem, written in Phalaecean hendecasyllables:

Has supplex famulus preces dicauit
responsum opperiens pium ac salubre.
ut reddas patriam simulque uitam
Lugdunum exonerans suis ruinis,
hoc te Sidonius tuus precatur:
sic te Sidonio recocta fuco
multos purpura uestiat per annos;
sic lustro imperii perennis acto
quinquennalia fascibus dicentur;
sic ripae duplicis tumore fracto
detonsus Vachalim bibat Sigamber.
quod si contuleris tuo poetae,
mandem perpetuis legenda fastis
quaecumque egregiis geris triumphis.
nam nunc Musa loquax tacet tributo,
quae pro Virgilio Terentioque
sextantes legit unciasque fisci,
Marsyaeque timet manum ac rudentem,
qui Phoebi ex odio uetustiore
nunc suspendia uatibus minatur.

This petition thy suppliant servant has offered, waiting for a kind of life-giving answer. That thou mayest give him back his native town and his life withal, releasing Lugdunum from its fallen estate—this thy Sidonius craves of thee: so may the purple, redipped in Sidonian dye, clothe thee for many a year; so, when thou hast completed a lustre of thine everlasting reign, may a quinquennial festival be consecrated to thy rule; so may the Sygambrian, when the commotion on both banks has been quelled, drink the waters of Vachalis with head shorn in humiliation. If thou grant this to thy poet, I will commit to history's undying records, to be read of mankind, all the exploits of thy glorious triumphs. For now my talkative muse is silenced by the tax, and culls instead of Virgil's and Terence's lines the pence and halfpence owed to the Exchequer, and fears the hand and rope of Marsyas, who from his old-time hatred of Phoebus now threatens bards with hanging.

Unlike the first one, the second part of the poem can be perfectly understood only by readers who already know the content of ll. 1–20. Its metre, however, is the more widespread after elegiacs in Martial's epigrams. But the Phalaecean hendecasyllable is a lyrical metre, which suits Sidonius's half-serious supplication perfectly, and the poet can play on the meaning of his own name, *Sidonius*, an adjective alluding to the imperial purple, and on his past activity as a panegyrist to promise to celebrate Majorian in his verses. The change of metre divides the poem in two parts of the same length; the first one has a more mythological character, the second is more connected to the person of Sidonius.[37] Majorian dominates in the first, and Sidonius in the second.[38] The very fact that a perfect understanding of the second half of the poem depends on the knowledge of the first could in my opinion underline the subordinate position of the poet, who is the protagonist of the second half, towards the emperor, who is the protagonist of the first.

2.9. Ennodius

With his four polymetric pieces, Ennodius demonstrates that he is quite attracted by the possibilities that polymetry offers a skilled poet. The least complex piece is the first on our list, an epigram on the *lauacra Aponi*, the hot springs of Abano (*ep.* 5, 8 = 224 V, 6), which had been celebrated in fifty elegiacs by Claudian (*carm. min.* 26). Ennodius distances himself from Claudian by developing his theme in the shorter text of an epigram that plays on the paradox of water and fire co-present and cooperating in the river.[39] After illustrating in six elegiac couplets the contradiction of water not extinguishing the fire and drying up the bodies with its vapours, Ennodius closes the epigram with two hexameters on the paradox of these opposite principles, which are able to coexist, and on the water, whose presence is the very condition for the fire to survive (ll. 13–14 *Ne pereat, Nymphis Vulcanus mergitur illis. / Foedera naturae rupit concordia pugnax*).

In the last two verses, the hexameter replacing the expected pentameter is a slight surprise, alerting the reader to the singularity of this natural phenomenon. Ennodius came from Arles, and it is not impossible that Hilary's epigram inspired his recourse to a couple of hexameters to emphasize by the change of metre the existence of a phenomenon conflicting with the laws of nature.

---

37. Santelia 2005: 198–9: "è in distici elegiaci, infatti, la parte 'mitologica' (vv. 1–20) e in endecasillabi falecei la parte che riguarda più da vicino Sidonio (vv. 21–40), un espediente cui l'autore ricorre, probabilmente, per rendere il più possibile chiara la 'separatezza' tra i due momenti del componimento."

38. See Hernández Lobato 2007b, particularly 76–95 = Hernández Lobato 2012: 200–21.

39. Cf. Kennell 2000: 96–8 and, more recently, Majani 2006. References to Ennodius give the correspondence between the two editions of Hartel 1882 and Vogel (V) 1885.

120   *The Poetics of Late Latin Literature*

Unlike Hilary, who had placed the two verses at the beginning of his composition, Ennodius places them at the end.

Ennodius's other short polymetric poem is an epitaph he composed for Cynegia, the late wife of Flavius Anicius Probus Faustus iunior Niger, consul in 490.[40] The text, transmitted by *ep.* 7.29 (362 V), consists of two elegiac couplets followed by three Phalaecean hendecasyllables:

> *Optinui pretium uotorum munere Christi:*
> *   quae mihi uita fuit, crux dedit hanc tumulis,*
> *dissoluens carni subolem sine uolnere mentis,*
> *   quod faustum et felix coniuge praemorior.*
> *Disiecit lacrimas medela cordis.*
> *Quae seruat meritis torum fidelem,*
> *exoptet similem matrona sortem.*

By the gift of Christ I obtained the reward of my prayers: the cross gave to the tomb the life which was once mine, dissolving what belongs to the flesh without any wound to my soul, because—which is fortunate [*faustum*: the adjective recalls the name of her husband] and prosperous—I die before my husband Faustus.

The healing of the heart has dissolved the tears. Hope a similar fate for herself every matron who for her merits keeps faithful her bed.

The text of this short poem is preserved in the letter with which Ennodius sent it to his young friend Beatus, who noticed the prosodic error of l. 7, consisting in the long *a* of *mātrona* instead of the short vowel required.[41] The poet relates to Beatus how Cynegia herself had reproached him for not honouring her sepulchre with a poem. As God does not despise this kind of offer or require the gems of verbal elegance from those he endowed with a rough talent, our poet decided to dedicate his verses to the composition of the epitaph (§3: *his ergo uersibus scribendum epitaphium destinaui*), which he is now sending to Beatus. The singular *epitaphium* testifies that the poet considered the distichs and the hendecasyllables as different parts of the same epigram.

In the two distichs, the convinced profession of Christian faith in the immortality of the soul (ll. 2–3) is framed by verses 1 and 4, which draw the portrait of a loving wife preferring her husband's survival to her own. The motif of the wife ready to sacrifice her life for her husband is a very old one, going back to the Greek

---

40. Cf. *PLRE* II, 454–6.
41. After reacting aggressively to the critics of Beatus (*ep.* 8, 29= 406 V), Ennodius felt later forced to a painful palinody in *ep.* 8.21 = 398 V.1–3): see Polara 1993: 223–4.

myth of Alcestis, which is alluded to by Propertius in his *regina elegiarum*. In the first section of the poem Ennodius gives a Christian version of it, presenting Cynegia's untimely death as a gift of God, who heard her request to die earlier than her husband. The same motif returns in the last two Phalaecean hendecasyllables with a variation, very Roman in spirit, which emphasizes the conjugal fidelity of Cynegia, whose destiny every faithful *matrona* should wish for herself. Line 5, which introduces the second part of the epitaph with a new metre, summarizes and comments upon the theme of ll. 3–4, because the healing of the heart (*medela cordis*) can come only from the certainty that Cynegia has been rewarded by God.

The change in metre underlines two different ways of considering the same event. In the elegiac couplets, Cynegia's death is seen through her own eyes, while the Phalaecean hendecasyllables consider it from a more social and profane point of view, as is proved by the final *sententia*, which underlines the exemplary nature of the late matron, proved by her life as well as by her death. With all the differences in situation and in extension, we have, as in the case of Sidonius's poem to Majorianus, a first part in elegiac couplets which could be read and understood as an autonomous epigram, while the second section comments upon the content of the first and cannot actually be understood without previously reading the first.

Apart from underlining the transition from the facts to a commentary on them, the change of metres could also have other, more practical functions. *Ep.* 5.7 (219 V) has transmitted yet another epitaph for a noblewoman called Cynegia, who may or may not be the same as the one in our epitaph but very probably is.[42] If so, the use of two metres could be an element which distinguishes our epitaph from the other, which is made of five elegiac couplets. There is also another, more certain reason, which could explain the change of metre. From a letter of Ennodius (*ep.* 7.28= 361 V) we learn that he intended to have this epitaph copied on Cynegia's funeral monument, while in another letter to Beatus (*ep.* 8.29= 406 V.2) the poet tells him that he had presented the epitaph to Cynegia's husband, the very cultivated and influential Faustus Niger, who had appreciated it. We might therefore suppose that by changing the metre Ennodius wanted to impress him, as he had done (or would do in the future) with the major virtuoso performance of *carm.* 1.7 (= 26 V), a poem dedicated to Faustus, who was a relative of Ennodius and a poet in his own right.[43]

Introduced by a prose preface, this poem alternates four different metres: elegiac couplets (ll. 1–32), hexameters (ll. 33–44), elegiac couplets again (ll. 45–8),

---

42. For an up-to-date discussion of this question, see Consolino 2014.
43. On Ennodius's relationship with Faustus and his family, cf. Kennell 2000: 141–6.

lesser Sapphic strophes (ll. 49–68), and Adonics (ll. 69–80). The first thirty-two verses praise Faustus as a poet gifted with *ingenium* (ll. 1–10); his technical ability gives shape and life to words and he obtains from his studies what God does from his divine nature (ll. 11–20); the force of his song could transform an old corpse into a living young man and achieve *adynata* of every kind (ll. 21–30). Because of Faustus's skills, Ennodius himself has already become the prey of the passion for the Muses (ll. 31–2). As should be clear from this summary, the first thirty verses are completely devoted to the exaltation of the dedicatee. It is therefore rather strange that such a committed encomium is celebrated in elegiacs, which generally introduce poetic compositions (in our case the real introduction is written in prose), while the hexameter is normally preferred for solemn praise or panegyrics.

Lines 31–2 mark the passage from Faustus to Ennodius, whose attempts at poetry are the subject of the following section, written in hexameters (ll. 33–44). To characterize the poetry he has practised, Ennodius employs and develops the metaphor of the ship: as his own ship is very frail (*sutilis cumba*), the poet will be very cautious, avoiding the perils of the open sea. Nautical metaphors are very frequent in poetry[44] and not especially connected to epics. So the use of the hexameter might be explained by the intention of magnifying the risks of great poetry, as Paulinus of Périgueux had quite recently described them in the prologue to the second book of his *Vita Martini* (ll. 1–14).[45] The choice of a lighter and safer kind of poetry is underlined by the transition to the elegiacs of ll. 45–8, which openly declare the direction of Ennodius's navigation towards the seashore. This time elegiac couplets are employed, which also have the function of introducing the new song, institutionalized in prefaces by Claudian.[46]

Ennodius's new song consists of five lesser Sapphic strophes in which he asks the Muse to plead with Faustus on his behalf and to convince him to carefully examine the poet's modest verses. As Vandone (2004: 44–5) remarks in his commentary to the poem, this section is particularly inspired by a poem composed in the same metre by Sidonius Apollinaris (*ep.* 9.16.3.1–20). In this composition, Sidonius, who has now embarked on the ecclesiastical life, recalls the stages of his past political and poetical career and successes. The use of Sapphic strophes helps the reader to recognize the model and appreciate Ennodius's *uariatio in imitando*.

---

44. Cf. Curtius 1990: 128–30.
45. On the poets echoed or alluded to in this section of Ennodius's poem, see Vandone 2004: 38–40 and his detailed commentary.
46. See Felgentreu 1999.

The last part of the poem, written in continuous Adonics, contains the dedication to Faustus of Ennodius's humble poem and ends with the wish that Christ be propitious to Faustus's offspring and keep them as illustrious as they now are. The use of Adonics kata stichon is witnessed before Ennodius by Mart. Cap. 2.125 in the laudatory address of Euterpe to philology.[47] The eulogistic character assumed by Adonics in Martianus Capella could have influenced Ennodius in the choice of this metre for the final address to Faustus, but Ennodius also employs it at the end of *paraenesis didascalica*, where a few Adonics are addressed to the dedicatees Ambrosius and Beatus; Lapidge (1977: 256) has the credit pointing out "Ennodius' innovation in using Adonics for epistolary purposes."

No less ambitious, perhaps more so, than *carm.* 1.7 is *carm.* 1.4 (= 388 V), the epithalamium of Maximus, another of Ennodius's influential and cultivated friends.[48] Composed in five different metres, this poem opens with twelve elegiac couplets (ll. 1–24), followed by four catalectic trochaic tetramers (ll. 25–8). Then come six lesser Sapphic strophes (ll. 29–52), followed by seventy hexameters (ll. 53–122) and six Phalaecean hendecasyllables, which close the poem. The opening in elegiac distichs is consistent with the poetical tradition of late Latin epithalamia, which twice in Claudian and once in Sidonius are preceded by a preface in elegiac distichs.[49] The choice of this metre is particularly significant, all the more so if we consider that Ennodius's poem has no preface and starts with the description of a radiant nature paying her homage to the dedicatee.

The transition to a different metre introduces Ennodius's invocation of everything that can elevate his verses, for nothing trivial must occur in the praises of the Maximi. In late Latin poetry catalectic trochaic tetramers are present in Christian hymnody as well as in the profane *Peruigilium Veneris*, whose themes are quite close to those of epithalamia. Yet they had never been used before in a proper epithalamium, and by this innovation Ennodius makes it clear that he is attempting to compose an original and unprecedented poem. Equally unprecedented, at least in Latin epithalamia, is the use of Sapphic stanzas, which could perhaps be justified by the connection existing between Sappho and this literary genre. Moreover, the change of metre can also draw attention to the content of these verses, which describe the meeting—usual in epithalamia—of Venus and Amor but inverts their traditional roles, for this time it is Amor who invites his mother to act in defence of her threatened power.

---

47. On further use of continuous Adonics in Latin poetry, see Lapidge 1977.
48. For a detailed analysis of this poem, see Consolino 2009.
49. CLAUD. *carm.* 9 and *carm. min.* 25; SIDON. *carm.* 10.

The bulk of the poem, however, is in hexameters, which had been the normal metre for epithalamia since Statius. The closing Phalaecean hendecasyllables are certainly an innovation, but they are not completely new in epithalamic tradition, for Sidonius Apollinaris had employed them in the preface of his epithalamium for Polemius and Araneola. Apparently, Ennodius's alternating different metres have the double function of marking the connection of his poem to the literary genre it belongs to, as well as underlining its own innovative features. As in the case of *carm.* 1.7, here too all the metres employed are also present in the *paraenesis didascalica*, and this shows that, quite apart from any single explanation of their use, there is also a more general preference of Ennodius for these metres.

At the end of our analysis, we may be able to draw some conclusions. Late Latin polymetric poems turn out to be a phenomenon limited in extension but neither negligible nor devoid of interest. It is a kind of poetry almost exclusive to Gaul, whose diffusion certainly depended on Ausonius's prestige and influence and probably on Gallic schoolteaching. Yet apart from the common feature represented by the exhibition of virtuosity, there are (more or less great) differences in the way this device is used.

In some cases it is employed simply to emphasize a single fact or circumstance, as often happens in short epigrams (often but not always, as is proved by Cynegia's epitaph). In longer and more elaborate poems it can help to enhance the importance of a personal decision (as in the letters of Paulinus to Ausonius), of a particular event (as in Paulinus's *carm.* 21 or in the epithalamium of Maximus), or of the author's situation in relation to his dedicatee (as in the case of Sidonius in his problematic relationship with Majorianus or in Ennodius's letter to Faustus). The change of metres can also underline the exemplary nature of an existential situation: this happens in the *poema coniugis ad uxorem* and in the *de obitu Baebiani*.

The reasons that may have inspired the choice of each metre are the most problematic question, but a poem's belonging to a canonic literary genre can make it more perspicuous, as happens beyond any doubt in the case of Cyprianus Gallus and, with a reasonable degree of certainty, in the epithalamium of Maximus. At any rate, the overall examination of polymetric poems presents us with a wealth of solutions and nuances worth exploring and casts a brighter light on the relationship of the authors concerned, both with each other and with the rest of the Latin poetic tradition.

3

Words Pregnant with Meaning

The Power of Single Words in Late Latin Literature

ISABELLA GUALANDRI

Disregarding Horace's famous warning, "Select a subject, you writers, befitting your strength,"[1] I have chosen a subject that cannot easily be fitted into a few pages. Therefore, making a virtue of necessity, I use some examples to explore a topic involving almost every aspect of late Latin literature in the fourth and fifth centuries AD. The features I analyze, although present in the earlier tradition, developed in richness, strength and boldness in Late Antiquity.

My starting point is a passage from Augustine, since he investigated in depth many problems related to language and words.

3.1. THE TRUE MEANING OF WORDS

In the first of his sermons on Saint John's Gospel,[2] when commenting on its famous incipit, *In principio erat Verbum et Verbum erat apud Deum et Deus erat Verbum*,[3] Augustine faces the difficult task of explaining to his audience, most of whom were probably uneducated, the pregnant meaning of *Verbum* (God's Word, God). This is a common word, he says, and likely to escape notice, because words which are used every day lose their significance and are perceived only as sounds that pass away and vanish.[4] But while the sounds of words, made up of letters and syllables, may fade away, the meaning they convey remains, both in the speaker's and in the hearer's mind.[5] Thus, for instance, when we say *Deus* (God), we pronounce a very short word, made of only two syllables and four letters,[6] whose sound disappears, while we

---

1. *Sumite materiam uestris, qui scribitis, aequam / uiribus* (*ars* 38–9).
2. *In euang. Ioh.* 1.8 (CC XXXVI 51, 1954, ed. R. Willems); the sermons were written in the years 414–17.
3. "In the beginning was the Word, and the Word was with God, and the Word was God"
4. *Quotidie dicendo uerba uiluerunt nobis, quia sonando uerba et transeundo uiluerunt*.
5. *Quaecumque dicuntur et transeunt, soni sunt, litterae sunt, syllabae sunt. Hoc uerbum transit, quod sonat: quod autem significauit sonus, et in cogitante est qui dixit, et in intellegente est qui audiuit, manet hoc transeuntibus sonis*.
6. *Ecce uerbum dico, cum dico "Deus." Quam breue est quod dixi, quatuor litteras, et duas syllabas . . .*

125

keep in our heart the idea of an omnipotent, eternal, infinite being.[7] In a simple way and with characteristic didactic clarity, Augustine is here hinting at two different problems. Words for him are simply *signa* (signs) of the *res* (things) they refer to: "A word is a sign of any sort of thing. It is spoken by a speaker and can be understood by a hearer."[8] Meanwhile, "a sign (*signum*) is a thing which causes us to think of something beyond the impression the thing itself makes upon the senses" as he explicitly states in *de doctrina christiana* (2.1.1).[9] In words there is something not perceived by the ears, but by the mind, and held within the mind itself.[10] *Signa* refer to *res* but do not coincide with them, and Augustine explicitly warns his audience to avoid identifying words with things (*signa pro rebus accipere, doctr. christ.* 3.5.9). The issue is of particular relevance in religious matters:[11] at a higher level, for instance, in Neoplatonic theology (as in Porphyry's school), the names of the gods are themselves considered to be divine and to share the divinity's sacred essence (Mastandrea 1979: 180–92), while in common practice the widespread belief that names reflect the nature of the things they refer to prompted the pagans to mistake what were just names for the gods themselves, in cases like *Pietas* (Piety), *Concordia* (Concord), *Felicitas* (Fertility, Happiness), *Virtus* (Virtue), *Salus* (Health), where they converted *nomina* (names) into *numina* (gods).[12] When Symmachus wrote, "at least grant the name the honour that has been denied to the god" in his petition for the restoration of the altar of the Victory in the Senate (*rel.* 3.3),[13] Prudentius used a similar wordplay and contemptuously remarked (*c. Symm.* 1.220) that a mere name, in this case the name of a place (Rome), was being taken for a divinity: *nomenque loci ceu numen habetur*.[14]

Besides, as a skilled teacher,[15] Augustine feels the need to draw attention to words, their meanings, their wasting away in daily use. Grammarians

---

7. *Quando cogitas quandam substantiam uiuam, perpetuam, omnipotentem, infinitam . . . hoc est uerbum de Deo in corde tuo.*

8. *Verbum est uniuscuiusque rei signum, quod ab audiente possit intellegi, a loquente prolatum* (*dialect.* 5) (trans. from *de dialectica* by Jackson 1975; elsewhere, unless otherwise stated, they are my own).

9. *Est . . . res praeter speciem, quam ingerit sensibus, aliud aliquid ex se faciens in cogitationem uenire* (trans. Robertson). Of the huge bibliography about Augustine's linguistic theories I shall quote only a few items: Markus 1972, 1995; Jackson 1969; Baratin and Desbordes 1982; Bettetini 1993; Stock 1996; Long 2005.

10. Cf. *dialect.* 5 *quidquid . . . ex uerbo non aures sed animus sentit et ipso animo tenetur inclusum.*

11. Jackson (1969: 25) points out the importance of moving from the sign to the thing designated in interpreting scripture (which is Augustine's main concern).

12. As Christian authors frequently complained: see, e.g., ARN. *nat.* 4.1–4.

13. *Reddatur saltem nomini honor qui numini denegatus est.*

14. "The name of the place is reckoned as a divinity" (trans. Thomson).

15. "Il resta toute sa vie un grammairien," Marrou 1958: 15.

were accustomed to breaking up texts to study them with a strongly analytical approach and to explain them line by line and word by word,[16] putting them, as it were, under a microscope[17] and focusing on lexical details. Augustine's remark that words, when used daily, lose their significance (like coins lose their value, if you put too many of them on the market), betrays the grammarian's interest in the original meaning and form of words, which had been "obscured by incrustations of time and language change" (Amsler 1989: 17), as well as the habit of trying to recover this meaning through etymology. In the long history of etymology, which extends from the ancient Greek world to the Latin Middle Ages,[18] the confluence of the classical tradition and the language of the Bible enhanced the interest in words.[19] On the one hand, Christian writers transferred the analytic techniques they had applied to classical texts to the exegesis of scripture; on the other hand, the Bible itself powerfully heightened the importance of words, through which God created the world (Gen. 1:3; 6; 9; etc.) and Adam, naming the animals (Gen. 2:19), asserted his dominance over them. The main difference was that the Fathers, in their exegesis of the Bible, exploited it as a model for their discourse, absorbing its language and appropriating its words (Gualandri 1995: 171).

Augustine takes a number of different attitudes towards etymology in his works. In *dialect.* 6,[20] he is rather sceptical, maintaining that to inquire about the origin of a word is "more a matter of curiosity than necessity,"[21] "an occupation that could go on for ever."[22] "Like the interpretation of dreams, it is a matter of each man's ingenuity."[23]

---

16. An example of this method is in Priscianus, *Partitiones xii uersuum Aeneidos principalium* (GL Keil III Lipsiae 1959: 459–515).

17. Roberts 1989a: 55, "it was as though texts were put under a microscope, magnifying the constituent parts at the expense of the whole"; on the influence of this habit on literary taste, see also Gualandri 1995.

18. For an exhaustive survey of etymology in the ancient world, see Opelt 1966; for the Latin world, Curtius 1953: 495–500 and O'Hara 1996. Den Boeft 1979: 244–5 rightly remarks on the difference between "scientific etymology" and "the use of etymology as a rhetorical device."

19. From a grammarian's point of view, etymology is a fundamental tool to understand a name's power (*uis*), as pointed out by Isidorus of Seville (*orig.* 1.29), whose encyclopaedic work based on etymologies describing the whole world is a sort of "grammar of the universe" (Henderson 2007: 24). But already Varro's *de lingua Latina* (books V–VII) was a great inventory of the world through words and their etymology (Hinds 2006: 56, 61).

20. I agree with Jackson's assumption (1975; see introduction) about the authenticity of the treatise.

21. *Res . . . nimis curiosa et minus necessaria.*

22. *Quod persequi profecto infinitum est.* By contrast Hinds 2006: 48 finds in this method "not a movement towards infinite deferral and unfixity of meaning, but a movement towards plenitude and perfection of meaning."

23. *Vt somniorum interpretatio ita uerborum origo pro cuiusque ingenio iudicatur.*

But in practice, his behaviour conflicts with these assertions: Maltby's lexicon (Maltby 1991)[24] offers a long list of words explained by him,[25] related either to peoples and places[26] or to Christian or philosophical vocabulary (sometimes of Greek origin: e.g., *Christus*, from *chrisma*, viz. "anointing"; *angelus*, from the Greek word meaning "messenger," etc.)[27] or pertaining to grammar and other disciplines (e.g., *coniugatio, grammatica, musica, uersus*) or to a variety of topics: e.g., *adulterium* (adultery), *quasi "ad alterum"* (i.e., "when a woman or a man goes to another" scil. partner); *balneum* (a bath) from the Greek *balaneion*, from *ballei anian*, that is, "dispels the anxiety" from the soul; *egregius* (distinguished), explained as "separated from the flock" (*grex*); *horreum* (barn), so called because it contains *hordeum* (barley); *serui* (slaves), that is, "prisoners who were not killed but saved" (*seruati sunt*).[28] This is a huge number, in part explained by the fact that preachers frequently needed to use explanations and etymologies, in order to be understood by everybody in the congregation.[29]

As for proper names, whose etymology was approved by Quintilian (*inst.* 1.4.25),[30] Augustine focuses on Roman deities in *de ciuitate Dei*, where, in his critical survey of pagan religion, he lists the many gods related to every aspect of daily life:[31] for instance, *Agenoria* (a goddess who "prompts to action," whose

---

24. I merely quote Maltby's entries; some additions have been provided by Adkin 2005 and Marangoni 2007. On the limits of some etymological interpretations (since it is sometimes difficult to distinguish between etymological wordplay and mere paronomasia), see Maltby 1993 and Hinds 2006 (with a bibliography on etymological puns in Latin poetry). A more complex use of etymology in some passages from *de civitate Dei* is highlighted by Den Boeft 1979.

25. Whose etymologies sometimes go back to Varro.

26. Such as *Areopagus, Argi, Argiui, Auentinus, Hebraei, Ianiculum, Iudaea, Niniue, Pygmaei*.

27. Cf. also *caritas, catechumenus, catholicus, circumcellio, clericus, cynici, daemon, diabolus, diuinitas, dominicus, dominus, elemosyna, encaenia, episcopus, euangelium, gratia, martyrium, monachus, orthodoxus, parabola, parasceue, pascha, philosophus, religio*.

28. Cf. also *asbestos, aspis, cadauer, caeles, caelicola, campester, clangor, competens, consors, consul, cuneus, cynomya, enchiridion, eques, exclusor, fallax, fatum, fictilis, fidelis, fides, figulus, fiscella, foedus, frugalitas, furtim, genius, gratia, heros, holocaustum, infamis, inferus, infirmus, innocentia, inquilinus, intempesta, inuenio, inuentio, lex, liberalis, libero, meridies, metreta, misericordia, modicus, moechia, morio (-onis), mythicus, negotiatio, nequitia, oculus, oenophorum, opulentia, orbis, organum, ostentum, paedagogus, palatum, potestas, rex, salutatio, sapientia, sententia, speciosus, superstitiosus, uirtus, uis, uoluntas*. But the list is far from exhaustive.

29. See, e.g., in Ambrose (also from Maltby 1991) the etymologies of *accola, aduena, aequor, Aethiopia, amphibius, antrum, caelum, concubina, coniugium, diuitiae, exlex, faenus, fides* (musical instrument), *firmamentum, hippopotamus, homo, incola, innocentia, mergulus, modestia, obstetrix, officium, paedagogus, perdix, reptile, serpens, thymallus, uespertilio*; cf. also Bartelink 1979: 194–202 and Pizzolato 2000.

30. *Scrutabitur ille praeceptor acer atque subtilis origines nominum*: "the really sharp and subtle teacher will look at the origins of names" (trans. from Quintilian by Russell). Quintilian is mostly dealing with proper names often derived from bodily characteristics, places of birth, and so on. Donatus, commenting on Terentius (*ad Adelph.* 1.1.26) remarks that the names of the various characters must "have a reason and an etymology" (Petrone 1988: 40).

31. See Opelt 1966: 833 for the same topic in other Christian authors.

name comes from *agere*, "to put in motion"); *Collatina*, who "oversees the hills" (*colles*); *Iuno Iterduca*, "Juno who guides" (*ducere*) on "the road" (*iter*); *Iuppiter Iugatinus*, "Jupiter who oversees the summits of mountains" (*iuga*), etc.[32]

3.2. Playing with Words

While the Hebrew Bible had stressed the meanings of some proper names,[33] a Christian precedent was set by this key passage from Matthew's Gospel 16:18-19: "I am telling you that you are Peter, and on this *petra* (stone) I shall build my church."[34] This gave a Christian model for the ancient *nomen/omen* play ("a name that is a presage"), and Augustine uses the name of a martyr or a saint to enunciate a prophecy of the spiritual life or holiness that the saint had manifested or would manifest in his or her behaviour.[35] *Paulus* is explained as *modicus, paruus*: Saint Paul changed his original name (Saul) and called himself *Paulus*, because *paulus* means "small" and he considered himself "the smallest" among the Apostles;[36] while *Vincentius* (a martyr under Diocletian) is portrayed as "victorious" from *uinco* ("to conquer"), because of the pains he endured;[37] the two martyrs *Felicitas* and *Perpetua* enjoy "eternal" (*perpetua*) "happiness" (*felicitas*);[38] Saint Stephan (*Stephanus*), whose name in Greek means "crown," won a victory crown,[39] and so on. This kind of amphibological play can be found at many levels of late antique literature, as a favourite and widespread feature, for instance in a poet like Ausonius, whose style was deeply influenced by his

---

32. See also *Altor, Attis, Barbatus, Bubona, Catius, Centumpeda, Deuerra, Educa, Egeria, Forculus, Fortuna, Frutesea, Honor, Hostilina, Intercidona, Inuictus,, Lacturnus, Liber, Libera, Limentinus, Matuta, Mellona, Mena, Mercurius, Numeria, Opis, Pecunia, Prema, Proserpina, Quies, Ruminus, Runcina, Rusina, Rubor, Saturnus, Sentia, Sentinus, Spiniensis, Statilinus, Stercutius, Stimula, Subigus, Supinalis, Tigillo, Tritonia, Vallonia, Venus, Vesta, Victoria, Virginensis, Vitumnus, Volumna, Volumnus, Volupia, Volutina*. To these names, all included in Maltby 1991, I should add, from *civ.* 4.11 *Camena, Consus, Cunina, Fortunius, Leuana, Nodutus, Pauentia, Potina, Strenia*; from 7,22 *Salacia* and *Venilia*; from 7,24 *Mater Magna*.
33. E.g., Gen. 16:11 Ismael; 17:19 Isaac; Is. 7:14 Emmanuel; 3 Kings 13:2 Iosias. See Opelt 1966: 819–20.
34. *Et ego dico tibi quia tu es Petrus et super hanc petram aedificabo ecclesiam meam.*
35. On such wordplays, cf. McCartney 1919, O'Hara 1996, and Booth and Maltby 2006. Mohrmann 1961: 325 points out that nobody after Plautus used wordplays so frequently as Augustine in his *sermones*. See also Mohrmann 1961: 327–30.
36. *Serm.* 315.5.7.
37. *Serm.* 274.1 *spectamus . . . Vincentium ubique uincentem. Vicit in uerbis, uicit in poenis, uicit in confessione, uicit in tribulatione; uicit exustus ignibus, uicit submersus fluctibus; postremo uicit tortus, uicit mortuus* ("we see that Vincentius was everywhere victorious. He won with his words, he won amidst pains, he won acknowledging Christ, he won in tribulation; he won when he was burnt by fire, he won when he was overwhelmed by waters; at last he won when he was put to the torture, he won when he died"). The idea of victory is stressed by the strong iteration (*uicit . . . uicit . . . uicit*) and the rhymes.
38. *Serm.* 282.1.1.
39. *Serm.* 314.2; 318.3.

habits as a teacher and who loved verbal puns and jokes. Ausonius plays on his grandmother's name (*parent.* 5.3–6):[40] Aemilia Corinthia was nicknamed *Maura* (Moorish) by her friends when she was a girl, because of her dark skin;[41] while his grandson was called Pastor (shepherd), because when he was born a pipe happened to be playing a pastoral air (*parent.* 11.5–8), which turned out to be a bad omen, since his life was short and passed away as quickly as the breath passes from a pipe. Again he writes of a professor who suffered the name Lascivus ("playful," but also "lustful") even though his life was virtuous (*prof.* 7.5–8); of the Homeric hero Protesilaus (*epitaph.* 12.1–8), the first of the Greeks to perish in the Trojan war, as had been prophesied by his name (in Greek "the first of the people").[42] The same kind of word pun is used with rhetorical skill to praise the mighty Sextus Petronius Probus,[43] in a letter written to accompany copies of books Ausonius had been asked to send him for his son's education.[44] In this case (*epist.* 9b.42–50) the *libellus* itself (i.e., the letter) addresses Probus, asking him to explain the origin of his name (Probus meaning "virtuous"): was it given to him as an acknowledgement of his virtues, or did he make his behaviour conform to the name or, perhaps by God's will, was he graced with a name expressing his nature and character?[45]

Similarly, several examples of this kind of wordplay are found in Paulinus of Nola.[46] Baptized by *Delphinus* (dolphin), bishop of Bordeaux, Paulinus himself is like *illi pisces, qui perambulant semitas maris* (Psalm 8:9, "fish who walk through the sea's paths"), that is, the fish that Peter hooks (see *epist.* 20.6.20–22).

---

40. I am quoting Ausonius according to Green 1991.

41. *Nomen huic ioculare datum, cute fusca quod olim / aequales interuocata fuit. / sed non atra animo, qui clarior esset olore / et non calcata qui niue candidior*: "her name was given her in play, because of her dark complexion she was called Maura in old days by her girlfriends. But she was not dark in her soul, which was whiter than a swan and brighter than untrodden snow" (trans. from Ausonius by Evelyn-White 1919, occasionally slightly modified).

42. For similar jokes, cf. also *epigr.* 41; 42; 81; 111.2; *epist.* 16.5.

43. Consul in 371: for his career, cf. *Sextus Claudius Petronius Probus*, PLRE I, 1971: 736–40.

44. *Epist.* 9b: the first part of the letter is in prose, while the second is in verse.

45. And the answer is (51–2) *nomen datum praeconiis / uitaeque testimonio* ("the name was given in his praise and for a token of his life"). Cf. the careful analysis by Mondin 1995; on the link between words and things in Ausonius and Rutilius Namatianus, see Hernández Lobato's contribution to this volume.

46. For Paulinus, see Guttilla 1990; 2004; 2007. Cf. also Rut. Nam. 1.311–12, who points out that the house of the Lepidi led Rome to ruin, although *lepidus* means "friendly," "amiable"; and the wordplays in Sidonius *carm.* 14, *epist.* 2 *uiro uere Magno*, "a man as great as his name"; *carm.* 9.5 to Magnus Felix, who is *Felix nomine, mente, honore, forma*, etc., "felicitous in his name, in his intellect, in his eminence"; *carm.* 16.127–8 (playing with the names of Faustus, bishop of Riez, and of Honoratus and Maximus, his predecessors as abbotts of Lérins) *semper mihi Faustus, / semper Honoratus, semper quoque Maximus esto*, "I wish thee for evermore the blessings of the three names, Fortunate, Honoured, Greatest"; *epist.* 8.11.3 v. 35–6 *satis facetum et / solo nomine Rusticum uideo*, "and look in on that most elegant man who is Rustic only in name" (trans. from Sidonius by Anderson, occasionally slightly modified).

In *epist.* 38.9.7–10, *Aper*, formerly brilliant lawyer and governor of a province, converts to monastic life: his name may mean "wild boar," yet he is a boar for the world but a lamb for God (*aprum saeculo, agnum deo*). In *carm.* 21.312–21 *Asterius* ("who is like a star"), "whom his parents dedicated to God when he was a child" (*quem . . . parentes / infantem Christo constituere sacrum*), "gleams with his starry name and his starry face" (*sidereo pariter et nomine et ore micat*). Of course Felix, the patron saint of Nola, is *felix* (felicitous) "in his deserts and in his name" (*meritis et nomine, carm.* 12.1 and elsewhere).[47]

In a more formal and public context, etymological play is used in the verse funerary inscriptions of high aristocrats. In the poem dedicated to the same Probus (*CIL* VI 1756 b 3), after his death and free from mortal ashes, the great man travels a sure path in the skies, and since he reproduced what his name proclaims through his behaviour in life and is purified by the baptismal waters, he has now become a better Probus.[48] One may perhaps add the funerary epigram on the sarcophagus of Junius Bassus (low), the urban prefect who died in 359, which plays on his name as he ascends "higher" (*celsius*).[49]

That this kind of word pun was popular in funerary inscriptions in every period, and even for common people, can be gathered from the examples collected by M. T. Sblendorio Cugusi (1980, 2007).[50] There is much play on names that are said to mirror the character of the deceased, like *Benignus* (kind, friendly); *Celsa* (eminent); *Sacerdos* (priest); *Hedistes* (most sweet, from the Greek word *hedys*); *Vitalis* (vital); *Pulcheria-pulchra* (beautiful); *Amans* (loving); *Seuera* (serious, austere); *Celer* (swift); *Adeodatus* (Godsend), etc.[51]

3.3. Words and Sounds

Many word puns are achieved by placing words whose meaning is different but whose phonic structure is the same next to one another.[52] In Augustine one

---

47. Cf. also *carm.* 21.308–9 *Pinianus* ("like a pine tree"); *epist.* 32.6.1–2 *Clarus* ("illustrious"); *carm.* 17.61–2 *Nicetes* ("victor" in Greek); *carm.* 31.42 *Celsus* ("high"); *carm.* 25.240–1 *Memor* ("who remembers").

48. *Exuuiis resolutus in aetheris aequore tutum / curris iter cunctis integer a uitiis. / Nomine, quod resonans, imitatus moribus aeque / Iordane ablutus nunc Probus es melior*. For the same pun with the name Probus, Green 1991: 621 compares two passages from *Historia Augusta* (Vopisc. *Prob.* 4.1 and 4.4–5).

49. See Cameron 2002. For similar wordplays, cf. the verse epitaph of Bassa (ICVR 6, 14076), where two acrostics highlight her name and the name of her husband, Gaudentius (Trout 2010: 338–9).

50. For a more general assessment of literary influences on funerary inscriptions in verse, see Cugusi 1996.

51. And also *Amoena, Grata; Glyconis, Stephanus, Proba, Sanctus, Turtura, Deusdedit, Clearchus, Eusebius, Dextrianus, Rhodantion, Fortunata, Pyladen, Callistratus, Pamphilus, Anastasia*, and many others.

52. See, e.g., in Augustine, Mohrmann 1961: 334–7 and Moretti 2009 focused on the text of *confessiones*.

thinks of the play between *mundus* "world" and *mundus* "clean,"⁵³ between the verb *amare* (to love) and the adverb *amare* (bitterly),⁵⁴ between the noun *uenia* (mercy) and the verb *ueniam* (I shall come).⁵⁵ Mohrmann (1961: 342) assembled countless examples of wordplays where only one letter is changed in Augustine's sermons:⁵⁶ for instance, *rota* (wheel) and *nota* (known), *onerant* (they load) and *honorant* (they honour), *negaturi* (who will deny) and *necaturi* (who will kill), *militia* (warfare) and *malitia* (malice), *reus* (culprit) and *Deus* (God), *amores* (loves) and *mores* (manners, character), *errores* (mistakes) and *terrores* (fears), *fatidicos* (prophetic) and *falsidicos* (speaking falsely, lying).

Such sensitivity to sounds⁵⁷ can affect the choice of words, so that one synonym may be preferred to another just because it produces a rhyme or a phonic resonance (even Cicero, *orat.* 49.163 advised choosing *uerba bene sonantia*, i.e., "euphonious words").⁵⁸ Sometimes this even leads to the creation of new words, as A. Traina pointed out (1999: 52), quoting Avg. *ciu.* 14.26 *omnipotenti Deo summo ac summe bono creatori omnium naturarum, uoluntatum autem bonarum adiutori et remuneratori, malarum autem relictori et damnatori, utrarumque ordinatori non defuit utique consilium*,⁵⁹ where the neologism *relictori* (who abandons) is introduced to complete, with the same rhyme, the series *creatori, adiutori, remuneratori, damnatori, ordinatori*, and particularly to create a new pair with *damnatori*, connected by the article and matching the couple *adiutori et remuneratori*.⁶⁰ One might also cite Ambrose for the new word *inexcepta* (without exception: *exc. Sat.* 2.6), which in the sequence *mors aequalis est*

---

53. *Serm.* 216.2.2 *si despicitis mundum, habebitis cor mundum, et uidebitis eum qui fecit mundum; et sicut ille uicit, ita et vos in eius gratia uincetis hunc mundum* ("if you despise the world, you will have a clean heart and see the One who created the world; and as He won, so you too by His grace will win this world"); cf. also *serm.* 96.4.4; *serm.* 177.3.

54. *Serm.* 295.3.3.

55. *Serm.* 114.2 *Et quid praecepit? Dari fratri tuo ueniam. Tamquam diceret tibi: Tu homo da homini ueniam, ut ego Deus ad te ueniam* ("and what did He command? That mercy be given to your brother; as if he would say to you: man, be merciful with another man so that I, who am God, shall come to you").

56. It should be noted that the loss, addition, and transposition of single letters, according to Varro *ling.* 5.6, are to be taken into account when searching for etymologies.

57. Comeau 1930: 12 rightly points out that "Augustine, théoricien du rythme comme le prouve son ouvrage *de musica*, devait être extrêmement sensible à la musique de la phrase."

58. Cf. Qvint. *inst.* 1.5.4 *sola est quae notari possit uelut uocalitas, quae euphonia dicitur: cuius in eo dilectus est, ut inter duo, quae idem significant ac tantundem ualent, quod melius sonet malis*, "the only detectable virtue is 'vocality', what is called in Greek 'euphony'; this is the basis of the choice by which the better-sounding word is preferred when there are two which mean the same and have the same connotations."

59. "God almighty, who is the supreme and supremely good creator of all things, who supports and rewards all good will but abandons and condemns all bad will and orders both alike, surely did not lack a plan" (trans. Levine).

60. Besides the rhymes in *–ori*, the ones in *-arum* (*naturarum, bonarum, malarum, utrarum*) should also be noticed.

omnibus, indiscreta pauperibus, inexcepta diuitibus[61] is identical to *indiscreta* in its number of syllables (Traina 1999: 161).

One of the structural consequences of this procedure is that both Ambrose and Augustine, when commenting on scripture, often connect different texts not according to their meaning but because they share the same words.[62] All these features intensify the pleasure of listening to words and enhance their sweetness (*dulcedo, suauitas*), a quality Cicero had prescribed as crucial in epideictic eloquence[63] and which for Christian authors came to be of fundamental importance in the project of presenting Christian truth in a way that can move souls.[64] After all, the sweetness of Ambrose's words had been momentous in its attracting of Augustine.[65]

In a well-known section of *de dialectica* (5–6), Augustine expounds the Stoics' theory of words and etymologies, which he probably knew through the lost parts of Varro's works on grammar (Long 2005: 37).[66] According to the Stoics, whose ideas spark Augustine's criticism, if you want to find the origin of a word, you must search:

> until you arrive at some similarity of the sound of the word to the thing, as when we say "the clang of bronze," "the whinnying of horses," "the bleating of sheep," "the blare of trumpets," "the rattle of chains." For you clearly see that these words sound like the things themselves which are signified by these words.[67]

---

61. "Death is the same for all, without difference for the poor, without exception for the rich."

62. Cf. for Augustine, Comeau 1930: 12; for Ambrose, Fontaine 1976: 147 on the "apparente gratuité de ses enchaînements."

63. *Orat.* 42 *dulce igitur orationis genus et solutum et adfluens, sententiis argutum, uerbis sonans est in illo epidictico genere, quod diximus proprium sophistarum, pompae quam pugnae aptius ...* ("the epideictic oration, then, has a sweet, fluent, and copious style, with bright conceits and sounding phrases. It is the proper field for sophists, as we said, and is fitter for the parade than for the battle"; trans. Hubbell).

64. Cavadini 1995: but sweetness can also be dangerous, as Augustine warns in *doctr. christ.* 4.5.8 (a passage which is in itself a good example of the "sweetness" of the words it speaks about): *qui enim loquenter dicunt suauiter; qui sapienter salubriter audiuntur ... sicut autem saepe sumenda sunt et amara salubria, ita semper uitanda est perniciosa dulcedo. Sed salubri suauitate vel suaui salubritate quid melius?* ("For those who speak eloquently are listened to with pleasure; those who speak with wisdom are heard with profit ... but as often even bitter medicine must be taken, so always harmful sweets must be avoided. Still, what is better than wholesome sweets or sweet wholesomeness?"; trans. from *doctr. christ.* book IV by Sullivan).

65. AVG. *conf.* 5.13.23 *et delectabar sermonis suauitate* ("I was delighted by the sweetness of his sermons").

66. Long 2005: 55 suggests that chs. 5 and 6 of *de dialectica* ought to be included in a future collection of Stoic material on language.

67. *Donec perueniatur eo, ut res cum sono uerbi aliqua similitudine concinat, ut cum dicimus aeris tinnitum, equorum hinnitum, ouium balatum, tubarum clangorem, stridorem catenarum. Perspicis enim haec uerba ita sonare ut ipsae res quae his uerbis significantur.*

The passage describes what we usually call onomatopoeia,[68] a popular figure of speech among ancient teachers and writers of Latin, who not only discuss it but like to list the words related to animals' voices.[69] One of the more curious examples, from the *Historia Augusta* (SPART. *Geta* 5.4–5), portrays the emperor Geta, who seems to have been mad about grammar,[70] asking grammarians questions about animal sounds:

> to characterize the cries of the different animals, as for example: the lamb bleats, the pig squeals, the dove coos, the hog grunts, the bear growls, the lion roars, the leopard snarls, the elephant trumpets, the frog croaks, the horse neighs, the ass brays, the bull bellows; and in proof he would cite the ancient writers.[71]

While this passage has the unmistakable mark of a school exercise, we find series of onomatopoeic verbs integrated into sophisticated contexts, as parts of rich descriptions which epitomize "the artificializing of the natural" (Hernández Lobato 2012: 254). In a famous letter, Sidonius Apollinaris describes his country estate of Avitacum and lingers on its charms and pleasures, among which are the animal voices that merge with shepherds' songs and music (*epist*. 2.2.14):

> *hic iam quam uolupe est auribus insonare cicadas meridie concrepantes, ranas crepusculo incumbente blaterantes, cycnos atque anseres concubia nocte clangentes, intempesta gallos gallinaceos concinentes, oscines coruos uoce triplicata puniceam surgentis aurorae facem consalutantes; diluculo autem Philomelam inter frutices sibilantem, Prognem inter asseres minurientem! cui concentui licebit adiungas fistulae septiforis armentalem Camenam, quam saepe nocturnis carminum certaminibus insomnes nostrorum montium Tityri exercent, inter greges tinnibulatos per depasta buceta reboantes. quae tamen uaria uocum cantuumque modulamina profundius confouendo sopori tuo lenocinabuntur.*[72]

---

68. For onomatopoeia in the ancient world, see Bettini 2008: 66. VARRO *ling*. 5.75 maintains that many birds are named after their cries; e.g., *upupa* (hoopoe), *cuculus* (cuckoo), *coruus* (raven), *hirundo* (swallow), *ulula* (screech owl), *bubo* (horned owl) (trans. Kent). Cf. Bettini 2008: 64.70–4.

69. See the passages collected by Bettini 2008: 265–83.

70. Cf. also below.

71. *Vt dicerent singula animalia quomodo uocem emitterent, uelut:* (5) *agni balant, porcelli grunniunt, palumbes minurriunt, porci grunniunt, ursi saeuiunt, leones rugiunt, leopardi rictant, elephanti barriunt, ranae coaxant, equi hinniunt, asini rudunt, tauri mugiunt, easque de ueteribus adprobare* (trans. Magie). For the catalogue structure, see below.

72. One cannot help wondering whether it was actually possible to sleep amidst all that noise. See the careful analysis by Squillante 2012: 155–6 and Hernández Lobato 2012: 254–5.

How charming it is here to have echoing in one's ears the midday chirp of cicadas, the croaking of the frogs as evening comes on, the honking of swans and geese in the early hours of slumber, the crowing of cocks in the small hours; to hear the prophetic rooks greeting with thrice-repeated cry the red torch of rising dawn, Philomela piping in the bushes in the half-light, and Procne twittering amid the rafters! To this concert you may add if you please the pastoral muse with seven-holed flute, which often many a Tityrus of our mountains, forgoing sleep, keeps sounding in a nocturnal competition of song, among the belled sheep whose cries echo through the pastures as they crop the grass. Yet all these changeful tones of music and cries will but fondle and coax your slumber and make it all the deeper.

In the same passage from Augustine's *de dialectica*, Stoic theories of etymology connect word sounds with different sensations in a fascinating way: not only they can be harsh or pleasant on the ear, but they can almost be perceived by touch, as it were, suggesting smoothness (*lenitas*) or roughness (*asperitas*);[73] and by taste, suggesting flavour: for instance the word *mel* (honey) is as sweet as the thing it refers to. In short, words seem to have a sort of material nature, and the synaesthetic delight they convey is in part a physical one: analyzing the text of Psalm 118, Jerome (*epist*. 30.13) explains the pleasure (*uoluptas*) he feels while perusing the scriptures by means of a comparison to the pleasures of food: "What is more delightful than this pleasure? which food, which honey is more sweet than to understand God's intelligence, to penetrate into his sanctuary[?]"[74]

What *de dialectica* reveals with theoretical awareness appears to have been widely perceived, judging from what we can infer from other writers, either through their own practice or through their comments on performances by skilled orators (see AVG. *doctr. christ.* 4.3.4 on the pre-eminence of practice over theory) or as a result of school teaching.

The unusual patterns of sounds created by rare and foreign words, for instance, were particularly appreciated. They are like lights which brighten a

---

73. *Quis item "asperitatem" non et ipso nomine asperam iudicet? Lene est auribus cum dicimus "uoluptas," asperum cum dicimus "crux." Ita res ipsae afficiunt, ut uerba sentiuntur. Mel, quam suauiter gustum res ipsa, tam leniter nomine tangit auditum.* "Likewise, who does not by the name itself judge *asperitas* (roughness) to be rough? It is gentle to the ears when we say *uoluptas* (pleasure); it is harsh when we say *crux* (cross). Thus the words are perceived in the way the things themselves affect us. Just as the honey itself affects the taste pleasantly, so its name, *mel*, affects the hearing smoothly."
74. *Quid hac uoluptate iucundius? qui cibi, quae mella sunt dulciora Dei scire prudentiam, in adyta eius intrare* ...

text, as Augustine says about Hebrew names in *doctr. christ.* 4.7.17,[75] commenting on Amos 6:1–2:[76] "in this passage the language is adorned by the names of places, as though by lights, to wit, Sion Samaria, Chalanne, Emath Magna and Geth of the Philistines."[77]

3.4. Lists of Words

The same appreciation, although without Augustine's philosophical background, is to be found in Ausonius *epist.* 17, who quotes some verses from Paulinus of Nola's epitome of Suetonius's lost books *de regibus* (about kings), full of names of barbarian kings and of their peoples:

Illibanum Numidamque Auelim Parthumque Vononem
et Caranum, Pellaea dedit qui nomina regum,
quique magos docuit mysteria uana Nechepsos,
et qui regnauit sine nomine mox Sesoostris.

Illibanus, Numidian Avelis, Vonones the Parthian,
Caranus who founded the dynasty of Pella,
and Nechepsos who taught the wizards unavailing mysteries,
and afterwards Sesostris, who reigned and left no name.

Here the task was more difficult, because foreign names had to be inserted into Latin verses, and Ausonius's comment is enthusiastic: "How skilfully and neatly, how harmoniously and sweetly have you delivered these names, conforming at once to the character of our Roman accent, yet not allowing the true and original sounds to lose their proper stress!"[78] This judgment by one poet on another betrays Ausonius's experience as a grammarian, since lists of words, frequently

---

75. Hebrew names of course aroused Christians' interest in the complex issue of their meaning, which raised the question of how to translate them (or in some cases why not to translate, as the Greek translators of the Septuagint had already chosen to do in order to preserve the power of the original words): cf. above all Hier. *de nominibus Hebraicis* (PL 23.771–858); *de situ et nominibus locorum Hebraicorum* (PL 23.859–928); *tract. in Psalm.* 114,4; *in Hieremiam prophetam* (PL 25.787–9), and the various remarks scattered in his letters (*epist.* 20; 25; 26; 30; 34).

76. *Vae qui opulenti estis in Sion et confiditis in monte Samariae optimates capita populorum ingredientes pompatice domum Israhel transite in Chalanne et uidete et ite inde in Emath magnam et descendite in Geth Palaestinorum,* etc. "Woe to you that are wealthy in Sion, and to you that have confidence in the mountain of Samaria, ye great men, heads of the people, that go in with much state into the house of Israel. Pass ye over into Chalanne, and see, and go from thence into Emath the great, and go down into Geth of the Philistines."

77. *Cum ista dicuntur, locorum nominibus tamquam luminibus ornatur eloquium, quae sunt Sion, Samaria, Chalanne, Emath magna, et Geth Palaestinorum.*

78. *Haec tu quam perite et concinne, quam modulate et dulciter, ita iuxta naturam Romanorum accentuum enuntiasti ut tamen ueris et primigeniis uocibus sua fastigia non perirent.*

of proper names (mythical or historical) assembled according to their subjects, were among the typical aids used by teachers.[79]

Among several other examples from different authors, in verse and prose,[80] I mention Sidonius Apollinaris, who is particularly fond of catalogues and is a master of exploiting this feature. Sometimes more than one catalogue recurs in the same composition: for instance, in the long speech that a personified Rome delivers in the *Panegyric on the Emperor Avitus*, the rivers of foreign countries trembling before the Tiber (i.e., Roman power) are listed at ll. 74–6:

Indorum Ganges, Colchorum Phasis, Araxes
Armeniae, Ger Aethiopum Tanaisque Getarum
Thybrinum tremuere meum.

Ganges of the Indians, Phasis of the Colchians, Araxes of Armenia, Ger of the Ethiopians, Tanais of the Getae, all trembled before my Tiber .

Then (ll. 79–82) three different lists of names are intertwined: Roman leaders, the enemies they overcame, and the punishments imposed on the latter:[81]

qualis eram cum per mea iussa iuberent
Sulla, Asiatogenes, Curius, Paulus, Pompeius
Tigrani, Antiocho, Pyrrho, Persae, Mithridati
pacem ac regna, fugam, uectigal, uincla, uenenum.

---

79. See the evidence from papyri in Kramer 1983, where fish names are recorded; e.g., at n. 5, 61 (a papyrus from second century AD); n. 6, 63–6 (first/second century AD); n. 7, 67–8 (third century AD); Morgan 1998: 100 and appendix II, 275–87. Cavarzere 2003: 76 (quoting E. S. Dulabahn) mentions Polemius Silvius's *Laterculus* (fifth century AD; MGH AA IX 544). The habit of learning lists of synonyms is recalled by Quintilian (*inst.* 10.1.7), who considers it *puerile* (childish). Examples of catalogues have been collected by Wedeck 1960, Kyriakidis 2007, and Hernández Lobato 2012: 398–9.

80. See, e.g., Venantius Fortunatus, who in the preface to his poems (4; ed. Reydellet), dedicating them to Pope Gregory, describes his long journey: *de Rauenna progrediens Padum Athesim Brintam Plauem Liquentiam Teliamentumque tranans, per Alpem Iuliam pendulus montanis anfractibus, Drauum Norico, Oenum Breonis, Liccam Baiuaria, Danuuium Alamannia, Rhenum Germania transiens ac post Mosellam, Mosam, Axonam et Sequanam, Ligerem et Garonnam, Aquitaniae maxima fluenta transmittens, Pyrenaeis occurrens* . . . ("starting from Ravenna, going through the rivers Po, Adige, Brenta, Piave, Livenza, Tagliamento, hanging down from mountains' crooks in the Julian Alps, I proceeded to Norico through the river Drava, through Inn in the country of Breuni, through Lech in Bavaria, through Danube in Alamannia, through Rhenum in Germania, and then crossing the Mosella, Mosa, Aisne and Sequana, the Liger and Garonna, the biggest rivers of Aquitania, coming to the Pyrenaeans"); cf. Squillante 2005: 71.

81. This is an (imperfect) example of *uersus rapportati* ("correlative verses"): a structure which became popular in the Middle Ages and required that every line exhibit one different series of elements and that each element of the first line correspond to one placed in the same position in every other line.

> Alas for what I was when at my bidding
> Sulla, Asiaticus, Curius, Paulus, Pompeius,
> demanded of Tigranes, Antiochus, Pyrrhus, Perseus, and Mithridates
> peace and realms, banishment, tribute, chains and poison.

Single names synthesize famous events, emphasizing the words' strength and power of suggestion.

The names of barbarian tribes are frequently listed in catalogues by Sidonius: in the *Panegyric on Maiorianus* 474–7, different peoples fight in Emperor Majorian's army:

> *Bastarna, Suebus,*
> *Pannonius, Neurus, Chunus, Geta, Dacus, Halanus*
> *Bellonotus, Rugus, Burgundio, Vesus, Alites*
> *Bisalta, Ostrogothus, Procrustes, Sarmata, Moschus*
> *post aquilas uenere tuas.*[82]

> Bastarnian, Suebian,
> Pannonian, Neuran, Hun, Getan, Dacian, Alan,
> Bellonotan, Rugian, Burgundian, Visigoth, Alites,
> Bisalta, Ostrogoth, Procrustian, Sarmatian, Moschan
> have ranged themselves behind thine eagles.

These clusters of names, compressed in asyndeton, are effective in suggesting the image of enormous crowds of peoples and also a sense of acceleration in the narrative tempo (Kyriakidis 2007: xvii); even more so in the *Panegyric on Auitus* 321ff., where Sidonius describes the incursions of Attila, whose hordes had gathered so many tribes that the whole North poured into Gaul and where, in the climactic end of the catalogue, Attila himself is centre stage:

> *pugnacem Rugum comitante Gelono*
> *Gepida trux sequitur; Scirum Burgundio cogit:*
> *Chunus, Bellonotus, Neurus, Bastarna, Toringus*
> *Bructerus, uluosa quem Nicer alluit unda*
> *prorumpit Francus; cecidit cito secta bipenni*
> *Hercynia in lintres et Rhenum texuit alno;*
> *et iam terrificis diffuderat Attila turmis*
> *in campos se, Belga, tuos.*

---

82. We may add *pan. Mai.* 335–8, where the barbarian peoples who fight under the Vandal king Geiseric are listed.

After the warlike Rugian, with the Gelonian close by
comes the fierce Gepid; the Burgundian urges on the Scirian;
forward rush the Hun, the Bellonotian, the Neurian, the Bastarnian, the Thuringian,
the Bructeran, and he whose land is washed by the sedgy waters of Nicer,
the Frank. Straightway falls the Hercynian forest,
hewn to make boats, and overlays the Rhine with a network of its timber;
and now Attila with his fearsome squadrons has spread himself in raids
upon your plains, Belgian.

But elsewhere the catalogue scheme seems to be aimed merely at displaying erudition:[83] for instance, in the passage from *Panegyric to Majorian* (ll. 279–90) that stresses Aetius's loyalty to Majorian, Sidonius deploys a series of *adynata*, full of geographical and mythological names. Even lists formed by less exotic nouns can make a striking impression on the reader, as in the famous passage where Ausonius speaks of the fish that live in the crystal waters of the Mosella (*Mos.* 85–140), using small and incisive touches to describe their shapes, colours, and flavours. He lists the *squameus . . . capito* (the scaly chub); the *salar, purpureis stellatus tergora guttis* ("the trout, whose back is starred with purple spots"); the *rhaedo, nullo spinae nociturus acumine* ("the roach without pointed bones to do mischief"); the *barbus* (barbel); the *salmo* (salmon) with red flesh; the *mustela* (eelpout); the *perca* (perch); the *mullus* (mullet); the *lucius* (pike); the *tinca* (tench); and the *alburnus* (bleak); the *alausa* (shad); the *gobio* (gudgeon); the *silurus* (sheatfish).[84]

3.5. Painting with Words

In this passage,[85] Ausonius seems to take pleasure in displaying his rich vocabulary, as Symmachus perfectly understands, claiming with admiration (*epist.*

---

83. Cf., e.g., *epist.* 4.3.7, on the style of Claudianus Mamertus, who *sentit ut Pythagoras dividit ut Socrates, explicat ut Platon implicat ut Aristoteles, ut Aeschines blanditur ut Demosthenes irascitur, vernat ut Hortensius aestuat ut Cethegus, incitat ut Curio moratur ut Fabius, simulat ut Crassus dissimulat ut Caesar, suadet ut Cato dissuadet ut Appius persuadet ut Tullius*, etc. ("he makes judgements like Pythagoras, distinguishes like Socrates, unfolds like Plato, and enfolds like Aristotle; he cajoles like Aeschines and storms like Demosthenes, luxuriates like Hortensius, and seethes like Cethegus; incites like Curio, holds back like Fabius, simulates like Crassus and dissimulates like Caesar, advises like Cato, dissuades like Appius, and persuades like Cicero").

84. Cf. also *epist.* 13.59–62 *referuntur ab unda / corroco, letalis trygon mollesque platessae, / urentes thynni et male tecti spina ligatri / nec duraturi post bina trihoria corvi* ("from the waves are brought home sturgeon, the deadly sting ray, soft tender plaice, bitter tunnies, spindle fish ill-guarded by their spines, and grayling which will not keep above twice three hours").

85. For a detailed commentary, see Cavarzere 2003: 75–93; Hernández Lobato 2012: 391–4 highlights the deconstructing and parodistic character of this catalogue.

1.14): "Where did you find those shoals of river fish, as varied in colours as in names, as different in size as in savour, which you coloured with your poem's paint beyond nature's gifts?"[86] Symmachus is clearly attracted by the way that the suggestion of words is able to depict so many fish, enhancing their natural colours. This not only has a visual appeal (Roberts 1989a: 76–8 rightly recalls mosaics where fish were a popular subject), but also displays the poet's ability to compete with nature and to surpass it.[87]

That words can have a visual potential of their own is explained by Augustine, who maintains, in his sophisticated way (*in euang. Ioh.* 33.11), that when we look at something, we store what we perceive through our eyes in our memory, as a sort of hoard of treasure, and as long as our thoughts are directed elsewhere, we do not see it any more: but if a word turns our attention to it, we can see it once again. Augustine appears to be describing the stylistic effects of *enargeia*, that is the vivid nature of words in appealing to the listener's senses and turning him into an eyewitness (Zanker 1981: 297). From a different and simpler point of view, referring to the Sophists' style (of which he does not approve, as its only purpose is to show off) Cicero, *orat.* 65 (Roberts 1989a: 47–8) says that they use words as painters use various colours (*uerba ... disponunt ut pictores uarietatem colorum*).[88] Catalogues can enhance this visual effect, even if (or sometimes, at least in my opinion, particularly if) they are much compressed, so that the attention is drawn to the single word or name, which stands out like a single colour or image.[89]

To clarify this, I quote two different examples. The catalogue of Hercules's labours was a very common topic (Green 1991: 432). Ausonius (*ecl.* 17) lists the twelve most famous ones, summarizing each of the hero's exploits in a single verse, skilfully condensing—not without stylistic variation—circumstances, places, chronology,[90] into a whole whose didactic purpose is clearly to help

---

86. *Vnde illa amnicorum piscium examina repperisti quam nominibus uaria tam coloribus, ut magnitudine distantia sic sapore, quae tu pigmentis istius carminis supra naturae dona fucasti?* (trans. Evelyn White).

87. Roberts 1989a: 70: "in late antiquity, as opposed to their classical period, both art and literature are expected not merely to imitate nature, but to exceed it"; cf. also Nugent 1990: 243.

88. On the comparison between poetry and the visual arts in Late Antiquity, cf. Roberts 1989a: ch. 3.

89. Or like "unidades esteticas autosuficientes" (Hernández Lobato 2012: 384). From this point of view, I disagree with Kyriakidis's opinion (2007: xvii), that the importance of a name in a catalogue "depends largely on the density of names the verse has; the greater the density the smaller the significance each name has in the catalogue."

90. *Prima Cleonaei tolerata aerumna leonis. / proxima Lernaeam ferro et face contudit hydram. / mox Erymantheum uis tertia perculit aprum*, etc. ("the first toil endured was that of the Cleonaean lion. The next with sword and brand crushed the Lyrnaean hydra. The third exploit presently destroyed the boar of Erymanthus," etc.).

memory.[91] Sidonius develops the same theme more than once[92] and, with the most striking compression, in his *Epithalamium for Polemius and Araneola*, where the scene is set in Athens in two different temples, both consecrated to Minerva: one is a home for philosophers, the other is dedicated to the textile arts, over which she presides. In the latter Sidonius describes two different garments next to each other, both richly embroidered with mythical scenes, one depicting Jupiter's might (represented in the image of his thunderbolt) and the other Hercules's labours. In the former, a brief passage (126–31) exhibits some descriptive details that show a taste for colours.[93] The second ekphrastic textile concentrates a list of mere names related to Heracles's exploits in only three verses (141–3), outnumbering the twelve canonical labours:

sus, leo, cerua, Gigans, taurus, iuga, Cerberus, hydra,
hospes, Nessus, Eryx, uolucres, Thrax, Cacus, Amazon,
Cres, fluuius, Libs, poma, Lycus, uirgo, polus, Oete.

The boar, the lion, the deer, the giant, the bull, the yoke, Cerberus, the hydra,
the host, Nessus, Eryx, the birds, the Thracian, Cacus, the Amazon,
the Cretan beast, the river, the Libyan, the apples, the Lycian, the maid, the sky, Oeta.

Heroes, monsters, animals, places, are put together in a disjointed series which seems to multiply their number. Contrasting this synthetic passage to the more descriptive account of Jupiter's garment, Sidonius is stressing the evocative visual power of single words, as if pictures in their own right condensed into only one image.[94]

This feature is particularly noticeable when catalogues, referring to things which are in themselves rich in colour, create patterns of words and phrases

---

91. As in the other *eclogae* which deploy similar didactic topics, i.e., the names of the seven days in a week, the months and the number of days in each of them, the seasons.

92. In *carm*. 13.1–20, where the emperor Majorian is humorously compared to Hercules; besides, Hercules's labours (more than the twelve traditional ones) are squeezed into seven verses in *carm*. 9.94–100.

93. 127ff. *palla Iouis rutilat, cuius bis coctus aeno / serica Sidonius fucabat stamina murex, / ebria nec solum spirat conchylia sandyx; / insertum nam fulgur habet, filoque rigenti / ardebat grauidum de fragmine fulminis ostrum* ("here the robe of Jupiter first shows its ruddy gleam; Sidonian purple twice boiled in the cauldron coloured the silken threads, and the deep-dyed red showed not only the sheen of purple, for the gleam of lightning was intermingled, and a blaze came from the broken levin-shaft"). Cf. the analysis by Ravenna 1990: 77–81.

94. See Gualandri 1994: 341. I obviously do not agree with Gerbrandy's (2013: 74–5) totally dismissive judgement about this kind of poem.

whose polychromatic effect appeals to the reader's eye, as Roberts (1989a: 10) brilliantly shows, starting from Cyprianus's *heptateuchos* 1098–1103, a verse paraphrase of Exod. 28:17–20, where the twelve precious stones in Aaron's breastplate are listed.[95]

I shall choose just one example: the description of Venus's palace, built by Vulcanus, in Sidonius's *Epithalamium for Ruricius and Hiberia*, 17–28: [96]

> *hic lapis est de quinque locis dans quinque colores*
> *Aethiops, Phrygius, Parius, Poenus, Lacedaemon,*
> *purpureus, uiridis, maculosus, eburnus et albus.*
> *postes chrysolithi fuluus diffulgurat ardor;*
> *myrrhina, sardonyches, amethystus Hiberus, iaspis*
> *Indus, Chalcidicus, Scythicus, beryllus, achates*
> *attollunt duplices argenti cardine ualuas,*
> *per quas inclusi lucem uomit umbra smaragdi;*
> *limina crassus onyx crustat propterque hyacinthi*
> *caerula concordem iaciunt in stagna colorem.*
> *exterior non compta silex, sed prominet alte*
> *asper ab adsiduo lympharum uerbere pumex.*

Here is stone from five regions, giving forth five hues,
Aethiopian, Phrygian, Parian, Punic, Spartan,
purple, green, mottled, ivory, white.
The yellow glow of topaz flashes through the doorpost;
porcelain, sardonyx, Caucasian amethyst, Indian jasper,
Chalcidian and Scythian stones, beryl and agate,
form the double doors that rise upon silver pivots,
and through these doors the shadowy recess beyond pours out the sheen
    of the emeralds that are within.
Onyx thickly encrusts the threshold, and hard by the blue colour
of amethyst casts upon the lagoon a harmonious hue.

---

95. *Sardia prima loco, topazo adiuncta smaragdus; / sapphirus hanc sequitur, cum qua carbunculus ardet, / iaspisque uiret fuluoque intermicat auro: / tertia ligurio sedes: hic iunctus achati / atque amethysto, fulgens quem purpura tingit. / Chrysolithus quartus, beryllo adnexus onychnus.* "First in position is the carnelian, and emerald along with the topaz; then comes the sapphire, with which the carbuncle blazes, and the jasper is green and shines with tawny gold. Third place is taken by amber, and along with it the agate and amethyst, with its bright purple hue. Fourth the chrysolite, and onyx next to the beryl" (translation by Roberts).

96. The model is the description of Venus's palace in Claudian's *Epithalamium for Honorius and Maria* 87–91. For Claudian and Prudentius see Roberts (1989a: 13, n. 9).

Outside is no dressed stone, but towering walls
of rock that has been roughened by the constant lashing of the waters.

Exotic names of precious stones and foreign countries—some evoking an indistinct and fabulous remoteness—are mixed here with words hinting at shades of colours and gleams of light, as in a painter's palette.

3.6. FRAGMENTING THE WORDS

Words can also be fragmented, as was customary in school. The grammarian known as Sergius (fifth century AD?) states that "every discourse can be broken down into words, words again into syllables and syllables into letters,"[97] and Augustine, discussing a passage in Saint John's Gospel (*in euang. Ioh.* 37,4) and using a derogatory tone, calls the grammarian who dares to find fault with the Word of God *uerborum appensor et syllabarum examinator* ("a weigher of words and examiner of syllables"). But a careful analysis of Augustine's prose (Moretti 2009: 33ff.) shows that he himself was extremely sensitive to the intertwinement of syllables and letters echoing each other in the words' texture, independently of their meaning (cf., e.g., *conf.* 1.19.30 cu*piditate*/au*cupabar*; 2.2.2 lum*inosus*/lim*es*/lim*osa*; 52.2 in*quieti*/in*iqui*; 8.12.29 ar*ripui*/a*perui*; 1.10.15 nu*gae*/ne*gotia*; 8.5.12 superati/soporis). In a strikingly scholastic form of poetics, Publilius Optatianus Porfyrius, a contemporary of Constantine, composed a poem (*carm.* 15) whose first line is wholly made up of disyllables, the second of trisyllables, the third of tetrasyllables, the fourth of pentasyllables (Levitan 1985: 247).[98] Ausonius in his *Technopaegnion* (Green 1991: XXV) plays with syllables or, more precisely, with monosyllabic words, which he calls "small particles, as it were, of the discourse" (*quasi quaedam puncta sermonum*),[99] composing a series of small poems whose lines all end with one of them[100] and where in some cases the same monosyllable which is the ending of a verse becomes the beginning of the next one.

---

97. But "the letter alone cannot be split: that's why it is called 'atomos' ('indivisible') by philosophers": *cum omnis oratio soluatur in uerba, uerba denuo soluantur in syllabas, rursum syllabae soluantur in litteras, littera sola non habet quo soluatur. ideo a philosophis atomos dicitur* (GL Keil IV 475.7, Lipsiae 1864); cf. Dionigi 2005: 33–8. Children actually followed the opposite way and began learning letters, then syllables, then words.

98. QVINT. *inst.* 1.1.30 insists on the importance of learning and repeating syllables; examples of exercises where words are divided into syllables (monosyllables, disyllables, and so on) in Cribiore 2001: 173–4; Ahl 1985: 35–40 focuses on syllables to discuss the complex interplay of sounds in Latin poetry.

99. In the preface letter to Pacatus. Evelyn White, following Lorimer, translates "monosyllables which serve, if I may put it in that way, as so many full-stops"; I prefer "small particles, as it were, of the discourse."

100. As Green 1991: 583 points out, Ausonius "uses almost all the monosyllabic nouns in the language." As to syllables, Ahl 1985: 35 remarks that ancient grammarians assigned them more importance than we do and that "Varro's etymologies are based on syllables rather than on whole words."

Above all, the practice of perceiving syllables and letters as word fragments, since fragments can be moved and reassembled, opens the way to multifarious manipulations of language, in the form of anagrams, acrostics, mesostics, telestics, palindromes, where the emphasis is on single letters more than syllables.

In the passage mentioned above from the grammarian Sergius (*GLK* IV 475.5),[101] the word *littera* (letter) is explained as perhaps coming from *legitera* (which is a ficticious noun), since, like a kind of guide, it shows *legentibus* ("to the readers") *iter ad legendum* ("the way to reading"). And Augustine (as he himself recalled in *retract.* 1.20), when he composed in simple language his *Psalmus contra partem Donati* ("Psalm against the Donatists"), chose the Latin alphabet as a guide to arrange the incipits of different stanzas, so that his audience (including the ignorant and the uneducated) might better follow them and impress in their memory the theological matter at issue.[102] He was influenced by the biblical tradition, above all by the precedent set by texts such as Psalm 118 (119), which is divided into twenty-two stanzas of eight verses and where in each stanza each verse begins with the same Hebrew consonant, progressing in alphabetical order. Needless to say, this feature attracted the interest of Latin Christian authors such as Jerome (*epist.* 30.5) and, most of all, Ambrose, who composed an impressive *Explanatio psalmi 118 (119)*, that attempted to find a spiritual and allegorical explanation in each Hebrew letter[103] and remarked that the abecedarian sequence (*prol.* 1) had been chosen so that through letters, like children getting accustomed to learning, we too may learn how to live. In a more frivolous and jocular way it is recorded that the emperor Geta, whose mania for grammar was mentioned above, fixed the menus of his meals according to letters of the alphabet.[104]

In word manipulation, acrostics were among the most popular features. The practice had a long and ancient history, beginning from the Sumerian, Egyptian, Hebraic, Phoenician, and Greek worlds.[105] The earliest known occurrence in a

---

101. In the wake of Serv. *gramm.* IV 421 (*comment. in artem Donati*).
102. See Gillian Clark's contribution to this volume. For the abecedarian structure, cf. also Hilary of Poitiers, *hymn.* 1 and 2; Venantius Fortunatus *carm.* 1.16. Cf. Dornseiff 1922: 26–7.
103. On Ambrose's sources, see Pizzolato 1987 I: 26–31.
104. *Habebat etiam istam consuetudinem, ut conuiuia, et maxime prandia, per singulas litteras iuberet, scientibus seruis, uelut in quo erat anser, aprugna, anas; item pullus, perdix, pauus, porcellus, piscis, perna, et quae in eam litteram genera edulium caderent; et item fasianus, farta, ficus et talia* (Spart. *Geta* 5.7–8). "He was accustomed, moreover, to have skilful slaves serve meals, and especially dinners, according to a single letter of the alphabet, as, for instance, one in which there was goose, gammon, and gadwall, or, again, pullet, partridge, peacock, pork, poisson, pig's thigh, and other kinds of food beginning with this letter, or pheasant, farina, figs and so forth."
105. See Guarducci 1978; Graf 1894; an impressive collection of acrostics, many of them accidental, was made by Hilberg 1899 and 1900; cf. also Pease 1963: 529; Courtney 1990 (with bibliography); Cameron 1995: 37–8; Squire 2011: 216–28.

Latin literary text seems to be in Ennius, whose acrostic, *Q. Ennius fecit* (*Inc.* 53 Vahlen³), probably made up from the first letters of subsequent verses, is recorded by Cicero (*div.* 2.111). This is a typical kind of acrostic that contains the name of the author, who exploits it as a seal and mark of authenticity.[106] Acrostics (and telestics) are common in inscriptions, where they can give prominence to the name of a deceased (Courtney 1990: 6) or of an honorand; while in dedications (of buildings or objects), they highlight the name of the dedicatee: in such cases the initial or the final letter composing the acrostic or the telestic can be marked out from the rest of the line by some device, either by spacing or by colour. A good example is a small poem from Africa (now in *Anthologia Latina*, 120 Riese = 109 Shackleton Bailey; Cameron: 1992) which describes the baths built by Filocalus, whose name appears in the acrostic (*Filocali*), and paid for by Melania, whose name is spelt out in the telestic (*Melaniae*).[107]

But the best and most astonishing examples of manipulation of language and of the "atomistic" nature of letters (to recall Sergius's definition)[108] are the poems composed by Optatian, whose remarkable technical skill, after Polara's critical edition and seminal studies (1973, 1987, 1996), has aroused scholars' interest in recent years (Levitan 1985, Edwards 2005, Squire 2011: 219–28, 2015a, Hernández Lobato 2012: 307–11, 471–5, Squire and Wienand, forthcoming).[109] The poems, mostly in hexameters, are set out in square grids so that, alongside the verses written as usual in horizontal lines, there are others in vertical lines as acrostics, mesostics, telestics. Moreover, as an entirely new feature, previously unknown in the Latin tradition but entirely in keeping with the aesthetics explored in this chapter, in the main body of the poems verses are hidden (*uersus intexti*) which create graphic designs. These are not only geometric patterns, sometimes quite intricate, but also very complex images, as in *carm.* 19, where the hidden verses draw a Roman trireme whose mast is formed by the Christian chi-rho monogram (cf. figure 1.23). Beyond this, the poems can have a sort of "protean" character, like *carm.* 15 (Levitan 1985: 246–9), where the position of the words can be changed in a single line without disrupting the metre; a hexameter can be read forward or backward retaining its metrical

---

106. For Greek acrostics used to establish the authenticity of a work, cf. Courtney 1990: 7–9; for their presence in Sibylline oracles, see Pease 1963: 529–32; Courtney 1990: 4–5.

107. Cameron 1992: 141–2 persuasively identifies them with well-known persons: Melania the Elder and Furius Dionysius Filocalus, the famous "calligrapher," who "was not in fact a man who earned his living by his skills. He was a man of respectable (if not aristocratic) origins and comfortable means who simply chose to spend his time doing what he did so well."

108. But in a more complex and fascinating way, Lucretius (cf. 1.196–7; 2.682–99) had already drawn the comparison between atoms and letters: cf. Squire (this volume), 91–2.

109. On Optatian, see now Michael Squire's exhaustive contribution to this volume. On figure poems and acrostics in Venantius Fortunatus, see Graver 1993.

form or, when inverted, become a pentameter, and so on. In this manner, a limited set of words can be rearranged to produce an incredible number of variations.[110] Scholars agree in stressing the pre-eminence of the drawing and the picture of the written words over their meaning in these features:[111] that is, to use Augustine's language, of *signa* over *res*. Even in Ausonius we can find a passage where the poet's eye is particularly attracted by the letters drawn with pen and ink on the surface of the papyrus (*epist*. 14b.48–52):

fac campum replices, Musa, papyrium
nec iam fissipedis per calami uias
grassetur Cnidiae sulcus harundinis,
pingens aridulae subdita paginae,
Cadmi filiolis atricoloribus.

See that thou abridge, my Muse, thy acreage of paper,
and no longer get the furrow of the Cnidian reed
to proceed along the paths of the cloven-footed pen
painting the surface of my poor parched page
with Cadmus' dark-hued little daughters.

But in Optatian's poems the letters' visual appeal must actually have been truly impressive since, as shown in medieval manuscripts, while the text was written in black ink, the *uersus intexti* were highlighted in brilliant colours,[112] thus catching the reader's attention to the detriment of the context. I doubt whether Augustine would have approved of these "letter games." In *in euang. Ioh*. 24.2 he specifically says that when we see letters beautifully written, it is not enough to admire them and to praise the calligrapher. We must read and understand what they say (*aliter enim uidetur pictura, aliter uidentur litterae*, "the drawing and letters are different things"). Thus he admonishes us to move from *signa* to *res*; in Optatian there is always the danger that *res* may be completely forgotten.[113]

---

110. As to the total number, see the discussion in Levitan 1985: 251–2—along with Squire (this volume), 85–92.
111. Most of which go back to the Hellenistic tradition: Squire 2011: 224.
112. E.g., in purple, as Optatian himself points out (*carm*. 19.1): cf. figure 1.1.
113. Cf. Squire (this volume), 75–6. I am grateful to the editors for the careful revision of the language of this paper.

PART II

Late Antique Intertextuality

4

Intertextuality in Late Latin Poetry

HELEN KAUFMANN

1. INTRODUCTION

condicio optima est ultimi: parata uerba inuenit, quae aliter instructa nouam faciem habent. (SEN. *epist.* 79.6)

The situation of the last is the best: He finds the words ready and they take on a new shape once they are put together in a different way.

IN HIS SEVENTY-NINTH LETTER SENECA ENCOURAGES LUCILIUS TO write a poem on Aetna and explains that Lucilius will be in the best possible situation as the subject had already been treated by other poets before him.[1] Extending Seneca's argument to Late Antiquity, the poets of that period should be in an even better position, as they had a much longer tradition of Latin poetry to rely on than Lucilius. However, their reliance has not always been appreciated; indeed, intertextuality in late Latin poetry has often been described as inferior to that of earlier, especially Hellenistic and Augustan, poetry—for example, as less sophisticated or with fewer allusions to Greek models.[2] While some of these characteristics are correct, they are not by themselves negative. The negative evaluation has been largely due to the assumption that intertextuality in Late Antiquity works according to the same principles as that of Hellenistic or classical literature as well as to the view that deviations from those principles must express lack of quality.[3] In this chapter I question the assumption of the same principles and replace the decline and deficiency model by one that shows the range of intertextuality modes used in late Latin poetry. In particular, I argue that while in late Latin poetry the classical mode of intertextuality continues to be used, there are other modes in which allusions do not, or not necessarily, make up content; in these modes, instead, the allusions are formal features and represent ideas of literary tradition, particularly genres, status, even Roman culture, which in turn

---

1. Cf. McGill 2012b: 200–1.
2. E.g., Anderson 1936: liii, in the introduction to his Loeb edition of Sidonius Apollinaris: "If imitation is the sincerest flattery, never [...] were previous writers honoured with a more thorough-going adulation. But the imitation does not go beneath the surface. Some of it is merely mechanical."
3. The two do not necessarily go together. A number of scholars of late Latin poetry would sign up to the former while disagreeing with the latter, e.g., Charlet 1988 and 2008, who describes late Latin poetry as neo-classical and neo-Alexandrian, Kelly 2013.

makes them a useful means to negotiate values and identities, especially in multicultural and multireligious contexts.

2. Definitions and Terminology

Intertextuality can be discussed in various ways, and the terms used often indicate the ideological position or theoretical framework behind the discussion. For example, the use of the terms "reference" or "allusion" may express that the user considers authors to intentionally refer or allude to an earlier text, whereas the terms "parallels" and "intertexts" may point to the idea of intertextuality as something that is created by readers following their discovery of similarities in two texts.[4] While I favour the view that meaning is created by the reader at the moment of reading, I nevertheless want my readings to be, at least potentially, historical. Therefore, I seek to identify parallels that are historically possible references from one text to the other and which allow for an interesting interpretation. For stylistic reasons, the terms "parallels," "correspondences," "references," and "allusions" are used interchangeably in this chapter and without implying authorial intention.[5]

Fowler (1997: 19–20) describes intertextuality in the following way: "We require a correspondence to stand out and to make sense: that is, if someone wants to convince the interpretative community of a particular intertextual relation, s/he must say how the correspondence between the source- and target-texts is special, and s/he must do something interesting with it, make it mean." This definition includes two dimensions of intertextuality: its visibility ("we require a correspondence to stand out") and its meaning ("and to make sense"). While the focus in this chapter is on the latter, it is also important to understand what happens to the former in late Latin poetry. In general, visibility has two components: the degree of linguistic similarity between two passages and the degree of signposting allusions. Without linguistic similarities it would not be possible to identify allusions in the first place, and the poets of Late Antiquity clearly used many expressions of previous poets, particularly of Vergil, for example *iuncturae*, line endings, half-lines. Even the idea of multiple references, expressions which allude to two or more older passages,[6] seems to

---

4. Conte 1986: 67 and passim, for example, distinguishes between "integrative" and "reflective allusions," Thomas 1986: 174 uses "parallels" for "accidental confluence" and various types of "references," e.g., "apparent reference" or "multiple reference" for other types of correspondences (1986: 175–98), and Thomas 1999: 2 "intertextuality." Cf. also Hinds 1998: 17–51 on "allusion," "reference," and "intertextuality."
5. Cf. Hinds 1998: 47–50 on accepting authorial intention even in a reader-centred approach to intertextuality.
6. Thomas 1986: 193–8.

be a matter of inevitability rather than choice. In this respect, intertextuality in late Latin poetry does not differ much from that of earlier poetry, nor are the examples chosen for further discussion in this chapter very different from each other in linguistic similarity. Late Latin intertextuality, however, does differ from earlier poetry in the second component of visibility: signposting. Explicit markers of allusions such as "Alexandrian footnotes," that is, expressions such as *fama est, ferunt, dicitur*,[7] do not seem to be as common as in earlier poetry, though other ways of signposting, for example, the use of (near-)complete lines or centos, make some allusions more heavily marked than others. The following discussion, however, is not about the visibility of allusions, linguistic similarity or signposting, but about their meaning. For it is in this second of Fowler's dimensions in which some late Latin poets differ significantly from the practices of their classical colleagues, not just in degree but also in kind.

The meaning of intertextuality could be described as lying between two poles, one at which allusions are an essential part of the content and the other at which they are formal features. Hellenistic and classical intertextuality tends to be found around the first pole: meaning is created by engagement with a passage from an earlier text and the changes made to the passage or its context. Likewise in late Latin poetry, allusions can make up content even if the intertextual engagement tends to be a less essential part of it, but more importantly, they can also be used just as formal features. This extension of meaning of intertextuality in late Latin poetry has so far not generally been recognized, not even by those scholars who have pointed to differences between late Latin and classical intertextuality. Among such scholars some have studied allusions in individual poets,[8] whereas others have described late Latin allusions in general as "nonreferential" (Pelttari 2014: 131–7) and "fragments of earlier poets" (Roberts 1989a: 57–8) and the process of alluding as "inclusion" (Rijser 2013). Furthermore, Pelttari (2014: 154–60) as well as Hernández Lobato (2012: 562–80) have proposed that late Latin intertextuality differs from classical allusivity as a whole, Pelttari by arguing that it does not engage in *aemulatio*, Hernández Lobato by describing it as a 'poetics of simulation' (in contrast to the classical 'poetics of representation'). The reading of late Latin intertextuality that I propose differs from these approaches in two ways: Firstly, instead of considering it as different from classical intertextuality as a whole, I suggest that classical intertextuality continues to be employed but that

---

7. Cf. Hinds 1998: 1–5. The term was introduced by Ross 1975: 78 based on the description of the phenomenon by Norden 1957: 123–4. Wills 1996: 30–1 calls such allusions "externally marked."

8. In addition to the scholarship discussed later, see, e.g., Posani 1962, Görler 1969, Newlands 1988, Nugent 1990, and Williams 2010, all on Ausonius; Lühken 2002 on Prudentius; Ware 2012 on Claudian; Tizzoni 2014 on Dracontius.

the range of intertextuality modes has been expanded in late Latin poetry to include the use of allusions as purely formal features. Secondly, despite describing the allusions used in a non-classical way as formal features, I do not consider them to be "nonreferential," in my view a rather misleading term, nor would I want to draw any conclusion from the poets' deviating uses of allusions on their (missing) engagement in *aemulatio*.

3. Classical Intertextuality

In classical intertextuality, as we know, a passage from an earlier text is integrated in a new context and the meaning of the new passage depends very heavily on the recognition of the model passage and changes made to it in and by the new context. A *locus classicus* in twentieth-century intertextuality scholarship is Ariadne's lament after Bacchus's departure in pursuit of an Indian woman from Ovid's *Fasti*.[9]

> *en iterum, fluctus, similes audite **querell**as.*
>   *en iterum lacrimas accipe, harena, meas.*
> *dicebam, **mem**ini, "periure et **perfide Theseu**!"*
>   *ille abiit, eadem crimina Bacchus habet.*
> *nunc quoque "**nulla uiro**" clamabo "**femina credat**"*
>   *nomine mutato causa relata mea est.* (Ov. *fast.* 3.471–6)

Again, waves, hear my like complaints. Again, sand, receive my tears. I kept saying, I remember, "falsely sworn and faithless Theseus!" He went away, and Bacchus incurs the same charge. Now again I will cry, "no woman shall trust a man"; the name has changed, but my case has been repeated.

In his discussion of the passage Conte (1986: 60–2) has highlighted the strong intertextual signposts *iterum, memini, dicebam* as well as the close linguistic parallels to Ariadne's lament in Catullus 64.

> *atque haec extremis maestam dixisse **querell**is*
> *frigidulos udo singultus ore cientem:*
> *"sicine me patriis auectam, **perfide**, ab aris,*
> ***perfide**, deserto liquisti in litore, **Theseu**?*
> *sicine discedens neglecto numine diuum*
> *im**mem**or a! deuota domum periuria portas?*
> *[…]*
> *nunc iam **nulla uiro** iuranti **femina credat**."* (Catull. 64.130–4, 143)

---

9. Conte 1986: 60–2, Miller 1993: 153–5, Hinds 1998: 3–4.

And this, [they say] is what she, distressed, said in her last laments while chilly sobs were running over her wet face: "Is this how you have left me on the deserted beach, faithless Theseus, after you had taken me away from the altars of my father, faithless you? Is this how going away without heeding the will of the gods, forgetful, alas, you take your cursed falsely sworn oaths home with you? [. . .] No woman shall trust a man and his oaths any more."

Indeed, the allusions are highly visible and point to Ariadne's (literary) past, relying on the reader's familiarity with them. If we knew nothing about Ovid and did not have Catullus's epyllion either, we could read Ariadne's lament in a biographical fashion: *iterum* would then refer to her former abandonment by Theseus, as the surface of the text suggests. However, since we know Ovid and Catullus 64, we would probably all agree that such a reading would miss at least half of the content of the passage. For Ovid does not seem to be so much interested in Ariadne's suffering as in competing with earlier poets and showcasing his poetic genius. It is therefore indisputable that the allusions to Catullus 64 are an essential part of the content of Ariadne's lament in *Fasti* 3.

4. Late Latin Intertextuality

4.1. Allusions as Essential Part of the Content

In late Latin poetry, the classical mode of intertextuality, in which allusions form an essential part of the content, continues to be employed. While no poet has used the same intertextuality mode throughout his work, the classical mode is particularly favoured in the poetry of Ausonius, Claudian, and Sidonius Apollinaris. In the following example, as in Ovid, the interaction with earlier passages and contexts is essential for the understanding of the new passage. As this mode of intertextuality is very well known, one example shall be enough, but others can easily be found in the scholarship.[10]

My example comes from Sidonius Apollinaris's *Carmen* 22, in which the poet praises the *uilla* of his friend Pontius Leontius. Among many other things, he commends the columns in the lower bath complex implicitly by a catalogue of different kinds of marbles not used there.

ipsa autem quantis, quibus aut sunt fulta columnis!
*cedat puniceo pretiosus **liuor** in **antro***
***Synnados**, et **Nomadum** qui portat eburnea saxa*

---

10. For Claudian cf. e.g., Wheeler 2007 and Ware 2012: passim; for Ausonius O'Daly 2004; for Sidonius Stoehr-Monjou 2013a and Hernández Lobato 2012: 536–605.

collis, et herbosis quae uernant marmora uenis;
*candentem iam nolo Paron, iam nolo **Caryston**;*
uilior est rubro quae pendet purpura saxo. (SIDON. *carm.* 22.136–41)

But how many and what columns support them [i.e., the baths]! May precious spots [i.e., spotted marble] in the purple cave of Synnas, may the Numidian hill, which carries ivory stones, and may the marbles that are green due to their grassy veins yield; I do not now want white Parian or Carystian marble; of lower quality is the purple that hangs down from the red rock.

These lines are a catalogue of six foreign kinds of marble that are absent from Leontius's baths: marble from Synnas in Phrygia, from Numidia, Sparta, Paros, and Carystos, and porphyry.[11] Very curiously, the marble that has been used is not mentioned in one word.[12] A hint of what it might have been can be found in the intertextual references. Catalogues of kinds of marbles are a recurrent feature of poetic architectural descriptions, and the closest parallel can be found in Statius's praise of Claudius Etruscus's baths, which has a catalogue of marbles and other stones including four missing kinds.[13]

*non huc admissae Thasos aut undosa **Carystos**;*
maeret onyx longe queriturque exclusus ophites:
*sola nitet flauis **Nomadum** decisa metallis*
*†purpurat†, sola cauo Phrygiae quam **Synnados antro***
ipse cruentauit maculis lucentibus Attis
†quoque tyri† niueas secat et Sidonia rupes. (STAT. *silu.* 1.5.34–9)

Thasos or billowy Carystos have not been admitted here; alabaster mourns far off and serpentine laments its exclusion: [marble] cut out from the yellow mines of Numidia shines alone, alone the stone from the hollow cave of Phrygian Synnas, which Attis himself made red with drops of his gleaming blood and the snow-white rocks that Sidon cuts.

This parallel opens up various new ways of reading Sidonius's praise, for example, as a poem grounded in the Roman imperial tradition of praising buildings and as such turning Leontius's baths in rural Gaul into Roman imperial ones

---

11. Cf. Delhey 1993: 134–8.
12. For Sidonius's use of negative catalogues omitting the positive cf. Hernández Lobato in this volume.
13. Cf. Delhey 1993: 134.

or as questioning the speaker's choice and reliability, since Apollo, who speaks the praise in Sidonius's poem, has been banned in *Siluae* 1.5.3 as a source of inspiration.[14] But it does not help us find the marble used in Leontius's baths, as in Statius (33–4) the four missing kinds of marble (from Thasos and Carystos, alabaster and serpentine) are counterbalanced by the four kinds of marbles used (from Numidia, Phrygia, Tyre [?], and Sidon, 36–9). To identify the marble used in Leontius's *uilla*, the catalogue in Statius's *Siluae* 2.2.85–94, the praise of Pollius Felix's *uilla*, might be more useful. For that catalogue concludes with all the kinds of marbles present (from Syene, Phrygia, Taygetus, Numidia, Thasos, Chios, and Carystos) greeting the Chalcidian towers (*omnia Chalcidicas turres obuersa salutant*, 94). *Chalcidicas turres* is itself an allusion to Vergil's description of the citadel at Cumae (cf. VERG. *Aen.* 6.17: *Chalcidicaque ... arce*), a Chalcidian colony in origin.[15] If the foreign marbles in Pollius Felix's *uilla* salute Cumae across the bay of Naples, perhaps the foreign marbles in Leontius's *uilla* have given way to a local one, too, for example, marble from Aquitaine.[16] If this is the case, the references to the marble catalogue in *silu.* 1.5 might also implicitly mock Leontius's choice of local marble over more prestigious foreign kinds. So, reading Sidonius's *Carmen* 22 without Statius's *Siluae* 1.5 and 2.2, we would not only miss out on the implied comparisons with Claudius Etruscus's baths but not be able either to move beyond puzzlement at the list of missing kinds of marbles.

4.2. Allusions as Optional Part of the Content

Unlike the references discussed in the previous section, many other allusions in late Latin poetry are not essential to establish the content of the new passage. In other words, their recognition is not necessary for the understanding of a new passage (in fact, it may sometimes be felt to rather distract from it), even though they still contribute to the content by adding another layer of meaning through their intertextuality. The examples chosen here come from Juvencus and Proba, but this mode of intertextuality was used by other poets as well.[17]

In the preface of his *Libri Euangeliorum IV*, an epic version of Saint Matthew's Gospel, Juvencus explicitly draws a comparison between Homer,

---

14. But cf. Mathisen 1991: 30–6 on Apollo as a nickname for Sidonius himself.
15. On marble catalogues in Statius and, in particular, in *silu.* 2.2 cf. Newlands 2011: 142–5.
16. Delhey 1993: 134–5 believes that the local marble used for the columns of Leontius's bath is from Aquitaine and had also been used in Sidonius's own *uilla*.
17. E.g., Prudentius (cf. Lühken 2002), Sedulius (cf. *carm. pasch.* 5.4–10). On Juvencus see also Roberts 2004.

Vergil, and himself (praef. 9–10), and his language is thoroughly Vergilian.[18] Linguistic similarity thus clearly provides the dimension of visibility in intertextuality. In discussions of such close linguistic imitation combined with content new to Latin poetry (like episodes from the Bible), the term "Kontrastimitation" (Thraede 1962: 1008) has often been used. It implies total reversal in content despite the linguistic parallels. One such example has been identified in the scene in which Jesus is led to Pontius Pilate as a captive:[19]

> *insultant uerbisque omnes et **illudere certant*** (IUVENC. 4.568)
>
> Everyone insulted him with words and competed in mocking him.

> *iamque e concilio Christum **post terga reuinctum**
> praesidis ad gremium **magno clamore trahebant*** (IUVENC. 4.588–9)
>
> And already, with great shouting they were dragging Christ, with fetters behind his back, from the council to the palace of the governor.

This scene shows obvious linguistic parallels to the capture of Sinon in Vergil's *Aeneid* 2:

> *ecce, manus iuuenem interea **post terga reuinctum**
> pastores **magno** ad regem **clamore trahebant**.* (VERG. Aen. 2.57–8)
>
> See, in the meantime, with great shouting some shepherds were dragging a man with his hands tied behind his back before the king.

> *circumfusa ruit **certantque inludere** capto.* (VERG. Aen. 2.64)
>
> [The young Trojans] came running, gathered around and competed in mocking the prisoner.

In addition to the linguistic parallels, the captives of the two scenes, Jesus and Sinon, have also both been arrested voluntarily. However, if understood as a contrast imitation, the scene emphasizes that Jesus is completely different from Sinon: Jesus speaks the truth, not a lie, he will actually die, not escape death as Sinon, and his death will bring salvation to humankind instead of destruction for the people, as in Sinon's case. Moreover, in his lying tale Sinon has even been

---

18. Borrell Vidal 1991, quoted by Roberts 2004: 50, studied IUVENC. 1 and showed that 92% of Juvencus's vocabulary is Vergilian and that all but two lines of Book 1 contain identical words in the same position.

19. Cf. Green 2006: 63–4.

seen as prefiguring or mirroring Jesus in the role of the human sacrifice killed to bring salvation to others.[20] This is an interesting reading, but, in fact, Sinon is not indispensable for our understanding how Jesus was brought before Pontius Pilate. That Jesus speaks the truth, is killed, and brings salvation to others is clear from the narrative of Juvencus's epic. The allusions to Sinon are therefore an optional part of the content. They are not necessary to follow the plot, though they may add an extra layer of meaning if taken into account.

The second example comes from Proba's *Cento*. In formal terms, a cento is by nature the most intertextual text possible, as it consists entirely (except, in Proba's case, for the preface) of Vergilian lines and half-lines.[21] On the other hand, a cento is a poem in its own right, with its own story and argument: Proba's *Cento*, for example, in the form of a biblical epic, brings together stories from the Old and the New Testament.[22] The following passages describe Mary's flight to Egypt shortly after Jesus's birth (372–9) and Jesus's first appearance in public (384–7).

> *at mater gemitu non frustra exterrita tanto,*
> *ipsa sinu prae se portans, turbante tumultu,*
> *infantem fugiens plena ad praesepia reddit.*
> *hic natum angusti subter fastigia tecti*
> *nutribat teneris inmulgens ubera labris.*
> *hic tibi prima, puer, fundent cunabula flores,*
> *mixtaque ridenti passim cum baccare tellus*
> *molli paulatim colocasia fundet acantho.*
> [. . .]
> *illum omnis tectis agrisque effusa iuuentus*
> *attonitis inhians animis prospectat euntem,*
> *turbaque miratur matrum: "qui spiritus illi,*
> *qui uultus uocisque sonus uel gressus eunti est!"* (PROBA cento
>   372–9, 384–7)

But the mother, not terrified for nothing by such great wailing, herself carrying the baby in the fold of her dress in front, in the midst of agitated uproar, fled and brought him to full mangers. Here she nurtured her son under the roof of a narrow hut, milking her breasts into his tender lips. Here, child, flowers will pour forth your first cradle, and the earth, everywhere mixed with laughing-eyed baccar, will gradually produce Egyptian beans with soft acanthus. [. . .]

---

20. Roberts 2004: 54–5.
21. Cf. Pollmann 2004, McGill 2005: 23–30, and Formisano and Sogno 2010.
22. Cf. Herzog 1975: 14–51 and McGill 2007b.

The whole youth, pouring forth from the houses and fields, were watching him as he came, agape and wondering in their minds, and the crowd of mothers said admiringly: "What spirit he has, what face and sound of voice, and what steps when he walks!"

In the first passage, clusters of half-lines from the account of Camilla's youth in Vergil's *Aeneid* and from his fourth *Eclogue* have been identified, with another two and a half lines from Camilla's first description in the *Aeneid* in the second passage:[23]

at mater gemitu non frustra exterrita tanto,	
***ipsa sinu prae se portans**, turbante tumultu,*	VERG. *Aen.* 11.544 (Metabus)
***infantem fugiens** plena ad praesepia reddit.*	VERG. *Aen.* 11.541 (M. & C.)
hic natum angusti subter fastigia tecti	VERG. *Aen.* 11.570 (Camilla)
***nutribat teneris inmulgens ubera labris**.*	VERG. *Aen.* 11.572 (Camilla)
*hic **tibi prima, puer,** | **fundent***	
***cunabula flores**,*	VERG. *ecl.* 4.18 | 4.23
mixtaque ridenti** | **passim cum	
baccare tellus	VERG. *ecl.* 4.20 | 4.19
***molli paulatim** | **colocasia fundet acantho**.*	VERG. *ecl.* 4.28 | 4.20
[. . .]	
illum omnis tectis agrisque effusa iuuentus	VERG. *Aen.* 7.811 (Camilla)
***attonitis inhians animis prospectat euntem**,*	VERG. *Aen.* 7.812
***turbaque miratur matrum**: "qui spiritus illi,*	VERG. *Aen.* 7.813
qui uultus uocisque sonus uel gressus eunti est!"	

As literal quotes, the parallels are heavily signposted. In addition, there are similarities in situation: for instance, both Jesus and Camilla flee as babies with one of their parents and are later admired by other people. Likewise, the magnificent landscape in *Eclogue* 4 surrounding the birth of the wonder child sets a perfect scene for Jesus to grow up in (and the Christian interpretations of *Eclogue* 4 may have facilitated this identification).[24] In the half-lines selected from *Eclogue* 4, line 20 stands out as it mentions *colocasia*, Egyptian beans, the only plant of those listed in the *Eclogue* that does not grow wild in Italy.[25] It thus indirectly indicates the destination of Mary's flight.[26] On the other hand, Camilla is also rather different from Jesus: a woman, a warrior, devoted to Diana, reared in the wilderness, and so on, and Jesus's flight with Mary as well as the admiration he

---

23. E.g., Harich-Schwarzbauer 2009: 341–2; cf. also Sineri 2011: 219–25.
24. On the Christian interpretation of VERG. *ecl.* 4, cf. Benko 1980: 670–8.
25. Cf. Coleman 1977: 136.
26. Sineri 2011: 221.

attracts later are all found on the surface level of Proba's *Cento*. Even the hint to Egypt (*colocasia*), indirect as it may be, is explicit: If we can infer the destination of Egypt from *colocasia*, we can also do so without remembering it as the odd one out in a list of plants growing wild in Italy in *Eclogue* 4. Thus, the allusions to Camilla and *Eclogue* 4 are an optional part of Jesus's characterization.[27]

4.3 Allusions as Formal Features

Already with the examples just discussed, one might have wondered what functions the allusions had if they did not make an essential contribution to the content. This question becomes even more urgent in cases such as the examples presented in this section, where knowledge of the model text not only is not essential to understand a late Latin passage but makes it in fact more difficult to do so. The solution that I propose is to consider allusions of this kind as purely formal features, that is, elements of the texture of the poem, by themselves expressing adherence to the classical poetic tradition but irrelevant for the content of the new poem. This is the mode that is most difficult to describe as it relies on the argument that a (classical-intertextual) reading of a specific line or passage is not the best or even an appropriate reading, which will never meet everyone's approval.[28]

The first example comes from the last book of Corippus's *Iohannis*. In the scene described, John is confronted with a mutiny and addresses the mutinous soldiers in a brief speech which shows clear linguistic parallels to Caesar's speech in a similar situation in Lucan 5.

[...] *propera, **si bell**a uetari*
me pereunte putas, si Martis causa Iohannes (CORIPP. *Ioh.* 8.117–8)

Hurry, if you think that the war can be prevented by killing me, if John is the reason for war.

*hic fuge, **si bell**i finis placet, ense relicto* (LUCAN. 5.321)

Here [i.e., in my body] leave your sword and flee if an end to war pleases you.

[...] ***certe iam** gentibus istis*

---

27. But cf. Schottenius 2010 for an example of how intertextuality supports typology in Proba's *Cento*.
28. Cf. Pelttari's 2014: 133 n. 38 acknowledgement of a classical intertextual reading for CLAUD. *rapt. Pros.* 2.250, with which he disagrees.

bella geram. [. . .] (CORIPP. *Ioh.* 8.120–1)
*uos **ignaua** manus nostris **discedite castris**!* (CORIPP. *Ioh.* 8.123)

Now I at least will fight wars with these peoples. [. . .] Leave my camp, you lazy corps!

iam certe *mihi **bella geram. discedite castris**,*
*tradite nostra uiris **ignaui** signa, Quirites.* (LUCAN. 5.357–8)

Now I at least will fight wars for myself. Leave the camp, lazy Roman civilians, and give our standards to men.

Both speeches rely on the same rhetorical strategies: Caesar and John first offer their own life to the mutineers and later shame them by dismissing them. As a result of the dismissal, the soldiers in each case are even more eager to follow their commanders. Clearly, the speeches also characterize Caesar and John, respectively, and the parallels suggest that they, at least partly, share personal attributes or rhetorical training. However, John is characterized as a positive leader and does not have any of Caesar's cruelty and abusive use of his power, and the difference in the personalities becomes obvious in the soldiers' respective reaction to the speeches: While Caesar's soldiers are terrified by the speech and offer the ringleaders for execution (LUCAN. 5.364–3), the mutineers in John's army yield not just because they are afraid of John but also in obedience to their wise commander Ricinarius (CORIPP. *Ioh.* 8.133–6). Thus, despite the parallels in the arguments of Caesar's and John's respective speeches, (Lucanian) Caesar has little to add to the praise of John—and Ricinarius—whose praise is the main concern of the *Iohannis*. On the other hand, the contrasts between John and Caesar are not exploited either, as we would expect them to be if this was a "Kontrastimitation."[29] Thus, the references to Lucan 5 do not enhance the understanding of the content of the passage in *Iohannis* 8, though they help characterize the poetic texture of the epic: A passage such as this infuses the predominantly Vergilian epic of John's war against the Moors with a flavour of (Lucanian) historiography and civil war.[30]

The second example is taken from Dracontius's short epic on *Medea* (*Romul.* 10).[31] After killing Creon, Glauce, Jason, and her children towards the end of the narrative, Medea departs on a chariot drawn by snakes (*Romul.* 10.562–6). This

---

29. Cf. Riedlberger 2010: 181–2.
30. Riedlberger 2010: 75–7. Cf. also Tommasi Moreschini 2007 for different ways of reading intertextuality in Corippus.
31. Cf. Kaufmann 2006b: 109–11.

scene can be described as a negative apotheosis: Medea, more powerful than the gods, gets herself a chariot on which she disappears into the sky while the chariot burns like a torch emitting venomous smoke, which nearly extinguishes the sun.[32] The following passage describes her departure on the chariot.

> ***occupat ill**a grauem funesto **corpore currum**,*
> *ire furore sidens taetros simul imperat angues.*
> *tolluntur celeres, mox se tellure leuabant,*
> *iam nutant per inane rotae hinc inde **labante**s,*
> *aera saeua petit uolitans quadriga uenenis.* (Drac. Romul. 10.562–6)

She got on the chariot, which her fatal body made heavy, and at the same time she ordered the foul snakes to depart while she sat down. They swiftly raised themselves, now they took off from the ground, now the wheels nodded through space, shaking on both sides, and the flying chariot was heading to the air among poisonous fumes.

There is a very close parallel to the scene in Ovid's *Metamorphoses* 2, when Phaethon gets onto the chariot of the sun (2.150):

> ***occupat ill**e leuem iuuenali **corpore currum**.* (Ov. met. 2.150)

He got on the chariot, which was light because he had the body of a boy.

At the same time, the differences between the two scenes are obvious: Medea's body is "fatal" (*funestum*), that of Phaethon simply "youthful" (*iuuenale*), and, more strikingly, Medea's chariot is "heavy" (*grauis*), whereas that of the sun is "light" (*leuis*). If we read *funesto* and *grauem* as "Kontrastimitationen," we would be keen to explore further contrasts with Ovid's account of Phaethon's ride on the chariot of the sun. There is, indeed, another allusion to this part of the *Metamorphoses*, specifically to the simile comparing the sun chariot driven by Phaeton to unsteady ships:

> *sed leue pondus erat, nec quod cognoscere possent*
> *Solis equi, solitaque iugum grauitate carebat,*
> *utque **labant** curuae iusto sine pondere naues*
> *perque mare instabiles nimia leuitate feruntur,*
> *sic onere adsueto uacuus dat in aëre saltus*

---

32. Cf. Kaufmann 2006a: 437–9.

succutiturque alte similisque est currus inani. (Ov. met. 2.161–6)

> But the weight was light, one that the horses of the sun could not recognize, and the yoke lacked its usual heaviness. And as curved ships are unsteady without the right weight and are carried unsteadily through the sea if they are too light, in this way the chariot makes jumps in the air as it lacks the usual weight and is tossed up high as though it was empty.

However, this linguistic parallel reveals an incompatibility between the two passages: In both of them, *labant/labantes* describes the instability of Phaeton's/Medea's chariot as it flies through the air. In the *Metamorphoses* it is clear that the chariot of the sun is unsteady because Phaethon is too light (cf. *leuem* in 150): The horses think that there is no charioteer and pull the chariot through the air in all directions. By contrast, Medea's chariot is heavy (*grauem*) and should therefore be steady, not totter as Dracontius describes it. In this case, the model text not only is irrelevant for the content of the new passage, but also creates a paradox that makes it harder to understand it.[33] At the same time, given the close linguistic parallels, it would be absurd to deny the allusions altogether. Therefore, reading them as formal elements allows us to acknowledge them without having to force them to contribute to the content. We can appreciate the Ovidian texture of the passage and at the same time focus on the specific characteristics of Medea's chariot without interferences by Phaethon or Ovid.

4.4 Discussion of the Modes of Intertextuality

I have presented examples from late Latin poetry to show the range of modes used at the time in interacting with previous poetry. However, even though I have referred to them as three distinct modes, I do not conceive of them as such nor as the only modes at work in late Latin poetry. Instead, the modes stand for the two extremes and a rough middle on a *continuum* of possible intertextual relationships (figure 4.1).

Most of the passages discussed above could be shifted further towards either of the poles to allow for a different reading. In addition, the two poles "essential part of the content" and "formal features" should be considered not to exclude but to complement each other: The more essential an allusion is for the content, the less it is perceived as a formal feature—but it is still a formal feature—and the less essential an allusion is for the content, the more it

---

33. To avoid this paradox caused by allusions to Ovid's *Metamorphoses* 2, Stoehr-Monjou 2013b: 169 suggests taking *grauem* as a reference to the bad smell of the burning chariot: "empesté."

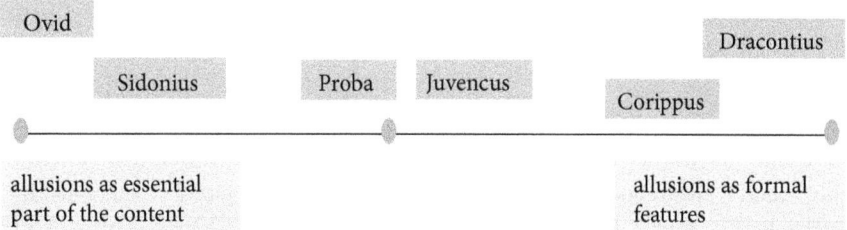

Figure 4.1. The late Latin intertextuality modes as a *continuum*.

functions as a formal element while at the same time also contributing something to the content.

Texts in which allusions function as formal elements and those in which they constitute an essential part of the content differ in their main concern: A text of the former kind is mainly concerned with literature, its position in the literary tradition, with literary roles and identities. Thus, the passage from *Fasti* 3 quoted earlier focuses on Ariadne's literary identities, on Ovid's own position in the history of Latin poetry, and his relationship to Catullus and Hellenistic poetry, not (primarily) on Ariadne's miserable situation. On the other hand, texts whose form is enriched by allusions tend to engage in non-literary matters and situations on the level of content: Medea's flight on her chariot in Dracontius's *Romul.* 10, for example, is about the end of a former priestess of Diana who committed terrible crimes because she served a goddess, not (primarily) about how Ovid's Phaethon could be outdone.

Accordingly, formal allusions can express new content in a traditional way, which makes this mode particularly fitting for Christian poets, as it allows for a straightforward combination of a form that would attest the poets' knowledge of classical literature with a Christian content, itself alien to classical literature. Paulinus of Nola's verse letter to Ausonius (*carm.* 10) exemplifies this: Here Paulinus distances himself and his poetry from the Muses and Apollo while at the same time writing in classical metres (elegiacs [1–18], iambics [19–102], and hexameters [103–331]) and with allusions to Catullus, Vergil, Horace, Ovid, and other poets.[34] Thus, on the level of form the poem expresses the values of classical education, which links the writer to the addressee, the poet's former teacher, while in content it conveys a Christian aversion against traditional poetry. The same combination of traditional form (hexameter epic, Vergilian language) and new content (biblical stories) can be observed in the poetry of Juvencus

---

34. Witke 1971: 56–65. Cf. also Amherdt 2004.

164 *The Poetics of Late Latin Literature*

and Proba, though the two elements combine in a less antagonistic way, which enables allusions to Vergilian content to blend with the biblical account.

Furthermore, the two extreme modes correspond to the very different concerns of the poets' audiences. For example, for Sidonius's highly educated audience, his allusions, which contribute essentially to the content, would have confirmed traditional values of Roman elite culture and helped create a distance to the less sophisticated one of the barbarian invaders.[35] On the other hand, Dracontius's and Corippus's allusions, which do not add or subtract from the content, were ideal for audiences, at least part of whom were non-native speakers of Latin: the Vandal elite (even if keen to Romanize themselves) in Dracontius's case and the Byzantine general John with his adjutant Ricinarius (presumably a Goth from Spain, to judge from his name)[36] as well as the Berber commander Cusina, all praised in Corippus's epic.[37] These audiences, less familiar with the Latin literary tradition, would have been able to follow the plots in Dracontius's or Corippus's poetry without being alienated from it by allusions they did not understand, whereas the more educated members of these audiences might have enjoyed acknowledging the poets' and their own superior literary knowledge.

By linking the examples discussed with the audiences of the poets, I argue that the proposed modes of intertextuality not only are useful categories by themselves but also allow for potentially historical readings. This case is now to be strengthened by external evidence. For such I have drawn on contemporary (i.e., late antique) literary scholarship and metapoetics as well as colonial and postcolonial literature. In the former I have found support both for taking allusions as formal elements and, in some metapoetical statements, for reading them as an essential part of the content. On the other hand, the cross-cultural comparison inherent in drawing on colonial and postcolonial literature for late Latin intertextualty confirms the link between the modes of intertextuality and the audiences of the poets by way of revealing modes of reception that largely correspond to the modes of intertextuality proposed.

5. Reading Intertextuality in Roman Late Antiquity

A considerable amount of literary criticism has survived from Roman Late Antiquity, for example, commentaries on classical works (e.g., Servius,

---

35. Mathisen 1993: 105–18 describes the Gallo-Roman literary circles as a reaction to the invasions. Rijser 2013: 89–90, on the other hand, assumes that Sidonius's audience would not have been able to appreciate his allusions though they would have understood the (Roman) cultural capital they implied.

36. Riedlberger 2010: 194–5.

37. Cf. Kaufmann 2006a: 22–3 and Riedlberger 2010: 86–7 for Dracontius's and Corippus's respective audiences.

Lactantius Placidus) and on parts of the Bible (e.g., by Hieronymus and Saint Augustine), discussions of literary criticism, such as Macrobius's *Saturnalia*, and other interpretations—for instance Fulgentius's *Expositio Virgilianae continentiae*. Furthermore, some late Latin poets have themselves commented on their works in prefaces and accompanying letters. Since, however, the late antique scholars are concerned with the works of classical poets, most importantly of Vergil, not with late Latin poetry, they can at best be used as indirect evidence for how intertextuality in late Latin poetry would have been read, though such evidence would still seem promising and, in combination with the metapoetical statements of the late Latin poets, certainly good enough. But regrettably the material is rather disappointing for our purposes, as there does not seem to have been a straightforward late antique discourse on intertextuality, which in itself is perhaps not entirely surprising given that earlier periods lacked such as well.[38] Nevertheless, late antique scholarship is still relevant for the understanding of intertextuality at the time, not least exactly because it lacks a straightforward discussion of it.

After an analysis of the material the first point to note is the general awareness and explicit acknowledgement of model texts and the literary tradition by late Latin poets and scholars alike. For example, Juvencus (praef. 9–10), Corippus (*Ioh.* praef. 1–15) and Dracontius (*Romul.* 8.16–23) all compare themselves, with due modesty, to Vergil and Homer, and Sidonius Apollinaris mentions Statius's *Siluae* as his model (*epist.* [*carm.* 22] 6). In Macrobius's *Saturnalia* the comparisons between passages by Vergil and his models take up all of Book 5 and parts of Book 6, and Servius (*Aen.* 1 praef.) describes *Homerum imitari* (to imitate Homer) as one of the *Aeneid*'s two purposes. However, with the exception of commentators on the Bible,[39] the scholars (commentators, Macrobius) on the whole show little interest in the meaning of parallels or allusions. Instead, most of their discussions relate to the production of poetry. For example, Servius explains the model of *Aeneid* 4 in the following way:

Apollonius Argonautica scripsit et in tertio inducit amantem Medeam: inde totus hic liber translatus est. est autem paene totus in affectione, licet in fine pathos habeat, ubi abscessus Aeneae gignit dolorem. (Serv. *Aen.* 4 praef.)

Apollonius wrote the *Argonautica* and in Book 3 introduced Medea in love: This whole book has been taken from there. It is, however, nearly

---

38. See Pucci 1998: 83–108 and McGill 2012b: 18–30.
39. Biblical commentaries invariably try to explain what the passage in question means, no matter whether it contains allusions or not; e.g., in *in Rom.* 26.1–3 St Augustine explains that *Romans* 6:6 refers to *Deuteronomy* 21:23 and how the latter helps to understand the former. On biblical commentaries cf. e.g., Pollmann 2009.

completely given over to affection even if there is passionate feeling at the end when Aeneas's departure causes pain.

Servius focuses on Vergil's composition of *Aeneid* 4 on the model of *Argonautica* 3 and only very briefly and implicitly, by describing the emotional tone of *Aeneid* 4, compares the two texts themselves. For Servius, then, intertextuality took place when Vergil wrote the *Aeneid*, not when it was being received by an audience or readers later on. Likewise, the discussions of parallel passages in Macrobius's *Saturnalia* centre on Vergil and his composition. Most passages are listed without an in-depth discussion. Of those parallels examined in more detail, many are quoted to evaluate Vergil's poetry in one way or another, some, for example, to demonstrate Vergil's superiority (or inferiority) to Homer. Quoting the respective passages from the *Aeneid* (3.622-5) and the *Odyssey* (9.288-94), in which the Cyclops eats some of Odysseus's companions, Eusthatius, for instance, makes the following judgement:

> *narrationem facti nudam et breuem Maro posuit, contra Homerus πάθος miscuit et dolore narrandi inuidiam crudelitatis aequauit.* (MACR. *Sat.* 5.13.17)
>
> Maro rendered his narrative of the episode bare and short; Homer, on the other hand, added some strong feelings and matched the indignation at the cruelty by pain expressed through the narrative.

Here, Eusthatius gives preference to Homer's passage, and this is all he has to say. He does not try to understand or appreciate the changes that Vergil made to his model. The connection between intertextuality and value judgements is, in fact, typical of the late antique discourse, and the third point to note (after the general awareness of literary models and the focus on the production of poetry). A later passage in Macrobius shows the connection between intertextuality and evaluation of Vergil's poetic skills in combination with a focus on the production of poetry:

> *etsi uereor ne dum ostendere cupio quantum Vergilius noster ex antiquiorum lectione profecerit et quos ex omnibus flores uel quae in carminis sui decorem ex diuersis ornamenta libauerit, occasionem reprehendendi uel imperitis uel malignis ministrem, exprobrantibus tanto uiro alieni usurpationem nec considerantibus hunc esse fructum legendi, aemulari ea quae in aliis probes, et quae maxime inter aliorum dicta mireris in aliquem usum tuum opportuna deriuatione conuertere, quod et nostri tam inter se quam a Graecis et Graecorum excellentes inter se saepe fecerunt.* (MACR. *Sat.* 6.1.2)

Intertextuality in Late Latin Poetry 167

> Yet I fear that, while I wish to show how much our poet has benefited from reading earlier poets and which flowers he took from all or which ornaments from various poets for the beauty of his poetry, I will present the unlearned and malicious with the opportunity to find fault with him—they will reproach such a great man for making use of someone else['s poetry] without considering that this is the benefit of reading: to emulate what you like in others and to turn to your own use the words which you admire most among those of the others by derivation when the opportunity presents itself. This is what our poets have done among themselves as much as with the Greeks and what the best of the Greeks have often engaged in as well.

Here, Rufius Albinus details Vergil's intertextual practices by metaphorically describing how the poet enhances the beauty of his poetry by blossoms and ornaments from earlier poets with the aim to emulate them.

While the emphasis on the production of poetry is not directly relevant to the reader-oriented perspective on intertextuality taken here, the link between allusions and poetic excellence is important to note, as it is also found in comments on the reception of poetry and its allusions. According to the same Rufius Albinus in Macrobius's *Saturnalia*, for instance, Vergil's excellence in intertextuality causes readers to attribute the material entirely to him or to admire the poet for improving on the model:

> *Denique et iudicio transferendi et modo imitandi consecutus est, ut quod apud illum legerimus alienum aut illius esse malimus aut melius hic quam ubi natum est sonare miremur.* (MACR. *Sat.* 6.1.6)

> Finally, through his judgement in transposition and manner of imitation he succeeded to make us prefer what we read in his poetry which is not his to be his or to admire it for the fact that it sounds better here than at its original place.

In another passage, Eusthatius links Vergil's poetic excellence with his knowledge of Greek learning, which will only be appreciated by those who are equally well versed in the Greek tradition:

> *sed de his hactenus, quorum plura omnibus, aliqua nonnullis Romanorum nota sunt. ad illa uenio quae de Graecarum litterarum penetralibus eruta nullis cognita sunt, nisi qui Graecam doctrinam diligenter hauserunt. fuit enim hic poeta ut scrupulose et anxie, ita dissimulanter et quasi clanculo doctus, ut multa transtulerit quae unde translata sint difficile sit cognitu.* (MACR. *Sat.* 5.18.1)

But enough of these, of which most are known to all, others to at least some Romans. Now I come to the things taken from the sanctuary of Greek literature, not known to anyone except those who have seriously taken up Greek learning. For our poet was as scrupulous and diligent in his learning as he was hiding and secretive so that the sources of many of his borrowings are hard to recognize.

In much more general terms, Avienus, finally, highlights the pleasure of the listeners when they hear the very best poets convey the same in their respective ways.[40]

"perge quaeso," inquit Auienus, "omnia quae Homero subtraxit inuestigare. quid enim suauius quam duos praecipuos uates audire idem loquentes?" (MACR. *Sat.* 5.3.16)

"Please go on," said Avienus, "look into everything that he took from Homer: For what could be more pleasant than to hear two outstanding poets expressing the same?"

Thus, pleasure at and admiration of the poet's intertextual skills, including his knowledge of earlier literature, are the key reactions to the reading of poetry attested by late Latin scholars. How, if at all, does this correspond to the modes of intertextuality presented above? While there is no obvious link between the two and while the late Latin scholars would presumably have been puzzled, at best, by my modes of intertextuality, the evidence supports the proposed general difference between late Latin intertextuality and classical intertextuality: The interlocutors in Macrobius's *Saturnalia* do not read allusions as essential to the meaning of the poetry; in fact, they seem to take the meaning of the passages for granted and, by expressing pleasure and admiration, read the allusions as elements constituting the texture of the poetry. This accounts fairly well for the third mode of intertextuality discussed above and the presence of elements of that mode within the other two modes, but less well for the other modes themselves, especially the first, in which allusions are essential for the content. Evidence for this, on the other hand, can be found in metapoetical statements of late Latin poets. Ausonius, for example, preventively tones down the readers' expectations in the prose letter accompanying his wedding cento, stating that the cento is unlikely to elicit praise and more likely to evoke laughter: *solae memoriae negotium sparsa colligere et integrare lacerata, quod ridere magis quam laudare possis* ("it is a task for the memory alone to bring together what is [found] scattered and make whole what is [found] torn, which you could laugh at rather

---

40. Cf. also Pucci 1998: 64–9 on this passage.

than praise") (*epist.* [*Cento*] 132, 4–5 [Green]). As Pollmann (2004: 82) notes, the poem's "content as such is not funny at all [...]; the humour comes in only when the readers recognize that the poetic material used is entirely taken from Vergil." Thus, Ausonius envisages a reception of the poem in which the recognition of the allusions will override the content on the surface, the wedding, and so make an essential contribution to it. This confirms an awareness of the first mode of intertextuality. Sidonius Apollinaris's metapoetical statements are more ambivalent: Like Ausonius, he is concerned to temper the readers' expectations and for these purposes recommends a reception of the poem amidst plenty of wine in the letter framing the praise of Leontius's *uilla* (*carm.* 22, discussed above): *ecce, quotiens tibi libuerit pateris capacioribus hilarare conuiuium, misi quod inter scyphos et amystidas tuas legas; subueneris uerecundiae meae, si in sobrias aures ista non uenerint* ("see, I have sent you something to read among your cups and bumpers, whenever you like to cheer up your dinner party with larger bowls; you would respect my shyness if these lines never reached sober ears") (*epist.* [*carm.* 22] 5). It is rather unlikely that Leontius and his guests would have been able to appreciate Sidonius's intertextuality if they were drunk, but it is perhaps equally unlikely that Sidonius is serious here. Rather, the reference to drinking could be read as an allusion to Leontius's nickname, Dionysus,[41] which might in turn direct Leontius back to the poem, in which Bacchus figures prominently. A similar discrepancy between the surface meaning and a hidden message may be behind the last paragraph in the letter (*epist.* [*carm.* 22] 6), in which Sidonius quotes Statius's *Siluae*, listing four titles as examples of long descriptive poems in case Leontius should object to the length of *Carmen* 22. Three of these four *Siluae* are not even half as long as *Carmen* 22, and the only one that is of a similar length is *silu.* 3.1: the praise of a shrine that Pollius Felix built for Hercules. This is the same Pollius Felix whose *uilla* is praised in *silu.* 2.2, the knowledge of which, as discussed above, contributes in an essential way to the understanding of the negative catalogue of marbles in *carm.* 22.136–41. Finally, a metapoetical statement by Proba offers evidence for the second mode of intertextuality, in which allusions are an optional part of the content. In the preface to her cento she unites Vergil's poetry with her proposed work: *Vergilium cecinisse loquar pia munera Christi* ("I will show that Vergil sang of Christ's pious gifts," PROBA *cento* 23). This could mean either that she will bring out the Christian in Vergil or, perhaps more likely, that through her cento Vergil will seem to have sung of Christ.[42] Either way, the statement combines her language model (Vergil) and her subject matter (Christ) in a way that leaves open how essential her allusions will be.

---

41. Mathisen 1991: 36.
42. Cf. McGill 2007b: 175–6, who prefers the former.

All in all, while the late Latin scholars show far more interest in intertextuality during the production of poetry, the (comparatively few) passages in which they refer to the reception of the poetry and of its allusions may confirm their awareness of the mode of intertextuality in which allusions are formal features, since they note that the audience's main concern is to praise the poet and his poetic expressions on the basis of his allusions, not to investigate what these mean. On the other hand, the metapoetical statements by Ausonius, Sidonius Apollinaris, and Proba may speak for the other two modes of intertextuality, in which allusions are, or can be, part of the content. Finally, support for the link between intertextual readings and the learnedness of the audience has also been found in Macrobius *Saturnalia*.

6. Late Latin Intertextuality and (Post-)Colonial Classical Reception

With the support of the proposed modes of intertextuality found in late Latin scholarship and metapoetics, I now strengthen my case from a very different angle: by comparing the modes of intertextuality proposed for late Latin poetry with the modes of reception used in a sample of colonial and postcolonial texts which refer to classical (and, in one case, classical English) literature. For while colonial and postcolonial literatures obviously differ in many respects from late Latin poetry, the environments in which the two kinds of texts were produced have various features in common: They were places where different languages, cultures, literary traditions, and audiences came together, and writers had to make choices about them. Furthermore, even though in reception the references to the model tend to be more general than in intertextuality, the modes of reception discussed below can be described in the same way as the modes of intertextuality proposed for late Latin poetry and are likewise used to negotiate and assert identities and to communicate with particular groups of readers.

At one end of the spectrum, for example, is the Eton boy and Cambridge man Henry Nelson Coleridge, who wrote *Six Months in the West Indies* in 1826. In this narrative full of learned allusions, Coleridge describes his impressions of the Caribbean islands for an English readership.[43] In the following excerpt he describes a "rite de passage" just before the ship crosses the equator:

> [Neptune] said; the conchs Tritonian sounded again, the god rushed by in a flaming chariot like unto a tar barrel, which the sailor heaves upon the forecastle, what time he tars the newly twisted yarn. (Coleridge 1826: 39)

43. Cf. Williamson 2010.

The references to Roman religion (Neptune, a fiery chariot driven by the god) and, presumably, Latin word order ("conchs Tritonian") are obvious; in fact, the classical references and the description of what really happens on the ship are intertwined to such a degree that it is difficult to separate them from each other. This preserves the text for readers of an identical cultural and educational background and asserts and promotes Coleridge's culture against that of the West Indies. In another passage (on slavery) Coleridge uses the metaphor of a "mirror shield of knowledge" to detach himself from the West Indians: "[The philanthropist] must hold steadily before him the mirror shield of knowledge and cause the brutified captives to see themselves therein" (Coleridge 1826: 102). This mode of reception, in which the classical references are inseparably interwoven with the new text and which bars readers of other cultures from making sense of it, resembles the mode of intertextuality in which allusions are an essential part of the content. In both Sidonius's and Coleridge's texts the classical learning is a means to express the authors' identities in multicultural environments and to communicate with readers of the authors' own cultures.

An example of the mode of reception in which classical references are an optional part of the content can be found in Hugh Clifford's sketch "Up Country" (1897), in which he advises British colonial officers about life in the colonies:

> He is Frankenstein's monster, yearning for love and fellowship with his kind, [. . .] yet knowing [. . .] that he is indescribably repulsive to the people among whom he lives. Add to this that he is cut off from all the things which, to educated Europeans, make life lovely. [. . .] His few books are for a while his companions, but he reads them through and through [. . .] till the best sayings of the best authors ring flat on his sated ears [. . .]. He has not yet learned that there is a great and marvellous book lying beneath his hand [. . .] which, though studied for a lifetime, is never exhausted. [. . .] This knowledge comes later; and it is then that the Chapter of the Great Book of Human Nature, which deals with natives, engrosses his attention and, touching on the grayness of his life, like the rising sun, turns it into gold and purple. (Clifford 1897: 249–51)

In this text, the classical English reference to Frankenstein's monster underlines the content, the importance of books in the colonies, fits the style of the essay, and again addresses readers of a cultural and educational background similar to that of the author. On the other hand, towards the end of the passage, it becomes clear that for Clifford "the Great Book of Human Nature" has replaced his other books and has made their content insignificant. Thus, while the style, including the classical English reference, is traditional and suitable to communicate with readers familiar with it, it is here used to communicate a new experience.

This mode of reception is like the mode of intertextuality used by Juvencus and Proba, by which they communicate a new truth in traditional style familiar to and appreciated by their audiences.

Finally, Derek Walcott's *Omeros* (1990), an epic on contemporary life on the Caribbean island of Saint Lucia,[44] is an example of the mode of reception at the other end of the spectrum. In this work, Walcott etymologizes Omeros, the version of Homer's name used for a character and also as title of the epic:

[...] I said, "Omeros,"

and *O* was the conch-shell's invocation, *mer* was
both mother and sea in our Antillean patois,
os, a grey bone and the white surf as it crashes

and spreads its sibilant collar on a lace shore. (Walcott 1990: 14 [II.iii])

In this mode of reception the plot can be understood without the classical reference even if that adds significantly to the poetic texture of the work. Homer becomes Omeros, the name in turn is explained by references to various native Caribbean features of nature (shell, sea, bone, surf) and language (*mer* for mother and sea), and the etymology of Omeros does not presuppose knowledge of Homer by the reader. As in Coleridge's text the classical reference is inseparably merged into the texture, but here it is used to create a hybrid text equally representing classical learning and new content. This use resembles the mode of intertextuality in which allusions are used as formal features, demonstrated above by examples from Dracontius and Corippus.

Thus, the comparison with the modes of reception at work in a sample of colonial and postcolonial texts reveals similarities with the proposed modes of intertextuality: In these texts as in the late Latin examples, classical references/allusions can be an essential part of the meaning (as in Coleridge and Sidonius), an optional part of it while also being a means of communication in traditional style (as in Clifford, Juvencus, and Proba) and formal features to enable departure from the tradition as well as innovation on the level of content (as in Walcott, Corippus, and Dracontius). Finally, the modes have also proved similar in their promotion of identities in multicultural environments as well as in communication with specific audiences or groups of readers.

---

44. Cf. e.g., Burkitt 2007.

7. The End of Intertextuality in Late Latin Poetry

The late Latin modes of intertextuality presented in this chapter work (within late Latin poetry) outside a chronological framework or development. In other words, any passage from a late Latin poem could be found to employ any of the modes. Nevertheless, a clear endpoint to late Latin intertextuality can be identified in Venantius Fortunatus's poetry. When Fortunatus arrived in Merovingian Gaul in the mid-sixth century, he wrote an epithalamium for the wedding of King Sigibert and Brunhild, probably shortly after his arrival. This epithalamium (*carm.* 6.1) follows the tradition of mythological epithalamia, which goes back to Statius, *Siluae* 1.2,[45] but it is Fortunatus's only poem in such a clearly defined literary tradition. According to Roberts (2009: 8), Fortunatus "realized that the formal and semiotic resources of late antique epideictic poetics were only of limited utility in the Merovingian cultural context."[46] For our purposes this means that it is not only hard to say something interesting about allusions in the rest of Fortunatus's work; it is even difficult to find them. The following extract from his panegyric on King Charibert may give a flavour of this.

> **omnia laeta** *canunt* **felicia tempora regis**
> *cuius in auspiciis floret opima quies,*
> *per quem tranquille terrarum frugis abundat:*
> *deuotis populis est tua uita seges.*
> *cum* **te nascentem** *meruerunt saecula regem,*
> *lumine maiori* **fulsit in orbe dies**.
> *posteritate noua tandem* **sua gaudia** *cernens*
> *crescere se dixit prolis honore pater.* (Ven. Fort. *carm.* 6.2.41–8)

Everything sings joyfully of the happy times of the king, under whose auspices fruitful peace prospers, through whom the fruit of the lands abounds in tranquillity: your life is your faithful people's crop. When the centuries deserved that you were born as king, daylight shone with more brightness in the world. Perceiving joy for himself at last in his new offspring, your father said that he was rising in status because of his son's honour.

---

45. Roberts 1989b: 345; cf. also Blomgren 1950: 62–4.
46. Cf. also Roberts 2007: 156–8 and Consolino 2011 for a comparison of Sidonius Apollinaris's and Venantius Fortunatus's uses of intertextuality and audiences.

It has been argued that this passage shows parallels to Christian interpretations of Vergil's *Eclogue* 4.⁴⁷ However, a closer look at the linguistic parallels reveals the following models (if such they are):

for 6.2.41: *aspice uenturo **laet**antur ut **omnia** saeclo!* (Verg. *ecl.* 4.52)
    *atque ita subridens: "**felicia tempora**, quae te* (Iuv. 2.38)
    *delapsa attactu nudauit **tempora** regis* (Sil. 16.269)
for 6.2.45: *at **te nascentem** gremio mea prima recepit* (Stat. *silu.* 1.2.260)
for 6.2.46: *cum uoluit, puro **fulget in orbe dies*** (Ov. *am.* 1.8.10)
for 6.2.47: ***sua gaudia*** [in the same position]: e.g., Verg. *Aen.* 10.652; Ov. *ars* 2.419; 481; *met.* 4.350; Stat. *Ach.* 1.183

There are hardly any echoes from *Eclogue* 4—*tu modo **nascent**i puero, quo ferrea primum* (*ecl.* 4.8), which is likely to be behind the Stat. *silu.* 1.2.260 quoted above, for Ven. Fort. *carm.* 6.2.45 is as close at it gets—certainly none from its Christian interpretations⁴⁸ even though the passage as a whole may reflect the mood of Vergil's fourth *Eclogue*, including its Christian interpretation. So if we want to read this passage through *Eclogue* 4, we would have to assume an intertextuality mode beyond visibility, that is, one that does not rely on close linguistic parallels. On the other hand, it might seem more appropriate to read this text in a non-intertextual way, to consider all resemblances to earlier texts to be irrelevant for its meaning, and to focus on the picture of timeless prosperity and abundant nature associated with Charibert's reign without worrying about potential allusions. Such a reading would allow us to note the prominence of landscape and nature descriptions in Fortunatus's poetry (as in Walcott's *Omeros*) as if those were to fill the gap left by the abandonment of intertextuality and were to mark the end of intertextuality in late Latin poetry in highly poetic terms.

8. Conclusion

In this chapter I have described a *continuum* of modes of intertextuality, presenting as three cases the two extreme modes and the mode roughly between the two poles. I have argued that the main difference between late Latin and classical intertextuality lies in the last mode, in which allusions are understood as elements of the form or texture of the poetry. As shown, this mode is particularly

---

47. George 1992: 45.
48. E.g., Lact. *inst.* 7.24.7 or Prud. *cath.* 9.8.57–70; the most famous, attributed to the emperor Constantine (Const. *or. s. c.*), is Greek and thus unable to provide close linguistic parallels with Venantius Fortunatus's poem.

suitable to communicate new content to audiences of various educational levels as it draws attention away from the model texts to the new text and allows the less educated (and/or non-native speakers of Latin) to follow a poem just as well as the highly educated members of the Roman elite. Evidence from late Latin metapoetical statements and literary scholarship has—indirectly—confirmed awareness of allusions which make essential contributions to the content and those that act as formal features, and a cross-cultural comparison with some modes of reception used in colonial and postcolonial literature has strengthened the case of the intertextuality modes as such as well as the proposed link between the modes and the poets' audiences. Finally, Venantius Fortunatus's poetry has been argued to constitute the endpoint of late Latin intertextuality.

Throughout this chapter I have pretended that interpreting allusions happens in a straightforward and objective way. This is, of course, not the case. Most readers, certainly if they are classicists, will have an expectation of the modes of intertextuality used in late Latin poetry and will often make an allusion (and by implication, the poet who made it) live up to their expectations.[49] For example, Ware (2012: 10–17 and passim) states "Claudian's intertextual relationship with the literary past is intrinsic to his work" (10), Hernández Lobato (2012: 541–51) claims that Sidonius 'is perfectly able to allude and emulate in passages that require the confirmation of his poetic stance' (541; my English paraphrase), and Stoehr-Monjou (2013a) has set out "to establish a corpus of intertexts which do not make intertextuality 'a question of faith,' so to speak, but a trustworthy methodological tool for [...] illuminating [Sidonius's] writing and his intentions" (133). On the other hand, Riedlberger (2010: 181) in very general terms advises caution against attempts to 'reconstruct Corippus' literary engagement with his model texts' (my English paraphrase) and Pelttari (2014: 159) thinks that "when late antique poets want to write an allusion, they often appropriate directly the words of their classical predecessors while ignoring their original context." Likewise, my own perception and this discussion of late Latin intertextuality have come out of reading expectations formed by my culture, education, and person. This seems worth considering in future studies on late Latin intertextuality.

49. Cf. Edmunds 2001: 39–62.

Late Narcissus

Classicism and Culture in a Late Roman Cento

JAŚ ELSNER

> *The narcissistic satisfaction provided by the cultural ideal is among the forces which are successful in combating the hostility to the cultural unit. . . . Art offers subjective satisfaction for the oldest and still most deeply felt cultural renunciations, and for that reason it serves as nothing else does to reconcile a man to the sacrifices he has to make on behalf of civilization. On the other hand, the creation of art heightens his feelings of identification, of which every cultural unit stands in so much need, by providing an occasion for sharing highly valued emotional experiences. And when those creations picture the achievements of his particular culture and bring to mind its ideals in an impressive manner, they also minister to his narcissistic satisfaction.*
>
> Sigmund Freud (2001: 13–14)

LONG BEFORE FREUD TIED THE LOVE OF ART AND THE UPHOLDING OF civilized values to the idea of cultural narcissism, I argue here, a poem probably composed in the fifth or sixth century AD used the image of Narcissus in a strikingly similar vein.[1] It will be my proposition that the Latin Narcissus cento (and indeed the cento form within late antique poetics) is a creation designed to picture the achievements of classical culture and to bring its ideals to mind, even as so many of the key aspects of Classical Antiquity were being sacrificed and renounced in the Christian present of Vandal North Africa, where the poem was probably written and certainly anthologized.[2] In addition to the complex of narcissistic satisfaction, the poem's evocation of Narcissus—made up of the cultural units of Vergil's verse and speaking to a highly educated elite with a deep command of Latin literature—is an interrogation of feelings of identification and highly valued emotional experience in a moment when the once vibrant presence of the ancient past was receding into the distance of a series of figures reflected in a pool.

---

1. Acknowledgements: Thanks are due to my fellow editor, Jesus Hernández Lobato, to Averil Cameron, and especially to John Henderson, Irene Peirano, and Michael Squire, who commented on an earlier draft. A version read at the Corpus Classical Seminar received valuable responses from Ewen Bowie, Kate Cooper, Eric Dugdale, Dan Jolowicz, and Gavin Kelly.

2. For an archaeologically nuanced account of the end of paganism in Africa in this period, see Leone 2013.

One set of specific questions raised by considering an ekphrastic cento as an exercise in cultural "narcissicism", is to probe the nature of its reflections on the classical tradition. Does the desire to love the self-image of its protagonist, an empty reflection in the waters, forged from the lines of Vergil, intimate affection and love for Antiquity or worries about its dangers and destructiveness (e.g., from a Christian-centred perspective) or concerns about the vanity of the self-conscious erudition it so effortlessly displays? What are the appropriate limits to put around the extraordinary chasm of metapoetic implications which this short poem from the twilight of Latin poetry so brilliantly opens? By exploring the poetics of the cento and the larger cultural politics of the cento aesthetic in late antique Latin literature through a close-focused discussion of a single poem, of course I succumb to one of the fallacies and fantasies of the medium of the cento in focusing on miniatures to elucidate larger questions, on parts of a bigger picture to enhance a sense of the whole.

5.1. The Cento: A Distinctively Late Antique Form of Classicism

The history of Latin literature is a history of classicism. That is, it is a process of quotation, borrowing, rewriting the canon, both the chosen Greek classics and, by Late Antiquity, the major Latin classics. Classicism of this kind—dense in allusion, playful, intertextual—is a defining quality of the finest Roman writing[3] and indeed arguably a fundamental aspect of Roman culture as witnessed by the ways its visual arts appropriated, remade, and hence canonized chosen works from the past.[4] Late Antiquity is no exception (although this has not always been accepted), except that the new line between the dominant, exclusivist, Christian culture and what had now become the *pagan* past, cast a new frame around the canon and redefined the process of classicism. Instead of a kind of free play of dialogue with the past—of the sort Vergil conducts with Homer and Ovid conducts with both Homer and Vergil—the present, for all its indebtedness to and affection for the classics, was now definitively different. Alongside the fantasy of a dialogue with Homer went the clear fact of fundamental religious difference. The process of establishing that difference—both through the selection of texts that would now count as classic in Christian culture and through the imitation of them with some panache in the major writers of the fourth to the sixth centuries—is a fundamental aspect of Late Antiquity in both the eastern and western

---

3. For a general account, see Hinds 1998; for late antique Latin poetry, see now Pelttari 2014: 115–60.
4. For the theoretical model in relation to the visual arts, see Elsner 2006a; on early Christian appropriations, see Elsner 2011.

halves of the Roman Empire, in both Greek and Latin literature.[5] One might resist the use of the term "Classicism" to describe this process in Late Antiquity, and indeed in its context it has ramifications of anxiety about the past, of ideologically motivated appropriation, of copy-and-paste homage, of the exercise of cultural nostalgia as narcissism; but the term has the merit of insisting on the deep continuity of late antique Latin poetics with the classical past and the use of that continuity as a key agent for cultural change.

The invention of the particular poetic form of the cento—a form used by both Greek and Latin writers—is a peculiar and, in certain ways, remarkable gesture within classicism, both in its wholesale, virtually monumental, appropriation of fragments from old poems for new purposes and in the density of allusions this could conjure.[6] In one sense, centos are themselves eminently anti-classical forms of literature, as they substitute the imitation of nature with a series of ready-made artefacts (from Homer and Vergil) while often subjecting the past to ironic or playful commentary and flagrantly parading a refusal of the poet's traditional task of creating new and original works. The ways that centos valorize a lost and unattainable or palpably passing classicism necessarily entails a certain distance from the tradition as well as immersion in it: this is their particular value to helping us understand the larger question of the transformation of the classical tradition within late ancient culture.

Like the use of *spolia* in monuments of material culture, the cento takes fragments from earlier poetry—above all from the canonical works of Homer and Vergil—to create new poems which operate on a double level.[7] They are poems in their own right and their poetics simultaneously evokes the associations of the quotations selected so as to conduct an audacious intertextual commentary from the past (the corpus of Vergil, say) on the present (e.g., Ausonius's wonderful poem of sexual intercourse on the marital bed, the *cento nuptialis*, written according to its preface at the behest of the emperor Valentinian) or by the present on the past (Ausonius's lascivious spoof on the *Aeneid*).[8] Like, for instance,

---

5. There are similarities of course with the visual arts—both in the process of collecting or preserving old statues and monuments and in that of imitation in new works.

6. On the cento as a poetic form, see Polara 1989, Salanitro 1997: 2314–24, Paolucci 2006: xxxviiii–cxii, Salanitro 2007: 9–24, Moretti 2008, Okáčová 2009a, Bažil 2009: 43–71 and 79–85, Prieto Domínguez 2010: 13–86 (on the Greek tradition), Formisano and Sogno 2010, Ehrling 2011: 11–64, Rondholz 2012: 1–40, Pelttari 2014: 96–112, and Galli 2014: 1–42.

7. For a comparison of the late antique culture of *spolia* with the literary culture of the cento, see Elsner 2000: 175–7 and Hernández Lobato 2012: 289–97. The literature on *spolia* in the last thirty years has become vast but remains firmly archaeological and architectural, skirting the larger issues of comparison with the literary products of the same cultural moment. See, however, with some comparison to literature and a meditation on issues of appropriation, Kinney 2012.

8. On Ausonius's *cento nuptialis*, see, e.g., Pollmann 2004: 83–7, McGill 2005: 92–114, Ehrling 2011: 148–79, Hinds 2014: 190–6.

the sculptural *spolia* of the arch of Constantine (see figure I.1, Introduction, p. 9),[9] the fragments of Homer or Vergil betray themselves and can bring their original contexts to mind (one thinks of the portrait of Antinous on the Hadrianic hunting roundels of the arch, where the emperor's head was recut with the portrait of Constantine).[10] But like the architectural *spolia*, column shafts, capitals, sculptural ornament (out of which so much of the arch's fabric was composed),[11] the original lines and half lines may hide in the shape of the new poem. On the arch, a number of the reused pieces were touched up over time—both specifically for their employment on the arch (as in the recutting of imperial heads to turn them into Constantine and at least one other tetrarch, over whose identity arguments continue to rage)[12] and before they were attached to the arch.[13] Likewise in the cento form, small accommodations in the borrowed lines or half lines are sometimes necessary to make the grammar and syntax work for the new poem,[14] while the segments borrowed—especially from the canonical works of Vergil— may acquire the further resonance of those phrases' earlier intertextual reuse by such epic poets as Ovid, Valerius Flaccus, and Silius Italicus.[15]

Of crucial value for any critical reading of the cento as a form of poetics is the introductory letter to Paulus, appended by Ausonius to his *cento nuptialis*.[16] There, with mock modesty, the poet speaks of his book as trifling and of little value (*"friuolum et nullius pretii,"* pref. 1)—a disastrous move in the history of receptions since his humorous *captatio beneuolentiae* has been taken at face value by the vast majority of the scholarship.[17] Ausonius calls

---

9. For comparison of the *spolia* on the arch of Constantine with the "*spolia*" gathered in late Roman mathematical collections, see Cuomo 2000: 1–2.

10. Recut heads: e.g., Prusac 2012: 138–50 with bibliography. Antinous: Meyer 1991: 218–20; note that the scholarship is divided on whether to identify Antinous in the tondi (though I do not see the problem myself: e.g., Boatwright 1987: 190–202 with bibliography).

11. At length: Pensabene and Panella 1993–4 and Pensabene 1999.

12. For a bibliography of suggestions, see Elsner 2000: 163, n. 22.

13. Notably the *liberalitas* relief on the north side of the attic storey, which once belonged to an arch of Marcus Aurelius and Commodus and from which the figure of Commodus appears to have been carefully excised after his fall from power and *damnatio memoriae* in 193 AD. See, e.g., Koeppel 1986: no. 33, 72–4.

14. E.g., in vv. 3 and 11 of the Narcissus cento.

15. For the significance of Vergil in Late Antiquity, see MacCormack 1998, Rees 2004b, Bažil 2009: 97–105. On the long history of "faking" Vergil as part of his ancient reception, see Peirano 2012: 74–116, 173–204, 242–53.

16. I use the text of Green 1991: 132–4 with his line numbering. This, alongside all the ancient theoretical and commentarial literature on the cento, appears in Prieto Domínguez 2010: 201–10. For discussion of Ausonius's letter, see, e.g., Polara 1989: 247–51, Pollmann 2004: 80–3, McGill 2005: 1–30, Hinds 2014: 188–90, Pelttari 2014: 70–1 and 104–7.

17. There was support for this kind of dismissal in Antiquity itself—see Jerome's *letter* 53 to Paulinus of Nola (written in 394), which discusses the puerilities of the Christian centos. See, e.g., Cameron 2011: 336–7, Curran 2012: 339–41, Pelttari 2014: 108–11, Cullhed 2014. Yet this game of verse as trifling is at least

the form a "compilation" (*concinnatio*, pref. 3), a collection of fragments and a fitting together of lacerated scraps (*sparsa colligere et integrare lacerata*, pref. 4).[18] And he stresses the problems of doubleness and paradox inherent in the form: "continuous though from disconnected parts, one but from diverse sources, ludicrous though from serious origins, mine but from another's work" (*de inconexis continuum, de diuersis unum, de seriis ludicrum, de alieno nostrum*, pref. 20–1). This opening dismissal—which takes in the degrading of Vergil's majestic verse, the writing to (imperial) command, the claim that his "little work" (*opusculum*, pref. 20) was hurriedly composed in a day—is then undermined by the very careful presentation of the rules for writing a cento. For a cento is made sound (*solidatur*, pref. 25) out of a variety of passages and different meanings (*uariis de locis sensibusque diuersis*, pref. 24–5) by the joining of half lines or one line and the following half with another half. "For to place two whole lines side by side is inept (*ineptum*) and three in succession trifling" (pref. 26–7).[19] The lines can be fitted at any of the caesuras, so that the result "you may say is like the puzzle (*ludicro*) which the Greeks call *stomachion*" (pref. 31–2), in which little pieces of bone are fitted together in various ways to form the appearance of a thousand objects—"a monstrous elephant, a brutal boar, a goose in flight, a gladiator in armour, a huntsman crouching down, a dog barking, a tower, a tankard and innumerable other things" (pref. 38–40) In this game, the skilful make something wonderful (*miraculum*, pref. 41), the unskilful something absurd (*ridiculum*, pref. 42). The little work of the cento (*centonis opusculum*, pref. 43) is handled just like this game: to make different meanings cohere and to make what has been appropriated from elsewhere seem naturally connected, to let no foreign elements shine through (*sensus diuersi ut congruant, adoptiua quae sunt, ut cognata uideantur, aliena ne interluceant*, pref. 44–5).

Much can be made out of this programmatic prose introduction in the form of a letter—the emphasis on play,[20] on dismemberment and unity,[21] on paradox,[22] on puzzles,[23] for example—but the claim of ownership despite the overt

---

as old as Catullus, and no one seeks to dismiss his poetry because he himself called it "inept" (CAT. 14b.1) or Martial's because he quotes Catullus in jokingly calling his own verses "inept" in the opening poem of his eleventh book (MART. 11.1.14).

18. Among the elegant jokes is the comparison of a cento to the son of Thyone and Virbius—"the first re-shaped (*reformatum*) out of Dionysus, the second out of Hippolytus," where of course Dionysus is himself responsible for sparagmos in the case of Pentheus. See also McGill 2005: 18–19.

19. On these rules, in relation to the corpus of surviving Vergilian centos, see Bright 1984.

20. See McGill 2005: 4–9.

21. See McGill 2005: 10–23.

22. See Pollmann 2004: 81.

23. See Malamud 1989: 35–7.

plagiarism (*de alieno nostrum*, pref. 21) is arresting. For spoliation is the creation—through contiguous placement and according to complex rules—of a new work of art, something quite different from the segments from which it is built, even if it may resonate constantly against the original contexts out of which it has been constituted. That new surface, in the Christian culture within which Ausonius was writing, allowed the potential for a radically new text to be written out of the fragments of Antiquity—in the Christian centos that were composed in both Latin and Greek.[24] Even in what have been termed the secular and mythological centos, the poetic method of spoliation and reconstitution forms a new relationship with the classical tradition—a new form of literary classicism.

Most of our surviving Latin centos (but not that of Ausonius) appear as a group in the Codex Salmasianus, an anthology of poems in Latin,[25] which was—in its current form—compiled in the last years of Vandal rule in North Africa (between 523 AD, when one of the poems must have been written, and before the fall of the Vandal kingdom to the Byzantines in 534).[26] Some poems in the collection (as well as others not in Salmasianus) survive in later manuscripts, but the earliest and most significant is MS Paris Lat. 10318, known as the Codex Salmasianus (after its humanist owner in the seventeenth century), which was probably copied about 800 in Italy.[27] The centos, magnificently despised by generations of modern readers,[28] have even been excluded from the most

---

24. On the Greek material, see esp. Usher 1998 and Whitby 2007; on Proba in Latin, see Shanzer 1994, Pollmann 2004: 87–92, McGill 2007b, Bažil 2009: 111–97, Curran 2012, Hinds 2014, Cullhed 2015 with much further bibliography.

25. The poems of the codex are published in the order of their appearance there by Riese 1894: 33–269, from which poems will be cited by Riese's number in the form AL 9R; and by Shackleton Bailey 1982: 28–295, although this idiotically omits the centos, from which poems will be cited by Shackleton Bailey's number in the form AL 9SB. On the codex as anthology, especially memorable is John Henderson's comment: "never an anthology . . . but always and forever an agglutination of agglutinations, snowballed from other codices by editorial *studium augendi*" (http://bmcr.brynmawr.edu/2011/2011-09-54.html). The first critical edition and commentary of the centos in the Codex Salmasianus appeared only in 2014: Galli 2014.

26. The date is given by Luxorius's epigram for Hilderic, king of the Vandals from 523, AL 194 SB (= AL 203 R); see Heusch 1997: 13–19 and McGill 2005: xix and 158, n. 37. For historical accounts of Vandal Africa, see Heather 2006: 264–99, Merrills and Miles 2010, Sarris 2011: 89–97. On cultural and literary contexts, see Hays 2004, George 2004, Kay 2006: 7–13, Merrills and Miles 2010: 204–27, and Conant 2012. For an archaeological conspectus, see Bockmann 2013, and on North Africa generally but including the Vandal kingdom, Leone 2013.

27. See Baumgartner 1981: 7–9, 67, Spallone 1982: 36–49, Socas 2011.

28. It is revealing that Farrell and Puttnam 2010 find no room for discussion of the centos in five hundred pages. For some of the opprobrium, see McGill 2005: xvii, n. 21; for more on late antique Latin literature in general, see Roberts 1989a: 1–3. Typically, the one comprehensive treatment of Narcissus in Western literature, Vinge 1967, fails even to mention the Narcissus cento.

recent critical edition of the *Latin Anthology* on the historically absurd grounds of their poetic awfulness.[29] In this essay, I focus on one cento, that describing Narcissus—which appears early in the Anthology (AL 9 R)—and whose content, I argue, represents an acute reflection on the classical tradition.[30] Indeed, insofar as the centos look as if they were an anthology made in Late Antiquity, the placement of the Narcissus poem, with all its metaliterary and self-reflexive potential as the first in the mythological sequence, looks like a deliberate and even programmatic act.

5.2. The Narcissus Cento

I begin with the text and a translation of the cento, including, in parentheses, the Vergilian origins of its borrowed lines.[31]

Narcissus (*Anthologia Latina* 9 R)
candida per siluam (A. 8.82) *primaeuo flore iuuentus* (A. 7.162)
adsidue ueniebat: ibi haec (E. 2.4) *caelestia dona* (G. 4.1)
et fontes sacros (E. 1.52 [*fontis*]) *insigni laude ferebat* (A. 1.625)
insignis facie (A. 9.583, cf A 9.336) *longumque bibebat*[32] *amorem* (A. 1.749)
intentos uoluens oculos, (A 7.251, cf A. 4.363 and 12.939) *securus amorum.*
    (A. 1.350, cf. 10.326)   5
dum stupet (A 1.495) *atque animum pictura pascit inani,* (A. 1.464)
expleri mentem nequit ardescitque tuendo (A 1.713)
egregium forma iuuenem, (A 6.861, 12.275; cf. 7.473) *quem nympha*
    crearat: (A. 10.551)
sic oculos, sic ille manus, sic ora ferebat. (A. 3.490)
his amor unus erat, (A 9. 182) *dorso dum pendet iniquo,* (A. 10.303)   10

---

29. Shackleton Bailey 1982: iii: "Centones Vergiliani (Riese 7–18), *opprobia litterarum, neque ope critica multum indigent neque is sum qui uati reuerendo denuo haec edendo contumeliam imponere sustineam.*" "The Virgilian centos (Riese 7–18), a disgrace of literature, hardly call for scholarly labour, nor am I one to insult a poet who ought to be worshipped, by editing those poems again(!)."

30. To my knowledge, the only discussions of this poem longer than a paragraph are McGill 2005: 76–9 and Okáčová 2009b. For text and commentary, see Galli 2014: 73–91.

31. The information on Vergilian ur-texts is taken from Schenkl 1888: 534 and printed also by McGill 2005: 76–7, Okáčová 2009b: 179, and Galli 2014: 73–4. I have added a few instances missed by these scholars.

32. This word is an interesting case where the codex in fact gives *uiuebat* for *bibebat*—an easy error given the closeness of *b* and *v* sounds in Late Antiquity. The codex has a series of spelling mistakes, all restored by the editors (Riese in 1894, followed by Galli in 2014) to the Vergilian original. But here the "error" (potentially a misremembering of Vergil's original or even a deliberate riff on it) makes sense as "he would have lived a long love," that life playing against Narcissus's imminent death.

oblitusue sui est (A 3.629) *et membra decora iuuentae* (A. 4.559
   [*iuuenta*])³³
miratur rerumque ignarus imagine gaudet. (A. 8.730)
ilicet ignis edax (A. 2.758) *secreti ad fluminis undas* (A. 3.389 [*undam*])³⁴
ipsius in uultu (G. 1.452) *uana spe lusit amantem,* (A. 1.352)
et praeceps animi (A. 9.685) *collo dare bracchia circum* (A. 2.792/
   6.700)   15
ter conatus (A. 2.792/6.700/10.685) *erat* (A. 6.32) *nec, quid speraret,
   habebat* (E. 2.2).

Gleaming white through the wood, a youth³⁵ in early bloom
Would come repeatedly. There, with his exceptional face,
He would give those heavenly gifts and sacred springs
Exceptional praise, and would drink long draughts of love,
Moving his eyes in deep thought, careless of love.   5
While he is stupefied and feasts his mind on an empty image,
He cannot satiate his soul and takes fire through gazing
At a youth of outstanding form, whom a nymph had borne—
Such eyes, hands and face did he bear.
Theirs was one love, while it hangs upon an uneven ridge,   10
Or has been forgetful of itself, and at the beautiful limbs of youth
He³⁶ wonders, and rejoices in the image not knowing the truth.
Forthwith the burning flames [having brought him] to the waters of a
   secluded stream
Deluded the lover with a vain hope in the sight of his own face,
And reckless of heart, to throw his arms around the image's neck   15
Thrice he tried nor grasped anything to hope for.

---

33. In the last word of ll. 11 and 13, the centonist makes a minor change to what is the current text of Vergil's original. In l. 11 *iuuentae* is necessary to make grammatical sense, but it is also a well-attested late antique reading (in both Servius and the fourth- to fifth-century Codex Palatinus of Vergil) and is indeed the reading chosen by R. G. Austin in his Oxford edition of *Aeneid* 4 (1955): ad loc. and 167, though not in Mynors's OCT of 1969.

34. In l. 13 editors of the cento have preferred *undas*—e.g., Galli 2014: 87–8, 91—but *undam*, which is what Vergil wrote in *Aeneid* 3.389, may be what the centonist wrote and the scribe miscopied.

35. I translate as if *iuuentus* can be taken as a singular youth (an implication of Narcissus's solitary love); but the generic and collective meaning of the word, as "youth per se" or "all the youths" in a given context, resonates here not only with Vergil's original but against the many boys and girls who loved Narcissus at Ovid *met.* 3.353–5.

36. I translate "he" (meaning Narcissus), but technically the subject remains "love" (*amor*) from v. 10. Both must be right—my version describing the boy and the pool, but the grammatical version meaning roughly "love wonders and rejoices in its unknowing self-oblivion" is also true. Just as the theme slides between two lovers and a single self-love, the collective "youth" of *iuuentus* and the specific youth called Narcissus, so the grammar stitching the cento discombobulates.

This is a strange text, more an ekphrastic gathering of lines evocative or descriptive of a state and place than a narrative. While many centos, notably Ausonius's *cento nuptialis* and also the Christian narrative centos, tell a story through someone else's lines, creating a paranarrative, the Narcissus cento—by significant contrast with the canonical Narcissus narrative in Latin verse (OVID *met.* 3.339–510)—simply evokes the boy by the pool, without any lead-up or conclusion. The Vergilian lines that the text gathers and out of which it is constructed, effectively constitute a commentary on the image they render. The segments of the cento are from canonical set pieces and classic moments within Vergil, and the resonances of the Vergilian originals are brought to bear on the new poetical construct. As will become clear below, I believe the choices of segments to cull to be erudite and indeed commanding not only of Vergil's texts but also of the ways they are quoted by Ovid.[37] Moreover, those choices construct a brilliantly marshalled pattern of intertextual allusion to a series of specific passages in both Vergil and Ovid, one on which the Narcissus theme is a powerful commentary and which are themselves commentarial on the image of Narcissus in love by the pool. Were that simply all the cultural work this poem performs, then it could perhaps fairly be dismissed as a clever kind of crossword puzzle, a trite, pointless piece of antiquarianism from the late (indeed the Vandal) decadence of Roman poetry. This kind of judgement is on the generous side of the usual way this cento has been read. But insofar as the poem is a cultural commentary in its own right on the relation of its world with the classical past, it is, I argue, much more powerful and significant than it has seemed. I approach the poem from a number of the themes it extracts and recombines from within Vergil's corpus—sexual desire and homoerotics, intimations of disaster and mortality, ekphrasis and the metapoetic meditation on the ghostly emptiness of images, its politics of African identity—as well as the text's play with Ovid's Narcissus through the conceit of only citing Vergil directly.

5.2.1. Desire Queering the Waters

Clearly the Narcissus theme is about love. The centonist relentlessly stresses the depth and heroic grandeur of his hero's passion by reference to Vergil's most powerful love affair, that of Dido and Aeneas. The final part of v. 3 quotes from the first speech Dido makes to Aeneas in Carthage (*Aen.* 1.625), while the last part of v. 4 and all of v. 7 are drawn from the passage where Dido feasts Aeneas at the end of book 1 and falls hopelessly in love with him (with some help from

---

37. In other words I think it much more subtle than Bažil's characterization as "pastiche": Bažil 2009: 56.

Cupid, *Aen.* 1.695–755, the quotations being from 1.749 and 713, respectively). Beside the immensity of Dido's passion is its failure and its conclusion in death. V. 11 of the cento quotes the description of Mercury (at *Aen.* 4.559) when he warns Aeneas (who is acting as a madman in his love, *demens*, 4.562) that he must escape Dido or be doomed. That warning is not heeded of course by Narcissus, who will perish for his love as Aeneas does not but as Dido will. V. 5, *intentos uoluens oculos*, while quoting directly from Latinus's welcome to Aeneas at *Aen.* 7.251, refers also to Dido's last speech to her lover at *Aen.* 4.365–87, as she gazes at him with her eyes dancing (*uoluens oculos*, 4.363) and not least to Aeneas's own eyes at *Aen.* 12.939, when he resolves finally to strike the death blow to Turnus and bring the epic to its close. The choices from the Dido narrative are striking: direct quotations culled from the first meeting, the falling-in-love banquet, and the last confrontation. It is as if a mini Dido epyllion has been performed in miniature in the frozen space of Narcissus's gaze, where there is virtually no action or plot development. The dynamic pattern in the Dido story, whose entire development is alluded to, is set in direct contrast with the lack of movement in the Narcissus cento. At the same time, Narcissus is built from lines that in the original, define Dido. He is effectively feminized through being constructed as a female lover (admittedly one of great passion) who conceives a love (like his) that cannot be achieved (though for very different reasons).[38] Yet at the same time, there is a potential cultural politics in the Dido theme in sixth-century Africa; for it plays into a contemporary reflection on the likely African context of the cento's composition and its anthologization at the Vandal court (on which, see further below).

The homoerotic, but from Antiquity's point of view non-normative, undertones of the Narcissus narrative are insistently stressed through the Vergilian intertexts.[39] The myth of Narcissus is sexually transgressive not only because his love is for himself but also because it is for one of the same age as opposed to being for a younger boy (in the classic *erates/erômenos* model of Greek love).[40] The second half of the poem's opening line is culled from *Aen.* 7.162, where boys and youths (i.e., the normative male homoerotic pattern) exercise outside the walls of Latinus's city.[41] Narcissus is, of course, at rest rather than in action, and he is solo—so that his narrative and the account within the cento are effectively in denial of the allusions of the passage through which he is evoked. Lines 2 and 16

---

38. The feminization of Narcissus is a common theme in the Greek ekphrastic accounts of paintings and statues of the theme; see Elsner 2007: 147.
39. The homosexual theme is noted but not developed by Okáčová 2009b: 182–3.
40. See Elsner 2007: 147–8 and 151 on the age transgression, with Dover 1978: 16, 85–7.
41. See Horsfall 2000: 142, ad. loc: "Virgil nowhere names Latinus's city."

(the last) of the cento open and close respectively with quotations from early in Vergil's Second *Eclogue*,[42] a classic account of unrequited homosexual love, whose failure echoes that of Narcissus himself. [43] Beyond the gay theme, the ring composition that frames the cento with *Eclogue* 2 refers twice to the prelusory frame of Vergil's poem and the way the solitary Corydon flings his "artless song to the mountains and the hills":

... ibi haec incondita solus
montibus et siluis studio iactabat inani (*Ecl.* 2.4–5)

This passage is precisely not one selected for inclusion in the cento, but it is the lead-in to Corydon's lament from the five-line opening to the poem from which the cento quotes twice. Corydon's lament, which forms the rest of Vergil's poem, effectively makes present in the cento, through its absence and through lack of quotation, the call of Echo in Ovid's classic treatment of the Narcissus theme in *Metamorphoses* 3. 356–401. Notably at *met.* 3.400, Echo is no longer seen in the mountains and the woods (*latet siluis nulloque in monte uidetur*), just as she does not appear at all in the Narcissus cento except in the non-reference to (but implicit evocation of) the lover's voice from *Eclogue* 2.

Within this homoerotic cyclic structure, the Narcissus cento finds space for a further quotation from Vergil's other most famous homosexual passage, the account of the love and tragic deaths of Nisus and Euryalus in book 9 of the *Aeneid* (vv. 176–449).[44] The "one love" of Narcissus (*amor unus*, v. 10) is the "common love for each other" of Nisus and Euryalus at *Aen.* 9.182, *erastes* and *erômenos* at *Aen.* 9.176–81. The *Aeneid*'s hymn to homosocial companionship—which concludes with the poet's own apostrophe to the fallen pair as "both fortunate" (*fortunati ambo, Aen.* 9.446)—becomes the solitary self-love of one who will wilt away, dying alone neither in the heroic heat of battle nor in the chase nor at exercise.[45] Yet the spur of the homoerotic can itself be a signal of doom: v. 4 opens with *insignis facie*, quoting, among other lines, *Aen.* 9.336, the description of young Serranus, slain by Nisus in his *aristeia* at *Aen.* 9.314–66. As with the play on *Eclogue* 2, the centonist quotes directly from the opening of an extended narrative in his source, but evokes—through his quotation and through the implicit commentarial play of the Vergilian source on his own text—a much wider set of resonances than are explicit. In the case of the allusion but non-reference to Corydon's song in relation to Echo's absence from his

---

42. See Galli 2014: 78 and 91 on "Ringkomposition."
43. On sexuality in Vergil, see Oliensis 1997.
44. For a summary, see Hardie 1994: 23–34 and also Fowler 2000a and Reed 2007: 6–43.
45. For parallels between the (differently) love-spurred deaths of Dido and Nisus, see Reed 2007: 80–1.

Late Narcissus 187

text, the centonist explicitly plays on the choices he does not make as themselves in certain respects constitutive of his poetics and the claims his poem is making.

5.2.2. Intimations of Doom

Arguably the theme of doom can hardly be overestimated in the narrative of Narcissus, but the centonist cannot be said to have failed to rise to the challenge of overstating it. The Narcissus poet seizes on one of the key features of the later books of the *Aeneid*—the long line of ephebic youths sketched in the promise of their futures and then slaughtered in battle as the poem progresses.[46] There has been some discussion of the way Vergil feminizes these youths,[47] and this—alongside their age and lack of a fulfilled life—works very effectively as a series of types for Narcissus, although ironically so since they die in glory and in action, not wilting away by a pool. The opening of v. 4 (*insignis facie*) evokes two deaths at once—quoting not only that of Serranus at *Aen.* 9.336 but also that of Arceus's son at 9.583, slain by Mezentius at 9.586–9. The last half of v. 5 (*securus amorum*) quotes the description of Clytus at *Aen.* 10.326, who is "forgetful of his loves" when killed in battle by Aeneas. The opening of v. 8 (*egregium forma iuuenem*) again hits two doomed youths with one half line: Augustus's nephew and adoptive son, Marcellus, who has the shadow of death over him even as Aeneas meets him in the Underworld (at 6.861, cf. 6.866 for the shadow)[48] and the unnamed son of Gylippus, who is skewered by Tolumnius's spear when the truce is broken at *Aen.* 12.275. Arguably it also evokes the description of Turnus, inspired with rage to defend Italy from Aeneas at *Aen.* 7.473 (*decus egregium formae mouet atque iuuentae*). V. 8 closes with reference to the nymph's son Tarquitus (*Aen.* 10.551), who is slaughtered by Aeneas at 10.552–60. Finally in this relentless catalogue of intertextual death, the first half of v. 15 (*et praeceps animi*) refers to Tmarus, "reckless at heart," who falls to the Trojan brothers Pandarus and Bitias at 9.685, themselves to perish by Turnus's hand later in the same book. In all these cases, it is not the heroic death but the ekphrastic evocation of the doomed hero—usually a short description giving an intimation of character—that is selected. In a sense Narcissus stands as a permanent symbol of what has been called "the pregnant moment" before all such catastrophes but redolent of the suggestion of disaster.[49] At the same time, his passivity and lack of action is in direct conflict with the repeated pattern of the *Aeneid*'s deaths

---

46. See, e.g., Hardie 1997: 320–1 and Rossi 2004: 73–4.
47. See Fowler 1987: 188–91 on Euryalus and 194–5 on Pallas.
48. On Marcellus, see Reed 2007: 148–72.
49. The concept is Lessing's from his classic work of 1766: Lessing 1984: 19–22, with, e.g., Bergmann 1996: 199.

out of which he is confected. Again, a particular quality of the poetics of the Narcissus cento is the poem's frequent reversal of the most obvious meanings evoked by allusion to the passage from which the chosen element is plucked.

Alongside the theme of death, one might hazard that the repeated emphasis on body parts thematizes a poetics of dismemberment. At v. 5 (*oculos*), v. 9 (*oculos, manus, ora*), v. 11 (*membra*), v. 14 (*uultu*), v. 15 (*collo, bracchia*), the cento proffers a persistent splitting of any sense of the whole body into part objects. This resonates against Narcissus's own doomed splitting of self and reflection in his division of himself into lover and beloved, but it also comments on the spoliate poetics of the cento's own formal construction out of segments of other poems and another poet's words. In the theme of epic death which the poem exploits in contrast to Narcissus, dismemberment is the mark of a hero's fall and the fame of his conqueror, but in the case of Narcissus it is a performance of self-fracture that reflects the poet's own work in fragmenting Vergil in order to put together his Narcissus out of the parts.

Beside the litany of epic deaths, perhaps ironizing his unheroic, pastoral tragedy through their relentless message of war and glory, is a group of less directly hero-focused resonances of foreboding. At v. 10, Narcissus's love rests on an uneven, indeed a hostile, ridge (*dorso dum pendet iniquo*) – a quotation from the shipwreck of *Aen.* 10.303, when Tarchon's boat is dashed against the shoals and its crew flung into the waters. In a poem which repeatedly plays fire against water,[50] this image of death by drowning (very apposite to at least some versions of the Narcissus myth)[51] may be set against the opening of v. 13, where the voracious fire of Narcissus's love is that of the flames that engulf Troy from *Aen.* 2.758. At v. 14, the opening borrowed from *Georgic* 1.452 (*ipsius in uultu*) is an image of the setting sun—a reversal at the end of the cento (but from the first *Georgic*) of its quotation at v. 2 from the first line of *Georgic* 4, which promised "heavenly gifts" (*caelestia dona*) of honey from the skies. Even the text's framing ring composition through the *Georgics* offers only intimations of doom. The anthropomorphism of the sun in Vergil's original text is itself used to foreshadow the death of Caesar (at *Georgic* 1.461–8), which presages the fear of "eternal night" (*aeternam . . . noctem*, 1.468). The descent to darkness is not only a reflection on Narcissus's fate but may also be the doom of an impious age (*impia . . . saecula*, 1.468) as the bright sun of classicism sets in the dusk of Late Antiquity.

---

50. On fire and water, see Okáčová 2009b: 181; on the debt of this to Ovid's intertextual uses of Lucretius in his Narcissus, see Hardie 2002: 159–60.

51. Notably Plotinus in *Ennead* 1.6.8.

5.2.3. Image and Imagination

One of the key dynamics of the Narcissus theme is the way that the pool's reflection of its viewer functions as a work of art—fascinating, enchanting, compelling, ultimately perilous. This is not only the case in the prose works of the Greek side of the tradition, especially the ekphrases of Philostratus and Callistratus,[52] but also Ovid's memorable comparison of Narcissus to a statue of Parian marble (*ut e Pario formatum marmore signum*, met. 3.419; cf. *marmoreis . . . palmis*, met. 3.481) and as a kind of image fashioned in ivory, like that made by Pygmalion (*eburnea colla*, met. 3.422).[53] The centonist seizes on this theme with the words *pictura* at v. 6 and *imago* at v. 12[54] and develops it by means of a repeated borrowing of quotations from some of the great ekphrastic passages from the *Aeneid* that explicitly deal with works of art.[55] The whole of v. 6 draws from two lines in the first great ekphrasis of the *Aeneid*, where the hero observes the decorations of Dido's new-built temple in Carthage, which show the narrative of the Trojan war (*Aen*. 1.453–95). *Dum stupet* (the opening of the line) is culled from the very end of the passage (1.495) and describes Aeneas's dumbfounded wonder at the pictorial narratives of his own past, just before Dido approaches; *atque animum pictura pascit inani* comes from near the opening of the ekphrasis (1.464) and describes the way Aeneas's soul is fed by a set of pictures, empty of substance but resonant of so much memory and so many tears (he weeps at 1.459, 462, 465, 470, 485). In the *Aeneid* the emptiness is reiterated at 1.476 with Troilus's empty chariot (*curru . . . inani*), and of course that emptiness of the image, coupled with its emotive power to fuel desire, is key to Narcissus. In both quotations, what matters is not the image itself but its subjective effects—its ability to move, stupefy, cause wonder. In the cento, where the image in the pool is literally empty (being but a reflection in the water), the Vergilian trope is pushed still further by literalizing what was a metaphor in the original. One may note that the second half of 1.495 (not quoted but evoked intertextually through *dum stupet*) reads, very appropriately in the case of Narcissus, "he hangs wrapt on one fixed gaze" (*obtutuque haeret defixus in uno*). The irony is that the poet builds the wonderment of his passive non-hero, Narcissus, out of the canonical text of a hero gazing at his own deeds (1.488) and those of his kinsfolk in the defining war of the entire classical tradition.

---

52. See Webb 2006: 128–32 and Elsner 2007: 137–46.
53. Cf. OVID met. 10.248, 255, 275–6 for Pygmalion and ivory.
54. See McGill 2005: 77–8 and Okáčová 2009b: 181–2.
55. Ekphrasis in the *Aeneid* is a big theme. See, e.g., Dubois 1982, Putnam 1998, Dufallo 2013: 142–60, and Elsner 2007: 78–87 for an argument about their incremental effect.

While the cento performs an act of dual vision in fashioning the image of Narcissus gazing from Aeneas's gaze (here at v. 6, later at v. 12 and v. 16), Aeneas himself—throughout the ekphrasis at the temple of Carthage—performs an act of double vision. He slides from image to person, animating the *pictura inanis* (of the Vergilian quotation at v. 6) by filling the empty iconography with the heroes of his memories. The ekphrasis climaxes with Penthesilea at Troy (*Aen.* 1.491–3), before she is loved and killed by Achilles, in a passage that may be said to prefigure and segue into Dido (at *Aen.* 1.496), who will be loved and whose death will be caused by Aeneas (though not in battle). Vergil's concluding line of the temple description—*dum stupet obtutuque haeret defixus in uno* (*Aen.* 1.495, from which v. 6 in the cento quotes the opening)—brilliantly encompasses the theme of doubling (image to person, Penthesilea to Dido) through its hendiadys of *stupet . . . haeret* and its verbal repetition *ob-tu-tu*, which resonate against the line's firm closure on the word "one" (*in uno*). The centonist exquisitely uses Vergil's evocation of doubling in relation to the unity of the work of art to underwrite his theme of the imagined doubling of lover and beloved out of the singularity of one boy in Narcissus and the governing aesthetic of his own poetics in being not only the classic voice of Vergil as refracted through a theme of Ovid but also simultaneously classic and contemporary in a single poem.

The whole of v. 12 is borrowed from the penultimate line of book 8 of the *Aeneid*, which sums up the long description of the shield that Venus brings her son (itself the Latin version of Homer's shield of Achilles at *Iliad* 18.478–608), whose visual narratives are a mythological summary of Rome's history leading up to Augustus himself (*Aen.* 8.625–731).[56] Again the centonist quotes not the epic's account of the object nor what the shield depicts but Vergil's focus on the subjective affect in the viewer's mind. In this case, Aeneas—who lives before the stories that the shield foretells and cannot know them—wonders and rejoices in their representation but is ignorant of them. That Vergilian play on Aeneas as a viewer who is moved by what he sees but is fundamentally ignorant of its intentions (which resonates also in the temple images of book 1, where the Trojan war is depicted from a triumphalist Greek point of view but is interpreted in tragic Trojan mode by Aeneas)[57] is brilliantly marshalled by the poet for its relevance to Narcissus, who is much more deluded throughout his tragic viewing even than Aeneas.[58] In the course of Vergil's epic, Aeneas moves as a character from one who stands back and experiences multiple levels and contradictory

---

56. On the shield of Aeneas, see, e.g., Gransden 1976: 161–3, Hardie 1986: 336–76, Putnam 1998: 119–88, Feldherr 2014.

57. See Dubois 1982: 32–5, Boyd 1995: 76–9, Dufallo 2013: 142–7.

58. On Narcissus and the problems of knowledge, see, e.g., Janan 2009: 120–55.

resonances in response to art to one who sees the belt of Pallas on the fallen Turnus and at that point does not hesitate to kill (in a passage explicitly quoted by the centonist at v. 4: *uoluens oculos, Aen.* 12.939);[59] but Narcissus's character fails to move at all and is simply lost in the eddies of his own desire.

Finally, in the flurry of Vergilian ekphrastica at the opening of the last line of the cento (v. 16), the poet borrows and transforms a passage from the description of the great doors of the Sibyl's temple at Cumae, fashioned by Daedalus himself (*Aen.* 6.14–37). Here the focus is on the artist. Vergil tells us that Daedalus twice tried to fashion in gold the image of his son Icarus falling from the sky and twice he failed, as his hands fell from the task (6.32–3). Some things are beyond art, some tales too tragic for the artist to tell. The centonist, borrowing from elsewhere in the *Aeneid*, changes "twice" (*bis*) to "thrice" (*ter*) but keeps the full half line that ends *conatus erat*, which occurs only at 6.32.[60] He alludes here to grief, failure, and also—in shifting to the great Vergilian self-reflection on the limits of the artist—to the idea that Narcissus is his own artist, author and sufferer of his own woes.

The ekphrastic frame of the cento—in keeping with its own effectively ekphrastic rather than narrative force—feeds into a repeated emphasis on ghostly shadows and images.[61] Notably the last part of v. 15 and the opening of v. 16 take texts from two such moments in the *Aeneid*. First, this section picks on Aeneas's attempt to embrace the ghost of his wife Creusa at 2.792–3:

ter conatus ibi collo dare bracchia circum;
ter frustra comprensa manus effugit imago . . .

Thrice there I strove to throw my arms about her neck,
thrice the image, vainly clasped, escaped my hands . . .

Second, it quotes the exact repetition of these lines at 6.700–1, where they describe Aeneas attempting to embrace the ghost of his father, Anchises, after their conversation in the underworld. Both these failed moments, with their twice voiced *ter*, themselves echo Odysseus's three frustrated attempts to grasp the phantom of his mother at *Odyssey* 11.206–7. In Vergil, Aeneas's loss of wife and father is a kind of familial fulfilment of Odysseus's loss of his mother; in the very last line of the cento—at any rate, for the reader learned in Greek as well

---

59. Elsner 2007: 85–6.
60. One may wonder if the *ter* is in part borrowed from the ekphrasis of *Aen.* 1, where Achilles drags Hector three times around the walls of Troy (*Aen.* 1.483).
61. This theme draws on Ovid's own intertextual play with shadows and ghosts in his Narcissus, on which see Hardie 2002: 156–8.

as Latin literature—the *mise-en-abîme* of ghostly refractions is made to spiral out of control in a vortex of allusion that points to the earliest moments in the classical canon.

The very fact that the centonist shifts the *bis conatus* of *Aen.* 6.32 to *ter conatus*, is not only a capping of two Vergilian moments of ghostly vision (like reflections glimpsed in water) with his own anti-hero straining for the boy in the pool, but a fulfilment of these two Vergilian passages (with their Homeric resonances) in Vergil's own third evocation of the failure to grasp such an image—namely, that of Daedalus to make the *imago* of Icarus. All these failures culminate in Narcissus's failure to grasp the image at the pool, despite help from all the words in Vergil. Meanwhile at v. 9 of the cento, the line *sic oculos, sic ille manus, sic ora ferebat* is culled from a further powerful evocation of the dead in the *Aeneid*. The line comes from *Aen.* 3.490, where Andromache gives Ascanius a gift from her loom, woven for the now dead Astyanax, her son with Hector, whom Ascanius exactly resembles. Indeed at 3.489 Ascanius is the sole surviving image of Astyanax (*o mihi sola mei super Astyanactis imago!*). Here the evocation is not of a ghost or of a memory that cannot be put into art but of an image of a boy exactly alike to Ascanius—a perfect type for Narcissus and his reflection, both in the matter of resemblance and in the thematics of doom.

5.2.4. In Play with Ovid

Twice, the Narcissus cento borrows lines from Vergil's account of Dido's flight from Tyre, where her beloved husband, Sychaeus, was killed for love of gold by her own brother, Pygmalion (v. 5, *securus amorum* from *Aen.* 1.350, and v. 14, *uana spe lusit amantem* from 1.352). The fact that Vergil's Pygmalion, king of Tyre, is *not* the same as Ovid's Pygmalion, king of Cyprus, at *met.* 10.243–92, is a good joke, since Narcissus's beloved is not after all the boy he thinks he is but only his own reflection. The thematic connection of Narcissus and Pygmalion is deep in the *Metamorphoses*, signalled by Narcissus's ivory neck (*met.* 3. 422),[62] and it is one of a series of oblique references through Ovidian quotations of Vergil's lines as included in the cento to a well-chosen selection of vision-related moments in Ovid's *Metamorphoses*. Notably, *dum stupet* at v. 6 is itself quoted from Vergil twice in the *Metamorphoses*:[63] at 10.287, where Pygmalion stands amazed that the ivory woman has turned into flesh, and at 5.205, where Astyages stands amazed at the sight of Aconteus—turned to stone by the Gorgon's gaze—and then is himself turned to "a marble face" (*marmoreo . . . ore*)

---

62. See Rosati 1983: 58–67.
63. One may also add Valerius Flaccus 5.96, where Mopsus stands amazed at the ghost of Sthenelus.

by the sight of Medusa's head.⁶⁴ These oblique references, carefully targeted to Ovid's major accounts of art (mainly statuary) and the gaze—playing on themes of self-investment and deception (so that Pygmalion sculpts the girl of his desires, Narcissus is trapped by self love, Astyages and Aconteus become statues of themselves)—circle around the centonist's genuflections to Ovid's Narcissus narrative itself. At v. 15 the half line *collo dare bracchia circum* is not a quotation from Ovid, but it certainly evokes Echo's final attempt to throw her arms around Narcissus's neck (*bracchia collo, met.* 3.389) and Narcissus's own visual echo of her failure, as he seeks to embrace the neck of the image in the pool at *met.* 3.428–9 (*collum/bracchia*).⁶⁵

In a sense, Ovid's Narcissus text may itself be read as a commentary on Vergil,⁶⁶ especially on the viewer viewing himself (as in the case of Aeneas at Dido's temple),⁶⁷ on falling in love (in relation to Dido),⁶⁸ in the text's repeated imagery of flames and love at *met.* 3.372–4 and 490 (in relation to the flames in Dido's heart, *Aen.* 1.660, 673, 713—a line fully quoted in the cento—and 4.300). It is this intertextual, we may also say commentarial, tradition, now refracted as a pure synthesis of quotations and reduced to the minuscule of a sixteen-line cento but referring with panache and clear intent to a series of key passages in both Vergil and Ovid, that our anonymous Vandal poet enacts and transforms in Late Antiquity.⁶⁹ We may even argue that the cento's deliberate and repeated quotation of Vergil, when its governing theme is from Ovid, alongside its refusal to refer directly to Ovid's Narcissus while circling this text knowingly, is a brilliant reflection on the Narcissus theme. The boy's love is for another person in the pool—one who is himself but whom he does not see as such. The poem's love is for Ovid's theme, but it fails consistently to find the specific words Ovid finds for that theme and instead uses Vergil's words (as all centos do, of course), which inevitably fail to realize the Ovidian goal.

A powerful example of this is the cento's cyclical structure revolving around quotations from the opening of *Eclogue* 2 (at vv. 2 and 16). In the Vergilian poem (*ecl.* 2.25–7), Corydon—aflame for Alexis—looks into the still waters of

---

64. See Hardie 2002: 179–81 on this passage ("Astyages as the Narcissistic viewer") with 145–46 in relation to Narcissus; Rimell 2006: 61–2 and her more general reflections on Narcissus and Medusa at 1–40; von Glinsky 2012: 36–7.

65. For further narrative and verbal echoes of Ovid's Narcissus, see Okáčová 2009b: 183–5 and Galli 2014: 14–15.

66. Generally, see Janan 2009: 174–9.

67. See Hardie 2002: 146 and Glinsky 2012: 120–1.

68. See Hardie 2002: 148.

69. For shifts between Vergilian and Ovidian resonances in Ausonius's cento-like poem *Cupido Cruciatus*, see Rees 2011b: 146–9.

the sea to judge that he is not unsightly (*informis*), "unless my image deceive me" (*si numquam fallit imago, ecl.* 2.27). The entire idea is of course central to Ovid's Narcissus, with the Vergilian phrase used in the key passage where Ovid's Narcissus (by deep contrast with the cento's hero) is clearly aware that he is himself the boy in the pool:

> *Iste ego sum! sensi, nec me mea fallit imago.*
> *uror amore mei . . . met.* 3. 463–4.
>
> Oh I am he! I have felt it, and my own image does not deceive me.
> I burn with love for myself . . .

The centonist quotes the Vergilian poem, knowing—one presumes—precisely how it related to Ovid's Narcissus, and deliberately fails to quote the passage that would unambiguously establish the link—missing the Ovidian goal but at the same time tentatively alluding to it in Vergilian terms.

5.2.5. *The Transformation of Vergil*

The cento is overwhelmingly a poem that mines the *Aeneid*. But it deliberately refers to both the *Eclogues* and the *Georgics* as part of its ring-compositional structure and it insists (by contrast with the basic setting of the *Aeneid*) on a pastoral frame. Notably this is evoked by the references to the opening of *Eclogue* 2 at v. 2, by the *fontes sacros* of *ecl.* 1.52 at v. 3, and by the divine gifts of honey from the opening of *geo.* 4 at v. 2. Pastoral is key to Ovid's *Metamorphoses* (it is one of the major differences between *Metamorphoses* as an epic poem and the *Aeneid*),[70] and in reframing the poetics of war and heroic love borrowed from the *Aeneid* within a landscape of woods and water, the centonist conducts an Ovidianization of his source (in conformity with his Ovidian theme).

More potent still, in terms of the religious dynamics governing Vergil and their reflection in a late antique Christian cultural context, is the opening half line of the poem, *candida per siluam*. Of course, this is a smooth insistence on the pastoral theme. But it is also a quotation of *Aen.* 8.82, where the white sow—a miraculous portent (*mirabile monstrum*, 8.81)—appears to Aeneas and which he sacrifices to Juno with all her young (8.81–5). The monstrous aspect—not quoted by the poet but within his web of allusion—is a good commentary on the Narcissus theme, while the act of sacrifice conducted on the sow is yet another doleful portrait of the protagonist's fate. But the theme of the sow is reiterated at v. 14 of the cento in the closing half line *secreti ad fluminis undam*, which is lifted

---

70. See Segal 1969.

from Phoebus's prophecy, through Helenus's lips at *Aen.* 3.374–462. At *Aen.* 3.389, "by the waters of a secluded stream" the white sow and her litter of thirty piglets are foretold as the sign for the site of Aeneas's new city.[71] Arguably, this double reference to sacrificial pigs itself evokes the pigs sacrificed on the shield of Aeneas (to make the treaty between the Romans and the Sabines, 8.639–41) and the treaty between Aeneas and Latinus at 12.169–215, passages not themselves cited in the cento but close to lines culled (8.730 and 12.275). One might wonder at the double reference to the sacrifice—both the foundation of ancient Rome in its classic literary mythology and the aspect of the past most insistently left in the past by the new Christian appropriation of the Roman world. Even as the centonist evokes Antiquity through the brilliant, targeted spoliation of his erudite classicism, so he leaves the past—Narcissus, Vergil, Ovid, and all—in the pool of mirroring memories, a *mirabile monstrum* and a receding ghost of images, which one can no longer fully grasp.

5.2.6. African Politics

We may presume most of the centos of the Codex Salmasianus were composed in Vandal North Africa. This is not the case, however, for at least one of them—Hosidius Geta's *Medea*, of the late second or early third century AD. Whether the Narcissus cento was itself first created in the Vandal kingdom, certainly in an elite milieu and very likely for the court, or was only selected for anthologization there, it is well suited to its context of reception in Africa. Beneath the poem's mythological surface, there lurks a panegyric of Africanism as constituted from the conscious choice to cull many of the poem's lines from earlier passages about Africa. As we have seen vv. 3, 4, 5, 7, 11, and 14, all borrow from the narrative of Dido, with lines 3, 4, 5, and 7 all set in the Vandal capital of Carthage as envisaged during its founding moment. To these lines we may add a series of Vergilian quotations from the *Punica* of Silius Italicus, the other great African epic poem in the Latin tradition. At v. 1, *primaeuo flore iuuentus* evokes *primaeuo flore iuuentae* at *Punica* 1.376, which is a description of the heroic Murrus, who kills many Carthaginians, challenges Hannibal, and is eventually slain at 1.515–21 in the first great *aristeia* of the poem during the siege of Saguntum. The verse not only echoes the Vergilian poetics of youths doomed to perish in battle but recalibrates the theme as one of African triumph. At v. 2, *caelestia dona* quotes the account of Synhalus the healer, son of Ammon, "famed through the cities and shores of African (Paraetoniae) Syrtis," from *Punica*

---

71. On the relation of the prophecy at *Aen* 3.389–93 to its enactment in book 8, see N. Horsfall, *Vergil, Aeneid 3. A Commentary*, Leiden, 2006, xxxiii–iv and 296 ad. loc.

5.360, who cures Hannibal's brother, Mago. At v. 5, *uoluens oculos* evokes Dido among other Vergilian referents but also two moments in Silius—when Syphax, King of Massylia, welcomes the rival generals Hasdrubal and Scipio to his court at 16.189 and when Hannibal gazes at the sea storm at 17.259. Finally, v. 13, *ad fluminis undas* occurs at *Punica* 13.66, in the account given to Hannibal by Dasius of how Diomedes met Aeneas by the Tiber and returned the Palladium to the Trojans, an elegant evocation of the original poem from which all the cento's lines are borrowed through a secondary reference.

This means that out of sixteen lines, nine—more than half and including the first five—have an African resonance in their earlier usages. That set of associations need not be noticed by a reader (and has not been by any modern commentator), but it remains open to any learned member of the Vandal elite to appreciate. The cento's Africanism has a double purpose. It is an implicitly encomiastic celebration of the place of the Vandal kingdom as an apogee of the deep African tradition of Roman culture and Latin literary life. But it also offers potential subversion of the normative narrative of Roman triumph over Carthage (whether mythologized as Aeneas's escape from Dido or historicized as the epic version of Scipio's defeat of Hannibal) by emphasizing the vibrant Latin culture of the new Carthage, the Vandal capital after 439.[72] It is worth noting that the Vandals considered their realm a kingdom only from the date of the capture of Carthage and its establishment as their capital.[73] It was from Carthage that the job Hannibal never accomplished was finally achieved in 455, when the Vandal king Geiseric sacked Rome.[74] The cento in its Vandal context of reception appropriates the poetics of Roman defeat of the Carthaginians, as presented in the classic literary works of Vergil and Silius, and spins them into a mythological meditation whose backdrop, as understood in Africa, would have been contemporary Carthaginian triumph over Rome (a story at any rate sustainable until 533 when Justinian's armies under Belisarius reconquered the Vandal kingdom for Byzantium).

5.2.7. The Late Antique Poetic Context

Before turning to some broader cultural observations, it is worth placing the Narcissus cento in its late antique poetic context. The poem appears as one of a collection of Vergilian centos, selected and compiled together at what is now the opening of the Codex Salmasianus.[75] The beginning of the codex is missing

---

72. On Vandal Carthage, see Bockmann 2013: 23–129.
73. See Conant 2012: 20–1.
74. On the sack of Rome and the "Fourth Punic War," see Merrills and Miles 2010: 116–24.
75. The group is published by Riese 1894:, nos. 7–18, 33–82.

(and may have included other centos, as well as other poems). The first two surviving centos are on "everyday life" topics, perhaps with parodic intent—the end of a poem on bread making (*de paneficiis*, AL 7R) and an obscure piece on dice and dice players (*de alea*, AL 8R).[76] Then there is the mythological series, opening with Narcissus (AL 9R), followed by the *Judgement of Paris* by Mavortius (AL 10R), *Hippodamia* (AL 11R), *Hercules and Antaeus* (AL 12R), *Progne and Philomela* (AL 13R), *Europa* (AL 14R), and *Alcesta* (AL 15R). Most of these—functioning like specific mythological snapshots within a broader tapestry of cultural antiquarianism (parallel to what we find on mosaic floors or on cloth)[77]—are short, except for *Hippodamia* and *Alcesta*, which are both 162 lines.[78] These are succeeded by a Christian cento, *de ecclesia* (AL 16R), the only Christian example in the *Latin Anthology* (although others survive), followed by Hosidius Geta's third-century dramatic cento on Medea (AL 17R),[79] and finally the *epithalamium Fridi*,[80] a marriage poem by Luxorius—probably a Vandal poet of the late fifth or early sixth century, whose book of epigrams is separately anthologized as a whole in the Codex Salmasianus as poems 282–370 SB. That is, a formal logic about the type of poem (a Vergilian cento) governs the choice for the grouping of pieces on disparate themes in which the Narcissus poem sits as a largely non-narrative mythological work at the head of a sequence of other centos on mythological themes in a total collection that includes marital-honorific, parodic, tragic, and Christian material. But a number of these poems, from Narcissus, via the *Judgement of Paris, Progne and Philomela*, and *Europa*, to the climax of the *epithalamium Fridi* (vv. 61–6), have strongly erotic and even explicit sexual content.

Within Codex Salmasianus, there are seven other poems (all short epigrams) on the subject of Narcissus.[81] Two (AL 26 SB and 210 SB) are isolated, but the others (AL 134–6 SB and 259–60 SB) are grouped in larger mythological sequences within what may well be prior collections of poems subsequently included in the codex.[82] The phenomenon of a Narcissus sequence within a mythological

---

76. See McGill 2005: 53–70. Note that dice are the subject of a number of late antique texts—Agathias's poem on the table game of the emperor Zeno (*anth. Pal.* 9.482), Sidonius's letter to Trygetus (*ep.* 8.12.5), and some aphorisms from Codex Vossianus in Riese 1870: nos. 496, 503, 504, with Purcell 2004: 197–8, 204. Dice are also a favourite theme of Hellenistic epigram, with Goldhill 1994: 199–204.

77. E.g., on the second- to third-century AD mosaic floor at Orbe, see von Gonzenbach 1961: 184–92.

78. For some discussion of the mythological centos, see McGill 2005: 71–91, although he does not follow the order of the codex, and Okáčová 2010.

79. See McGill 2005: 31–52 and Hardie 2007: 169–76.

80. For some discussion, see McGill 2005: 98–114 and Ehrling 2011.

81. See McGill 2005: 73.

82. Notably, AL 78–188 SB have been suggested to be a collection by a single author, perhaps writing in the early sixth century; see Kay 2006: 1–7.

farrago is apparent also in Ausonius's epigrams (nos. 108–110), which are grouped together in the manuscript tradition.[83] In two of these three epigrammatic groupings of late antique Latin verse, the Narcissus poems—like the cento—are placed alongside other (and arguably thematically related) mainly mythological topics. In Ausonius, for instance, the Narcissus poems follow two on Hylas (nos. 106–7) and precede two on Hermaphroditus (111–12)—a group that mixes themes of love and death by water (Hylas, Narcissus) with issues of sexuality and sexual indeterminacy. In the anonymous collection within Codex Salmasianus (poems AL 78–188 SB), the three Narcissus poems (AL 134-6 SB) sit between quite explicit sexual accounts of Leda (AL 129–31 SB) and Europa (AL 132-3 SB) and the strikingly obscene pair on the lawyer Filager and his act of sex with a horse (AL 137–8). All this is to say that in its late Roman context, the cento was anthologized to sit within a sequence whose workings can be paralleled by other poetic collections, several closely connected by being preserved in the same codex. Of course, the cento's intertextual and allusive powers are far greater than anything in the Narcissus epigrams, but its positioning and presentation belong firmly in its era.

In thematic terms, several of the epigrams in the Codex Salmasianus (AL 134 SB, 135 SB and 210 SB) emphasize the fire/water dynamic, which is part of the cento's argument.[84] Two epigrams (AL 26 SB and AL 259 SB, by Pentadius) impose a strong cyclic structure, where the opening of the hexameter uses the same words as the close of the pentameter.[85] This circular poetics for modelling the representation of Narcissus mirrored by his image in the pool is paralleled by the circular structure of the cento in using both the *Eclogues* and the *Georgics* for its ring composition. Moreover, like the cento, there is a ludic element to this kind of composition where the poem self-consciously advertises its manner of construction.[86] The epigrams in general (in part because of their elegiac form) do not quote Vergil particularly nor offer larger developments of the subject than brief reflections on such themes as reflection (e.g., AL 134 SB, 136 SB, Ausonius 109) and solitude (AL 26 SB, 135 SB, Ausonius 108). Insofar as there is a riddling element in the aesthetics of the cento, challenging readers to remember which lines relate to which bits of Vergil, the Narcissus cento may resonate with the collection of *aenigmata* (or riddle poems) in the Codex Salmasianus, attributed to Symphosius and probably dated to the late fourth or fifth century, of which one is on the theme of a mirror and another on Echo.[87] In any case, one

---

83. See Kay 2001: 32 for sequences in the MSS.
84. See McGill 2005: 78 and Okáčová 2009b: 185.
85. These are *uersus serpentini*; see McGill 2005: 73–4 for parallels with the centos.
86. See McGill 2005: 74.
87. These are AL 286R nos. 69 and 98 = AL 281SB, nos. 69 and 98. For some discussion, see Leary 2014.

may surmise that the cento, especially in its sixth-century placement within the florilegium of the *Latin Anthology*, was meant to resonate against these poems (and these poems in their contexts) as well as to relate intertextually to the works of Vergil and Ovid.

5.3. The Poetics of Classicism

I hope I have shown that, however awkward the stitching of the Narcissus cento may appear to modern readers, it is very carefully culled from a series of well-chosen Vergilian sources that make for a complex play between the sixth-century poem and its many pasts.[88] Ovid's story is retold through the lines of Vergil, and very particular themes within Vergil's texts are highlighted. The cento's Narcissus is entirely the product of Vergil's words (implicitly of the canonical centre of the great Latin tradition) but through the prism of an Ovidian topic. What the Narcissus created by the cento *sees*—what makes him burn (vv. 7 and 13), the ghostly figure whose neck he three times tries to embrace (vv. 15–16) but can never grasp—is likewise entirely the product of Vergil's words refracted through Ovid's story (and sometimes humorously evoking other parts of Ovid's text, as in the two passages that come from discussion of Pygmalion). The cento's snapshot of a viewer frozen in self-desire and yet oblivious to the self for whom he yearns brilliantly captures a key predicament of late Roman culture (no less than Freud's cultural interpretation of narcissism captures a key problematic in modernity).

The cento's Narcissus is caught in a love affair with the canonical classics, which are nonetheless in a process of receding to a ghost-like embrace. While the cento's quotations from the *Aeneid* have its hero looking into his own past (*Aen*. 1. 453–95 in Dido's temple, at v. 6) and gazing with incomprehension at Rome's future and that of his own line (*Aen* 8.730, at the shield, v. 12), Narcissus gazes at the entire classical tradition refracted through the words of Vergil. The way to articulate art (the poem before us, the ancient theme of the dangers of viewing that this theme evokes), in the centonist's archetypally late antique form of writing, is through the words and the poetic forms of a canonical past. What Narcissus sees, in the eddying waters of his desire, is the classical tradition itself, shimmering uncertainly before him—cut up and reconfigured, ghostly, unachievable, a string of disparate poetic memories redolent of a string of untimely deaths, an ekphrasis of itself and never the real thing. The ripples

---

88. For a late antique parallel on the Greek side, see MacIver 2012: 39–86 on ekphrasis in Quintus Smyrnaeus and its engagement with the literary past.

of his pool are many: the poem's subject and predicament are the result of an Ovidian narrative that frames the spolia taken from Vergil and from later poets themselves appropriating Vergil. That spolia evokes Vergil's own borrowings, themselves already ghostly in his own work—from Homer (especially the ekphrasis of the Trojan war in *Aeneid* 1 at v. 6 of the cento, Andromache's lament for Astyanax at v. 9, the way Aeneas's attempts to grasp the phantoms of his father and wife evoke Odysseus in the Underworld at v. 16), from the tale of Daedalus (v. 16), from the myths of Aeneas's past (the ghosts of Creusa and Anchises at vv. 15–16) and from what is—in the cento's perspective—the myth-history of Rome's past (Anchises's prophesy of Marcellus at v. 8, the prophetic imagery of the shield at v. 12). And they ramify further in the citations to and borrowings from Vergil in the Roman epic tradition of such as Ovid, Valerius Flaccus, and Silius Italicus.[89] Yet the cento, in its miniature form and epigram-like scope, is a boiling down of this great and almost wholly epic tradition *in nuce*. The canonical past—present in the poem as whole segments of Vergil disparately gathered and juxtaposed—is something quite different from this bricolage of its remaking.

The cento's emphasis on specifically ekphrastic passages from the *Aeneid* stresses the construction of the beloved as an art object[90] and via these allusions brings the reader as viewer of this construct into the conversation. Narcissus not only evokes the author of the cento, staring at the elusive past that looks much the same (textually) as his own writing (with only the arrangement of his lines different from Vergil), but also its readers in staring at a self-conscious artefact. In doing so, in collapsing author and reader as figures mesmerized by the image of one himself mesmerized by his own image, all fashioned in the words of Vergil through the narrative of Ovid, the centonist offers a wonderfully suggestive picture of the predicament of late Roman classicism and the place of elite learning in fifth- and sixth-century North Africa. But we may also ask if there is potential for a form of perhaps Christian distantiating subversion of the tradition—for instance, in the recasting of the gaze of Aeneas and indeed the evocation of Augustan history (in the references to Marcellus from *Aen.* 6 at v. 8 and to the shield of Aeneas in v. 12) as homoerotic self-absorption. The Christian theme—never explicit in the poem—is only present if the reader wishes to introduce it. But one is reminded of Paulinus of Nola's riff on Vergil's

---

89. So, e.g., v. 1 *primaeuo flore iuuentus* almost quotes at Silius Italicus, *Punica*, 1.376; v. 2 *caelestia dona* appears at Manilius 5.21, Ovid, *met.* 13.289, Silius Italicus 5.360; v. 5 *uoluens oculos* (in addition to its range of Vergilian uses) reflects Silius 16.189 and 17.259; v. 6 *dum stupet* occurs at Ovid, *met.* 5.205 and 10.287, as well as Valerius Flaccus, *Argonautica*, 5.96; v. 13 *ad fluminis undas* evokes Silius 13.66.

90. A key theme in its own right in Roman literary culture; see Bettini 1999.

pascit pictura inani (*Aen.* 1.464, Narcissus cento v. 6), when he presents a viewer craning his neck to look at Christian images in a portico (itself surely a play on Aeneas at Dido's temple) looking on the empty figures but feeding his mind on them since they are not empty to him.[91]

In part the relationship of the centonist's Narcissus with his Vergilian sources is one of typology. Just as the arch of Constantine uses the sculptures—indeed, the imperial bodies—of a number of Constantine's major predecessors (Trajan, Hadrian, Marcus Aurelius) into which to place the persona of Constantine (through his portrait, replacing that of his predecessors), so the cento uses the bodies of some very specific Vergilian themes into which and against which to confect Narcissus. The cento's theme and hero are feminized through the repeated use of Dido, whose feelings and emotions Narcissus feels (vv. 3, 4, 5, 7). He is created through the repeated descriptions of doomed youths from the *Aeneid*'s long litany of death (vv. 4, 5, 8, 15). His dilemma is homosexualized in its evocations of the Second Eclogue and the Nisus and Euryalus episode from the *Aeneid* (vv. 2, 10, 16). His act of viewing as love is conceived through a range of Vergilian ekphrases, as if his narrative was one of being beguiled by art (vv. 6, 12, 16). Most powerfully, perhaps, in this catalogue of types against which the cento's Narcissus is constructed, is the brilliant theme of ghost-like figures inadequately grasped. The three attempts to catch hold of the image in the pool at v. 15 reflect three such moments of failure in Vergil—Aeneas's inability to embrace Creusa and Anchises, as well as Daedalus's failure to fashion the image of Icarus for grief. That triple failure plays against the tripartite articulation of *sic* at v. 9, itself a sparagmos of part objects (eyes, hands, face) that evoke the spectre of the dead Astyanax, who is so exactly like Ascanius—out of whom both Narcissus and his beloved reflection have been formed.

These different Vergilian themes form a plethora of types against which the cento's Narcissus is measured and out of whom he is constructed. Normally, we understand typology in Late Antiquity as the model by which Old Testament themes are made to prefigure those from the Gospels in both art and exegesis in the early Christian period.[92] But in the cento, as on the arch of Constantine, the images of the present—the poem of Narcissus, the various representations of Constantine in action—are effectively culled from and so implicitly mapped against specific texts from chosen sections of Vergil or reliefs that depicted a series of lauded earlier emperors. The typological potential is rife, although it is

---

91. Paulinus, *Carmen* 27.511-5, esp.:
    Qui uidet haec uacuis agnoscens uera figuris
    non uacua fidam sibi pascit imagine mentem.
92. For a summary and bibliography, see, e.g., Malbon 1990: 127-53 and Tkacz 2002: 51-62.

not in any sense Christian in these cases, and the earlier model always resonates as an intertextual or material commentary on its current reappropriation.[93] In the cento form in general this is rich territory for irony and humour but also for a contemporary cultural claim that embeds modernity in the ancient Graeco-Roman (as opposed to Old Testament) past—something with ideological potency, especially in the Christian centos both Homeric and Vergilian. In the Narcissus poem, the typological selections are, as we have seen, not only strongly enriching but also potentially exegetic, even subversive, as well as being virtuosically learned and well chosen. Above all, the passivity and frozen pastoral setting of Narcissus in the Vandal present is in stark contrast with the heroic action of Rome's glorious epic past out of which he is fashioned.

At stake in the Narcissus poem are fundamental issues in the poetics of the cento as a form. Identity (the identity of passages of Vergil with lines in the Narcissus cento) is anything but resemblance, since the poem resembles Ovid more than Vergil (and arguably neither), just as Narcissus—although he and his image may be identical (through quotation) to Astyanax and Ascanius—does not resemble these epic heroes in any way at all. To formulate this topic—a profound theme for a world that claimed both to be the Roman past and to be constitutively different from that past (especially in respect of Christianity)—in a cento devoted to the theme of Narcissus is a spectacular means of focusing issues of the confusion of identity and resemblance, alterity and mimesis, in a superbly self-reflective and critically targeted interpretative act. It is a meditation not only on the poetics of the cento quite as thoughtful as Ausonius's introduction to his *cento nuptialis* but much more broadly an interrogation of the predicament of late Roman culture in relation to its past.

As we have seen, in his introduction to the *cento nuptialis*, Ausonius compared the process of cento writing to the puzzle of *ostomachia*. The ludic aspect of poems as games is deep in his corpus (one thinks of the *technopaegnion* or the *griphus* on the number three)[94] and is perhaps a significant aspect of the way late antique Latin verse attempts both to stand on the shoulders of the past and proffer a (surely ironic) disclaimer about how little invested it is in matching the heights of the canon. The cento is a fundamentally (although, I have attempted to argue, a seriously) playful medium,[95] and the ways it relates to what it reworks has similarities to, for instance, the pictorial poems composed by Optatian

---

93. For discussion of this in respect of the arch of Constantine, see Malbon 1990: 150–2 and Elsner 2000: 169–75.

94. Green 1991: nos. 15 and 25.

95. For an overview of the tradition of Latin *technopaegnia*, or playful verses, including centos, see Alvar Ezquerra 2011: 243 on Palladius's Narcissus verse (AL 259 SB) and 246–50 on centos.

Porfyry in the fourth century⁹⁶ and—deeply within the tradition of short poems like the Narcissus cento—to the kinds of riddle poems found in book 14 of the Palatine anthology,⁹⁷ the Hellenistic calligrams,⁹⁸ and the kinds of magic squares found on the backs of the *Tabulae Iliacae*, which were made in Rome in the early Imperial period,⁹⁹ let alone the kinds of play the obverses of these objects make between epic text and pictorial cycle.¹⁰⁰ That is, all the cento's complex artifices of scale, quotation, fragmentation, recombination with varieties of allusion and reference in play, are about as deep and committed a statement of continuity within the tradition and its methods as could be made.

While the mythical theme of the Narcissus cento preserves the fiction of an Antiquity untouched by Christianity and avoids the games of bathos at play in the centos on dicing, bread making and sexual intercourse, the choice to focalize the problem of the canon—which one can cull, or quote, or emulate but never surpass—through the topic of Narcissus, is acute. The issue is whether the great texts of Antiquity can be in dialogue with the late antique world of sixth-century Christian Africa in the way one might fantasize that Vergil "spoke" with Homer or Ovid with Vergil or whether the late antique world must always gaze through a Christian prism, a pool made of ghosts, phantoms, and pale reflections whose repeated subtext signals doom. The question becomes how to translate the *iuuentus* of v. 1 and the *iuuenta* of v. 11. Are they references to a single youth by a pool, in love with his own image, or to the youthfulness of modernity as it gazes fascinated into the ramifications of a canon it knows so well yet cannot escape, a set of epics it loves so deeply yet transforms to near-parodic miniature, a classical grandeur it can quote, recapitulate and reconstitute but can never access? The very ubiquity of spoliation in the more significant buildings, monuments, and composite artworks of Late Antiquity—from before the arch of Constantine but most perfectly epitomized by that monument for the first Christian emperor—speaks to the relevance and acuity of the cultural commentary on classicism written into the cento. The Narcissus cento is effectively a complex take from within Late Antiquity on the (much-discussed critical) question of whether spoliation is a form of backwards-looking classicism or an innovative act of appropriation that constructs a modern aesthetic.¹⁰¹ It is noncommittal in its response to this issue but rather suggests an impasse of

---

96. See, e.g., Hernández Lobato 2012: 307–11, 471–9, Pelttari 2014: 75–84, Squire 2015a—and, above all, Squire's contribution to this volume (with further bibliography).
97. For some discussion of such puzzle poems, see Goldhill 1994.
98. E.g., *anth. Pal.* 15.21–2 and 24–7, with Squire 2011: 231–5 with bibliography.
99. See Squire 2011: 197–246, 305–10.
100. E.g., Squire 2011: 127–196 and 303–70.
101. For a summary of the issues with rich bibliography, see Bosman 2013: 72–4 and 77–8.

Narcissus-like introspection and a nostalgia that comes close to mourning in its thinking on the present's access to the past.[102]

I began with reference to Freud, one of the great adherents of the classical tradition in the German-speaking world, and the narcissism of culture. Let me end, at the beginning of that German tradition of the reception of Antiquity, with Winckelmann. Winckelmann famously concludes his great *History of the Art of Antiquity* with the image of a maiden on the seashore following with tearful eyes her departing sweetheart, with no hope of seeing him again.[103] That feminized image of modernity's relations with an Antiquity, which is "only a shadowy outline of the subject of our desires" draws on the great theme of Ariadne looking out at Theseus as he sails away, so potent in both ancient art and text.[104] The cento, one of the early and great products of a post-antique nostalgic classicism—so much closer to the world that it mourns than either Winckelmann or Freud, yet already so close to them and to modernity in its nexus of desire, distance, nostalgia, and mourning for the classics—chooses Narcissus as its theme of spellbound immersion yet failure to access the thrice-grasped phantom. The wonder of late antique Latin poetics, in the cento's vision, is that it is already fully modern in its relations to the classics. That is perhaps why this poetics has so frequently been unfairly condemned.

---

102. In other words, I suspect that late antique literature is more ambivalent about its innovations than some of the positive claims made for it in recent discussions—see, e.g., Formisano 2007: 282–4.
103. Winckelmann 2006: 351.
104. See, e.g., Elsner 2007: 67–77, 88–109.

PART III

Programmatic Reflections

A Metaliterary Twist

6

Displacing Tradition

A New-Allegorical Reading of Ausonius, Claudian, and Rutilius Namatianus

MARCO FORMISANO

In this chapter I argue that three of the best known and most studied texts from late Latin literature—Ausonius's *Mosella*, Claudian's *De raptu Proserpinae* and Rutilius Namatianus's *De reditu suo*—exemplify a typical late antique literary feature that in the context of the general critical enthusiasm for this period over the past decades has largely escaped notice. It is my suggestion that, rather than display the absolute veneration of tradition which scholars tend to attribute to late Latin texts, these poems pervasively thematize the relationship to the literary tradition precisely by undermining it, and I describe a way of interpreting these texts that complements but differs from the intertextual mode that has understandably (and profitably) dominated studies of late antique literature. In particular, I describe a common thread in these texts (and by no means only these texts), detectable at the level of both content and language: the theme of *displacement*. I suggest that displacement invites an allegorical reading, allegoresis itself being a typically late antique hermeneutic strategy, both in classical pagan and in Christian texts. In particular, I argue that an allegorical reading of displacement in these texts points to the theme of departure from a distant and absent classical tradition, which turns out to be no longer attainable. The most obvious historical factor in the textual displacement I describe is the radical cultural and above all textual shift produced by Christianity and its novel hermeneutic approaches, among which allegory and allegoresis play a prominent role.

The identification of a specifically literary aesthetic of Late Antiquity is the merit of Michael Roberts, who in a series of articles and above all in his monograph *The Jeweled Style* (1989a, repr. 2010) was able to define some characteristic traits. "Taste has changed," Roberts writes. "In order to appreciate late antique poetry properly, it is necessary to view it *on its own terms* rather than from the perspective, conscious or not, of classical aesthetics" (Roberts 2010: 3; my italics). As is well known, Roberts describes as the main mark of late Latin texts a tendency to fragmentation: in the case of Ammianus's, Claudian's, and Rutilius's narrative techniques, for example, he observes their "episodic nature," showing how their texts are made up "of a series of self-contained vignettes, which derive their unity from a principle which operates at a higher level of abstraction than the literal level of the narrative" (Roberts 1988: 187). This approach has the great merit of encouraging or insisting on readings of late antique texts in their specificity rather than under the aegis of the classical canon. Yet as often happens, while Roberts's work has become a standard reference point, regularly cited and quoted, it is often simply accepted as dogma and not discussed any further, and Roberts's monograph itself does not explore all of the methodological and theoretical implications it raises. While current critical trends in the study of late Latin poetry rightly acknowledge the importance of Roberts's statements on the aesthetical otherness of late antique literature, they generally continue to use precisely the hermeneutic tools which have been so successful for the interpretation of classical Latin poetry: those of allusion and intertextuality. The paradoxical result is that precisely the otherness of late Latin poetry which is emphasized by Roberts is frequently neutralized. Similarly, the insistence on the fact that Christian and pagan authors share one and the same literary language deriving from the classical tradition is a refrain in scholarship,[1] and while there is obviously truth to this assertion, an overemphasis on it has also had the effect of normalizing the otherness of late antique textuality.

A number of questions suggest themselves. Are Roberts's observations on the episodic nature the only common or salient characteristic of late antique texts? To what extent can readings of the "jewelled style" be combined with intertextual hermeneutic practices? Are intertextuality and allusion universal instruments suited for the interpretation of any text written in any age (particularly on the understanding of the concept of "intertextuality" as described by Bakhtin and Kristeva) or are they more specifically suited to certain kinds of texts, such as canonical Latin poetry, whose authors overtly and systematically adopt intertextual and allusive modes?[2] Is this also true of late antique texts? What would it mean to read any ancient text "on its own terms"? How might we reconcile this goal with an awareness of the unavoidable alterity of our own critical position as modern readers and interpreters?[3]

On the assumption that it is possible to look at late antique texts "on their own terms," my central question is what might happen if we were also to activate some other hermeneutic strategies that are characteristic of the late antique literary aesthetic: in particular, the discourse of allegory; that is, not only allegory

---

1. Cameron 2011 represents the summa of this tendency.
2. For one answer to this question, see Kaufmann in this volume.
3. As Martindale 1993: 3 memorably puts it, "the meaning is always realized at the point of reception."

as hermeneutic instrument but the entire background that made allegory a cultural mark of Late Antiquity. As Jesús Hernández Lobato has recently pointed out, allegorical readings of the Bible and of classical pagan texts generated an "authentic semiotic explosion" in Late Antiquity,[4] yet the very practice of allegorical reading has been progressively marginalized within Western literary criticism because, in a word, it is not "scientific" enough.[5] Allegory—and allegoresis—in fact had a powerful impact in Late Antiquity, not only at the level of learned circles of literati but more widely within culture and society. David Dawson (1992: 2) very clearly shows that late antique debates about allegorical reading "stemmed from efforts by readers to secure for themselves and their communities social and cultural identity, authority, and power." What is relevant for the kind of discussion I would like to develop in this chapter is that allegorical interpretation can be seen as a strategy that aims to subvert an established meaning, which in most cases is the literal meaning of a given text. Moreover, allegorical reading is a search for the "true" meaning of the text, a meaning that, quite paradoxically perhaps, is not located within the text itself and yet is tightly connected with the literal meaning as it appears in the text. For allegorical reading accompanies, revises, or displays literal meaning (Dawson 1992: 7). As the etymology suggests, "'to say other' implies an antithetical stance towards a previous 'saying'" (Dawson 1992: 8), so allegorical reading ends up being a hermeneutic practice based on resistance to and denial of previously asserted and established meanings. As Robert Lamberton points out, behind allegory is another way of conceiving of texts, and its ancient and late ancient usage is much broader and more complex than its strict rhetorical meaning (Lamberton 1986: 20). What is striking about allegory is its intrinsic contradictory quality and its capacity of reversing textual meanings. This aspect very clearly emerges in the reading of Homer by one of the most active Christian allegorical readers, Clement of Alexandria, who "saw in Homer an authoritative theological source for an inimical tradition who might be turned against that tradition and mustered to the new cause" (Lamberton 1986: 80). The broader valence of allegory has more recently been rediscovered, and deconstruction, by generalizing and amplifying the original meaning of allegory, sees in it the most evident proof for the absence of meaning that every text, qua text, represents. Typically, Paul de Man, in his influential essay "The Rhetoric of Temporality" (1969), discusses allegory as the complete loss of any extratextual referent,[6] and in *Allegories of*

---

   4. Hernández Lobato 2012: 105 (see the paragraph entitled "Consecuencias hermenéuticas: el triunfo alterizador de la alegoría," 103–6).
   5. On the history of resistance to allegory, see Whitman 2003.
   6. The essay is contained in de Man 1983. See also Tambling 2010: 130.

Reading (1979) he shows that allegory and reading coincide, so every text is allegorical, no matter whether explicitly or implicitly, since it can never refer to itself without allegorizing its own meaning. Within the short space of this chapter it is not possible to discuss the long history of such an important concept.[7] At this stage, however, it is important to note in advance that I do not intend to launch an allegorical interpretation of the texts I discuss. By referring to allegory I would like to insist on the emergence of a different textuality, which in my opinion characterizes the literary universe of Late Antiquity but, for various reasons, struggles to be fully recognized. For not only is allegory a hermeneutic technique, but also, and more importantly, it represents the most innovative aspect of late antique literature and culture, which adopts it as a striking instrument which, by means of reinterpreting past traditions, eventually ends up resisting or denying them.

Scholarship on Ausonius's *Mosella*, Claudian's *De raptu Proserpinae*, and Rutilius Namatianus's *De reditu suo* has frequently been concerned with questions of genre: Claudian's text can be uncontroversially classified as epic poetry, but there has been no universal agreement on how to generically classify the *Mosella* and *De reditu suo*. The first has been described as a sort of hymn to the river, the latter as a narration of a journey (*Reisegedicht*) or a *nostos*, that is, a return home, but both present many points of contact with other genres; and in any case the attribution to a specific genre is, as so often, less a quality of the texts themselves than a scholarly preoccupation. Otherwise, much of the scholarship has concentrated on external circumstances of composition: for Claudian's *De raptu* there is the notorious problem of the date, on which the text itself gives contradictory indications,[8] while in the case of the *Mosella* and *De reditu* there has been much interest in determining whether Ausonius and Rutilius really visited the places they describe and to what extent their texts are trustworthy for historical reconstruction. Scholars more interested in literary questions have above all been preoccupied with identifying and describing the influence of classical authors such as Ovid, Vergil, Horace, and Statius. In the following pages I take a different approach, unabashedly leaving aside both historical aspects and intertextual and allusive references, not because I consider them

---

7. For allegory within Neoplatonism, see Lamberton 1986 and Struck 2010. Markus 1996 discusses the role of allegory in the hermeneutic work of Augustine. The impressive book by Dawson (1992) focuses on the use of allegory by pagan, Jewish, and Christian interpreters in Late Antiquity, but it also offers a very broad discussion of the concept both in Antiquity and within modern literary criticism.

8. For a compact overview of the debate around the date of composition of *De raptu Proserpinae*, see Felgentreu 1999: 157–60.

unimportant or irrelevant to interpretation (on the contrary), but because this will allow me in the short space of this chapter to analyse in closer detail some of the themes and motifs of the texts which often end up being overshadowed. In particular, I focus on a macrotheme which is in my opinion relevant for each of the three texts and at the same time opens the way to a new interpretation.

As I will show, this approach is aimed at shedding light on some aspects which can be considered both text-immanent (i.e., in which meaning is located within the text itself) and "allegorical" at the same time. For this reason I call this approach "new allegoresis." More specifically, the meaning of the text which I emphasize here is not (necessarily) the same as the literal meaning of the words but results from the combination and/or juxtaposition of words. Independently of the primary and logical function of the words in their own linear, logical context, a new and different meaning emerges, a meaning which is still located in the text but at another level. This other level may even be in contradiction with the logical meaning of the individual words within a given sentence or line. This meaning is not necessarily aligned either with the intentions of their author as expressed or implied in the texts themselves or with the historical circumstances of the text's composition.[9] It is precisely the manifestation of this *other* meaning that I call "new allegoresis." A similar approach to the text is theorized by Roland Barthes in S/Z, where he pleads for a kind of analysis which dismembers the text in order to find a unity beyond the literal or "natural" meaning:

> The commentary, based on the affirmation of the plural, cannot therefore work with 'respect' to the text. The tutor text will ceaselessly be broken, interrupted without any regards for its natural divisions (syntactical, rhetorical, anecdotic). [...] The work of the commentary, once it is separated from any ideology of totality, consists precisely in *manhandling* the text, *interrupting* it. What is thereby denied is not the *quality* of the text (here incomparable) but its 'naturalness'. (Barthes 1974: 15)

A further theoretical input is offered by Michael Riffaterre in his treatment of syllepsis, which he describes as "the literary sign par excellence" (Riffaterre 1980: 638). Syllepsis is a rhetorical figure that refers to the simultaneous presence of two meanings within the same word: the first is produced by the context within which that word is situated, while the second is given precisely by the absent context, i.e. a potential context which can only be evoked in absentia. Riffaterre describes the first meaning as "contextual", the second as

---

9. Cf. Quilligan 1979: 46: "The 'other' named by the term *allos* in the word 'allegory' is not some other hovering above the words of the text, but the possibility of another, a polysemy, inherent in the very words on the page."

"intertextual"; the latter is "another meaning the word may possibly have, one of its dictionary meanings and/or one actualized within an intertext," and "this intertextual meaning is incompatible with the context and pointless within the text, but still operates as a second reference" (Riffaterre 1980: 638).

By "new" I do not want to emphasize the novelty of this approach. I wish rather to underline the connection with allegory as a method of reading and approach to textuality privileged in Late Antiquity. Moreover, I seek also to establish a more solid connection with reception theory, which generally emphasizes the role of the reader more than authorial intentions and historical contexts.[10] The term allegoresis draws attention to the possibility of later allegorical readings of a given text which might be written without any allegorical intentions.[11] Finally, a distinction is important: while the concepts of allegory and allegoresis are usually employed in order to detect a moralizing meaning mostly through personifications, the new allegoresis to which I refer here neither is conveyed through personifications of concepts nor bears a moral or religious meaning. Rather, according to deconstructive criticism, I use the term as a tool for analysing how a text thematizes within itself its own status as text.[12]

6.1. Displacement and Absence

As is well known, the theme of the voyage abundantly characterizes late antique literature. But this is far from being merely a superficial motif, since the language of travel often defines a conceptual constellation that indicates displacement, separation, and novelty.[13] All these aspects not only reflect the new geography of the Roman Empire, but more relevantly, they map out a design for a new textual discourse which originates precisely within the general climate of political and cultural destabilization of traditional spaces. As has been shown by Catherine Chin (2007: 101), for instance, Jerome in his correspondence with the Christian poet Paulinus of Nola draws "imaginative 'spaces,' containing landscapes that the reader could enter and explore by reading." The space traced by the church father is an imagined Christian landscape in which remote places and events are coexistent, and so both history and geography are reconfigured in an original way (Chin refers here to the Foucauldian concept of "heterotopia").

---

10. The work to read here is of course Martindale 1993.
11. Dawson 1992: 4 distinguishes in principle between a "compositional" and "interpretative" allegory, although this distinction in the discussion of the texts analysed in his work ends up being "an act of resistance against the radically revisionary consequences of an unfettered allegorical imagination."
12. See de Man 1979. For a good overview on allegory, see Tambling 2010, esp. chs. 5–7, and Copeland and Struck 2010.
13. See Soler 2005 and Squillante 2005.

Reconfiguration of traditional sites and spaces and the discovery of new ones is by no means a prerogative of Christian authors. In fact, as we will see, the poems discussed here also significantly thematize, though in different ways, displacement, separation, and novelty.

The macrotheme I explore in the three texts selected consists of two intertwined motifs: on the one hand the dialectic between centre and margins, that is, between centralization and distancing or displacement, and on the other hand the sense of absence informing the texts at several levels. In the *Mosella*, as has been already pointed out by Jacques Fontaine, readers find no conceptual centre: the text presents itself as a *flowing* poem, and exactly like a river it reproduces nothing but reflected images.[14] Claudian's poem focuses on the abduction of Proserpina and, as we will see, on a series of movements which indicate a distancing process and an abrupt break. In the *De reditu suo* the narrating voice of the travelling poet describes the separation from Rome, which represents both the conceptual and textual centre, in the terms I will shortly present. Thus in each of the three texts "absence" is thematized: the *Mosella* thematizes the absence of several things which can be only reflected in the water; *De raptu Proserpinae* thematizes both the absence of Ceres and of her daughter Proserpina; *De reditu suo* thematizes the absence from Rome.

6.2. MOSELLA

The short hexametric poem *Mosella* can be considered the most successful work of Ausonius. He composed it in 371, when he was an established member of Valentinian's court.[15] A universally agreed-upon generic definition for the poem has proved impossible: the poem has been read respectively as *hodoeporicon*, hymn, encomium, epyllion, and so on, but it has also been argued this poem refers to all these genres but does not belong to any of them (Scafoglio 1999: 267–9). This generic instability is in my opinion not only a formal characteristic; it radically substantiates the nature of the work, which, as we will see, both thematizes and destabilizes precisely the Latin poetic tradition. The theme of displacement characterizes the text at many levels, both thematically (the journey) and conceptually (absence of a centre, continuous references to other places). The subject matter itself, as revealed in the poem's title *Mosella*,

---

14. Fontaine 1977: 440 uses the adverb "fluvialement" in order to describe the poetic quality of the poem.
15. For this reason the poem has been interpreted in the past as a piece of political propaganda (see above all Marx 1931, Ternes 1970, Szelest 1997). More recently, scholars (e.g., Kenney 1984, Roberts 1984, Newlands 1988, Green 1989, Fuoco 1993, Scafoglio 2004, Taylor 2009) have given a more nuanced interpretation by driving more attention on the literary construction of the text.

transfers the reader's imagination to the borders of the Roman Empire by indicating a river well away from the Italian environment which represents the usual background in Latin poetry.

Precisely the transition to another geographical dimension, which at the same time symbolizes the passage to a different poetical dimension, is powerfully marked at the beginning:

Transieram celerem nebuloso flumine Nauam (1).[16]

The first word *transieram* ("I had crossed") describes an abrupt transition, emphasized by the verbal form of the pluperfect, rather unusual in poetry,[17] which represents the break as having already happened when the narrative begins. The abruptness is also underlined by *celerem*, referring to the river Nava, which is the first of the long list of rivers named by the poet. The opening contains many other aspects which will be developed later in the poem:

Addita miratus ueteri noua moenia Vinco,
aequauit Latias ubi quondam Gallia Cannas (2–3).[18]

Two features are relevant here. Firstly, *miratus* describes the admiring and stupefied gaze of the poet. More in general, the gaze and the visual quality of the *Mosella* represent a characteristic feature of the poem.[19] The expressions related to the semantic area of seeing/admiring punctuate the text. For instance, at line 51, *naturae mirabor opus*, *miror* again appears, and at line 55, *spectaris* and *uitreo profundo*, the river is observed through its crystal clear surface. At line 43 the river observes itself with admiration: *ipse tuos miraris recursus*. The nature described in the poem as well as the river itself are in general the object of the admired vision but also the sign of "the fallibility of appearances" (Roberts 2010: 62), one of the most recurrent motifs present throughout the poem. The contrasting juxtaposition *ueteri noua*[20] as well as *aequauit* creates a sense of synchronicity whereby past events and present time are put on the same level and two different

---

16. "I had crossed over swift-flowing Nava's cloudy stream." All translations of the *Mosella* are by Evelyn White 1988.
17. See Cavarzere 2003 ad loc. for the classical reminiscences.
18. "And (I had) gazed with awe upon the ramparts lately thrown round ancient Vincum, where Gaul once matched the Roman rout at Cannae."
19. As Fontaine 1977: 443 pointed out, "Kaléidoscope de 'visions,' cette Moselle poétique nous est bien présente, mais dans l'ordre d'une réalité *spectaculaire*." See also Green 1999, 458: "The visual impact of the river and its gorge is obviously the poet's principal concern." Fuoco 1993 thematizes the vision as the key concept of the poem (see in particular 330).
20. See also 208: *excludit ueteres noua gratia curas*.

events from the past are compared.²¹ To the mechanism of synchronicity corresponds that of bringing together different places, here *Gallia* and *Cannae*, which is also a characteristic of this text. For instance, a little later the poet will compare the natural spectacle of the Moselle landscape to his hometown Burdigala (ll. 19–20), and astonishingly, in the last line of the poem not the Moselle but the Garonne is named as the last word: *aequoreae . . . Garumnae* (l. 483). And even the Garonne is not described with an epithet suiting a river but as "sea-like."

In the following lines another important aspect emerges:

Vnde iter ingrediens nemorosa per auia solum
Et nulla humani spectans uestigia cultus. (5–6).²²

The poet is now alone on his way,²³ the new (poetical) dimension which he is entering does not show any human trace: *uestigia* is a key word in this sense. At line 47 they are *sicca* and indicate the solid sand which cannot be pressed by the feet (the same concept is repeated at lines 53–4: *nec retinent memores uestigia pressa figuras*). After having walked through the lonely fields the poet finally reaches Nouomagum (today Neumagen):

Purior hic campis aer Phoebusque sereno
Lumine purpureum reserat iam sudus Olympum;
Nec iam consertis per mutua uincula ramis
Quaeritur exclusum uiridi caligine caelum;
Sed liquidum iubar et rutilam uisentibus aethram
Libera perspicui non inuidet aura diei.
In speciem tum me patriae cultumque nitentis
Burdigalae blando pepulerunt omnia uisu. (12–19).

Here the air is not only pure but *more* pure (*purior*): the comparative marks again the passage to another dimension or atmosphere, which is no longer foggy (l. 1, *nebuloso*) or woody (l. 5, *nemorosa*).²⁴ Moreover, here the poet can admire

---

21. The mechanism of synchronicity, i.e., of rendering the past present, is a typical feature of many late antique texts which would deserve further discussion. See, e.g., Formisano 2003 (on Vegetius) and 2013 (on Orosius).
22. "Thence onward I began a lonely journey through pathless forest, nor did my eyes rest on any trace of human inhabitants."
23. Gruber 2013 in his commentary ad loc. emphasizes the "Zivilisationsferne" as the most important aspect here beyond the fact that the poet might have been alone or not.
24. Görler 1969: 97, followed by the commentators, refer here to *Aen.* 6. 640–1: *largior hic campos aether et lumine uestit purpureo*, which is the description of Elysium.

the splendid sky in all its brightness and purity because there are no branches which obscure the view. The branches described here are interlaced; they form a sort of *tex*t*ure* which blocks the view of the sky. The poet wants to be freed of them in order to enjoy the spectacle without any obstacle. He wants to catch a new reality which is far away from the centre, which requires to be admired in a more visible form, *purior*, than the Italian landscape characterizing the Latin poetic tradition and its textual language.

Another recurring image in the *Mosella* which deserves attention from the perspective I am developing is that of reflexion. In the central section of the text the poet first thematizes the *secretum* of the river, which cannot be disclosed by human eyes and therefore indicates the impossibility of properly describing it:

> *Sed non haec spectata ulli nec cognita uisu*
> *Fas mihi sit pro parte loqui: secreta tegatur*
> *Et commissa suis lateat reuerentia riuis* (186–8).[25]

He then describes some images reflected on the river which reproduce both objects surrounding the river and past events. Those images, in contrast to the *secreta*, are *fruenda palam* (l. 187); that is, are available and can be openly enjoyed. Yet they are nothing but reflections of the real thing:

> *Tota natant crispis iuga motibus et tremit absens*
> *Pampinus et uitreis uindemia turget in undis.* (194–5)[26]

The vine is "absent" and yet the grapes seem bigger, overblown, in the reflection in the glassy river. In the following lines the motif receives a more extensive treatment and is enriched with a comparison which works as a sort of *mise en abyme* of reflection itself and its fallacy (I print in boldface the relevant terms referring to the theme of reflection):

> *Non aliam **speciem** petulantibus addit ephebis*
> *Pubertasque amnisque et picti rostra phaseli.*
> *Hos Hyperionio cum sol perfuderit aestu,*
> ***Reddit** nautales uitreo sub gurgite formas*
> *Et redigit pandas inuersi corporis **umbras**.*
> *Vtque agiles motus dextra laeuaque frequentant*

---

25. "But of this thing which no man has looked upon and no eye beheld, be it no sin for me to speak in part: let things secret be kept hid, and let Reverence dwell unspied upon, in the safe-keeping of her native streams."

26. "Whole hills float on the shivering ripples: here quivers the far-off tendril of the vine, here in the glassy flood swells the full cluster."

Et commutatis alternant pondera remis,
*Vnda **refert** alios, **simulacra** umentia, nautas:*
***Ipsa suo** gaudet **simulamine** nautica pubes*
***Fallaces** fluuio **mirata redire figuras**.*
Sic ubi compositos ostentatura capillos,
*Candentem late **speculi** explorantis honorem*
Cum primum carae nutrix admouit alumnae,
*Laeta ignorato fruitur uirguncula **ludo***
*Germanaeque putat **formam spectare** puellae:*
Oscula fulgenti dat non referenda metallo
Aut fixas praetemptat acus aut frontis ad oram
Vibratos captat digitis extendere crines:
*Talis ad **umbrarum** ludibria nautica pubes*
***Ambiguis** fruitur **ueri falsique figuris**.* (220–39)[27]

The sailors are described in the moment when they are puzzled by their own reflection in the water of the river. They are then compared with a young girl looking at herself in a mirror, who thinks she is seeing her sister and shows affection by giving her kisses. Both the sailors and the girl are amused by the play of the reflected shadows, which turn out to be true and false at the same time.[28]

The theme of reflection well represents the displacement staged in the poem. As I was arguing before, every place described in the *Mosella* is either the reflection of something else or is compared to another place which is far away historically or geographically. A few examples of this textual device will suffice. At lines 345–7 there is a comparison between the baths along the Moselle and those in Baiae:

Quod si Cumanis huc afforet hospes ab oris,
Crederet Euboicas simulacra exilia Baias
His donasse locis.[29]

---

[27] "Such the appearance which youth, river, skiffs with painted prows, lend to these merry lads. But when Hyperion pours down the sun's full heat, the crystal flood reflects sailor-shapes and throws back crooked pictures of their downward forms. And as they ply their nimble strokes with the right hand and the left, and throwing their weight in turn now upon this oar, now upon that, the wave reflects a watery semblance of sailors to match them. The boys themselves delight in their own counterfeits, wondering at the illusive forms which the river gives back. Thus, when hoping soon to display her braided tresses ('tis when the nurse has first placed near her dear charge the wide-gleaming glory of the searching mirror), delighted, the little maid enjoys the uncomprehended game, deeming she gazes the shape of a real girl: she showers on the shining metal kisses not to be returned, or essays those firm-fixed hairpins, or puts her fingers to that brow, trying to draw out those curled locks; even so, at sight of the reflections which mock them, the lads afloat amuse themselves with shapes which waver between false and true."

[28] Fontaine 1977: 443 considers l. 239 "la clé du poème."

[29] "But if a stranger were to arrive here from the shores of Cumae, he would believe that Euboean Baiae had bestowed on this region a miniature copy of its own delights."

And at 374–7 there is another interesting remark:

Quod si tibi, dia Mosella,
Smyrna suum uatem uel Mantua clara dedisset,
Cederet Iliacis Simois memoratus in oris,
Nec praeferre suos auderet Thybris honores.[30]

The concepts are of course different on the level of the literal meaning. In the first quotation there is a reminiscence of Statius (*Silu.* 1.5.60–1). Interestingly enough, Green (1999 ad loc.) in his commentary points out that "the comparison was trite." But precisely because the idea was well known, the addition *simulacra exilia* has the effect on the one hand of alienating the concept and on the other, and more relevantly here, of recalling both the themes of reflection and –by means of syllepsis in Riffaterre's terms - displacement: In the phrase *simulacra exilia*, the neuter plural of the adjective *exilis*, "thin, slender, meager," suggestively recalls the plural of the noun *exilium*, "exile".

In the second quotation the reader may be puzzled by the series of famous names within the same sentence. The obvious references are to Homer (Smyrna) and Vergil (Mantua); but we then read that the Moselle would surpass the Simois and the Tiber if only those two cities would have given their prestigious poets to the Moselle. But those cities do not lie on those rivers: here again displacement is thematized. In both cases Ausonius maps himself and the landscape of the Moselle on the landscape of the Latin literary tradition, emblematized here by Homer and Vergil, but the poem has no true centre, not even the river Moselle, which is never entirely itself, which is always displaced and compared to other rivers and places. Absence, echo, and reflection pervade the text but also the impossibility of escaping precisely the traditional poetical language.

An aspect of the *Mosella* to which some earlier scholarship drew attention is its internal dichotomy, which has been treated in various ways, sometimes also by implicitly taking it for granted and not taking it seriously as a fundamental mark of the text. In a much quoted article from 1969, Woldemar Görler points out the reference in the *Mosella* to the sixth book of the *Aeneid*. In particular, he argues for a comparison consciously established by Ausonius between the Moselle valley and Elysium, between the Hunsrück and the "dark regions of the underworld" (Görler 1969: 96). Görler sees the Vergilian reminiscence not only as a formal aspect but also as an explicit thematic reference

---

30. "But if thee, O divine Moselle, Smyrna or famed Mantua had given its own poet, then would Simoïs, renowned on Ilium's coasts, yield place, and Tiber would not dare to set his glories above thine."

to the context—the passage of the poet to the Moselle landscape is comparable to the passage of Aeneas to Elysium—and his observations on the intertextual relationship with Vergil draw out a political message in the poem (Görler 1969: 114). But this same point can be applied perhaps even more productively to the literary dimension of the text, reading the passage from one dimension to the other as an allegory of literary displacement. In his 1984 study, Michael Roberts also bases his interpretation on the poem's dichotomous quality but from another perspective. He identifies one theme in particular: the relationship between super- and subaqueous realms which characterizes the key moments in the *Mosella*. Crossing from one dimension to the other is seen, according to Roberts (1984: 348), as a crime against nature: "the boundary between the two realms must remain inviolate." The key passage in this sense is roughly located in the middle of the poem: the description of a fish which dies for having trespassed the natural boundary, represented by the antithesis *sub amne suo* versus *aere nostro* (l. 261; Roberts 1984: 350). Another kind of violation which Roberts (1984: 351) sees happening in the "horizontal level" is less aggressive and more positive. This other level is present towards the end of the poem and can be well represented by the catalogue of tributaries of Moselle (ll. 349–80).

Responding to an article by E. J. Kenney (1984) which argues that the Statian reminiscences present in the *Mosella* are used by Ausonius in order reaffirm the superiority of men over nature, Carole Newlands (1988: 404) sees the reference to Statius in the opposite way: "[Ausonius] praises nature for qualities that are independent of man and his works and are superior to them"; and the imitation of Statius is applied "in order to revise classical values, not to perpetuate them." For Newlands (1988: 406, 408), "man in this river landscape is a peripheral character," and his arts, such as fishing and architecture, have the function of disrupting "the harmony of the landscape." In particular, she focuses on the villas surrounding the river. They are "the hallmark of Roman culture," and the subtle critique by Ausonius "suggests a new set of values that question one of the most visible signs of the Pax Romana on the German frontier" (Newlands 1988: 410). The aim of the poet, according to Newlands, is not to praise human skills but, on the contrary to assert the potency of nature. I have dwelled on these studies among others in order to show that my interpretation of the *Mosella* as a text which allegorizes displacement—more precisely, literary distancing from the Latin poetic tradition—can be harmonized with a significant tendency in the scholarship, which attributes to this text in different ways and for different purposes a basic conceptual dichotomy between two levels or two places, something which, as we will shortly see, also characterizes Claudian's and Rutilius's texts.

6.3. DE RAPTU PROSERPINAE

Many of the aspects of the *Mosella* that I have just highlighted are to be found also in Claudian's epic poem *De raptu Proserpinae*, narrating the abduction of Ceres's only child, Proserpina, by Pluto, eager for a wife. We do not know anything about the circumstances of the composition of this poem. The text is incomplete, and the narration ends while Ceres is looking for her daughter; most scholars infer from the second prologue that Claudian wrote the text in two phases with a considerable break in between.[31] Traditionally the scholarship has concentrated its efforts on reconstructing intertextual relationships with classical texts, in particular Ovid, who in *Metamorphoses* 5 tells the story of the rape of Proserpina. Claudian's poem has been recently discussed in terms of 'displacement' by Stephen Hinds, who in his 2012 Housman Lecture identifies many important aspects of the poem. Here the term "displacement" refers to phenomena of intertextuality, with particular reference to Ovidian resonances in Claudian's poem, but (although he does not use the term) Hinds does read the text allegorically, when he sees the story narrated by Claudian as a grand metaphor of the split of the Roman Empire between East and West.

> Claudian both operates within and newly reanimates the topoi of epic dualism: in a universe of split-imperial poetry, the *DRP* asks: how *does* the Upper-to-Nether narrative of a fraternally divided cosmos map on the West-to-East narrative of a fraternally divided cosmos? (Hinds 2012: 7)

In what follows I deepen this kind of discussion by enriching and slightly modifying Hinds's reading and aim to shed light less on the "geopolitical" aspects than on the "geopoetical" ones.[32] The dualism to which Hinds refers can in my opinion be expanded to another sphere: precisely, as in the case of Ausonius's *Mosella*, in the allegorical terms of a confrontation with the Latin poetic tradition. In particular, I focus on a set of themes familiar from the *Mosella*: dualism, distancing and separation, absence and loss. It would be impossible here to analyse the entire text; I offer instead a brief selection of passages where these themes emerge with particular clarity.

One of the most discussed passages from the *De raptu Proserpinae* has been the preface, which more or less directly invites an allegorical reading.

> *Inuenta secuit primus qui naue profundum*
> *et rudibus remis sollicitauit aquas,*

---

31. See Charlet 2002: xx–xxxiii.
32. Hinds actually refers here to Alessandro Barchiesi's terms.

qui dubiis ausus committere flatibus alnum
    quas natura negat praebuit arte uias:
tranquillis primum trepidus se credidit undis
    litora securo tramite summa legens;
mox longos temptare sinus et linquere terras
    et leni coepit pandere uela Noto.
ast ubi paulatim praeceps audacia creuit
    cordaque languentem dedidicere metum,
iam uagus inrumpit pelagus caelumque secutus
    Aegaeas hiemes Ioniumque domat. (pr., 1–12)[33]

The most common interpretation is poetological in nature: comparing himself to a sailor who gradually learns how to achieve distance from the coast in order to venture on a more risky journey into the sea, Claudian alludes to his own poetic career. After having written smaller texts he is now ready to confront the most ambitious literary genre, epic poetry.[34] This approach implicitly depends on the belief that this allegorical meaning was Claudian's intention;[35] without necessarily questioning it, I would like to push the allegorical reading a step further by reading this passage as a thematization of the confrontation with the poetic tradition. The entire passage—indeed I would argue the entire poem—thematizes *nouitas* through the metaphor of displacement in different ways: the word *inuenta* symptomatically opens the poem, followed by *secuit* (signalling an abrupt cut of some kind) and then *primus*, which brings us back to the theme of novelty. In the exact middle of the preface the word *legens* has particular relevance. Its surface meaning is of course that of "touching" the edge of the coast (*summa litora*). And yet if we activate an allegorical reading, a type of reading which the passage as a whole seems to invite, we could also understand the word as "reading."[36] The poetic tradition is here the landscape; more precisely it is represented by the dry land, while

---

33. "He who first cut the deep with the ship he had invented and disturbed the waters with rough-hewn oars, who dared to commit his vessel of alder-wood to the unreliable blasts and made available by his art ways which nature denies, at first trusted himself trembling to the calm waves, coasting along the edge of the shores on a safe course; soon he began to try out vast bays, to leave the land and spread his sails to the mild south wind; but when, little by little, his impetuous boldness grew and his heart forgot sluggish fear, roving now far and wide he burst upon open water, and, following the sky, mastered Aegean storms and the Ionian Sea." All translations of *De raptu Proserpinae* are those of Gruzelier 1993.

34. On the different nuances and implications of this interpretation, see Charlet 1991: xx–xxii. See also Felgentreu 1999: 157–68, Bureau 2009, and Harrison in this volume.

35. One potential difficulty with this reading is that there is no clear connection between the topic of the prefaces and that of the poem (see Felgentreu 1999).

36. I am pleased to see that Aaron Pelttari also reads this preface as thematizing the conflict between tradition and originality in similar terms (Pelttari 2014: 6, which I saw only after completing this article).

the courageous attempt (*trepidus, temptare, audacia, metum*) to conceive of a different textuality is represented by the journey to the open sea away from the coast (*linquere terras*). And later, perhaps even more overtly, *legere* invites being perceived as having a double meaning, in other words as an instance of syllepsis. In the famous *anthologia* in book II, Venus invites Proserpina and other goddesses to "gather" (2.119: *legant*) the flowers from the meadow. Soon thereafter (2.137) we read that Proserpina in particular, more than her fellow goddesses and nymphs, burns with the desire to gather: *aestuat ante alias auido feruore legendi*. The context is highly metaphorical, and in addition to the various intertextual implications that have been described, for instance, by Stephen Hinds (2012), I would argue that *legere* as a syllepsis here suggests both "gather" and "read."

Moreover, the sailor has to "unlearn his fear" (*dedidicere metum*): unlearn something which cannot be learned, fear being a natural feeling in this context. Although not discussed by commentators, the verbal form *dedidicere* is striking both in sound (the internal alliteration) and in sense: the new poet actively unlearns the language of the poetic tradition.

The thematization of a new landscape, in allegorical terms, of a new poetic language, which was present in the *Mosella*, re-emerges also later in Claudian's text. In the second book, when Pluto seeks to console his beloved Proserpina, he praises the good qualities of the new world over which she will reign:

> *Desine funestis animum, Proserpina, curis*
> *et uano uexare metu. Maiora dabuntur*
> *sceptra nec indigni taedas patiere mariti.*
> *Ille ego Saturni proles, cui machina rerum*
> *seruit et immensum tendit per inane potestas.*
> *Amissum ne crede diem: sunt altera nobis*
> *sidera, sunt orbes alii, lumenque uidebis*
> *purius Elysiumque magis mirabere solem*
> *cultoresque pios. Illic pretiosior aetas,*
> *aurea progenies, habitat semperque tenemus,*
> *quod superi meruere semel. Nec mollia desunt*
> *prata tibi. Zephyris illic melioribus halant*
> *perpetui flores, quos nec tua protulit Henna.*
> *Est etiam lucis arbor praediues opacis,*
> *fulgentes uiridi ramos curuata metallo.*
> *Haec tibi sacra datur, fortunatumque tenebis*
> *autumnum et fuluis semper ditabere pomis.* (2.277–93)[37]

---

37. "Stop troubling your heart with mournful cares and empty fear. A greater sceptre will be granted you, and you will not endure marriage with an unworthy husband. I am that child of Saturn whom the

In his reading of this passage, Hinds argues that the duality of the Western and Eastern empires is reproduced in the duality of Upper and Nether world; Claudian's strategy is to harmonize the two parts. Not surprisingly, Hinds (2012: 26) sees here an intertextual relationship with Ovid: "other stars, another sun, a purer light [...]: in short (and with traces of Ovidian language) *another Enna, but a better one*." [38] In addition to such connections *back* with Ovid, I would draw attention to some possible *lateral* connections with late antique poetry; for instance, between Pluto's description of what his kingdom resembles and Ausonius's description of the Moselle valley. In both cases the displacement and the passage to another dimension are thematized. In both places—the Moselle landscape and in the Plutonian Underworld—the air is *purior* (*Mos.* 12 and *rapt.* 284). Both places are characterized by alterity and represent *another* textual dimension, which requires to be read in *another* way: allegory is the term. As we will shortly see, comparable analogies are also detectable in *De reditu suo*.

De raptu Proserpinae is a poem not only of displacement but also of separation, detachment, and interruption. In the preface, as we have seen, the sailor-poet is eager to disconnect himself from the coast. When Lachesis tries to turn Pluto from his rebellious intents, she says:

ne pete firmatas pacis dissoluere leges,
quas dedimus neuitque colus, neu foedera fratrum
ciuili conuerte tuba. (1.63–5)[39]

A little later there is the description of the place where Ceres decides to keep her daughter safe, Sicily, depicted by Claudian precisely in the moment when it was separated from the mainland:

Trinacria quondam
Italiae pars una fuit, sed pontus et aestus

---

framework of nature serves, and my power extends through the limitless void. Do not believe that you have lost the daylight. We have other stars and other worlds, and you will see a purer light and wonder rather at the sun of Elysium and its righteous inhabitants. There dwells an age of greater worth, a golden generation, and we possess for always what those above have obtained but once. Nor shall you be without soft meadows; there ever-blooming flowers, such as not even your Aetna has produced, breath to kindlier Zephyr breezes. In the shady groves there is also a most precious tree, whose curving branches gleam with verdant metal: this is appointed as sacred to you –you will possess the blessed harvest and will ever be enriched with its tawny-gold fruit."

38. He also argues that the Underworld representing *another* Enna activates a sort of intertextual *aemulatio*: "This (scil. Enna) is a *locus* which is always being measured against other rhetorical and geographical versions of itself, against other *loci* and *loca*."

39. "Do not seek to dissolve the established laws of piece which we have given and our distaff has spun, nor overturn the bonds of brothers with the trumpet blasts of civil war."

mutauere situm. Rupit confinia Nereus
uictor et abscissos interluit aequore montes
paruaque cognatas prohibent discrimina terras.
Nunc illam socia ruptam tellure trisulcam
opposuit natura mari. (1.141–7).[40]

As Marie-France Guipponi-Gineste (2010: 45) points out, this passage invites being interpreted symbolically: The mainland and the island are presented as *cognatae terrae*, as relatives (as we will shortly see, the rhetoric of the family plays an important part in the poem) separated (*rupit*) by Nereus; this prefigures the separation of Proserpina from her mother, which will happen later in the poem.[41] I would add a further dimension: in the preface as well as here, the mainland allegorizes the poetic tradition as such.

Moreover, there is in this poem a tendency of going back to the origins of poetic language. Commenting on another interesting passage which cannot be discussed here (the *anthologia*, 2.131–5), Hinds (2012: 24) notes that Claudian seems to reconnect "with the earliest origins of the story he tells anew." This movement directed towards the origins is noticeable also in another famous passage, the description of Proserpina's weaving (1.248–65). Here two things are relevant for my reading. First, the reference to the origins of the universe, which Proserpina represents in her embroidery (248 *sedes paternas*, 249 *ueterem tumultum*, 250 *Natura parens*) brings us back to a period *ante litteram* in the true sense of the word; that is, before the creation of a poetic language. Her work, as has been noticed, reiterates the original creation by Nature (Guipponi-Gineste 2010: 35). On the other hand, and more importantly, what Proserpina weaves is actually an impossible *ekphrasis*: the original movements of the creation of the universe cannot be statically represented in a picture.[42] The passage is pervaded by verbs indicating movement (251 *discessere, fertur,* 251 *cadunt,* 252 *egit, fluxit, pependit,* 254 *accendit, fundit, attollit,* etc.), but this sense of

---

40. "Trinacria was once a conjoined part of Italy, but sea and time have changed the lie of the land. Victorious Nereus burst his boundaries and washed between the severed mountains with his waters, and a small division keeps apart these kindred countries. Now Nature has set against the sea that three-pronged island that is broken from its related ground." See Gruzelier 1993 ad loc.: "the description is loaded—or rather overloaded—with words evoking savagery and rage, to create a mental picture of violence."

41. A little later (1.197–201), Sicily is depicted as a land enjoying a perennial golden age, "en dehors de l'histoire et du temps," more apt for a natural state and of course so similar to the Underworld in the terms it will be depicted in later by Pluto (Guipponi-Gineste 2010, 69)

42. This aspect seems not to have caught the attention of the critics, who usually refer to the Classical models. See, e.g., Von Albrecht 1989, who nonetheless recognizes that Claudian defamiliarizes the description of "the other worlds" by depicting the Underworld as a paradise (390).

impossibility is accompanied by the fact that Proserpina's piece is defined as *inrita munera* (247), a "vain present" for her mother.[43] She uses a medium of representation, weaving, which is not apt to describe the subject she has chosen: her language cannot match the subject, her work is *inritum*.[44]

Disruption is also thematized at another level: precisely that of interruption. In the eyes of modern readers, the text per se is an example of interruption par excellence, since Claudian never brought it to an end. This coincidence seems to find a sort of prefiguration in the passages in books 1 and 3 where the interruption of Proserpina's weaving is thematized. At the end of book 1 she leaves her work unfinished (*imperfectum laborem*, 1,271) because of the sudden and unexpected arrival of Venus, Minerva, and Diana. Later, her desperate mother, Ceres, is described as she enters the unguarded house in order to look for Proserpina and finds nothing but the unfinished work:

foribusque reclusis,
dum uacuas sedes et desolata pererrat
atria, semirutas confuso stamine telas
atque interruptas agnoscit pectinis artes. (3.153–6)[45]

Interestingly enough, a particular figure emerges at this point:

Diuinitus perit ille labor, spatiumque relictum
Audax sacrilego supplebat aranea textu. (3.157–8)[46]

It should not come as a surprise that it is the Ovidian *audax aranea* (*met*. 6.1–145) which completes the work unfinished—perhaps incapable of being finished—by Proserpina. Guipponi-Gineste (2010: 27) notices that in this passage Arachne represents through her transgressive action a sort of a *Doppelgänger* of Proserpina, since both enter a confrontation with an intrusive divine power (Minerva in one case, Jupiter in the other). Following my interpretation, the Ovidian Arachne represents imitation of the poetic tradition itself: it intervenes where Proserpina is not able to compete her work, and it fills the gaps (*spatium relictum*). Her text is "sacrilegious" precisely because, by reactivating a

---

43. Charlet 1991 ad loc. seems to put the meaning of *inrita* in relationship with 1,271 *imperfectumque laborem* and 3,156 *interceptas artes*. Is Proserpina's work *vain* because it is *unfinished*?
44. On the equivalence of weaving and poetic language, see Guipponi-Gineste 2010: 26–8.
45. "Opening the doors, as she passed through the empty rooms and deserted halls, she recognized the half-ruined weaving with its disordered threads and the work of the shuttle that had been broken off."
46. "That wonderful task of the goddess had gone to waste and the bold spider was completing the gap left behind with her sacrilegious web."

traditional poetic language, it subverts the sense of what Proserpina was doing at the moment when she had to leave her embroidery unfinished. In the end, the "impossible" ekphrasis has been outdone.

I have suggested that both the *Mosella* and the *De raptu Proserpinae* not only display an attempt to create a new poetical language but thematize, in new-allegorical terms, the tension with the traditional language of Latin poetry. If this interpretation is plausible, the implications are significant on a double level. First, a specific trait of late Latin poetry emerges, which perhaps unexpectedly subverts the common scholarly assumption that late antique textuality is pervaded by a stubborn respect for literary tradition. Second, the kind of intertextual reading so *en vogue* among Latinists (and so well suited to texts from other periods) cannot alone catch the complexity of late Latin poetry, which perhaps tends to dismantle or even subvert the practice of intertextuality itself. Before coming to *De reditu suo*, I would like to discuss another feature of Claudian's poem which has not yet received any attention but which is in my opinion relevant, above all because it exemplifies in a very clear way the *new-allegorical* reading I am sketching here.

From a certain perspective, Claudian's poem tells the story of a family. A mother wants to protect her daughter from a wicked uncle who, with the help of an authoritarian grandfather and assisted by a treacherous aunt and naive cousins, succeeds in abducting her to a place far away from her mother. And even though Claudian's poem is unfinished, the end of the story is well known: the creation of a new family. The language of the family in *De raptu* is literally ubiquitous; references to the familial constellation appear regularly. At the beginning of the story, Pluto is described as a man eager to become a husband and a father (1.35–6), and Lachesis implores him to not break the *foedera fratrum* (1.64). Mercury, son of Maia (1.76) and grandson of Atlas (1.88) has to bring a message to Iuppiter, "the most cruel of brothers" (1.93, *saeuissime frater*). As we already saw, Sicily and Italy once were *cognatae terrae* (1.146), and Proserpina represents in her embroidery the achievements of *Natura parens* (1.251). In book 2, Venus, Diana, and Minerva manifest themselves to Proserpina, and they are referred to as *sorores* (2.10; again at 2.119). Gruzelier (1993, ad loc.) in her commentary points out: "Claudian is keeping an unobtrusive but insistent emphasis upon family relations to heighten the tragedy of Proserpina's fate: not only betrayed by her father into the power of her uncle in the absence of her mother, but from the very arms of her sisters." It does not come as a surprise that the structural and thematic core of the poem, that is, the scene of the rape itself, is dotted with references to the family: 2,207 *patruo*, 216 *deterrime fratrum*, 219 *te coniuge*, 220 *fratris*, 230 *socerum*, *hymenaeus*, 231 *conubia*, 234 *patris*, 237 *genitor*, 238 *sorores*, 246 *fratris*, 251 *pater*, 254–255 *paternae mentis*, 265 *matris*. On the one hand one can agree with the instrumental function of this insistence: the familial terminology has the function of emphasizing the bitter disappointment of Proserpina being betrayed by her own family members. On the other, this aspect is insufficient to explain its presence in other parts of the poem where, as we have now seen, Proserpina herself plays no role. Endogamic practice in ancient mythology is per se not surprising, and yet the hammering presence of family terms might have another meaning, which is at the same time text-immanent but also transcends the text itself, and therefore I define it allegorical. The narration of the creation of a "new family" (Pluto and Proserpina) takes place within an older and pre-existent familial order. The family allegorizes a tradition which is impossible to escape and within which every new event cannot be anything else than a reproduction of the same order.[47]

Again, in Claudian's poem as in the *Mosella*, the very concept of tradition, that is, the language of Latin poetry, is directly thematized and problematized through figures of displacement, disconnection, decentralization, and separation but also through the very impossibility of escaping precisely that language.

6.4. DE REDITU SUO

Rutilius Namatianus's *De reditu suo* was composed between 416 and 418, probably after the author arrived in his home country, Gallia, having felt obliged to leave his beloved Rome in order to rescue his estates. The poem narrates the journey from Rome to Gallia in various steps, and many scholars have focused on the question whether it is possible to treat the text as a source for historical and topographical reconstruction.[48] More recently scholars have looked at the poem in a more strictly literary way by discussing two interrelated issues above all: genre and models. Attention has been also drawn to the theme of the journey and its tradition within ancient literature, as well as its metaliterary implications (Soler 2005, Squillante 2005). As in my discussion of Ausonius's and Claudian's poems, instead of insisting on the relationship between the poet and his classical models or on genre, here I emphasize the contradictory quality of Rutilius's text itself; the predominance of the intertextual approach has generally led to a neutralization of the poem's contradictory qualities by presupposing a typical late antique "mélange de genres."[49]

---

47. The interpretive connection—*from* family *to* tradition—is nowhere explicit, but then again, Claudian's readers have generally and unquestioningly made the interpretive connection *from* seafarer *to* poet an element in an allegorical reading of the *praefatio*.

48. To this tendency reacted Paschoud 1978.

49. The concept was launched by Jacques Fontaine in the path-breaking article of 1976 and has rather dogmatically been accepted without any further discussion or revision. Soler 2005: 256 seems to question the application of this concept to Rutilius's poem.

The most evident aspect of this is the fact that the "return" of the poet to his homeland is actually represented in terms of an exile from Rome. The *nostos*, previously always represented as the positive outcome of the peripeteia of an epic hero following the prototype of the Homeric Odysseus, here becomes a negative experience. In this regard the choice of the elegiac couplet plays a significant role. As Étienne Wolff (2007: xxxii) points out, in Late Antiquity this meter generally works as a medium in order to break with rather than to support the tradition. In more general terms *De reditu suo* puts on the stage a confrontation between a traditional form or genre (the *iter* and the *nostos*) and a new content; that is, the clash between the concept of "return to the homeland" and sentiment against this return, expressed in elegiac couplets.[50]

The questions of generic affiliations (*iter*, *Reisesatura*, *nostos*, etc.), as well as of intertextual relationships with Ovid, Vergil, Homer, and Juvenal, among others, have been thoroughly discussed by many scholars.[51] As in the case of Ausonius's and Claudian's works, here I focus on the text itself in order to highlight some aspects which on the one hand characterize Rutilius's poetry and on the other establish a common ground with the *Mosella* and *De raptu Proserpinae*. For obvious reasons "displacement" is in this text even more relevant and obvious a theme than in the others: the journey is not only an isolatable aspect but informs the poem in its totality. Here I would like to draw attention to how the text is constructed around this central idea of displacement. Commenting on the characteristic recurrence of narrative digression in Rutilius, Soler (2005: 301–2) has noticed that no matter what these digressions contain, even if they have the effect of distracting the reader during the narration of the journey, all together they fully support the "voyage intertextuel," which has the effect of bringing back the text and its readers to Rutilius's beloved adoptive home, Rome, always present as the true destination of the poet despite his decision to return to his native Gallia.

This is an important point, but the intertextual aspect is in my opinion only the surface of what happens within the text itself. How are movement and displacement *textually* represented? The textual movement in *De reditu suo* has two directions, which I define as centripetal and centrifugal, the centre being represented by Rome. The two kinds of movement have different but complementary characteristics. The centripetal movement indicates the proximity of

---

50. In this regard, Soler 205: 297–301 notes that Rutilius, by retracing his journey on the model of the *Aeneid*, brings himself to the very origins of Rome. By doing so he orients his text to a discourse of the original sources of Roman civilization and consequently of regeneration. This strategy is supported by a general archaic patina in the text, expressed by ancient toponyms and their particular histories.

51. See Doblhofer 1972–7; Fo 1989, 1992; Tissol 2002; Squillante 2005; and in particular Soler 2005, who reorients the text towards a more genuinely literary discussion.

Rome and is characterized by a language pervaded by multiplication, cohesivity, familial terminology, repetitions—all figures that emphasize centrality and compactness but produce at the same time a sense of saturation. The centrifugal movement indicates the process of separation from Rome and is characterized by dispersion, fragmentation, deformation, and a massive presence of water and ruins. Since nearly every line of Rutilius's poem contains language indicating one or the other kind of movement, I would argue that the poem as a whole allegorizes displacement as such. Here I can give only a few examples.

The opening lines of the poem in its surviving form place both kinds of movement on display:[52]

> *Velocem potius reditum mirabere, lector,*
> *tam cito Romuleis posse carere bonis.*
> *Quid longum toto Romam uenerantibus aeuo!*
> *Nil umquam longum est, quod sine fine placet.*
> *O quantum et quotiens possum numerare beatos,*
> *nasci felici qui meruere solo,*
> *qui Romanorum procerum generosa propago*
> *ingenitum cumulant urbis honore decus!*
> *Semina uirtutum demissa et tradita caelo*
> *non potuere aliis dignius esse locis.*
> *Felices etiam, qui proxima munera primis*
> *sortiti Latias optinuere domos!* (1.1–12)[53]

Interestingly enough we find here two elements also present in the *Mosella*: with *uelocem reditum* compare *celerem Nauam* (*Mos.* 1), with *mirabere* compare *miratus* (*Mos.* 2).[54] Within the first couplets there are repetitions of identical words or similar concepts: *uelocem* and *tam cito, tam* and *toto, Romuleis, Romam,* and *Romanorum longum* (ll. 3 and 4), and *sine fine, uenerantibus,* and *placet.* The sense of multiplication is also given by *o quantum et quotiens, numerare,* and

---

52. Given the comparative *potius*, the poem very probably began differently. See Fo 1992 ad loc. On the other hand, if this is the (original) opening line, *potius* itself can be interpreted as a marker of "displacement."

53. "Rather will you marvel, reader, that my quick return journey (to Gaul) can so soon renounce the blessings of the city of Romulus. What is too long for men who spend all time in venerating Rome? Nothing is ever too long that never fails to please. How greatly and how often can I count those blest who have deserved birth in that happy soil! Those high born scions of Roman nobility crown their honourable birth with the lustre of the Capital! On no other land could the seeds of virtues have been more worthily let fall by heaven's assignment. Happy they too who, winning meeds next to the first, have enjoyed Latin homes!" All translations of *De reditu suo* by J. Wight Duff and A. M. Duff 1982.

54. The motif of wonder or marvel (*miror, mirus* vel sim.) characterizes both the *Mosella* (e.g., Newlands 1988) and *De reditu suo* (Soler 2005: 302).

cumulant. Another repetition consists in the sequence *beatos, felici,* and *felices*, while the theme of generation is marked by many terms: *nasci, generosa* (etymologically deriving from *genus*), *propago* (in alliteration with *procerum, proxima,* and *primis*), *ingenitum*, and *semina. Honore, decus* (in alliteration with *demissa*), *uirtutum*, and *dignius* belong to the same semantic field. *Solo, urbis, (non aliis) locis,* and *Latias domos* all refer to the city of Rome. The very core of the city, the venerable curia, is named in the following line:

> *Religiosa patet peregrinae curia laudi*
> *nec putat externos, quos decet esse suos.* (1.13–14)[55]

Peregrinae and *externos* both refer to foreigners, and the pentameter symmetrically repeats the same concept in each of the two hemistichs. The insistence on the concept of "generation" returns in a few subsequent passages, especially in the so-called hymn to Rome, representing the city as the centre of the world.

> *Exaudi, regina tui pulcherrima mundi,*
>   *inter sidereos, Roma, recepta polos,*
> *exaudi, genetrix hominum genetrixque deorum;*
>   *non procul a caelo per tua templa sumus.*
> *Te canimus semperque, sinent dum fata, canemus;*
>   *sospes nemo potest immemor esse tui.*
> *Obruerint citius scelerata obliuia solem*
>   *quam tuus e nostro corde recedat honos.*
> *Nam solis radiis aequalia munera tendis,*
>   *qua circumfusus fluctuat Oceanus;*
> *uoluitur ipse tibi, qui continet omnia, Phoebus*
>   *eque tuis ortos in tua condit equos;*
> *te non flammigeris Libye tardauit arenis,*
>   *non armata suo reppulit ursa gelu:*
> *Quantum uitalis natura tetendit in axes,*
>   *tantum uirtuti peruia terrae tuae.*
> *Fecisti patriam diuersis gentibus unam;*
>   *profuit iniustis te dominante capi;*
> *dumque offers uictis proprii consortia iuris,*
>   *Vrbem fecisti, quod prius orbis erat.*
> *Auctores generis Venerem Martemque fatemur,*

---

55. "The Senate-house, though fenced with awe, yet stands open to foreign merit, nor deems those strangers who are fittingly its own."

>   *Aeneadum matrem Romulidumque patrem;*
> *mitigat armatas uictrix clementia uires,*
>   *conuenit in mores nomen utrumque tuos;*
> *hinc tibi certandi bona parcendique uoluptas,*
>   *quos timuit superat, quos superauit amat.* (1.47–72)[56]

This passage is perhaps the most typical illustration of what I call the centripetal movement of this poem. Repetitions (*exaudi* and *exaudi*, *canimus* and *canemus*, *genetrix* and *genetrix*, *superat* and *superauit*, etc.) and two intertwined motifs almost obsessively mark it: the centrality of Rome and its generative power. Rome is both *genetrix* and generated by Venus and Mars, *mater* and *pater*. Here the familial terminology emerges similarly to *De raptu Proserpinae* but with a different nuance. The entire world is contained in Rome, the *orbis* is made *urbs* (66) and hence it includes and renders "familiar" what is normally located outside. Even Roman architecture symbolizes this inclusivity (1.111: *inclusas inter laquearia siluas*). Rome is central both in geographical and in political terms, but it is as if its power implodes in itself (see l. 58 *e tuis in tua*). Rome erases every difference: *patriam diuersis gentibus unam* (63). Its inclusivity is continually expressed through the massive recurrences of the prefix *con-* (15 *collegarum*, 18 *concilium*, 35 *complexis*, 57 *continet*, 65 *consortia*, 70 *conuenit*, 77 *complexa*, 78 *communi*, 83 *conectere*, 101 *conduntur*, 102 *consumunt*), through the almost tautological expressions (e.g., ll. 91–2: *quod regnas minus est quam regnare mereris / excedis factis grandia facta tuis*) and of course figures of multiplication (1.93–4: *percensere labor densis decora alta trophaeis / ut si quis stellas pernumerare uelit*). A similar language re-emerges in other passages in which the image of Rome plays, though indirectly, a relevant role, such as the episode on Rufius Volusianus (1.415–28) and in particular the arrival of the poet in Pisa, where he can admire a statue erected in honour of his father Lachanius (1.559–96). Pisa is also represented through figures of geographical centredness and inclusivity (566: *cingunt geminis Arnus et Ausur*

---

56. "Listen, O fairest queen of thy world, Rome, welcomed amid the starry skies, listen, thou mother of men and mother of gods, thanks to thy temples we are not far from heaven: thee do we chant, and shall, while destiny allows, for ever chant. None can be safe if forgetful of thee. Sooner shall guilty oblivion whelm the sun than the honour due to thee quit my heart; for benefits extend as far as the sun's rays, where the circling Ocean-flood bounds the world. For thee the very Sun-God who holdeth all together doth revolve: his steeds that rise in thy domains he puts in thy domains to rest. Thee Africa hath not stayed with scorching sands, nor hath the Bear, armed with its native cold, repulsed thee. As far as living nature hath stretched towards the poles, so far hath earth opened a path for thy valour. For nations far apart thou hast made a single fatherland; under thy dominion captivity hath meant profit even for those who knew not justice: and by offering to the vanquished a share in thine own justice, thou hast made a city of what was erstwhile a world. As authors of our race we acknowledge Venus and Mars—mother of the sons of Aeneas, father of the scions of Romulus: clemency in victory tempers armed strength: both names befit thy character: hence thy noble pleasure in war and in mercy: it vanquishes the dreaded foe and cherishes the vanquished."

aquis, and 569: *communi in gurgite*), while the father symbolizes, analogously to Venus and Mars in the praise of Rome, the generative power previously attributed to Rome (575 *genitoris*, 577 *parentis*, 579 *pater*).

The centrifugal movement indicates the direction of the journey which brings the narrating voice of the poet away from the centre, Rome. In an analogy to Ausonius's *Mosella*, the transition to another dimension is described in terms which indicate abruptness: compare 1.1 *uelocem reditum* and 19 *reuellitur*. Other motifs include deformation (1.21 *deformia*), falling apart (1.27 *longas ruinas*, 29 *laceris fundis*) and separation (1.35 *laxatis complexibus*). Within this constellation an important role is played by water. Rutilius decides to travel on the sea because travelling through Italy could be dangerous (1.37–42), and so, after the praise of Rome, Rutilius begins his journey on the Tiber:

> *Tum demum ad naues gradior, qua fronte bicorni*
>   *diuiduus Tiberis dexteriora secat*
> *laeuus inaccessis fluuius uitatur arenis* (1.179–81).[57]

A sense of dismemberment is given by the ramification of the river (*fronte bicorni, diuiduus, secat*) and by the verb describing the very act of setting sail (1.217, *soluimus*). Even a toponym can contribute to the fragmentation taking place when the poet leaves Rome: *Centumcellas* (1.237). The water symbolically breaks the spatial continuity given by the ground on the dry land.

In this sense, the three poems discussed in this chapter have also this aspect in common: even if each in a different way, they all thematize precisely through water the separation from a centre, represented by the ground, which allegorically represents the tradition of Latin poetry. In the preface of *De raptu Proserpinae*, as we have seen, a sailor learns how to gradually leave the coast. The same caution is demonstrated by Rutilius and his men when they begin their journey (1.199 *progredimur paruis per litora proxima cymbis*). Finally, before departing, Rutilius gives another look at his Rome and he observes:

> *Illic perpetui soles, atque ipse uidetur,*
>   *quem sibi Roma facit, purior esse dies* (1.200–1)[58]

Purior referred to an atmospheric agent is also used, as we have seen, by Ausonius and Claudian in passages where they also narrate the particular

---

57. "Then at length I proceed to the ships, where with two-horned brow the branching Tiber cleaves his way to the right. The channel on the left is avoided for its unapproachable sands."
58. "There 'tis lasting sunshine: the very daylight which Rome makes for herself seems purer than all else."

moment of passing from one dimension to another: in *Mosella* 13 *purior hic campis aer*, when the poet for the first time sights the Moselle valley, and in *De raptu Proserpinae*, as part of Pluto's description of his kingdom to his new wife, we read: *lumenque uidebis purius* (2.283–4).[59] In the same passage (2.289) Pluto qualifies the flowers in the Underworld as *perpetui*; the adjective is used by Rutilius here in order to describe the eternal presence of the sun in Rome. In both cases, the adjective works as a marker of a temporal distinction.

6.5. Conclusion: "the other place"

King: Where is Polonius?
Hamlet: In heaven: send thither to see: if your messenger
find him not there, seek him i' the other place yourself.

Shakespeare

I have focused on three of the most read of late antique poems in order to consider the possibility of reading them allegorically. A macrotheme emerges with great clarity: that of displacement. This characterizes the poems both in narrative and stylistic terms. In the *Mosella* the celebrated river creates both a distance from the Italian landscape and a proximity to Ausonius's home city, Burdigala, and its river, the Garonne. *De raptu Proserpinae* is of course the story of the abduction of Proserpina from the Upper to the Underworld, but it also refers to other displacements, like the separation of Sicily from the mainland and the wandering of Ceres. Finally, *De reditu suo* by means of the double movement, which I have defined here centripetal and centrifugal, allegorizes *displacement* itself. From my reading of three poems emerges the presence of *the other place*, which is thematized in various ways through the constant appearance of a dichotomy of two levels. This "other place" is always better (*purior*) than the usual one, and it brings the text back to an original or *generative* phase: Ausonius through his subject, the river Moselle, goes back to Burdigala and the Garonne; Claudian applies a familial language in key passages; Rutilius recaptures the origins of Rome by recalling a pre-Roman atmosphere and also using a familial terminology (see 1,67–8). Despite the similarities, an important difference emerges: if in Ausonius's and Claudian's texts, *the other place* is located outside but is nonetheless constructed on the model of the *usual* place (Rome and Italy for Ausonius, the Upperworld for Claudian), in *De reditu suo* the other place is astonishingly

---

59. While praising Rome's magnificent architecture, which even contains all the natural elements, Rutilius again uses the comparative: *frigidus aestiuas hinc temperat halitus auras / innocuamque leuat purior unda sitim* (1.105–6).

represented by Rome itself: it is there that the air is *purior* and the sun eternal. And as we have seen, the motif of water plays in all three poems the important role of conveying the passage from one to *the other place*. Therefore the change in the historical situation certainly plays a role. Rutilius in fact thematizes in his poem precisely the loss of centrality of the city after Alaric's sack in 410. Rome, while losing its political and geographical centrality, acquires a symbolic and ideal status, an *allegory* of itself and of its own past.

It is certainly legitimate to look at historical circumstances and relevant changes both in politics and culture in order to reconstruct the background in which these texts originated. But interpretation cannot merely reconstruct and describe historical circumstances, it has also to identify and discuss the new meaning of the emerging new poetics of Late Antiquity. For this reason the question cannot only be to *which* other place these poems refer. The *other place*, in the terms I have been describing, allegorizes precisely an absence of that very place; that is, the search for a new language but at the same time the impossibility of escaping the language of the Latin poetic tradition.[60] As already indicated above, deconstruction sees in allegory the key concept of the essence of any text, since it refers to the absence of a referent outside of the texts themselves. But de Man (1983 [1969]) shows also that allegory is generated within a general loss of meaning of literary language, within which presence is replaced by absence. The late Latin poems discussed in this chapter, although they were conceived in a very different age from ours, if read according to the new allegoresis sketched above, thematize absence and loss. The *other place* is not a real place, it does not indicate a particular poetic direction, but rather it allegorizes the departure from past tradition, and it also refers to the *other* level of interpretation I have been attempting to demonstrate.

I also have argued for the importance of a hermeneutic technique which considers late Latin texts not (only) from the perspective of the classical canon. In particular, I have been analysing and discussing these texts by explicitly bracketing the usual intertextual approach, which sometimes turns out becoming an obsessive chase for references to canonical authors as an end in itself. This is not to say that this approach has not made valuable contributions to the study of late antique texts; but of course it does not exhaust the interpretive possibilities. The new allegoresis I have briefly introduced here could fruitfully be applied not only to the late antique literary context more generally but also to a broad spectrum of texts of other kinds and periods. Rediscovering allegory as a hermeneutical

---

60. In this sense, my approach to the texts I discuss can be seen as complementary to Hernández Lobato's discussion of the "poetics of silence" elsewhere in this volume.

possibility brings two benefits. It allows us to read late antique texts within their own interpretive frame since, historically, allegory is a prominent product of this period. And since allegory by definition emphasizes the role of the reader, this approach underscores the particular importance of reception for the interpretation of late antique texts.[61]

61. My deep gratitude to Jesus Hernández Lobato, Jaś Elsner, Craig Williams, and Stephen Hinds for their invaluable suggestions and to Orla Mulholland for having carefully corrected my English.

7

Metapoetics in the Prefaces of Claudian's De raptu Proserpinae

STEPHEN HARRISON

7.1. Introduction

Recent scholarship[1] has rightly stressed the creativity of the poetic output of Claudian (writing ca. 395–405 CE) and has persuasively argued that his texts are as rich and sophisticated as many of those commonly admired in earlier Latin literature.[2] This is part of a welcome larger tendency: as with their equivalents in the Neronian and Flavian ages, the Latin poetic texts of Late Antiquity in general have increasingly been rehabilitated from previous prejudice against "uncanonical" periods and from the charge of being merely "imitative," and their characteristically decorative aesthetics, innovative poetics, and vivid cultural and historical contexts have been effectively appreciated.[3] In what follows, I argue that the two extant prefaces to books of the *De raptu Proserpinae*, Claudian's major mythological poem, engage in the kind of creative allusion and metapoetic play usually associated with much earlier works in Latin literature and that they show new features connected with their late antique cultural setting, such as a clear association with elements of prose rhetoric.

More than half of the books in Claudian's major hexameter poems have attached to them brief verse prefaces in the less elevated metre of elegiacs.[4] Such prefaces are themselves a post-Augustan development in the history of Roman literature as we have it: the first extant poetic preface formally separate from the actual opening/programmatic poem of a collection or work is the epigram preceding Ovid's *Amores* (late first century BCE), which refers to their shortening

---

1. My thanks to Jesús Hernández Lobato and Jaś Elsner for their editorial guidance and patience and to Gavin Kelly for some useful comments and bibliography and an early sight of Kelly 2013. The text of Claudian used is that of Hall 1985; English translations are my own.

2. Cf., e.g., Gruzelier 1993, Dewar 1996, Ware 2004, Gioseffi 2004, Hinds 2012.

3. See, e.g., Roberts 1989a, Herzog 2002, Cameron 2006.

4. Of the seventeen hexameter books of *carmina maiora* other than the *De raptu* in Hall's Teubner edition, the following nine are preceded by prefaces: *in Rufinum* 1 (3 Hall), *in Rufinum* 2 (5), *Tert. Cons. Hon.* (7), *epithal. Hon.* (10), *Pan. Mall.* (17), *in Eutrop.* 2 (20), *Cons. Stil.* 3 (24), *bell. Get.* (26), *Sext. Cons. Hon.* (28). On Claudian's prefaces in general, see Ware 2004, which has brief but useful comments on both the prefaces treated here, Perrelli 1992, which looks at the prefaces in the political poems, and Felgentreu 1999, which considers the whole range of prefaces.

from five books to three, while those attached to all the five books of Phaedrus's iambic fables a generation later (first half of first century CE) provide more substantial introductions generally addressed to real-life individual dedicatees: in terms of content, those to book 1 (seven lines) and book 5 (ten lines) claim Aesop for model and that to book 2 (eleven lines) appeals to the reader to appreciate both fidelity to Aesop and Phaedrus's own original contribution, while that to book 4 (twenty lines) is both a more personal dedication to the addressee and a self-defence by the poet. The preface to book 3 is a rather more substantial enterprise, sixty lines of flattery, a history of the genre of Aesopic fable and self-commendation. In both Ovid and Phaedrus the prefaces are in the same metre as the poems they introduce. It is in the Neronian period that we find the first Latin verse preface in a different metre—the fourteen choliambic lines which precede Persius's book of hexameter satires from the 60s CE, an ironic, comic, and self-deprecating introduction. In the later Flavian period (80s and 90s CE) we again find separate prefaces to books in a different literary format, which share with Phaedrus the function of dedicating poetic books to real individuals but which differ from his work in being in prose: a number of Martial's books are introduced by dedicatory prose epistles to friends (I, II, VIII, IX, XII), while each book of Statius's *Silvae* has the same (see White 1974).

Between the late first century and the late fourth there is little evidence, but the practice of Ausonius (d. 394), perhaps the most important Latin poet of the generation before Claudian, follows these precedents: apart from the liminary verses in various metres gathered at the head of what seems to have been a collected edition of his poems (*I Praefationes Variae* in Green's edition; see further Green 1991: xliii–iv), we find introductory prose epistles to verse works (*VIII Protrepticus ad Nepotem, XII Epitaphia, XV Griphus, XVII Bissula, XVIII Cento Nuptialis, XIX Cupido Cruciatus, XXV Technopaegnia*), separate dedicatory poems in the sole or predominant metre of the work or collection introduced (*XI Commemoratio Professorum Burdigalensium*: a six-line elegiac preface to twenty-six poems, fourteen in elegiacs; *XXIII Caesares*, a five-line hexameter preface to a largely hexameter book), and once a mixture of the two (*X Parentalia*: a prose epistle and a short elegiac preface to a largely elegiac book); in only one work do we find a poetic preface in a metre unconnected with the collection, *XXVI Ludus Septem Sapientum*, a notionally theatrical work in the dramatic metre of iambic senarii, which is prefaced by eighteen lines of elegiacs.[5] Ausonius's liminary verses and his prose prefaces contain metapoetic reflections and interesting self-presentations of the poet, which form an

---

5. See Cazzuffi 2014.

important precedent for Claudian's practice: the first of the *Praefationes Variae* is an Ovidian-style elegiac autobiography, the third a witty recall in hendecasyllables of Catullus's collection-opening dedication to Nepos (first century BCE), the fifth a witty elegiac dialogue with one of his own books.[6]

In Claudian's own period, we find another poet who resembles him in attaching substantial verse prefaces in different metres to longer hexameter works. Claudian's older contemporary Prudentius (writing before 405) prefaces his *Apotheosis* in 1,084 hexameters not only with a twelve-line hexameter hymn to the Trinity but also with 56 epodic iambics (trimeter and dimeter, the main metre of Horace's *Epodes*) defending the Christian orthodox view of the divine nature which the poem sets out, prefixes his *Hamartigenia* in 966 hexameters against gnostic dualism with 63 iambic senarii particularly attacking the Marcionite form of this heresy, and introduces his *Psychomachia* in 915 hexameters on the allegorical battle of virtues and vices with 68 iambic senarii which take the struggle back to Abraham; likewise, his two books against the paganism of Symmachus (657 and 1,132 hexameters) are prefaced with 89 stichic asclepiads (cf. Horace *Odes* 1.1) and 66 stichic glyconics (used regularly in the lyrics of Senecan tragedy), respectively. But none of these prefaces focuses on the person of the poet or metapoetic issues: all are really miniaturized introductions to the main matter of the larger works to which they are attached.

Claudian's prefaces, on the other hand, like those of Ausonius, can be seen at least sometimes to reprise the literary reflections on the poet, his work, and his role which appear in Ovid, Phaedrus, and Persius, as well as being in different metres from the works to which they are attached. The distribution of these prefaces is sometimes uneven within the individual hexameter works, sometimes perhaps as a result of losses in transmission.[7] The *De raptu Proserpinae* has elegiac prefaces to books 1 and 2 (see below) but not book 3; the *In Eutropium* has no preface to its first book but a long elegiac one to its second; the first two books of the poem on Stilicho's consulship have none but the third book does (in elegiacs); and the single-book panegyrics for Honorius's third and sixth consulships have elegiac prefaces but not that for his fourth. These prefaces have much more significance than almost all of those which have just been considered in previous poets; they sometimes seem to reflect important political changes since the last book (e.g., *In Eutropium* 2, which reflects the subject's fall;

---

6. It is not clear which book this poem was originally attached to (see Green's commentary); here I follow the sequence of texts and analysis of Green 1991. For recent work on Ausonius's self-presentation, see Kleinschmidt 2013.

7. For the loss of parts of Claudian's prefaces in some lines of transmission, see Hall 1969: 54, Dewar 1996: 47–8.

Cameron 1969: 136–8, Gioseffi 2004: 299–300) and reflect substantially on the poet's writing (e.g., *Tert. Cons. Hon., Sext. Cons. Hon.*; for the latter, see Dewar 1996: 47–63); as we shall see, this is the case for *De raptu Proserpinae* 1. Such prefaces can also relate to rhetorical (*pro*)*laliai*—short narrative introductions to prose declamations (e.g., in Lucian); as we shall also see, this is the case for *De raptu Proserpinae* 2.

7.2. DE RAPTU 1 PRAEFATIO

Inventa secuit primus qui nave profundum
  et rudibus remis sollicitavit aquas,
qui dubiis ausus committere flatibus alnum
  quas natura negat praebuit arte vias:
tranquillis primum trepidus se credidit undis
  litora securo tramite summa legens;
mox longos temptare sinus et linquere terras
  et leni coepit pandere vela Noto.
ast ubi paulatim praeceps audacia crevit
  cordaque languentem dedidicere metum,
iam vagus inrumpit pelagus caelumque secutus
  Aegaeas hiemes Ioniumque domat.

He who was the first to invent the ship and cleave the deep,
  and stir the waters with virgin oars,
he who dared to trust his boat to the uncertain winds
  provided by his skill routes nature denies:
first fearfully he consigned himself to quiet waters,
  coasting the edge of shores in a safe route:
then he began to cross long bays and leave land,
  and spread his sails to the gentle south-west wind.
but when rash boldness slowly grew, and his heart
  unlearned the fear that made him slow,
now freely ranging, seeking ocean and heaven,
  he tames the Aegean storms and the Ionian sea.

Gruzelier in her commentary (1993: 80) has rightly described this preface as "an extension of the metaphor of poetic endeavour = sea-going into a stylized allegory of Claudian's poetic career up to the point where he began the *DRP*"; a short article by Minissale (1975–6) has pointed in outline to some links with well-known Augustan poetic programmes. I would here like to explore and extend these brief formulations. The preface begins with what appears to be the familiar analogy between first sailing and first poetry, well established in Latin literature before Claudian (see, e.g., Harrison 2006); the use of the ship and its cleaving of waves with the ship as a metapoetic symbol is found already at VERG. *georg.* 2.50: *ac prius ignotum ferro quam scindimus aequor*, "and before we cleave the unknown ocean with iron"; while the same passage confirms the equivalent of the deep sea and hexameter verse (Claudian's *profundum* clearly picks up the Vergilian *aequor*). The invention of the ship mentioned by Claudian irresistibly recalls the story of the Argonauts, itself of course an epic plot.[8] As an expert Homeric reader (Cameron 1970: 306), Claudian would no doubt recall the famous allusion in the *Odyssey* to "the Argo everyone knows" (Ἀργὼ πᾶσι μέλουσα 12.70), implying to Homer's readers that the Argonaut saga preceded that of the *Odyssey* as a primal epic topic; for Claudian as a reader of Catullus (Cameron 1970: 305), the line *et rudibus remis sollicitavit aquas*, "and stir the waters with virgin oars," surely looks back to the context and phrasing of the maiden voyage of the *Argo* at CAT. 64.11: *illa rudem cursu prima imbuit Amphitriten*, "that [ship] first initiated the virgin Amphitrite with its course." Likewise *audeo* is a verb used in Catullus's description of the first voyage of the *Argo*, where the Argonauts *ausi sunt vada salsa cita decurrere puppi*, "dared to run over the salty shallows with swift ship" (64.6);[9] in both passages it also surely has overtones of audacious poetic enterprise, of boldly going where no one has gone before. This is confirmed once again by a passage from Vergil's *Georgics* (1.40–1), *da facilem cursum atque audacibus adnue coeptis / pelagoque uolans da uela patenti*, "grant an easy course and assent to my bold enterprises,"[10] where the poet asks the future god Caesar to approve his new work, using both the first navigation metaphor and the idea of boldness. As Ware (2004) has acutely noted, Claudian's oblique reference to the voyage of the Argo here in his first four lines also picks up the first four lines of the *Argonautica* of Valerius Flaccus (1.1–4), the key Latin source for the story available to Claudian.[11]

The description of the poet's quiet coasting before venturing on the open sea (*tranquillis primum trepidus se credidit undis / litora securo tramite summa legens*) recalls the use of the same metaphor in other famous expressions of poetic caution: in the proem of the second book of the *Georgics*, already echoed in this preface, Vergil calls on Maecenas to follow the shore at the start of the book's poetic voyage (VERG. *georg.* 2.44 *primi lege litoris oram*, "coast the rim of

---

8. So, e.g., Felgentreu 1999: 161, in the course of a useful account of this preface (157–68).
9. The parallel was already noted by Minissale 1975–6: 496 n. 2, without comment.
10. Again already noted by Minissale 1975–6: 496 n. 1, without comment.
11. VAL. Fl. 1.1 *prima* ~ 1.1 *primus*, 1.3 *ausa* ~ 1.3 *ausus*, 1.4 *rumpere* ~ 1.4 *inrumpis*.

the edge of the shore"), while Propertius evokes the same image for his shore-hugging elegiacs in contrast with ocean-going epic in Phoebus's address to the poet at PROP. 3.3.23–4, *alter remus aquas alter tibi radat harenas, / tutus eris: medio maxima turba mari est*, "if one of your oars grazes the water, the other the shore, you will be safe: the greatest disturbance is in mid-ocean" (a clear figure for the elegiac couplet's uneven metrical combination of "oceanic" epic hexameter and less ambitious pentameter).[12]

The gradual growth of *audacia*, like *ausus* earlier, plainly refers to growing epic ambition (*ast ubi paulatim praeceps audacia crevit*: note how the phrase is headed by the emphatically epic phrase *ast ubi*—cf., e.g., VERG. *Aen*. 3.410), while the move to the open ocean is (as we have already seen) a metaphor for epic itself (*iam vagus inrumpit pelagus caelumque secutus / Aegaeas hiemes Ioniumque domat*). Here both the weather and the geographical locations have symbolic significance: *hiemes* looks to the frequency of storms in epic from the *Odyssey* onwards,[13] while the naming of the Aegean and Ionian seas picks out waters associated with Homer, who was thought to come either from the Ionian coast of Anatolia or from an Aegean island (cf. ANTIPATER *anth. Plan*. 296, listing Colophon, Smyrna, Chios, Ios, or Salamis as possible Homeric birthplaces).[14] *Caelumque secutus* might suggest a search for poetic immortality to match that of Homer and also perhaps the impending "heavenly" subject of the *De raptu* itself. We should also recall that the key Greek source for the story of the kidnap of Proserpina, the *Homeric Hymn to Demeter*, was in Antiquity thought to be a genuinely Homeric work: the poet is gearing up for a Homeric topic in the work which this preface introduces.

As Minissale has noted, the key innovation Claudian makes here to the "sailing = poetry" topos is the introduction of autobiography: the image here is made into "un pretesto prezioso per introdurre l'elemento autobiographico" (Minissale 1975–6: 499). Here we have a case of the poet self-consciously constructing his own ascent within the subgenres of hexameter poetry: the *De raptu Proserpinae* is Claudian's only surviving multibook mythological narrative poem and can be construed as a step up from his encomiastic and political poetry in its use of traditional "Homeric" subject matter. The idea of such career progression within hexameters was already familiar in Antiquity: Statius presents his *Silvae* in his preface to its first book as a kind of prelude to his forthcoming *Thebaid*, suggesting that they are worth reading despite their light nature,

---

12. Both parallels are already noted by Minissale 1975–6: 496 n. 1, without comment; for the metapoetic symbolism of the Propertian passage, see Heyworth and Morwood 2011: 120.
13. Cf., e.g., Friedrich 1956.
14. For discussion and further evidence for Homer's supposed origins, see Gow and Page 1968: 2, 75–6.

and compares his future progression from *Silvae* to *Thebaid* with the supposed upward moves of Homer and Vergil from the parodic *Batrachomyomachia* and *Culex* to their serious poems (STAT. *Silv.* 1 *praef.*): *Sed et Culicem legimus, et Batrachomyomachiam etiam agnoscimus: nec quisquam est illustrium poetarum, qui non aliquid operibus suis stilo remissiore praeluserit*, "but we read the *Culex*, and even recognise the *Batrachomyomachia*: nor is there any one of the great poets, who has not made some prelude to his works in a more relaxed style." We can thus add Claudian to the list of Latin poets who reflect on their own literary careers.[15]

This apparent construction of a poetic career provides some limited evidence for the dating of the *De raptu*, since it implies that the poet is moving on to a higher form of hexameter poetry after some experience in a lower one. This fits the general view that the *De raptu* comes after some at least of the other hexameter poetry, with the first book being followed after a gap by the second and third, the delay being explained by the preface to the second book. In what follows I argue that this second preface must be dated before the end of the year 397, in other words in the early days of Claudian's presence in Rome (where he is attested as present for the first time in 395: cf. Cameron 1970: 30–5). The first preface would therefore be written at a date even earlier than this and even closer to Claudian's arrival in the imperial capital from Alexandria; its emphasis on journeying by ship, even its allusions to the Ionian and Aegean seas, might then have some autobiographical colour given the real long journey that the poet had undertaken in the search to advance his poetic career.

7.3. DE RAPTU 2 PRAEFATIO

Otia sopitis ageret cum cantibus Orpheus
  neglectumque diu deposuisset ebur,
lugebant erepta sibi solatia Nymphae,
  quaerebant dulces flumina maesta modos.
Saeva feris natura redit metuensque leonem   5
  implorat citharae vacca tacentis opem.
Illius et duri flevere silentia montes
  silvaque Bistoniam saepe secuta chelyn.
Sed postquam Inachiis Alcides missus ab Argis
  Thracia pacifero contigit arva pede   10
diraque sanguinei vertit praesepia regis
  et Diomedeos gramine pavit equos,

---

15. For this tradition see, e.g., Hardie and Moore 2010.

tunc patriae festo laetatus tempore vates
  desuetae repetit fila canora lyrae
et resides levi modulatus pectine nervos   15
  pollice festivo nobile duxit ebur.
Vix auditus erat, venti frenantur et undae,
  pigrior astrictis torpuit Hebrus aquis,
porrexit Rhodope sitientes carmina rupes,
  excussit gelidas pronior Ossa nives.   20
Ardua nudato descendit populus Haemo
  et comitem quercum pinus amica trahit,
Cirrhaeasque dei quamvis despexerit artes,
  Orpheis laurus vocibus acta venit.
Securum blandi leporem fovere molossi   25
  vicinumque lupo praebuit agna latus.
Concordes varia ludunt cum tigride dammae,
  Massylam cervi non timuere iubam.
Ille novercales stimulos actusque canebat
  Herculis et forti monstra subacta manu,   30
qui timidae matri pressos ostenderit angues
  intrepidusque fero riserit ore puer.
"Te neque Dictaeas quatiens mugitibus urbes
  taurus nec Stygii terruit ira canis,
non leo sidereos caeli rediturus ad axes,   35
  non Erymanthei gloria montis aper.
Solvis Amazonios cinctus, Stymphalidas arcu
  appetis, occiduo ducis ab orbe greges
tergeminique ducis numerosos deicis artus
  et totiens uno victor ab hoste redis.   40
Non cadere Antaeo, non crescere profuit Hydrae,
  nec cervam volucres eripuere pedes.
Caci flamma perit, rubuit Busiride Nilus,
  prostratis maduit nubigenis Pholoe.
Te Libyci stupuere sinus, te maxima Tethys   45
  horruit, imposito cum premerere polo.
Firmior Herculea mundus cervice pependit,
  lustrarunt umeros Phoebus et astra tuos."
Thracius haec vates. Sed tu Tirynthius alter,
  Florentine, mihi, tu mea plectra moves   50
antraque Musarum longo torpentia somno
  excutis et placidos ducis in orbe choros.

When Orpheus was engaged in rest with his songs put to sleep
    And had put down his ivory instrument for some while in neglect
The Nymphs lamented for their stolen solace
    And the rivers sadly missed his sweet measures.
Their natural savagery returned to the beasts, and the cow,
    In fear of the lion, implored the aid of the lyre that was now still.
His silence was lamented by the tough mountains
    And by the forest that had often followed the sounding Thracian shell.
But after Hercules, sent from Argos, city of Inachus,
    Touched the fields of Thrace with peace-bringing foot,
And overturned the terrible stables of the bloody king
    And pastured the horses of Diomedes with grass,
Then the bard, cheered by his country's happy times,
    Sought again the sounding strings of his long-left lyre,
And, tuning the dormant notes with a polished plectrum
    Played the noble ivory with joyous joint.
Hardly was he heard when the winds and waves were bridled,
    Hebrus slowed more sluggishly with restricted stream,
Rhodope stretched out its rocks all athirst for songs,
    And Ossa, bending down, threw off its coat of frozen snow.
The lofty poplar came down from a denuded Haemus
    And the friendly pine-tree dragged along the oak as companion,
And, though she had rejected Apollo's arts,
    The bay-tree came, impelled by the voice of Orpheus.
The Molossian hounds fawningly licked the hare, free from fear
    And the lamb presented her side as neighbour to the wolf.
Hinds played in happy concord with the striped tiger,
    And the stags felt no fear of the African mane.
Orpheus sang of the stepmother's goading and the deeds
    Of Hercules, and the monsters quelled by his mighty hand,
Of how the boy showed the strangled snakes to his fearful mother,
    And laughed fearlessly with his fierce mouth.
"You were not frightened by the bull that shook
    The cities of Crete with his roaring, or the rage of the hound of Hell,
Nor by the lion, doomed to return to the starry vaults of heaven,
    Nor by the boar, the boast of Mount Erymanthus:
You can loose the girdle of the Amazon, hunt down the monsters
    Of Stymphalus with your bow, lead herds from the sun's setting,

And cast down the numerous limbs of the three-bodied leader,
    Returning home victorious so many times from a single enemy.
It was no use for Antaeus to fall, for the Hydra to grow again,
    And nor could its speedy feet carry the hind in escape.
The flames of Cacus came to naught, the Nile blushed for its Busiris,
    Mount Pholoe was soaked under the bodies of the cloud-born Centaurs.
At you the bays of Libya were taken aback, at you mighty Tethys
    Trembled, when you bore the weight of the heavens upon you.
The universe hung more securely from the neck of Hercules,
    Phoebus and the stars passed your shoulders in their courses."
So sang the Thracian bard. But you, Florentinus, are a second Hercules
    For me, you stir the plectrum of my lyre,
And shake the Muses' grottoes sluggish with long sleep,
    And lead in peaceful dances in a circle.

(a) Dating and political references

This preface is addressed to Florentinus, who was prefect of the city of Rome in the years 395–7 CE. Two issues arise: the length of the gap between the first and second books of the *De raptu* given the opening allusion here to Orpheus's silence (clearly a reference to a pause in Claudian's own poetry; see (b) below); and the occasion and date of the address to Florentinus, elaborately praised through a comparison with Hercules. Given that Claudian compares his main patron, Stilicho, himself to Hercules (21.140–7) and that Stilicho's many military victories in several parts of the world and triumphant returns to Rome make him a natural analogue for the Greek hero, some have thought that Florentinus is another name for Stilicho here; but this is very unlikely given the clear presence of another character named Florentinus at the very top of Roman politics in this period (see Cameron 1970: 453–5). Some have also thought that the preface is misplaced and belongs to a lost panegyric of Florentinus himself; this would be unparalleled in the transmission of Claudian and seems an extreme solution. Both in terms of Florentinus's career and in terms of the figure of Orpheus (see (b) below), this preface can be made to fit the date and content of *De raptu Proserpinae*.

Though Cameron (1970: 455) argues that there is no reason to suppose that the *De raptu* was dedicated to Florentinus during his prefecture of Rome, it is hard to find another point in the latter's career where the elaborate comparison with the deeds of Hercules is appropriate. Though I do not think we need to find closely fitting parallels between the Herculean labours and the particular achievements of Florentinus as prefect,[16] the reference to Hercules's taking up the burden of the globe itself, which forms the climax of Orpheus's song, would be a neat general allusion to Florentinus's control of the *urbs* of Rome, so often compared to the *orbis* of the world in Roman literature from the late Republic to Late Antiquity (cf., e.g., Bréguet 1969, Eigler 2008). Florentinus served as city prefect for a longer term than the normal year or so; and he was dismissed from the post at the end of 397 CE as the consequence of a dispute with Stilicho, apparently going into retirement in Gaul (Cameron 1970: 392). It seems unlikely that Claudian would have addressed him so fulsomely after this event, and as already noted, the Herculean analogy works best if Florentinus is currently engaged on a large task which benefits his country.[17]

I agree with the case made by Charlet (1991: xxvii) for a dating of the *De raptu* in the period 392–4 for the first book and 395–6 for the other two books; a gap of a year or even two years between poems was quite a considerable period for a prolific poet like Claudian, most of whose extensive output can be securely dated to the period 395–404 CE at the rate of several poems per year. In the preface to the *Bellum Geticum* of 402 we find a reference to delay similar to that in *De raptu* 2 (25.1–4):

Post resides annos longo velut excita somno
  Romanis fruitur nostra Thalia choris.

After years of rest, as if roused from long slumber,
  My Muse now enjoys the measures of Rome.

The "years of rest" are a maximum of two, since Claudian's last major poem on Stilicho's consulship must have been written in the latter's consular year of 400; and this is to discount the two lesser poems, the *Epistula ad Serenam* (*carm. min.* 31 Hall) and *In Jacobum* (*carm. min.* 50), which belong to the years 400–2. The considerable chronological gap between books in the same poem is, however, unusual. Charlet's arguments to show that the first book was composed in Claudian's home city of Alexandria and that the other books may have been added on his arrival in

---

16. In particular, I am sceptical about the link between Hercules's return of Diomedes's horses to a normal equine diet and Florentinus's achievement in provisioning Rome during the Gildonic crisis—see Cameron 1970: 453–5; it is notable that Florentinus is not mentioned in Claudian's account of Gildo's threat in *De bello Gildonico*. The further idea of Dutsch 1991, that the *De raptu Proserpinae*, a poem which narrates the origin of wheat growing, alludes in general terms to Florentinus's sustaining of the corn supply, is interesting but unprovable.

17. For another view, see Felgentreu 1999: 172, suggesting a date of 402, in a significant account of this preface (169–81).

Rome are attractive (Charlet 1991: 32). Book 2 addresses the most important man in Rome other than the emperor during Stilicho's constant absence on campaign (395–7 CE); he might naturally be the recipient of extensive flattery from a recently arrived poet trying to establish his position in the city; Stilicho himself is not mentioned in a datable passage of Claudian until the *In Rufinum* of 396 (1.259), though after that date he is plainly Claudian's central patron (Cameron 1970: 45).

(b) Metapoetic references and links with De raptu

It seems clear that Orpheus stands for Claudian himself here; Orpheus's break from song matches the gap between *De raptu* 1 and 2, and both poets might be viewed as coming from the exotic edges of the known Mediterranean world: Claudian from Egypt, Orpheus from the distant land of Thrace. Furthermore, as noted by Kelly (2013), the specific comparison between Orpheus and Claudian is found in the *Epistula ad Serenam*, where the supposed advocacy of Serena, cousin and mother-in-law to the boy emperor Honorius, for Claudian's own marriage is compared at some length to Juno's support for the marriage of Orpheus (*carm. min.* 31 Hall, esp. 33–4), as well as in a number of other passages (see Bureau 2009).[18] Schmitz (2004) has further suggested that Orphic imagery can be found in the preface to book 1 in its references to the imposition of poetic order on unruly nature and that Claudian in his usual role of panegyrical poet can be generally compared with Orpheus as an agent of harmony. I am a little sceptical of these rather general interpretations, but her further argument that Orpheus embodies a principle of order to be found elsewhere in the *De raptu*, especially in the figure of Proserpina, is more attractive, and I would like to follow her lead and that of Bureau (2009: 55–60) in arguing that the Orpheus of the second preface picks up important themes of the *De raptu* as a whole.

Here we need to recall the plot of the poem at the point where this preface occurs. Book 1 of *De raptu* concludes with the description of the tapestry woven by Proserpina, describing the world and its creation, which evidently looks forward to her kidnapping and forced marriage in the next book of the poem (1.246–72). A key element towards the end is a depiction of Hades and its ruler, where she is destined to spend at least some of her future life (1.265–7):

nec non et patrui pingit sacraria Ditis
fatalesque sibi manes. nec defuit omen;
praescia nam subitis maduerunt fletibus ora.

---

18. Kelly 2013 has also attractively argued that Claudian's self-identification with Orpheus is picked up by Sidonius's later use of Orpheus as a figure for Claudian.

Further, she depicted the sanctuary of her uncle Pluto,
And the shades that were her destiny. An omen intervened,
For her foreseeing face dampened with sudden tears.

Here it becomes clear that the ekphrasis of Proserpina's weaving is proleptic, anticipating the future of its own narrative, a technique which goes back to Homer (see Harrison 2001); the girl weaves her own future kidnap, imminent in the next book. The mention of the Underworld reminds us that the *De raptu*'s narrative of contact with the world below is parallel to the story of Orpheus, who descends to the Underworld and either does or does not retrieve Eurydice according to which of the two mythological versions one adopts (Vergil notoriously has both, *georg*. 4.453–527 [failure] and *Aen*. 6.119–20 [success]).[19] Just so Ceres, though without actually descending to the Underworld herself,[20] both does and does not retrieve her daughter, famously condemned to spend half the year with Hades and half in the world above, so that Proserpina, like Eurydice, can be seen as someone who both breaks the bonds of Hell and is held by them in the face of a rescue attempt by a loved one.

Finally, as Ware has plausibly suggested (2004: 185), the focus on Orpheus in the preface to *De raptu* 2 links neatly with the preface to *De raptu* 1 as analysed above: Orpheus was famously an Argonaut, which picks up the Argonautic theme of initiatory voyaging, which is the central topic of the earlier preface.

(c) Link with rhetorical prolaliai

Finally, I consider the connection of this preface with the rhetorical prose tradition of *prolaliai*, short spoken prefaces on mythical or other subjects with some relevance to the main performance which they introduced. In Latin literature the second-century *Florida* of Apuleius may well contain some, whether whole or in part (the work presents twenty-three excerpts from Apuleius's speeches, some of which may be complete).[21] A constant theme in these pieces is the description of a great literary or philosophical performer, which seems likely to have functioned as a point of comparison for Apuleius himself in his careful self-fashioning in front of audiences. *Florida* 3 is a case in point: Apuleius introduces the mythological theme of the poetic contest between the god Apollo and the satyr Marsyas:

Sed Marsyas, quod stultitiae maximum specimen, non intellegens se deridiculo haberi, priusquam tibias occiperet inflare, prius de se et Apolline

---

19. For the various versions of the myth of either ending, see Gantz 1993: 2,722–5.
20. Though she threatens to descend to Hades permanently to live with Proserpina in the account at Ov. *fast*. 6.612, just possibly a reflection of a katabasis in an earlier version of the story.
21. Cf., e.g., Nesselrath 1989: 113–14, Harrison 2000: 133, Hunink 2001: 15.

quaedam deliramenta barbare effutivit, laudans sese, quod erat et coma relicinus et barba squalidus et pectore hirsutus et arte tibicen et fortuna egenus: contra Apollinem—ridiculum dictu—adversis virtutibus culpabat, quod Apollo esset et coma intonsus et genis gratus et corpore glabellus et arte multiscius et fortuna opulentus. "Iam primum," inquit, "crines eius praemulsis antiis et promulsis caproneis anteventuli et propenduli, corpus totum gratissimum, membra nitida, lingua fatidica, seu tute oratione seu versibus malis, utrubique facundia aequipari. Quid quod et vestis textu tenuis, tactu mollis, purpura radians? quid quod et lyra eius auro fulgurat, ebore candicat, gemmis variegat? quid quod et doctissime et gratissime cantilat?"

But Marsyas (and this is the greatest proof of his folly), not realising that he was being made fun of, blurted out some delirious rubbish about himself and Apollo, before he began to blow the pipes, praising himself because he had curly hair, a shaggy beard, a hairy chest, was a piper by profession and unencumbered by wealth. On the other hand (how ridiculous it is to speak of it!) he found fault with Apollo for the opposite characteristics: that Apollo did not cut his hair, that he had pretty cheeks and a smooth body; that he knew many arts and was of wealthy fortune. "Firstly," he said, "his hair sticks out and hangs down in front, with cowlicks and forelocks licked down and slicked forward; his whole body is very pleasing; his limbs are glossy, his tongue foretells the future, and he is equally eloquent whether you choose prose or verse. What about the fact that his clothes are finely woven, soft to the touch, and glowing with purple? What about his lyre shining with gold, gleaming with ivory, and sparkling with gems? What about the fact that he croons most eruditely and most entertainingly?" (trans. Hilton 2001)

Modern commentators are agreed that Apuleius presents himself as resembling the divine singer while his rivals are analogous to the inferior opponent and that this passage is likely to have come from an introductory speech or section attached to a longer performance.[22] Similar examples are *Florida* 9, where Apuleius compares himself with the versatile sophist Hippias, or *Florida* 15, where he draws an analogy with the philosopher Pythagoras, or *Florida* 16, which sets up a similarity between the speaker and the playwright Philemon, or even *Florida* 18, which could parallel Apuleius and the doctor Asclepiades of Prusa.[23] Just as Apuleius in *Florida* expands in prefatory mode on his similarity to Apollo as performer, so Claudian in the preface to *De raptu* 2 explores

---

22. See Hunink 2001: 71, Lee 2005: 72–3.
23. For detailed analysis of each piece mentioned with this perspective, see Harrison 2000: 89–135.

parallels between himself and Orpheus as singer. Though there is no evidence that Claudian knew Apuleius, he would be acquainted with the same rhetorical techniques.

Also close to Claudian's preface are two brief *prolaliai* of Apuleius's contemporary Lucian, where extensive parallels with mythological figures are used to characterize the speaker and to talk about his own performing career.[24] In the *Dionysus*, Lucian compares himself humorously to Dionysus in his military victory over the Indians, where the enemy thought that the god would be effeminate but found him and his forces irresistible, just as Lucian's hearers expected light and comical material but were in fact misled, while in the *Heracles* Lucian compares himself to a portrait of the ageing Heracles as one who is getting old and may now be inadequate for performance, alluding to a previous performance to the same audience. These rhetorical links are relevant for Claudian, since it is clear that the poet was a performer, analogous to a Sophist who consistently recited his works in public, and was well acquainted with Greek rhetorical theory (Cameron 1970: 321–3). Thus this preface in Claudian may actually owe something to the practice of rhetorical prose of the Imperial period. This matches a tendency noted in an important survey of Latin poetry in Late Antiquity as a whole by Alan Cameron, where he points to an interesting cycle between prose and verse: from the middle of the second century CE the literary role of poetry was increasingly taken over by that of prose,[25] while one of the markers of the renaissance of literary culture in Late Antiquity from the end of the third century was the opposite, with poetry appropriating elements associated in the previous century with prose. Thus Claudian's preface can be seen to provide interesting evidence both about the status and self-presentation of poetic performers in Late Antiquity and their proximity to rhetorical performers in prose, whose prestige had risen in the period of the Second Sophistic and continued to be substantial in Late Antiquity.[26]

7.4. CONCLUSION

This paper has argued that both the extant *De raptu* prefaces are rich in allusion and metapoetical symbolism and that they are good evidence for the sophistication of Claudian's literary texture and for the contact in late antique literary

---

24. For a useful treatment of Lucian's *prolaliai* see Nesselrath 1990; for the technique in Greek imperial rhetoric in general, see Russell 1983: 77–8.

25. Cameron 2006; see also Harrison 2013: 39–44, 55–6.

26. See, e.g., Russell 1983.

culture between the writing and performance of texts in verse and prose. These prefaces fulfil a literary function well beyond those of mere dedication and introduction and as such look back to earlier texts rather than the more perfunctory poetic introductions of Claudian's recent predecessors and contemporaries, even if they echo the latter in their use of a different verse form from that of the main poem itself. Interestingly, this focus on the nature of the poet's production may look both forward and back, evoking both an Augustan-style interest in metapoetics and a late antique interest in the figure of the poetic and rhetorical public performer. I have suggested that the symbolic ship of poetry in the preface to *De raptu Proserpinae* 1 represents a transition from encomiastic poems to traditional mythological narrative, marking an upward progression through the hexameter genres in the manner of Vergil, and that it alludes in detail to similar Augustan and indeed earlier metapoetical contexts. In particular, the reference to geographical locations linked with Homer suggest the Homeric ambition of the *De raptu Proserpinae*, both in form (using the hexameter of Homer) and in content (emulating the mythological plot of the *Homeric Hymn to Demeter*). Similarly, I have argued that the evocation of Orpheus in the preface to *De raptu Proserpinae* 2 is integral to the plot of the poem rather than an alien insertion (picking up the katabasis of *De raptu Proserpinae* 1 by allusion to Augustan poetry), as well as presenting an interesting self-characterization of the poet which has clear links with the performance of prose rhetoric in the Roman Empire. The poems of Claudian thus play their full part in the revival of poetics in Late Antiquity and the metatextual and intertextual perspectives discussed in this volume.

Rewriting Ausonius

SCOTT MCGILL

How long does it take to write a poem? For the fourth-century CE poet Ausonius, an answer was not much time at all. In prefaces and prefatory remarks to certain poems, he calls attention to how quickly he wrote the piece—in a little more than a day, in just a part of a day, or as a spontaneous effusion.[1] However accurate his descriptions are, Ausonius uses them for purposes other than revealing his working methods. In every example, he aims to mark a poem as minor and ludic and to disparage the work while striking a conventional pose of affected modesty.[2] Beneath that veneer of modesty is its opposite, self-promotion: Ausonius wishes to impress his addressee and his general reader with his speed of composition.[3] In one instance, too, he tells Paulinus of Nola that he is sending a poor, because hastily written, playful poem to show his commitment to the frequent exchange of poetry with him—an exchange that both demonstrates and nourishes their elite friendship.[4]

It is difficult to look beyond this fast-writing Ausonius, because he matches up so closely with the image of the poet that until recently predominated in the critical imagination: he is a nugatory dabbler who writes facilely, without any real labour or struggle, as he skims the surface of things.[5] But a very different image of the poet also emerges in his work. At varied points, Ausonius counterbalances his references to rapid authorship with glimpses of more deliberate writing, either by claiming to have revised his work or by asking others to edit

---

1. Examples appear in the prefaces to the *Cento nuptialis* and to the *Griphus*, as well as in letters to Petronius Probus (*epist.* 9a) and Paulinus (*epist.* 19a). For Ausonius, I use the text of Green 1999 unless otherwise indicated.

2. The pose belongs to the *captatio beneuolentiae*, the effort to secure the goodwill of an audience; rhetorical theory prescribed the *captatio* for orators, and authors of all stripes commonly pursued it in their prefaces. It seems altogether likely that audience members familiar with the convention would understand that the modesty of the *captatio* was a traditional script rather than an expression of sincere emotion. On affected modesty, see Curtius 1953: 83–5. On Ausonian affected modesty, see Nugent 1990: 44 and Knight 2006: 375–6.

3. Knight 2006: 376 observes that Ausonius's modesty "is at once self-deprecating and boastful."

4. For extended discussion of these topics, see McGill 2014: 123–48.

5. Examples of that viewpoint include Raby 1934: I.56, Rose 1936: 528, Isbell 1974: 41–2, and Browning 1982b: 701. The work of Green 1991 has been instrumental in the Anglophone world in moving criticism of Ausonius past reflexive dismissiveness and hostility. Recent scholarship in continental Europe has also broadened understanding of the poet; Dräger 2002, 2011, 2012 is a notable example.

it. His remarks on both authorial revision and collaborative revision portray literary creation as a process that extends over a period of time and that includes plural acts of authorship: different drafts reveal an author who revisits a text and changes his mind about it, while calls for editing make composition a social act that unfolds in stages.[6] The references to revision create a picture of an author who does not rely upon a flitting muse. Ausonius's attention and efforts are ongoing even when he writes light poetry; the verses do not simply float to life but rather are exposed to self-criticism and the critical eyes of others.

As is the case when he conveys that he wrote a poem in little time, Ausonius utilizes nearly all his references to revision and editing to do things other than capture the circumstances of textual genesis.[7] In fact, it is unknown if he actually revised every time he said he did and clear that he did not always hope or expect his addressees to edit his work when he asked them to do so. The purpose of this chapter is to bring out what Ausonius sought to accomplish by connecting his poetry to those modes of rewriting.[8] His aims do not include espousing a neo-neoteric poetics of perfectionism governed by the principles of polish and refinement, which revision and editing would help to achieve.[9] Ausonius instead adapts his remarks to the rhetorical purposes of his different prefaces. Again, a concern in every instance is to express authorial modesty; the examples show how Ausonius varied an important prefatory theme. In addition, the poet generates messages that are specific to the individual addressees of each preface and to the rhetorical conditions that prevail in each text. To explore how Ausonius uses revision and editing as topics in his prefaces is to contribute to our understanding of how a late antique author could write about writing poetry. It is also to cast light upon the discourse and functions of Ausonius's paratexts, or the prose and verse material—mainly prefatory letters and dedications—that accompanies his poetry.[10]

---

6. Relevant is Martelli 2013: 4–6, who examines how authorial revision and collaborative revision "share a commitment to dismantling" (5) the assumption of final authorial intentions.

7. I echo Gurd 2012: 3, an important source on revision in ancient Rome and a significant influence on this chapter.

8. In this, my approach is in line with Genette 1997: 2, who emphasizes the communicative functions of paratexts.

9. Gurd 2012: 7–8 discusses perfectionism as a goal of revision. As he observes, scholarship has focused on the link between revision and Hellenistic/neoteric poetics, while overlooking other dimensions of Roman discussions of revision. I take his point, and I extend his examination chronologically—he ends with Pliny the Younger—and thematically by identifying new ways that references to revision functioned in later Roman literature.

10. Genette 1997 uses the term "paratext" to describe all accompanying material to a main text. That material includes prefaces. On the paratext in ancient Rome, see Jansen 2014. On paratextual prefaces in late antique Latin poetry, including those written by Ausonius, see Pelttari 2014: 45–72.

8.1. THE POET AND THE EMPEROR

Revision is something that can be hard to stop, even in the face of diminishing returns. Such is the experience of Ausonius, at least as he describes it in an exchange with the emperor Theodosius. The communication begins with a letter from Theodosius to Ausonius written at some point between 388 and 394.[11] After relating that he wrote the letter in his own hand because of the affection and respect he had for Ausonius, Theodosius asks the poet to send him some of his poetry.[12] No matter how close the two actually were,[13] it is clear that Theodosius emphasized his feelings for Ausonius in order to tie his request to the obligations of long-standing *amicitia*. The realities of power give way to the rhetoric of friendship: Theodosius downplays the differences in status between him and Ausonius and implies that the poet should send his work as a friend to a friend. What he seeks specifically are two types of poems—those that he once read but has forgotten with time and those that Ausonius has added to his corpus, as "wide report" (*fama celebris*) tells Theodosius the poet has done. The two men had people in common who might have brought that word to the emperor, including perhaps Pacatus Drepanius, the Gallic rhetor and Ausonius's friend, who delivered a panegyric on Theodosius in 389.[14]

Theodosius goes on to cite poets under Augustus as precedents for Ausonius: just as they endlessly produced texts for the esteemed Augustus (*nullo fine in eius honorem multa condentes* [writing many works without end out of regard for him]), so, it is implied, Ausonius should send his work to Theodosius.[15] The emperor looks back to the Augustan Age as a model for the

---

11. As Green 1991: 240 recognizes, we cannot be any more precise in dating the poem. Sivan 1992: 85, however, suggests that the poem was written "between 389 and 392, during Theodosius's longest stay in the west."

12. *Amor meus qui in te est et admiratio ingenii atque eruditionis tuae, quae multo maxima sunt, fecit, parens iucundissime, ut morem principibus aliis solitum sequestrarem familiaremque sermonem autographum ad te transmitterem, postulans pro iure non equidem regio, sed illius priuatae inter nos caritatis, ne fraudari me scriptorum tuorum lectione patiaris* ("my love for you and my admiration for your talent and learning, which are by far the greatest they could be, causes me, my most congenial father, to follow the wonted custom of other princes and to send a friendly word in my own hand to you, insisting—not, indeed, by regal right but from our private mutual affection—that you not allow me to be cheated of a reading of your writings"). The text is Green 1991: 707, app. B, 1–5. This translation and all others are my own.

13. Green 1991: 240 questions the extent of the friendship between the two. Ausonius had been close to the emperor (and his former pupil) Gratian, and he would have appreciated Theodosius's defeat of the usurper Magnus Maximus, who had revolted against Gratian. Whether this resulted in any particular friendship is uncertain.

14. Sivan 1992: 85. On Pacatus and his panegyric, see Nixon and Rodgers 1994: 437–516.

15. *Quae tu de promptuario scriniorum tuorum, qui me amas, libens imperties, secutus exempla auctorum optimorum, quibus par esse meruisti, qui Octauiano Augusto rerum potienti certatim opera sua tradebant, nullo fine in eius honorem multa condentes* ("as you love me, freely share the poems from the storing

present; the relationship that Augustus had with contemporary poets is an ideal that Theodosius claims to want to revive. By so relating his situation to the early Imperial past, the emperor both aligns himself with a great exemplar and conveys that he wishes to have Ausonius regard him as poets regarded Augustus. So, too, Theodosius must have been aiming to flatter Ausonius by suggesting that he was equivalent to the Augustan luminaries Vergil and Horace, among others.

A twenty-two-line elegiac poem from Ausonius answers Theodosius's request. Roger Green suggests that the poem is nothing more than a promissory piece in which Ausonius claimed that he would honour Theodosius's wishes and send him sometime in the future the work he wanted.[16] Yet grounds for believing that the text did in fact preface a poetry collection extend beyond the circumstantial evidence that elegiac prefaces were common in Late Antiquity and appear frequently in Ausonius and that no other examples of elegiac promissory pieces exist in his corpus. At the conclusion of his text, Ausonius imitates a prefatory poem in Martial describing the publication of his first book of epigrams and a line in Pliny the Elder's dedicatory preface to the *Historia naturalis*.[17] It is possible that Ausonius adapted Martial and Pliny's introductory matter when writing a poem that was not itself a preface but was rather just a promise to send Theodosius future compositions. But this reading creates excess complexity when Occam's razor would do: the simpler and, to my mind, more plausible explanation is that Ausonius turned to those models because he was writing a prefatory text, just as they did.[18] The classical prefaces informed Ausonius's late preface and gave him paratextual content with which to work when writing his dedicatory poem to the emperor.[19]

---

place of your writing cases, following the example of the best authors, with whom you have earned equal status—they who vied to hand over their own works to Octavian Augustus when he ruled, writing many things without end out of regard for him"). Green 1991: app. B, 7–11.

16. This is the position of Green 1991: 240, although he suggests elsewhere (1991: xliii–xliv) that Ausonius's reply "may have accompanied, or preceded" a collection. Green still includes the poem among Ausonius's *praefationes uariae* (*praef. uar.* 3) in his editions of 1991 and 1999. See also Pastorino 1971: 73.

17. See 258–60 for Ausonius's imitation of Martial and Pliny.

18. Other critics who maintain that the poem served as a preface to a collection are Evelyn White 1919–21: 1:xxxvi and Sivan 1992: 86–7. No sure conclusions have been reached or are likely to be reached about the number of editions of Ausonius's poetry published in Antiquity. See Nardo 1966–7: 321–82 and Sivan 1992: 84.

19. Lines 11–14 of the poem pose no problem for this reading. In the lines, Ausonius asserts that Theodosius will instil *ingenium* in him where there is none (*non habeo ingenium, Caesar sed iussit— habebo*, 11) and that he stirs Ausonius's feeble powers and assists him by ordering him to write (*inualidas uires ipse excitat et iuuat idem / qui iubet*, 13–14). The future *habebo* and the present *excitat* and *iuuat* need not suggest that Ausonius is preparing to produce his volume for Theodosius rather than send it to him with the poem and that he is taking from the emperor the impetus to meet the future task. In fact, the tenses appear to be used for vividness, to describe with immediacy how Ausonius felt upon receiving Theodosius's request.

In his piece, Ausonius responds not as a personal friend of Theodosius but as his obedient subject. This was to adopt a rhetorical stance with deep roots in Roman culture. It was long customary for an author to describe a request to write and send a text as an order.[20] Among the examples are those in which the initiator of the request stands above the recipient in status.[21] Such was the case with Theodosius and Ausonius, as the poet makes very clear in his preface. Ausonius devotes the first sixteen lines of the preface to Theodosius's superiority: not only does he compare the emperor to a god, but he also repeats the point several times that the call for poetry is a command that he must obey. The alternative is a request among equals, which Ausonius sets up as a contrast to Theodosius's order. Thus in lines 9–10, he states that Theodosius bade him to write, although nearly asking him to do so (*scribere me Augustus iubet et mea carmina poscit / paene rogans; blando uis latet imperio*).[22] The verses include key terms for literary requests, *rogare*, which implies "no other relation than equality" between the initiator and author, and *iubere*, which can indicate "that the person demanding was so influential that the author had no choice."[23] In lines 15–16, meanwhile, Ausonius states that he cannot safely refuse a god, whereas delay due to modesty is praiseworthy when dealing with an equal (*non tutum renuisse deo; laudata pudoris / saepe mora est, quotiens contra parem dubites*).[24]

The amount of space that Ausonius gives to framing Theodosius's request as a superior's command is an example of his rhetorical maximalism. Ausonius develops a conventional theme to an extreme degree, as he does elsewhere in his prefatory paratexts, particularly when disparaging his own poetry in displays of modesty. The extended focus on Theodosius's *iussum* highlights hierarchy and emphasizes Ausonius's inferiority to the emperor. The poet observes a kind of imperial ceremonial, in which he shows deference to his *dominus*, who, in

---

20. Curtius 1953: 85, Janson 1964: 117–20, and White 1993: 64–71. For other examples in Ausonius, see *epist.* 5a.16 and 18, a letter to Axius Paulus, and *Cento nuptialis praef.* 10–11, as well as ll. 10–11 of the cento itself. For further late antique Latin examples, see SEDULIUS *epist. ad Mac.* 2 and 7 (*CSEL* 10.171) and SIDONIUS APOLLINARIS *carm.* 9.11 and 14.

21. I echo White 1993: 67 on the status differences between the initiator of a literary request and the recipient.

22. "Augustus commands me to write and demands my poems, though almost asking; force lies hidden under an ingratiating order."

23. Janson 1964: 119–20. Ausonius similarly plays on the difference between *rogare* and *iubere* in connection with an emperor (Valentinian) in *Cento nuptialis praef.* 10–11.

24. "It is not safe to refuse a god; often delay due to modesty has been praised, whenever you hesitate in response to an equal." It is tempting to conclude from ll. 15–16 that Ausonius did indeed comply with Theodosius's request and send him a collection of poems; by stating that he must not deny a god and distancing himself from *mora* (delay), he suggests that the elegiacs accompany a volume that has quickly satisfied the emperor's wishes.

Ausonius's terms, was like a god among mortals.[25] This calls sharp attention to what Theodosius had suppressed in his letter: the power he wielded over Ausonius as the emperor. Indeed, Ausonius seems to be responding precisely to Theodosius's claim that he made his request simply on the basis of friendship, and not "by regal right" (*pro iure . . . regio*, Green 1991: app. B, 4). The poet corrects the emperor by grounding the request in the exercise of imperial authority. In the process, he paints a very different picture of their relationship from that presented by Theodosius.

After devoting the first sixteen lines of his preface to conveying that Theodosius compelled him to send his work, Ausonius shifts gears and states that his poetry was long eager to get out to the emperor. It is at this point that he refers to revision (17–20):

quin etiam non iussa parant erumpere dudum
    carmina: quis nolit Caesaris esse liber,
ne ferat indignum uatem centumque lituras,
    mutandas semper deteriore nota?

And indeed, the poems have long been ready to burst forth unbidden; what book would not want to be Caesar's, so that it not endure a worthless poet and a hundred erasures that are always changing it with a worse mark?

Like Roman authors generally, Ausonius would have surely revised drafts of his poetry before publication as a matter of course.[26] One apparent product of revision is a poem on oysters and mussels that Ausonius sent to his friend Theon. According to the poet, the piece was a careless effusion in his youth that he had now revised as an older man.[27] It is possible that he also produced a second edition

---

25. On late antique ceremonial, see Roberts in this volume, 385–6.
26. I echo Sivan 1992: 86.
27. *Cuius rei munus reciprocum quoniam in me colendo fastidisti, inuenta inter tineas epistula uetere, quam de ostreis et musculis affectata obscuritate condideram, quae adulescens temere fuderam iam senior retractaui* ("since you have disdained to send me a reciprocal gift for this [a letter from Ausonius], having found an old letter among my worm-eaten ones, which I wrote about oysters and muscles in affected obscurity, [I send a poem from it] that I as a youth poured out rashly and, now as an older man, have revised," *epist.* 14a.3–7). Worth mentioning, too, is an editorial note that introduces Ausonius's poem *Pater ad filium*. The note relates that the poem, begun but never finished, was found among Ausonius's drafts (*liturarii*). While there is no talk of revision in this instance, it stands to reason that a poet who kept *liturarii* was one who retained drafts that he revised or intended for revision. Ausonius himself claims that he found the *Cento nuptialis* among his drafts (*cent. praef.* 22) and the *Griphus* from a pile of dusty paper (*griph. praef.* 3–4). See McGill 2014: 139–45 on the cento and Hernández Lobato 2007a: 455–62 on the *Griphus*.

or at least a touched-up version of the published *Moselle*.[28] Likewise, he might have revised the *Professores*, poems commemorating the teachers of Bordeaux, years after the initial publication of the collection. At that point, he could have added a piece on himself that he placed after the original conclusion.[29]

But in this instance, had Ausonius really revised his poetry as he described? The question arises because, to build upon an earlier observation, his account derives from Martial's *ep.* 1.3.9–12. While Ausonius might have turned to Martial to give poetic form to his personal experience, it is very possible that the detail was a purely literary one, a product of *imitatio* alone.

Martial's lines read as follows:

sed tu, ne totiens domini patiare lituras
 neue notet lusus tristis harundo tuos,
aetherias, lasciue, cupis uolitare per auras:
 i, fuge; sed poteras tutior esse domi.

But so that you not endure your master's frequent erasures and so that the stern reed pen not mark your play, you want, naughty one, to fly through the lofty breezes. Go, take flight; but you could have been safer at home.

Ausonius's debt to this passage seems certain given the similarities between the poems: both describe a poetry collection that seeks to leave behind its author's constant revisions, and both contain the word *lituras* and negative purpose clauses. Ausonius then adds the detail that he only makes his work worse by revising it. This is to fit Martial and the theme of revision to a staple of his paratextual rhetoric, the affected modesty of the *captatio beneuolentiae*.[30] Whereas Martial's poetry wants to escape its stern master, who, it is implied, is working hard to improve it, Ausonius's poetry merely wishes to be free of the author, who, in the pose of the *captatio*, haplessly damages and degrades the work with his revisions.[31]

---

28. Sivan 1992: 91, which repeats Sivan 1990: 383–4. See also Shanzer 1998, 231–2, as well as Gruber 2013: 18.

29. Sivan 1992: 94. I do not believe, with Evelyn White 1919–21: 1:xxxv, that the different prefaces to the *Technopaegnion* imply alterations and, thus, revision (although they certainly show that Ausonius added to the poem at different stages). See also Nardo 1966–7: 323–4. The circumstances of the composition of the *Fasti*, which Ausonius addresses once to Hesperius and once to Gregorius, are also uncertain.

30. The affected modesty is of course consistent with the idea that Ausonius was writing a preface rather than a promissory poem, given that humble poses mark his prefaces generally.

31. Cf. the analogous thoughts on revision from Quintilian, who in *inst.* 10.4.4 states that it could make a work worse (*cura peiora*). Quintilian also notes that "correction itself must have a limit" (*ipsa emendatio finem habeat*, 10.4.3) and compares obsessive revisers to doctors who cut bodies that are healthy (*similes medicis etiam integra secantibus*, 10.4.3).

Ausonius also personalizes Martial by assigning it the destination he does. Taking his cue from Horace's *ep.* 1.20 and addressing his book as a rambunctious slave, Martial describes the dangers that his epigrams will face among the fickle and hypercritical readers of Rome.[32] The city is a demanding mistress and its citizens too knowing, and they will very quickly turn on the book after applauding it.[33] Things are altogether different for Ausonius's poetry. Rather than journey to the public, it seeks a private addressee; and rather than move on a horizontal plane out to the general reader, it travels on a vertical one up toward an imperial reader.

That imperial reader, moreover, is very much a desired destination for the *carmina*. Ausonius relates that his poems have long sought to "burst forth" (*erumpere*) and—so the train of thought implies—come into the hands of Theodosius. This is to depart from the dominant picture of how Theodosius had ordered Ausonius to write. Now the poet relates that his work would have come to the emperor unbidden (*non iussa*), if only Ausonius would have stopped revising it. In so reconstructing the history of his text, Ausonius makes his reference to revision do more than just express the modesty of a *captatio*. His approach is to explain via refined irony why he had not sent Theodosius his poetry. He had long wanted to do so—or so he conveys when describing his eager collection, which stands in for the eager author. Yet his compulsive urge to revise had prevented it. The suggestion is that the *carmina* only wished to go to Theodosius to escape Ausonius' revisions. It would be wrong, however, to suppose that this was a way of slighting Theodosius, by suggesting that the urge was conditional. Ausonius is not insulting the emperor. He is instead using self-deprecating humor to excuse the absence of poetry sent to Theodosius while also indicating in what he surely considered an appropriately witty manner that he had for some time wanted to reach out to him.

Given its destination, Ausonius's poetry does not face the unprotected peril that Martial's epigrams do. While Martial asserts that his book would have been safer at home (*sed poteras tutior domi*) because of how severe the urban audience is that it will face, the only threat in Ausonius's preface is to his own safety if he denies Theodosius his request (*non tutum renuisse deo*, 15). Rather than expose his over-revised poetry to the dangers of anonymous criticism, Ausonius

---

32. For discussion, see Fitzgerald 2007: 74–5.
33. "Demanding mistress" is the translation of Fitzgerald 2007: 75 for Martial's *dominae fastidia Romae* in *ep.* 1.3.3, while "all too knowing" comes from his translation of *nimium Martia turba sapit* in *ep.* 1.3.4.

concludes his preface by requesting indulgence from the emperor for the faults his work possesses (21–2):

Tu modo te iussisse, pater Romane, memento
  inque meis culpis da tibi tu ueniam

Remember only, father of the Romans, that you gave the order and forgive yourself for my faults.

An allusion to Vergil's *Aeneid* deepens the call for Theodosius's leniency. The line *tu modo te iussisse, pater Romane, memento* reworks *Aen.* 6.851, *tu regere imperio populos, Romane, memento* ("you, Roman, be sure to rule the nations with your power"), where Anchises famously exhorts Romans to govern mankind. Anchises continues with the equally well-known exhortation to "spare the submissive and subdue the proud" (*parcere subiectis et debellare superbos, Aen.* 6.853). Because Ausonius had taken such a compliant stance toward Theodosius, it seems reasonable that he sought to refer to both Vergilian lines; the allusion not only activated *Aen.* 6.851 but also called to mind the subsequent command at 6.853 in order to convey an implicit message about the need for imperial mercy toward the submissive poet. Ausonius plants a reference and, in the process, sets the conditions for Theodosius to identify himself with Vergil's *Romane* and Ausonius with the spared *subiectis*.[34]

Ausonius follows up the allusion to Vergil in line 21 with one to Pliny the Elder in line 22: *inque meis culpis da tibi tu ueniam* recasts *in nostra culpa tibi ignosces* ("you will forgive yourself for my fault"), which Pliny includes in the preface to the *Historia naturalis* (*praef.* 4). Whereas Pliny asks his addressee, the Flavian emperor Titus, to take the blame for Pliny's presumption in treating him with great familiarity, Ausonius calls upon Theodosius to recognize that he is responsible for the flawed work he receives because he commanded Ausonius to send it. The contrast with Pliny is pointed: Ausonius has not taken Theodosius's cue and treated the emperor with the familiarity of a friend, and he continues to the end to call attention to the emperor's power over him, as exemplified in the important thematic verb *iubere* (*tu modo te iussisse*, 21).[35] Obviously, Ausonius's

---

34. Ausonius's *pater Romane* might also respond to *pater Romanus* in *Aen.* 9.449. But the dominant model is clearly *Aen.* 6.851. It seems not at all far-fetched that Ausonius hoped Theodosius would catch the meaning of his allusions to Vergil. Certainly the emperor could have been expected to know the lapidary statements on the exercise of Roman power in the most famous poem in the Latin tradition.

35. In *HN praef.* 4, Pliny is apologizing for treating Titus with such familiarity. Still, the contrast is in place between an author in Pliny who had addressed an emperor familiarly, as a companion, and an author in Ausonius who turns away from an emperor's friendliness and focuses on his power and authority.

final line is meant to amuse. But it still serves to highlight imperial authority, as the preface as a whole emphatically does.[36]

The close of Ausonius's poem both recognizes Theodosius's power and directs him on how to use it. The emperor is to be the opposite of the demanding, unsatisfied reader that the revising Ausonius is by definition; he is the escape from the poet's unrelenting critical eye, the haven from unhappy authorial judgement who accepts the flaws that revision did not correct, but rather increased. This is, of course, a way of asking Theodosius not to approach the poetry with the exacting standards that Ausonius ascribes to himself but instead to give it a friendly reading. As Roman authors did in prefaces generally, including through the use of the *captatio beneuolentiae*, Ausonius shapes his message to secure a favourable response, whether or not he felt there was real need to solicit it.

We do not know what or how many poems comprised the collection that Ausonius sent to Theodosius. But it is reasonable to suppose that he designed it to meet Theodosius's wishes, at least as a first instalment in what the emperor might have hoped would be an ongoing process.[37] Certainly that would have been the politic approach to take. As his letter makes clear, Theodosius sought an anthology of older and newer poems; by sending and, it follows, dedicating that collection, Ausonius would show the emperor Augustan regard. Ausonius, I suggest, not only complied with that wish but also conveyed his eagerness to meet it and took care to explain his inability to do anything similar at an earlier point.

We cannot know if Theodosius believed Ausonius' statement that his urge to revise kept him from sending his poems. In fact, belief might well have been immaterial. Flattering praise and elaborate expressions of deferential respect were customary and pervasive elements in late antique elite communication, and they were natural when an addressee/dedicatee was an emperor or other social/political superior.[38] No doubt the speaker and recipient alike usually understood

---

36. The tone of the line suggests that Ausonius felt at least some comfort with Theodosius and, therefore, that they had some kind of relationship. A person will tend to joke, after all, with someone who is at least an acquaintance. It remains the case, however, that the line continues to emphasize Theodosius's sway over Ausonius: the poet is focused on power and hierarchy to the end.

37. When Theodosius wrote that Augustan poets composed many works without end in honour of the emperor, he might have envisioned a situation where Ausonius presented him with more than one collection of verse. By all appearances, Ausonius did not do that. This need not suggest that he was grudging toward Theodosius's request, assuming that the emperor wanted more poetry from him and that Ausonius recognized this. It is possible that Ausonius was, in fact, happy to dedicate one collection but no more to Theodosius and that he believed this was enough to satisfy the emperor's wishes. It is also possible that, at his advanced age (see n. 67), Ausonius simply did not have the wherewithal to produce as much for Theodosius as the emperor might have liked.

38. Ausonius himself provides many examples; perhaps the most extreme is his letter to the praetorian prefect Petronius Probus (*epist.* 9a and b).

that the blandishments moved beyond literal truth. Still, as a rule the sentiment behind the exaggeration was to be considered real and true. This allowed a person not merely to satisfy a convention but to convey respect, if not affection, and to work to establish or confirm a tie. Ausonius operates under that principle in his preface. Although he eschews Theodosius's language of friendship, the poet's attitude is anything but ambivalent or hostile toward the emperor.[39] Instead, the stress he lays on hierarchy and command enables him to use his constructed Self—that is, the image of the author in the text—to acknowledge and honour Theodosius's position. Theodosius is to see the real author in the constructed author, to recognize how Ausonius demonstrates his regard for him through the version of the author he creates in his preface.[40]

When Ausonius presents himself as a compulsive reviser in order to justify the lack of poetry from him, the gesture itself could, thus, well have been enough. Whether or not it was true that the drive to revise kept Ausonius from sending his work, and whether or not Theodosius considered it factual, the poet shows respect by including the detail; in explaining why he had sent no work to Theodosius, the author acknowledges that he should have done so. At the same time, Ausonius conveys that the emperor had long been in his thoughts. The statement that his poetry wished to burst forth and get to Theodosius, because it was suffering under his revising hand, reveals his attentiveness to the emperor *in absentia* and his esteem for him.

Presumably, Ausonius expected Theodosius to circulate the collection with its prefatory poem and understood that the emperor gave him liberty to do the same. Only if the work were so published—that is, copied and put into circulation—would Theodosius receive the credit he so clearly sought for having had Ausonius address a volume to him.[41] This suggests that Ausonius invested the preface with a further function: to advertise his ties to Theodosius and to earn esteem from the connection. Even if the emperor's own letter did not circulate with the text and survived only because, later, Ausonius or his posthumous editor included it in another collection of Ausonius's poetry, the preface demonstrates that Theodosius considered the author to deserve his attention and held him in enough regard to seek a collection from him. This

---

39. Green 1991: 240 describes Ausonius's reply to Theodosius as "ambivalent."

40. This constructed Self resembles the implied author of Booth 1983: 70–6 or the author's "second self" presented in a text; see also Schmid 2010: 37–51, who uses the term "abstract author." I resist the term "implied author," however, because it is a very contested concept in narratology. See Genette 1983: 135–54 and de Jong 2014: 19. The constructed author is to be distinguished from the real author; but particularly in a personal preface, a real author will be apt to communicate things about himself through his projected Self, that is, through the image of the author that he creates.

41. On the processes of making texts public in Roman Antiquity, see Starr 1987: 213–15.

implied the existence of a personal connection, since "commands belong[ed] to the sphere of personal obligation."⁴² Emphasizing the emperor's position and authority elevates Ausonius by association; the proximity to power renders him a powerful poet, someone significant enough to receive Theodosius's request and, therefore, someone worthy of respect. What is more, Ausonius' remarks on his poetry's eager desire to travel to Theodosius indicate that he long considered the emperor to be part of his network as a potential recipient (and dedicatee) of his work—and his use of revision to explain why he had sent Theodosius no *carmina* only reinforces the point, since it implies an expectation of contact. To recognize these messages is to see all the more that the paratextual preface was not an afterthought or ancillary politesse, no matter how conventionally modest or flattering it was. It was instead an active agent in the construction of authorial identity and textual function.

8.2. A Family Affair

Ausonius's own authority is an essential subject in another of his references to revision. This appears in a prefatory letter in prose attached to the *Protrepticus ad nepotem*, a hundred-line hexameter poem exhorting his grandson, also named Ausonius, to be a good and unafraid student in school. Ausonius addresses the letter to his son Hesperius, who is the younger Ausonius's uncle. (Hesperius's sister was the boy's mother; the boy's father was Thalassius and not Euromius, the woman's first husband.) In it, he tells Hesperius that he has sent the poem ahead for him to read before Ausonius himself arrives for a visit. This, he continues, is preferable to reciting the work, in that Hesperius will feel more able to offer his frank criticism (*hoc enim malui quam ipse recitare, esset ut tibi censura liberior*, "I preferred this to reciting it myself, so that your criticism might be freer," 3–4).

What Ausonius describes is the restricted circulation of a poem before publication, so that the author receives comments from a genetic reader, or one who takes part in the genesis of a work by responding with critical comments that the author could then incorporate into his revisions.⁴³ This form of active reading was an established pursuit long before Late Antiquity that endured into that period.⁴⁴ Sending work out for feedback was one of the things that made

---

42. White 1993: 70. A personal connection is of course not necessarily the same thing as the affectionate friendship that Theodosius describes in his letter.
43. Gurd 2012: 108.
44. Starr 1987: 213 and Fedeli 1989: 352.

literature a social practice in Roman Antiquity.⁴⁵ Writers looked to members of their families or their communities for comments on their works and, in doing so, turned the act of producing a text into a collective enterprise. While attributed single authorship was the norm, authorial isolation was not, and there were various means—private readings, semi-public recitations, and letter exchange—through which those connected to a writer could offer him criticism and suggestions that helped to shape his text.⁴⁶

In the case of Ausonius's *Protrepticus*, the apparent idea is that Hesperius will write out his *censura* and give Ausonius his comments when he sees him, which the poet will then take under advisement when he revises.⁴⁷ How sincere Ausonius was in his call for criticism is impossible to determine: he may indeed have wanted the kind of feedback that Roman authors commonly sought, or he may have asked for it as a rhetorical gesture, without really expecting Hesperius to provide it.⁴⁸ In either scenario, his request for edits portrays Hesperius in a positive manner. The underlying idea is that Ausonius could enlist his son to make meaningful suggestions about his poetry and therefore that he viewed Hesperius as a valued editorial collaborator.

As the letter continues, Ausonius identifies two things that impede the free airing of criticism. The first, which might take its cue from Quintilian (*inst.* 10.1.17–19),⁴⁹ is that "things heard pass by our ears more quickly than things read" (*aures nostras audita uelocius quam lecta praetereunt*, 5). This means that the potential critic cannot accurately appraise an oral text because he does not have the time to examine it adequately. The second is that "the frankness of the critic is burdened by the presence of the reciter" (*sinceritas iudicandi praesentia recitantis oneratur*, 6). Because Ausonius sends his poem in advance of his

---

45. I take the phrase "social practice" as applied to literature from Gurd 2012: 9.

46. For similar remarks, see Gurd 2012: 128. Semi-public recitations of the sort described by Pliny the Younger, however, are not part of the literary landscape in Late Antiquity, at least as the evidence allows us to reconstruct it.

47. Presumably, therefore, we are to understand that Hesperius will mark the copy that Ausonius sent him with corrections and suggestions and then give that marked copy back to his father. For if Hesperius were to try to offer his criticism orally, the *uerecundia* to which Ausonius refers in his letter (see below) would logically be operative.

48. While Ausonius sent poems that he wanted published to dedicatees with conventional directions to correct those texts (more on this to come), the detail about his pending visit separates this request from those calls to edit. The detail has the specificity of the real, and I am inclined to believe that Ausonius really did send his poem ahead to his son as he said he did. Whether he actually wanted feedback is a separate question. It is altogether uncertain if the version of the *Protrepticus* that Ausonius sent to his son was the draft poem that got out against Ausonius's wishes, as he complains in a letter to Symmachus (*epist.* 12.35-7; cf. Symm. *epist.* 1.31).

49. McGill 2007a: 332–5.

arrival, however, Hesperius will be able to avoid those hindrances and to be open in his *censura* (7–8):

*nunc tibi utrumque integrum est, quia et legenti libera mora est
et iudicaturo non obstat nostri uerecundia.*

Now each thing does not touch you, because there is both a free duration of time for you as you read and the respect you feel toward me does not stand in your way when you will come to criticize.

As a reader rather than a listener, Hesperius will be able to linger over Ausonius's text and give it the careful attention that produces useful criticism. At the same time, he will not be confined by the *uerecundia* that, Ausonius implies, he would feel if Ausonius were present. By *uerecundia*, Ausonius means the emotion that causes Hesperius to grant his father due respect. A person guided by *uerecundia* in Roman Antiquity acted with circumspection, acknowledging his place in a social transaction and behaving accordingly.[50] Our sources mention the emotion with particular frequency in connection with sons; the "*uerecundia* of the Roman child before a parent" and "above all, of the son before the father"[51] is of deep and abiding cultural interest. Sons were to subordinate themselves to their fathers and, as the inferior party, were to show respectful self-restraint in their dealings with them.

By ascribing Hesperius's potential reticence to *uerecundia*, Ausonius has him acting precisely as a good Roman son should act. The detail builds upon the earlier remark that the presence of the reciter inhibits the critic by laying out a more precise scenario in which the presence of the reciting father inhibits his son. Hesperius recognizes his position below Ausonius and, when in his presence, does not freely voice his criticism out of paternal respect. The further suggestion is that Hesperius will not be so burdened by *uerecundia* when separated from his father, because the constraints that obtain when he is with Ausonius loosen when they are apart. This does not mean that he will show disrespect. Rather, he will simply be able to overcome his praiseworthy observance of an appropriate emotion and to be honest about the *Protrepticus* in the way that Ausonius says he wants him to be. Again, Ausonius may not have been sincere in his call for criticism. Yet even in that scenario, there would be more to Ausonius's discussion than an empty pose. By voicing his request as he does, he sets out to represent Hesperius as a good son, someone who meets cultural standards of proper filial conduct.

---

50. I follow Kaster 2005: 15, an important source on Roman *uerecundia*.
51. Kaster 2005: 24.

Another form of *uerecundia* appears later in the prefatory letter, now as something that Ausonius himself might feel. When explaining with customary ironic modesty why he awaits Hesperius's criticism when he himself admits that the poem is flawed, Ausonius states that he blushes to send such verses out to the public but is less ashamed (*minus uerecundari*) when keeping them between the two of them (17–20).[52] *Verecundia* moves from something that Ausonius elicited to something that he feels, and it is a different emotion from Hesperius's respectful deference and restraint: it is now the embarrassment Ausonius would suffer at revealing his poetry to others.[53] While the poor quality of Ausonius's work would cause him to lose face with his general reader, he asserts that he will not be subject to the same disgrace with Hesperius.

Ausonius here uses conventional modesty to make another substantive point about Hesperius. Now the concern is to show how comfortable Ausonius feels with his son, and how confident he is that Hesperius will treat him with more generosity of spirit than a general reader would because of the bond that the two have. What Ausonius describes is an intimacy with Hesperius that allows him to share things with him that he would not with others. For Ausonius, stating that he will not fear the same judgement from Hesperius that he would from the public is a way of figuring their closeness and good relations as father and son.

I would suggest that Ausonius circulated the letter we have to Hesperius with the published *Protrepticus* and that he understood that his representation of their relationship anticipated an important theme in the poem.[54] Ausonius's text was a playful variation on a *protrepticus*, or an exhortation to salutary conduct. Not only does he describe the poem in his prefatory letter with the words *libellum ... instar protreptici luseram* ("a small work in the form of an exhortation with which I trifled," 1–2), but he also invests it with humorous details, verbal wit, and rhetorical expansion that hardly suit a child or a merely practical function.[55] The text has a narratee, the young Ausonius, and an abstract, ideal reader

---

52. *Superest igitur ut dicas, "quid moraris iudicationem meam de eo quod ipse pronuntias esse mendosum?" dicam scilicet me huiusmodi uersibus foris erubescere, sed intra nos minus uerecundari* ("it therefore remains for you to say, 'Why do you await my criticism about that which you yourself proclaim is faulty?' I will of course answer that I blush for verses of this kind in public but feel less embarrassment between us").

53. Kaster 2005: 19 discusses the connection between *uerecundia* and embarrassment: "*Uerecundia* ... [was] marked not by the pallor associated with *timor* or *metus* but by the blush associated with *pudor*."

54. Even assuming, as I do, that Ausonius sent a letter with a draft of the *Protrepticus* to Hesperius ahead of a visit, we cannot know for certain how much that letter looked like the one we now have. Yet it is entirely plausible that Ausonius saved a copy of it, which he then reproduced and sent out with the published poem, thereby turning what had been a private letter into a dedicatory one. Be this as it may, my concern centres on the letter we possess and how it functioned with the poem.

55. Green 1991: 287. On the poem, see also Dräger 2012: 394–419.

who has the sophistication and sensibility to appreciate the poet's treatment—its codes and aesthetics. The presence of that reader indicates that Ausonius intended the *Protrepticus* for an adult, educated public whose tastes were in sympathy with his; in presupposing a particular kind of reader, he indirectly reveals whom he expected his actual audience to be.[56]

Yet Ausonius also uses his poem to do more than to entertain. First, he promotes a vision of culture and politics in which the classics play a central role.[57] Second, he advertises his achievements and those of his family members. Thus in lines 41–4, he urges his grandson to study so that he might strive for the prizes of the Muses and proceed to where Ausonius had gone, as well as to where the boy's father, a proconsul, and Hesperius, a prefect, had advanced.[58] The passage implies that education and the culture it brings will put the boy in position to rise as high as his forbears did.[59] Ausonius then devotes *prot.* 66–95 to autobiography: he relates that he himself was long a schoolmaster (in Bordeaux) before he was called to the imperial court to tutor Gratian, and that, under Gratian and his father, Valentinian, he rose to great political prominence. His own achievements, he concludes, are the things to which his grandson should aspire (*prot.* 96–100). That way, he will follow in his grandfather's footsteps, as his father and uncle had done, and use his education as a springboard for advancement into the political elite.[60]

The *Protrepticus* is thus a piece of ludic entertainment, a call to cultural arms, and a work celebrating Ausonius and his family, for whom learning and culture, Ausonius suggests, had laid the foundation for great success in the world. Probably written and published ca. 380 or soon thereafter,[61] the poem

---

56. On this abstract reader, or the audience presumed by a text, see Schmid 2010: 52–6, who notes (55) that the "ideal" abstract reader "understands the work in a way that optimally matches its structure."

57. As Amherdt 2010: 43–60 convincingly argues. Amherdt is good as well on how Ausonius uses humour to convey that serious message.

58. *Ut patris utque mei non immemor ardua semper / praemia Musarum cupias facundus et olim / hac gradiare uia, qua nos praecessimus et cui / proconsul genitor, praefectus auunculus instant* ("so that, not unmindful of your father and of me, you in your eloquence desire the hard-won prizes of the Muses and proceed along the path where I went first and your father the proconsul and your uncle the prefect press on").

59. Ausonius was summoned to Valentinian's court ca. 367 CE to tutor the emperor's son Gratian. He had then risen to political prominence under Gratian's rule in the 370s. On the status of Ausonius's family and his political rise, see now Brown 2012: 187–9.

60. Ausonius states that his dotage has made him forgetful of the literature he once knew (*prot.* 51–5). This of course is not to suggest that his learning had been in vain. The talk of his failing memory is on one level a variation on the modesty pose. But the theme also connects grandfather and grandson, in that Ausonius suggests that the boy will lead him to relearn what he once knew so well (*prot.* 56–65). The sense is of continuity across the generations: the grandson Ausonius, as a student, will come to teach his grandfather, who himself was once a teacher.

61. Green 1991: 288.

highlights their recent rise to prominence while also looking to the future through Ausonius's grandson and raising the possibility of continued political glory.[62] Such subject matter points to readers who need to be told how much the Ausonian family achieved. Within the poem, the grandson, as narratee, occupies that role; the conceit is that the youth needs to be instructed in the ways of his family. But since the poem was clearly meant to circulate widely, there are behind the didactic *tu*-figure further targeted readers, to whom Ausonius wishes to leave a record of his and his family members' accomplishments. The *Protrepticus* is significantly commemorative. It presents from the perspective of an old man a look back on a distinguished political life, while also expressing the hope that his family will continue to achieve great things. There is a natural public orientation to that content, as there is to commemoration generally. Ausonius wants himself and his family recognized and remembered by those outside it, and he gives the requisite details to allow that to happen.

Ausonius's picture of his relationship to Hesperius in the prefatory letter to the poem offers an initial glimpse into that family. As we have seen, the glimpse is a flattering one; Ausonius and Hesperius are men of culture who engage in a form of collective revision, and they have a relationship marked by right conduct and intimacy.[63] This is to establish the merits of the family in one way before Ausonius advertises them in a different way in the poem itself. The dedicatory letter promotes its dedicatee, but it also joins with the poem to show, with different emphases, that the family to which he belonged was worthy of admiration—and it seems altogether likely that Ausonius would have wanted the two texts to circulate together, since both contributed to that message.[64] This, in turn, provides a further example of the rhetorical work that Ausonius had his prefaces do. More than introducing a poem, the paratext introduces a family in a favourable light, and it sets up a reading of the *Ludus* that continues to discover how exemplary that family was.

---

62. In this, Ausonius would apparently have been disappointed, since there is no evidence that his grandson had a political career; see *PLRE* I.139, s.v. Ausonius 3.

63. The portrait of Ausonius and Hesperius as collective writers naturally implies that they had embraced the culture of the classics that Amherdt 2010: 43–60 sees Ausonius promoting in the poem.

64. If Ausonius had sent the letter as we have it (or very close to what we have) to Hesperius when dispatching a draft of his poem, it would have obviously offered the same messages about father and son. Ausonius would have just understood that Hesperius and the public would receive those messages from different vantage points. Ausonius's point when sending the letter to his son would not have been to advertise their family (Hesperius would not have needed that done) but would have anticipated that function, assuming that Ausonius planned to publish the letter with the poem.

8.3. Revision among Friends

Two other prefaces of Ausonius solicit feedback from dedicatees. Both are addressed to Pacatus Drepanius, the Gallic friend who delivered a panegyric on Theodosius. The multiple dedications to Pacatus—and Ausonius also dedicates the *Technopaegnion* to him[65]—and the warmth displayed in the prefaces indicate the extent to which the poet was attentive to Pacatus, shared interests with him, and felt affection for him. One of the dedicatory pieces to him is an eighteen-line elegiac preface to the *Ludus septem sapientum*, a poem in iambic senarii that purports to be a *fabula palliata*; the seven wise men each come "on stage" and explain the sayings ascribed to them.[66] The *Ludus* was quite possibly written very late in Ausonius's life, during or close to Pacatus's term as proconsul in 390.[67]

The preface opens with Ausonius asking Pacatus to read through the poem carefully in order to decide if it should be "pardoned or perused" (*ignoscenda istaec an cognoscenda rearis, / attento, Drepani, perlege iudicio*, "Drepanius, read this through with attentive consideration of whether you think it should be pardoned or perused," 1–2).[68] The wordplay in *ignoscenda/cognoscenda* follows Terence, and it displays a verbal exuberance that continues in 3–4 (*siue legenda / siue tegenda putes carmina*, "whether you think the poems should be read or hidden") and 18 (*optabo ut placeam; si minus, ut lateam*, "I will hope that I please you; failing that, that I lie hidden").[69] The opening varies the convention Ausonius uses elsewhere in which he leaves it up to his dedicatee to decide if a work is to be published or not.[70] Yet Ausonius is asking more of Pacatus, as lines 5–18 of the preface make clear. The poet invites him to read the work as a critic and to mark what he considers substandard. This is to solicit editing from a genetic reader, whose suggestions would leave Ausonius with revisions

---

65. I do not include the first prose preface to the *Technopaegnion*, also to Pacatus, which seems to me not to be soliciting feedback. See n. 95.

66. I follow the summary of Green 1991: 597.

67. In the heading to the preface (as well as to the preface of the *Technopaegnion*), Pacatus is described as a proconsul. As Green 1991: 242 observes, if this is not an editorial addition, then the work would have to date to 390 or soon thereafter, when Ausonius was around eighty. Green 1991: 597, however, proposes that the *Ludus* "may have been devised for classroom purposes much earlier" than Ausonius published it with a dedication to Pacatus. If that was the case, we might suspect that Ausonius revised the poem before publication.

68. "Pardoned or perused" comes from the translation of Evelyn White 1919–21 1:311.

69. Green 1991: 598 notes that the play on *ignosco* and *cognosco* appears in Terence at *Eun.* 42 and *Heaut.* 218. He also remarks on the continued verbal play with *legenda/tegenda* in ll. 3–4 and *placeam/lateam* in 18.

70. On the convention, see Janson 1964: 108–9, Pavlovskis 1967: 539 and 554, Fedeli 1989: 346, Sivan 1992: 89, and McGill 2014: 132.

to incorporate into a later draft; Pacatus would send his marked copy back to the author so that he could work from it. What Ausonius describes is a kind of peer review. Either Pacatus will find things that need improvement and will, therefore, not put the poem into general circulation, or he will publish a work that has passed muster with him.

Ausonius's call for criticism was itself conventional, and of course he expected Pacatus to publish the poem rather than to send it back with corrections.[71] Still, the gesture is more than a "polite farce."[72] One of its functions is to call attention to Pacatus's duties as a dedicatee. While Ausonius overstates matters by giving Pacatus such a privileged role in the publication of the *Ludus*, his words still indicate that Pacatus occupied a lead place among Ausonius's readership, and they figure the responsibilities he had to circulate and champion the poem.[73] Ausonius would have assumed that Pacatus was familiar with the convention and that he could read below it to recognize the indirect message that it contained.[74]

Through his use of the topos, Ausonius also provides a glimpse into a circle of cultured elites that is "critical but intimate."[75] Even though Ausonius does not actually seek the collaboration that he requests, his gesture signals that he and Pacatus had a meeting of literary minds, and it suggests that they could and did call upon each other for feedback on their compositions in acts of collective revision and authorship. The call for corrections is unreal, but it projects an image of a relationship in which that call had a place.

The idea that poets formed a community marked by collegiality had itself a long history in Roman literature, to which requests for criticism contributed.[76] Yet for Ausonius as for others, to call attention to a literary partnership was not to ape a topos but to construct the poet's cultural reality. The paratextual theme was designed to guide readers to identify Ausonius's place within a textual community where poetry was, again, a social practice that brought men together.[77]

---

71. For examples of requests for criticism, see Janson 1964: 141–3, Pavlovskis 1967: 542, White 1993: 20 and 76, and Salzman 2011: 12 and 18.

72. Evelyn White 1919–21: 1:xxxv.

73. The topos "publish or suppress" operates similarly; for an example, see McGill 2014: 132–3, which this discussion follows. Mathisen 1993: 112–13 discusses the responsibilities of dedicatees and other friends in the process of publication in Late Antiquity.

74. Ausonius's theme would thus operate like an indirect speech act, on which see Searle 1975: 59–82.

75. Gurd 2012: 96, on Albius, the "candid judge" (*candidus iudex*) of Horace's *Satires* (HOR. *ep*. 1.4.1). Ausonius points to Pacatus's learning not only by comparing him to great critics of the past (see below) but also by applying the word *doctus* to him (*docti uiri*, 16).

76. On that history, see White 1993: 47–8. Pacatus was not only a rhetor (and probably a teacher of rhetoric in Bordeaux) but also a poet (see the lines cited in n. 94).

77. I derive the notion of "textual communities" from Stock 1990: 140–58, although his interest lies in Christian communities and orality/textuality.

To proceed in that manner was to celebrate literary fellowship, specifically its collaborative spirit and practices.[78] Composing and sharing poetry bound men in intellectual sodality, and requests for edits were one of the paratextual themes that provided a language for describing social relations.[79] By including the verbal play he does, Ausonius demonstrates as well how he and another member of his circle took delight in their cultured life.[80] The suggestion is that he and Pacatus shared a playful literary sensibility and enjoyed entertaining each other with displays of it—and the content of the poem confirms the point.[81]

But Pacatus is not just a partner in literary play: he is also someone suited to the role of literary arbiter because he has superior judgement. Indeed, Ausonius goes so far as to equate Pacatus with the Homeric critics Aristarchus and Zenodotus (11–12).[82] The comparison, which has precedents in Cicero (*Att.* 1.14.3) and Horace (*ars p* 452), endows Pacatus with the authority of those paradigmatic strong readers. We have no reason to suspect that Ausonius was being ironic when touting Pacatus's critical faculties, even though his flattery is exaggerated and even though the poem on which he was called to exercise his judgement was a minor one. By all appearances, light poetry had value in Ausonius's and Pacatus's literary culture and was a legitimate form of composition. Since such ludic verse had cultural capital as an accepted part of elite literary life, it follows that Pacatus could display his merits when responding to an example of it. As we have seen him do elsewhere, Ausonius celebrates his dedicatee and does so in the inflated strains that were normal in the code of communication with which he worked.[83] Yet the purpose now is not only to praise him but also to idealize further their literary world by relating that it contained such an admirable figure as Pacatus. Ausonius's ties to that figure, meanwhile, reflect well on him. As someone connected to Pacatus, he is by extension a person who, late in life (assuming he was writing in or soon after 390), still had impressive cultural contacts and credentials.

---

78. When sending the *Ludus* out into general circulation, Ausonius must have expected it to come to those who belonged to his literary world and to those who stood outside it. For the former, his preface would idealize a world that they knew, while for the latter it would provide a glimpse into that world.

79. I vary Trout 1999: 79, on the relationship between Ausonius and Paulinus of Nola.

80. My language echoes Green 1980: 197, who uses the phrase "joys of cultured life" when discussing poetic or artistic *querellae* in Late Antiquity, in which an author requests longer letters from his addressee.

81. That Ausonius also dedicated the *Technopaegnion* to Pacatus, a poetic game (i.e., one governed by strict ad hoc rules that centred on the manipulation of the verbal surface), indicates further that the two shared light and playful tastes. On Ausonius and the poetic *lusus*, see La Penna 1993: 731–51.

82. *Maeonio qualem cultum quaesiuit Homero / censor Aristarchus normaque Zenodoti* ("what polish did the critic Aristarchus and the standard of Zenodotus require for Maeonian Homer").

83. For similar praise of an addressee's skills as a critic, see SIDONIUS APOLLINARIS *carm.* 8.11–14.

The strengths of Pacatus as a reader are again highlighted in a second dedicatory verse preface where Ausonius calls for his criticism.[84] In the manuscript V, the text precedes one of the poems among Ausonius's *Eclogues* (*ecl.* 19). The editors Peiper and Prete believed that it was an introduction to the entire collection of *Eclogues*, which is made up of two groups of poems found separately in V (*ecl.* 1–18 and 19–25).[85] This is, of course, speculative, and the preface could introduce just the smaller set of poems that it introduces.[86] But however that may be, I follow the manuscript evidence and suppose that the text was attached to some number of the *Eclogues* rather than maintain with Green that it originally preceded a separate work entirely and then migrated somehow to its position in V.[87] Green sees incompatibility between the *Eclogues*, which are "serious and sometimes sophisticated,"[88] and Ausonius's self-deprecation in the preface, which is extreme even by his standards. But it is a mistake to consider his words evaluative—that is, to suppose that they need to reflect on or actually capture the character and quality of his poetry. As we will see, Ausonius's disparagement in fact fits with the rhetorical purposes of the preface, which are separate from the content of the work it accompanies; his stance contributes to a message about his addressee Pacatus rather than about the poetry he introduces.[89]

A quotation of Catullus 1.1, *cui dono lepidum nouum libellum* ("to whom do I dedicate this charming new volume") occupies the first line of the preface and establishes that the dedicatory poem will be in a meter, hendecasyllabic, that is very rare for Ausonius.[90] After then citing Catullus as his source and explaining

---

84. A concluding extrametrical *uale* marks the poem as a verse prefatory epistle.

85. In response to the location of the preface, Peiper and Prete place *Ecl.* 19–25 before 1–18. The title *Eclogues* comes from the heading that appears before the group 1–18 (*incipit eclogarum*, [the book] of *Eclogues* begins). On the textual history of the collection, see Green 1991: 420–1.

86. Green in his 1991 and 1999 editions presents all twenty-five poems together, however, under the title *Eclogues*.

87. Green thus includes the piece among Ausonius's *praefationes uariae* (4).

88. Green 1991: 242.

89. Assuming, as I do, that Ausonius expected his audience to consider the self-deprecation insincere, moreover, there was nothing to keep him from writing in such strains when introducing serious and at times sophisticated poetry. Indeed, it is plausible that he supposed the extreme humility would lead to heightened irony and, thus, would set off the seriousness and sophistication of the poetry more vividly. The date of this preface is more uncertain than those of the other two prefaces to Pacatus, because there is no heading that refers to him as a proconsul and because the date of the *Eclogues* is uncertain. It is certainly possible, however, that the date of the preface is close to 390. The similarities between the text and the preface to the *Ludus*, which I will address, are certainly consistent with the idea that they were written near in time to each other.

90. Hernández Lobato in this volume (279–83, esp. n. 9) discusses Ausonius's preface and another intertextual nod to Catull. 1.1 in Sidonius Apollinaris's *carm.* 12. The only other place that hendecasyllables appear in Ausonius's corpus is in *epist.* 13, a verse letter to Theon containing different meters (70 lines of hexameter, 11 of iambic dimeter, and 23 of hendecasyllables). Consolino in this volume explores polymetry in late antique poetry and discusses Ausonius's *epist.* 13.

that Catullus addressed the verse to Cornelius Nepos (2–3), Ausonius contrasts Catullus's "charming volume" (*lepidum libellum*) with his own "charmless, rough little work" (*illepidum rudem libellum*, 4). This is to adopt the familiar modest pose, which Ausonius subsequently amplifies by describing his poetry as "fluff, trash, and trifles" (*burras, quisquilias ineptiasque*, 5). At the same time, the word *ineptiae* suggests that Ausonius plays a more involved game. Catullus uses *ineptiae* to describe his own poetry (*si qui forte mearum ineptiarum / lectores eritis*, "if you who perhaps will be readers of my trifles," 14b.1–2). Perhaps Ausonius was aware of this, in which case he would have echoed Catullus's self-deprecation while distancing himself from that poet. Ausonius's foremost aim is to establish a contrast, but he also might have complicated the irony and set the conditions for a knowing reader to conclude that Ausonius was not as far from Catullus as he stated he was. While the affected modesty is emphatic, there is within it an indication of a different design: to relate that Ausonius writes similar "trifles" to those of Catullus, which is a way of elevating Ausonius's poetry.

After Ausonius compares his work to Catullus's, he goes on to proclaim Pacatus a superior figure to the Catullan Nepos (7–9):

inueni—trepidae silete nugae[91]—
nec doctum minus et magis benignum
quam quem Gallia praebuit Catullo.

I have found—silence, my anxious trifles—a man no less learned and more kind than he whom Gaul provided Catullus.

As in the preface to the *Ludus*, Ausonius portrays Pacatus as an ideal reader and dedicatee. His goal, he says, is to find someone who, entrusted with his *libellus*, will caress the work in his bosom (*credemus gremio cui fouendum*, "to whose bosom will we entrust it to be nurtured," 6). That person is Pacatus, who is *doctus*, as in the preface to the *Ludus* (16), and more *benignus* than Catullus's Nepos. Once Ausonius begins to describe Pacatus, the extreme self-deprecation in lines 4–5 takes on rhetorical purposes beyond the *captatio beneuolentiae*. While the abject humility is patently insincere, the juxtaposition it creates between the poets (Catullus > Ausonius) casts into relief the opposite juxtaposition between

---

91. The word *nugae* echoes Catull. 1.4, *meas nugas*. Here, Ausonius clearly uses a verbal echo to link his poetry with that of Catullus even as he sharply distinguishes between them. This can be seen to elevate Ausonius's poetry in the same way as his use of *ineptiae* does, although the main purpose is to create a situation like that in Catull. 1: Ausonius, like Catullus, sends his *nugae* out to a dedicatee. This, in turn, sets up the comparison between Pacatus and Nepos.

the dedicatees (Nepos < Pacatus).⁹² The aim is to make an actual point about Pacatus's merits: endowed with Nepos's learning and more than Nepos's kindness, Pacatus stands above his classical model. By explicitly identifying Nepos as a man from Gaul (*quem Gallia praebuit Catullo*, 9), moreover, Ausonius deepens the contrast between that figure and Pacatus. The understood message is that Ausonius is even more fortunate in his Gallic friend than Catullus was in his.⁹³

Ausonius proceeds to praise Pacatus all the more as his dearest friend and as an author whom the Muses favour above all others but Vergil.⁹⁴ Addressing his work as he had done in line 7 (*trepidae silete nugae*), he then concludes the preface by enjoining the text to fearlessly take safe shelter with Pacatus, who will look after it while he gives it a critical reading (13–18):

> "*Pacatum haud dubie, poeta, dicis?*"
> *ipse est. intrepide uolate, uersus,*
> *et nidum in gremio fouete tuto.*   15
> *hic uos diligere, hic uolet tueri;*
> *ignoscenda teget, probata tradet.*
> *post hunc iudicium timete nullum.*

"Without doubt, poet, you mean Pacatus?" That is the very man. Take flight fearlessly, verses, and nestle in his safe bosom. He will wish to hold you dear, to protect you; he will hide the things that are to be pardoned, will hand on the things that are to be praised. After him fear no judgement.

The use of *ignoscenda* signals that Ausonius has in mind the same process of editing for revision that he describes in the preface to the *Ludus* (recall *ignoscenda* in *lud. praef.* 1).⁹⁵ The genetic reader Pacatus is to cover over the shortcomings

---

92. I thus disagree with Conte 1986: 60 that there is no "tension" established between Ausonius and Catullus, no "'expropriation" of the older text, because the new verbal segment does not rework the old one dialectically. While the quotation certainly operates differently from allusion (and, in fairness, this is Conte's point), the lines that follow it recast and respond to Catullus to create original textual meaning. Pelttari 2014: 148–9 analyzes how Ausonius "plays on the difference between himself and Catullus" and "juxtaposes Catullus's poem and his own" (148), but not in the terms that I do. Pelttari also considers the quotation allusive while recognizing the differences between it and conventional allusion.

93. Nepos was from Cisalpine Gaul, whereas Pacatus was from the south of France and educated at Bordeaux. But Ausonius elides those distinctions and identifies both men simply as Gallic.

94. *Hoc nullus mihi carior meorum, / quem pluris faciunt nouem sorores / quam cunctos alios Marone dempto* ("none of my friends is dearer to me than he whom the nine sisters esteem more than they do all others with the exception of Vergil", 10–12).

95. We do not find *ignoscenda* or some equivalent in the first preface to the *Technopaegnion*, mentioned earlier. The talk there is only of approval: Ausonius appears to suggest that Pacatus will endow the verses with value if he approves of them (10–11). Without any reference to editing, there is no reason to find the theme of collaborative revision in the preface. Ausonius focuses instead on the hope that Pacatus might look favourably on the poem and, consequently, publish it with his imprimatur.

of the poem by marking them in his copy, which he is to send back to the poet. That act stands in tacit contrast to the publication that *tradere* describes in line 17. Once more, the talk of editing is conventional. Once more, too, its function extends beyond investing the preface with customary modesty. As he does in the *Ludus* preface, Ausonius uses the theme to touch on Pacatus's role as dedicatee. While Pacatus is not to edit the poem, he is to "cherish" it; that is, to provide it with support and, if needed, protection.[96] In addition, Ausonius advertises his enjoyment of ideal fellowship with an admirable member of the Gallic cultural elite. The word *doctus* and the reference to Catullus's Nepos establish Pacatus's credentials within that elite, while the talk of his closeness to Ausonius and of their collective authorship situates the poet there as well. The request for edits from a genetic reader is not real, but it illustrates the kind of relationship Ausonius and Pacatus had and represents the sort of thing that went on in the textual community they inhabited.

The strength of that relationship allows Ausonius's initially fearful text to proceed to its dedicatee without trepidation.[97] What Ausonius describes is a friend's kind and constructive criticism, which acts as a buffer against the potentially frightening responses of others (*post hunc iudicium timete nullum*, 18). The reading that takes place within their relationship will enable the poetry to face without fear whatever it encounters outside of it; if Pacatus likes what he sees, then the general reader—whose judgement, it is understood, is inferior to Pacatus's—will present no valid criticism to disturb Ausonius.[98] In this vision of elite friendship, it is the guarantor of good poetry (*probata tradet*, 17) and a source of security.[99] Ausonius expresses anxiety about the reception of his work at the hands of both Pacatus and the general reader. But after recognizing Pacatus's benignity, he draws a stark contrast between him and the public. Pacatus is the right kind of reader whom Ausonius could trust to read him in the right way, and he is someone whose criticism is in fact protective. Ausonius uses the theme of editing for revision to figure the value of literary *amicitia*, the benefits that the in-group of cultured elites provides.

Again, then, Ausonius utilizes his preface and the subject of editing in it to celebrate his dedicatee and the cultured life that they shared. Ausonius's

---

96. It is tempting to think that Ausonius wished to draw a connection between his poetry, which is to fly to Pacatus's *gremium*, and Catullus's *passer* in 3.8, which did not move from Lesbia's *gremium* (*nec sese a gremio illius mouebat*). I thank Joshua Hartman and Ian Fielding for calling my attention to this.

97. The use of *intrepide* in l. 14 recalls *lud. praef.* 10, where Ausonius compares himself when he submits his poem to Pacatus's judgement to a horse that learns to endure the lash fearlessly (*nouit et intrepidus uerbera lenta pati*).

98. Sidonius Apollinaris offers a version of the same idea in *carm.* 9.329–46. Quite similar, too, is Sidonius's *carm.* 24.10–15.

99. Relevant is Gurd 2012: 123, on authors' fears of their reception by the public (with an emphasis on Pliny the Younger) and the way that those fears spur them to revise.

commitment to that life was profound; it was the currency of so many of his relationships, including those with Symmachus and Paulinus of Nola. It would be wrong to view that commitment as peculiar to him in his era, despite the snide remarks of Ammianus Marcellinus on the meagre literary interests of late fourth-century CE aristocrats.[100] Certainly Symmachus and Paulinus (at least until his turn to committed Christianity), as well as others in Ausonius's orbit, cultivated and valued classical learning and letters.[101] Ausonius is, however, a powerful example of that wider phenomenon. His prefaces demonstrate as much and, in the process, display how an author in the period could reveal and sustain his elite identity. Poetry was a binding agent in the world in which Ausonius operated. For him, to dedicate a poem to someone, or even just to send a person a piece or a collection, was to offer a kind of gift that generated social contact and demonstrated regard and, in some instances, personal affection.[102] His prefaces reinforce the social dimensions of his poetry, while they also provide messages about the author, his dedicatees and addressees, and their relationship that situated Ausonius within the cultural and political elite.

Late Antiquity was an age of the preface. Many poets and prose authors alike used them especially to sketch their literary programs and to make gestures toward securing goodwill.[103] But even in this preface-heavy period, Ausonius stands out for the number, variety, and rhetorical richness of his introductory and dedicatory passages. Affected modesty is a salient and, to some critics, tedious feature of the texts.[104] Yet Ausonian modesty is not a one-note topos, and expressions of it have rhetorical functions that move far past conventional

---

100. AMM. 14.6.18 and 28.4.14, a clearly biased perspective.

101. Salzman 2011: xliv and xlvi.

102. I echo McGill 2014: 129. This is part of the late antique "world of erudite interchange" that formed bridges between men, which Knight 2005: 364 discusses. Dedicated poetry in Antiquity can be seen as a gift, but one, as I have noted, with responsibilities attached. Cf. Culpepper Stroup 2013: 108, who observes that when a book becomes a gift, it is "no longer merely a book [and] becomes a material expression of social [contact] . . . [and] an 'object of affection' that may initiate, confirm, reinforce, or seek to heal a relationship between approximate (or ideally) social equals."

103. To confine things to Latin poets like Ausonius, a partial list of late antique authors who attached prefaces to their works (some dedicatory, some not) includes Proba, Claudian, Prudentius, Paulinus of Nola, Sedulius, Sidonius Apollinaris, Avitus, Dracontius, and Corippus. For other examples of late antique prefaces, see Janson 1964: 116–58. See also Pelttari 2014: 45: "In late antiquity, prefaces played a significant role in mediating the presence of their texts."

104. Isbell 1974: 40–1 is representative: "Throughout the corpus of his writing Ausonius habitually adopted a humble and suppliant pose which seems to have disparaged his own production and invited the mocking laughter of his reader. The reader, on the other hand, quite quickly determines the real intent of these remarks. It seems an exercise in vanity; by appearing humble, he invited if not compelled the reader to insist that the poems are not tedious. In the end, however, a charming ingenuosity becomes finally cloying." See also Nugent 1990: 44–5 for examples of other critics impatient with Ausonius.

self-deprecation. Examinations of his references to authorial and collective revision prove the point. The passages and the prefaces in which they appear show how Ausonius wrote to and about imperial authority, advertised his and his family's virtues, called attention to the duties that dedication brought, and produced favourable portraits of the literary fellowship that he enjoyed with his dedicatees. Along the way, they reveal a poet who adapted his message, depending on his relationship to each addressee and the purpose of his text, to present different versions and visions of elite authorial identity.

9

To Speak or Not to Speak

The Birth of a "Poetics of Silence" in Late Antique Literature

JESÚS HERNÁNDEZ LOBATO

—Samuel Beckett once said: "Every word is like an unnecessary stain on silence and nothingness."
—Yes.
—On the other hand, he said it.

Art Spiegelman, *Maus: A Survivor's Tale*

Ecce non possumus dicere, et non permittimur tacere . . . Quid ergo faciamus, non loquentes et non tacentes? Iubilemus.[1]

AVG. *in psalm.* 102.8

After years studying the poetics and aesthetics underling late antique literature, I have come to realize that there is a key factor which, though rarely mentioned and often misunderstood, allows us to explain some of its most prominent features. This factor is a striking and ubiquitous problematization of notions of language and representation, something I will call the "poetics of silence."[2]

The generic label of "poetics of silence" refers to a phenomenon that was new to the ancient world in Christian Late Antiquity, a kind of propaedeutic problem extending far beyond—or more accurately, far before—the conventional metaliterary reflections that we tend to find in classical poetry. It poses a sort of preliminary question: is it possible really to say anything? If not, wouldn't it be better to remain silent? Is there any reason to continue speaking and writing at the edge of Antiquity? The problem is no longer whether to say this or that (the *what*) or whether to say it in this way or another (the *how*); it is the very act of saying that becomes intrinsically problematic, regardless of its content and its form. To speak or not to speak, that is the question—or at least it was a problem

---

1. "We cannot speak and we are not allowed to be silent. [. . .] Therefore, what can we do without speaking and without being silent? We can rejoice." My translation.

2. I have borrowed the expression from Yves Bonnefoy's universally acclaimed "poétique du silence," on which cf., e.g., Pereira Romero 1993. The first time that I applied this notion to the study of late antique literature was in a paper on the poetical programme of Sidonius Apollinaris (Hernández Lobato 2010b), which is discussed in detail later (see sec. 9.2). See also Hernández Lobato 2012: 401–49.

that troubled late antique Hamlets. This novel attitude problematizes something that had until then been simply taken for granted: the very notion of literature and the pertinence of speech.

This phenomenon is not restricted solely to the field of literature but can be defined as an omnipresent element in almost every manifestation of late antique culture; one needs only to recall Augustine's semiotics, Evagrius Ponticus's hesychasm, Gregory of Nyssa's apophatic theology, or Pseudo-Dionysius's negative mysticism, all strikingly reminiscent of our postmodern "linguistic turn."[3] However, given the limitations of this chapter and the specific aim of this volume, I focus almost exclusively on the literary side of the question, leaving the rest for a forthcoming study.

Clearly, a broad cross-cutting phenomenon such as this knew very different literary expressions based on different authors' perspicacity and the conventions of the various literary genres in which it emerged: parody, exegetical treatise, lyric, philosophical dialogue, occasional poetry, programmatic statement, Menippean satire, epistle, and so on. In the following pages I limit myself to an overview of some of the highlights, to reveal its fundamental significance to the study and understanding of late antique poetics.

9.1. *Nunc Musa loquax tacet*: Creating Poetry in a Crumbling World

Let us begin by considering an apparently humoristic piece of poetry: Sidonius Apollinaris's *carm.* 12, also known as the "Satire on the Burgundians":[4]

> *Quid me, etsi ualeam, parare carmen*
> *Fescenninicolae iubes Diones*
> *inter crinigeras situm cateruas*
> *et Germanica uerba sustinentem,*

---

3. As is well known, the so-called linguistic turn was a major development in twentieth-century philosophy and humanities, characteristically focusing on the relationship between philosophy and language and on all kinds of metalinguistic issues. The term was popularized by Richard Rorty's 1967 anthology *The Linguistic Turn*, in which it refers to the turn towards linguistic philosophy.

4. For more on the life and historical context of the fifth-century poet Sidonius Apollinaris, see Harries 1994, which updates and reformulates the classical Stevens 1933. On his sophisticated style, see the reference work by Gualandri 1979, which extends beyond the pioneering and still useful study by Loyen 1943. For Sidonius's poetics within the broader context of late antique aesthetics, see my monograph, Hernández Lobato 2012. Cf. also in this respect Condorelli 2008. For more on Sidonius's reception during the Middle Ages and the Renaissance, see Hernández Lobato 2014. A comprehensive and updated intoduction to Sidonius will be provided by Kelly and van Waarden, forthcoming. The Latin text of Sidonius's poems is taken from Loyen's reliable edition (1960). Translations are always those of Anderson 1936.

280 *The Poetics of Late Latin Literature*

> 5   laudantem tetrico subinde uultu
>   quod Burgundio cantat esculentus,
>   infundens acido comam butyro?
>   Vis dicam tibi quid poema frangat?
>   Ex hoc barbaricis abacta plectris
> 10 spernit senipedem stilum Thalia,
>   ex quo septipedes uidet patronos.
>   Felices oculos tuos et aures
>   Felicemque libet uocare nasum,
>   cui non allia sordidumque cepe
> 15 ructant mane nouo decem apparatus,
>   quem non ut uetulum patris parentem
>   nutricisque uirum die nec orto
>   tot tantique petunt simul Gigantes,
>   quot uix Alcinoi culina ferret.
> 20 Sed iam Musa tacet tenetque habenas
>   paucis hendecasyllabis iocata,
>   ne quisquam satiram uel hos uocaret.

Why—even supposing I had the skill—do you bid me compose a song dedicated to Venus the lover of Fescennine mirth, placed as I am among long-haired hordes, having to endure German speech, praising oft with wry face the song of the gluttonous Burgundian who spreads rancid butter on his hair? Do you want me to tell you what wrecks all poetry? Driven away by barbarian thrumming the Muse has spurned the six-footed exercise ever since she beheld these patrons seven feet high. I am fain to call your eyes and ears happy, happy too your nose, for you don't have a reek of garlic and foul onions discharged upon you at early morn from ten breakfasts, and you are not invaded even before dawn, like an old grandfather or a foster-father, by a crowd of giants so many and so big that not even the kitchen of Alcinous could support them.

But already my Muse is silent and draws rein after only a few jesting hendecasyllables, lest anyone should call even these lines satire.

The title of this brief and openly comic composition (*Ad Catullinum*) immediately informs us of the identity of its addressee: the influential Gallo-Roman senator Catullinus.[5] Apparently, it was Catullinus himself who commissioned his

---

5. For more on Catullinus's life, see Loyen 1943: 67–8 and Kaufmann 1995: 289. His name also figures quite prominently in SIDON. *epist.* 1.11.

childhood friend Sidonius to compose an epithalamium for his upcoming wedding. Needless to say, the request could well have been merely a fictional device, intended to provide Sidonius with a credible excuse to indulge in a caustic satire on the Burgundians. The reason for addressing this short piece to Catullinus was probably twofold: on the one hand, a private joke existed between them regarding the impracticability of the satiric genre, as demonstrated by a curious incident at Arles in 461 (SIDON. *epist.* 1.11), directly involving both Sidonius and Catullinus;[6] on the other hand, it can be seen as an intertextual clue to the reader, based on the appealing paronomasia Catullinus/Catullus. Not surprisingly, Catullus's famous dedicatory poem (CATVLL. 1, in particular its ll. 1–3) appears to have been the principal model for the interrogative beginning of Sidonius's *carm.* 12:[7]

Cui dono lepidum nouum libellum
arida modo pumice expolitum?
Corneli tibi . . .

To whom do I give my pretty new book,
freshly polished with dry pumice?
To you, Cornelius . . .[8]

A careful comparison of the texts can enlighten Sidonius's witty strategy, containing an ironic inversion of his Catullan precedent. When Catullus decided to write his programmatic *carmen*, he held in his hands a brand-new book of poetry, perfectly completed, lavishly ornate, and thoroughly polished (*lepidum nouum libellum / arida modo pumice expolitum*), for which he was desperately

---

6. Harries 1994: 93–4: "An anonymous satire had been circulated at Arles, which attacked, among others, the former prefect Paeonius. Catullinus, Sidonius's friend, also from the Auvergne, had been shown the satire by Paeonius and naïvely expressed admiration, saying it should be immortalized in letters of gold. Paeonius had seized on this as proof of Sidonius's authorship: Catullinus was, after all, Sidonius's friend and clearly had inside knowledge. Sidonius therefore arrived at Arles to find the population in ferment, stirred up by Paeonius's demagogic arts, and himself as a marked man." The next day, both Sidonius and Paeonius were invited to dinner with the emperor Majorian. Sidonius was able to gain the emperor's favour by reciting at his request an impromptu epigram which claimed his innocence and subtly humbled his false accuser, there present. Despite the apparent triviality of this episode, the risk of writing satire at that time should not be underestimated. According to Harries 1994: 93, "writing satire could be construed as defamation, and that merited punishment by 'the avenging sword.'" For more on the political and literary implications of this episode, see Hernández Lobato 2012: 145–55.

7. As demonstrated by Consolino 1974: 423–6, Sidonius also referred to Catullus's famous incipit in his own programmatic poem, the *carm.* 9 (cf. sec. 9.2), whose beginning (ll. 9–13) is also interrogative. In addition to this explicit intertextual link, Sidonius's *carm.* 12 is also subtly reminiscent of other Catullan sources, such as CATVLL. 36, a curious satire whose Phalaecian hendecasyllables are paradoxically called iambs by the poet himself, thus denying the very nature of the piece.

8. The translation is taken from Goold 1989: 31.

searching an addressee (*Cui dono . . .?*). Sidonius, on the other hand, had nothing but an addressee (Catullinus) and was engaged in a vain quest for an elusive poem that never materialized (*carm.* 12.1: *parare carmen*). Thus, this ironic piece is no more than a tragicomic chronicle of a failed poem, a prologue to a non-existent work, since Catullinus's long-awaited wedding song would never be composed. Such shrewd intertextual dialogue aims to draw our attention to a second implicit contrast: in Catullus's world, poetry was still feasible; in Catullinus's world, it no longer was.[9]

It is not surprising that Sidonius opted to compose a non-poem, a poem having the sole purpose of metapoetically denying its own existence (or at least the existence of the very piece which had been really commissioned). Its raison d'être is to reveal—or rather to denounce—the ultimate absence of a poem and even the impossibility of writing any poem in the prosaic and grotesque context of the Germanic invasions. This shameful absence is not the result of a sheer lack of talent (*etsi ualeam*) but of certain unfavourable environmental conditions: the vulgarity and ugliness of Sidonius's world destroy any attempt to write a poem (*quid poema frangat*), making the very survival of literature impossible. Therefore, this poem-which-is-not-a-poem was conceived as a satire, aimed at denouncing a world deprived of poetry, a world in which only silence reigned: *iam Musa tacet* (l. 20). But not even this barely articulate satire, a pale substitute for the real unwritten poem, can openly confess itself as such (l. 22: *ne quisquam satiram uel hos uocaret*), since satires were strictly prohibited at the end of the Western Empire.

To summarize, we are examining a poem which claims not to exist, a satire which carefully denies being such. Poetry fails, there is no epithalamium,

---

9. It is not the first time that a late antique author has chosen Catullus's poetic programme to model by contrast a new programmatic statement of his own. Most famously, the fourth-century Gallo-Roman poet Ausonius literally quoted Catullus's first line in order to highlight both the insurmountability of his predecessor's poetry and the moral equivalence of their respective addressees (AVSON. *praef.* 4.1–9 [Green]): *"Cui dono lepidum nouum libellum?" / Veronensis ait poeta quondam / inuentoque dedit statim Nepoti. / At nos illepidum rudem libellum, / burras quisquilias ineptiasque, / credemus gremio cui fouendum? / Inueni—trepidae silete nugae— / nec doctum minus et magis benignum / quam quem Gallia praebuit Catullo*. In Evelyn White's translation (1919: 163): "'To whom do I give my pretty, new book?' quoth the poet of Verona long ago, and, straightway finding Nepos, presented it to him. But this ugly, rough little book junk, trash, and drivelling to whose bosom shall I commit it to be cherished? I have it! (Peace, my anxious trifles!) 'Tis one not less learned and more generous than he with whom Gaul furnished Catullo." Ausonius's emphasis on the idea of silence is noteworthy: his trivialities are not only unpleasant and clumsy (*illepidum rudem*), but had they not had such an illustrious protector, they should have also been condemned to keep an eternal silence (*silete*). In his own playful and ironic manner, Ausonius is questioning for the first time the very pertinence of writing poetry after the end of Roman classicism. Sidonius's situation is even more desperate: whereas Ausonius had a bad book of poetry and an excellent addressee, Sidonius has nothing but his addressee, since the poem which had been commissioned to him would never be composed.

a miscarriage occurred before the poem was born. These few broken lines that together form a kind of self-aware *poema fractum* (cf. l. 8) are useful only for pointing out the painful absence of a real poem, the failure of poetry and the vicious expulsion of the once venerated Muse from the fifth-century scene (ll. 9–11: *Ex hoc barbaricis abacta plectris / spernit senipedem stilum Thalia, / ex quo septipedes uidet patronos*). Sidonius's impracticable poem confines itself to denouncing how the brutality of the world's prose, incarnate in the coarseness of the barbarians, had ended up silencing the Muse, condemning the poet to a renunciation of poetry, or in other words, to the most absolute of silences (l. 20: *iam Musa tacet*). But the core of Sidonius's bitter denouncement was not the contingent entities—Burgundians, war, vulgarity, lack of interest, or others—which wrecked poetry (*quid poema frangat*) but the very fact that the ship of poetry was definitively wrecked (*quod poema frangitur*).

The clear-cut vulgarity of the surrounding world as the ultimate cause of the Muse's silence is a recurring motif in Sidonius's poetry. It emerges with strength in even the most apparently unsuitable or unexpected places. This is the case, for instance, in *carm*. 13, in which the poet, displaying his usual set of rhetorical fireworks, addresses a plea to Emperor Majorian for tax exemption, in response to the punitive damages sanctioned on the rebellious city of Lyons, Sidonius's native city.[10] The poem closes with a surprising turn to the literary consequences of this situation:

> 35 *Nam nunc Musa loquax tacet tributo,*
>   *quae pro Vergilio Terentioque*
>   *sextantes legit unciasque fisci,*
>   *Marsyaeque timet manum ac rudentem,*
>   *qui Phoebi ex odio uetustiore*
> 40 *nunc suspendia uatibus minatur.*

For now my talkative muse is silenced by the tax and culls instead of Vergil's and Terence's lines the pence and halfpence owed to the Exchequer, and fears the hand and rope of Marsyas, who from his old-time hatred of Phoebus now threatens bards with hanging.

Once more, Sidonius, with his usual mixture of bitter humour and ironic distance, expounds on an idea, displaying a tragic lucidity about the spirit of his time: the unfeasibility of poetry in a crumbling world. The arrogant satyr Marsyas, whose ignorance was so audacious as to challenge Apollo, the most

---

10. A detailed analysis of this poem can be found in Hernández Lobato 2012: 159–221.

refined god of the Greek pantheon, to a musical contest, represents the rudeness and roughness which Sidonius was so desperately trying to combat, although to no avail. Unlike what happened in the classical myth, in this case it is the rude Marsyas that has defeated and humiliated the cultured god of poetry, who must resign himself to being strung up from a tree and flayed alive. In accordance with Sidonius's irrepressible penchant for humorous contrasts and the frustration of readers' expectations, the once hieratical classical deities are vividly depicted as having the most degrading of attitudes: the Muse, forced out of her beloved Parnassus, must now sit down without her fellow sisters to do the accounts of her exiguous income, and she struggles to pay off her many debts; Apollo has become a fearful outcast, persecuted by the law and sentenced to the gallows for fraud. In the new world order, the kingdom of the rude Marsyas, the path of Vergil and Terence ceased to be passable. The poet's heavy tax burden ended up silencing the most loquacious of the Muses (l. 35: *nunc Musa loquax tacet tributo*), imposing Marsyas's brutal tyranny on the delicate reign of Apollo (l. 38–40: *Marsyaeque timet* [sc. Musa] *manum ac rudentem, / qui Phoebi ex odio uetustiore / nunc suspendia uatibus minatur*). Thus, Sidonius's *Musa loquax* (*carm.* 13.35) is extremely prone to become a *Musa tacita*, as a result of the vulgarity of a world that is becoming less and less suitable for poetry.[11]

9.2. Silence as a Literary Programme: The Strategy of Negation

Perhaps the most striking and radical exponent of the new poetics of silence is Sidonius Apollinaris's extravagant *carmen* 9 (written ca. 461), which heads his voluminous *carmina minora* or *epigrammata* collection.[12]

The poem, consisting of 346 Phalaecian hendecasyllables, has a perfect three-part structure, consisting of a prologue, a centre (the negative catalogue), and a concluding epilogue. This dialogic architecture is perfectly delimited by the rhetorical-semantic links established in the respective beginnings of each of the three main sections: the prologue (l. 4: *dic, dic*), the central body (l. 16: *non nos*) and the concluding epilogue (l. 318: *nos*). The largest part, taking up some 300 lines, is the central body (ll. 16–317). It consists of an interminable catalogue of

---

11. A similar statement can be found in Sidonius's *carm.* 5.371-2: *iam tempus ad illa / ferre pedem, quae fanda mihi uel Apolline muto.* ("Now it is the time to advance to deeds which must be told, even were Apollo dumb.") For more on this passage, see Condorelli 2008: 50–7.

12. See Hernández Lobato 2010b. A revised and expanded version of this paper has been reissued as a book chapter in Hernández Lobato 2012: 401–49.

negations, a virtually monotonous litany of everything that Sidonius is *not* going to discuss in his poem. In light of these numbers, the overall structure of *carmen* 9 may be summarized as one immense "no" with a prologue and epilogue. But undoubtedly, the most striking feature of this poem is the absence of a positive term after the unending *recusatio*, a blatant violation of the most basic rules of programmatic poetry. I have suggested interpreting its three-part structure in dialectic terms, based on the following scheme (Hernández Lobato 2012: 440):

THESIS	ANTITHESIS	SYNTHESIS
(ll. 4–15)	(ll. 16–317)	(ll. 318–46)
Dic, dic . . . dic ("Tell, tell . . . tell")	*Non nos:* ("I am not . . .") *non* . . . ("I shall not . . .") *non* . . . ("I shall not . . .") *non* . . . ("I shall not . . .") *non* . . . ("I shall not . . .") *non* . . . ("I shall not . . .") *non* . . . ("I shall not . . .") etc	*Nos* (= *sterilis Camena*): ("I [= barren muse]") *nullus scit / nescit* ("nobody knows / doesn't know")

Following a long literary tradition which dates back to the famous Homeric beginnings μῆνιν ἄειδε θεά (*Il.* 1.1: "the wrath sing, O Goddess") and ἄνδρα μοι ἔννεπε Μοῦσα (*Od.* 1.1: "of that man, O Muse, tell me the story"),[13] the first word of the poem—reduplicated, in our case, in an emphatic *dic, dic* ("tell, tell")[14]—serves to point out the fundamental theme of the work, that is, the essential object of Sidonius's quest, which is none other than the act of speech

---

13. Both translations are mine. Cf. VERG. *Aen.* 1.1 *arma uirumque cano* ("arms and the man I sing").

14. After a three-line epistolary heading (a kind of versified paratext), Sidonius opens his programmatic *carmen* with an insistent imperative in anadiplosis, which is repeated a total of three times in the brief space of a single line (l. 4: Dic, dic *quod peto, Magne,* dic, *amabo,* "Come *tell* me, *tell* me what I want to know, *tell* me, Magnus, please"). This provides an image of the poet's obsessive need to reach a revelation concerning language that seems never to arrive. Indeed, taken as a whole, this first line boils down to a single word: *dic*, a simple but unobtainable monosyllable, which the poet confines himself to adorning and amplifying by means of an emphatic formula of extolment (*amabo*), which underscores the imperative nature of the sentence, a vocative addressed to the receiver of the work (*Magne*), which reveals its openly dialogic nature, and an expletive development of the object already implicit in the very semantics of the verb *dicere* (*quod peto*), which reveals the personal involvement of the lyric subject in the search for the deeply desired answer. In addition, this initial line, as demonstrated by Consolino 1974: 424–6, is a conscious rewriting of a passage from Martial (8.76.1: *dic uerum mihi, Marce, dic amabo,* "tell me the truth, Marcus, please, tell it to me"), through which is filtered the well-known dedication written by Catullus, which inspires and impregnates the whole of Sidonius's poetical programme. On the ultimate meaning of this rewriting of Marcial, see Hernández Lobato 2012: 430–4.

(*dicere*) itself; in other words, language and poetry[15] (the thesis). The next dialectic step (the antithesis) radically frustrates the elocutive longings of the lyric subject with a long chain of negations, capable of collapsing the work's anticipated development and thereby ruining the speech act that was so ardently desired, which is postponed sine die due to the lack of a *what* that would justify it. The poem, in rebellion, is not willing to *say* (*dicere*); what is more, it manages patiently to negate everything that poetry—which is to say the totality of the classical tradition of which it is consciously part—had previously proffered and all of the literary roads opened by its predecessors. What conclusion does the poem finally reach? What is the synthesis of this dialectical process of self-deconstruction or even "poetical apophasis"? Sidonius, put on the ropes by this torrent of negations and without an affirmative space for his poem, is obliged to confess the sterility of his Muse (l. 318: *nos ualde sterilis modos Camenae*, "As for these measures of my sadly barren muse"), who, despite her unbridled loquacity, deployed in the almost 350 lines of the work, or perhaps because of it, is thoroughly incapable of saying anything at all. Sidonius's Muse speaks but does not say anything; she therefore shares the paradox inherent in the *praeteritio* that animates the entire poem. The poem's final revelation, the synthesis of its dialectical process, is of an immense epistemological pessimism (ll. 345–6)

345   *uerum si cupias probare, tanta*
      nullus scit, mihi crede, quanta nescit.

If you would get at the real truth, believe me, nobody knows as many things as he doesn't know.

It is not possible for us to know or communicate, there is no access at all to that slippery *what* that the poem has attempted in vain to grasp in its over 300 lines. The final sentence is doubly negative: *nullus scit* and *nescit* are two ways of expressing a single concept. What humankind is capable of knowing is very meagre and unimportant when compared to what is beyond our understanding. Language and poetry is no more than a mere game, *tenerae iocus iuuentae*

---

15. The verb *dicere* refers us to two perfectly bounded semantic spheres: on the one hand, that of the oral expression of a thought, that is, language; on the other, that deriving from the technical uses, both ritualistic and poetic, of the verb *dicere*, that together link it directly to poetry, understood as inspired speech (Cf., e.g., VERG. *ecl.* 2.95–6: *quo te carmine dicam / Rhaetica?*; HOR. *carm.* 4.9.21: *dicenda Musis proelia*). The verb *to say, to tell*, conceived as the establishment of a representative relationship (whether poetic or of another type) with an extralinguistic referent, is revealed from the very beginning as the great theme—and certainly the great problem—of *carm.* 9. The imperative form of the verb and its pressing reiteration (*dic, dic . . . dic*) unequivocally reveal to us that the speech act demanded by the poet has not taken place, nothing has yet been uttered: rather, it is a desideratum that the poem hopes to achieve and not a consummated reality that can happily be taken for granted.

(l. 10) or *nostrae Terpsichores iocum* (l. 340), with no connection to reality, and incapable of producing either knowledge or meaning. In summary, Sidonius's *carm.* 9, with its audacious use of negation and cataloguing, establishes a surprising equation: poem = Ø, poetry = silence. The almost 350 lines of the work, the hundreds of pages of works by Sidonius, are equivalent to a prolonged silence.

Given this panorama, we must finally ask ourselves: what sense does it make to write? Why break this all-embracing silence with verses that are equivalent to it? *Carm.* 9, which explicitly poses this question, offers us the only conceivable answer in the times of Late Antiquity: poetry must exist in order to reveal its own futility, to open our eyes to a tragic truth that, ironically, is only accessible through poetry. Only poetry can produce the paradoxical knowledge of our inability to know; only language can unmask its own opacity. *Carm.* 9, therefore, is a kind of path of initiation that leads to the final understanding of its own uselessness (and, hence, of literature itself): only after having ascended the poetical ladder of *carm.* 9, to use Wittgenstein's apt metaphor,[16] can we observe its lack of meaning and throw it into the abyss. The novelty of Sidonius's poem (cf. l. 16: *non nos currimus aggerem uetustum*, "I am not speeding over the old road") lies precisely in having reached such a conviction—that of the inexpressibility of reality and the futility of poetry—and in wishing to communicate it to us as if it were a kind of initiatic revelation. The wounding realization of the real is absolutely inaccessible to our minds and therefore unrepresentable: poetry can aspire only to wrap up in words a reality that it is already incapable of representing. That is why, freed from any connection to reality, poetry cuts itself off forever from its traditional didactic aspirations and gives itself over entirely to the pleasure of pure form, to aesthetic play. In this way, awareness of the fundamental fissure in the link between words and things (which emerged with painful clarity in Late Antiquity) led directly to a formal baroque style, which we should not consider as something merely accessory and gratuitous but as the radical expression of a new *episteme*[17] of singular complexity.

9.3. The Age of Silence: Making Literature after the End of Literature

The precarious situation of the once talkative Muse, so bitterly depicted by Sidonius, was not just a temporary phenomenon but a growing trend. Only a

---

16. *Tractatus logico-philosophicus* 6.54: "My propositions serve as elucidations in this way: he who understands me eventually recognizes them as nonsensical, when he has used them—as steps—to climb up over them. (He must, so to speak, throw away the ladder after he has climbed up it.) He must overcome these propositions, and then he will see the world aright."

17. On the notion of *episteme*, see Foucault 1966.

few decades after Sidonius's death, the African writer Fulgentius,[18] living under the Vandals, lucidly characterized his time as a genuine age of silence (FVLG. *Virg. cont.* 83.1–4):

Expetebat quidem, Leuitarum sanctissime, nostri temporis qualitas grande silentium, ut non solum mens expromptare desisset quod didicit, quantum etiam obliuionem sui efficere debuit quia uiuit;

The spirit of this epoch of ours, oh most saintly of Levites, required a big silence, such that our mind should not only cease to disclose what it has learnt, but it should also attain to a state of self-forgetfulness, to an oblivion of its very existence;[19]

According to this passage, containing the very first words of Fulgentius's *Expositio Virgilianae continentiae*, a bizarre allegorical interpretation of Vergil's *Aeneid* put in the mouth of Vergil himself,[20] the new world order required complete oblivion of speech. Such oblivion entailed not only silencing what we had learned up to that moment (*mens expromptare desisset quod didicit*), that is, the unending chain of words, reflections, theories, and myths bequeathed to us by our forefathers, but it also required forgetting the very existence of our thinking mind, with its unstoppable plethora of concepts and ideas (*mens . . . obliuionem sui efficere debuit quia uiuit*). The human mind and its rampant mental noise had to be quietened, domesticated, silenced, almost in the same way that contemporary hesychasts, Neoplatonic philosophers, and apophatic theologians persevered in their indefatigable quest for wordless enlightenment.[21] The so-called age of silence, eloquently symbolized by Jesus's refusal to speak at his trial before Pilate, had arrived to stay, thus becoming an emblem of the triumph of

---

18. The works of Fulgentius will be quoted from Helm's 1898 edition (indicating page number and lines), which remains unequalled. Unfortunately, the only extant translation into English of his complete works (Whitbread 1971) is utterly unreliable and of little use. For more on Fulgentius's life, context and style, see the comprehensive and well-informed introductions by Manca 2003: 7–70, Wolff 2009: 7–39 and Wolff and Dain 2013: 7–41. An extensive annotated bibliography on Fulgentius, compiled and updated by Gregory Hays, can be found at http://people.virginia.edu/~bgh2n/fulgbib.html#mit (accessed January 16, 2015).

19. This is my translation, since the English renditions of this sentence proposed by Whitbread 1971: 119 and Hardison 1974: 329 are inaccurate, and Hays's abridged translation of the *Expositio Virgilianae continentiae* (2008: 666–72) does not include this passage. As Wolff 2009: 167 n. 3 correctly points out, "le subjonctif plus-que-parfait *desisset* est mis pour un subjonctif imparfait."

20. For more on this work, see the remarkable fully annotated bilingual editions by Rosa 1997 and Wolff 2009. For a brief introduction, see Wolff 2008.

21. Cf., e.g., AVG. *in psalm*. 146.11: *Conticescant humanae uoces, requiescant humanae cogitationes; ad incomprehensibilia non se extendant quasi comprehensuri, sed tamquam participaturi; participes enim erimus* ("Let human voices be hushed, human thoughts still: let them not stretch themselves out to

Christianity and the defeat of pagan logocentrism.[22] But why did Fulgentius's era so radically demand this absolute silencing?

9.3.1. A World Unsuitable for Poetry

First, there is what may be referred to as the practical reason. As Sidonius already denounced in his caustic non-poems, the very vicious ugliness of the times, obsessed with mundane concerns and besieged by raids and taxes, was perceived as thwarting any serious attempt to create literature. Fulgentius also frequently deplored the dreadful state of affairs in his oeuvre, most notably at the beginning of his extravagant lipogrammatic work *De aetatibus mundi et hominis*[23] (FVLG. *aet. mund.* 129.1–7):

> *Oportuit quidem, uirorum excellentior, hoc nostro quo nuper regimur temporis cursu perenni potius studere silentio et non dicendi studio, praesertim ubi nihil plus nisi de nummi quaestu res uertitur et conquirendi lucri perennis sollicitudo cotidie mentibus suppuretur; cupido etenim sensui non sermo dicentis comptior, sed offerentis est dulcior.*

In this time of ours which has been recently ruling our lives, it would have been advisable, oh excellent among men, *to devote oneself to an everlasting silence rather than strive to speak*, especially now that nothing but the pursuit of money moves the world and an unremitting concern for making

---

incomprehensible things, as though they could comprehend them, but as though they were to partake of them, for partakers we shall be.") On Augustine's debt to Neoplatonism, see Cary 2000. Another paradigmatic example of this inner silencing is provided by the sixth-century apophatic theologian and mystic Pseudo-Dionysius the Areopagite (*myst.* 1.997b–1000a): "My advice to you as you look for a sight of the mysterious things, is to leave behind you everything perceived and understood, everything perceptible and understandable, all that is not and all that is, and, with your understanding laid aside, to strive upward as much as you can toward union with him who is beyond all being and knowledge. By an undivided and absolute abandonment of yourself and everything, shedding all and freed from all, you will be uplifted to the ray of the divine *darkness* which is above everything that is." The translation is taken from Luibheid 1987: 135 (with a minor amendment in italics).

22. On the cultural and religious significance of Jesus's choice of silence, see Elsner 2009: 679–83. As Elsner interestingly points out (2009: 681–2), "even more than his sayings, Jesus's silence at the point where the entire burden of the antique tradition called for eloquence speaks for a fundamental break with tradition in one who is beyond the relativities of competing rhetoric, one who is uniquely divine." Cf. Sidonius's allegorical interpretation of Zechariah's imposed muteness (Luke 1:20) as a symbol of the end of the "age of Law" (the Old Testament) and the beginning of the "age of Silence/Grace"—the new world order brought about by the arrival of Jesus Christ: SIDON. *carm.* 16.38–9: *edita significans iusso reticere propheta, / gratia cum fulsit, nosset se ut lex tacituram* ("who in bidding the prophet [Zechariah] to be silent about thy message didst give token that with the dawn of Grace the Law must know that silence was coming upon it").

23. For more on this work, see Manca's 2003 edition, which provides the reader with an extensive introduction, facing-page Italian translation, and notes. For more on the quoted preface, see Manca 1998.

profits rots every day our minds. In fact, the feeling of greed does not deem the words of the speaker to be more elegant but deems those of the giver to be sweeter.[24]

A similar statement can be found in the prologue of his famous *Mythologies*[25] (FVLG. *myth*. 3.3–10), where the hunger for our daily bread (*fames domestica*) is depicted, by means of a witty play on words, as something much more pressing than the classical quest for poetic fame (*fama poetica*):

> *hoc uidelicet pacto, quia nostri temporis erumnosa miseria non dicendi petat studium, sed uiuendi fleat ergastulum nec famae adsistendum poeticae, sed fami sit consulendum domesticae—cito itaque nunc aut quod amiseris fleas aut quod edas inquiras quam quod dicas inuenias uacatque hoc tempore potentibus opprimere, prioribus rapere, priuatis perdere, miseris flere . . .*

for this very reason, that the lamentable misery of our time does not pursue the goal of eloquence but only weeps over the sweatshop of life, nor does it defend the reputation of poetry, but it must look out for the hunger at its doorstep, and thus you would rather weep for what you have lost or look for something to eat than find the right topics to declaim, even though at this time the powerful have the leisure to oppress, the rich to steal, the private citizens to lose all they have, and the wretched to wail . . .

9.3.2. A Knowledge Unsuitable for Words

On the other hand, Fulgentius occasionally adduces other considerations of a more abstruse and speculative nature concerning the boundaries and dangers of human knowledge in his sort of world. This is particularly evident in the prologue of his aforementioned *Expositio Virgilianae continentiae* (FVLG. *Virg. cont*. 83.6–12 and 84.17–19):

> *Virgilianae continentiae secreta phisica tetigi uitans illa quae plus periculi possent praerogare quam laudis. Vae inquam nobis, aput quos et nosse aliquid periculum est et habere. Ob quam rem bucolicam georgicamque omisimus, in quibus tam misticae interstinctae sunt rationes, quo nullius pene artis in isdem libris interna Virgilius praeterierit uiscera . . .*

---

24. This is my translation.
25. For a fully annotated Latin-French edition of Fulgentius's *Mythologies*, see Wolff and Dain 2013. For more on this work's prologue, which is extensively discussed in the coming pages, see Relihan 1993: 152–63 and Venuti 2009. This chapter reproduces Relihan's accurate translation (1993: 203–10) with some minor amendments.

> *Ergo doctrinam mediocritatem temporis excedentem omisimus, ne, dum quis laudem quaerit nominis, fragumen repperiat capitis.*
>
> I have touched on the natural secrets contained in Vergil's writings, avoiding those things which might invite risk rather than praise. Woe betide us, I say, for whom both knowing and possessing something is a risk! For this reason I have passed over the *Eclogues* and the *Georgics*, so bestrewn with mystical matters that in them Vergil has concealed the innermost heart of almost every art . . .
>
> I have therefore left out the teaching which goes beyond the mediocrity of our time, lest someone like me, while seeking the reputation of a great name, should merely end up with a broken head.[26]

According to this passage, certain subjects are somehow thorny and even risky to tackle, not only due to the cultural and political constraints of the era but also because of the unsuitability of words and definitions to convey them. There is a hidden knowledge that is too deep to be attained and expressed by words, a secret insight into reality which goes far beyond the barren combination of verbal signs that we call human language. Fulgentius, at least in theory, seems to align himself with the categorical conclusive remark of Wittgenstein's *Tractatus logico-philosophicus*: "Wovon man nicht sprechen kann, darüber muss man schweigen" ("Whereof one cannot speak, thereof one must be silent"). In practice, however, it is precisely this unutterable realm beyond words and concepts that constitutes the core subject matter of most of his works, in clear contradiction with all of these programmatic cautions. I explore this blatant inconsistency later on. For now, it is sufficient to remember the humoristic and playful overtones of Fulgentius's prologues, modelled on the ironic rules of Menippean satire.[27]

Interestingly enough, Fulgentius draws a parallel between the material and the cultural realms: in that time of uncertainties, knowing, he points out, was as dangerous as possessing (*et nosse aliquid periculum est et habere*). Thus, both possessor and knower are continuously menaced by the unscrupulous avidity of undeserving usurpers: greedy looters, tax collectors, or mere dilettanti, as avid of knowledge as they are unprepared to gain access to higher revelations. Both knowing and having make you vulnerable, an easy prey to envy and plunder, to criticism and punishment.

---

26. This is my translation.
27. For a general view of Fulgentius's prologues, see Manca 2002. For more on the presence of the literary conventions of Menippean satire in the prologue of Fulgentius's *Mythologies*, see Relihan 1993: 152–63 and Venuti 2013.

At this point, one may reasonably ask: if the qualities of the era compelled thinkers and authors to maintain an absolute silence, why did Fulgentius compose such a vast oeuvre? Was not it much safer to refrain from writing or even to avoid speaking? Fulgentius fails to offer readers a sincere answer. His indisputably unsatisfactory reply merely adjusts to the well-known conventions of programmatic statements: his works, he adduces, were reluctantly written down only to abide by the wishes of his patron and not by his own will (FVLG. *Virg. cont.* 83.4–7 and *aet. mund.* 129.10–15):

> *sed quia nouo caritatis dominatui fulcitur et in amoris praecepto contemptus numquam admittitur, ob hanc rem Virgilianae continentiae secreta phisica tetigi . . .*

Yet in view of the fact that it [sc. our time] is now based on the rule of Charity and a refusal is never permitted in the commandment of Love, for this only reason, I have touched on the natural secrets contained in Vergil's writings . . .

> *Et crede, teste Deo nostro confiteor, uolui tuum in his opusculis praeceptum spernere, nisi hoc meo indixissem ingenio, tuo nullo modo inoboediens inueniri imperio. Esto ergo contentus huic oneri, quod tibi florulentis Pieridum decerpsimus hortulis et sicut Euristeus mihi inponendo sudori Herculeo praefuisti.*

And believe me, as God is my witness, I confess that I would have wanted to ignore your request for these opuscules, had I not enjoined my wits never to be caught disobedient to your command. Be therefore satisfied with this load, which I have garnered for you from the flowery gardens of the Muses, daughters of Pierus, and which you, like Eurystheus, have imposed on me, making me sweat like Hercules.[28]

The idea of equating himself with Hercules, forced to carry out the labours demanded by his cousin Eurystheus (mythological counterpart to Fulgentius's unidentified *dominus*), is another constant in his prologues, as noticed by Manca (2002: 320–2, 333–5).

9.3.3. Words Threatened by Silence: Critics as Gravediggers

Even after the hesitant Fulgentius decided to pick up his quill and break the silence, no result can be taken for granted. His would-be book is still besieged by

---

28. Both translations are mine.

a final threat of silence, which seriously menaces its very survival: the criticism of readers (FVLG. *aet. mund.* 129–130.16–1).

> *Sic quoque nostris opusculis intentus quaesumus incubes lector, ut, si—quod minime puto—iniunctum opus tuo non displicuerit legendum iudicio, poeticum felix gessi negotium, sin uero obscuro stultitiae nubilo tenebrescit inconditus sermo, in silentii cinerem sepultae migrentur necesse est tot lucernae peruigiles et sine effectu honoris productae usque in crepusculum noctes.*

> Also I beseech you, oh reader, to rest your eyes on these opuscules of mine with full attention, so that, if the reading of this inflicted work does not offend your judgement (what I do not believe at all), I will have successfully achieved a poetical enterprise; but if my clumsy expression darkens into a sombre mist of foolishness, all the lamps of my late-night work will have to fade away, *buried into the ashes of silence*, and all those nights prolonged till dawn will have attained no worthwhile result.[29]

Consequently, every word that Fulgentius, though unwillingly, dared to utter is in danger of immediately returning to the ashes of silence (*in silentii cinerem sepultae migrentur*), as if it had never existed. The mere expression of slight disapproval by readers of this newborn piece of literature would be sufficient to bury Fulgentius's unending nights of work by candlelight (*tot lucernae peruigiles et . . . productae usque in crepusculum noctes*) into the dust of oblivion. In this context, the literary word is always an anomaly, a kind of incidental—and often unnecessary—exception in the midst of an overwhelming ocean of silence.

9.3.4. Silence as the Birthplace of Words

As we have seen, the motif of silence clearly dominates Fulgentius's prologues, where it is consistently related to all sorts of metaliterary issues. But silence was not only a fearsome danger or an impending threat to be carefully avoided by the poet in order to make a bit of space for his menaced words. The metaphor of silence in Fulgentius's texts, like the texts themselves, is always contradictory, problematic, and to a large extent reversible. Over and beyond the dark connotations that it often entails, it also has a positive side that should not be overlooked in any serious attempt to reconstruct the complex poetics of Fulgentius. This is especially evident in the prologue of his *Mythologies*, where silence represents the idea of a yearned-for oasis of tranquillity in the midst of a crumbling

---

29. This is my translation.

world, a peaceful countryside retirement, joyfully consecrated to the otherwise impossible practice of literature (Fvlg. *myth.* 4–5.7–1):

> *Me interim discedentem a te domine dum quasi urbanis extorrem negotiis ruralis otii torpor adstringeret, et euitans erumnosa calamitatum naufragia quibus puplicae uexantur incessabiliter actiones, arbitrabam agrestem secure adipisci quietem, ut procellis curarum celantibus, quo in turborem urbana tempestas exciderat, uelut Alcione niduli placidam serenitatem uillatica semotione tranquillior agitassem; sopitisque in fauilla silentii raucisonis iurgiorum classicis quibus me galagetici quassauerant impetus defecatam silentio uitam agere creditabam, ni me illuc quoque memorum angina inprobior sequeretur felicitatisque nouerca fortuna, quae amarum quiddam humanis interserit semper negotiis, me quasi pedisequa sectaretur.*

> While I was apart from your presence, lord, when the sloth of rural boredom held me tight, as it were an exile from city business, and while I was avoiding those damnable shipwrecks of disaster which relentlessly upset public affairs, I thought that I would try to get in peace to some country quiet; so that, after the gales of anxiety had calm down after the crisis in the city devolved to mass confusion, I might, like Halcyone, enjoy at ease the quiet serenity of the nest, in the indolence of a country estate. After the blaring trumpets of war had been lulled into the ashes of silence, the trumpets of the barbarian invasions which had so shaken me, I was thinking that I could lead a life made perfect by silence, were it not that the wicked heartache of my grief was following me there as well, and Fate, the stepmother of happiness, who always sprinkles something bitter upon human affairs, was dogging my footsteps like a lackey.

The reversibility of the metaphor of silence may be easily recognized in the recurrent expression "ashes of silence" (Fvlg. *aet. mund.* 129.20: *silentii cinerem*; Fvlg. *myth.* 4.14: *fauilla silentii*). While in the prologue of *De aetatibus mundi et hominis* (129.20) it was used to describe the oblivion to which unfavourable criticism could consign any literary work, regardless of its quality (resulting, by extension, in the silencing of literature itself),[30] it now referred to the peace resulting from the long-awaited cessation of barbarian raids, a new state of tranquillity in which literature could once again flourish. Fulgentius's almost monastic ideal of life consisted of an existence "made perfect by silence" (*defecatam silentio uitam agere*). In was only in the still of the night, placidly sitting

---

30. The text is analyzed in sec. 9.3.3.

by candlelight, or enjoying the inspiring calm of a natural environment, that the author felt compelled to compose a new poem (FVLG. *myth.* 6–7.22–4):

Nam me auium quaedam uernulitas, quae fragili quadam dulcedine crispantes sibilos corneis edunt organulis, ad hoc opus allexerat et laboris tam subita requies melos quoddam carminis expectabat.

For a certain native charm of the birds who were giving forth their chirping voices from their instrumental beaks in a sort of brittle sweetness drew me to the following effort, and such an unexpected rest from labour fairly demanded some sort of song and poem.

In summary, it is silence and only silence that allows for the existence of literature. Without silence there can be no literature, since it is the very space where creativity is made possible, far from the confusing noise of so-called civilization. Therefore, in Fulgentius's metaphoric vocabulary, silence may be used in a broader positive sense as a synonym for night, candlelight, *secessus mundi* (seclusion from the world), countryside, peace, creativity, revelation, and even word.

9.3.5. Words as a Gateway to Silence: Language beyond Language

But silence is much more than just that. It is the unattainable goal that every page of Fulgentius's works ultimately pursues: the deep, unexpressed, and inexpressible meaning underlying—and surpassing—human language. In his own words (FVLG. *myth.* 11.15–18):

Certos itaque nos rerum praestolamur effectus, quo sepulto mendacis Greciae fabuloso commento quid misticum in his sapere debeat cerebrum agnoscamus.

And so I aim for the real *essence* of things, so that once the *fanciful invention of deceitful Greece has been buried into silence* we can recognize what mystic things our understanding ought to grasp in them.[31]

Fulgentius's works aim to make emerge the inaudible and intangible truth that words have concealed for centuries with their hollow and confusing noise.[32]

---

31. In this passage I depart from Relihan's translation (1993: 208) in several points, highlighted in italics for the sake of clarity.
32. See Mastrangelo in this volume on the connection between *fabula* and moral truth in Boethius's poetics.

Words, always deceitful (*mendacis Greciae fabuloso commento*), must be silenced—buried, as Fulgentius puts it (*sepulto*)—in order to allow our dull and limited understanding (*cerebrum*) to have a taste (*sapere*) of the non-discursive truth hidden behind them, constituting a sort of ineffable revelation (*quid misticum*).[33] In other words, the paradoxical mission of the new Christian writer is to unearth the silent truth by unmasking the lies and deceits of language, to silence words by giving a voice to the silence behind them.[34] In order to gain a deeper insight into this rather obscure text, it is worthwhile to put it into a broader context.

The passage is part of a humorous dialogue between Fulgentius and the recently appeared Muse Calliope, displayed at the beginning of his *Mythologies*.[35] In this revealing conversation, modelled on the conventions of Menippean satire, the African writer decidedly embraces Sidonius's poetics of silence by means of a deliberate imitation of his programmatic *carm.* 9—in particular, its three-part dialectic architecture, already discussed.[36] This debt to Sidonius's *carm.* 9, which enlightens many aspects of Fulgentius's poetics in its complex intertextual underpinning, has thus far gone unnoticed and requires in-depth examination.

In a first dialectic movement (the *thesis*), the talkative Muse Calliope, having recognized Fulgentius as a genuine initiate in the art of poetry, characterized as "mysteries" (*myth.* 10.11–12: *Anacreonticis iamdudum nouus mistes initiatus es sacris* "you have for some time now been the latest initiate in the Anacreontic mysteries"), enthusiastically volunteers to help him master his verbal skills and thus become a classical poet. Calliope's speech repeatedly emphasizes the centrality of words in a writer's task. She speaks of "her pupil" Fulgentius (*myth.* 10.12–13: *meo* ... *tirunculo*) as having being struck by Satire's "wanton dew of words" (*myth.* 10.14: *lasciuienti uerborum rore*). Lest he lack any poetic gift

---

33. Similar statements can be found almost throughout Fulgentius's *Mythologies*: *myth.* 54.9 *Sed haec fabula mistici saporem cerebri consipit*; *myth.* 74.8–9 *Nunc ergo huius misticae fabulae interiorem cerebrum inquiramus*; *myth.* 78.18–20 *uocis ergo pulchritudo delectans interna artis secreta uirtutem etiam misticam uerborum attingit*. Cf. within this very prologue *myth.* 12.3–4 *Tam secretis misticisque rebus uiuaciter pertractandis*; *myth.* 12.12 *misticae artes*; *myth.* 15.1–2 *misticis* ... *rationibus. Neque enim illos de his exspectas effectus*.

34. This is particularly evident in the writings of Augustine of Hippo, credited in his own right as the father of semiotics. As Mazzeo 1962: 192 correctly points out, "for St. Augustine all dialectic, true rhetoric, and thought itself were but attempts to reascend to that silence from which the world fell into the perpetual clamour of life as fallen men know it." A similar point of view can be found in Gregory of Nyssa, as recently proposed by Hernández Lobato 2016a. As the contemporary philosopher Giorgio Agamben has rightly observed (1991: 63), "the mythogeme of a silent voice as the ontological foundation of language already appears in late-antique Gnostic and Christian mysticism." For further discussion with several examples, see Agamben 1991: 63–5. On Augustine's theory of knowledge, see below.

35. An interesting analysis of this prologue can be found in Relihan 1993: 152–63.

36. See sec. 9.2.

(*myth.* 10.12–13: *ne quid . . . tibi desit*), she willingly grants him the power of tale telling (*myth.* 10.17–18: *historiae quilibet effectus*), which he may urgently need in order to undertake his literary venture.

But Calliope's expectations were soon to be frustrated. The reluctant Fulgentius was quick to provide her with a surprising reply (the *antithesis*), clearly modelled on the unending *recusatio* at the core of Sidonius's *carm*. 9: though the title, even the superficial content, of Fulgentius's book might invite anyone (including the Muse) to assume that he would be talking about different episodes of Greek mythology, he categorically denied having ever had such intentions. Fulgentius would *not* deal with the superficial aspects of those verbal accounts known as myths (*historiae effectus*) but rather with the inner truth, the unseizable "thing," which they all conceal (*certos rerum effectus*).

> *Tum ego: Index te libelli fefellit, generosa loquacitas; non mihi cornutus adulter arripitur nec imbre mendaci lusa [Danae] uirgo cantatur, dum suo iudicio deus sibi pecudem praetulit et hanc auro decepit quam potestate nequiuit; non suillo canimus morsu depastum amantis iuuenis femur nec in meis libellulis sub falsa alite puerilis pependit lasciuia; non olorinis reptantem adulterum plumis, oua pulligera uirginibus inculcantem quam semina puerigena uisceribus infundentem, nec lignides puellas inquirimus, Ero atque Psicen, poeticas garrulantes ineptias, dum haec lumen queritur extinctum, illa deflet incensum, ut Psice uidendo perderet et Ero non uidendo perisset; nec referam uirginali figmento* Nonacrinam *lusam uiraginem, dum quaereret Iuppiter quod magis esse uellet quam fuerat. Mutatas itaque uanitates manifestare cupimus, non manifesta mutando fuscamus, ut senior deus innitus exerceat et sol fulgoris igne deposito malit anilibus exarari rugis quam radiis; certos itaque nos rerum praestolamur effectus, quo sepulto mendacis Greciae fabuloso commento quid misticum in his sapere debeat cerebrum agnoscamus.*[37]

Then I said: "The title of my book deceives you, your noble garrulousness. I have taken up no horned adulterer, nor sung of a maiden deceived by treacherous rain, while a god through his own judgement preferred a beast to himself and deceived by gold the girl whom he could not gain by force. We do not sing of the thigh of the young lover eaten by the boar's bite, nor in my little chapters childish wantonness hang from a transformed bird; nor do we seek after the adulterer sneaking about in swan's

---

37. FVLG. *myth.* 10–11.19–18. Following Ellis's (1904) well-founded conjecture (based on the parallel with Ov. *met.* 2.409–10), I substitute *Nonacrinam* for Helm's problematic *Aricinam*.

plumage, quickening fowl's eggs in a virgin's womb rather than pouring in human seed; nor after the girls with the lamps, Hero and Psyche, who babble poetic nonsense as the former laments the lamp extinguished and the latter weeps for the lamp lit (for Psyche lost by seeing, and Hero, by not seeing died). Nor will I tell of the Arcadian maiden deceived by a fictitious maiden, when Jupiter was looking for something that he more desired to be than what he was. Therefore *I want to make clear these transformed vanities, not to obscure clear things by transformation*, so that an elder god can practice his neighing and the sun can put aside the fire of his brightness and prefer to be furrowed with an old woman's wrinkles instead of his own rays. And so I aim for the real *essence* of things, so that once the *fanciful invention of deceitful Greece has been buried into silence we can recognize what mystic things our understanding ought to grasp in them*."[38]

This negative catalogue, closely following Sidonius's deconstructive procedure, carefully enumerates what thus far appeared to be the content of the book but only in order to deny it point by point, thereby destroying the reader's—and even the Muse's—horizon of expectations.[39] It is worth remembering that some of the myths included here are effectively treated to differing degrees in Fulgentius's *Mythologies*, clearly underlining the paradoxical nature of this enumeration. This apparent contradiction invites the reader to resolve it on a higher plane of decodification by philosophically abstracting it. Fulgentius's book may indeed be considered mythological, but it is definitely *not* a book about mythology (at least not in the same way as those of Hesiod and Ovid are).[40] Its meaning extends far beyond its words.

Unlike Sidonius's *carm.* 9, here we do find, at least apparently, a positive term or *pars construens* after the prolix negative enumeration of all the things that Fulgentius is *not* going to speak about. But we also soon realize that this allegedly unproblematic affirmative statement is decidedly dominated by paradox. In fact, far from dispelling the paradoxical aspects of the Sidonius-style *recusatio*, it enhances them by making explicit the underlying reflections, implicit in Sidonius's poem, on the inability of language to convey reality. Fulgentius makes the effort to list the superficial content of his book only in order to deny it, thereby implying that what really matters is precisely what the words do not say, that *quid misticum* that emerges only when the lies of language are silenced (*sepulto mendacis Greciae*

---

38. This is Relihan's translation (1993: 207–8), except for the parts highlighted in italics.
39. On the seminal notion of "horizon of expectations" (*Erwartungshorizont*), coined by Hans Robert Jauss, see Jauss 1982.
40. For more on the anti-Ovidian undertones of this prologue, see Relihan 1984 and Venuti 2011.

fabuloso commento). Fulgentius uses language against language, as a means to overcome the blindness produced when its hypnotic tricks go unnoticed and are rashly assumed to be reality. After all, it virtually makes no difference what words superficially convey: be it the Holy scripture or a chef's recipe, a pagan myth or a sibyl's oracle, everything must ultimately mean the same, since the ultimate reality, unexpressed but in some mysterious way intuited beneath the words, is only one. The text, any text, is only an excuse to gain deeper revelations. Everything is allegory, since the ultimate meaning of words, what every Christian commentator should make appear, extends far beyond the vicious circle of semiotics (signifier/signified/referent). It is no wonder that Robert Edwards eloquently described Fulgentius's modus operandi as a "collapse of meaning."[41]

According to Fulgentius, the apparent message of any text, founded upon a stable association between signifier and signified, is nothing but an illusion, since any imaginable linguistic sequence ultimately speaks of the same thing: what is beyond all discourse, that is, the ungraspable and inexpressible essence underlying all communication, which, paradoxically, sustains and makes possible the act of speech itself. In other words, what Fulgentius is proposing is an abolition of the system of differences upon which language is based, meaning the complete destruction of the symbolic and the obliteration of the very ideas of sign and representation. Or in the words of Roland Barthes (1974: 215), "the transgression of the Antithesis, the passage through the wall of opposites, the abolition of difference." And that is precisely the unwanted outcome attained by the ubiquitous allegorical reading which characterizes late antique literature as a whole. In fact, the success and diffusion of allegory and all sorts of metonymical procedures within the cultural fabric of Late Antiquity stem from and contribute to the challenge to the classical notions of language and representation that is at the very heart of that era's tottering *forma mentis*. As Barthes (1974: 215–16) correctly pointed out in his analysis of Balzac's *Sarrasine*:

> This catastrophic collapse always takes the same form: that of an unrestrained metonymy. By abolishing the paradigmatic barriers, this

---

41. Edwards 1976: 32–3: "The collapse of meaning in Fulgentius' allegorical writing involves three phases. The initial problem derives from a view that separates language from its intended meaning. Although Fulgentius is not dealing with a religious text, he tends to accept the exegetes' distinction between proper and figurative senses. Consequently, his allegories raise the issue of treating a secular text as if it were Scripture. Fulgentius does not claim divine inspiration for the pagan myths, but he does seek a philosophical truth beneath the surface of language. [...] Because he is concerned with deriving an added significance from the myths, Fulgentius can equate the perception of meaning with its reality. However, his description of Minerva's iconography shows that any such understanding must be fragmentary and incomplete. As a result, the structure of philosophical truth collapses, and a technique of association takes over the allegories."

metonymy abolishes the power of *legal substitution* on which meaning is based: it is then no longer possible regularly to contrast opposites, sexes, possessions; it is no longer possible to safeguard an order of just equivalence; in a word, it is no longer possible to *represent*, to make things *representative*, individuated, separate, assigned; *Sarrasine* represents the very confusion of representation, the unbridled (pandemic) circulation of signs, of sexes, of fortunes.

This phenomenon extends behind the deep and unfathomable silence which looms over late antique culture in its entirety, giving it its distinctive character. That is what ultimately makes of this period a genuine "age of silence" (and by logical extension an "age of interpretation"),[42] a kind of apophatic and self-deconstructive coda to the unrestrained verbosity of the classical world. Thus Late Antiquity witnessed the emergence of an unheard-of apophatic theology aimed at revealing the inefficiency of language to convey the inner reality of things.[43] The ultimate goal of mysticism is precisely the abolition of the apparent oppositions underlying the physical and the logical realms—what has come to be known as the *coincidentia oppositorum*, that is, the overcoming of the duality implicit in all forms of language and conceptual knowledge.[44] Similarly, Fulgentius, acting as a lay mystic of literature, embraces the wordless mystery of reality by deliberately dismantling the intrinsically dualistic notion of sign, the cornerstone of the very idea of representation.

To conclude, let us now return to the final statements of our text of reference: the prologue of *Mythologies*. After Fulgentius's paradoxical speech, which has just been discussed, the Muse is inclined to draw her own conclusion; that is to say, the long awaited *synthesis*. Just like Sidonius's enigmatic closing statement (SIDON. carm. 9.345–6: *uerum si cupias probare, tanta / nullus scit, mihi crede, quanta nescit*. "If you would get at the real truth, believe me, nobody knows as

---

42. For more on this epithet, based on Vattimo's "età dell'interpretazione" (2005), see Hernández Lobato 2012: 91–107. A lucid reflection on this phenomenon can be found in Gualandri 1995.

43. This is the case of Gregory of Nyssa's quasi-postmodern philosophy of language. For more on this, see Mosshammer 1990, Karfíková 2007, Ludlow 2007: 231–91, Zupi 2007, and Hernández Lobato 2016a. On Augustine's seminal position on this matter, see below. On his huge influence on twentieth-century philosophy of language (Wittgenstein, Gadamer, Ricoeur, Jung, Lacan, Derrida, Lyotard, etc.), see Alici, Piccolomini, and Pieretti 2002.

44. In the words of Pseudo-Dionysius the Areopagite (*myst.* 1.1000b): "Since it is the Cause of all beings, we should posit and ascribe to it all the affirmations we make in regard to beings, and, more appropriately, we should negate all these affirmations, since it surpasses all being. Now we should not conclude that the negations are simply the opposites of the affirmations, but rather that the cause of all is considerably prior to this, beyond privations, beyond every denial, beyond every assertion." The translation is taken from Luibheid 1987: 136.

many things as he doesn't know"), here we find a vindication of the power of unknowing, of the prevalence of silence (the wise ignorance of mystics)[45] over words (discursive worldly knowledge):

> *Tum illa: Vnde haec tibi, inquit, homuncule, tantam ignorantiae scientiam, unde tam ratum ordinem ignorandi? Dum enim saeculis intacta exquiris, ostendis te sapienter scire quod nescis. Cui ego: Si his, quibus ignorare aliquid contingit, ne ipsut quidem nescire suum scire contingerit, quanto satius erat eis etiam non nasci contingere quam nasci inefficaciter uenire. Primum itaque ego scientiae uestibulum puto scire quod nescias.*[46]

Then she said: "How, homunculus, do you come by these things, this great knowledge of ignorance, this so-thought-out ordering of unknowing? For when you seek out things untouched by the ages you show that you in your wisdom know *that* you do not know."

I answered her: "If those who happen not to know something do not even happen to know their own ignorance, how much better would it have been for them not to happen to be born than to come to be so uselessly! And so *I think that the most important entryway of knowledge is to know that you do not know.*"[47]

This dialectic structure can be convincingly summarized in a three-part scheme, which graphically reveals the strong parallelism between Sidonius's programmatic poem (*carm.* 9) and Fulgentius's programmatic prologue, two unsurpassed masterpieces of this new and extremely self-deconstructive "poetics of silence":

---

45. Cf., e.g., Avg. *ord.* 2.16.44 (speaking about God): *qui scitur melius nesciendo,* "who is better known by not knowing." My translation. Similar thoughts can be found almost everywhere in the works of Gregory of Nyssa and Pseudo-Dionysius the Areopagite. See for instance the latter's *myst.* 3.1033b-c (translated by Luibheid 1987: 139): "The fact is that the more we take flight upward, the more our words are confined to the ideas we are capable of forming; so that now as we plunge into that darkness which is beyond intellect, we shall find ourselves not simply running short of words but actually speechless and unknowing. [...] But my argument now rises from what is below up to the transcendent, and the more it climbs, the more language falters, and when it has passed up and beyond the ascent, it will turn silent completely, since it will finally be at one with him who is indescribable."

46. Fvlg. *myth.* 11–12.18–2.

47. My rendition of the last sentence, highlighted in italics, differs significantly from that of Relihan 1993: 208—"And so I think that I know the most important entryway of knowledge, a thing you may not know"—whose otherwise reliable translation is faithfully reproduced elsewhere. As aptly noted by Hays 1998: 128, "in reality, *quod* introduces *oratio obliqua,* as often in later Latin. Fulgentius is merely harking back to the Socratic paradox: 'I think that the threshold of knowledge is to realize that you do *not* know.'" Similarly Wolff and Dain 2013: 143 n. 65.

THESIS (The Muse) *myth.* 10.8–19	ANTITHESIS (The poet) *myth.* 10–11.19–18	SYNTHESIS (The Muse + the poet) *myth.* 11–12.18–2
lasciuienti uerborum rore ("wanton dew of words")	*non mihi...* *nec ... cantatur* *non ... canimus* *nec in meis libellulis* *non ... inquirimus* *nec referam ...*	*ignorantiae scientiam* ("knowledge of ignorance") = *sapienter scire quod nescis* ("you in your wisdom know that you do not know") =
historiae effectus (the power of tale telling)	*certos ... rerum ... effectus* ("real *essence* of things") *sepulto mendacis Greciae fabuloso commento* ("once the fanciful invention of deceitful Greece has been buried into silence") *quid misticum* ("what mystic things")	*scire quod nescias* ("to know that you do not know")

Based on the synthesis of his prologue, it is clear that the author's idea of true knowledge consists fundamentally of being aware of the vast ocean of "unknowing," ignorance and silence, concealed under the apparent knowledge provided by words. Fulgentius, obsessive collector of lexical rarities and sophisticate rhetorical structures, may therefore be credited in his own right as the most verbose prophet of silence of the ancient world.

Interestingly enough, Augustine's semiotic, epistemological, and even mystical concerns seem to share a great deal of Fulgentius's distrust of human language as a valid means to convey reality.[48] Words, Augustine states, can speak only about themselves and are therefore unable to produce any real knowledge of the outer world: *uerbis igitur nisi uerba non discimus, immo sonitum strepitumque uerborum* ("Through words we do not learn [anything] but words, or I should rather say the sound and noise of words").[49] That is why even "those who speak the most are ultimately mute" (AVG. *conf.* 1.4.4: *loquaces muti sunt*).[50] Words function as mere "pointers" to the inner silence

---

48. Cf. the conclusion of Mastrangelo's contribution to this volume, where he discusses the different ways in which Prudentius and Boethius dealt with the gap between words and things, so vividly experienced in Late Antiquity. On Augustine's attitude towards literature (particularly poetry), see Clark in this volume.

49. AVG. *mag.* 11.36 (my translation). On the "negative" epistemology underlying Augustine's semiotics, see Cary 2008: 87–120.

50. This is my translation.

in which the wordless teacher reveals the hidden nature of things.⁵¹ As Mayer (1969: 241) puts it:

> So widersprüchlich das klingt, die Zeichen haben keine semantische Funktion. [...] Worin bestehet die *utilitas uerborum (signorum)*? Die Antwort Augustins—sie ist im ganzen Dialog [*De magistro*] verstreut—lautet: Im *admonere*. Die *signa* sind Warner und Mahner; ihre gnoselogische Funktion bestehet in der *commemoratio sensibilis* des *homo interior*.

The ultimate reality, unutterable by definition, is always concealed beyond language and conceptual knowledge, in the non-discursive and timeless realm of eternal silence⁵² (Avg. *conf.* 9.10.25):

> *Si cui sileat tumultus carnis, sileant phantasiae terrae et aquarum et aeris, sileant et poli, et ipsa sibi anima sileat et transeat se non se cogitando, sileant somnia et imaginariae reuelationes, omnis lingua et omne signum, et quidquid transeundo fit si cui sileat omnino (quoniam si quis audiat, dicunt haec omnia: "non ipsa nos fecimus, sed fecit nos qui manet in aeternum"), his dictis si iam taceant, quoniam erexerunt aurem in eum qui fecit ea, et loquatur ipse solus non per ea sed per se ipsum, ut audiamus uerbum eius, non per linguam carnis neque per uocem angeli nec per sonitum nubis nec per aenigma similitudinis, sed ipsum quem in his amamus, ipsum sine his audiamus, ... si continuetur hoc et subtrahantur aliae uisiones longe imparis generis et haec una rapiat et absorbeat et recondat in interiora gaudia spectatorem suum, ut talis sit sempiterna uita quale fuit hoc momentum intellegentiae cui suspirauimus, nonne hoc est: "intra in gaudium Domini tui"?*

> If to any man the tumult of the flesh were silenced—silenced the phantasies of earth, waters, and air—silenced, too, the poles; yea, the very soul be silenced to herself, and go beyond herself by not thinking of herself—silenced fancies and imaginary revelations, every tongue, and every sign, and whatsoever exists by passing away, since, if any could hearken, all

---

51. Avg. *mag.* 11.38: "Regarding each of the things we understand, however, we don't consult a speaker who makes sounds outside us (*non loquentem, qui personat foris*), but the Truth that presides within over the mind itself (*intus ipsi menti praesidentem ... ueritatem*), though perhaps words prompt us to consult Him (*uerbis fortasse ut consulamus admoniti*). What is more, He Who is consulted, He Who is said to dwell in the inner man, does teach: Christ—that is, the unchangeable power and everlasting wisdom of God, which every rational soul does consult, but is disclosed to anyone, to the extent that he can apprehend it, according to his good or evil will." See also Avg. *mag.* 14.46: *Ego uero didici admonitione uerborum tuorum nihil aliud uerbis quam admoneri hominem, ut discat*; "I have learned from the prompting of your words that words do nothing but prompt man to learn." Translations of *De magistro* are taken from King 1995.

52. Cf. Mastrangelo in this volume on Boethius's distinction between God's "mode of cognition" (synchronic and eternal) and that of humans (diachronic and time-bounded).

these say, "We created not ourselves, but were created by Him who abideth for ever." If, having uttered this, they now should be silenced, having only quickened our ears to Him who created them, and He alone speak not by them, but by Himself, that we may hear His word, not by fleshly tongue, nor angelic voice, nor sound of thunder, nor the obscurity of a similitude, but might hear Him—Him whom in these we love—without these. [...] If this could be sustained, and other visions of a far different kind be withdrawn, and this one ravish and absorb and envelop its beholder amid these inward joys, so that his life might be eternally like that one moment of knowledge which we now sighed after, were not this "Enter thou into the joy of Thy Lord"?[53]

This seems to be the ultimate epistemological horizon of Late Antiquity as a genuine age of silence. Only when words are paradoxically employed to reveal their own futility (as Sidonius, Fulgentius, Augustine, and many other late antique authors did), can we begin to embrace the abyss of unknowing and silence underlying them, thus gaining access to the unutterable realm of true knowledge. After all, "what can be properly *said* about God?" asked Augustine (*serm.* 341.7.9). "On the contrary, those who transcend words [...] will find a silence to be praised with the ineffable voice of their hearts."[54]

9.4. Ausonius and Rutilius Namatianus on the Death of Names

Rutilius Namatianus, the renowned early fifth-century Gallo-Roman poet, felt trapped in a blurring world. In the extant 712 lines of verse of his mutilated *De reditu suo*,[55] a single idea prevails: everything around him is a monochromatic blur (Rvt. Nam. 1.432: *concolor umbra* "matched in colour, the mass of shadow"), an indiscernible mist that obscures perception and makes knowledge

---

53. The translation is taken from Schaff, Pilkington, and Cunningham 1886: 137–8. On the mystical dimension of this passage, see Kenney 2005: 73–86 (esp. 83–6).

54. *Quid ergo de deo digne dicitur? ... Qui autem et ista transcenderit ... inueniet silentium ineffabili cordis uoce laudandum*. The translation is mine.

55. The poem describes a sea journey made by its author in 417 AD. For more on the arguments for this dating, see Cameron 1967. As for its genre, it could be ultimately considered a *nóstos*, a kind of late antique *Odyssey* with undertones of sadness, defeat, and disenchantment. Thus, its hero, Rutilius Namatianus himself, is forced to return to his native Gaul after Alaric's sack of Rome, in order to help his countrymen to reconstruct their cities, also devastated by barbarian invaders. Nevertheless, it is difficult to assign the poem to a specific genre, since it shows a vast variety of heterogeneous formal and thematic features. For a qualified approach to this difficult question, see Brocca 2003. When quoting the poem, I shall make use of Castorina's reliable edition (1967) and Duff's translation (1934: 753–829), also taking into consideration Wolff 2007.

impossible. Unlike Fulgentius and the new apophatic theologians, he is quite sceptical regarding the possibility of grasping anything, of accessing an underlying reality beyond words and concepts. In Namatianus's world, nothing can be clearly recognized (1.409: *agnosci nequeunt* "cannot be recognized"). His eyes are exhausted (1.434: *defessis oculis*) from trying to discern shapes in the confusing dimness and turmoil that dominated the entire empire after Alaric's still fresh sacking of Rome.[56] Namatianus constantly doubts the accuracy of his senses: he does not know whether he is really seeing Rome on the horizon or if it is just his nostalgic desires playfully deceiving his "impaired eyes" (1.190: *uisu deficiente*): . . . *duces oculi grata regione fruuntur / dum se, quod cupiunt, cernere posse putant* ("and look where the guiding eyes feast on that dear scene, fancying they can see what they desire to see").[57] Even his ears are both sceptical and surprised (1.201: *attonitae . . . aures* "spellbound ears") when they perceive the distant hurly-burly of the city with its crowded theatres and circuses—are those sounds real or is it just a fiction created by his love for Rome?: *pulsato notae redduntur ab aethere uoces, / uel quia peruerniunt, uel quia fingit amor* ("familiar shouts are sent back by the echoing air, whether it is that they really reach us or that affection fancies so").[58] All in all, senses should never be trusted. Nothing is certain: not even what you are seeing with your own eyes. Therefore, *De reditu suo* should be ultimately regarded as a poem about blindness.

In view of Namatianus's obsession with the limits of human knowledge/perception, it is not unreasonable to assume that the problem of naming must have also come to the foreground of his poetical reflection. Apparently this was the case: if, according to Georgia Nugent (1990:36), "statistically, *nomen* appears far more frequently in Ausonius's works than any other noun and almost twice as often as the next most commonly used noun," it should be noted that, according my own count, the same lexical law is also valid for Namatianus's extant work. Sure enough, *nomen* clearly appears to be Namatianus's favourite word, having fourteen occurrences, followed by the author's second biggest concern: *Roma* (mentioned eleven times throughout the poem).[59] Both words seem to be deeply interrelated in Namatianus's personal imagery: Rome is desperately considered to be the last chance of signification, the old centre of a collapsed system capable of putting together "words and things" under the illusion of

---

56. As is well known, Alaric's sacking of Rome occurred on August 24, 410.
57. RVT. NAM. 1.191–2.
58. RVT. NAM. 1.203–4.
59. *Nomen* appears in RVT. NAM. 1.70; 169; 226; 231; 249; 309; 310; 419; 453; 476; 569; 574; and 2.10; 64. As for *Roma*, it appears in RVT. NAM. 1.3; 48; 116; 167; 200; 298; 416; 467; 550; and 2.40; 49.

coherence.⁶⁰ Because Rome, the principle that used to guarantee the ideal link between words and their referents, is irremissibly fading away into a blur, as Umberto Eco would gladly say quoting a medieval poem, only "the bare names" remain (*nomina nuda tenemus*):⁶¹ it is merely words speaking of other words that we can handle.

Namatianus clearly questions the fundamental link between "les mots et les choses,"⁶² or the very idea of representation, in passages like this: *Nominibus certos credam decurrere mores? / Moribus an potius nomina certa dari?* ("Am I to believe that definite characters descend from names or rather that definite names are given to characters?").⁶³ He does not offer any solution to this essential question; once again the surrounding mist prevents him from getting any answers or cognitive illumination. The origin of this passage should be found in an intertextual recall of Ausonius, whose concern about language and representation has opened the door to a major topic of late antique aesthetics: *utrumne mores hoc tui / nomen dedere, an nomen hoc / secuta morum regula?* ("Was it thy conduct earned thee this name, or to this name hath thy rule of conduct conformed?").⁶⁴ Curiously enough, the starting point of both reflections is not a noun but a name (Lepidus for Namatianus, Probus for Ausonius) according to a type of onomastic play that is quite characteristic of late antique literature and thought.⁶⁵

Moreover, the primacy of the incorporeal, ephemeral, empty words over the supposedly solid monuments of the past is lavishly defended in Namatianus's verses.⁶⁶ But he goes even further in his reflection: not even the names are destined to endure, even they—and the poetry created from them—shall die with the

---

60. On the centripetal (Rome-centred) and centrifugal movements coexisting in *De reditu*, see Formisano's contribution to this volume.

61. BERNARDVS CLVNIACENSIS, *De contemptu mundi* 1.952. This poem closes Eco's world-famous novel *The Name of the Rose*.

62. I have borrowed the expression from Michel Foucault's influential 1966 essay, to which this chapter is greatly indebted.

63. RVT. NAM. 1.309–10.

64. AVSON. *ep.* 9b.44–6 [Green]. The translation is taken from Evelyn White's bilingual edition 1921: 37.

65. Cf., e.g., in Sidonius's poems *carm.* 7.26–7: *ibique / glaucus, Glauce, uenis*; ibid. 32–3: *Phoebus ephebus, / Pan pauidus*; *carm.* 9.5 [AD FELICEM]: *Felix nomine, mente, honore, forma*; *carm.* 13.25–7: *Hoc te Sidonius tuus precatur: / sic te Sidonio recocta fuco / multos purpura uestiat per annos*; *carm.* 16.127–8 [AD FAVSTVM EPISCOPVM]: *quidquid agis, quocumque locus es, semper mihi Faustus, / semper Honoratus, semper quoque Maximus esto*, etc.

66. Namatianus seems to be highly persuaded by the paradox that only the ephemeral, incorporeal and contingent has a chance of lasting over time—it is only the incorporeal words and not the material monuments that can remain. The image of Alaric's devastating entry into Rome, which seriously threatened the official *aeternitas* of the city, was indelibly etched in his memory and underlies the entire work: *non indignemur mortalia corpara solui: / cernimus exemplis oppida posse mori*, "let us not chafe that

passing of time: *aeuo deposuit nomen Agylla uetus* ("the ancient Agylla has lost its name through time");⁶⁷ *multa licet priscum nomen deleuerit aetas* ("although long years have blotted out the earliest name").⁶⁸ The origin of this type of reflection, clearly refuting Horace's famous celebration of the eternity of poetry over the material world,⁶⁹ is of course to be found in Ausonius—and not precisely in his *Moselle* (which should itself be considered one of the finest exponents of the "poetics of silence," as I have recently suggested elsewhere)⁷⁰ but in some other "minor" pieces like his eloquent and highly metalinguistic *epigr.* 37 (Green). This short piece aims to describe a marble epitaph with an almost unreadable inscription, a starting point for further considerations on time and human language:

> *Lucius una quidem, geminis sed dissita punctis*
>   *littera; praenomen sic nota sola facit.*
> *Post M incisum est. Puto sic, non tota uidetur;*
>   *dissiluit saxi fragmine laesus apex.*
> *Nec quisquam, Marius seu Marcius anne Metellus*
>   *hic iaceat, certis nouerit indiciis.*
> *Truncatis conuulsa iacent elementa figuris,*
>   *<u>omnia confusis interiere notis.</u>*
> *Miremur periisse homines? monumenta fatiscunt,*
>   *<u>mors etiam saxis nominibusque uenit.</u>*

human frames dissolve: from precedents we discern that towns can die" (Rvt. Nam. 1.413–14). Having seen the most impressive and solid monuments in Rome—and consequently, the social values attached to them—fall and vanish within a few hours made him doubt the possibility of the material reality around him (409–12) surviving this "voracious time" (l. 410: *tempus edax*). Therefore, the reborn eternal Rome continuously invoked in his poem is clearly characterized not as a material entity but as an abstract and intangible one. For Namatianus, Rome seems to be primarily a way of thinking, a political and cultural institution, an ordering and guiding principle, a set of inherited values that he longs to perpetuate in the future, as it is already impossible to safeguard the materiality of a city that is no longer recognizable: *agnosci nequeunt aeui monumenta prioris*, "the memorials of an earlier age cannot be recognized" (Rvt. Nam. 1.409). This idea is perfectly put into words in a seventeenth-century sonnet by the Spanish poet Francisco de Quevedo, whose last lines read as follows: "¡Oh, Roma!, en tu grandeza, en tu hermosura, / huyó lo que era firme, y solamente / lo fugitivo permanece y dura."

67. Rvt. Nam. 1.226.
68. Rvt. Nam. 1.231.
69. Hor. carm. 3.30.1–2: *Exegi monumentum aere perennius / regalique situ pyramidum altius*. In Kaimowitz's translation (2008: 142): "I have achieved a monument more permanent than bronze and higher than the royal pyramids."
70. See Hernández Lobato 2016b. This paper reinterprets Ausonius's *Mosella* as a "complex and many-layered depiction of a sui generis epiphanic experience, ultimately triggered by an unmediated encounter with nature. This sudden 'revelation,' be it real or merely an artful literary device, did not only provide Ausonius with a deeper insight into the world around him, but also raised many epistemological issues on the limits of human knowledge and the (in)ability of language to convey reality."

"Lucius" is one letter, but it is separated by twin points: in this way a single sign indicates the <entire> praenomen. After an "M" is inscribed, at least I think so—it is not all visible. The top has been damaged by the stone breaking and has fallen off, nor could anyone know through certain clues whether a Marius, a Marcius, or a Metellus lies here. The letters lie disturbed with their shapes truncated, all have perished in a confusion of signs. Are we surprised that men die? Monuments gape apart, death comes even to stones and names.[71]

The presence of this brief piece in Namatianus's poetical imagery is not restricted to the level of content: there is also a probable intertextual recall of its final verses in Namatianus's categorical *sententia: non indignemur mortalia corpora solui: / cernimus exemplis oppida posse mori* ("Let us not chafe that human frames dissolve: from precedents we discern that towns can die").[72] Regardless, the tragic but dispassionate verification of the perishable character of words and objects pervades all the late antique literature and culture and could perhaps explain many of its extant features. Namatianus, by picking up and increasing all of these lucid reflections of Ausonius, makes it a central concern of his poetical and, at the same time, political activity. The true name of things (*Optarem uerum complecti carmine nomen*, "I'd fain include your true name in my poem")[73]—just like Rufius's name in this passage from Namatianus—no longer fits in a poet's verse.

9.5. In Search of Spring: The Bitter Loquacity of a Silent Poet

It is perhaps in a text such as the enigmatic *Peruigilium Veneris*, a perfect expression of the late antique aesthetics,[74] where we find a formulation of the poetics of silence closer to that of Sidonius or Fulgentius, uttered poetically in all its radicalism and forcefulness.[75] The poet, after singing of the resurgence of springtime and love over nearly one hundred lines of verse, concludes with an unexpected twist in which he paradoxically affirms that he has been silent all along. Despite desiring a spring resurrection of language and poetry with all his heart, he is

---

71. This translation is taken from Fowler 2000b: 193. For some brief reflections on this poem and on the topic of the ruin of time in Latin literature, see Fowler 2000b: 193–217.

72. Rvt. Nam. 1.413–14.

73. Rvt. Nam. 1.419.

74. Today, most scholars look to the fourth century as the most likely date of composition of the work, whose late antique sensibility seems unquestionable. For a synthesis of the different hypotheses and possibilities, see Cucchiarelli's introduction (2003: 19–27).

75. Despite sharing this trait (so rarely taken into account), the frustrated attempt by Raquettius 1905 to attribute *Peruigilium Veneris* to Sidonius Apollinaris has no basis.

aware that his Muse has gone mute after years of silence and that speaking, in that context, is an impossible enterprise:

> *et canoras non tacere diua iussit alites.*
> 85 *Iam loquaces ore rauco stagna cygni perstrepunt,*
> *adsonat Terei puella subter umbram populi,*
> *ut putes motus amoris ore dici musico*
> *et neges queri sororem de marito barbaro.*
> *Illa [sc. Terei puella] cantat, nos tacemus. Quando uer uenit meum?*
> 90 *Quando faciam uti chelidon, ut tacere desinam?*
> *Perdidi Musam tacendo nec me Phoebus respicit.*
> *Sic Amyclas, cum tacerent, perdidit silentium.*

and tuneful birds that the Goddess has bidden not to be mute. Now hoarse-mouthed swans crash trumpeting over the pools; the maid of Tereus makes descant under the poplar shade, that you would think tunes of love issued trilling from her mouth and not a sister's complaint of a barbarous lord. She sings, we are mute: when is my spring coming? when shall I be as the swallow, that I may cease to be voiceless? I have lost the Muse in silence, nor does Apollo regard me: so Amyclae, being mute, perished by silence.[76]

Some sixteen hundred years later, one of these lines would come to form part of the colophon of one of the most influential poems of the twentieth century: *The Waste Land* by T. S. Eliot, first published in 1922. The modernist poet, cultivator of a poetics of the fragment which is not very distant from that of Late Antiquity,[77] identifies with the lyric subject of the *Peruigilium Veneris* in his anxious desire to find a renaissance of language and poetry amidst a context of silence and ruin (ll. 429–34):

> *Quando fiam uti chelidon*—O swallow swallow
> *Le Prince d'Aquitaine à la tour abolie*
> These fragments I have shored against my ruins
> Why then Ile fit you. Hieronymo's mad againe.
> Datta. Dayadhvam. Damyata.
> Shantih shantih shantih.

---

76. This translation is by Mackail 1921: 361–2.
77. The late antique aesthetic trend that I propose calling "poetics of fragment" is explained in detail with abundant examples in Hernández Lobato 2012: 257–317.

9.6. The Rest Is Silence (Final Remark)

Throughout these pages we have witnessed a curious parade of late antique texts dealing in one way or another with the topics of the (im)possibility of speaking and the (in)ability of human language to convey reality. Some of them were funny satires of the precariousness of a time which left no room for poetry; others were bitter political complaints; others were Sunday homilies; others were allegorical commentaries on pagan literature; others were self-deconstructive literary programmes; others were frivolous epigrams; others were highbrow philosophical treatises; others were spring-like love songs; others were autobiographical reflections with a mystical flavour; and others were nostalgic travel books. At times, silence was the long-awaited haven of tranquillity which enabled literary creation; at other times, it was a threat of dissolution hovering over the always fragile poets' work; most often, it was the deep ultimately unknowable reality beyond the annoying murmuring of words. Despite this disconcerting variety, there was something common to all of them: their problematizing approach to human language and their inner distrust of the classical idea of representation, teetering on the brink of collapse amidst the crisis of certainties that shook the very foundations of late antique society. This panoramic overview of such a varied range of texts, exponents of very different genres, tones, and intentions, may be sufficient to offer a taste of the overwhelming presence of this powerful "poetics of silence" at the very core of late antique culture, a promising and largely neglected research field still deserving further study.

PART IV

Literature and Power

10

The Poetics of Latin Prose Praise and the Fourth-Century Curve

ROGER REES

10.1. Introduction

Details of the surviving Latin prose panegyrics from the fourth century are set out below in Table 10.1.[1] The majority were anthologized, probably in that century's final decade, in the collection now known as the *XII Panegyrici Latini* (Pichon 1906: 285–91). Symmachus's three panegyrics, now all fragmentary, were published with the rest of his orations (Sogno 2006: 28–30); presumably, Ausonius's *Gratiarum actio* ("speech of thanksgiving for the consulship") was published with the rest of his oeuvre (Green 1991: xliii–xlvi). The *Panegyrici Latini* (*PanLat*) are here presented in their chronological sequence, although the manuscript sequence is indicated in the left-hand column.[2]

Table 10.1. Surviving Latin prose panegyric before 400[3]

	Date	Author/Emperor	Location
[*Panegyricus*	100	Pliny to Trajan	Rome]
PanLat X(2)	289	Anon. to Maximian	Trier
PanLat XI(3)	291	Anon. to Maximian	Trier
PanLat VIII(4)	297	Anon. to Constantius	Trier
PanLat IX(5)	298	Eumenius to Constantius	Autun (?) Lyons (?) Trier (?)
PanLat VII(6)	307	Anon. to Constantine + Maximian	Trier
PanLat VI(7)	310	Anon. to Constantine	Trier
PanLat V(8)	311	Anon. to Constantine	Trier
PanLat XII(9)	313	Anon. to Constantine	Trier

1. As the earliest surviving example of Imperial Latin prose panegyric and the head of the *Panegyrici Latini* in manuscript and chronological sequence, Pliny's *Panegyricus* features here, but its aesthetics are not addressed below. See Gamberini 1984 and various discussions in Roche 2011. All the other speeches, including Ausonius's and Symmachus's, were delivered in Gaul or by a Gallic orator.

2. Conventional Anglophone scholarship cites a speech in the *PanLat* collection by its position in manuscript sequence in Roman numerals and, in parentheses, by its position in chronological sequence in Arabic numerals; for example, the speech of 289 is cited X(2). On the manuscript sequence of the collection, see Barnes 2011, Rees 2012; for the dates, see Nixon and Saylor Rodgers 1994 ad loc., with Barnes 1996.

3. For details of the date, location, and political context for the speeches, see Nixon and Saylor Rodgers 1994, Pabst 1989, Callu 2009, and Green 1991.

313

Table 10.1. Continued

	Date	Author/Emperor	Location
PanLat IV(10)	321	Nazarius to Constantine	Rome (?)
PanLat III(11)	362	Claudius Mamertinus to Julian	Constantinople
orat I	368	Symmachus to Valentinian I	Trier
orat III	369/70	Symmachus to Gratian	Trier
orat II	370	Symmachus to Valentinian I	Trier
gratiarum actio	379	Ausonius to Gratian	Trier
PanLat II(12)	389	Pacatus Drepanius to Theodosius	Rome

Broadly understood, the late antique treatise by Menander Rhetor, *Basilikos Logos*, provides a template for what to say in a speech to the emperor and in what order to say it (home country, birth, education, war and peacetime achievements, virtues, etc.; Russell and Wilson 1981). Accordingly, the "fit" between what Menander suggests and what surviving speeches actually do, is an interesting topic for study (Kehding 1899: 4–16; Del Chicca 1985; Nixon and Saylor Rodgers 1994: 10–14; Russell 1998; de Trizio 2009: 25–7).[4] But Menander offers only rare and oblique glimpses of *how* to say it; for example, when recommending inclusion of the figure of prosopopoeia, he suggests that an orator say, "If the Ister had been poetical like the poetical Scamander, I think it might have said as follows . . ." (374).[5] Earlier Latin treatises are more forthcoming on the appropriate style of such oratory: Cicero wrote of the "middle style" of his *Pro lege Manilia*, with *suauitas* ("pleasantness") as its goal (*orat.* 91, 102);[6] and Quintilian distinguished between appropriate styles of delivery for different types of epideictic speech, *igitur in laudationibus, nisi si funebres erunt, gratiarum actione, exhortatione, similibus laeta et magnifica et sublimis est actio* ("Therefore, in speeches of praise, unless they are for funerals, the delivery for a speech of thanksgiving, encouragement and the like, is upbeat, magnificent and sublime," *inst.* 11, 3, 153). This enquiry into panegyrical poetics cannot unveil something to be conveniently mapped against contemporary or historic instruction but it might instead reveal some other literary qualities or tendencies which were considered suitable in late antique Gaul to grace prose works of political ambition.

---

4. That is not to suggest, however, that the *Basilikos Logos*, a Greek text, was circulating among Latin orators in fourth-century Gaul; rather, that text is indicative of the general practice of instruction in oratorical composition in Late Antiquity, which, we might extrapolate, flourished in Greek in the East and in Latin in the West.

5. "very much a poetical device"; Russell 1998: 31.

6. See also *part.* 72–3; FRONTO 3.17.2.

In an essentially synchronic study of the aesthetics of Greek and Latin panegyric of Late Antiquity, Donald Russell observed that "Neither of the other two main branches of rhetoric [forensic and deliberative] was in any way a substitute for poetry, but epideictic was" (1998: 23); concerning panegyric in particular, Russell went on: "it was ... in direct competition with poetry; accordingly, it used poetical vocabulary and ornament freely" (1998: 39). Accepting Russell's characterization, this analysis insists on the chronological sequence of the speeches, as I seek to trace development in literary aesthetics in Latin prose panegyric in the century from 289 to 389. In particular, I identify and evaluate examples of poetic colour in those fifteen speeches. "Poetic colour" is a slippery concept, but for the purposes of this chapter I understand it to include citation or quotation of poets, other intertextual engagement with poetry, lexis which in Late Antiquity may still have retained associations with its origins in poetry, and lexical adventure in the form of neologism; in certain cases, I consider too passages of sustained poetic character, such as natural simile, ekphrasis, prosopopoeia, and apostrophe.[7] What the study has the potential to illuminate is both the aesthetic range of a genre across a century and, in the case of the *PanLat* in particular, the dynamics of that range within a literary collection.[8] That the issue of the suitability of association with poetry generally in panegyric was of keen interest to the orators themselves is suggested by an opening remark in the earliest speech. In the first paragraph of the speech of 289, the orator says: *neque enim fabula est de licentia poetarum nec opinio de fama ueterum saeculorum, sed manifesta res et probata* ... ("For this is not a story taken from the licence of poets or opinion from the reputation of past centuries, but a manifest and proven matter," X(2), 1, 3).[9] That is, as an index of his own credibility, the earliest orator emphasizes the gap between his own epideictic prose and poetry.[10] This opening protestation invites consideration of the extent and function of poetic discourse in panegyric from the late third to the late fourth century.

---

7. Rees 2013a: 244 with some bibliography on the problems of definition. Analysis of other aspects of stylistic character is not undertaken here, such as grammatical and syntactical variation, text as "live" transcript, intertextual engagement with earlier oratory (for Cicero, see Klotz 1911 or intratextual dynamics within the *PanLat* collection; for Pliny's *Panegyricus*, see Gibson and Rees 2013).

8. Scholarship to date has not considered poetics as a component of the critical trajectory of the *PanLat*: but relevant studies have addressed questions of authorship (Seeck 1888; Gotze 1892; Pichon 1906; Rees 2002: 193–204), sequencing within the collection (Barnes 2011; Rees 2012), and intertextual engagement with Pliny's *Panegyricus* (Garcia Ruiz 2013)

9. On the *fabula poetarum* trope in panegyric, see Ware in this volume.

10. See below for the scholarly orthodoxy that Pacatus Drepanius was the editor of the *PanLat*, a hypothesis which clearly has implications for appreciation of the anthology's collective dynamics.

But particularities can always defy or deny general conclusions: having said his material was not drawn from fabulous poetry but "manifest and proven by the Pinaria family, guardians of the cult of Hercules," the orator immediately uses language which recalls Vergil's *Aeneid* (de Trizio 2009: 28, 58–9), rendering interpretation difficult. And the same example also demonstrates how intertextual practice can wrong-foot chronological reading, as it collapses the time difference between the hypotext and hypertext: *licentia poetarum* ("licence of poets") in 289 echoes in Symmachus's first panegyric to Valentinian in 368 (*aut licentia poetarum dearum aliquam dixerim destrictos a uitalibus tuis detorsisse mucrones*, "nor would I say with poetic licence that some goddess had turned drawn swords away from your vital organs," *or.* 1,4) and Ausonius's speech to Gratian in 379 (*nec iam miramur licentiam poetarum qui omnia deo plena dixerunt*, "Now we do not wonder at the licence of poets who have said that everything is full of god," *Grat. act.* 1, 5). Ausonius's direct allusion is to Vergil, *ecl.* 3, 60, *omnia Iouis plena* ("everything is full of Jupiter," also at *PanLat* XI(3), 14, 2; see below). Poetic accounts are either to be not believed, unlike the addressee emperor's achievements, or to be believed because of the addressee emperor's achievements—"licence of poetry" seems to have been a topos to be manipulated for advantage, and poetic discourse is presented as a foil to better demonstrate the credibility of the current discourse. However disingenuously, here we have prose texts involved in a process of self-definition by evocation of poetic commonplaces, but the fact that the phrase *licentia poetarum* occurs in three texts in similar circumstances across ninety years complicates its classification on a linear trajectory. Such backward arcs of intertextuality (or in the case of the *PanLat*, intratextuality) are very common in panegyrical prose and defy chronological plotting; at the outset, therefore, it is important to bear in mind that "poetic colour" is only a single component in the full panoply of literary effect.

I use Mynors's *PanLat* OCT (i.e., Oxford Classical Text series; reprinted in Nixon and Saylor Rodgers (1994)),[11] Callu's Budé for Symmachus, and Green's *Ausonius* OCT. I have gleaned philological data from many sources but must acknowledge particular debt to Schenkl (1881), Gotze (1892), Chruzander (1897), Klotz (1911), and the commentaries of Galletier (1949–55), Gutzwiller (1942), Nixon and Saylor Rodgers (1994), De Trizio (2009) and Laudani (2014).[12]

---

11. Note that late nineteenth-century scholars generally refer to the text by page and line number of the 1874 (Teubner) edition of A. Baehrens, whose ignorance of clausulae and MS Harleianus 2480 and propensity to emendation led to its rapid replacement by the edition of his son William in 1911 (also Teubner).

12. Additional material has come from the ongoing collaborative *Panegyrici Latini* project, http://www.st-andrews.ac.uk/classics/panegyric/.

Poetics of Latin Prose Praise 317

The parallels cited for poetic origins are representative rather than exhaustive. The assemblages, therefore, combine quantitative and qualitative data, and the methodological pitfalls must immediately be acknowledged: for example, lexical analysis must needs be limited to the literature we have (and so, for example, there may be more Ennius lurking in the speeches than we can know about); what are hapax legomena to moderns might not have been in their original context; and although some intertexts are more recognizable than others, fine calibration will be a matter of controversy. But despite these considerable limitations, I hope the data prove interesting in themselves and sufficiently rich to allow conclusions about generic evolution.

10.2. *PanLat* X(2), 289 CE, Anon to Maximian, Trier

Despite what is said about the "licence of poets" in its opening chapter, Greek poetic discourse is later invoked in cautious validation: *si non frustra Graeci poetae hominibus iustitiam colentibus repromittunt binos gregum fetus et duplices arborum fructus, nunc* ...("if it's not in vain that Greek poets promise for men who cultivate justice, double the offspring for flocks and a double harvest of fruit, now," 11, 3). Although no further detail is attested, the orator is probably alluding to Homer *Od.* 19,107–114 and Hesiod *op.* 232–5.[13]

The examples of poetic colour tend to be restricted to a single word or short phrase:

1, 3 *Herculei sacri custos familia Pinaria* ("Pinaria family, guardians of the cult of Hercules"): Verg. *Aen.* 8.270–1.
2, 1 *occidui* ("setting"; see also Symm. *or.* 1.5.3.11): Ov. *fast.* 4.832, 5.558; *met.*1, 63, 14, 416; Sen. *Thy.* 822; Manil. 3.367; Sil. 1.145 (*TLL* IX.2.353.27).
2, 1 *trino* ("triple"): Sen. *Thy.* 676; Stat. *Silv.* 4.9.15.
2, 4 *armorum sonitus* ("sounds of weapons"): Lvcr. 2.49; Verg. *Aen.* 2.301; Sil. 5.433.
3, 1 *faciam ... compendio orationis ...* ("with an abbreviation of my speech, I will make"): Plavt. *Most.* 60 (see also VI(7), 1, 4; de Trizio 2009: 70, Müller-Rettig 1990: 45).
3, 3 *terras omnes et maria despicias* ("you gaze down on all lands and seas"): Verg. *Aen.* 1.224.
3, 4 *perpeti* ("everlasting"; see also XI(3), 3, 4): Pacvv. *Trag.* 188, 208; Plavt. *Amph.* 280, 732 (*TLL* X.1.1624.59–60).

---

13. On the identity (name) of the author (and for XI(3)), see Rees 2002: 193–204 and de Trizio 2009.

4, 2 *Terrigenarum* ("earth-born"; see also SYMM. *Or.* 2, 21): LVCR. 5.1411, 1427; OV. *met.* 5.325, 7.36, 7.141; LVCAN 3.316, 4.553; VAL. FL. 7.505, 629, 8.107; SIL. 6.254.

4, 3 *cultorum* ("cultivated land"): LVCR. 1.164; VERG. *Aen.* 8.63, 10.141, *georg.* 2.196, 4.126, 4.372 [LIV. 5.5.2, 38.49.7] (*TLL* III.1692.78).

4, 3 *uastator* ("devastator"): VERG. *Aen.* 9.772; OV. *met.* 9.192, 11.395; STAT. *Ach.* 2.32, *Silv.* 2.5.1, *Theb.* 7.565.

5, 2 *astu* ("cunning"): PACVV. *Trag.* 186, 377, 378; ACC. *Trag.* 414, 475; PLAVT. *Capt.* 222, *Poen.* 111.1223; TER. *Eun.* 924, 987; VERG. *Aen.* 10.522, 11.704; OV. *met.* 4.776, 13.193 [PLIN. *Paneg.* 81.2].

7, 4 *serena tempestas* ("calm weather"; see also 3,3): ENN. *Ann.* 446, 541 (Skutsch), VERG. *Aen.* 1.255.

7, 5 *nutu illo patrio, quo omnia contremescunt* ("at that paternal nod, at which everything trembles"): VERG. *Aen.* 10.115.

10, 1 *imperium non terrae sed caeli regionibus terminatis* ("you limit your empire not by the regions of the earth but of the sky"): VERG. *Aen.* 1.287.

11, 7 *sorbuerunt* ("have swallowed"): PLAVT. *Mil.* 818–20, *Most.* 791; LVCR. 6.1130; VERG. *Aen.* 3.422.

12, 1 *refugum* ("receding"): LVCAN 8.526, 10.132; STAT. *Theb.* 12.634 [PLIN. *Paneg.* 30.4].

12, 4 *naualia texerentur* ("ships be built"): VERG. *Aen.* 11.326.

12, 5 *temperiem* ("mildness"): OV. *met.* 1.51, 430, 4.344; LVCAN 1.647, 9.435, 10.231; STAT. *Theb.* 6.324 [PLIN. *Paneg.* 5.8, 15.3].

12, 6 *largos imbres* ("heavy rainfalls"): LVCR. 1.282; VERG. *georg.* 1.23; OV. *met.* 4.282, 11.516; HOR. *ep.* 16.53–4; LVCAN 4.76; STAT. *Theb.* 4.91.

Galletier (1949: 17–20) commends the author's powers of description. One bright example of poetic flourish by topos, lexis, and intertext stands out: *toto quippe proelio ferebare, non aliter quam magnus amnis solet hibernis imbribus auctus et niuibus passim fluere qua campus est* ("Indeed, in the whole battle, you were borne like a great river, swollen by the winter rains and snows, tends to flow everywhere the plain reaches," 5.3). Natural similes generally have epic association, and likening warriors to rivers in particular is a hallmark of the hexameter *aristeia*: for example, HOM. *Il.* 5.85–8; VERG. *Aen.* 12.523–25, STAT. *Ach.* 2.143–5, *Theb.* 8.456–65 [AMM. 14.1.10] (Fenno 2005; Rees 2013b: 106–8). In this prose reprisal (one of only two in Latin panegyric), the simile incipit *non aliter quam* might also suggest its poetic origins (VERG. *Aen.* 4.669, *georg.* 1.201; OV. *met.* 3.373, 483, 4.122, 348, 6.516; VAL. FL. 5.407; SIL. 7.500; STAT. *Theb.* 1.421).[14]

---

14. The *incipit* also appears twice in Livy (6.41.6 and 24.16.10) and frequently in Seneca, e.g., *clem.* 1.5.1, 13.2, 21.4.

10.3. PanLat XI(3) 291 CE Anon to Maximian, Trier

This orator twice quotes famous Latin poetry. The first quotation comes from Vergil's *Eclogues*: *itaque illud quod de uestro cecinit poeta Romanus Ioue, Iouis omnia esse <plena>*, ... *id nunc ego de utroque uestrum audeo praedicare* ("and so, that which the Roman poet sang about your Jupiter—that "everything is full of Jupiter"— ... I myself now dare to proclaim about each of you," 14, 2).[15] Given Vergil's status, perhaps more surprising is the later quotation from Ennius: *etenim, quod ait ille Romani carminis primus auctor*: *a sole exoriente usque ad Maeotis paludes id nunc longius longiusque protendere licet* ("for that which the first founder of Roman poetry says— 'from the rising sun to Lake Maeotis'—can be extended further and further," 16.3). The quotations are introduced, given and elaborated in similar ways, to formulaic effect.[16] In the Ennian example in particular, the quotation hardly illuminates the orator's point—its inclusion might be thought contrived: it also seems quite likely that his source was not the poetry text directly but an intermediary, such as Cicero or a grammarian (Enn. *Frg. uar.* 21 [Vahlen]; Cic. *Tusc.* 5.49; Klotz 1911: 538–9);[17] but despite any such laboured pretentiousness, the quotations bring new colour to the genre.[18]

Elsewhere in the speech, poetic lexis is less conspicuous: Vergil dominates what colouring there is.

- 2, 3: *annis uoluentibus* ("the rolling years"; see also VIII(4), 3, 1): Verg. *Aen.* 1.234.
- 3, 4: *tantam molem* ("such a mass"; see also VIII(4), 6, 4, XII(9), 24, 2, IV(10), 18, 2, II(12), 3, 5): Verg. *Aen.* 1.33.
- 3, 6: *nemora pacauit* ("pacified the groves"): Verg. *Aen.* 6.803.
- 3, 6: *caelitum* ("of the gods"; see also Symm. *or.* 1, 13): Enn. *Trag.* 171, 270; Pacvv. *Trag.* 232; Acc. *Trag.* 298, 593 (Ribbeck); Plavt. *Rud.* 2; Cat. 61, 49; Ov. *met.* 5.322, 6.151; Sen. *Ag.* 21, 392, 520 (*TLL* III.67.20–21).
- 4, 2: *arces Monoeci* ("the summits of Monaco"): Verg. *Aen.* 6.830.
- 6, 6 *aequanimitate* ("equanimity"): Ter. *Ad.* 24, *Phorm.* 34 (*TLL* 1.1005.20).
- 8, 3 *ueliuola nauis* ("a ship flying with sails"): Enn. *Ann.* 380, *Trag.* 111 (Jocelyn); Lvcr. 5.1442; Verg. *Aen.* 1.224.
- 17, 1 *gens effrena* ("the unbridled tribe"): Verg. *georg.* 3.382.

---

15. For *plena*, see Mynors ad loc.; Rees 2004a: 38.
16. Cf. *quod* ... *cecinit poeta* ... *id nunc*; *quod ait* ... *auctor* ... *id nunc*; in neither case is the poet named.
17. The quotation's leverage is laboriously explained at 16, 4.
18. See also John Henderson's speculation (2013: 191–3) that Pindar's text might have underlain some of this speech's argument, although not in its style.

10.4. *PanLat* VIII(4) 297 CE Anon to Constantius, Trier

More than XI(3), this speech has a consistent texture, with the poetic colours assuredly integrated in its parole, as the Ennian intertext at 18,5 exemplifies—the same phrase as appears at XI(3), 16, 3, but here, without being headlined, it is less conspicuous (Klotz 1911: 548). A similar impression of stylistic poise can be seen in the celebration of the springtime origin of Tetrarchic government: *o felix beatumque uer nouo partu, iam non amoenitate florum nec uiriditate segetum nec gemmis uitium nec ipsis tantum fauoniis et luce reserata laetum atque uenerabile, quantum ortu Caesarum maximorum!* ("O Spring, happy and blessed with its new birth, now joyous and venerable not so much for the delightfulness of flowers, nor the verdure of crops, nor the buds of vines, nor the west winds themselves and the opening light as for the rise of the greatest Caesars!" 3, 1) Exclamatory syntax is common in panegyric (Rees 2010a: 115–18), but the carefully choreographed sentence resonates with but does not quote poetic celebrations of springtime, such as Lucretius (5,737–47), Horace (*carm.* 1.4, 3.7), and Vergil (*georg.* 2,319ff.) (Russell 1998: 45–6).

Elsewhere, the orator regularly deploys poetic lexis, usually with epic association:

- 2, 2 *originem mundi nascentis* ("the origin of the world at its birth"): VERG. *georg.* 2.336, *ecl.* 6.34.
- 2, 3 *rerum tenera primordia* ("tender beginnings of matter"): LVCR. 1.55.
- 3, 1 *annorum uoluentium* ("the rolling years"; see also XI(3), 2, 3): VERG. *Aen.* 1.234.
- 4, 3 *beatis* ("you bless"): PLAVT. *Amph.* 643, *Cap.* 137; HOR. *carm.* 4.8.29 (*TLL* II.1908.65).
- 5, 2 *intremuit* ("trembled"; cf. *PanLat* IV(10), 3, 5, 19, 2; AVSON. *Grat. act.* 3, 13): VERG. *Aen.* 3.581, 5.505; OV. *met.* 1.284, 2.180; VAL. FL. 2.519, 3.73; SIL. 3.437, 5.330, 11.518 ; STAT. *Theb.* 12.381 (*TLL* VII.248.25).
- 6, 4 *tanta mole* ("with such a great mass"; see also XI(3), 3, 4, XII(9), 24, 2, IV(10), 18, 2, II(12), 3, 5): VERG. *Aen.* 1.33.
- 8, 2 *pedum pulsu* ("the tread of feet"): ENN. *Ann.* 1.1; VERG. *Aen.* 7.722; HOR. *Carm.* 1.4.7.
- 9, 1 *adfari* ("to address"; see also V(8), 9, 1, 4): ACC. *Trag.* 538; VERG. *Aen.* 1.663, 2.700, 4.284, 12.138; OV. *met.* 1.350, 5.268, 9.696 ; VAL. FL. 1.299, 5.352; STAT. *Achill.* 1.251, 383.
- 9, 1 *attonita feritate* ("astonished wildness"): of inanimate subjects, VERG. *Aen.* 6.53; VAL. FL. 1.45; SIL. 4.7 [PLIN. *Paneg.* 38.3].

10, 4 *proculcata* ("trampled"): Lvcr. 5.1235; Verg. Aen. 12.534; Ov. met. 8.290, 12.374 (*TLL* X.2.1565.72).

11, 1 *frugum ubere* ("rich in crops"): Verg. Aen. 1.531.

16, 4 *puluere et cruore foedata* ("fouled with dust and blood"): Verg. Aen. 2.272–3.

18, 5 *usque ad Maeotias paludes* ("up to the Maeotic swamps"; see above on XI(3), 16, 3): Enn. *frg. uar.* 21.

10.5. *PanLat* IX(5) 298 CE, Eumenius's *Pro Instaurandis Scholis* (to Constantius) Trier? Autun? Lyon?

Ennius again features, although not by name but as the *summus poeta* ("highest poet," 7,3); he is not quoted. Eumenius occasionally ventures a simile or metaphor (Galletier 1949: 119), once, even twice, in one sentence: *neque aliter quam si equestri turmae uel cohorti praetoriae consulendum foret* ("just as if they had to give thought to an equestrian squadron or praetorian cohort") is quickly succeeded by *ueluti repentino nubilo in mediis adulescentiae fluctibus deprehensi* ("as if seized by a sudden cloud on the open waves of youth," 5, 4); if the simile *incipit* has poetic origins (see above, X(2), 5, 3), the subjects do not. In his other examples, Eumenius avoids extended similes.[19] In general, the speech lacks poetic colour.

2, 4 *puluere sordidus* ("dirty with dust"): Hor. *Carm.* 2.1.22.

10, 1 *praescius futurorum* ("prescient of the future"): Verg. Aen. 6.66.

17, 4 *eloquio* ("in eloquence"; see also Symm. *Or.* 2, 29): Verg. Aen. 11.383; Ov. *ars. p.* 1.462.

19, 2 *pari cura* ("with equal care"): Verg. Aen. 6.159.

21, 1 *cornua* ("horns," of river branches): Ov. met. 9.774; Val. Fl. 8.186; Sil. 3.405 (*TLL* IV.971.45).

10.6. *PanLat* VII(6) 307 CE Anon to Maximian and Constantine, Trier

This short speech, delivered on the occasion of Constantine's marriage to Maximian's daughter Fausta, is organized into two halves, addressed to Constantine and Maximian, respectively. The first is elevated by a formal

---

19. 2, 4, 4, 3, 9, 4, 15, 2, 18, 3.

ekphrasis of a fresco in Aquileia (6), the second by a scene of prosopopoeia in which Roma personified appeals to Maximian (11). Of course, both ekphrasis and prosopopoeia are epic topoi, although the style of neither passage in the speech is distinctively heightened by poetic lexis. Elsewhere, with one notable exception, examples of poetic diction are occasional and isolated.

- 2, 5 *germine* ("offshoot"; see also IV(10), 3, 4; Symm. *or*. 1, 3, 3, 6): Lvcr. 4.1083; Verg. *georg*. 2.76; Stat. *Theb*. 2.280 (*TLL* VI.1923.32).
- 4, 1 *maritalem* ("marital"): Ov. *ars p*. 2.258.
- 4, 1 *uxorius* ("devoted to his wife"): Verg. *Aen*. 4.266.
- 6, 2 *radiantem* ("gleaming"): Acc. *praetext*. 28, *frg. trag*. 588 (Ribbeck); Cat. 63.39; Lvcr. 4.213; Verg. *Aen*. 8.23, 616.
- 12, 8 *posuere uenti* ("the winds dropped"): Verg. *Aen*. 7.27, 10.103.
- 12, 8 *fugere nubes* ("the clouds fled"): Verg. *Aen*. 1.143.
- 12, 8 *immurmurat* ("murmurs"): Verg. *georg*. 4.261; Ov. *met*. 3.646, 6.558, 11.567; Val. Fl. 7.312; Sil. 5.332, 7.146 (*TLL* VII.1.509.21).
- 14, 1 *indefessum* ("tireless"; see also VI(7)18, 2): Verg. *Aen*. 11.651; Ov. *met*. 9.199; Sil. *Pun*. 13.127, 15.576 [Plin. *paneg*. 14.5] (*TLL* VII.1.1130.57).[20]

The exception is the cluster of epic intertexts at 12.8, where the context is the immediate aftermath of an interview between Maximian and Jupiter at a dramatic date of 306, in which the god instructed Maximian to take up the reins of imperial office (again). Here, unusually, the orator combines epic situation and intertext to generate elevating poetic colour (Rees 2004a: 38–9).

10.7. PanLat VI(7) 310 CE Anon to Constantine, Trier

The speech of 310 has proved a key text in analyses of Constantinian religion.[21] A central passage in this controversy has been 21.5: *uidisti teque in illius specie recognouisti cui totius mundi regna deberi uatum carmina diuina cecinerunt* ("you saw and recognized yourself in the appearance of him to whom the divine poems of bards have sung that commands over the whole world are owed"). Details of political and religious interpretations aside, it is notable that in this difficult subject, the orator invokes poetic discourse (*uatum carmina diuina*, "the divine poems of bards") as the key authority in determining the legitimacy

---

20. The images of weather and sea bring tidy conclusion to the metaphor of the "ship of state," which Maximian is variously said to have steadied, 9.3–4, 11.4, 12.7, recalling Hor. *carm*. 1.14 (Galletier 1942: 11; Nisbet and Hubbard 1970: 178–82).

21. Saylor Rodgers 1980 and Nixon and Saylor Rodgers 1994: 249–50, with bibliography.

Poetics of Latin Prose Praise   323

and nature of Constantine's government. This represents a significant distancing from the ideological position of the collection's opening paragraph (see above); it also chimes with its orator's general deployment of poetic lexis and intertext.

- 5, 2 *hostium classe feruentem* ... *oceanum* ("the seething ocean ... enemies' fleet"): VERG. Aen. 8.676.
- 7, 2 *Thylen ultimam* ("furthest Thule"): VERG. georg. 1.30.
- 8, 1 *Cydonumue tela* ("the weapons of Cydonia"): VERG. ecl. 10.59; HOR. carm. 4.9.17–18
- 9, 2 *lacte distenta* ("distended with milk"): VERG. ecl. 4.21, 7.3.
- 10, 4 *oderint hostes dum perhorrescant* ("let our enemies hate you, provided they are terrified of you"): ACC. 168 (Warmington) (CIC. Sest. 102), *oderint dum metuant*.
- 11, 4 *flumina ... potatis* ("live beside rivers"): SEN. Med. 373, Phaed. 57–8; SIL. 8.367, 13.676, 14.227 (TLL X.2.360.27–8).
- 11, 5 *bicorne* ("two-branched river"; see also SYMM. or. 2, 4): VERG. Aen. 8.727; Ov. met. 11.763 (TLL II.1971.81).
- 15, 4 *transcripsit* ("transfer," "yield"; L&S IIB2): VERG. Aen. 7.422; Ov. met. 7.173.
- 18, 2 *indefessis* ("tireless"; see also VII(6), 14, 1): VERG. Aen. 11.651; Ov. met. 9.199; SIL. Pun. 13.127, 15.576 [PLIN. paneg. 14.5] (TLL VII.1.1130.57).
- 18, 4 *incubuere remigiis* ("fell to their oars"): VERG. Aen. 5.15.
- 18, 6 *praeuertere* ("they outstripped"): CAT. 64.341; VERG. Aen. 7.807, 12.345; STAT. Ach. 2.111, Theb. 4.271, 5.691 (TLL X.2.1110.34).
- 18, 6 *flabra* ("gusts"): LVCR. 1.275, 5.217, 742, 6.428, 719, 730; VERG. georg. 2.293, 3.199; VAL. FL. 6.665 (TLL VI.832–33).
- 19, 1 *refluit* ("flows back"): VERG. Aen. 8.87, 240, 9.32; Ov. met. 7.267, 8.163; LVCAN 4.428; VAL. FL. 8.90; SIL. 2.307, 5.624, 7.417; STAT. Theb. 4.705, 7.333.
- 20, 2 *ueniam precarentur* ("they pray for pardon"): PACVV. Trag. 296; VERG. Aen. 3.144; Ov. met. 9.765.
- 21, 4 *Apollinem tuum* ("your Apollo"): VERG. ecl. 4,10.
- 21, 6 *salutifer* ("healthbringing"): Ov. met. 2.642, 15.632, 744; STAT. Ach. 1.117.

10.8. PANLAT V(8) 311 CE ANON TO CONSTANTINE, TRIER

- 6, 7 *solibus perurendam* ("scorched by the sun"): LVCR. 5.251.
- 7, 2 *squalentia* ("neglected"): VERG. georg. 4.13; Ov. met. 2.760, 4.656; SIL. 1.674, 3.275; STAT. Theb. 1.152.

7, 2 *tenebrosa* ("gloomy"): VERG. *Aen.* 5.839, 6.107; Ov. *met.* 1.113, 5.359, 7.409; LVCAN 2.79; VAL. FL. 3.400; SIL. 14.240; STAT. *Theb.* 1.351, 6.382, 7.118, 10.119.

9, 1, 4 *adfari* ("to address"; see above VIII(4), 9, 1): VERG. *Aen.* 1.663, 2.700, 4.284, 12.138; Ov. *met.* 1.350, 5.268, 9.696 ; VAL. FL. 1.299, 5.352; STAT. *Achill.* 1.251, 383.

10, 2 *ingenui largique fontes* ("natural and large springs"): LVCR. 1.230.

This is a relatively meagre display of poetic colour, with Vergil in particular uncharacteristically inconspicuous. There is, however, some lexical adventure apparent in the collection's first example of neologism—*separate* ("separately" 11.1), elsewhere only attested in the comparative form in Cicero *inu.* 2.51 (156) (Chruzander 1897: 69–70).

10.9. PANLAT XII(9) 313 CE ANON TO CONSTANTINE, TRIER

Both the speech of 313 and that of 321 take as their point of departure Constantine's victory over Maxentius in the Battle of the Milvian Bridge in 312. Both speeches make frequent turns to Vergil (Nixon and Saylor Rodgers 1994: 289, 338; Rees 2004a: 39–43). The anonymous orator of 313 is the more direct:

> *magnus poeta, dum bellorum toto orbe surgentium discursum apparatumque describit, "et curuae" inquit "rigidum falces <conflantur in ensem>." triste nimium tempus illud, cum instrumenta cultui pecudum praeparata in caedem hominum uerterentur. at nunc rigidi illi mortiferique mucrones in salutaria uincla curuantur, et exarmatum hominem non interimunt sed coercent, deditosque hostes gladii sui conlisi obtunsique tutantur, qui nihil illis prodesse integri acutique potuerunt.*

> When he describes the extent of the wars rising up throughout the whole world, and their preparation, the great poet says, "And curved sickles are melted down into hard swords." It was an enormously sad time, when tools prepared for the cultivation of herds were turned to the slaughter of men. But now those hard and death-bearing blades are curved into salutary chains, and do not kill but restrain disarmed men, and their own battered and blunted swords, which could be of no advantage to them intact and sharpened, protect the surrendered enemy. (12.3–4)

In total, discussion of the Vergilian text occupies three full chapters (11–13).[22] Although, of course, allusions to Vergil have been frequent up to this point in

---

22. See Mynors ad loc. for the text.

the collection, the extent of the quotation and its elaboration are unprecedented. If this indulgence has not inspired confidence among his modern commentators in the orator's sense of discretion (Galletier 1942: 118–19; Nixon and Saylor Rodgers 1994: 313), other examples of his engagement with Vergil reveal a lighter touch—see, for example, 4, 2 and 14, 2, where the intertext is conspicuous, but without signposting or elaboration.

- 4, 2 *sua enim cuique prudentia deus est* ("for each person, their own prudence is a god"): VERG. *Aen.* 9.185.
- 8, 4 *congredi* with the dative ("to engage with"): e.g., PLAVT. *pseud.* 560; VERG. *Aen.* 1.475; Ov. *met.* 12.76 (*TLL* IV.287.34–35).
- 9, 4 *in media hostium tela* ("into the middle of the enemies' weapons"): VERG. *Aen.* 2.353, 10.237.
- 10, 3 *anhelum pectus* ("breathless chest"; see also *PanLat* IV(10).26.4): VERG. *Aen.* 6.48; SIL. 12.418–19; [SEN.] *Herc. O.* 1414.
- 13, 4 *reparabilia* ("reparable"): Ov. *am.* 1.14.55, *her.* 5.103, *met.* 1.379; CALP. *ecl.* 5.20; LVCAN 10.429; VAL. FL. 6.562.
- 14, 2 *degeneris, ut dictum est, animos timor arguebat* ("fear revealed the degenerate's spirit, as the saying goes"): VERG. *Aen.* 4.13.
- 17, 3 *hostium corpora et arma praeceps fluuius uoluendo deuexit* ("in its flow, the river carried off the bodies and weapons of the enemy"): VERG. *Aen.* 8.538.
- 18, 1 *sancte Thybri, quondam hospitis monitor Aeneae* ("sacred Thybris, one-time advisor to your guest Aeneas"): VERG. *Aen.* 8.31ff., 72.
- 21, 5 *Albula* (= the river Tiber): VERG. *Aen.* 8.332.
- 22, 2 *cessat terra noualibus* ("the land gives way to fallows"): VERG. *georg.* 1.71.
- 23, 4 *letalibus* ("lethal"): VERG. *Aen.* 4.73, 9.580; Ov. *met.* 2.827; LVCAN 4.559; SIL. 1.286, 2.92, 4.172; STAT. *Theb.* 6.40 (*TLL* VII.2.1183.61).
- 24, 2 *quantae molis sit* ("how great a mass" ; see also XI(3).3.4, VIII(4).6.4.IV(10).18.2, II(12).3.5): VERG. *Aen.* 1.33.
- 26, 1 *sator* ("one who sows"): PACVV. *Trag.* 295; LVCR. 2.1168; VERG. *Aen.* 1.254, 11.725; SEN. *Herc. f.* 357, *Oed.* 1028; VAL. FL. 1. 505; SIL. 3. 364, 4. 430; STAT. *Theb.* 1.179, 3.218, 488.
- 26, 1 *toto infusa mundo omnibus miscearis elementis* ("infused in the whole world, you are mixed with all the elements"): VERG. *Aen.* 6.726–7.

The poetic colour is almost exclusively Vergilian, working particular leverage from the circumstances of Maxentius's death in the Tiber. There is also a debt to the epicizing river simile of X(2).5.3 (see above), this time with its own Vergilian signature: *toto quippe impetu ferebare, torrenti similis amni quem abruptae radicitus siluae et conuulsa funditus saxa sequerentur* ("Indeed, in your whole momentum, you were borne like a river in torrent, followed by trees torn from their roots and rocks wrenched from their foundation," 9.5), recalling *Aeneid* 2.305-7 (Rees 2013b: 106-8). The river simile and the apostrophe to the Tiber (18.1) are joined together in an affirming Vergilian lustre.

Further ground is broken by the only appearance in Classical Latin of *abusiuus* ("misapplied," 4.3), used of *appellatio* ("name"; Chruzander 1897: 69-70); satisfying interpretation of the historical detail underlying this continues to defy commentators, but we can reasonably assume some stylistic adventure to heighten the orator's sneering tone.

10.10. PANLAT IV(10), 321 CE NAZARIUS TO CONSTANTINE, ROME

For its style, the only surviving speech by Nazarius, a distinguished rhetorician (Jer. *chron.* 324 and Ausonius *prof.* 14.9) has had its detractors; criticisms have highlighted its structural indiscipline and excessive use of rhetorical figures (Galletier 1952: 158-9; Etienne 1962: 258-9; Nixon and Saylor Rodgers 1994: 336-8). It is particularly of note, therefore, that Nazarius twice discusses his own oratory. The first is a tidy if rather formulaic version of the sort of *captatio beneuolentiae* Menander Rhetor (*Basilikos Logos* 368) recommends for a speech's early stage: *sentio nullam eloquentiam nec optari nec concipi posse quae dignam adferat aut tempori gratiam aut materiae copiam aut uestris studiis facultatem* ("I realize that no eloquence can be desired or grasped to bring a grace worthy of the situation or a fullness worthy of the subject, or an ability worthy of your enthusiasm," 1.1).[23] Less conventional is Nazarius's return to the topic, some thirty chapters later: *o si nunc mihi facultas daretur sermonis pro rerum <modo> figurandi! adhiberem omnes flosculos et abuterer exquisito quodam lepore ac uenustate dicendi* ("O if I were now given the power to adorn a speech according to the measure of its subject! I would apply all the blossoms and use an exquisite charm and grace of speech," 30.3).[24] The exclamation is difficult to evaluate for two reasons. The first is that although in literary criticism, *lepor* ("charm") and *uenustas* ("grace") could be commendable, provided they were deployed with discretion, in surviving sources *flosculus* ("blossom") generally has a tone of disapprobation.[25] The second reason is that Nazarius clearly reached for eye-catching literary style in his speech.

---

23. The latter perhaps addressed to the Senate.

24. Galletier 1952: 163 is at his wits' end when he says of Nazarius's wish, "Il eût mieux fait de demander aux dieux la sobriété et le gout" ('He would have done better to ask the gods for restraint and taste'). See Mynors ad loc. for the text.

25. Laudani 2014: 348-9. On *lepor/lepos*, see CIC. *de orat.* 2.98, 3.67, *orat.* 96; on *uenustas*, QVINT. *inst.* 4.2.118, PLIN. *ep.* 4.18.2; on *flosculus, non sum tam ignarus, iudices, causarum, non tam insolens in dicendo, ut omni ex genere orationem aucuper et omnis undique flosculos carpam atque delibem* ("Judges, I am not

Like some of his predecessors, Nazarius also invokes poetry as an authority *ut poetae ferunt* ("as poets say," 11, 5); but he reaches further into poetic flourish. Within a few sentences of the second passage of rhetorical self-reflexiveness, for example, a passage describing Constantine's triumphal entry into Rome sustains a Vergilian character:

> *duci sane omnibus uidebantur subacta uitiorum agmina quae Vrbem grauiter obsederant: scelus domitum, uicta Perfidia, diffidens sibi Audacia et Importunitas catenata. Furor uinctus et cruenta Crudelitas inani terrore frendebant; Superbia atque Arrogantia debellatae, Luxuries coercita et Libido constricta nexu ferreo tenebantur.*

Certainly everybody thought that the train of vices which had blockaded the City grievously had been conquered: Crime was tamed, Treachery conquered, Impudence which cannot trust itself, and Insolence in chains. Fettered Fury and bloody Cruelty gnashed their teeth without causing fright; Haughtiness and Arrogance were subdued, Luxury held back and Lust held tight in iron bonds. (IV(10).31.3)[26]

To similar effect as that in XII(9), Vergil generally dominates the poetic intertextuality in Nazarius's speech.

- 3, 4 *germen* ("seed"; see also *PanLat* VII(6).2.5, SYMM. *or.* 3.6): LVCR. 4.1083; VERG. *georg.* 2.76; STAT. *Theb.* 2.280 (*TLL* VI.1923.32).
- 3, 5 *intremuit* ("trembled"; cf. *PanLat* VIII(4).5.2; below 19, 2; AVSON. *Grat. act.* 3 (13)): VERG. *Aen.* 3.581, 5.505; OV. *met.* 1.284, 2.180; VAL. FL. 2.519, 3.73 ; SIL. 3.437, 5.330, 11.518 ; STAT. *Theb.* 12.381 (*TLL* VII.248.25).
- 7, 1 *bellorum euentus . . . uarios* ("various outcomes of wars"): VERG. *Aen.* 10.159–60.
- 7, 1 *Mars dubius* ("uncertain Mars"): VERG. *georg.* 2.283.
- 7, 1 *adglutinat* ("glues"): PLAVT. *Aul.* 801, *Men.* 342 (*TLL* I.1313.25).
- 7, 4 *illa maiestas fandi ac nefandi discriminatrix* ("that majesty who distinguishes between right and wrong"): VERG. *Aen.* 1.543.

---

so ignorant of the case, not so immoderate in my talking, that I give chase to speech from every genre and grasp and pluck all blossoms from every quarter," CIC. *sest.* 56 (119); of earlier philosophers, Seneca noted *non fuerunt circa flosculos occupati* ("they were not detained by [stylistic] blossoms," *ep.* 33.1); Quintilian is variously scathing: a warning to young orators is that *ne recentis huius lasciuiae flosculis capti uoluptate praua deleniantur* ("they should not, won over in depraved pleasure, be enticed by the blossoms of this recent lasciviousness," *inst.* 2.5.22). See also Aulus Gellius 17.21.1. On the other hand, supposed highpoints of rhetorical elegance are said by Ammianus to have been called *flosculos Tullianos* ("Ciceronian blossoms") by Modestus (29.1.11).

26. *Aen.* 1.294–6, 6.853; Rees 2004a: 42–3. See below for some details of the diction.

7, 4 *fulmineus miles* ("brilliant soldier"): VERG. *Aen.* 9.812.
8, 4 *incestet* ("pollutes"; see also II(12).25.3, 29.3): VERG. *Aen.* 6.150 (*TLL* VII.1893.7–8).
12, 3 *caligastis* ("you were in darkness"; see also 14.2): LVCR. 3.156; STAT. *Silv.* 5.3.238 (*TLL* III.157.33–34).
14, 2 *caligantem* ("darkened"): see 12.3 (*TLL* III.157.34).
14, 2 *mortalis uisus* ("mortal vision"): VERG. *Aen.* 4.277.
14, 2, 25, 4 *contagium* ("contagion"): LVCR. 3.345, 3.740; Ov. *met.* 15.195 (*TLL* IV.627.12–13).
14, 3, 29, 5 *corusci* ("flashing"): PACVV. *Trag.* 413; CIC. *Arat.* 96; LVCR. 5.295, 6.283; VERG. *Aen.* 1.164 (*TLL* IV.1077.1–2, 8–9).
15, 3 *contente* ("with restraint"): PLAVT. *As.* 78 (*TLL* IV.712.48).
17, 2 *asperata* ("sharpened"): LVCAN 6.801; STAT. *Theb.* 1.138, 9.1 (*TLL* II.827.38–39).
17, 3 *inoffensus* ("without hindrance"): VERG. *Aen.* 10.292; SEN. *Herc. f.* 928 (*TLL* VII.1.1735.27–28).
18, 2 *tantam belli molem* ("so great a mass of war"; XI(3).3.4, VIII(4).6.4, XII(9).24.2, II(12).3.5): VERG. *Aen.* 1.33.
18, 6 *conlatiuam* ("combined"): PLAVT. *Curc.* 231 (*TLL* III.1580.18).
19, 2 *intremuerit* ("trembled"; cf. *PanLat* VIII(4).5.2; IV(10).3.5; AVSON. *Grat. act.* 3 (13)): VERG. *Aen.* 3.581, 5.505; Ov. *met.* 1.284, 2.180; VAL. FL. 2.519, 3.73 ; SIL. 3.437, 5.330, 11.518 ; STAT. *Theb.* 12.381 (*TLL* VII.248.25).
19, 3 *caecos euentus* ("blind outcomes"): VERG. *Aen.* 6, 157–8.
23, 4 *arietauerint* ("they butted"): ACC. *Praetext.* 24 (Warmington) [CIC. *Diu.* 1.44] PLAVT. *Truc.* 256; VERG. *Aen.* 11.890; SIL. 4.149 (*TLL* II.574.39–40).
23, 4 *immunes uulnerum* ("free from wounds"): VERG. *Aen.* 12.559; Ov. *met.* 8.690–1.
25, 7 *lassa* ("exhausted"): PLAVT. *As.* 873; VERG. *georg.* 4.449; Ov. *met.* 14.120 (*TLL* VII.2.991.55–56).
26, 4 *anhelus* ("breathless"; see also XII(9).10.3): VERG. *georg.* 2.135; LVCAN 9.587.
29, 5 *trabalis* ("beam-like"): VERG. *Aen.* 12.294; STAT. *Theb.* 4.6.
30, 1 *fuga turpis prodidit* ("foul flight betrayed"): VERG. *Aen.* 10.592–3.
31, 3 *catenata* ("in chains"): HOR. *epod.* 7.8; STAT. *Silv.* 2.1.110 (*TLL* III.607.75–76).
31, 3 *frendebant* ("they were gnashing their teeth"): SEN. *Herc. f.* 693 (*TLL* VI.1287.53–54).
32, 8 *defaecatum* ("cleaned"): PLAVT. *Aul.* 79, *pseud.* 760 (*TLL* V.285.27–28).
33, 5 *facilior . . . est uia* ("the road is easier"): VERG. *georg.* 1.122.
33, 6 *feralis* ("funereal"): VERG. *Aen.* 4.462; LVCAN 1.86 (*TLL* VI.487.35–36).

33, 7 *publicitus* ("for the State"); PLAVT. *Amph.* 162, *Bacc.* 313 (*TLL* X.2.2472.65–66).

This constitutes a sizeable catalogue of poetic lexis—Nazarius's speech is longer than any of the collection's eight earlier late antique speeches, but the incidence of such lexis per page is still considerably greater. Nazarius might also be thought to be venturing association with poetry when he elaborates an extended simile: *nam ut fistulae, cum diu intersaeptae sunt, exitu dato quo largiores eo crassiores aquas euomunt, sic uota hominum metu interclusa turbidi aliquid egerunt cum cumulata ruperunt* ("for, just as when pipes have been stopped up for a long time, and an outlet is presented, they spew out water as more plentiful as swollen, so when the wishes of mankind, shut up with fear, break the accumulation, they effect something turbulent," 32.9); the vocabulary is hardly typically poetic, but the graphic quality of the burst-pipe simile recalls Pyramus's suicide as told by Ovid, *met.* 4.122–4 (NB: *fistula ... aquas ... rumpit*). Nonetheless, as the description of virtues and vice in triumphal procession (31, 3, discussed above) exemplifies, Nazarius's claim to be incapable of literary *flosculus* ("blossom") is most resoundingly undermined when poetic colour in lexis and topos work in combination. Another example of this is a scene of Constantine's military activity. The orator of 289 used a simile of a rushing river for Maximian in battle (X(2).5.3, discussed above), the detail and conceit of which were applied to Constantine in 313 (XII(9).9.5, discussed above). Nazarius does not use a simile but heightens his stylistic register by combining poetic echoes from various Latin epics:

cuius rei cum imaginem cepi, dicturus horresco. inuadis primus aciem, solus inrumpis. obumbrant euntem telorum inriti iactus, sonat ictibus umbo securus. his, quos trabalis hasta deiecit, insultans equus proterit. fulget nobilis galea et corusca luce gemmarum diuinum uerticem monstrat. auro clipeus, auro arma conlucent.

On the point of speaking I shudder as I seize upon an image of this episode. You attack the enemy line first, you alone burst into it. Weapons thrown uselessly cast their shadows over him as he goes, his safe shield boss resounds with blows. His horse jumps at and crushes the men he felled with his beam-like spear. His noble helmet gleams and shows his divine head with the flashing light of jewels. His shield, his weapons, shine with gold. (IV(10).29.5)

In addition to some of the vocabulary detailed above, this passage is a tissue of Ennian, Vergilian, and Statian resonances: *dicturus horresco* ("On the point of speaking I shudder"; VERG. *Aen.* 2.204), *inuadis primus* ("You attack the enemy line first"; VERG. *Aen.* 10.310), *obumbrant ... telorum* ("[casts] of weapons shadow him"; VERG. *Aen.* 12.578); *sonat ictibus umbo* ("shield boss resounds with blows"; ENN. *Ann.* 15.392; LVCAN 6.192); *trabalis hasta* ("beam-like spear"; STAT. *Theb.* 4.6-7), all casting Constantine as an epic hero.[27]

As a closing observation on Nazarius, in addition to his reprisal of established poetic expression and topos, another distinctive feature of his stylistic register is his lexical innovation (Laudani 2014: 48-9) For, against the total of only two lexical hapax legomena / first occurrences in the eight earlier speeches, Nazarius boasts eight: *deflexio* ("detour," 5, 6; in a tropical sense, *TLL* V.360.83), *discriminatrix* ("she who distinguishes," 7, 4, *TLL* V.1362.63), *recondite* ("secretly," 13, 1),[28] *inconcretus* ("bodiless," 14, 2, *TLL* VII.1.999.13-15)), *superegredi* ("to surmount," 16, 2),[29] *robuste* ("firmly," 17, 2), *clibanarius* ("mail-clad soldier, 22, 4, *TLL* III.1341.80-82), *constipatio* ("thickly packed crowd," 28, 5, *TLL* IV.509.38-39). This attests an extraordinary ambition to increase the aesthetic elasticity of the genre.

10.11. PANLAT III(11) 362 CE CLAUDIUS MAMERTINUS TO JULIAN, CONSTANTINOPLE

Like Nazarius (11, 5) and the orator of 289 (X(2).11.3), Claudius Mamertinus grants poets cultural authority. He equates Julian's effect on his people with that of the highest god: *poetae ferunt altissimum illum et cuncta potestate cohibentem deum, qui ditione perpetua diuina atque humana moderatur, cum despiciat in terras, habitu oris tempestatum incerta mutare, eius nutu mundum tremescere, illius hilaritate turbines abigi, nubes fugari, nitentia per orbem serena diffundi* ("poets say that the highest god who holds everything in his power and in universal authority governs human and divine affairs, alters the changing weather by the expression on his face when he gazes down upon the earth; at his nod the world shakes, when he is happy storms are driven away, clouds are put to flight, shining calm is spread throughout the world," 28, 5). No poets are named or quoted, but Ennius's *Annales* (446-7) and Vergil's *Aeneid* (1, 254-5) seem the

---

27. See Menander Rhetor, *Basilikos Logos* 374: "You will also describe the king's armour and campaigns, focusing on the moment of his *aristeia* and engagement." On the ekphrastic quality of the scene, see Rees 2013b: 108-9.

28. The reconstructed text of M (Magontius) reads *recondite*: I accept this reading, against *recondita* of Mynors et al., which is based on the text of the first printed edition; Chruzander 1897: 70, Laudani 2014: 185-6.

29. Taking the text of M and Bertinensis, accepted by Baehrens 1874, against *supergredi* of the correctors, accepted by Mynors 1964; Chruzander 1897: 70.

likely inferences, in keeping with the collection's tendency (Garcia Ruiz 2006: 151). By invoking poetic discourse in affirmation of his claims about Julian's nature, Claudius Mamertinus asserts its value as analogous to his own discourse. Examples of poetic lexis are relatively evenly distributed across the speech:

3, 2 *inclementer* ("harshly"): PLAVT. *Amph.* 742, *Poen.* 1323, *Rud.* 734 (*TLL* VII.1.937.77–78).
4, 3 *luctamen* ("struggle"): VERG. *Aen.* 8.89; VAL. FL. 2.234, 3.39, 6.510 (*TLL* VII.2.1727.28–30).
6, 4 *tremulae* ("trembling"): ENN. *Ann.* 1.34; PLAVT. *Curc.* 160; TER. *Eun.* 336; CAT. 61.51; LVCR. 2.976.
6, 4 *anhelitum ... crebriorem, sudorum riuos* ("more frequent panting, streams of sweat"): VERG. *Aen.* 5.199.
6, 4 *sidereis* ("starry"): OV. *met.* 1.780, 4.169, 6.341, 10.140; VAL. FL. 2.104, 4.490; STAT. *Silu.* 1.2.141.
8, 3 *hospitas* ("host"): VERG. *Aen.* 3.539; OV. *met.* 3.637 (*TLL* VI.3032.51–53).
9, 1 *ad incitas* ("to a standstill"): PLAVT. *Poen.* 907, *Trin.* 537; LVCIL. 101 (Marx) (*TLL* VII.1.933.64–65).
9, 2 *lacrimabiles* ("lamentable"): VERG. *Aen.* 3.39, 7.604; OV. *met.* 2.796 (*TLL* VII.2.843.57).
9, 2 *lacerae* ("torn"): OV. *met.* 2.318; STAT. *Theb.* 5.254; SIL. 1.232 (*TLL* VII.2.821.12).
10, 1 *terrarum ingeniis* ("the earth's qualities"): VERG. *georg.* 2.177.
10, 1 *lata camporum* ("broad expanses of fields"): VERG. *Aen.* 1.422, 2.332, 725.[30]
10, 1 *balatu ... mugitibus* ("with bleating ... lowing"): VERG. *georg.* 3.554; *Aen.* 9.62; OV. *met.* 7.319–20, 540.
10, 1 *persona* ("resounding"): PETR. 120.72; STAT. *Achill.* 1.208 (*TLL* X.1.1736.7–8).
10, 2 *dispendium* ("expense"; see also AVSON. *Grat. act.* 2.9, 16.72): PLAVT. *Poen.* 163; TER. *Eun.* 929 (*TLL* V.1395.65–66).
11, 4 *picturatae* ("variegated"): VERG. *Aen.* 3.483; STAT., *Silu.* 5.1.104 (*TLL* X.1.2084.51–52).
15, 2 *adoreis* ("glory"): PLAVT. *Amph.* 193; HOR. *carm.* 4.4.41 (*TLL* 1.813.61).
17, 1 *reserabo* ("I will unlock"): OV. *met.* 15.145; VAL. FL. 2.438; SIL. 7.436.
17, 2 *canitiem* ("grey hair"; see also SYMM. *or.* 3.12): VERG. *Aen.* 10.548; HOR. *carm.* 1.9.17 (*TLL* III.261.6–7).

---

30. For the construction, see also III(11), 11, 3, 12, 1, 12, 3, 28, 5 with Gutzwiller 1942: 151–2.

19, 4 *adulabant* ("they adulated"): Acc. *Trag.* 390; Lvcan 5.1070 (*TLL* I.879.63–64).
21, 5 *tantillum* ("such a small" [adj.]): Plavt. *Poen.* 273; Ter. *Ad.* 563; Lvcr. 3.189.
23, 1 *grauatur* ("burdened"): Verg. *Aen.* 8.220; Lvcan 5.628 (*TLL* VI.2311.1).
27, 2 *regnator* ("ruler"): Naev. *Carm. frg.* 14.17 (Warmington); Acc. *Trag.* 32; Plavt. *Amph.* 45; Verg. *Aen.* 2.557, 779, 4.269.
28, 5 *tremescere* ("to tremble"): Lvcr. 6, 548; Verg. *Aen.* 5.694; Ov. *met.* 7.205.
30, 1 *usurpata* ("perceived"): Plavt. *Cas.* 631; Lvcr. 1.301, 4.975.
31, 6 *festinae* ("hasty"): Val. Fl. 6.472 (*TLL* VI. 622.25).

After the eight neologisms in Nazarius's speech, Claudius Mamertinus has three: *inflammatrix* ("she who inflames," 3, 3),[31] *stimulator* ("instigator," 5, 2),[32] and *deambulacrum* ("a walkway," 9.4, *TLL* V.81.50). However, it is notable that despite Claudius Mamertinus's acknowledgement of poetry's authority and his considerable deployment of poetic and innovative lexis, the speech lacks poetic set pieces such as extended simile, prosopopoeia, and formal ekphrasis. In one passage of unusually imaginative flight (10.1), a rich cluster of poeticisms ornaments an elaborate rhetoric[33]; but generally lexis and topos do not coincide to generate highpoints of conspicuous and sustained poetic colour. Rather, while committing to the deployment of poeticism, Claudius Mamertinus adopts a measured aesthetic.

10.12. Symmachus *orationes I–III* to Valentian and Gratian, 368–70 CE, Trier

10.12.1. Or. 1

In his first panegyric, after his reprisal of the *licentia poetarum* ("licence of poets") topos (*or.* 1, 4; see above) and some Vergilian allusions (*Aen.* 5.810, 9.746, 12.477–80),[34] Symmachus asserts *sint haec figmenta carminum, nos habemus exempla factorum* ("let these be the figments of poems, we have examples of facts"). Nonetheless there are instances of poetic lexis.

2 *Scythiae regna* ("kingdoms of Scythia"): Verg. *Aen.* 6.798.
2 *glacialem* ("glacial"): Verg. *Aen.* 3.285; Ov. *met.* 2.173, 9.582; Lvcan 1.18, 5.23, Sil. 12.1.
3 *germina* ("offshoots"; see also VII(6).2.5; IV(10).3.4; Symm. *or.* 3.6): Lvcr. 4.1083; Verg. *georg.* 2.76; Stat. *Theb.* 2.280 (*TLL* VI.1923.32).

---

31. Later found in Amm. 14.1.2.
32. Later found in Clavd. *In Ruf.* 2.501.
33. On sentence length, see L'Huillier 1992: 435; this sentence is outdone only by 13.3. Gutzwiller 1942: 150 also observes that the syntax of *aquas oppidis influentes* ("waters flowing into the towns") is a poeticism.
34. Callu 2009: 43.

5 *occidui* ("setting"; see also *PanLat* X(2).2.1, SYMM. *or.* 3.11): Ov. *fast.* 4.832, 5.558; *met.* 1.63, 14.416; MANIL. 3.367; SEN. *Thy.* 822; SIL. 1.145.

5 *radiabat flamma* ("the flame was spreading"): Acc. *praetext.* 27–8 (Ribbeck) (CIC. *diu.* 1.44); GERM. 604; SIL. 2.586.

9 *robore . . . pubis electus* ("strength . . . youth, chosen"): VERG. *Aen.* 8.518-19.

10 *obluctatus* ("struggle"): VERG. *Aen.* 3.38; LVCAN 3.662; SIL. 8.10, 12.426 (*TLL* IX.2.117.18–19).

13 *caelitum* ("heaven dwellers"; see also *PanLat* XI(3).3.6): ENN. *Trag.* 171, 270; PACVV. *Trag.* 232; ACC. *Trag.* 298, 593 (Ribbeck); PLAVT. *Rud.* 2; CAT. 61.49; Ov. *met.* 5.322, 6.151; SEN. *Ag.* 21.392, 520 (*TLL* III.67.20–21).

14 *inpacati* ("not peaceable"): VERG. *georg.* 3.408; STAT. *Silu.* 5.1.137; SIL. 7.665.

Symmachus appears to indulge in lexical innovation with *usurpator* ("usurper," 22).

10.12.2. Or. 2

In his second speech to Valentinian Symmachus hints at the temptations of poetic heightening: *consulto multa praetereo, ne in poeticos flatus rerum ingentium cothurnus erumpat* ("I pass over many things on purpose, in case a high style breaks out into poetic exaggeration of great affairs," 26).[35] This point is reinforced by the suggestion that Homer (*Troiani carminis auctor*) be free to invent material (26). Again, despite this and similar protestations, Symmachus includes examples of poetic colour.[36]

4 *bicornis* ("two-branched"; see above *PanLat* VI(7).11.5): VERG. *Aen.* 8.727; Ov. *met.* 11.763 (*TLL* II.1971.81).

9 *nisus* ("exertion"): PACVV. *Trag.* 256; ACC. *Trag. f.* 239.

14 *inhospita* ("inhospitable"): VERG. *Aen.* 4.41, 5.627; Ov. *met.* 1.218, 11.284; LVCAN 1.367; SIL. 1.237, 2.23, 3.444; STAT. *Theb.* 5.715 (*TLL* VII.1.1603.16–17).

21 *Terrigenas* ("earth-born"; see also *PanLat* X(2).4.2): LVCIL. 1377; LVCR. 5.1411, 1427; Ov. *met.* 5.325, 7.36, 7.141; LVCAN 3.316, 4.553; VAL. FL. 7.505, 629, 8.107; SIL. 6.254.

29 *eloquii* ("eloquence"; see also *PanLat* IX(V).17.4): VERG. *Aen.* 11.383; Ov. *ars.* 1.462.

A possible neologism is *contextio* ("a joining," 26, *TLL* IV.694.10–11); *occentatio* ("sounding," 5, *TLL* IX.2.342.69–71) is hapax legomenon.

Symmachus also deploys topoi often associated with poetry in the apostrophe *inhospita regio* ("inhospitable area," 14); and the extended simile *ut dammis pernicibus campus aperitur, ut agmina ignaua ceruorum latibus emota siluestribus*

---

35. Symmachus's metaphor for poetic elevation—*cothurnus*—was well known from poetic sources, such as VERG. *ecl.* 8.10, HOR. *carm.* 2.1.12, and so must have been deployed here with some irony.

36. See *or.* 2.8, on the Trojan War, and 21, on the "ancient story" (*uetus fabula*) of the Giants.

in plana coguntur, ita gratius uisum est discurrentem barbarum spectare quam caedere ("Like a plain is laid open to swift deer, like cowardly herds of stags, moved out from their woodland hiding places, are forced onto level grounds, so it seemed more welcome to watch the barbarian running to and fro than to kill him," 10).

10.12.3. Or. 3

In his third speech, to Gratian, Symmachus has a passage of reflection on literary discourse, reminiscent of Nazarius (30.3) in its rhetoric:

si mihi nunc altius euagari poetico liceret eloquio, totum de nouo saeculo Maronis excursum uati similis in tuum nomen excriberem. dicerem caelo redisse Iustitiam et ultro uberes fetus iam grauidam spondere naturam; nunc mihi in patentibus campis sponte seges matura flauesceret, in sentibus uua turgeret, de quernis frondibus rorantia mella sudarent. . . . nec poeticis utar indiciis

If now I could now wander higher with poetic speech, like a poet from a new age of Vergil I would set out a whole excursus in your name. I would say that Justice has returned to heaven and that nature, now burgeoning, promises rich offspring in return; that in the open fields the ripe corn was turning golden of its own accord, the grape grew heavy on the thorns, the dewy honey was sweating from the oak leaves. . . . But I will not use poetic examples. (9)

Vergil's fourth *Eclogue* glitters in this particular *praeteritio*. The conditional nature of the sentence maintains the gap between oratorical and poetic discourse, and the closing assertion is emphatic. Once again, however, a few poeticisms can be identified.

- 3 *aequaeuus* ("of equal age"): VERG. *Aen.* 2.561, 5.452; SIL. 13.191; STAT. *Theb.* 5.226 (*TLL* 1.993.26–27).
- 3 *insudas* ("sweat in"): HOR. *sat.* 1.4.72; CALP. *ecl.* 5.10; STAT. *Silu.* 3.1.126 (*TLL* VII.1.2029.35–36).
- 6 *germen includit* ("encloses a bud"; see also SYMM. *or.* 1.3): VERG. *georg.* 2.76–7.
- 6 *praesegmina* ("paring"): PLAVT. *Aul.* 313 (*TLL* X.2.836.1).
- 9 *bicornis* ("two-branched"); see above *PanLat* VI(7).11.5, SYMM. *or.* 2.4): VERG. *Aen.* 8.727, Ov. *met.* 11.763 (*TLL* II.1971.81).

11 *occidui* ("setting"; see above *PanLat* X(2).2.1 and SYMM. *or.* 1.5): Ov. *fast.* 4.832, 5.558, *met.* 1.63, 14.416; SEN. *Thy.* 822; MANIL. 3.367; SIL. 1.145 (*TLL* IX.2.353.27).

12 *obmurmurare* ("to murmur against"): Ov. *her.* 18.47 (*TLL* IX.2.119.25).

12 *canitiem* ("grey hair"; see also *PanLat* III(11), 17, 2): VERG. *Aen.* 10.548; HOR. *carm.* 1.9.17 (*TLL* III.261.6-7).

Symmachus also contrives an ekphrasis of an imaginary canvas (5) by a latter-day Zeuxis or Apelles, with *uix credenda miracula* ("scarcely believable miracles," 5), a figure to be traced back to epic poetry (Rees 2013b: 118-19).

10.13. AUSONIUS *GRATIARUM ACTIO* TO GRATIAN, 379 CE, TRIER

Ausonius's only surviving speech has several references to poetic discourse: *nec iam miramur licentiam poetarum qui omnia deo plena dixerunt*, "Now we do not wonder at the licence of poets who have said that everything is full of god," 1.5; VERG. *ecl.* 3.60; see *PanLat* XI(3).14.2 above), although the switch to the plural *poetarum* is peculiar; *Homerici oratores* ("Homeric orators," 4.19-20); *Homericos uersus* ("Homeric verses," 13.59); *mirabamur poetam*: "we wondered at the poet," 14.65: VERG. *Aen.* 4.41); *in audacibus Graecorum fabulis* ("in the daring stories of the Greeks," 18.81).[37] This seems a preferred rhetorical conceit, perhaps in keeping with what we might expect of a prolific poet himself—but a search for poetic colour yields surprisingly limited results.

2, 9 *dispendio* ("loss"; see also 16.72 and *PanLat* III(11).10.2): PLAVT. *Poen.* 163; TER. *Eun.* 929 (*TLL* V.1395.65-66).

6, 28 *aurea . . . mediocritas* ("golden mean"): HOR. *carm.* 2.10.5.

13, 61 *et tenuiore filo . . . deducta* ("spun out on a rather thin thread"): HOR. *epist.* 2.1.225; AVSON. *Griph.* 67.

13, 62 *ad plenum* ("fully"; see also *PanLat* II(12), 9, 2): VERG. *georg.* 2.244 and HOR. *carm.* 1.17.15.

16, 74 *uiuaci* ("vivid"; see also *PanLat* II(12).3.4): VERG. *ecl.* 7.30; HOR. *sat.* 2.2.132; Ov. *am.* 2.6.54, *met.* 3.194.

17, 77 *salutiferae* ("health-bringing"): Ov. *met.* 2.642, 15.744; STAT. *Achill.* 1.117.

---

37. Given the examples Ausonius then gives, he seems to have poetry in mind rather than prose.

Through the difficult manuscript tradition, there are signs of some lexical adventure:[38] *abolitor* ("he who abolishes," 1.4, *TLL* 1.120.29–30), only elsewhere in TERT. *Cult. fem.* 3; *palmatam*: ("a tunic embroidered with palm trees," 11.53, *TLL* X.1.150.75–76), an early occurrence, if construed as a noun (cf. Chruzander 1897: 45); *glomerosius* ("more roundedly," 15.68, *TLL* VI.2061.1–5), hapax legomenon;[39] *transmeabili* ("passable," 18.79) only elsewhere at OROS. *hist.* 6.9.6. But overall, despite being the work of a poet, this long speech is stylistically conservative.

10.14. *PanLat* II(12) 389 CE Pacatus Drepanius to Theodosius, Rome

Pacatus Drepanius, the author of the latest Latin prose panegyric of the fourth century, but also a poet in his own right (Turkan-Verkerk 2003; Rees 2013a; Clark in this volume, n. 5), makes several references to poetic discourse: *scio fabulas poetarum auribus mulcendis repertas* ... ("I know that tales of poets, made up to delight the ear," 4.4); *ut haec esse uera credamus quae mendaciis uatum in plausus aptata cauearum fidem tempori debent* ... ("Even supposing we believe to be true the things which, designed for the applause of theatres by the lies of poets, owe their trustworthiness to time," 17.2); *quis annalium scriptor aut carminum* ... ("which writer of annals or poems," 33.2); *germana illa pictorum poetarumque commenta* ... ("the related inventions of painters and poets," 39.1).[40] The references' consistent thread is poetry's tendency to exaggerate. Nonetheless, his modern readers have often commented on his own stylistic embellishments: "Pacatus' speech is one of the most stylish of the collection" (Matthews 1975: 229); *per uniuersum poetico ingenio orationem ornat* ("throughout, he embellishes his speech with a poetic instinct"; Scheffer, quoted in Valpy 1828: 1551); "La langue du panégyrique de Théodose manifeste d'ailleurs ce goût pour la poésie, son vocabulaire, ses cadences, et la tradition littéraire Antique" (Turcan-Verkerk 2003: 12).[41] Support for this characterization can be adduced in individual words and phrases of lexical and intertextual revival and in sustained topoi of typically poetic character. First, individual words and short phrases:

1, 3 *sinistrae* ("perverse"): CAT. 29.15; VERG. *Aen.* 11.347.[42]
2, 1 *inopina* ("unexpected"): VERG. *Aen.* 5.857, 6.104, 8.476; OV. *met.* 4.232 [PLIN. *paneg.* 30.2] (*TLL* VII.I.1751.65).

---

38. See Green ad loc.
39. If Green's text is accepted.
40. See below on 45, 6.
41. See also Étienne 1962: 259 and various favourable notices collected by Galletier 1955: 62–3.
42. Russell 1998: 44 identifies Pacatus Drepanius in particular for having "quotations and allusions out of Virgil."

3, 3 *diluuio* ("inundation"): VERG. *Aen.* 7.228; VAL. FL. 6.394 (*TLL* V.1191.60–61).
3, 4 *uiuax* ("vivid"; see also AVSON. *Grat. act.* 16.74):[43] VERG. *ecl.* 7. 30; HOR. *sat.* 2.2.132; OV. *am.* 2.6.54, *met.* 3.194.
3, 4 *fuscare* ("grows dark"): VAL. FL. 1.396; SIL. 11.268 (*TLL* VI.1652.72–73).
3, 5 *tantam molem* ("so great a mass"; see also XI(3).3.4, VIII(4).6.4, XII(9).24.2, IV(10).18.2): VERG. *Aen.* 1.33.
4, 3 *arctois* ("Arctic"): LVCAN 1.53, 10.250; SEN. *Oed.* 606 (*TLL* 11.472.31).
4, 4 *adde tot egregias ciuitates* ("Add so many outstanding cities"): VERG. *georg.* 2.155–7; AVSON. *Mos.* 454–8.[44]
4, 4 *prouentu* ("yield"): VERG. *georg.* 2.518 (*TLL* X.2.2314.28).
4, 5 *reptata* ("crawled"): STAT. *Theb.* 5.581.
5, 2 *sanguineus* ("bloody"): SIL. *Pun.* 4.593, 10.319.
7, 4 *aliquantisper* ("for a short while"): PLAVT. *pseud.* 571; TER. *Ad.* 639, *Heaut.* 572 (*TLL* 1.1602.59).
8, 3 *aeui maturus* ("mature in age"): VERG. *Aen.* 5.73; STAT. *Theb.* 5.90.
9, 2 *ad plenum* ("fully"; see also, AVSON. *Grat. act.* 13, 62): VERG. *georg.* 2.244; HOR. *Carm.* 1.17.14.
10, 2 *arma suspenderas* ("you had hung up your weapons"): VERG. *Aen.* 6.859; SIL. 6.446.
11, 1 *obnixe* ("determinedly"): PLAVT. *Stich.* 45; TER. *And.* 161 (*TLL* IX.2.123.45–46).
11, 3 *relapsa* ("fallen back"): HOR. *epist.* 1.1.18, *epod.* 17.18.
13, 3 *solantem* ("comforting"): VERG. *georg.* 1.159, 293; HOR. *carm.* 2.5.7.
14, 1 *gemmis* ("jewelled cup"): VERG. *georg.* 2.506; OV. *met.* 8.573 (*TLL* VI.1756.70).
18, 4 *subseruit* ("serve"): NAEV. *com.* 111; PLAVT. *Men.* 766; TER. *And.* 735.
19, 1 *externat* ("it terrifies"): CAT. 64, 71, 165; OV. *met.* 1.641, 11.77 (*TLL* V.2.1911.16–17).
19, 2 *deriguit* ("grew numb"): VERG. *Aen.* 3.260, 7.447; OV. *met.* 14.754; LVCAN 3.613 (*TLL* V.632.21–22).
20, 5 *osor* ("hater"): PLAVT. *As.* 859, *Poen.* 74; AVSON. *ep.* 13.24 (*TLL* IX.2.1116.41–42).
21, 1 *ambulacra* ("walkways"): PLAVT. *Most.* 756, 817 (*TLL* I.1869.13).
21, 4 *densissima ... testudine* ("very dense shell"): VERG. *Aen.* 9.514; LVCAN 3.474.
23, 2 *emicuit* ("broke out"): LVCR. 2.195; VERG. *Aen.* 5.319, 337; OV. *met.* 10.653 (*TLL* V.2.484.26–27).
24, 3 *iuuat meminisse* ("it is sweet to remember"): VERG. *Aen.* 1.203.

---

43. See above Green's emendation of Ausonius's *cum uiuaci recordatione* at *Grat. act.* 16, 74 1991: 592; if the emendation is upheld, this must be the source for Pacatus Drepanius.
44. Rees 2013a: 248–50.

24, 5 *contiguus* ("neighbouring"): Ov. *met.* 4.57; *ars* 3.410 (*TLL* IV.698.55–56).
25, 3 *incestat* ("pollute"; see also IV(10).8.4, II(12).29.3): VERG. *Aen.* 6.150 (*TLL* VII.1.893.7).
26, 4 *reiectare* ("to throw up"): LVCR. 2.328; SIL. 7.421.
26, 5 *reuomebat* ("vomited back"): LVCR. 2.199; VERG. *Aen.* 5.182; Ov. *met.* 13.731; SEN. *Ag.* 500, *Thy.* 581; SIL. 2.308; VAL. FL. 1.822.
29, 3 *incestauerant* ("they had polluted"; see also IV(10).8.4, II(12).25.3): VERG. *Aen.* 6.150 (*TLL* VII.1.893.3).
29, 3 *impiabant* ("they defiled"): PLAVT. *Rud.* 191, *Poen.* 384; SEN. *Phaed.* 1186 (*TLL* VII.1.620.29–31).
30, 1 *abrumpere* ("break"): VERG. *Aen.* 3.55; SIL. 1.296, 2.451; STAT. *Theb.* 3.655.
30, 2 *claustra laxaret* ("opened the barrier"): VERG. *Aen.* 2.259; SEN. *Oed.* 401, *Tro.* 430–1; SIL. 13.550, 14.185–6; Ivv. 8.261.
32, 4 *alternabat excubias* ("take turn on watch"): SIL. 9.93.
32, 5 *comparcendo* ("by making good provision"): TER. *Phorm.* 44 (*TLL* III.2050.25–26).
33, 2 *eborata* ("ivoried"): PLAVT. *Aul.* 168, *Stich.* 377 (*TLL* V.2.7.21–22).
33, 4 *suspirans* ("sighing"): CAT. 64.98.
34, 1 *puluereus* ("dusty"): VAL. FL. 4.608; STAT. *Silu.* 4, 3, 88, *Theb.* 6.7 (*TLL* X.2.2619.60–61).
34, 3 *imperuius* ("impassable"): Ov. *met.* 9.106; VAL. FL. 4.711 (*TLL* VII.1.594.80).
34, 3 *glomerantur* ("they were massed together"): VERG. *Aen.* 2.727, 9.440; STAT. *Theb.* 2.585 (*TLL* VI.2059.15–17).
34, 4 *decolor* ("discoloured"): CIC. (poet.) *Tusc.* 2.8, 20; Ov. *trist.* 4.2.42; STAT. *Theb.* 12.410 (*TLL* V.198.77–78).
35, 3 *horrebat* ("was bristling"): ENN. *Ann.* 285; VERG. *Aen.* 11.601–2 (*TLL* VI.2976.78).
37, 3 *exsequiale* ("funereal"): Ov. *met.* 14.430; STAT. *Theb.* 6.123, 11.610; AVSON. *par. praef.* B. 4, 21, 8, 25, 8 (*TLL* V.2.1849.8–9).
37, 4 *undantes* ("waving"): VAL. FL. 1.539; STAT. *Theb.* 1.449.
38, 3 *fatiscit* ("grows weak"): SIL. 2.315; STAT. *Theb.* 4.187, 8.705, 11.92 (*TLL* VI.353.48–49).
38, 4 *cassibus* ("snares"): VERG. *georg.* 3.371 (*TLL* III.518.48).
40, 1 *feriato* ("on vacation"): PLAVT. *Mil.* 1.7 (*TLL* VI.518.27).
41, 1 *abiuras* ("you repudiate"): PLAVT. *Curc.* 496, *Pers.* 478, *Rud.* 14; VERG. *Aen.* 8.263 (*TLL* I.102.27).
42, 3 *Diris . . . ultricibus* ("the avenging Furies"): VERG. *Aen.* 4.473, 610; VAL. FL. 5.445; STAT. *Theb.* 11.106.
42, 3 *crepitantia* ("rustling"): PLAVT. *Men.* 926; LVCR. 5, 229, 747, 6, 155; VERG. *georg.* 1.85, *Aen.* 3.70, 5.436, 459, 7.74.

43, 4 *funebris* ("deadly"): Ov. *trist.* 4.4.85; Hor. *epist.* 1.19.49 (*TLL* VI.1581.48–49).
44, 5 *anguipedum* ("snake-footed"): Ov. *met.* 1.184, *trist.* 4.7.17; Manil. 4.581 (*TLL* II.51.56–57).
45, 2 *auulsum humeris Maximi caput et sine nomine corpus* ("Maximus's head torn from his shoulders and the torso without a name"): Verg. *Aen.* 2.557–8.[45]

To confirm this list's characterization of Pacatus Drepanius as stylistically ambitious, his lexical innovation can be seen in three hapax legomena: *amplificatrix* ("she who amplifies," 8.5), *durator* ("hardener," 33.4), and *precabundus* ("prayerful," 36.3); *palmata* ("a tunic embroidered with palm-trees," 9.6) may be the word's first occurrence (see above, Avson. *Grat. act.* 11.53).

Some of the vocabulary above appears in a series of phrases and clauses which have a more sustained poetic turn, where Pacatus Drepanius reaches for novel expression: *geminis Delos reptata numinibus* ("Delos crawled by the twin gods," 4.5), *aestates in bella sudatas* ("summers sweated in campaigns," 8.3), *in gemmis capacibus* ("in voluminous crystals" [i.e., "drinking cups"], 14.1), *deriguit in mortem* ("she grew numb in death," 19.2), *ne morti sepultura contingeret* ("so that there would be no burial for the death," 34.4), *ut clausae cassibus ferae* ("like wild animals caught in snares," 38.4), *otioso feriatoque ferro* ("with weaponry leisured and on vacation," 40.1), *doctarum noctium* ("learned nights," 44.4).

In addition, some passages sustain poetic colour at greater length and/or adopt poetic topoi: for example, early in the elaborate description of Theodosius's home country of Spain, a distinct reprisal of Vergil's praise of Italy from the *Georgics* (perhaps also intended to trump Ausonius's adoption of the same passage in his description of Gaul, *Mos.* 454–8)[46] leads to a flamboyant catalogue of poetic commendations of geographical regions (4.4–5); the personified State addresses Theodosius in plaintive prosopopoeia (11.4–7); the River Save is discoloured and choked by the enemy dead in battle (34.3–4); in flight from Theodosius, Maximus utters a pathetic soliloquy (38.2–4); a council of personified virtues debate which of them contributed most to Theodosius's success (40.2–4) (Rees 2013a).

10.15. Conclusions

There are undeniable methodological problems in any attempt to plot poeticism in prose over time; the samples in this study are relatively small, both of the prose panegyrics and the verse source texts from which the data is generated;

---

45. Lunn-Rockliffe 2010: 329.
46. Rees 2013a: 249–50.

false positives may have emerged unnoticed from the accidents of survival or from the cultivation of a canon; and the judgements inherent in classification of literary phenomena as "poetic" or "prosaic," themselves ideological (consciously or not), can hardly yield reliable statistical values. Nonetheless, this study's survey method reveals difference and development over time, and so, after tendering some broad brush conclusions, I shall seek to relate them to the contexts of generic evolution and literary collectivity in Late Antiquity.

The Dyarchic (X(2), XI(3)), Tetrarchic (VIII(4), IX(5)), and early Constantinian speeches (VII(6), VI(7), V(8)) are not without poetic colour in trope (simile, ekphrasis, prosopopoeia) and lexis. There is some variety across these seven speeches, with X(2) of 289 presenting the most colour, and V(8) of 311 the least; but within the seven, the varying levels of poetic colour deny a chronological trajectory. Ennius ghosts in the first four speeches, Vergil in all of them; despite its relative lack of adventure, V(8) offers the anthology's first neologism. Without any material for comparison from the earlier third century, it is difficult to say how innovative the poetic colouring in these speeches was;[47] perhaps it is suitably cited in support of the "dilettantism" Christian Rönning identified emerging in the culture of inheriting, studying, copying, and composing oratory which flourished in the Gallic schools of Late Antiquity, such as Eumenius's Maenianae at Autun (2007: 139–51). From the evidence of these speeches it certainly seems to have been the case that poetic colour could comprise "noble ornament for the ritual praise of emperors" (Walker 2000: 308).

One event in particular in Roman history is given prominence in the *PanLat* collection by, uniquely, being the subject of two speeches; that is, the Battle of the Milvian Bridge (IV(10) and XII(9); Rees 2012); in their manuscript sequence, the two speeches tidily bookend the "diverse VII" (Mynors 1964: 174) and doubly celebrate Constantine's victory over Maxentius. This study demonstrates that the same two speeches are (perhaps not coincidentally) significant milestones too in the evolution of literary aesthetics in the Latin epideictic of Late Antiquity. First, they demonstrate an intensification in Vergilian colour (Rees 2004a: 39–44, 2013b: 216–7); it is tempting to attribute this to the Tiber battle setting shared by Aeneas and Constantine. And in some poetic features in XII(9), such as the reworking of a river simile from X(2)5.3 (9.5), and the laboured discussion of a Vergilian quotation (12–13), a marked sense of self-awareness can be identified, although in the latter case in particular, it may be accompanied by a little diffidence. But of these two speeches, linked by common

---

47. In parenthesis, Menander Rhetor, usually dated to the late third century, proves the detail that inclusion of prosopopoeia was a recent practice (*Basilikos Logos* 374).

subject matter and Vergilian register, it is the later orator, Nazarius, who works boldly with richer poetic colour. His self-referential remarks at 1, 1 may be dismissed as formulaic, but the more indulgent return to the subject of his own oratory and style at 30.3 confirms the impression, established by his narrative to that point, of sustained poetic lexis and trope working together in a steeper aesthetic trajectory; his count of hapax legomena (8, against 1 in each of V(8) and XII(9)) confirms this sense of a step change in ambition and adventure.

After the intensification of poeticism in the later Constantinian *Panegyrici*, the consular *gratiarum actio* of Claudius Mamertinus has a more measured aesthetic. Poetic colour through lexis is consistently applied in the speech but without conspicuous topoi.[48] There are fewer (3) neologisms than Nazarius's eight but perhaps enough to justify the conclusion that lexical innovation had consolidated its place in prose stylistics.

Although not in the *PanLat*, the panegyrics of Symmachus appear broadly to maintain the trajectory towards an increase in self-conscious poetic colour, in lexis, trope, and evocation of verse (although the fragmentary state of the speeches demands a degree of speculation here). Perhaps surprisingly, it is the consular *gratiarum actio* of Ausonius—the fourth century's most versatile Latin poet—with its generally plainer style, that is anomalous. However, there is some poetic colour (with a notable incidence of Horatian allusion) and lexical innovation. Ausonius's friend Pacatus Drepanius, generally assumed to be the editor of *PanLat*, gives most energy to the trajectory towards increased poetic colour. In lexis, topos, and reference to epic and tragic discourse, his speech self-consciously and repeatedly engages poetic adventure.

There is, then, considerable variety in the nature and intensity of poetic colour in late antique Latin prose panegyric. A trajectory can be plotted, which although far from linear, attests an intensification of this stylistic register over time. It would have developed in fits and starts, such as the speeches of 289, 313, and those of Nazarius, and Pacatus Drepanius', and would be largely resisted by some, such as in Ausonius's relatively monochromatic *gratiarum actio*. This chronological reading of late Latin prose panegyric presents its evolution as congruent with a general tendency in Latin prose, that is, in post-Augustan prose texts, such as Tacitus and Apuleius: a willingness to deploy poetic lexis and topos not attested in Republican prose, such as Cicero (Harrison 2005). In the panegyrics, the poetic lexis which tends to dominate is from Vergilian and post-Vergilian epic, although not to the exclusion of Republican texts, especially drama and epic. How consciously or otherwise each instance was deployed is

---

48. Browning was right to see stylistic variety in the collection but overlooked a great deal of evidence when he concluded, "Only Claudius Mamertinus . . . makes frequent use of poetic words" (1982a: 758).

moot, but a striking overall effect is how the poetics of early Imperial epic in particular features in a collection which tends to cite, as historical exempla, heroes and events from the Republican era.[49] Against the recommendations of progymnasmata and treatises, which might encourage the notion of a static, stagnating, ossified genre, panegyrical poetics were in flux, the general direction of which was to bring this prose closer to poetry.[50]

This trajectory in panegyrical poetics needs to be understood together with the speeches' alignment towards Ciceronian oratory (especially the *Pro lege Manilia* and the Caesarian speeches) and Pliny's *Panegyricus*, which scholarship has long recognized.[51] What is revealed is that along with the generic markers and ideological associations which situate the speeches within a tradition of political praise giving, there was a culture of, and appetite for, literary adventure. It was probably always thus: in the first century BCE, Publilius Syrus spoke of praise giving's inherent need to innovate in order to maintain its credibility: *nisi laus noua nascitur etiam uetus laus in incerto iacet ac saepe amittitur* ("unless praise is born afresh, even old praise becomes suspect and is lost"); in a letter discussing his consular *gratiarum actio* to Trajan (of 100 CE), Pliny spoke of the genre's tiredness *in ceteris enim lectorem nouitas ipsa intentum habet, in hac nota uulgata dicta sunt omnia* ("for in other [genres], the novelty itself holds the reader rapt, in this everything is known, familiar, already said," *ep.* 3.13.2).[52] As a subcategory of oratory, panegyric dealt in comparison and superlatives and so was intrinsically subject to inflation. To stand out, each new orator would be under pressure to say something that was new or differently conceived, and new ground was probably more easily broken aesthetically than thematically; and so poetic adventure would have its attractions. For the panegyricists of Late Antiquity, introduction of poetic colour was available as a means of renewing praise discourse: by reference to poetry and poets, intertext by quotation and paraphrase, lexical adventure in neologism, and incorporation of poetic lexis and topoi.

But in addition to panegyric's innate inclination to find novelty, the aesthetic trajectory of surviving speeches also needs to be understood within the context of literary collection. Anthologized, quite possibly in two or more stages, the *PanLat* invite comparison amongst themselves (Rees 2013a: 241–3; Formisano 2015); and although published separately, it seems likely, from their intertextual relationships with the *PanLat*, that the speeches of Symmachus

---

49. Nixon 1990.
50. For the concept of "intrasystemic hybridization," see Hernández Lobato 2012: 468–70.
51. See, e.g., Klotz 1911, Rees 2011a, and Gibson and Rees 2013.
52. Pliny addresses the issue in the speech itself, *Paneg.* 2, 2; see also Mart. 10, 72.

and Ausonius were written in awareness of them. Chronological resequencing does violence to editorial design but permits a clearer view of a generic evolution. From the survey above, the two crucial figures are Nazarius and Pacatus Drepanius. Whether or not he was the editor of an earlier collection, later to be absorbed within the *PanLat* (so Barnes 2011: 181–4), the bold stylistic adventure of Nazarius's speech seems to have been an inspiration to Pacatus Drepanius: Nazarius's enthusiasm for poetic lexis and topos, as well as for lexical neologism, is unprecedented in the genre but bears comparison with Pacatus Drepanius's later composition. Nazarius's influence is perhaps less conspicuous when the speeches are presented in manuscript sequence, where Pacatus Drepanius's sits second, sandwiched between the consular *gratiarum actiones* of Pliny and Claudius Mamertinus, with Nazarius's next; but nonetheless, threads such as the neologisms *discriminatrix* (*PanLat* IV(10).7.4), *inflammatrix* (III(11).3.3), *amplificatrix* (II(12).8.5), suggest a high degree of self-consciousness and awareness of the collection's chronology.

And Nazarius aside, another example of Pacatus Drepanius's awareness of his place on an aesthetic trajectory can be seen in his closing comments: we saw above how the opening paragraph of the first late antique speech emphasized the difference between poetry and panegyric: *neque enim fabula est de licentia poetarum* ("For this is not a story taken from the licence of poets," X(2).1.3), reprised by both Symmachus and Ausonius. In the final paragraph of the collection, Pacatus Drepanius says: *ad me longinquae conuenient ciuitates, a me gestarum ordinem rerum stilus omnis accipiet, a me argumentum poetica, a me fidem sumet historia* ("To me cities will come from afar, from me every pen will receive the sequence of events, from me poetry will take its subject matter, from me historiography will gain its reliability," II(12).47.6). And so, at the end of a speech with conspicuous poetic colour, Pacatus Drepanius narrows the gap between his epideictic prose and poetry. This highlights how far epideictic aesthetics had evolved since the opening paragraph of the speech of a century before and, as such, represents Pacatus Drepanius in his own time as the end and high point in the narrative of the aesthetics of political praise discourse but by no means its only innovator.

Pacatus Drepanius's closing ambition to inspire historiography and poetry, in combination with his speech's frequent turns to poetic locus and wide deployment of poetic lexis, could be testament to the resurgence of interest in Augustan and post-Augustan poetry in the late fourth century (Cameron 2011: 8); it could have been inspired to further poetic colour in prose by the ground distinctively broken by Nazarius especially; and its heightened poetic colour could be read politically as indicative of the magnetic brilliance of Theodosius, set, according to Pacatus Drepanius, to be the focal point of all literary endeavour thereafter. That is, if Theodosius was at the high point of panegyric's aesthetic curve, we might wonder if the curve was the product of the collection's editorial organization. If so, Latin prose panegyric's curve of heightened poetic colour was less a function of "organic" literary aesthetics than of the manipulation of aesthetics to advance a political petition.

But whatever its motivation, we should note that Pacatus Drepanius's high point was not Latin panegyric's end point. Prose did not function independently of poetry;[53] Ausonius and Pacatus Drepanius wrote both, for example. Although not the focus of this study, it is relevant to note that the gap of four decades between Nazarius's panegyric of 321 and the next surviving prose panegyric (362) leapfrogs various Latin *verse* panegyrics: the anonymous *Laudes Domini*, the works of Optatianus Porfyrius and the closing section of Juvencus's *Libri Euangeliorum*.[54] This concerted co-option of poetry for praise of the first Christian emperor proves an eye-catching complement to the developments in prose. And the next body of panegyrical Latin to survive after the *PanLat*, that is, from 395, and whose author seems to have known the prose collection, was the smooth hexameter poetry of Claudian (Kehding 1899; Cameron 1970; Ware 2012; Gillett 2012).[55]

---

53. Cf. "the conventions of poetry were not the same as those of prose," Cameron 1970: 195.
54. For some recent discussions, see Rees 2010c, Green 2010, Schierl 2010, and Squire in this volume.
55. With thanks to audiences at Oxford and Brussels.

The Lies the Poets Tell

Poetry in Prose Panegyrics

CATHERINE WARE

Phrases such as *fabulae poetarum* or *licentia poetarum*, the inventions or licence of poets, are a trope of late antique encomium, occurring in the *Panegyrici Latini* corpus, the panegyrics of Ausonius and Symmachus, and even in the poetry of Claudian.[1] On the surface, they are a figure of hyperbole, and not meant to be taken literally. Yet a disparaging reference to *fabulae*, the stories of myth, or to the inventions of the poets is very relevant to the study of prose panegyric, a genre which demands the appearance of sincerity. Poetry and panegyric were seen to have a shared origin, but Isocrates, the father of panegyric, had denied poetic licence to political orators whose use of language, he asserted, had to be precise and factual.[2] It is true that Latin panegyrics were classified as epideictic oratory, a genre with the aim of *delectatio* (delight), but by Late Antiquity, panegyric had acquired a significant political dimension. An orator voicing the requests of his city could not always afford the whimsy of poetic invention, and as a result the orators of the *Panegyrici Latini* repeatedly distinguish between their own works and the *fabulae poetarum*.

This chapter examines the trope as an introduction to the complex and interdependent relationship of panegyric and poetry. The educated audience knew well that the condemnation of *fabulae poetarum* was rhetorical misdirection, an apparent attempt to distract attention from the fact that panegyric and poetry had a great deal in common. Their knowledge enabled the conceit of the *fabula poetarum* to be maintained. By means of a critical reference to poetic licence, a panegyrist could offer one unlikely fact in place of another and could introduce the persuasion of poetry while maintaining an illusion of truth. Such a phrase as *ut poetae ferunt* might signal a direct allusion or, by means of a non-specific

---

[1]. My thanks are due to the Irish Research Council for their generous funding of my research, and to Bruce Gibson and Emily Kneebone for their helpful suggestions and advice.
  Greek abbreviations follow the style of DGE; Latin abbreviations follow the TLL with the exception of Ausonius, which follows Green 1991; the *Panegyrici Latini* collection, which Mynors 1964 (with the correction of 9(5) for 9(4) and 8(4) for 8(5)); and Claudian, which follows Cameron 1970.

[2]. *Eu.* 8–10; see Morford 1992: 579. On Isocrates and the relationship between poetry and oratory, see Johnson 1959.

reference, prompt the audience to think of the different variations of the myth with which they were familiar. In this way, although the formula appears the same, poetry is not condemned. The trope becomes ludic, almost paradoxical, and the educated audience, familiar with the conventions of panegyric and praise, would have appreciated this as it was intended.

In some cases, however, the trope has a more complex significance and serves to introduce some very real criticism of the role of poetry in Imperial encomium. The persuasive power of the poets had never been denied, but it was accepted as a positive power only in the case of Ennius and Vergil. These two alone were openly honoured by the panegyrists, and their work alone was explicitly cited as authoritative. The works of other poets and the use to which their poetry was put could not be trusted and was seen sometimes even as subversive since it offered an unworthy comparison for the emperor. This chapter looks at two such examples from prose panegyrics of the *Panegyrici Latini* collection in which the orators use the *fabulae poetarum* trope to examine and comment critically on the true relationship of poetry and praise. The chapter's final section looks at the trope in Claudian's verse encomia and argues that when writing as panegyrists, poets and orators alike had very definite expectations of the role of poetry in praise.

11.1. Poetry and Panegyric

The history of poetry and praise was a complicated one. Epic had been recognized as the medium of praise since Homer first sang of great men and their battles.[3] Ennius had honoured contemporary heroes, and his imitators had, in the words of Goldberg, "brought Republican epic to the brink of panegyric."[4] By writing of the mythic history of Rome and the ancestors of the Julian family, Vergil brought epic back from that brink and distanced his theme from explicit encomium, but the Julio-Claudian and Flavian emperors would be lauded to a greater or lesser extent in the epics of Ovid, Lucan, Statius, and Silius, and by the late fourth century, schoolchildren were routinely taught that the *Aeneid* had been written in honour of Augustus.[5] In that period also, court panegyric and

---

3. HOR. *ars* 73–4: *Res gestae regumque ducumque et tristia bella* ("the deeds and grim wars of kings and generals"), cf. VERG. *ecl.* 6.38.
4. Goldberg 2005: 15, with reference to such poets as Varro of Atax and Furius Bibaculus.
5. SERV. *Aen. pr.*, cf. DON. *Aen.* 1.2.19–25. Although the works themselves have not survived, there is evidence that epics celebrating contemporary events or individuals were written during the third and fourth centuries AD. Proba, e.g., in the prologue to her *Cento*, refers to an earlier work on the war between Magnentius and Constantius, *regum crudelia bella* ("the cruel wars of kings," *cento* 3), see Cameron 2011: 333–5; on the continuing tradition of encomiastic epic from the Hellenistic period to Late Antiquity, see Cameron 1995: 268–71.

heroic epic were formally reunited in the poetry of Claudian, who glorified the rulers of the Roman West in his short contemporary epics.[6] While the encomiastic element varied greatly in all of these, the genre itself conferred magnification. The subject of an epic panegyric was intertextually the heir to Achilles and Aeneas and could be extolled with all the techniques of poetic language and imagery available to the poet. As Hermogenes stated expansively in his treatise *Types of Style*, "[a]ll poetry is certainly panegyric, and is the most panegyric of all discourse. . . . If someone says that poetry is panegyric in meter, I shall not dispute it."[7] Hermogenes does not concern himself with the truthfulness of the content, nor would any such concern be relevant to poetic praise. Prose panegyrics, however, had evolved to suit rather different requirements.

Epideictic oratory had been seen initially as less serious than the other branches of rhetoric since it was not required for politics or law but designed only to give pleasure and delight to the listener.[8] On principle, the Romans had been opposed to flattery, but as Cicero admitted, sometimes such a speech was needed,[9] whether for a funeral oration or the *gratiarum actio*, the expression of gratitude from a newly appointed consul. The value in being able to deliver a ceremonial speech soon became apparent,[10] and it is evident from the writings of Fronto and Pliny that by the second century AD, the competent performance of a panegyric was an essential skill for those in public life. Mastering the decorative technique of the panegyric was not easy, as Fronto advised Marcus Aurelius, since there was no place for plain style and all must be adorned, *ubique ornandum* (3.17.2). The best way to acquire the stylistic techniques was by studying verse.[11] That Fronto's advice was followed is evident in the trend towards poeticization in the panegyrics of Late Antiquity.[12]

By the fourth century, panegyric had become an intrinsic part of court ceremonial, being delivered on all formal occasions.[13] An imperial *aduentus*, for example, was marked by a number of panegyrics[14] in which the most skilful

---

6. On Claudian and the invention of "panegyric epic," see most recently Schindler 2009, Gillett 2012, cf. Ware 2012: 18–20.
7. 2.10.3.89; see Walker 2000: 114.
8. *ad uoluptatem auditoris et ad delectationem*, CIC. *part*. 21,72, cf. QVINT. *inst*. 2.10.11.
9. CIC. *De or*. 2.341.
10. See Rees 2010b.
11. *Plerumque enim ad orationem faciendam uersus, ad uersificandum oratio magis adiuuat* (FRONT. 2.17.2); on studying the poets for help with the florid style, see Bloomer 2011: 104.
12. See Rees in this volume; cf. also Roberts 1991: 63. In its turn, panegyric would be very influential on medieval poetry, Curtius 1953: 154–66.
13. MacCormack 1976: 36–7. Further evidence of the importance of rhetoric is evident in the proliferation of oratorical treatises in this period; on Latin and Greek treatises, see Pernot 2000: 128–201.
14. The orator of 310 AD, for example, suggests that he did not know on what day he would be called on to speak, which suggests that his was not the only panegyric delivered to Constantine on that visit; *PL* 6(7)1–2.

rhetoricians from neighbouring cities, *homines disertissimi*, would speak the emperor's praises (*PL* 12(9)1.1) and address him on behalf of their cities. To what extent the panegyrist was also expected to articulate Imperial policy is a matter of debate, but the *Panegyrici Latini* make it clear that the orator was the ambassador for his city and his speech a medium for civic requests.[15] The late antique orator, therefore, faced a conflict of stylistic interests, having to present a very real request in a format and in language understood to be decorative only.

The vocabulary with which the orators contrast their own facts with another's fiction reveals much about their acknowledgement of this dichotomy. The existence of poetic licence was accepted since poetry was designed, as Pacatus Drepanius observes, to delight the ear.[16] That it was naturally mendacious was also accepted.[17] As the Emperor Julian asserted in his panegyric to Constantius, poets were given unlimited licence of invention by their Muse, and he himself dismissed all accounts of visions and prophecies as deriving from this licence (*or.* 1.1B, 10B). The Latin panegyrists were of the same opinion. Even if truth lay at the foundation of an anecdote, it was dressed up by the lies of the poets and given authority by the passage of time, (*quae mendaciis uatum ... fidem tempori debent, PL* 2(12)17.2).[18] The combined unreliability of poetry and Antiquity appeared again in Pacatus Drepanius's address to artists as he orders them to spurn the threadbare evidence of stories of old, *uulgata illa ueterum fabularum argumenta despicite* (2(12)44.5).[19] Whether a *fabula* is a poetic creation or

---

15. For example, *PL* 9(5) is a request for the restoration of schools, and 6(7)22 of 310 AD invites Constantinople to visit Autun (the benefits of this visit are clear from 5(8) of 311, which thanks him for the generosity he displayed on the visit). For the discussion as to the extent of the political aspect of these speeches, see MacCormack 1976: 53–4, Nixon 1983: 92, Grünewald 1990: 9, Nixon 1993: 232–3, Ando 2000: 127.

16. *PL* 2(12)4.4: *scio fabulas poetarum auribus mulcendis repertas* ("I know that the stories of the poets were devised to persuade the ear"); cf. SYMM. *or.* 1.4; see Rees 2004a: 36–7. This is an ancient idea in Greek and Latin literary criticism and found in PL. *r.* 601b. On this topic in relation to Christianity, see Mastrangelo in this volume, 393–400; cf. also Clark on Augustine.

17. The notion goes back to HES. (*th.* 26–8). As a variation on the topos, the scrupulous author acknowledged that verification was necessary: *utique si poetica recipiatur fabulositas* (PLIN. *nat.* 7.101).

18. Maguinness 1933: 135 refers to this as a variation of the formula of contemptuous acquiescence, by which "the orator refers to some tradition of history or legend, to which he flings a casual or disparaging assent, stating or implying that *he* has much greater things to tell."

19. Cf. also *PL* 10(2)1.3, *neque enim fabula est de licentia poetarum nec opinio de fama ueterum saeculorum* ("for this is neither an invention of the licence of poets nor a fancy from the rumour of past ages"). The combination of poetry and myth is posited as the opposite to true history in Livy's preface, *Quae ante conditam condendamue urbem poeticis magis decora fabulis quam incorruptis rerum gestarum monumentis traduntur* ("what is said to have happened before the city was founded or during its foundation is suitable more for the invention of poets than the genuine records of history," *pr.* 6). *Fabulosa* is used to describe the mythic history of the Mamertini (*PL* 5(8)3.1). Ammianus distinguishes between the truth and fiction of Antiquity in *fabulae* and *ueridicae antiquitates* (26,10,15).

a myth from Antiquity, it is by its nature improbable, and its improbability is emphasized by the vagueness of the reference; the sources of the *fabulae* are rarely made explicit. Occasionally, an orator may accept the truth of Antiquity but only because he has seen equal or greater contemporary miracles. Ausonius ceased to wonder at the licence of the poets, *nec iam miramur licentiam poetarum*, because he had experienced the might of Gratian,[20] while the power of Jupiter to change the weather and shake the world at a nod was proved by the power of Julian.[21] More usually, the fabrications of Antiquity serve to highlight the truth offered by the orator, whether it is the wealth of Spain, the providence of Constantine, or Julian's journey on the Danube.[22]

Panegyric attracted similar criticism to poetry. As it was intended for pleasure, *delectatio*, and its aim was magnification and adornment, praise could be concerned with truth only marginally, and in response orators duly made a parade of their sincerity.[23] In praising Valentinian, Symmachus rejects the fantastic *exempla* created by *licentia poetarum*. He selects instead his comparisons from history, which he saw as a more credible genre because less boastful, *credamus historiis minora iactantibus* (*or*. 1.4–5). To write panegyric may have been to write in the higher generic style, *maior stilus*, but the very adjective implied exaggeration.[24] *Extollere aliquid in maius* is to praise something beyond its deserts, and it is the phrase used by Mamertinus of the invention of the Greek poets.[25] Further, panegyric, *laudatio*, was by definition prejudiced and so untrustworthy. Speaking of the Roman custom of honouring family tradition by *laudationes*, Cicero decreed that encomia made the history of his time mendacious.[26] From this conflict of interests arose the sensitivity with which the orators

---

20. Avson. *Grat. act.* 5; see Green 1991: 540.

21. *PL* 3(11)28.5; cf. 4(10)15.5.

22. Spain stands out among other countries extolled by the *fabulae poetarum* (2(10)4.4), while the sight of Constantine surpasses that of Lynceus, whose abilities are described by poets, *ut poetae ferunt* (4(10)11.5). On the poets in question, see Nixon and Rodgers 1994: 355. Julian's journey on the Danube (3(11)8.104) is presented as an encomiastic challenge to poets of old.

23. Qvint. *inst.* 3.7.6 *proprium laudis est res amplificare et ornare*. See L'Huillier 1992: 98–101. Cic. *de orat.* 1.70 grants the poet more *licentia* in words but identical in freedom from boundaries and the same ability to claim what he will, *quo minus ei liceat eadem illa facultate et copia uagari, qua uelit*. For the accepted insincerity of panegyric, see Avg., *conf.* 6.6.9; Pliny makes it an important feature of his panegyric that under the good Emperor Trajan, an orator can speak freely, *Pan.* 3.5.

24. Amm. 31.16.9.

25. *PL* 3(11)8.1, cf. Clavd. *Get.* 14–15; cf. also Tac. *ann.* 15,30.

26. Cic. *Brut.* 62. A similar conflict can be perceived in historiography. For Cicero, the Sophists, who aimed to please by weaving stories (*fabulae*) elaborated with ornament and colour, are very like the historians whose narratives are told *ornate*, adorned with descriptions of places, events, and speeches (*orat.* 65–6), and who might even have more creative licence than the poets; see Russell in Laird 2006: 273. As Cic. *Brut.* 62 indicates, contemporary history may fall into the realm of panegyric; cf. Ivl. *ep.* 31, on which see L'Huillier 1992: 96; Amm. 31.16.9 and Evtr. 10.18.3, on which see Kelly 2007: 319–20.

handled poetry. The language with which they purported to weigh the evidence of the poets—*ut poetae ferunt, licentia poetarum, fabulae poetarum*—is that of grammarians and teachers and so gives didactic authority to their words.[27] By rejecting the poetic *fabulae* and *licentia*, the orators implied that their speeches were serious and reliable. This concept is clearly enunciated in Julian's panegyrics. In his oration to Constantius, he had allowed that the Muse had given the poets unlimited licence to invent but acknowledged also that orators too could "range the power of words against the nature of facts."[28] His second oration to Constantius is pointedly free from such licence (*or.* 2.74D–75A):

> These matters concerning the deeds of the emperor I have narrated in brief, adding nothing by way of flattery ... nor dragging in and forcing similarities from afar, just as they do who explain the stories of the poets and who interpret them in persuasive words which allow them to create fiction, starting from the smallest supposition ...

In reality, using the myths of poets to create fictions of their own is exactly what the panegyrists did, and it was a characteristic of the trope that the truth the orator presented was as unlikely as the myth it replaced. Maximian's descent from Hercules, for example, is not the invention of flatterers, *adulationibus fabulis*, but is proved by his virtues (*PL* 7(6)8.2). By means of this formula, gods could be put in their place (*finguntur haec de Ioue, sed de te uera sunt, imperator*, these things are made up about Jupiter but are told truly about you, emperor, 10(2)2.5),[29] and new fabrications could supplant old. Dismissing history as the transmission of errors regarding emperors of the past, *falso traditum de antiquis imperatoribus*, 7(6)8.4), the orator of 307 states that Maximian was the first emperor to move Roman standards across the Rhine against the barbarians, a verifiably false statement.[30] Varying the tone and adopting a didactic position, an orator could even rebuke the folly of those who believed in myth. In the panegyric of ca. 291 AD, the orator corrects those who believe that Maximian travels swiftly because he borrowed the chariots of day and night. This is the invention of the foolish, he states severely, but he himself will tell the truth: Maximian's *pietas*

---

27. Assessing the accuracy of information was one of the functions of ancient commentaries. Servius, e.g., advises his readers that the *secessus* of *Aen.* 1.159 is a poetic fiction, *id est fictus secundum poeticam licentiam locus*, although as discussed below, Vergil was considered to be generally free from such licence.

28. *or.* 1.1B, 1.1C. It has been argued that in this panegyric Julian assumes the persona of the philosopher who always tells the truth, and therefore the emphasis on truth and sincerity should not necessarily be taken at face value. On Julian and his encomiastic models for this pose, see Tougher 2012: 22–30.

29. This is perhaps a sly nod to the disputed traditions of Jupiter's infancy and claims of falsity in CALL. *Iou.* 4–8.

30. Nixon and Rodgers 1994: 201.

is the reason, *remoueamus istinc fabulas imperitorum, uerum loquamur: uestra uobis pietas* (11(3)8.4).³¹

11.2. PANEGYRIC AND POETIC COLOUR

Contrary to appearances, a reference to the imaginings of poets did not necessarily signify genuine criticism. Even a passing reference to the themes of poetry suggests that the honorand is deserving of epic aggrandizement. By extension, therefore, to dismiss poetry as an unworthy vehicle of encomium is to imply that the honorand is greater than the epic heroes of myth and history, an implication which was frequently voiced in the panegyrics.³² Further, a reference to the *fabulae poetarum* or the use of the tag *ut poetae ferunt* could in a variety of ways signal the insertion of poetry into the panegyric, by allusion or by poetic colour. When Pacatus Drepanius rejects the *uulgata illa ueterum fabularum argumenta*, the threadbare stories of old, he illustrates his point with examples intimately familiar to his audience through word and image, the labours of Hercules, the Indian triumphs of Dionysus, the wars of the snake-footed Giants (*Herculeos labores et Indicos Liberi triumphos et anguipedum bella monstrorum* 2(12)44.5).

In his analysis of allusion and intertextuality, Stephen Hinds discusses the complexities of the "Alexandrian footnote" and the use of such words as *ferunt* or *dicunt* to signal an allusion.³³ This can be seen in the condemnation of the cowardice of Maxentius at *PL* 12(9)14.2: *degeneris, ut dictum est, animos timor arguebat* (fear, as it is said, is proof of unworthy character), where *ut dictum est* prompts the audience to recall the familiar source, Dido's words regarding Aeneas, *degeneres animos timor arguit* (*Aen.* 4.13). The allusion is intended to be recognized, as it establishes Maxentius as lacking in the heroic qualities of Aeneas and by implication casts Constantine, the opponent of Maxentius, as Aeneas's heir. This almost exact quotation also prepares the audience for the highly allusive, Vergilian description of the battle of the Milvian Bridge, where the river Tiber, once protector of Aeneas, fights against Maxentius.³⁴

Such direct Alexandrian footnotes are rare in the *Panegyrici Latini*, but phrases citing *poetarum fabulae* do have an allusive function, if not necessarily

---

31. In the panegyric of 310, Constantine would also appear to travel in a divine chariot but without qualification (*PL* 6(7)7.5).
32. Theodosius, e.g., in youthful training surpasses Alexander, Scipio, or Hannibal (*PL* 2(12)8.4–5), while Maximian defeated a worse monster than Geryon (10(2)2.1).
33. Hinds 1998: 1–2; for the Alexandrian footnote, see Ross 1975: 78.
34. *PL* 12(9)18.1. On Vergilian allusion in this panegyric, see Rees 2004a: 39–40.

as specifically as the examples discussed by Hinds.[35] It is possible that the orators of the *Panegyrici Latini* had particular sources in mind when using the term *ut poetae ferunt*, but there are rarely verbal echoes to make this clear. When Nazarius praises the marvellous eyesight of Lynceus, the summary of his deeds, introduced by *ut poetae ferunt* (*PL* 4(10)11.4), does not seem to indicate a particular poet. The accompanying *exemplum*, the watchman on Sicily who could see ships in Italy, is said to belong to the same Antiquity, *eadem uetustas*, but *uetustas* seems to refer simply to the literary or mythic past rather than a shared literary origin. The listeners, therefore, depending on their familiarity with the *fabula*, are invited to think of a multitude of sources at once, the Lynceus of Horace or Valerius Flaccus or Ovid.[36] With an unspecified allusion, individual audience response supplies the intertext or intertexts, supplementing the deeds of Lynceus listed by the orator with those they remember from their own reading. Acting as a metaliterary signpost, the phrase *ut poetae ferunt* prompts not only the question "which poets say this?" but also "what exactly do the poets say?" The orator can give only a limited number of *exempla*, but the tag *ut poetae ferunt* leads to a multitude of others, limited only by the knowledge of the listener or the reader.

This is Ausonius's tactic in his praise of Gratian's speed: *quae enim umquam memoria transcursum tantae celeritatis uel in audacibus Graecorum fabulis commenta est*? (What recollection of such speed on a journey was ever mentioned even in the daring inventions of the Greeks? *Grat. act.* 81). The *fabulae* in question refer to mythical horses known for their speed: Pegasus, Cyllarus, and Arion. There is no single source apparent in this reference and the fact that Ausonius uses the plural, *fabulae*, suggests that he had no particular one in mind. The reader is free to choose Homer, Herodotus, Statius, or Vergil.[37]

The qualification of Ausonius's sources as Greek is unusual and merits consideration.[38] Green observes that commentators have seen a hint of Juvenal's *Graecia mendax* here,[39] a further disparagement of the unreliability of *fabulae*. This theory is borne out by a similar reference in Mamertinus's panegyric on

---

35. It is also possible that the orators had specific passages in mind but they have simply not yet been recognized by scholars. Considerable work remains to be done on the presence and role of intertextuality in this corpus since the work of Klotz 1911, although see, e.g., the recent short studies of Rees 2004a, Lunn-Rockliffe 2010, Ware 2014, and the collection of articles in Gibson and Rees 2013.

36. Nixon and Rodgers 1994: 355 suggest HOR. *epist.* 1.1.28, *sat.* 1.2.90; APOLLOD. 3.10.3, VAL. FL. 1.462–7; there are also references to Lynceus in Ov. *met.* 8.304 and in A.R. 1.151–5.

37. Pegasus appears in HDT 6.95.1 and HOM. *Il.* 6.201–2, Cyllarus and Arion in STAT. *silu.* 1.1.52–4.

38. Although cf. the citation of Greek poets at *PL* 10(2)11.3.

39. IVV. 10.174, Green 1991: 553, cf. SYMM. *or.* 2,8 and the citation of the Trojan war: *probabo Graeciam parua mentitam*. For this theme used rather differently, see Hernández Lobato 295–9 in this volume.

Julian in a passage which gives considerable insight into the nuanced relationship between panegyric and poetry. Mamertinus, unlike Ausonius or the writers of the *Panegyrici Latini*, was delivering a Latin panegyric to an emperor famous for his Greek writings, and in the emphatic *tuorum principum*, it is tempting to read a deliberate distinction between Greek and Latin encomium, the one poetic and fantastic, the other prosaic and sincere. If that was Mamertinus's intention, his rhetoric makes it clear that he is just as capable as any Greek of using the power of poetry (3(11)8.1–3):

> *O facundia potens Graecia! Omnium tuorum principum gesta in maius extollere sola potuisti, sola factorum glorias ad uerborum copiam tetendisti. Tu nauem unam propter aurati uelleris furtum et uirginis raptum in caelum usque sublatam sideribus consecrasti. . . . Quid tu, si ad scribendas celebrandasque res principis nostri animum adieceris, de Iuliani lembis liburnisque factura es?—quae non modo nihil cuiquam adimunt neque urbes hospitas populant, sed ultro omnibus populis immunitates priuilegia pecunias largiuntur.*

> O Greece, great in eloquence! You alone could augment the deeds of all your rulers, you alone could stretch out the glories of their achievements to equal the supply of your words. Because of the theft of a golden fleece and the abduction of a girl, you raised a single ship to the skies and honoured it as high as the stars. . . . If you were to give your attention to describing and extolling the achievements of our emperor, what would you make of Julian's cutters and galleys? Not only do they not plunder from anyone nor ravage cities but instead lavish immunities, privileges, and largesse on all peoples.

This is an epic interpolation in prose. The orator simultaneously criticizes poetry for exaggeration while incorporating poetic language and style. The passage begins with an epic invocation, the ship is elevated with the epic *unam*,[40] and in *aurati uelleris furtum et uirginis raptum*, the orator provides the colourful details of the myth. But the poetry presented here, the work of Greek eloquence, is clearly encomiastic epic. There is more than a suggestion here of Lucretius's address to Epicurus (3.1–3):

> *E tenebris tantis tam clarum **extollere** lumen*
> *qui primus **potuisti** inlustrans commoda uitae,*
> *te sequor, **o Graiae** gentis decus.*

---

40. Hardie 1993: 4–6. Note that *facundia* is also *sola*.

You who first were able to raise up so bright a light, illuminating the
advantages of life, I follow you, o glory of the Greek race.

but a more significant model, underlying *extollere* ... *tu nauem* ... *in caelum*,
is Ennius's promise of divinity to Romulus, *unus erit quem tu tolles in caerula
caeli / templa* (*ann*. 54–5). Ennius's lines would be identified with imperial encomium by Ovid, who quoted the lines to give Ennian authority to his version
of Augustan history.[41] Appropriately then, it is the task of Greek eloquence to
elevate the deeds of her emperors, *tuorum principum gesta in maius extollere*.
That she is erring on the side of flattery is suggested by *in maius* and also by
tetendisti. That the orator is unimpressed by her flattery is subtly conveyed by
his choice of vocabulary and his juxtaposition or even identification of *tuorum
principum gesta* with stories of myth. Is the listener to take the *gesta* as unrelated
to the story of the Argonautica, or does the orator mean to imply that Greek
eloquence (and epic poetry) did not differentiate between myth and reality?

Since the orator specifies Greek eloquence, the source is presumably the
Argonautica of Apollonius Rhodius, although it is unlikely that the orator knew
Apollonius at first hand and instead drew on Valerius Flaccus or the scholia
on Apollonius.[42] The summary he presents, however, suggests his own interpretation of the value of the myth. The details of the fleece and the stolen girl
are well known, but their insertion here does not add to the glory of the quest.
Apollonius had prefaced his work with an acknowledgement of Apollo as his
inspiration and his theme, the famous deeds of men of old, present here in *factorum glorias*, and the quest for the golden fleece (A.R. 1.1–4). In his preface,
Valerius had omitted the fleece and even postponed the deeds of the heroes, *uet-
erumque ... facta uirum* (1.10–11), devoting his opening lines to the glorification
and catasterism of the ship, *[quae] flammifero tandem consedit Olympo* (1.4).[43]
The orator here gives the ship its proper praise, *in caelum usque sublatam sideribus*, but the reasons for its elevations to the stars, the theft of a fleece and the
abduction of a girl, are unsatisfactory. The use of *furtum* to describe the quest is
unexpected, as the acquisition of the fleece was usually described in more neutral terms. Ennius's Argives simply sought it, *Argiui ... petebant pellem inaura-
tam*, and Hyginus describes it as being carried away, *pellem auratam auferri*.[44]

---

41. Ov. *met*. 14,814, also *fast*. 2.487; see Conte 1986: 57–9, Hinds 1998: 15–16; on the dissemination of the Ennian passage, see Elliott 2013: 354–5. Goldschmidt 2013: 129 sees this line as also influencing the apotheosis of Aeneas also at VERG. *Aen*. 1.259–60.

42. On the scholia, see Cameron 2004a: 63–4.

43. For Valerius's *Argonautica* and imperial encomium, see Stover 2013: 46–50; on the influence of Vergilian imperial invocation in this prologue, see Kleywegt 2005: 11.

44. ENN. *Med*. 212–13, HYG. *fab*. 22.2.

The undermining of the quest with the notion that the fleece was stolen comes from Juvenal and the list of hackneyed epic themes which opens his first satire: *unde alius furtiuae deuehat aurum / pelliculae*.[45] The intertext reinforces the orator's theme: the eloquence of the Greek poets has been used to flatter and exaggerate the glories of less worthy heroes and mythic quests. What would it make of the real Julian and his fleet, the specific *lembis liburnisque* challenging the mythic status of the *Argo*? By referring in such detail to the myth, the orator has bestowed the glamour of poetry on his own work while dismissing the genre of mythological epic as hyperbolic and the theme, for those who know Juvenal, as trite.[46] In its place, he offers a Latin intertext, the language of Roman imperial epic, which promises divinity to the founder of Rome and his heirs. *Facundia potens Graecia* can offer only exaggeration and trivial comparisons with myth: the Latin panegyrist offers true glory based on the words of Ennius and Vergil, who may have been poets but whose authority, as will be discussed below, was absolute.

11.3. Poetic Authority

The singular status of Ennius and Vergil in the *Panegyrici Latini* is obvious from the simple fact that they are the only poets mentioned specifically, albeit by epithet. Ennius is *summa poeta* (the greatest poet, 9(5)7.3), while Vergil is *poeta Romanus* (the Roman poet, 11(3)14.2) or *magnus poeta* (the great poet, 12(9)12.2), and quotations from their works are explicitly and directly inserted into the text. Their authority was absolute and self-reinforcing. The *Annales* and the *Aeneid* were seen as foundation texts, the Latin equivalent of Homer's epics. Both were used as teaching tools, and so their influence was reinforced by complete familiarity from childhood.[47] Vergil replaced Ennius as the most important school text, but it is evident from Macrobius's *Saturnalia* that even in the fifth century AD, the educated Roman possessed a thorough knowledge of the *Annales* as well as the *Aeneid*. The *Saturnalia* also supplies evidence of Vergil's importance for prose as well as verse. It is agreed that he is as great an orator as a poet, and while there are four distinct types of oratory, Vergil alone derives

---

45. Ivv. 1.10–11. On the complexities of this passage, see Henderson 1996.
46. Ammianus famously rebuked his contemporaries for reading nothing but Juvenal and Marius Maximus (AMM. 28,4,14).
47. On Ennius in Republican and Augustan Rome, see Goldschmidt 18–35. In his *Octauius*, Minucius Felix warns against the *fabulae* and *errores* which we learn from our parents and which we reinforce through our studies, particularly of poetry. The authority of the poets is harmful to the truth, he warns (*[poetae] qui plurimum quantum ueritati ipsi sua auctoritate nocuerunt* (23,1).

his eloquence from a combination of all four.[48] For the writers of panegyric in Late Antiquity, Ennius and Vergil also had the distinction of being the greatest exponents of panegyric in the Latin epic tradition. Cicero had revered Ennius for honouring the heroes of his time and the Roman people as a whole, while the aim of the *Aeneid*, according to Servius, was to praise Augustus.[49]

Some writers, however, felt that the question of *licentia poetarum* still had to be addressed. Ennius and Vergil might be *summus, magnus*, and *Romanus*, but they were still poets and therefore theoretically open to the charge of invention. Literary critics of Late Antiquity took care to dispel any such charge. When admitting that Vergil might be employing metonymy when he describes the wood of the Trojan horse as being made from maple, *trabibus acernis* (*Aen.* 2.211–13), Macrobius adds that Vergil usually dislikes the rashness of poetic licence, *solet tamen Vergilius temeritatem licentiae non amare*.[50] In this context, it is interesting to note that when orators are forced to accept the work of a poet as truth, the poet to whom they refer is Vergil. The widespread dissemination of Gratian's power convinced Ausonius not to marvel at poetic licence (*Grat. act.* 5):

ades enim locis omnibus, nec iam miramur licentiam poetarum, qui omnia deo plena dixerunt.

You are present in all places and no longer do I marvel at the licence of the poets, who said that all places were full of the deity

his source being Vergil's *Iouis omnia plena* (*ecl.* 3.60). Similarly the Vergilian anecdote greeted with initial doubt, *mirabamur poetam*, is proved true, and Mamertinus accepts the poetic description of Jupiter, taken from the *Aeneid*, as credible because he has seen the power of Julian.[51]

Vergil, therefore, was authoritative in a way that other poets were not, and this is made very clear in the panegyric of 313 on Constantine. This panegyric is almost entirely concerned with war, and not surprisingly, the orator turns to epic language and allusion to describe Constantine's campaign against

---

48. *unus omnino Vergilius inuenitur qui eloquentiam ex omni genere conflauerit*, Macr. *Sat.* 5.1.5.

49. On Ennius, Cic. *Arch.* 22; Servius sums up Vergil's intention as *Homerum imitari et Augustum laudare a parentibus* (*pr.*). Cf. *Arch.* 20; cf. also lavs Pis. 22–4.

50. Cf. Serv. avct 1.1.5: *et ingenti arte Vergilius, ne in rebus fabulosis aperte utatur poetarum licentia.* See Russell 2006: 273. However, Vergil is not immune to the charge of invention, and Symmachus cites three Vergilian passages which are clearly fantastic and the work of *poetarum licentia* when compared with the actual deeds of Valentinian (*or.* 1.4, see Callu 2009: 43).

51. Avson. *Grat. act.* 65, cf. *Aen.* 4.41; Nemesianus who cites the same story (*cyn.* 268) is proved true by the authority of the emperor and of Vergil; see Green 1991: 550. On Mamertinus, 11(3)28.5, cf. *Aen.* 1.223–4.255.

Maxentius and the final battle at the Milvian Bridge. The speaker is, as Nixon and Rodgers remark, "exceptionally fond of quoting, paraphrasing, or alluding to Virgil."[52] Shifting between praise of Constantine's valour as a warrior and his mercy as an emperor, the orator pauses after the victory at Aquileia to single out Constantine's stratagem of turning swords into manacles and does so in a direct quotation from Vergil, the *magnus poeta* (*PL* 12(9)12.3, *geo.* 1.508):

> *Magnus poeta, dum bellorum toto orbe surgentium discursum apparatumque describit, "Et curuae" inquit "rigidum falces <conflantur in ensem>."*

> The great poet, when describing the provisions and preparations for wars which were rising throughout the whole world, said, "Even curved scythes are being melted down into hard swords."

The Vergilian line is the starting point for a lengthy disquisition on the transition from destruction to salvation, Constantine's clemency, and the transmutability of iron. Then, suddenly, the orator turns on the evidence of *fabulae* (12(9)13.5):

> *Quid simile ad laetitiam fabulae ferunt? Conuersa esse humana corpora in fontes aut pecudes aut aues; foeda et degener talis conuersio. Gladius mutatus in manicas: hoc est quod securitas post timorem, quod umbraculum post calorem.*

> What stories bring equal pleasure? Human bodies mutated into streams or cattle or birds; such a change is shameful and unworthy. A sword transformed into shackles: this is safety after fear, this is shadow after heat.

The *fabulae* here can only be the *Metamorphoses* of Ovid, which opens with the changing of shapes *in noua corpora*.[53] The adjectives with which the orator condemns the *fabulae* deserve attention. *Degener* occurs only twice in the *Panegyrici Latini* corpus, both instances occurring in the same panegyric, here and shortly afterwards in the condemnation of Maxentius as noted above: *degeneris, ut dictum est, animos timor arguebat* (*PL* 12(9)14.2, *Aen.* 4.13). *Degener* seems an unusually strong term for literary disapproval, but it has linguistic as well as moral connotations, and in this case, very literally, it suggests generic failings.[54] Ovid's *fabulae* belong to the same genre as those of the *magnus poeta*, but they are *degeneres* and do not live up to the standard set by Vergil. In the same way (and in Vergil's

---

52. Nixon and Rodgers 1994: 289; for further examples, see Rees 2004a: 40–1.
53. Ov. *met.* 1.1–2, cf. 1.87–8: *tellus / induit ignotas hominum conuersa figuras.*
54. CVRT. 7.5.29 refers to bilingual speakers *paulatim a domestico externo sermone degeneres*; QVINT. *inst.* 12.10.19 uses the metaphor of seeds decaying, *degenerant*, to describe the corruption of Aeschines's Attic style.

words), Maxentius will be shown to be *degener* and unworthy of comparison with Constantine. *Foeda*, the adjective paired with *degener* in condemnation of Ovid, also attaches itself to Maxentius, who hides in the most shameful shadows, *foedissimis latebris* (12(9)16.2). In short, Vergilian epic, the foundation text for Roman history and *imperium*, offers the perfect match of theme and genre. Lesser poets, whose theme is unworthy of the Vergilian genre, are the creators of *fabulae*.

Many of the citations of Ennius and Vergil reflect the encomiastic interpretation of these authors. Constantine's entry into Rome after his victory at the Milvian Bridge draws on Jupiter's promise of peace under the Julio-Claudians,[55] while Ausonius's reference to *omnia deo plena* is an excerpt from a couplet in praise of Jupiter (*ecl.* 3.60–1):

> *Ab Ioue principium Musae: Iouis omnia plena;*
> *ille colit terras, illi mea carmina curae*

> From Jupiter the Muses take their inspiration: all things are full of Jupiter, he inhabits the earth, he is the subject of my song.

The reference to a plurality of sources, *poetarum licentiam*, may refer to Vergil's own sources, as the opening of the couplet as *ab Ioue principium* was known to have derived from ancient Greek sources and had provided inspiration to Latin encomiasts as well.[56] Certain passages are favoured. The description of Jupiter in book 1 of the *Aeneid* and the praise of Augustus in book 6 are particularly influential, as are the golden age passages from the *Eclogues*, *Georgics*, and *Aeneid*.[57] These are not introduced as being the works of a poet or even of *the* poet: verbal and thematic parallels are sufficient to establish the allusion, and Vergil does not need introduction. The *aurea saecula* under Diocletian and Maximian, described as that of the reign of Saturn, *quondam Saturno rege*, is clearly modelled on the age of Augustus in the *Aeneid* (*Aen.* 6.792–4):

> **aurea** *condet*
> **saecula** *qui rursus Latio regnata per arua*
> **Saturno quondam**.

---

55. PL 4(10)31.3 describes the vices being paraded before Constantine's chariot, **Furor uinctus** *et cruenta Crudelitas inani terrore frendebant*, a scene taken directly from Vergil's **Furor** *impius intus / saeua sedens super arma et centum* **uinctus** *aenis / post tergum nodis fremet horridus ore* **cruento** (*Aen.* 1.294–6).

56. Macrobius cites only Aratus's version as a source for many poets (*quod de Arato poetae alii mutuati sunt, somn.* 1, 17, 14), but the formula goes back to Alcman (see Coleman 1977: 117) and appears in, among others, Theocritus, Calpurnius Siculus, and at least one speech from the *Panegyrici Latini* corpus (6(7)2.1). The plural may also simply be poetic: Symmachus refers to the Trojan war with *aiunt* (*or.* 2.8).

57. On Vergilian allusion in the *Panegyrici Latini*, see Rees 2004a. For the focus on particularly encomiastic passages from Vergil in the panegyrics, see Ware 2017 (forthcoming).

>   He will establish
> a golden age in the fields of Latium where
> once Saturn reigned.

It is much more difficult to assess the extent of Ennian allusion, but the attributed line, *a sole exoriente usque ad Maeotis paludes* (from the rising sun to the marshes of Maeotis, 11(3)16.3), introduced as the work of the originator of Roman song, *ille Romani carminis primus auctor*, is certainly derived from panegyric.[58] To one unfamiliar with the quotation, the authority comes only from the distinction given to the author by the orator. An educated member of the audience would recognize it as half a couplet and could add the missing line: *nemo est qui factis aequiperare queat* (there can be none found on earth to equal my deeds). The whole is from Ennius's epitaph on Scipio, therefore encomiastic, and this particular quotation draws on Hellenistic themes of encomium in which the hero's deeds are celebrated over as much of the earth as possible.[59] The educated audience member might even recall the couplet being quoted by Cicero in a discussion of men who live great lives, a context which doubles the laudatory element.[60] In a similar fashion, Mamertinus doubled the weight of his praise to Julian with the following (3(11)28.5):

> *Poetae ferunt altissimum illum et cuncta potestate cohibentem deum, qui ditione perpetua diuina atque humana moderatur, cum despiciat in terras, habitu oris tempestatum incerta mutare ... nitentia per orbem serena diffundi.*
>
> Poets say that the highest god, the ruler of all, who has eternal dominion over divine and human affairs, when he looks down on earth, he changes the fickleness of the weather with the expression of his countenance, and that a bright calm is spread over the world.

The whole passage is a composite of allusions to Vergil.[61] Primed by *poetae ferunt*, the audience were invited to recall the familiar image of Jupiter watching over the world from the *aether* and in *despiciat in terras*, could recognize *despiciens ... terrasque* (*Aen.* 1.223–4). In this context, the less specific *habitu oris tempestatum*

---

58. ENN. *epigr.* v. 21 Vahl. On Ennian allusion in the *Panegyrici Latini*, see Klotz 1911: 538–9. On this author's use of poetic reminiscence, see Rees in this volume, 319.

59. Fears 1977: 89.

60. *et est in aliquae uita praedicabile aliquid et gloriandum ac prae se ferendum*, CIC. *Tusc.* 5.49. On these lines, see Walbank 1985: 123–4.

61. See Ware 2017 (forthcoming).

incerta mutare . . . serena could prompt the memory of lines from the same scene in the *Aeneid, quo caelum tempestatesque serenat* (with which he calms the sky and weather, *Aen.* 1, 255). And there is more, as behind the Vergilian lines is an Ennian allusion: *Iuppiter hic risit tempestatesque serenae riserunt* (here Jupiter laughed, and bright weather laughed, *ann.* 457–8) and so a double laudation of Julian.[62] It is not at all surprising that a panegyrist would look to panegyrical passages for inspiration, but the predominance of such citations suggests a continuing if unconscious anxiety about the charge of *licentia* even in such authorities.[63] Poetic licence could not be an issue if the lines concerned praise of a general or emperor or of Jupiter; such a context made the allusion beyond suspicion.

11.4. Poets and Poetry

The conflict between the generic expectations of panegyric and poetry was not confined to the orators and appeared even in the verse panegyrics and encomiastic epics of Claudian.[64] Like the prose orators, he had to deal with the tacit accusation of insincerity and, like them, contrasts the fables of Antiquity with his own truth. In the *Laus Serenae*, for example, which honours the wife of his patron Stilicho, Claudian praises Stilicho for being chosen by Theodosius to become Serena's wife and begins a long and detailed catalogue of famous suitors of myth with the line *antiquos loquitur Musarum pagina reges* (the page of the Muses tells of ancient kings, *Laus Ser.* 160), as a prelude to Stilicho, who surpasses all. There is no contempt in Claudian's reference to the Muses, but as in the prose panegyrics the stories they inspire are introduced to be dismissed as unequal to the glorious reality that is Stilicho.[65]

A second example from Claudian, however, is explicitly critical of the poets. On the surface it appears a rather presumptuous variation of the standard

---

62. To the layering of intertext here may be added Pliny's version at *PL* 1(1)80.4; see Garcia Ruiz 2006: 151.

63. On this philological anxiety and passages as *spolia*, see the Introduction to this volume, 8–11.

64. I prefer not to use the phrase panegyric-epic, although I agree with the recent work of Schindler 2009 and Gillett 2012 that Claudian's innovations gave new life to the encomiastic epic and inspired the panegyrics of Corippus and Sidonius. Except that the works labelled panegyric were written for a formal occasion (usually the inauguration of a consulship), there is no difference between Claudian's epics and his panegyrics. Stylistically and thematically they cover the same area and have the aim of praising Stilicho. *De bello Getico*, in spite of its epic title, is indistinguishable in style from, e.g., the *De consulatu Stilichonis*. On Claudian and genre, see Ware 2012: 18; on Claudian and Stilicho, see Cameron 1970: 37–45 (and passim).

65. For a similar example, cf. *si uerax narratur fabula* (if the story is told truly, *Get.* 442) and the sweeping *taceat superata uetustas* (let Antiquity, outdone, be silent, *Ruf.* 1.282), which dismisses a list of mythological *exempla*.

trope, but a close reading of the intertextual layering suggests that Claudian had very relevant observations to make concerning poetic licence. His criticisms have much in common with those of Mamertinus in his dismissal of the *Argonautica*, and it is interesting that both took their examples from the same myth which had provided epic poets in Greek and Latin with encomiastic themes.[66] Claudian gives the trope significant structural prominence, placing it at the end of his introduction so that it serves as a dismissal of the *fabulae* which have gone before and a guarantee of the truth that is to come.

The epic *De bello Getico* was written in 402 AD in celebration of Stilicho's recent victory over the Goths. The lengthy and vivid simile with which Claudian opens the poem is unparalleled in his work. Unlike Mamertinus, who introduced the Argonautic myth as a source of ridiculous poetic fancies, Claudian presents the reader with an epic vignette, giving full weight to the heroic qualities of *audacia* (*Get.* 2) and the dangers of the Symplegades (*Get.* 1–3):

intacti cum claustra freti, coeuntibus aequor
armatum scopulis, audax inrumperet Argo
Aeetam Colchosque petens

Through the confines of the untouched deep, a sea guarded by the clashing rocks, the daring *Argo* burst, seeking Aetes and Colchis . . .

The scene is set for a comparison between the skill and daring of Tiphys, the helmsman of the *Argo*, and the skill and daring of Stilicho, helmsman of the ship of state. It is a compelling epic backdrop for the real events Claudian is about to describe.[67] Yet with a sudden switch into the familiar trope of panegyric, Claudian diminishes the mythological hero in favour of Stilicho (*Get.* 11–14):

quodsi ardua Tiphyn
nauis ob innocuae meritum sic gloria uexit,
quae tibi pro tanti pulso discrimine regni
sufficient laudes, Stilicho?

But if lofty glory raised Tiphys so high because of the merit of saving one single ship, what praises could be enough for you, Stilicho, who saved so great an empire from danger?

---

66. On the Ptolemaic context of Apollonius's *Argonautica*, see Hunter 1993: 152–69, Newman 2011; on Vespasian and Valerius Flaccus, see Stover 2012.

67. On the Argonautic theme of this poem, see Schindler 2005.

This is the same formula as Mamertinus's version (*PL* 3(11)8.3):

> *Quid tu, si ad scribendas celebrandasque res principis nostri animum adiceris, de Iuliani lembis liburnisque factura es?*

> If you were to give your attention to describing and extolling the achievements of our emperor, what would you make of Julian's cutters and galleys?

Claudian continues to diminish the myth. After the persuasive and alluring opening, the voyage of the *Argo* turns out to be no more than the exaggerations of poets, *licet omnia uates in maius celebrata ferant* (*Get.* 14–15), invented simply in order to impress tender minds, *teneras uicturi carmine mentes* (*Get.* 21). By giving a poetic summary of the story, Claudian illustrates how enticing these details are, embellishing every scene with colour and movement so that the yoked bulls burn with scorching ash, *rapidis ambusta fauillis*, and the helmets of the earth-born warriors emerge from green furrows, *uirides ... sulcos* (*Get.* 24–5). It is clear therefore when he dismisses the story as unequal to the truth, *nil ueris aequale dabunt* (*Get.* 27), that he is making this judgement as a competent poet, one who could resort to such invention without difficulties. As the chronicler of Stilicho, however, he has no reason to do so but will instead praise the far nobler deeds of the man who alone defeated so many thousands of Goths, an enemy more rapacious than the Harpies and more violent than the earth-born soldiers (*Get.* 31–5).

To criticize the words of poets as exaggerated fiction may be a trope of panegyric, but in a poem so rich in allusion, this seems a very provocative remark indeed. Claudian's opening lines are strongly derivative of Valerius's proem, but the introductory *audax inrumperet Argo* also signals Seneca or Horace.[68] As Claudia Schindler observes, Claudian's acknowledgment of the literary history of this myth in *fertur* (*Get.* 6) may be a nod to Catullus's opening *dicuntur* (64.2)[69] and so also to Apollonius, Ennius, Varro of Atax, and any other Argonautic poets. The unspecified *fertur* offers up a world of poets and a world of *fabulae*, all to be set aside in favour of the praise of Stilicho.

The relevance of this particular myth to the war with the Goths is a matter of some debate. Schindler sees further thematic links with Valerius Flaccus, arguing that both celebrate the opening up of the East and the extension of Roman *imperium*. In this regard, she points to intertextual echoes which compare

---

68. VAL. FL. 1.3–4, *ausa sequi mediosque inter iuga concita cursus rumpere*; SEN. *Med.* 301–2, *audax ... rupit*; HOR. *carm.* 1.3.25–6 *audax ... ruit*.

69. Schindler 2005: 118–19.

Stilicho's journey over the Alps to the *Argo*'s passage through the Symplegades.⁷⁰ More convincing is her argument that Jupiter's master plan of *translatio imperii* in Valerius and the gradual transfer of power from Asia to Greece to Rome (1,531–60), becomes in Claudian a *reparatio imperii* (*Get.* 37), the restoration of power under Stilicho. Stephen Hinds also sees in this opening, and in the Argonautic beginning of *De raptu Proserpinae*, an association with "the hero's empire-straddling project with his praise-poet's ship of poetry and ship of state" and also a resonance with Claudian's preoccupation with the division between western and eastern halves of the empire.⁷¹ To these suggestions, I would add a further encomiastic theme, one which is intrinsic both to the Argonautic myth in Latin literature and to Claudian's poetry: the dawn of a new age. For the Romans, the primacy of the *Argo* was key to its iconic status: as the first ship it represented the daring, *audacia*, of mankind. Interpreted negatively, it stood for the end of the golden age of man, the moment when men took to the seas driven by their desire for plunder and booty.⁷² Interpreted positively and in imperial ideology, it represented the return of the golden age promised in Vergil's fourth *Eclogue*, an age fortified by the skills which man was forced to learn when Jupiter in the *Georgics* put an end to the Saturnian age.⁷³ In imperial ideology, the Saturnian *aurea saecula* was not replaced by a Jovian *ferrea aetas* but by an Augustan golden age, and in Latin epic, the *Argo* represented the drive towards civilization: exploration, commerce, and the expansion of Roman *imperium*.⁷⁴

Claudian follows Vergil in allowing for the restoration of the *aurea aetas*, but for him, the iron age is never banished. The two ages coexist, and the balance forever shifts as the *aurea aetas*, the age of peace and harmony established by Theodosius, is constantly challenged by threats from inside and outside the empire. Yet the golden age could always be attained by those who understood what it truly meant. For Claudian, the restoration and preservation of the *aurea aetas* depended on consciously embracing true Roman values, the qualities of endurance, hard work, and self-sacrifice which had made Rome great. Wisdom, *cognoscere*, was key. Mankind had to recognize the truth of the golden paradox, that gold was more harmful than iron, and that they had to turn away from greed and violence.⁷⁵ Under the guidance of such leaders as Stilicho, who put his *labor*

---

70. Schindler 2005: 116–17; for Stilicho as the hero who opens up the East (*Get.* 174–93), see Schindler 2005: 121.

71. Hinds 2013: 139.

72. For primacy, see ENN. *Med. ex.* 208–14, CATVLL. 64.11, LVCAN. 6.400–1; on the negative consequences, see CATVLL. 64, Ov. *met.* 1.94–5, 129–34. SEN. *Med.* 301–64. See Feeney 2007: 118–20.

73. *ecl.* 4.34–6, *georg.* 1.121–46.

74. Stover 2012: 51–60.

75. Ov. *met.* 1.141 *iamque nocens ferrum, ferroque nocentius aurum*; on this concept, see Feeney 2007: 134–7.

at the service of the state, and the consul Mallius Theodorus, who was the pupil of *Iustitia*, the golden age could be brought about for everyone.[76] In *De bello Getico*, the myth of the Argonautica stands for the bravery of the one man who restored true gold to the empire, but Claudian's readers must understand that this is a different story to the one familiar through the inventions of the poets.

Almost as soon as he dismisses the Argonautic motif as poetic exaggeration, *omnia ... in maius celebrata*, Claudian picks it up again through verbal associations. The strong opening lines of the poem (*Get.* 1–2):

> *intacti cum **claustra** freti, coeuntibus aequor*
> *armatum scopulis, **audax** inrumperet Argo*

are now redirected to Stilicho and his salvation of empire by leading justice out of confinement (*Get.* 36–7):

> ***claustrisque** solutae*
> *tristibus exangues **audent** procedere leges*
>
> freed from their grim confines
> bloodless laws dare to come forward.

With the *Argo* allusively re-established in the poem, the following words, *iamque potestates priscus discriminat ordo / iustitiae* (and now the ancient order of justice distinguishes between offices, *Get.* 38–9) introduces the theme of renewal. For Claudian the parallel between the Symplegades and Stilicho is in the restoration of the old age of justice[77] or, more specifically, the restoration of the golden age, *priscus ordo iustitiae*, the time when Justice walked among men.

The iron age crisis, through which the empire has just passed (Claudian, appropriately for a panegyrist, starts with the victory and works backward) was one in which the Romans had become soft through luxurious living and lack of challenge, *terrorum expers et luxu mollior aetas* (*Get.* 160). The Goths, on the other hand, were hardy barbarians, *ualidam gentem, quam dura niuosis / educat Vrsa plagis* (a strong race, which the harsh north stars have raised in lands of snow, *Get.* 134–5), whose simple existence, without possessions or laws, shared many characteristics of golden age man.[78] Lacking wisdom, however, they seek

---

76. For a detailed discussion of this, see Ware 2012: 171–230.
77. Note also the echo of *discrimine* (*Get.* 13) in *discriminat*.
78. For the differences between the "hard primitive" (realistic) and "soft primitive" (idealistic) interpretations of the golden age, see Lovejoy and Boas 1935: 23–102, Feeney 2007: 110–15.

plunder, and their Roman opponents, soft and flabby, are petrified and in peril. A new age of restoration is required, a second *Argo* led by a second Tiphys, a venture which will challenge the Romans to recover their true identity and restore to them their Roman golden age. It is the promise of Vergil's *Eclogue* (*ecl.* 4, 34–5):

> *alter erit tum Tiphys et altera quae uehat Argo*
> *delectos heroas*

Then there will be a second Tiphys and a second *Argo* which will carry chosen heroes.

Why then does Claudian reject the myth of the *Argo* as poetic exaggeration? The intertextual clue lies in the poets' intention of captivating foolish minds, *teneras uicturi carmine mentes* (*Get.* 21). The phrase *teneras mentes* is from Horace 3.24, a poem which condemns riches, arguing that it is better to live like the Scythians or the Goths (3.24.9–13):

> *Campestres melius Scythae,*
> *quorum plaustra uagas rite trahunt domos,*
> *uiuunt et rigidi Getae,*
> *inmetata quibus iugera liberas*
> *fruges et Cererem ferunt.*

The Scythians of the plains live better, whose wagons pull their wandering homes by custom, or the harsh Goths, for whom lands unsurveyed bring forth free fruits and corn.

The bounty of nature and the unmarked lands are typical of the golden age.[79] Horace then turns to laws, trade, and navigation, characteristics of the iron age (3.24.40–1), and asks what use they are if we abandon our virtuous ways (3.24.51–4):

> *Eradenda cupidinis*
> *praui sunt elementa et **tenerae** nimis*
> ***mentes** asperioribus*
> *formandae studiis.*

The elements of vicious greed must be eliminated, and our minds, too soft, must be strengthened by harsher studies.

---

79. See, e.g., Ov. *met.* 1.102, 136. As "hard primitives," Horace's Goths serve the same exemplary function as do the stern heroes of the early Republic in *carm.* 2.15; see Commager 1962: 87.

The rejection of greed, *cupido*, is critical to this lesson. Claudian did not praise the Argonauts for seeking the fleece but for driving away the rapacious Harpies, *rapaces Harpyias* (*Get.* 27–8). Over the course of the epic, the Romans learn that wealth cannot protect them; they find their riches a burden and their lust for gain is driven out by more serious cares (*Get.* 225–6):

> *iamque oneri creduntur opes tandemque libido*
> *haesit auaritiae grauioribus obruta curis*

> And now they think their wealth a burden and at last the lust for gain is halted, obliterated by more serious cares.

There are no direct verbal parallels, but the lines could be a response to Horace, *libido auaritiae obruta* answering *eradenda cupidinis elementa* and *grauioribus curis* the actualization of *asperioribus studiis*. Stilicho reinvigorates his army, urging the soldiers to restore the ancient glory of Rome, *Romanum reparate decus* (*Get.* 571). His appeal is successful. That the Romans have learned the lesson of Horace's ode is shown during the battle with the Goths, when the Romans prove that they have been restored to their former selves (*Get.* 604–8):[80]

> *inuisum miles sitiens haurire cruorum*
> *per uarias uestes onerataque plaustra metallo*
> *transit et argenti cumulos et caedis auarus*
> *contemptas proculcat opes; pretiosior auro*
> *sanguis erat*

> Thirsting to drink the hated blood of their enemy, the soldiers ignore the coloured fabrics, the wagons laden with metal, and the heaps of silver. Eager for slaughter they trample in contempt on the riches: blood is more precious than gold.

Claudian was not the first to see the *Argo*'s quest for gold as symbolizing man's moral downfall. In the myth of the ages of man, the quest for real gold led to spiritual corruption.[81] Although he does not make explicit the link between the restoration of the golden age and the myth of the Argonautica, the opening simile establishes the connection in the mind of the reader, who should be

---

80. The scene is an allusion to another Argonautic reference: Cicero's description of Mithridates's escape from Pontus (Cɪᴄ. *Manil.* 22–3).
81. Ov. *met.* 1.141–50, Seneca denounced as appropriate the rewards of the *Argo*'s quest, *aurea pellis / maiusque mari Medea malum* (*Med.* 362–3).

gripped at once by the vivid mythological imagery. The subsequent dismissal of the fabulous details as the exaggeration of the poets introduces a didactic element, and those who were enthralled by the story are now cast as children with *tenerae mentes*. Context and verbal echo lead to Horace's poem and the lesson that riches must be rejected. The rest of the poem shows that lesson in action.

In hindsight and with full knowledge of the theme of the poem, it becomes clear that Claudian is not rejecting the poets but their techniques of exaggeration, *celebrata in maius*. As with Mamertinus, the details are seen as nonsense and worse, a distraction from the deeds of the real hero, whether Stilicho or Julian, whose actions are so much more praiseworthy. The true and deserving object of poetic veneration, *celebrare*, the victory of Pollentia, is announced at the end of the poem: *O celebranda mihi cunctis Pollentia saeclis!* (Pollentia, to be glorified by me for all ages, *Get*. 635). Poets had to take their lead from the panegyrists.

11.5. CONCLUSION: FROM PROSE TO POETRY

Pacatus Drepanius, a poet as well as an orator, had foretold the future of panegyric. Having directed artists to avoid the hackneyed themes of Antiquity, *uulgata ueterum fabularum argumenta despicite* (2(12)44.5), he finished his oration by claiming that panegyric had authority over every genre: *a me gestarum ordinem rerum stilus omnis accipiet, a me argumentum poetica, a me fidem sumet historia* (from me, every genre will hear of your deeds, from me poetry will receive its themes, from me history will take its proof, 47.6).[82] The phrase, *a me argumentum poetica* has a double meaning: poetry will become verifiable with the evidence (*argumentum*) brought by the deeds of Theodosius, but also, poetry will receive its theme (*argumentum*) from panegyric.

Pacatus Drepanius's eulogy of Spain proves his point. He draws on the *laudes Italiae* of the *Georgics* for characteristics of the country and then continues (2(12)4.5):

> *Cedat his terris terra Cretensis parui Iouis gloriata cunabulis et geminis Delos reptata numinibus et alumno Hercule nobiles Thebae. Fidem constare nescimus auditis; deum dedit Hispania quem uidemus.*

> Let the land of Crete give place to this land, Crete, which boasts of being the cradle of the infant Jupiter, and Delos also, where twin divinities crawled,

---

82. Nixon and Rodgers 1994: 516 translate *stilus* literally as "pen," but appearing in the conclusion to a work, *stilus* often has a generic meaning, which would be very appropriate in Pacatus Drepanius's context (for *stilus* in a sphragis, see n. 28). On Pacatus Drepanius as poet, see Rees in this volume, 336–9.

and Thebes, famous for its foster-child Hercules. We do not know the truth of what we have heard, but Spain has given us a god whom we can see.

The authority of the ancient sources is barely questioned. The poetic details of the myths have now become an appropriate part of a prose panegyric and without much elaboration appeared in the verse encomia of Claudian a few years later (*IV Cons.* 132–6):

Herculis et Bromii sustentat gloria Thebas,
haesit Apollineo Delos Latonia partu
Cretaque se iactat tenero reptata Tonanti;
sed melior Delo, Dictaeis clarior oris
quae dedit hoc numen regio

The glory of Hercules and Bacchus uplifted Thebes, Latonian Delos stayed fixed after the birth of Apollo, and Crete boasts that the young Thunderer crawled there. But better than Delos, more renowned than Cretan shores, is this land which gave this god.

Claudian's debt to Pacatus Drepanius is clear in mythological exempla, direct verbal parallels (*gloriata* ~ *gloria*, *reptata* ~ *reptata*, *dedit hoc numen regio* ~ *deum dedit Hispania*), and *uariatio*: of Pacatus Drepanius's double divinities (*geminis numinibus*) only Apollo is mentioned, while Thebes's nurslings are doubled, Bacchus added to Pacatus Drepanius's Hercules. Pacatus Drepanius, in fact, supplies more than the poet's theme, providing him with poetic inspiration as well. Claudian's allusive techniques here are no different to those he applies to the work of Vergil or Lucan or Ovid: Pacatus Drepanius would also give themes to the poetic panegyrics of Sidonius.[83]

The relationship between poetry and panegyric, explored through the nuances of poetic intertextuality and allusion by Mamertinus, Pacatus Drepanius, and Claudian, had been summed up very simply in an early oration on Maximian. Dismissing the notion that the emperor had borrowed the chariots of day and night, the anonymous orator attributes imperial *celeritas* instead to imperial *pietas*. The wondrous speed itself is not in question. The orator disapproves only of the *fabulae* which mask the truth and which he will strip away, *remoueamus istinc fabulas imperitorum, uerum loquamur* (11(3)8.4). The orator of 313 makes his opinion of these *fabulae* even more pronounced, condemning as *foeda* and *degener* the transformations of Ovid's *Metamorphoses* but accepting the authority of Vergil as an exemplary source.

---

83. Brolli 2013: 97–9.

Stripped of its *fabulae*, what is left of poetry—or rather, what is left *for* poetry? The panegyrists do not say so in as many words, but the answer must be "praise." It is a very narrow definition and applies only in the context of panegyric, but it seems inarguable that when the orators speaking as panegyrists look at poetry, they do so from the premise that the proper subject of poetry is imperial encomia. Even Vergil, the *poeta Romanus*, may be challenged on poetic details, but his pronouncements on the power of Jupiter or of the emperor, Jupiter's representative on earth, are authoritative. The authority comes from praise, not from poetry. Challenging the *fabulae poetarum*, the panegyrists gradually reclaimed poetry from error and redirected it towards what they saw as its proper ends, the praise of the emperor.

PART V

A New Literary Space

The Challenges of Christian Poetry

Lactantius's Phoenix *and Late Latin Poetics*

MICHAEL ROBERTS

In his groundbreaking study of the Christian Latin poetry of Late Antiquity, Jacques Fontaine (1981: 65–6) concludes his chapter on Lactantius's *De aue phoenice* with the observation that the poem anticipates many of the features of late Latin poetry. He emphasizes both the stylistic qualities of the poem and its significance in legitimizing a classically based Christian poetics. (This in contrast with the irregular quasi-hexameters of the third-century poet Commodian, discussed in his previous chapter).[1] At the same time there is no reason to think that, in his stylistic qualities at least, Lactantius sets the pattern only for Christian poets.[2] The *De aue phoenice* displays traits shared with much of later Latin poetry, whether or not of Christian content. In this chapter I elaborate on Fontaine's insight, pointing out various features of Lactantius's poem that recur in later writers. My argument does not depend on the later poets in question knowing or directly imitating Lactantius. Instead they evidence common compositional features or thematic emphases first exemplified in the *De aue phoenice*.

The poem over the years has aroused a certain amount of scholarly controversy. Its attribution to Lactantius has been a matter of debate, though recently, despite occasional dissident voices, a firm consensus has developed for its authenticity. Gregory of Tours, in the sixth century, attributes the poem to Lactantius, as do two of the three earliest manuscripts.[3] Similarly it is now generally agreed that some passages in the poem refer covertly to Christian doctrines; that is, while being fully intelligible only from a Christian perspective, they would not be perceptible as Christian elements to a non-Christian reader.[4] The poem is generally dated to the period of the persecutions, roughly contemporaneous with Lactantius's *De opificio Dei* (303/4), which shows a similar concealed Christianity. Some have argued for a later date, typically connecting

---

1. Fontaine 1981: 41 follows the majority opinion in dating Commodian to the third century.
2. In his Fondation Hardt article (1977 = 1980: 25–81), Fontaine argues that the stylistic preferences of late antique authors transcend confessional differences.
3. For a review of the arguments, see Isetta 1980: 385–401 and more briefly Wlosok 1989: 400. Gregory of Tours summarizes parts of the poem in his *De cursu stellarum* 12.
4. Fontaine 1981: 56, 60 refers to the poem's crypto-Christianity. For a summary of the Christian elements in the poem, see Walla 1969: 129–31 and Fontaine 1981: 64–5.

it with the emperor's *Vicennalia* in 326, and seeing political symbolism in the phoenix theme, which they relate to Constantinian propaganda of renewal.[5] But it is difficult to understand why, in that case, Lactantius would be reluctant to make the Christian meaning of the phoenix myth explicit.

12.1. Meter, Genre, Narrative Structure

Lactantius's *De aue phoenice* is the first extended composition in elegiac couplets from the period of Late Antiquity. Before him elegiac compositions of any length are in short supply. Among surviving literature the extensive writings of Ovid, some three centuries earlier, provide the nearest antecedent. Although there is no evidence of direct influence of Ovid's elegies on Lactantius's poem, the classical poet's multifaceted corpus will have helped to legitimate that metre as an alternative to the hexameter for narrative compositions.[6] In fact the elegiac couplet had historically been something of a multipurpose metre. After Lactantius it becomes so again and in Late Antiquity is used for a variety of different subjects; for example, for a poem on the martyr Saint Hippolytus, for a journey narrative, for Christian moral instruction, and for a didactic poem on grafting.[7]

No single subject matter, then, was associated with the elegiac couplet. Instead the metre came to be defined against the dactylic hexameter. Paulinus of Nola addresses Ausonius, who has criticized him for neglecting the duties of friendship, first with greetings in nine elegiac couplets, before he turns to the substance of their differences in "the sterner tones of the hexameter" (*grauiore / heroi ... sono, carm.* 10.13–14). Prosper of Aquitaine begins his *De prouidentia Dei* with an elegiac preface, before switching to hexameters "so that [his] speech not be impeded by unequal verse" (*ne sermo moram patiatur ab impare uersu, De prouidentia Dei* 95–6). As with Paulinus, Prosper adopts the more solemn metre when it comes to the substance of his poem, in his case a disquisition on providence and divine goodness.[8] The habit of equipping substantial

---

5. For the early date, see Walla 1969: 132–5 and Wlosok 1989: 400. Fontaine 1981: 53–4, 66 and 1984: 106–11 argues for a later date and for political symbolism in the myth of the phoenix.

6. Fontaine 1981: 62 mentions specifically the *Fasti* and Propertius, book 4, as possible precedents. Ovid's only account of the phoenix myth is actually in his only hexameter work, the *Metamorphoses* (15.391–407), a passage Lactantius will have known. Of the Classical Latin elegists Ovid is far and away the best known in Late Antiquity, esp. his *Heroides* and exile poetry.

7. Respectively, Prudentius, *perist.* 12; Rutilius Namatianus, *De reditu suo*; Paulinus of Nola, *carm.* 25 and 31 (an epithalamium and a *consolatio*); and Orientius, *Commonitorium*; Palladius, *De agricultura*, book 15. Latin love elegy as a genre is absent from the period. The closest to it is the remarkable corpus of the sixth-century poet Maximianus, a group of elegies in which the poet looks back on a succession of erotic escapades from the perspective of old age.

8. See Roberts 2010: 86–7.

hexameter compositions with elegiac prefaces was common in Late Antiquity, evidence that the two metres were perceived as complementary in nature. In the cases of Claudian and Sidonius, prefaces often took the form of mythological vignettes, with some similarities to the compositional units that make up Lactantius's poem.[9]

It is understandable that Paulinus and Prosper would prefer the hexameter for the main body of their poems, since the tendency for the elegiac couplet to be a closed unit of sense, which becomes more pronounced in Late Antiquity, inhibits the ability to develop syntactical complexity or a complicated argument. Because Lactantius's narrative has a large descriptive element and description relies heavily on patterns of enumeration, the relative inhospitality of the elegiac couplet to more complex syntactical structures is not a handicap. In fact, in such passages, when a sentence extends beyond a single couplet, the successive couplets are normally joined by coordinating conjunctions or figures of speech (anaphora, polyptoton). The overall impression created by such passages depends on an accumulation of individual details, only loosely articulated syntactically.

Further light is shed on Lactantius's choice of metre by the practice of Claudian, who wrote on the same subject at the end of the century but in hexameters.[10] The Egyptian poet may well have known Lactantius's work, though the evidence is not conclusive. Alternatively both may be drawing on a common rhetorical tradition for writing about the phoenix.[11] The stylistic distinction between the two poems is already evident in the first lines, describing the bird's grove situated in the distant east.

1. Lactantius, 1–8
Est locus in primo felix oriente remotus,
   qua patet aeterni maxima porta poli,
nec tamen aestiuos hiemisue propinquus ad ortus,
   sed qua sol uerno fundit ab axe diem.
Illic planities tractus diffundit apertos,
   nec tumulus crescit nec caua uallis hiat,

---

9. Elegiac prefaces to hexameter works are written by Optatianus Porfyrius, Ausonius, Claudian, Prosper of Aquitaine, Sedulius, Sidonius Apollinaris, Corippus, and Venantius Fortunatus. For Claudian's prefaces, see Felgentreu 1999.

10. Ricci 1981: xv–xviii dates the poem to between 395 and 400.

11. This is the opinion of Gualandri 1974: 293–311. See most recently Colomo 2013 for two such rhetorical exercises partially preserved on papyri. (I am grateful to Professor Gualandri for drawing my attention to this article.) For the similarities between the two poems, see Walla 1969: 135–9. I quote Lactantius from the edition of Brandt 1893 and Claudian from Hall 1985.

> *sed nostros montes, quorum iuga celsa putantur,*
> *   per bis sex ulnas eminet ille locus.*

> There is a happy place set apart in the furthest east,
>   where the huge gate of the eternal heaven lies open,
> close to the source neither of summer nor of winter,
>   but where the sun sheds daylight from a springtime sky.
> There a plateau extends wide its open plains,
>   and no hill rises up or hollow valley gapes,
> but the place exceeds in height by twice six ells
>   our own mountains, whose peaks are thought to be lofty.

2. Claudian, *carm. min.* 27.1–6
Oceani summo circumfluus aequore lucus
trans Indos Eurumque uiret, qui primus anhelis
sollicitatur equis uicinaque uerbera sentit
umida roranti resonant cum limina curru,
unde rubet uentura dies longeque coruscis
nox adflata rotis refugo pallescit amictu.

Beyond India and the East is a green grove surrounded by the furthest waves of the ocean, which is the first to be roused by the panting horses and feels the nearby lashes when its watery threshold resounds to the dewy chariot, by which the coming day reddens and the night, feeling the breath of the far-glowing chariot wheels, grows pale and withdraws its dark cloak.

Lactantius begins with an eight-line passage framed by the repetition *est locus* (1) and *ille locus* (8). The whole falls into two sentences of four lines each, which rely on coordinating conjunctions and simple relative clauses to build up a picture from individual details. Most lines are complete units of sense; only in the case of the last couplet does the syntax of the hexameter need the pentameter for completion. By comparison the first six lines of Claudian's poem are a single sentence. The passage is articulated largely by a pattern of subordinate clauses (relative and temporal) that only in one case (4) coincide with a single line. Instead of building up a picture from a series of discrete details, Claudian lingers over the point that the grove is situated where the sun rises.

In Claudian's case the choice of metre is evidently dictated by a desire to treat the phoenix myth in epic fashion. His second line advertises this aspiration by echoing the first line of the *Aeneid* (*qui primus anhelis* ~ *qui primus ab oris*), and the metaphorical language he uses to describe sunrise derives from epic tradition.[12] His poem contains epic similes, likening the aging phoenix to a pine tree that is old and weather-beaten (31–5) and the birds that attend the restored phoenix to a Parthian army surrounding its king (83–8); an address in direct speech by Phoebus (= the Sun) to the phoenix, consoling it and urging it to seek rejuvenation on its funeral pyre (50–4); and a personification of *Natura*, who grieves, fearing for the phoenix's survival (62–3). All are features that lend the poem an epic colouring and find no equivalent in Lactantius's work.[13] To that degree Claudian's poem might be described as a small-scale epic or an epyllion—or, at least, an epic style fragment—a description that Fontaine applies to the *De aue phoenice*, where it is less appropriate.[14] The syntactically more complicated structure of the first lines of his poem, by comparison with Lactantius's, is a further index of its generic intent.[15]

Lactantius's poem, on the other hand, is hard to pin down generically. In this generic indeterminacy it anticipates trends in later Latin poetry. A narrative elegy, with substantial descriptive elements, it concludes with a *makarismos* praising the phoenix (161–4) and a series of lines playing with the paradoxes of the phoenix's self-parenting and its rebirth through death (165–70), a series of pointed *sententiae* that would not be out of place as the conclusion of a descriptive epigram.[16] Ausonius's *Mosella* shows a similar generic elusiveness: it begins as a travel narrative, mutates into a hymn to the river, with a catalogue of its fishy inhabitants suitable to didactic, though with a touch of humour, continues with a series of scenes of life on the riverbank, and concludes with a panegyric of the river and its inhabitants. The poem adopts a variety of subjects and tones that evade simple categorization. In a classic article on the mixing of genres in Prudentius, Fontaine detects similar tendencies in that Christian poet, comparing him with Ausonius.[17] Generic categories are shifting in the period,

---

12. See Ricci 1981: 7–10.

13. Lactantius's poem contains small-scale comparisons (47–50, 107–8, 143–6) but nothing of the dimensions of an epic simile. (Claudian also compares the phoenix's fading light with the moon when its face is covered by clouds, 37–9.) *Natura* does feature in Lactantius's poem (34, 99—in the latter case as an emendation), but without the attribution of human emotions.

14. Fontaine 1981: 62 speaks of "un *épos tytthon* (une épopée en miniature; les modernes disent: un épyllion)."

15. This is not to say that hexameter poetry avoided the enumerative, coordinating compositional structures exemplified here by Lactantius. Far from it, as many examples from late Latin poetry bear witness. On the other hand, elegiac poetry did not lend itself to syntactically complicated expressions and extensive enjambment. Claudius Marius Victorius's *Alethia* and Paulinus of Pella's *Eucharisticos*, both in hexameters, contain particularly lengthy sentences with complicated syntactical structures.

16. For the practice of ending epigrams with such *sententiae*, see Bernt 1968: 30–4.

17. Fontaine 1975: 755–77, repr. 1980: 1–23. On the genre or genres of Ausonius's *Mosella*, see Formisano 213–4 in this volume.

with new combinations of compositional elements and new genres or subgenres emerging.[18] Lactantius's poem is an early symptom of this process.

The poem is also typical of much that is to follow in the relative space it gives to narration and description. At the core of the phoenix myth is a narrative. In Lactantius's version the bird, when it feels itself aging, flies to Syria, where it constructs a nest / funeral pyre from which the new young bird will emerge. From there it travels to Egypt carrying the remains of its father, to lay them on the altar of the Sun in Heliopolis (*Solis ad urbem*, 121). Finally, that duty performed, it flies back to its homeland, accompanied by a retinue of attendant birds.[19] Despite this narrative core, if the final ten-line coda is discounted, descriptive passages occupy about 60% of the whole poem. The poem begins with an extended account of the location and features of the grove of the Sun, the phoenix's home (1–30), followed by the services the bird performs as the Sun's priest (31–58). Only then does the narrative proper begin, but the temporal progression twice comes to a halt for extended descriptions of the phoenix's pyre and the fragrances that constitute it (79–88) and the appearance of the reborn bird (123–50). This emphasis on the descriptive, with its accompanying enumerative patterns of composition, at the expense of the temporal progression of the narrative, is a recurrent feature of the poetry of Late Antiquity. The most striking example is Claudian's *De raptu Proserpinae*, in which the narrative of events provides the most tenuous of threads linking lengthy descriptive passages or speeches.[20] Because of this method of composition, Lactantius's poem breaks up into what Fontaine (1981: 61) calls "a series of medallions," self-contained units of composition, isolable from the narrative sequence of the poem, frequently of some artistic refinement. This pattern of composition was to become a characteristic feature of much late Latin poetry, with attendant jewel-like effects of the exquisite and small-scale.[21] Readers of such poems found their attention diverted from following a sequence of events to taking in spatially and sequentially ordered scenes, usually static in nature, presenting the content of the poem as a series of tableaux.

---

18. The Christian hymn is the most important new poetic genre. Panegyrical epic (epic panegyric) represents a new, or largely new, development in secular poetry, while biblical and hagiographical epic emerge as subgenres of the traditional epic.

19. Lactantius's version of the myth shows a number of unusual features. Most strikingly he combines two separate version of the bird's rebirth, regeneration by fire and emergence from a worm (*uermis*) that comes from the ashes, a process he likens to the emergence of a butterfly from a chrysalis (Van den Broek 1972: 157–8).

20. See Mehmel 1940: 106–7 and Fo 1982: 105–15, who estimates that the percentage of true narrative in book 2 of the poem does not exceed 15% and that in book 3 it is between 10% and 15%.

21. As described in Roberts 1989a.

12.2. Ekphrasis and Ceremony

Rhetorical treatises define the ekphrasis as a description that brings what is shown clearly before the eyes of the reader.[22] Visual immediacy is essential to the definition. By that criterion strictly only the description of the phoenix's appearance qualifies as an ekphrasis. It is the only one of the four passages that emphasizes the visual, insistently lingering over the colour and brilliance of the various parts of the phoenix's body. The bird's appearance is assimilated to that of precious metals and jewels: its tail is gold with purple markings (130–1), and its legs too are golden (141); its beak is picked out with green emeralds, and its eyes two hyacinths (135–7). Such precious stones and materials are, of course, frequently present in the art and literature of Late Antiquity, regularly associated with objects and settings that convey a high, sometimes divine or semi-divine, status. By the end of the period, in the poetry of Venantius Fortunatus, the dress of the Christian virgin, when she enters the heavenly bridal chamber, becomes largely an enumeration of jewels (ten in all) or other precious materials (*carm.* 8.3.263–76) that index her exalted status. Lactantius understands the appearance of the phoenix in a similar way: "it presents and offers itself as an object of wonder and veneration" (*mirandam sese praestat praebetque uerendam*, 125). Its beauty (*decor*, 124, 149) is royal in nature (*regali plena decore*, 149). It is telling that Lactantius chooses to place his description of the phoenix's appearance after its rebirth, when it has travelled to Egypt, where for the only time in its life it becomes visible to human eyes (*talis in aspectu se tenet usque hominum*, 150). In Claudian the equivalent passage comes much earlier (17–22), immediately after the description of the bird's location and diet, where to some it has seemed to fit more naturally.[23] The effect in Lactantius's poem is to translate the bird's appearance from simply an object of visual appeal to the embodiment of regal majesty, for which a human audience is essential; description becomes spectacle.

Affinities with the ekphrasis occur elsewhere in the poem but without the pronounced visual element essential to the rhetorical definition of that exercise. The phoenix's funeral pyre consists of a whole series of exotic gums and fragrances, enumerated in a manner not very different from the enumerative patterns of the ekphrasis (79–88). But here it is the sense of scent not sight that the

---

22. E.g., Aphthonius, *Prog.* 12.1 Ἔκφρασίς ἐστι λόγος περιηγηματικὸς ὑπ' ὄψιν ἄγων ἐναργῶς τὸ δηλούμενον.
23. Baehrens actually transposed the lines in Lactantius's poem to correspond to Claudian's sequence; see Walla 1969: 177–8.

poet appeals to. The nest / pyre brings together perfumes from various eastern nations in a bouquet of odours.[24]

The beginning of Lactantius's poem, his description of the grove of the Sun that is the bird's home, betrays a feature that perhaps also derives from the compositional patterns of the ekphrasis. Such descriptions often follow a simple organizing principle. Most clearly, for instance, a description of a person will proceed from head to feet.[25] (Lactantius's account of the phoenix's appearance is anomalous in following no such anatomical progression.) In the *De aue phoenice* the location of the grove is specified as remote both horizontally and vertically; it is in the furthest east and on a high plateau that overtops all other mountains (1, 5–8). The phoenix's grove occupies this marked off space, and within this grove, indeed in its centre, is a fountain of living water (25). Concentric organization takes over from linear, with the midpoint carrying a sacral charge. The description is constructed from simple spatial relationships, analogous to the head-to-toe progression in descriptions of the human body. This may be what Aphthonius has in mind when he recommends describing places ἐκ τῶν περιεχόντων καὶ ἐν αὐτοῖς ὑπαρχόντων, "from what surrounds them and what is in them."[26] Aphthonius's sample exercise describes the acropolis, actually the Serapeum, of Alexandria, which has the same quality as the phoenix's grove of being elevated above its surroundings.[27] Claudian again supplies a revealing comparison. His phoenix poem, it is true, does not emphasize the remoteness of the eastern grove to the extent that Lactantius's does, though it is imagined as situated on an island surrounded by the ocean (*Oceani summo circumfluus aequore*, 1). But his epithalamium for the marriage of the young Emperor Honorius and Maria, daughter of Claudian's patron Stilicho, contains an account of the palace of Venus that shows striking parallels with Lactantius's poem in its treatment of topography.[28] Venus's palace is doubly removed by being on an island, Cyprus, and set on a mountain inaccessible to humans (49–50). Like the

---

24. The association of perfumes with various different nations goes back in Latin poetry to Virgil, *georg.* 1.56–7. The fifth-century biblical poet Claudius Marius Victorius, in his *Alethia*, has a similar enumeration of locations and scents (1.237–42) in his description of paradise, though without any verbal parallels to Lactantius. His point is that the scents that elsewhere are separately located are all present together in paradise.

25. Aphthonius, *prog.* 12.1.

26. The phrase καὶ ἐν αὐτοῖς ὑπαρχόντων is omitted by some manuscripts and by the most recent editor of Aphthonius's work, Michel Patillon (Patillon 2008), but it accurately represents the procedure for descriptions of place.

27. The progression of the description is largely from the outside toward the middle but with less of the diagrammatic, instead tracing the course of a visitor to the site. For this practice, see Dubel 1997: 249–64.

28. Van den Broek 1972: 325, mentions the parallel in passing but does not pursue it. For the palace of Venus and its topography, see Guipponi-Gineste 2010: 161–6.

phoenix's grove, it occupies a mountaintop plateau and is untroubled by meteorological phenomena, enjoying an eternal spring (52–5; Lactantius 21–4). The concentric organization of Claudian's description is especially pronounced. On this plateau is a circuit wall of gold, containing an ideal landscape breathing the spirit of Venus, and within it the palace proper, where Venus sits enthroned in a context of bejewelled architecture and exotic fragrances reminiscent of the luxurious materials associated with the phoenix by Lactantius. Claudian, like his predecessor, relies on a schematic topography to create a circumscribed sacred space that transcends normal human experience and the everyday. Something similar applies also to the setting of Claudian's *De raptu Proserpinae*. The poet emphasizes the isolation of Sicily from the mainland, set off by the surrounding sea (1.142–52); in the middle of the island rises up Mount Etna (1.153), whose peaks are visible but inaccessible of approach (1.161–6). The description invests the location with a special sacral charge, appropriate for the setting of an event of transcendent cosmic significance: the carrying off of Proserpina by Pluto. In Lactantius's case Judaeo-Christian tradition may well have also informed the Christian poet's image, since in that tradition paradise is often imagined as a high mountain and the phoenix's grove has strong paradise-like elements.[29] But the comparison with Claudian suggests that the rhetorical tradition for describing locations of special sanctity (*loca sancta*, 63) plays at least as large a role.

The grove's sanctity derives from its consecration to the Sun. There not only is every sunrise celebrated anew (35–50), but the passing of the hours (55–6) and of the months (27–8) equally find commemoration. In the last case it is the spring at the centre of the grove that marks every month by bursting out with new water,[30] but in the other cases the celebration depends on the ritual actions of the phoenix, who is "the revered overseer of the grove and priestess of the forest" (*antistes luci nemorumque uerenda sacerdos*, 57). Lactantius describes in some detail the liturgical ceremony that marks the new dawn. At the first signs of the day's light the phoenix plunges into the waters of the spring three or four times and then drinks from it the same number of times.[31] It then settles on a tall tree awaiting the first rays of the sun, which it greets with a song that exceeds in its beauty the music of flutes and lyres, the voices of the nightingale and of the dying swan (39–50). Finally, as the sun rises into the heavens, it silently heralds it with a threefold beating of its wings (51–4). The passage shows a simple

---

29. Van den Broek 1972: 311–19.
30. The description recalls the tree of life in Revelation 22:2 that brings forth fruit every month.
31. The verb *libat* (38) could also mean "makes libations," which might well be the way a pagan reader would understand the word. Wlosok 1982: 144 understands these initial ritual acts of the phoenix as a reference to the sacraments of baptism and the Eucharist.

temporal progression, though with a large element of description. The ritual actions of the phoenix are coordinated with successive stages of the sunrise each morning.[32]

For the Christian reader the account of the phoenix's devotions must inevitably call to mind liturgical ceremonies in the service and praise of God. The phoenix is a *cultor D(d)ei*, devoted to the service of God just as, according to Lactantius (*inst.* 2.12.15), the first man was intended to be in the Garden of Eden.[33] Its liturgy follows a sequence of carefully scripted ritual performances, but at the core is the song of the phoenix that greets the new light of day, occupying about half the entire section on the phoenix's priestly functions. As Wlosok observes (1982: 150–1),[34] the centrality of song to this ritual practice lends itself to a metapoetic reading as an exemplary demonstration of the role of poetry in Christian literature, to praise and give honour to God. This suggestion derives support from the comparison Lactantius makes with the Cirrhaean (i.e., Delphic) strains of the flute (*tibia ... / musica Cirrhaeis ... modis*, 47–8) and the "tuneful strings of the Cyllenean [i.e., Arcadian] lyre" (*Cylleneae fila canora lyrae*, 50), a reference to the instrument's invention by Mercury. While avoiding mention of the gods Apollo and Mercury, the language suggests that Christian song, devoted to celebration of the divine, rivals and exceeds the pagan poetry that those gods embody.

The association of Christian poetry with liturgical ceremony and praise of God was to be taken up by many subsequent poets. Paulinus of Nola describes Christian poetry, in a letter to the young would-be poet Jovius, as "a sacrifice of praise" (*sacrificium laudis, epist.* 16.9), a phrase derived from Psalm 49.14; Augustine (*epist.* 26.5) directs another aspiring poet, Licentius, to take Paulinus as his model, to "learn with what resources of his intellect he offers sacrifices of praise (*sacrificia laudis*) to God."[35] The language has strong liturgical connotations. Christian poetry, though written in classical metres, is understood as a liturgical act. So, to take two more examples, Prudentius describes himself in his poetic corpus as "celebrating God with his voice" (*uoce Deum concelebret, praef.*

---

32. This is not inconsistent with the rhetorical ekphrasis, which often uses a simple chronological progression to organize its account.

33. *Deus hominem ... posuit in paradiso ...ut ex ... variis fructibus aleretur expersque omnium laborum deo patri summa devotione serviret.* See Wlosok 1982: 144–5.

34. In his *Institutiones diuinae* Lactantius shows himself unusually sympathetic to the value of poetry. His views helped to legitimate Christian poetry according to Classical models. See Van der Nat 1977: 191–234.

35. Paulinus, *epist.* 16.9, *Ingenii autem tui facultates et omnes mentis ac linguae opes deo dedica immolans ei, sicut scriptum est,* **sacrificium laudis** *ore facundo et corde devoto*; Augustine, *epist.* 26.5, *vade, disce quibus opibus ingenii* **sacrificia laudis** *ei offerat.*

36), and Sedulius, author of the New Testament biblical poem the *Carmen paschale*, draws an analogy between singing the psalms of David in a choir, that is, church song, and composing his poem on the miracles of Christ (*carm. pasch.* 1.23–6).[36] To write poetry was to honour God in song. In writing of the remarkable song of the phoenix as a liturgical act of celebration and as a poetic form that outdoes pagan lyric, Lactantius anticipates this understanding of Christian poetry that Paulinus, Prudentius, and Sedulius, among others, were later to give voice to.

In addition to comparing the phoenix's song to the music of the flute and lyre, Lactantius also compares it to the songs of two other birds, the nightingale and the dying swan. The notion of Christian poetry as birdsong also finds later echoes. In his seventh *natalicium* for the annual festival of Saint Felix at Nola in 401, Paulinus of Nola evokes the concert of birdsong that greets the arrival of spring and wishes that his own poetic voice could in like fashion herald Felix's *natalis dies* (*carm.* 23.1–2). He specifically mentions the swallow, turtle dove, and finch (9–12) but prays for inspiration from Christ, so that his own song may match that supreme avian songster (*auem ... canorum*, 28), the nightingale. Although he does not identify the nightingale by name, the reference is clear from Paulinus's account of the gentle modulations and varied tones of its song, which act as a model for Christian poetics.

In a poem for the celebration of Easter in the cathedral of Nantes, the sixth-century poet Venantius Fortunatus also likens his song to that of a bird. Like Paulinus he invokes the chorus of birds at the coming of spring, but in this case they are part of the universal rejoicing of nature at the resurrection of Christ (*carm.* 3.9.27–32). In this concert of joy Fortunatus joins the other birds as the humblest sparrow, making his own modest contribution of song (*has inter minimus passer amore cano*, 46). The Christian poet adapts the comparison of his poetry with birdsong to the expression of rhetorical humility, dwarfed as he is by the exultation of all creation. This concept of all nature joining in the praise of God's work derives ultimately from Psalm 148. It receives a virtuoso treatment in the *De laudibus Dei* of the late fifth-century African poet Dracontius (2.208–44). Earlier in the same poem, in his account of creation, the newly created birds alone sing a chorus of praise to their creator (1.241–5).

The ritual that the phoenix performs every day in the grove of the Sun is an individual performance. It serves to sacralize time by a repetitive, unvarying enactment of praise and worship that for Christian readers is a model of their duty to hymn and praise God. But the passages from Venantius Fortunatus and

36. See Roberts 2007: 148–50.

Dracontius remind us also of another form of ceremony, communal in nature, in which the praise is voiced by a form of choir, which expresses the admiration of that group for the *laudandus* or *laudanda*. Such passages of communal celebration, which regularly join various ranks of society or individuals of different status in a ritual of veneration or devotion, typically directed toward or centred on an individual of particularly elevated status, are ubiquitous in Late Antiquity in art and literature.

The phoenix myth traditionally incorporated such a moment of group veneration, directed toward the bird itself. The Hellenistic Jewish dramatist Ezechiel, in his *Exagoge*, makes reference to the birds who follow behind the phoenix in its train (265–9), as does the second-century CE novelist Achilles Tatius (3.25.5).[37] Tacitus, in his account of an appearance of the phoenix in 34 CE, recounts its flight to Heliopolis "with a large retinue of other birds admiring its remarkable appearance" (*multo ceterarum uolucrum comitatu nouam faciem mirantium, Ann.* 6.28). Claudian, then, describes in some detail this company of birds. Once again the comparison with Lactantius's treatment is revealing.

1. Lactantius, 155–60
Contrahit in coetum sese genus omne uolantum
    nec praedae memor est ulla nec ulla metus.
Alituum stipata choro uolat illa per altum
    turbaque prosequitur munere laeta pio.
Sed postquam puri peruenit ad aetheris auras,
    mox redit; illa suis conditur inde locis.

Every species of flying creature joined together in a group
    without any thought of predation or fear.
Surrounded by a chorus of birds the phoenix flew on high
    and the masses followed it in joy fulfilling their holy duty.
But after they reached the atmosphere of the pure heavens,
    they immediately turned back; then it settled in its own abode.

2. Claudian, 76–82
Innumerae comitantur aues stipatque uolantem
alituum suspensa cohors: exercitus ingens
obnubit uario late conuexa meatu.
Nec quisquam tantis e milibus obuius audet

---

37. The *Exagoge* is edited by Howard Jacobson 1983, who (5–13) dates the work to the second century BCE. Sidonius, *carm.* 7.353–6, and Corippus, *Iust.* 1.349–52, also describe a retinue of birds attending the phoenix but in slightly different contexts.

ire duci, sed regis iter fragrantis adorant;
non ferus accipiter, non armiger ipse Tonantis
bella mouet: commune facit reuerentia foedus.

Countless birds accompany the phoenix and a winged company crowds around it on high in its flight. A huge army conceals the wide vault of heaven, flying this way and that. From so many thousands no one dares to approach its leader, but they pay homage to their perfumed king's progress. Neither the fierce hawk nor the eagle, armour bearer of Jupiter, rouses up warfare. Their veneration secures a universal truce.

Claudian, like Tacitus, sets the aerial cortege immediately after the phoenix's rebirth, during its journey to Heliopolis. Lactantius alone moves it after the phoenix's appearance in Heliopolis, as it returns to its native abode in the grove of the Sun, a stage in the narrative that is unique to his version. (I return to this detail later.) The lines I have quoted from Claudian precede a simile that further emphasizes the regal majesty of the phoenix. It is compared to a Parthian ruler, richly attired with jewels, crown, and purple embroidered garments, riding a horse with golden bridle, and proudly lording it over his subservient troops (83–8).

For Claudian the phoenix is a king (80; cf. *regna*, 8), ruling over the other birds, who show the same reverence for their leader as a subject would in approaching the majesty of an emperor.[38] Although this is an account of a journey, the greater emphasis is placed on the relationship of subordinate birds to the high-status phoenix in their midst, imagined in spatial terms: they surround him (*stipat*, 76) but also keep their distance.[39] The passage concludes with an image of harmony (*commune . . . foedus*, 82). The reverence of the avian masses toward their lord provides a template of social and political order that both legitimates and derives from the hierarchical order it models.

This is a familiar pattern in late antique art and literature. It is not surprising that Claudian's *Phoenix* has sometimes received a political interpretation.[40]

---

38. See, for instance, the deference with which an imperial official approaches the emperor to receive his codicils of office on the Missorium of Theodosius in Madrid. For an illustration and description, see Weitzmann 1979: 74–6.

39. The tendency to present the movement of a high-status individual in terms of a constant, posed relationship between the central figure and his subordinates is widespread in Late Antiquity. In Ammianus Marcellinus's account of the *aduentus* of Constantius II to Rome in 357 the other participants are all located with reference to the central figure of the emperor, with whom they are in an unvarying spatial relationship; see Roberts 1988: 182–3. In Claudian's epithalamium for Honorius and Maria, Venus, travelling over the sea to Italy for the marriage, is the centre of a particularly rich posed tableau.

40. See Christiansen and Sebasta 1985: 204–24 and Lecocq 2011: 113–57. In Claudian's poem on Stilicho's consulship (*Stil.* 2.418–19), the birds gathering to salute the phoenix in Egypt are likened to the leading men who hurry to Rome to join in the celebrations for the new consul.

Lactantius's poem anticipates these developments to the degree that he too lingers over the company that accompanies the phoenix in flight. But his version is different in treatment and tone. As is the case in Claudian's account, the more predatory birds put aside all thoughts of aggression, so that their habitual prey need have no fear (156). There is, though, less emphasis on the spatial relationship of the birds to their leader; they are just represented as surrounding (*stipata*, 157) and attending on (*prosequitur*, 158) the phoenix. The mood is not one of reverent awe but of joyful celebration (*laeta*, 158). The passage has something of the quality of an *aduentus* ceremony, as the phoenix is escorted in triumph to the clear light of heaven and back to its homeland.[41] Similar passages are common in later Christian literature of the ascent of the individual soul or of Christ himself to heaven. In Ambrose's *De obitu Valentiniani* (77) angels form a retinue (*comitatus*) to accompany the young emperor's soul to heaven; in Prudentius's *Peristephanon* (5.373–4) choirs of saints (*sanctorum chori*) throng round (*stipant*) Saint Vincent's ascending spirit. Chromatius of Aquileia (*serm.* 8.4; *CCL* 9A: 36.83–4) describes Christ ascending to heaven with attendant angels (*famulatus debitus ab angelis deferebatur*), who go before and behind him (*alii enim praecedebant, alii sequebantur*). As Dufraigne says, similar texts describing the arrival of the souls of the just in heaven are frequent in Late Antiquity.[42] Lactantius's version differs in that the birds who attend the phoenix are not escorting the phoenix to their own abode; they do not live in heaven / the grove of the Sun. But in other respects they supply an avian equivalent of the company that surrounds the central figures in such Christianized *aduentus* ceremonies in later Christian literature. As a long-standing symbol of immortality, the phoenix is well suited to stand for the immortal soul or the resurrected Christ.[43] This perhaps is the reason why Lactantius transfers the account of the phoenix's winged retinue from its more common location as part of the journey to Heliopolis. It allows him to invest the flight of the phoenix with fuller Christian significance, since instead of just returning to Heliopolis to perform last rites for its father's remains, the phoenix now is ascending to heaven and returning home. In the final couplet of this section (159–60), heaven and the grove of the Sun are identified: the bird reaches heaven (159) and settles in its own abode (*suis . . . locis*; the

---

41. Fontaine 1981: 61 accurately describes the passage as a triumphal cortege.

42. For the Christian appropriation of the *aduentus* ceremony in accounts of death and of Christ's ascension, see Dufraigne 1994: 318–25 and 374–419. The quotation is from 320.

43. For Christological elements in Lactantius's treatment of the phoenix, see Wlosok 1982: 149. The Greek *Physiologus* (7), of uncertain date, develops the parallels with Christ's death and resurrection more systematically. Lactantius's choice of the phrase *animam commendat* (93) of the phoenix's death is significant, recalling as it does *commendo spiritum meum* of Luke 23:46.

phrase is studiedly ambiguous, equally applicable to both locations). To reach one is to reach the other. In a form of ring composition the reborn phoenix returns to its paradise-like home, as described at the beginning of the poem, a return that is absent from the non-Christian versions of the myth.

12.3. CHRISTIAN POETRY AND MIRACLE NARRATIVES

In significant respects the *De aue phoenice* points the way to subsequent developments in Christian Latin poetry. The phoenix's song in the grove of the Sun provides a model for Christian poetry as an expression of service and devotion to God, akin to liturgical performance. In adapting the traditional avian retinue that accompanies the phoenix in the ascent of the bird back to heaven / its homeland, Lactantius assimilates that escort to the welcoming company of the *aduentus* ceremony. In so doing he anticipates the theme of *aduentus* of the holy dead into heaven commonplace in subsequent literature, both prose and verse. It is also characteristic of Christian poetics that the poem is susceptible of a variety of different readings: the phoenix can be interpreted as standing for individual Christians who receive in heaven a reward for their holy life or for the resurrected Christ. The bird's devotions to the Sun can exemplify the life of service to God, but his song can also be a figure for the Christian poet and for poetry as an act of Christian devotion.[44]

In the concluding coda to the poem (161–4), Lactantius points to a further level of significance. He exults over the good fortune of the phoenix, which is born from itself and needs no sexual reproduction. The sex of the bird is consequently indeterminate; it may be male, female, or neither.[45] Whichever is the case, it enjoys a happy fate in that "it has no truck with the pacts of Venus" (*felix quae Veneris foedera nulla colit*, 164).[46] Lactantius's language here suggests a further level of meaning for the phoenix, as a symbol of Christian virginity. Indeed Van den Broek (1972: 381–9) considers that in the poem the phoenix "is primarily a symbol of the early Christian *uirgo*," citing Lactantius's praise of virginity in the *Divinae institutiones* as "a heavenly manner of life" (*caelesti genere uitae*, 6.23.37).[47] While the poem's concluding lines certainly suggest that the bird can

---

44. For the multiple levels of significance of the poem, see Fontaine 1981: 62 and Wlosok 1982: 147–50.

45. The text of the line on the phoenix's sex (163) is uncertain, though the meaning isn't. For a discussion, see Walla 1969: 180–2, who adopts the emendation of Brandt *femina<seu sexu> seu mas est siue neutrum*.

46. The phrase *Veneris foedera* is found in Seneca, *Phaedr.* 910, and Silius 2.83, where it refers to marriage, but here it apparently refers to sexual relations more broadly.

47. The quotation is from Van den Broek 1972: 381, who cites Lactantius, *inst.* 6.23.37, *plurimi beatam atque incorruptam corporis integritatem retinuerint multique sint qui hoc caelesti genere vitae felicissime perfruantur*.

carry this meaning, I see no reason to privilege it over the other possible readings, especially as the bird's asexual regeneration is not mentioned elsewhere in the poem.[48]

The *De aue phoenice* concludes with another passage that carries premonitions of what is to follow in Christian Latin poetry. In it Lactantius amplifies on the paradoxes of the phoenix's self-generation and life from death.[49]

> *Mors illi Venus est, sola est in morte uoluptas;*
>   *ut possit nasci, appetit ante mori.*
> *Ipsa sibi proles, suus est pater et suus heres,*
>   *nutrix ipsa sui, semper alumna sibi.*
> *Ipsa quidem, sed non <eadem est>, eademque nec ipsa est,*[50]
>   *aeternam uitam mortis adepta bono.* (165–70)

> For it death was its Venus, its only pleasure in death;
>   to be able to be born it sought first to die.
> It is its own offspring, its own father and heir,
>   nurse of itself, always its own nursling.
> It is itself, but not the same, the same and not itself,
>   achieving eternal life by virtue of death.

The passage has a riddling quality, communicated by the series of paradoxes that contradict normal human experience. Formally these are expressed primarily by antithesis (*nasci ~ mori; proles ~ pater; nutrix ~ alumna; ipsa ~ nec ipsa; non eadem ~ eadem; uitam ~ mortis*). The series of *sententiae*, reinforced by polyptoton (165) and a series of rhymes between the two halves of a line (166–8), find a kind of resolution in the final line—the only one not containing more than one clause—in which the reference to eternal life would immediately be fully intelligible only to the informed Christian reader.

The myth of the phoenix, particularly of its rebirth, constitutes a miracle of nature. It would fit perfectly well in the paradoxographical tradition, with that tradition's interest in such natural wonders.[51] Lactantius more than once

---

48. Later in the century Ambrose, *in psalm.* 118 19.13, treats the phoenix as a model of virginity and chastity. It is perhaps relevant that in Lactantius's poem the word *phoenix* is grammatically feminine (it is masculine in Claudian). According to the *ThLL* (10: 2049.53–6) the word is predominantly masculine. Pomponius Mela, first century CE, is the earliest citation for the feminine gender; most of the instances are from Late Antiquity.

49. See Uden 2012: 465–7.

50. I quote the line with Baehrens's emendation, adopted by Brandt.

51. For a summary of that tradition as it relates to a late antique poet (Claudian), see Guipponi-Gineste 2010: 201–3.

emphasizes the marvellous quality of his subject (*mira*, 46; *mirandam*, 123; *miracula*, 151). In Lactantius, though, quasi-scientific wonder at the marvels of the natural world gives way to admiration for a miracle that transcends normal human experience and in the Christian view of things communicates an important doctrinal truth. The clustering of paradoxical expressions at the end of the poem is not, or not just, a literary mannerism but a discursive idiom that does justice to the Christian understanding of the miraculous and the divine.[52]

In Lactantius we see the beginnings of the Christian miracle narrative, as it came to be practiced by later poets. When, in the second quarter of the next century, the poet Sedulius devotes the central books of his New Testament biblical epic to the miracles of Christ, episodes typically take the form anticipated by Lactantius: the narrative proper is followed by a line or lines that meditate on the remarkable nature of the miracle, often employing paradox and antithesis to bring out those features.[53] So, for instance, Sedulius concludes his account of the raising of Lazarus with paradoxical *sententiae*: Lazarus is "a living corpse" (*uiuens . . . cadauer*, 4.288), "a dead man [who] was his own successor and heir" (*ipse sibi moriens et postumus extat et heres*, 4.290). The compositional scheme occurs frequently in hagiographical epic, with its large miracle content, under the influence of Sedulius. Fortunatus, describing the raising of a catechumen in his *Life of Saint Martin*, adapts Sedulius's language of Lazarus to the Gallic saint's miracle. The revived catechumen "again comes to life, surviving himself, his own creator and heir" *ipse iterum post se uiuens, idem auctor et heres*, 1.176). Both passages exploit the possibilities resurrection offers for paradoxical expression, in a manner akin to Lactantius's treatment of the phoenix's rebirth. But whatever the circumstances of the miracle, Christian poets regularly employ paradox and antithesis, usually at the conclusion of a particular miracle episode, to elicit pious wonder at the nature-defying events.[54]

Reading Lactantius's *De aue phoenice* is a somewhat disconcerting experience for the student of late Latin poetry. In so many ways it seems familiar, not by evoking what has gone before—though it certainly has its fair share of

---

52. Lactantius had a prose forerunner in Tertullian (*De resurrectione mortuorum* 13.2), who cites the phoenix's self-survival as evidence for resurrection: *natali fine decedens atque succedens, iterum phoenix ubi nemo iam, iterum ipse qui non iam, alius idem.* It is worth noting that Claudian, although he refers to the paradoxical nature of the phoenix's rebirth (24–6, 50–2, 101), does not give it special emphasis or a prominent position in his poem.

53. Similar procedures can be found less systematically earlier. So Paulinus of Nola plays on the paradoxes involved in diabolic possession and exorcism (*carm.* 23.70–3).

54. For this compositional practice in Sedulius and Fortunatus, see Roberts 2009: 207–9 and 213–22. The same features are present in Paulinus of Périgueux's earlier (fifth century) hagiographical epic, also on Saint Martin, but not to the same degree as in Fortunatus's poem.

classical expressions—but by anticipating what is to come. The poem shows features that would be common to late antique poetry in general—generic indeterminacy, the increased emphasis on description at the expense of narrative, and the prominence of ceremony—but also specifically Christian features that point to a distinctive Christian poetics. In its crypto-Christianity it shows an adaptation to contemporary conditions of reception, when presumably overt expressions of Christian sentiments would be dangerous.[55] But in all other respects the *De aue phoenice* looks to the future, an important precursor of the poetic revival of Late Antiquity.

---

55. Compare Juvencus, who, when he came to write his New Testament biblical epic in 329/30, was entirely free to express Christian sentiments but had to make some concessions to a readership that was still not well informed about Christian doctrine by excluding almost all overt exegetical commentary. Squire in this volume sees a similar combination of secular and Christian meanings in the very different poetry of the near contemporary Optatianus Porfyrius.

The Early Christian Response to Platonist Poetics

Boethius, Prudentius, and the *Poeta Theologus*

MARC MASTRANGELO

13.1. INTRODUCTION

The literary tradition associated with Boethius's *consolatio philosophiae* is well known and crucial to Western literary history. As readers, we envision Boethius sitting in his cell, contemplating the injustice of his suffering and impending death.[1] *Philosophia* ("Lady Philosophy") comes to him to furnish a therapeutic cure that will change his perspective, bring him peace of mind and strength to face a fate that he does not control.[2] In the *consolatio*, Boethius revisits the age-old quarrel between philosophy (for Christians, theology) and poetry by drawing upon discrete forms of prose and poetry and by adopting the content of the ancient philosophical and poetic traditions—and even Christian traditions.[3] Poetry, the source of lies, stands side by side with its opposite, philosophy, the way of truth.[4]

I argue that Boethius offers a solution to the traditional quarrel between philosophy and poetry, which in the fourth-through-sixth-century Latin West had resulted in denying poetry's claims to truth, conferring upon poetry

---

1. On Boethius's life and imprisonment, see Helleman 2009: 96; Chadwick 1981: 48–56; Marenbon 2003: 7–10. For a summary of recent Boethian interpretation, see Helleman 2009: 110–24. Text and translations of Boethius are from Stewart, Rand, and Tester 1918 with changes; for Prudentius, see Thomson 1949 with changes.

2. See Helleman 2009: 110 for a summary of scholarship on the identity of *Philosophia*.

3. Mohrmann 1976: 54–61 argues that even though Boethius aims for "neutrality," the language of *consolatio* has Christian features concerning piety and the liturgy, i.e., Christian worship and ritual practice.

4. For prose forms the *consolatio* recalls the philosophical dialogue and theological treatise; for forms of poetry, elegy, lyric, and others. Boethius is steeped in the philosophical traditions of Plato and Aristotle (not to mention the Hellenistic schools, which may be represented by those who have torn *Philosophia*'s cloak, *cons.* 1.p1.22–5). He is also a sophisticated inheritor of Roman poetic tradition, including Vergil (Shanzer 2009: 229), Lucretius, and Horace (O'Daly 1991: 42, 49). Klingner 1966 and Courcelle 1967 are both excellent on Boethius's sources and influences. Donato 2013: ch. 4 argues that Boethius's attitudes toward philosophy in his writings take their cue from the Neoplatonists Iamblichus and Proclus, who understood philosophy as improvable and an important step to a superior form of knowledge.

consequently a secondary intellectual status[5] but also a challenge to reinvent itself. Moreover, from a literary and historical perspective, Boethius's use of poetry in the *consolatio* helps to clarify the poetics of early Christian poets, such as Prudentius. A renewed version of the old quarrel, articulated anew as a quarrel between poetry and theology, became fundamental to the conception of literature. By the end of the fourth century, patristic works sanctioned a devastating, Platonist critique of poetry, arguing that most poetry is divorced from truth and that the sole pleasure and truth of poetry therefore ought to subsist in chanting and singing hymns to God. For the church and its most eminent thinkers, poetry should avoid irrelevant allegories and metaphors and be committed to communicating doctrine directly to the masses. Theological and doctrinal prose had the upper hand, as it were, with poetry condemned to a subordinate position in the intellectual/religious debates of the day.[6] However, poetry did play a unique role in transmitting stories and doctrine and developing innovative forms. Christian poets did not merely conform to patristic strictures but engaged in a sustained project of reimagining poetry's use and purpose. Nevertheless, it remains the case that for the first three centuries of Latin Christian poetry, a revival of the opposition between prose and poetry obtained to the disadvantage of poetry as a cultural touchstone.

Given the results of the opposition between philosophy/theology and poetry, Prudentius and other early Christian poets, who wrote non-liturgical poetry, faced a profound problem of poetics: what was the function of poetry and what cultural role did it play? More specifically, what would be a response to the patristic, Platonist critique of poetry? Boethius's *consolatio* gives a comprehensive response, indications of which are also found in the work of Prudentius.[7] It is through the interaction of poetry and philosophy in the *consolatio* that Boethius achieves a rapprochement between the two, a new poetics that paved the way for the medieval *theologus poeta*. Long before Petrarch pronounced "theology is poetry that is from God,"[8] early Christian poets, like Boethius (and Prudentius as well), represent the beginning of a literary historical process in which Christian poets from Late Antiquity through Petrarch and right up to

---

5. Mastrangelo 2009: 313–20. See Ware in this volume on how the practitioners of prose panegyric attempted to appropriate and supersede poetry as a genre.

6. Mastrangelo 2009: 311; Lerer 1985: 3–4.

7. I am not arguing for a formal influence of Prudentius on Boethius, though there is some evidence (e.g., Klingner 1966: 54–5). Rather, Prudentius and Boethius are part of a literary historical trajectory, which originates in their attitudes toward poetry and philosophy, i.e., in their poetics.

8. *Le familiari*, 10,4 dicam theologiam poeticam esse de Deo; See Curtius 1990: 226. For Petrarch, "theology," whether in the form of prose or verse, is "poetry."

Milton settle the old argument between philosophy/theology and poetry and restore poetry's cultural and intellectual status.

In what follows I begin by sketching the nature of the Platonist-patristic critique of poetry that dominated the early Christian literary landscape. Secondly, I argue that Boethius responds to this critique in three ways: 1) by merging poetic and philosophical discourses; 2) by renewing poetry's claims to truth; and 3) by developing a dualist poetics in which poetry shares in unifying the human and the divine. Throughout, I suggest that the work of Prudentius reflects certain aspects of the Boethian response, especially when compared to other poets of the period. The works of Boethius and Prudentius reflect a rapprochement between the *poeta* and the *theologus*, a development that Dante, Petrarch, and Milton would take for granted.

13.2. The Platonist/Patristic Critique of Poetry

In the *Republic* and *Ion*, Plato nearly eliminates poetry's educational and cultural functions because of its inability to transmit knowledge and virtue to its readers. On this view, not only is poetry, as practiced in the Greek tradition, divorced from truth, it can shape bad character in its audience. Thus, Plato banishes poets from his ideal city, only allowing them to stay if they produce hymns to gods and virtuous men.[9] While classical and Hellenistic literary criticism followed upon this provocative thesis, it is not until the Roman Empire of Constantine and thereafter that this Platonist vision of poetry was to a certain degree enacted.

For early Christian poets, a patristic version of this doctrine became a central condition of artistic production.[10] Church fathers such as Lactantius, Ambrose, Augustine, and Jerome at different times either ignore or criticize (non-liturgical) Christian poetry. Their attitudes toward pagan poetry are clear: It is full of lies and is incapable of expressing truth. On the ground, this attitude translated into a lukewarm reception (and lack of recognition) of early Christian poetry by the church fathers. On the other hand, the patristic version of the Platonist view of poetry furnished a set of constraints that helped usher in, for example, the development of the genre of hymns in Ambrose and the experiment with pagan poetic forms in Prudentius and Paulinus of Nola, all the while transmitting Christian doctrinal content.

---

9. The bibliography is daunting on Plato's treatment of the poets. Moravcsik and Temko 1982 is still a good place to start. See also Asmis 1992.

10. The patristic critique of pagan poetic tradition developed a loose set of patristic conventions of poetic practice for Christian poetry. See Evenpoel 1993: 44–8, Mastrangelo 2009: 316–24, and Mastrangelo 2016. I wish to focus on specific Platonist-patristic themes to which the poetics of Prudentius and Boethius answers.

Lactantius, writing during the apologetic phase of early Christianity, is willing to give pagan poets credit for being close to the truth (*inst.* 1.5.11–14) and containing certain truths like the remoteness of justice in human affairs (*inst.* 5.5.1–2) and even resurrection (*inst.* 7.22.1–4). He laments that Orpheus, Vergil, and Ovid never fully express truth (*inst.* 1.5.14). Homer deals in falsities because, as Lactantius says at *inst.* 1.5.8, "he wrote on a human rather than a divine level." Even though he rationalizes the views of the pagan poets (see also *inst.* 1.11.30; 2.10.12), Lactantius plants the seeds in his patristic descendants of the rejection of pagan poets precisely because of their problem with telling the truth according to Christian doctrine: "Philosophy, oratory, and poetry are all pernicious for the ease with which they enslave incautious souls in beguiling prose and nice modulations of poetical flow. They are honey, hiding poison" (*inst.* 5.1.10).[11]

Lactantius wrote before Christian poetry constituted a body of work. However, Augustine, who could have commented on many Christian poetic texts, does so rarely, and when he does make a comment, it is only on liturgical works such as the *psalms* or Ambrose's *hymns*.[12] He begins from Lactantius's critique of the pagan poets, and like his contemporary, Jerome, he goes much further: *non audiendi sunt errores gentilium superstitionum* ("For we must not listen to the fictions of pagan superstitions," AUG. *doctr. christ.* 2.16.26–2.17.27). When not reading scripture, Augustine reads exclusively patristic authors,[13] and by the time of *City of God*, he has repudiated Vergil as a liar and discredited epic as source of (national) identity.[14]

---

11. *Nam et in hoc philosophi et oratores et poetae perniciosi sunt, quod incautos animos facile inretire possunt suavitate sermonis at carminum dulci modulation currentium* [*mella sunt haec venena tegentia*]. But Lactantius seems to have left the door open for a new kind of non-liturgical Christian poetry when he says that no poem is a "total fiction"; that is, poems harbour truths that are hidden and more difficult to find (*inst.* 1.11.30; 1.9.8–10; 1.11.23–5, 30, 36; 1.19.5; 1.21.44). All English translations of Lactantius are taken from Bowen and Garnsey 2003.

12. Westra 2007: 12 points out that Augustine offers no substantive comment on non-liturgical poetry as practiced by his contemporaries (see Roberts in this volume, on the importance of a liturgical purpose for Christian poetry.) E.g., the first explicit reference we have to Prudentius is Cassian in 426, and both Augustine and Jerome ignore him. Augustine does express admiration for Ambrose's hymn *deus creator omnium* (*conf.* 9.12.32; 10.35.52; 11.27.35). But could Augustine have *not* read an author like Prudentius? We know that Prudentian manuscripts show up early and often; and he is cited throughout the fifth century by people like Paulinus of Nola, Cassian, Claudius Marius Victor, Sedulius, and others. These citations cover Gaul to Greece, but Africa appears to lack this sort of Prudentian presence until Dracontius. *Civ.* 19.10 has been cited occasionally as a reference to the praise of peace in the *Psychomachia*. The philological evidence appears to be razor thin.

13. AUG. *doctr. christ.* 2.40.61; 4.5.8; 4.124.30; 4.21.45–8.

14. At *serm.* 105.7.10, Augustine attacks Vergil, the spokesman for all pagan Roman culture, as a liar. MacCormack 1998: 190, says: "This mode of interpretation reduced the subtle mingling of myth and history and of divine and human action that characterized epic poetry to a straightforward contrast of truth and invention." See also Mastrangelo 2009: 318–19.

Augustine stridently dismisses pagan poetry as worthless, especially when poetry views itself as a form of prophecy or theology. At *civ.* 6.5, he criticizes Varro's Platonist-inspired views on theological expression because he did not go far enough. Varro's three categories of theology form the basis of this critique: 1) the mythical, which "is especially used by the poets," 2) the physical (natural), "which the philosophers use," and 3) the civic, "which the people use." The bishop dismisses the first and third categories because they have poetry in common (the civil supports theatre that portrays the divine in unacceptable ways, *conf.* 2.24 and 4.27); poetry is "false, vile, and unworthy." While not giving an endorsement to physical or natural theology as practiced by philosophers, he does not criticize it as he does the other two. For Augustine, poetry is divorced from theology, at least poetry as traditionally practiced in Graeco-Roman culture. In Augustine's Christian (rhetorical) aesthetic, the pagan allegorical tradition of poets as theologians is unacceptable because of "the perception of poets as rivals to the Old Testament prophets."[15] The idea of poets as theologians places poetry as a textual rival to the scriptures.[16] Poetry is an activity limited to the human sphere, with little, if any, connection to the divine. Similar to Lactantius, Augustine seizes upon Hesiod's account of the Muses, whom he understands as human beings that became immortal by human invention (*doctr. christ.* 2.18.26–2.17.27). Poetry as a purely human production lacks a connection to the divine and is thus beyond the defence of "reasonable lies."

Augustine's silence on early Christian poets and his rejection of poetry as reflective of the divine compel the conclusion that non-liturgical poetry does *not* count as a legitimate reading or interpretation of the Bible.[17] Hence, a severe Platonist aesthetic results in which even poetry that celebrates God and proper theological and moral doctrines remains marginal because the moment the practice of poetry is severed from its divine connection and function of cultural and cosmic interpreter, it has no business concerning itself with the interpretation of scripture, a sacred text that is divine in origin and a guide for life. Thus Augustine moves away from pagan *and* Christian poets (for related but different reasons) to Ambrose, Cyprian, the scriptures, and other church fathers (*doctr. christ.* 2.40.61; 4.5.8; 4.14.30; 4.21.45–8). Combined with his explicit suspicion of

---

15. Westra 2007: 17. Augustine rejected poetry's association with hierophants, prophets, or others types of mediators of divine truth.

16. Stock 1996: 53 observes that for Augustine, spiritual progress is linked to the reading and interpretation of biblical texts.

17. See Clark in this volume for Augustine's (Platonist) view of a Christian poetics.

poetic pleasure,[18] which flows from the senses and emotions, Augustine constructs a Platonist aesthetic that separated the *poeta* from the *theologus* and poetry from (biblical) interpretation.[19]

Augustine is a prominent example in patristic literature wherein Platonist attitudes, such as poetry's fraudulent representation of the divine and its separation from prophetic knowledge, elicited reactions in the Christian poetry from Late Antiquity to the Renaissance.[20] Ambrose disparages both pagan poets and philosophers (Aristotle, in particular) by accusing them of having the same incorrect idea of God because both follow the same poetic *fabulae: et quomodo ipsi excludunt quos sequuntur poetas*? "And how is it that they [philosophers] reject the poets whom they follow?" (AMBR. *off.* 1.50). Jerome, who at one point in his life claims that he hadn't touched a pagan text in fifteen years (*in Gal.* 3), asserts the divorce of pagan poetry from things divine by criticizing clergy: "priests of God who slight the Gospels and the prophets, reading comedies, reciting love passages from bucolic verse, cherishing Vergil" (HIER. *epist.* 21,9).[21] One aspect of this legacy, crystallized in Augustine's *Confessions*—a prose work with poetic

---

18. See Westra 2007: 14. Augustine does accept certain kinds of cognitive pleasure like the contemplation of God. However, such an activity is best reserved for exegesis and theology, found in his more populist sermons and more scholarly treatises. As Westra 2007: 21 concludes, "the pleasurable element of Christian literature becomes subordinated to the didactic purposes of prose preaching."

19. Clark (432–8) in this volume rehearses Augustine's "Platonist objections to poetry." Clark in the same essay discusses Augustine's rejection of poetry's complicated vocabulary, syntax, and grammar as necessary in order to communicate with common people. A poem that is characterized by *sermo humilis* is best. Prudentius, on the other hand, was after an educated audience (Clark 444–5)

20. The separation of poetry from knowledge of or inspiration from the divine is apparent in both patristic literature and early Christian poetry. For example, the reputed teacher of Lactantius, Arnobius, who wrote his *adversus nationes* around the turn of the fourth century, denies that divine inspiration exists for the arts and similar crafts (*nat.* 2.19). At *nat.* 1.19, Arnobius recycles the argument of Plato's *Republic*, perhaps as filtered through Cicero (CIC. *nat. deor.* 1.16.42), in which poets' representation of the gods is criticized (cf. *nat.* 3.11 on poets and philosophers telling false stories about the gods and 4.32–6 on poets and dramatists). Another Christian author, the apocalyptic poet Commodianus (third century), discredits pagan poets who are seen as prophets and misrepresent the divine, *per vates historicae confictae* (*instr.* 6.15; see also 17.1). Commodianus sees himself as a *perdoctus* poet who is teaching the ignorant through reading of sacred texts (*instr.* 8.10–12, *accedite legis <codicem> et di<s>cete verum*—cf. Augustine's *tolle lege*!) Commodianus expresses the Platonist approach, in which the didactic and educative function of poetry determines what it can be used for (*disce Deum, stulte, qui vult te inmortalem adesse, instr.* 29,12; *lex docet* . . . , *instr.* 29,14).

21. Jerome's full critique of pagan poetry is explicitly Platonist. At *ep.* 21.4, he discusses further how this poetry penetrates the soul, causing a lack of truth, justice, and a character bereft of virtue (cf. *ep.* 22.30.4). His most famous statement against pagan literature at *ep.* 22.29.7 exploits 1 Cor. 8:10 and dismisses the two greatest pagan Latin poets: "What has Horace to do with the Psalter, Vergil with the Gospels, Cicero with Paul?" Notice that Jerome distinguishes between pagan poetry and liturgical poetry, Horace versus the Psalter. Also, Vergil is juxtaposed with the Gospels, the primary identity-forming text of Christianity. Poetry is of no use when put against these texts. Cicero and Paul are the spokesmen, apologists, and doctrinal sources of pagan Roman and Christian thought, respectively.

sensibilities, resulted in the discouragement of a theological poetry in favour of a poetry that highlights, for instance, an individual, spiritual journey, from earthly pleasures to heavenly contemplation.[22] Direct communication of the poet and, by extension, the reader with God would become a function of early Christian poetry.

Other personages from the early church, some of whom were poets, reflected the institutional and political role of the Platonist critique of reading and writing poetry. By the time of Avitus of Vienne (d. 517 CE), the freedom to experiment with form and style (meter, diction, tropes), a hallmark of fourth-century poetry, had come into question. In the dedicatory letter to his *de spiritalis historiae gestis* (507 CE), he says:

> However shrewd and learned a man may be, if in the representation of his Christian belief he follows the law of faith no less than the law of meter, he can hardly be a proper poet, since the seriousness of his subject requires that the freedom to lie ... be utterly banished. For in the composition of a secular poetry the more artistically, or rather ... the more improperly a man has introduced falsehoods, the more skilled he is acclaimed to be.[23]

Michael Roberts has described Avitus as taking an "unusually rigid" stance when compared to a poet like Dracontius, who engages in the tropes of metonymy or the mythological language of *tonans* for God.[24] Further, when posing the question of the source of Avitus's so-called rigidity, Roberts makes the point that he was a bishop, which added to his own restrictive, Platonist sense of what poetry could be.[25] In the *de virginitate* (275, 9–12, Peiper 1886) Avitus goes further by saying that only prose is appropriate for a bishop such as himself.[26]

---

22. Warner 2005: 2–5 observes that Petrarch was a main inheritor of this approach to poetry, but there is still the question of whether Augustine was the main or only purveyor of allegorical epic (2, 7) to Petrarch and other medieval and Renaissance poets.

23. Translation by Roberts 1980. The Latin text is as follows: *Quamquam quilibet acer ille doctusque sit, si religionis propositae stilum non minus fidei quam metri lege servavit, vix aptus esse poemati queat; quippe cum licentia mentiendi ... satis procul a causarum serietate pellenda sit. In saeculari namque versuum opera condendo tanto quis peritior appelatur, quanto elegantius, immo ... ineptius falsa texuerit.* Avitus cleverly discredits the fundamentally literary language of the *doctus poeta*; e.g., *doctus, elegantius, texuerit*. Other poets were endeavouring to package Christian doctrine in the more sophisticated pagan forms, but the purpose of this innovative and experimental work was to create, in the words of Jerome, a Christian literature *de scripturis sanctis*. See Vessey 2007: 33, 47.

24. Roberts 1980: 406.

25. Roberts 1980: 406 cites Avitus 202, 10–12 (Peiper), which shows the bishop rejecting the reading of pagan poetry because he is a member of the clergy.

26. Roberts 1980: 407 overstates when he says that "Avitus, alone of the Biblical poets of Late Antiquity, occupied an important position in the ecclesiastical hierarchy." While Avitus may have held a particularly powerful position in the church, the emphasis should be that Christian poets and other influential critiques of poetry were connected closely to the government and to the church. E.g., Juvencus

Avitus was not the only voice that re-energizes this overtly church-based Platonist critique. By the fifth century, Hilary of Arles is embarrassed that he had written poetry inspired by pagan poets.[27] Pierre Riché has gone as far as saying that in Gaul, the students of rhetors, who were under episcopal orders, had to account for the incompatibility between sacred and profane cultures.[28] Sidonius Apollinaris, who wrote masses and hymns, admits that he was not mindful enough of his profession as bishop (*epist.* 4.12) and recognizes that the reputation of a poet could stain the dignity of a member of the clergy (*clerici ne quid maculet rigorem fama poeta, epist.* 9.16).[29] One generation later, Ennodius, bishop of Ticinum, has a similar reaction to Sidonius, saying that his clerical status compels him to pursue simple (Christian) doctrine. He exclaims to his protégé, the poet Arator, that he hates the liberal arts, which included poetry (ENNOD. *epist.* 2.6 and 9.1).[30] Poets and rhetoricians are liars, which he cannot be obliged to follow (*a vera sapientia mentitam secutus abcesseram,* "Having followed lies I had gone away from the path of true wisdom," ENNOD. *euch. opusc.* 5). Finally, in the fifth century, church documents themselves reinforced this attitude that its clerics reject their Roman pagan literary inheritance, even instituting a probationary period for a year.[31] In fact, this impasse furnished a serious test of clerics ability to deal with the early Christian problem of education. This Platonist tension, in which an education program must be purged of its malevolent influences, could be resolved only by an intellectual conversion on the part of cleric-poets like Avitus, Sidonius, and others.

In the Rule of Benedict, written by Benedict of Nursia in the mid-sixth century, the monastic contribution to educational programming is

---

is said to have been a priest. Paulinus of Nola was a high-ranking senator and provincial governor as well as a presbyter (393 CE) and bishop of Nola (409 CE). Sedulius, who spent his early life studying pagan literature, becomes a priest, according to Isidore of Seville. Orientius appears to have been the bishop of Auch in the early fifth century. Ennodius of Arles (d. 534 CE) was bishop of Ticinum; and his protégé, Arator, who was a lawyer at the court of Ravenna, was a *subdiaconus* and entered the papal service. Sidonius (d. 485 CE) was prefect of Rome and bishop of Clermont. Both Augustine and Jerome, two of the most influential critics of poetry, held important positions in the church.

27. See Riché 1995: 83 for references.
28. Riché 1995: 83. Much of what follows in this paragraph is based on Riché 1995: 81–4.
29. See also SIDON. *epist.* 9.12.1: *Primum ab exordio religiosae professionis huic principaliter exercitio renuntiavi, quia nimirum facilitate posset accomodari, si me occupasset levitas versum. . . . Post mortem non opuscula sed opera pensanda.*
30. Cf. *epist.* 9.9, where Ennodius refuses to instruct his son in the liberal arts—in other words, the heritage of Graeco-Roman learning.
31. *Statuta ecclesiae antiqua* (sec. 13.5) says: *ut episcopus gentilium libros non legat* . . . ("so that the bishop not read the pagan books"). For the probationary period, see *Council of Sardique, PL* 56.407. Riché 1995: 84 says: "the cultured clergy felt the necessity to reject classical culture, but they did not resolve the problem despite council edicts."

manifest. Thus the reading list includes only prose: the New Testament, the Pentateuch, the church fathers, the *Lives of the Desert Fathers*, and Saint Basil. The *concilium vasense*, a clerical document from 529 CE outlining the responsibilities of priests asserts: "priests installed in the parish ... [should] ... bring up religiously, as good fathers, young readers" by teaching them psalmody, how to read sacred texts, and the Law of the Lord "in order to ensure the emergence of worthy successors"; and the *Toletana Synodus* (Second Council of Toledo) II.1 says that all children destined for the church should be taught in the church in the presence of a bishop.[32] By the sixth century, the church exerted nearly a total influence on education. Hymns and scripture constituted the reading list, all overseen by theologian authority figures—a scheme Plato could have only dreamed of in fifth- and fourth-century Athens.

Recent scholarship has confirmed that the period's environment for Christian poets was indeed challenging. Fontaine, for instance, has isolated two different but related factors: first, that after 406 CE the material destruction of civil war, invasions, the paralysis of public scholastic institutions, and the unintellectual forms of education of the German invaders damaged antique culture and the written word; and secondly, he argues that "Ciceronian culture" (i.e., the pagan inheritance, or *cultura animi*) undergoes a significant change. All cultural activity, including the "highest type," theology, exegesis, and literature, was integrated into a "specifically religious activity." Graeco-Roman culture "becomes a means toward a religious end which surpasses it: the personal encounter with God in the Holy scripture, which preserves His presence via His Word, and in the *vita communis* of a monastic or clerical community."[33] Christian doctrine and education as circumscribed by the monastic and clerical communities, the "philosopher kings," constitute the intellectual environment that Christian poets were working under.

Other modern scholars, such as R. Herzog and M. Vessey to different degrees, have commented on the reduction or displacement of poetry's interpretative function to biblical exegesis, which was being done authoritatively in prose by church fathers. When analyzing HIER. *epist.* 58,8–11, Herzog commented that "poetry, like every other genre, ha[d] forfeited its status as a

---

32. Fontaine 2005: 743–4 cites these texts.
33. Fontaine 2005: 737. See also Vessey 2007: 33 on the use of pagan poetry and prose as a means for exegesis and the view of Herzog 1975: 167–78 that Jerome was indifferent to poetry, contra Curtius who saw the saint as a promoter of Christian poetry. Vessey stakes out the middle ground by seeing in Jerome "a scripturally oriented poetics" (34). Both Vessey and Herzog are in line with the picture I am giving in this chapter.

distinct field of literary reception." In summing up Paulinus of Nola's contribution to literary history, Vessey concluded that he had "lent his hand to one of the most laborious acts in European literary history: the displacement of Roman poetry by biblical exegetical prose." Vessey's verdict is similar on Jerome's Christian *litteratus*, whose works should be "in prose on Holy scripture ... distinct from all previous poetry-as-versification, 'pagan' or Christian."[34]

Early Christian poets composed their works under an aesthetic regime in which exegesis of biblical texts and Christian doctrine was not seen as a distinguishing mark. Even with Herzog's pronouncement that a significant portion of early Christian poetry is exegetical,[35] the conventional wisdom has been that early Christian poetry was not innovative and nuanced, nor did it even achieve complete arguments, in the interpretation of biblical texts. For that, patristic treatises and sermons have been the gold standard. However, at different stages of the development of Christian poetry in the third to sixth centuries, one can indeed discern an engagement to varying degrees with the *poeta theologus* function. Green has recently sketched how the biblical epics by Juvencus, Sedulius, and Arator, for example, engage in a spectrum of exegesis, ranging from a default exegesis by the choice of biblical references to sophisticated commentary on biblical passages and stories.[36] For all the creativity in the exegesis of Sedulius and Arator, Curtius's conclusion continues to rankle: namely, that early Christian poetry's connection to Graeco-Roman tradition "falsifies" the meaning of scripture.[37] This state of affairs presented a challenge to Latin Christian poets of the third through the sixth centuries. Moreover, it also highlights the idea that the reception of early Christian Latin poetry before the early modern era ignores its theological efforts, or in the modern era, it is received as containing second-rate theology. Boethius's *consolatio* responds by arguing that poetry does not function like philosophical/theological prose, but nevertheless it is necessary in the quest for divine truth and for an understanding of the human predicament.

---

34. Both quotations are from Vessey 2007: 48 and 47, respectively.

35. See Charlet 1988: 82–4.

36. Green 2006, esp. 298–9, in the sections entitled "Exegesis" of the biblical poets Juvencas, Sedulius, and Arator, sums up this progressivist picture of the three poets. Green at 367 discusses Petrarch's negative judgement (*ecl.* 10. 311–26) of these biblical poets, as well as Prudentius, as having "rich material" but "poor style." However, Petrarch's critique goes further than mere style. He denies to them a connection to the Muses and a lack of quality; while he ascribes to them the metaphor of tired oxen and the pejorative "weak voice." Early Christian poetry has suffered in its reception from a secondary status as a poor imitator of scripture.

37. Curtius 1990 461–2, referenced by Green 2006: 384.

13.3. The Merging of Poetic and Philosophical Discourses

Boethius makes explicit comments concerning the status of poetry throughout the *consolatio*. At 1.p1.39–41 Lady Philosophy drives away the *poeticas musas* from the prisoner's bedside. The distinction between traditional poetry and philosophy is clear and raw. 1m.1 is an expression of the prisoner's highly emotional state, an elegy for his condition: he is friendless, old, and undergoing the worst fortune he has experienced. As she expels the "literary" Muses, *Philosophia* boasts that her own muses (*meisque musis*) will restore the prisoner to health (1.p1.40–1). Finally, she wonders how such an exemplary person, nurtured by the Eleatic and Academic schools of philosophy, could be reduced to such irrational, emotional confusion. Her intervention is programmatic in terms of the role that Platonist views of poetry play in defining the distinction between literary poetry and philosophical poetry operative at this early stage of Boethius's work.

This generic distinction is usually understood as turning on emotional versus rational discourse. The first example of what rational, poetic discourse would look like is 1.m2, in which *Philosophia* complains, similarly to Boethius, that he used to study the causes of things (*naturae varias ... causas*). The Greek naturalists (Thales, Empedocles, et al.) were his models, as they were Plato's, for finding answers to broad metaphysical questions. Rational and empirical methods used to satisfy the prisoner. But no longer does the light of his mind (*mentis*) provide answers. Early in *Philosophia*'s treatment of the topic, poetry appears to be useful only for expressing extreme emotion (even by *Philosophia*), but also that real health is achievable only through philosophical poetry or poetic philosophy. In the pejorative sense, poetry is a vehicle for expressing and eliciting extreme emotion; while in the ideal sense, poetry conveys knowledge of the universe. This understanding of poetry as either distracting emotion or a vehicle for pure reason (*affectuum* and *rationis, cons.* 1.p1.32–3) sums up the Platonist constraints on poetry that are established at the beginning of the *consolatio*.

Nevertheless, the first book of the *consolatio* provides a window into Boethius's modification of these Platonist strictures. At 1.m1, the Muses of poetry inspire Boethius to write emotional poetry, an elegy of sorts to express his grief over his situation. Poetry allows him to express his "tearful complaint" (*querimoniam lacrimabilem*, 1.p1.2). But as the first prose passage of book 1 proceeds, these Muses of poetry (*scenicas meretriculas*) are banished from the scene, but *poetry is not*. They are replaced by *Philosophia*, who carries a book and a sceptre. Philosophical poetry at this point of the *consolatio* appears to be the ideal, especially if we take into account 1.m.2's philosophical naturalism with its empirical and rational content. But by 1.m3 it is clear that this "ideal" is simply not enough for Boethius the prisoner to break free of his malaise. In that poem we encounter a ten-line simile about *Philosophia* lifting the mist of lethargy from the prisoner's eyes. Indeed, poetry enhances and clarifies the picture of his condition. *Philosophia* is the *magistra virtutum* (1.m7) who comes down from her high seat (*supero cardine*, 1m.3.8). Poetic discourse participates in describing Boethius's condition and indicates the beginning of a solution: moral and spiritual therapy.

The *consolatio* begins with an elegiac poem expressing the poet's tragic situation and ends with a complicated argument in prose about divine foreknowledge and free will. It would seem that Boethius has indicated that philosophical argument has won the day and is the most serious medicine that will cure his spiritual ills. However, the last ten lines of the work (5.p6. 166–76) are a remarkable complication of this picture. The passage is a combination of an exhortation, a kind of prayer, and a direct emotional appeal that concludes by circling back to the idea of necessity, the abstract idea parsed in the previous 165 lines of prose. Those lines argue that human free will exists even though God has foreknowledge (the corollary of which implies the necessary occurrence of all events).[38] But at lines 166–7, Boethius anthropomorphizes God as a *spectator desuper* ("observer on high") who dispenses justice to the good and bad (169–70). Lines 170–2 proclaim the importance of "hopes and prayers" (*spes precesque* and *humiles preces in excelsa porrigite*, 171, 173–4), which are vital to avoiding vices and acquiring virtues (*aversamini igitur vitia, colite virtutes*, "turn away, then, from vices, and cultivate virtues," 172). The final sentence addresses readers directly,[39] challenging them to use their free will for good while being watched by a human-like God, the judge (*cum ante oculos agitis iudicis cuncta cernentis*, "when you act before the eyes of a judge who sees all," 175–6). Boethius returns to the kernel of 5.p6's compatibilist argument that while God's foreknowledge constitutes one part of necessity (e.g., *cunctorum praescius*, 167), free will to choose good or evil is the other part (*magna vobis est . . . necessitas indicta probitatis*, "a great necessity is solemnly ordained for you to do good," 175).

Although the argument of the prose section and of the work as a whole is summarized in concentrated fashion within lines 166–76, the tone is distinctively "unphilosophical." The emphasis on God the final judge, virtues and vices, prayer, and the necessity of free will, coupled with a direct address to readers, represents a compilation of poetic, rhetorical, and philosophical discourses. These discourses represent a concord between or a consolidation of the rational

---

38. For the details of this difficult argument, see Marenbon 2003: 125–45.
39. Though note that the switch to the second person begins earlier at line 172 with "*aversamini . . .*"

and the revelatory, the human and the divine, and finally, poetry and philosophy/theology.[40] For Boethius the author, the categories of "the poetic" and "the philosophical" have interpenetrated one another. Prayer, an anthropomorphic God, and direct address to the reader, mainstays of poetic texts, invade the end of the apparently "philosophical" 5.p6. In these verses and lines of prose, reason and revelation and philosophy/theology and poetry do not form such discreet categories. Moreover, scholars have shown that poetry is integral to the work, whether considered separately or together with the prose passages.[41] Allegory, metaphor, and emotional expression, rhetorical features of verse, can express a philosophical position, while analytical arguments are validated when packaged in a poetic trope, including allegory, metaphor, or exemplarity.[42] Also, scholars oversimplify when they assert that Boethius finds solace to his dire situation more in a reasoned philosophical approach than in the revelation of individual salvation.[43] The end of the *consolatio* alludes to the final judgment with God as arbiter; the virtue/vice language, which Boethius uses in several places,[44] is a fixture of Christian discourse from Tertullian onward and appears most famously in Prudentius's *Psychomachia*.

A central aspect of the *consolatio*'s originality lies in its presentation of various discourses for an ideologically neutral result. The presentation of pagan philosophical discourse does not conflict with Christian philosophy or doctrine.[45] Also, prose and poetry work together, employing rational argument,

---

40. These factors along with others have led some scholars to argue that the *consolatio* is unfinished. See O'Daly 1991: 28–9. *Philosophia*'s voice dominates 5.p6 and for most of book 5. She does not engage in much dialogue with Boethius, her attention taken up by weighty philosophical and theological topics such as chance, providence, necessity, and free will. A. Donato has pointed to Boethius's immersion in late antique Neoplatonism, exemplified by Iamblichus and Proclus, who saw no conflict between prayer and philosophical inquiry (190). Moreover, Donato argues, revelation and philosophical investigation of the divine can work together, as in the Neoplatonists and as stated in Boethius's works *de catholica* and *de trinitate*. See Donato 2013: 181–3.

41. Helleman 2009: 200 (also 122 n. 80 on Marenbon); Dronke 1994: 6; Curley 1987: 358–64, 366; Sweeney 2006: 4, 39; O'Daly 1991: 52 and more restrained at 147.

42. See Elsner and Formisano in this volume on how certain late antique poems use allegory to meditate on the role of the classical inheritance; also see Hernández Lobato in this volume (295–304) for the centrality of allegory in the work of Fulgentius; see also Mastrangelo 2008.

43. One of the major interpretive challenges regarding the *consolatio* has been readers' tendency to separate poetic and philosophic discourse into the rational or philosophical versus emotional or poetical. Jaroslav Pelikan 1971: 44 has expressed the problem in the following way: "This orthodox theologian in the hour of utmost need, found solace more in philosophical contemplation based on natural reason than on Christian revelation to which his theological works point." Pelikan's formulation of the question assumes a binary opposition between reason and revelation in the *consolation*.

44. There is a tradition of virtue/vice language in the pagan philosophical tradition going back to Plato *Rep.* 392.

45. This is a general thesis of Donato 2013 expressed at 165–6, among other places.

mythological exempla, and emotional reflection to find the cure for the suffering prisoner's soul. Boethius presents a mixed approach to the prisoner's spiritual and moral malaise. The result is that Boethius is stretching the possibilities and limits of form. Poetic form is a product of reception; that is, of the repurposing of the Graeco-Roman tradition and the new use to which it is put: merging with, consuming, and consumed by other discourses, including philosophical discourse. Thus Boethius constructs a poetics that not only opens up the interpretation of the *consolatio* but also fosters connections to early Christian poetry such as can be seen in the works of Prudentius.

In the *apotheosis*, Prudentius explicitly comments on poetry's status and role in late fourth-century Roman letters.[46] He makes three points, the last of which connects to Boethius's poetics. First Prudentius makes a more formal and literary historical argument at *apoth.* 234–7, suggesting that he is part of a literary tradition going back to the Old Testament prophets (as he indicates at *pe.* 10.838 and *tituli* 19 with mention of the ur-psalmist, David). The revelatory discourse of the prophets merges poetry, prophecy, and theology. Secondly, he asserts poetry's cultural centrality: at *apoth.* 268, knowledge is passed on by tradition (*quod traditur esse Deum*), for which poetry and poets are integral. He enriches this idea with the claim that God gave knowledge directly to humans through his revelation (*apoth.* 301). Thus knowledge is divinely given and disseminated through human means; that is, poetry and literature. Both points counter the patristic rejection of non-liturgical poetry's connection to the divine and prophecy.

Prudentius's third point follows on from the first two and is expressed in three passages. He identifies the three major intellectual traditions, Hebrew (Torah), Greek (philosophy), and Roman (both secular and Christian literature), that all proclaim the truth and significance of Christ (*apoth.* 376–80).[47] In another passage, he goes even further, imagining that all three traditions are represented on the head of the cross: *agnoscat Iudaea legens et Graecia norit / et venerata Deum percenseat aurea Roma* ("Let Judaea, as it reads, recognize, and let Greece know God, and let golden Rome, as she worships God, examine," *apoth.* 384–5). The verbs associated with each tradition are instructive: *agnoscat* expresses the recognition necessary for reading Christ's

---

46. Prudentius discusses poetry elsewhere. See O'Daly 2016 with bibliography.
47. Apoth. 376–80: *nam quae iam littera Christum / non habet, aut quae non scriptorium armaria Christi / laude referta novis celebrant miracula libris? Hebraeus pangit stilus, Attica copia pangit, / pangit et Ausoniae facundia tertia linguae* ("For what literature does not contain Christ? What library is not filled with the praise of Christ and celebrates his wonderful works in new books? The Hebrew pen, the fullness of Athens, and third, the eloquent tongue of Italy are all composing them.")

story and doctrine throughout biblical history (in this section of the work Prudentius is attacking the Jews for their lack of recognition); *norit* emphasizes the epistemological approach of Greek philosophy through empirical and rational means; and *venerata* and *percenseat* represent Rome's Christian worship. All three areas of Mediterranean thought have not only proclaimed the legitimacy of Christ separately but appear inseparable when articulating proper Christian belief, doctrine, and practice. *Apoth.* 386–93 clinches the point that all traditions and genres of writing have proclaimed Christ and, what is more, that this function and role has been passed on to the poet Prudentius (*O nomen praedulce mihi!*).

For Prudentius, the fight amongst the three intellectual traditions is over. The *apotheosis* has got the trappings of a Christian apologetic work of the second or even third centuries. That is, it is a work which, at least on the face of it, is concerned with Christian identity in relation to the once dominant Hellenistic, Hebrew, and Roman traditions (for their political, intellectual, or religious authority).[48] An apologetic work demonstrates the value of the (Christian) ideology and refutes adversarial views.[49] However, by the end of the fourth century, the political, theological, and religious landscape had changed. Prudentius's tone is decidedly "post-apologetic." Christ's legitimacy can be confirmed by a combination of all three traditions, and for Prudentius, it is a straw man to assume that there are significant differences between them. This is not merely a syncretist view. When seen as a statement of poetics, it opens up a space for the merging of discourses, as seen in Boethius. For poetic composition and expression is fundamentally human and contains what can be said of the issues that both Prudentius and Boethius are tackling. At its best, poetry gives the human perspective on the divine, the world, and the universe. It is diachronic in its relationship to time, emotional in its orientation, and personal in its connection to the poet's real life situation. Philosophy and theology and their prose expressions are attempts to understand God's synchronic, universal perspective. They posit a God who sees all of time at once, presides over a rational universe, and is the judge of human action.

The *consolatio*'s poetics parallels Prudentius's view of poetry as the inheritance and expression of a grand metaphysical view; for example, a dualist (Platonist) distinction between human and divine perspectives on the world, traceable in the varieties of human discourse. This claim is shown in the use of

48. Rhee 2005: 21.
49. Rhee 2005: 24.

philosophical and poetic discourses in the *consolatio*. As we have seen, at the end of the *consolatio*, Boethius engages in poetic concerns in prosaic passages. The separation between prose and verse, theology and poetry, is ambiguous.[50] Finally, views on poetry's purposes and roles appear in both prose and verse passages.

13.4. THE RENEWAL OF POETRY'S CLAIMS TO TRUTH

Regarding his use of poetry, Boethius constructs a poetics that responds to the fate of poetry as seen in the *Republic* and the banishment of the poetic Muses seen in the beginning of the *consolatio*. This dualist-based poetics develops from the moment the *poeticas musas* are told to leave. At *cons.* 1.m2, *Philosophia*'s first spoken poem is a throwback to metaphysical pre-Platonic poetry in which natural philosophy is presented in meter. At first glance, one might conclude that Boethius is constructing a poetics in which poetry is philosophical in content, thereby remooring poetry to truth in an analytical way.[51] Recall that in her first speech, *Philosophia* expels the Muses of elegiac and emotional poetry only to call upon her own muses (*meis . . . musis*, 1.p1.40). However, as the work proceeds, a more sophisticated poetics emerges. Boethius realigns or repurposes several tropes throughout the *consolatio*, making significant changes to tropes such as 1) the Muses, 2) the honeyed pill, and 3) the status of fictional stories (*fabulae*).[52]

In general, the reception of the Muses in Late Antiquity posits the Muses as a source of lies and misinformation.[53] This attitude, which occurs at the beginning of the *consolatio*, begins to be reversed, as already mentioned, in 1.p1, when *Philosophia* lays claim to having her own muses. But further signs of this re-evaluation of the muses occur later as well. At 3.m11.15–16, *Philosophia*

---

50. Gualandri 1979: 85 had understood this ambiguity: "scomparsa ormai distinzione fra linguaggio poetico e linguaggio prosasticoche non sia quella pura e semplice del metro." On the merging of prose and poetry in Late Antiquity, see Hernández Lobato 2012: 466–70, whose term "intrasystemic hybridization" refers to the late antique practice of mixing, among other things, genres (e.g., the *Mosella* or Sidonius's *epistulae*) and aesthetic identities of poetry and prose.

51. Marenbon 2003: 162, Helleman 2009: 200, and O'Daly 1991: 52 have observed that the poetry in the *consolatio* is part of the search for truth.

52. In the context of this discussion, to repurpose is to reuse terms and concepts from literary tradition and history in new or different ways. On reuse, allusion, and intertextuality, see Kaufmann in this volume and Mastrangelo 2016.

53. See Walde 2006 on the ancient reception of the muses. For those who wished to disparage poetry, Hesiod's Muses at *theog.* 27–8 provided plenty of grist: "we know how to say lies that look like the truth, and whenever we wish, we can also speak the truth." However, poetry is still associated with truth. More to the point, for Boethius, it is language that is slippery, not the particular form of discourse.

says, *quod si Platonis musa personat verum / quod quisque discit immemor recordatur* ("If Plato's Muse rings true, what each person learns, though forgetting it, he remembers it"). *Philosophia* recalls Plato's theory of recollection in her own poem, a poem about the search for truth. The poem revises the Neoplatonic idea that the embodied soul is incapable of seeing truth. Rather, even when burdened by the forgetful weight of the body, the soul can see the light of truth through learning (*non omne ... depulit lumen / ... semen introrsum veri / quod excitatur ... doctrina*, "[the body] has not removed all light; inside there is the seed of truth, which excites through learning," 3.m11.9–12). Boethius the author appropriates the figure of the muse, repurposing it for an individual's spiritual therapy. This is not merely a muse of philosophy, but a muse that "excites through learning." The engagement with ideas at the level of the emotions belongs to poetry (and rhetoric). *Philosophia*'s muse achieves this engagement through the use of poetry, which helps to align feelings with true doctrine. This constitutes a readjustment of Platonist conditions on how a person learns the truth. Perhaps here the influence of Aristotelian ethics or Iamblichan ritual on Boethius's Platonist foundation is palpable.

In a second example of the repurposing of a trope, Boethius innovates on the familiar Lucretian topos of the honeyed pill, in which poetry is the sweet outer layer that permits the sick individual to swallow the bitter inner kernel of beneficial ideas.[54] At 3.p1.1–9, Boethius expresses great enthusiasm. He has been revived by *sententiarum pondere* ("the weight of [*Philosophia*'s] arguments," 5) and the *canendi iucunditate* ("the delight of [*Philosophia*'s] singing," 5–6). His spirit has been so strengthened that he is ready not only to face the blows of fortune but also to hear the more bitter remedies necessary for his progress. Boethius frames this passage with statements that he is eager to listen further (*me audiendi avidum*, 1; *audiendi avidus*, 9), and later, *Philosophia* herself describes him as *te audiendi cupidum* and *ardore flagrares* (15 and 16). The rhetorical effects of poetry are on display here: Boethius is motivated to listen; he is persuaded that he is up to the challenge of freeing himself from his spiritual malaise. Poetry causes him *to want* to listen

---

54. O'Daly 1991: 42 argues that several Boethian passages take their cue from Lucretius, LUCR. 1.945–7, where the bitterness of doctrine goes down more easily with the sweetness of poetry. The notions of sweetness and pleasure are invoked in several passages in the *consolatio* (4.p6.57; 3.p1.1–2; 4.p6.6). We have already discussed how Boethius reverses the metaphor of sweetness and bitterness to blur categories between poetry and prose; 3.p1.1–2 and 4.p1.1 appear to comfortably combine sweetness and gravity. See Rees in this volume on the crossover between prose and poetry in panegyric discourse.

to *Philosophia*. So both philosophical argument and poetic motivation are central to therapy.

In two passages that follow, one in prose, 3.p1.13–14, and the other in the companion poem, 3.m1.5–6, the boundaries between the roles of philosophical and poetic discourse become more interchangeable: *Talia [remedia] sunt quippe quae restant, ut degustata quidem mordeant, interius autem recepta dulcescant* (Such [remedies], which now remain, sting once tasted, but when taken in more deeply they are sweet") and *dulcior est apium mage labor, / si malus ora prius sapor edat* ("The honey of bees is far sweeter if at first a bitter flavor bites the mouth"). The second passage repeats in a way the message of the first but with the difference that the first passage in prose refers to the initial bitterness of the remedies but sweetness in the longer term, whereas the second passage in verse views the sweetness of the remedies as a result of the bitterness of unfortunate experiences. The reworking of the trope functions to transition from philosophical poetry to poetry proper. Remedies are bitter initially and connect the bitter and the sweet. They are not sweet and deceptive, as Lucretius's aphorism recommended. The poetic passage adds a further wrinkle to this topos by expressing the idea in verse that bitter experience can be overcome by the sweet cure. Poetry is not playing the role of deceptive persuader. In fact, through emotional engagement and enthusiasm, it provides the examples and inspiration so that *vera dehinc animum subierint* ("truths may get into your mind," 3.m1.13). Boethius has repurposed a hackneyed but important image in order to reinvigorate poetry's ability to make truth claims or, at least, be included in a discourse that makes truth claims.

The third example of aesthetic repurposing is found in the use of the term *fabula* (story), which occurs only twice in the *consolatio*. At 3.p12.69–70, Boethius engages in a typical use of the term: "*Accepisti*," inquit, "*in fabulis lacessentes caelum gigantas* . . ." ("You have read in stories," [*Philosophia*] said, "of the giants challenging heaven"). Here, *fabulis* refers to fictional stories that are typically represented in poetry. But here the *fabula* of the gigantomachy is a metaphor for the clashing of arguments, a process that brings to light the truth.

In the poem that follows, 3.m12, the well-known Orpheus poem, Boethius engages in some rich mythologizing, recalling the stories (*fabulae*) of Orpheus and Eurydice, Ixion, Tantalus, and Tityus.[55] By the end of the poem, *Philosophia*

---

55. Sweeney 2006: 47 summarizes 3m.1–5, 7, 9, 10, 12 as poems that define and refine the ideas of freedom and constraint.

focuses on the exemplarity of the Orpheus and Eurydice story and Orpheus himself.[56] The exemplarity of Orpheus forms the central *fabula*, which, *Philosophia* asserts, applies directly to the reader and Boethius himself:[57]

Heu, noctis prope terminus	Ah! By the very edge of night
Orpheus Eurydicen suam	Orpheus saw his Eurydice
vidit, perdidit, occidit.	lost and killed.
Vos haec fabula respicit	**This tale refers to you**
quicumque in superum diem	who seek to lead your mind
mentem ducere quaeritis.	into the upper day.[58]

These lines make clear the connection between *fabula* and moral truth.[59] Like the story of the gigantomachy, the tragedy of Orpheus's life elicits a truth; in the case of the former, the highest good and best arguments always prevail; in the case of the latter, to look back on one's failures can lead to grief, *quidquid praecipium trahit / perdit, dum videt inferos* ("Whatever excellence he takes with him, he loses, when he looks to those below," 57–8). The story of Orpheus forms the end of book 3 of the *consolatio*. That poet's example teaches Boethius (and readers, *vos*) the tragic limits of human endeavour; but it also inspires Boethius (and us) to go beyond Orpheus's (and Ixion's, Tantalus's, etc.) example of the human condition because turning inward can lead to clarity. Both Boethius and the reader are encouraged to turn back and reflect on the *fabula* of Orpheus, who

---

56. O'Daly 1991: 188–207 is a detailed and interesting study of 3.m12. Engaging mainly with Crabbe 1981 and Lerer 1985, as well as with the Platonic, Neoplatonic, and Latin literary traditions, O'Daly situates the interpretation of the poem in the following ways: "Orpheus is in some sense a type of the fallen and descended soul, captivated by the lower, and failing to achieve ascent towards the light of truth" (191); "It is both a paradigm for the soul's fall and flawed return or ascent, and at the same time it is a moral fable to be interpreted in the terms current in the poetic tradition—the power of love, whether it be flawed or 'true,' the conflict of feeling and rational control, and so on" (194); "he is not 'rewriting' any earlier poem. Rather, he is rewriting a complex tradition" that includes Greek and Roman philosophy and poetry (235).

57. It is worth emphasizing the parallels between Boethius and Orpheus. Both are represented as "complaining" about their fates: Orpheus at 3.m12.18, *inmites superos querens* ("complaining about the inscrutable gods above"), and Boethius at 1.p1.1, *querimoniam*, and at 1.p.2.1–2, *querelae*. Both are poets who boast of their early happy days in life and poetry, only to grieve and compose sad songs (*flebilibus modis*, 3.m12.7, and *maestos . . . modos*, 1.m1.2 and 3.m12.1–4; see 15–17 and 1.m1.1, 2–4). Both have had great success and failure in their lives. As O'Daly 1991: 192 has said concerning Orpheus, "[his] failure is complex, and includes considerable success." He adds, "the wondrous singer almost succeeds: he reaches the borders of darkness and light" (192). See Harrison in this volume for the association Claudian makes with Orpheus as a poet and a figure in the underworld.

58. *cons.* 3.m12.49–54.

59. See Hernández Lobato in this volume (295–304), where he discusses Fulgentius's idea of hidden truth underlying and transcending pagan *fabulae*. See also Ware in this volume on the tension between "generic expectations" of truth in prose and invention in poetry.

should not have turned back, in order to move forward themselves by returning to God.[60]

Moreover, the *fabula* of Orpheus provides a valuable model for reinterpreting Boethius's (Christian) poetics in light of pagan poetry and philosophy. The notions of turning back and returning are ideas that tap into the process of intertextuality. Just as a person looks back on his or her life to elicit truths about him or herself, so the poet looks back to his or her literary predecessors to express a truth in an original way (*vos haec fabula respicit*).[61] Boethius makes full use of his literary inheritance while discarding the debilitating opposition between philosophy and poetry. The *fabulae* of poetry are central to this project of the *consolatio*. Orpheus's failure, represented in poetry, does not correspond to a subordinate role of poetry in the work as a whole and is not part of Boethian poetics.[62] Poetry is not to be thought of as "in service" to philosophy. Rather, like philosophy, poetry operates on a human level, with all of its limitations, but nevertheless acts as a collaborator in the search for the truth. Books 4 and 5 carry on the therapy, focusing on the self-reflective turn within, further marshalling poetry and prose to achieve truth.

Far from a term that conjures up deceptive and mendacious storytelling in poetry, the application of *fabula* to the protagonist and the reader as a source of moral exemplarity that triggers inner reflection, a clear vision of the truth, even a connection to God, forms a fundamental part of the fabric of Boethian poetics. This approach functions as a response to the Platonist view of the falsity of myths that poets insert into their works. On the one hand, Plato can use poetic myths in order to articulate ideas that conventional prose (or philosophical argument) cannot, but on the other hand, myths in Plato can also be ambiguous and indeterminate, resisting clear-cut interpretations, such as the myth of Er. Boethius's use of mythic *fabulae* in poetry tends to eschew the ambiguous for a more determinate exemplarity.

His use of myth is strikingly similar to that of Prudentius. The theological side of poetry is manifest through Prudentius's idea of *fabula*, a Platonist and patristic byword for "false tale" that the poet transforms into a divinely sanctioned practice in which literary narrative and typological history complement

---

60. Sweeney 2006: 48. She cites 3.m11.1–5, which exploits fully the metaphor of turning back into oneself to find the truth. She is responding to Wetherbee 1974: 78, who interprets the Orpheus story as an "admonitory exemplum" that portrays Orpheus as imprisoned through an "attachment to earthly things."
61. The verb *respicit* invokes a looking back that is directly applied to Boethius and the reader.
62. Crabbe 1981: 316 argues that Orpheus's whole career "is to be viewed as a failure." Orpheus is like Boethius and all human beings: we forget and as a result we make mistakes.

each other.⁶³ A *fabula* is an allegorical vehicle that makes the reader think of things he or she already knows. This innovation is paralleled in Boethius's use of mythical narrative in the prose and poetry of the *consolatio*. For both Prudentius and Boethius, this aspect of their poetics represents a muscular response to a restrictive Platonist/patristic poetics through the utility of stories as vehicles of truth. However, both writers remain committed to the ultimate Platonist goal of achieving connection to truth, the good, and God.

If we briefly compare Paulinus of Nola's attitude toward poetic *fabulae*, it is clear that a much stricter view obtains in his work, one that is akin to the idea from Plato's *rep.* 10 that poetic fictions must be hymns to God or (for Paulinus, Christian) heroes:

Non adficta canam, licet arte poematis utar.
Historica narrabo fide sine fraude poetae;
Absit enim famulo Christi mentita profari.
Gentibus hae placeant ut falsa colentibus artes;
At nobis ars una fides et musica Christus

Though I use the poet's art, the song I sing will
not be invented. I shall tell it with a historian's
truthfulness and without the poet's deceit, because
a servant of God should not utter lies. Such
techniques may satisfy non-Christians who
cultivate falsehood, but our sole technique is faith,
and our song is Christ.⁶⁴

Paulinus circles the wagons, excluding all poetry except verse compositions dedicated to Christ's life and salvation history. His is a bold statement that draws clear lines between useful (Christian) poetry and mendacious (mostly pagan) poetry in order to articulate a new Christian poetics.⁶⁵ However, Paulinus's poetics remains mired in the opposition between Christian and pagan poetry. Boethius's more nuanced poetics underscores this observation, and Prudentius's work appears to be the tipping point at which early Christian poetics breaks free of this restrictive Platonist binary.

---

63. See Mastrangelo 2008: 46–9 on Prudentius's use of the term *fabula* and its role in typological exemplarity.
64. PAUL. NOL. *carm.* 20.28–32.
65. See PAUL. NOL. *carm.* 10.43–5 for a similar attitude. On both passages, see Mastrangelo 2009: 323.

13.5. POETRY, PHILOSOPHY, AND DUALIST POETICS

At *cons.* 1.p4.18–21, still bitter at his personal misfortune, Boethius demands that *Philosophia* reckon with what he sees as the failure of Plato's (and *Philosophia*'s) political project:

> *atqui tu hanc sententiam Platonis ore sanxisti: beatas fore res publicas, si eas vel studiosi sapientiae regerent vel earum rectores studere sapientiae contigisset. Tu eiusdem viri ore hanc sapientibus capessendae rei publicae necessarium causam esse monuisti, ne improbis flagitiosisque civibus urbium relicta gubernacula pestem bonis ac perniciem ferrent.*

> It was you who established through the thought of Plato the principle that those states would be happy where philosophers were kings or their governors were philosophers. You, through that same Plato, told me that this was why philosophers must involve themselves in political affairs, so that the rule of nations not be left to the base and the wicked, bringing ruin and destruction on the good.

The life of Boethius the prisoner was in fact an attempt at the Platonic experiment, not merely an example of an intellectual unjustly charged but a philosopher in politics who, for all his noble efforts, received a death sentence: *sed innocentiam nostrum quis exceperit eventus vides; pro verae virtutis praemiis falsi sceleris poenas subimus* ("But you see what the result of my innocence has been: instead of a reward for true virtue, I am punished for a false crime," 1.p4.120–3). Boethius's disillusionment with the Platonist view of politics is clear. The idea of the impossibility of the philosopher king as an ideal appears to have refocused Boethius's attention on injustice of the world, in which the true and the false are confounded, a state of affairs that poetry can represent in all its variety. Could it be that the failure of the ideal of the philosopher king has led Boethius to re-examine poetry as a vehicle of truth, at least for the world he lives in?

In his most emotional moments, Boethius the prisoner implicates *Philosophia* herself: *sed, o nefas, illi vero de te tanti criminis fidem capiunt atque hoc ipso videbimur affines fuisse malefici, quod tuis inbuti disciplinis, tuis institute moribus sumus. Ita non est satis nihil mihi tuam profuisse reverentiam . . .* ("But they are so wickedly impious that it is actually from you that they derive their proof of this great charge: I shall appear to have been a close party to such a misdeed precisely because I am steeped in your learning and trained in your ways. So it is not enough that reverence for you shall have done me good," 1.p4.149–54). While the passage embodies the laments of a nearly broken man in need of *Philosophia*'s therapy, the substance of the complaint remains true. In the real life of a human being in a political community, philosophy did not prevent Boethius's tragedy—nor should it have, as *Philosophia* argues later concerning the happiness of the good man and the never-ending desires of the bad man. The practice of philosophy/theology is not sufficient (*non est satis*, 152) for Boethius or any other human being to deal with earthly reality, especially a reality comprised of a church-state riven with philosophical/theological divisions. Although pure philosophical and theological knowledge remains slippery in the real world, the quest for such knowledge and truth for human beings, not to mention their moral health, requires philosophical *and* poetic tools. The *consolatio* reflects a dualism in its treatment of a series of existential problems that only both discourses, poetry and philosophy/theology, can hope to solve.

The need for both forms of discourse reflects this modified dualist conception that runs through the *consolatio* and is a pillar of Boethius's poetics. Boethius distinguishes between real life and the divine realm in several ways. For example, from a sense of political injustice, 1.m5 draws a distinction between God, creator and ruler of the universe, and a human ruler who acts alone, without any divine intervention (25–7). The result is that fickle *fortuna* becomes a major factor in the lives of human beings (*nam cur tantas lubrica versat / fortuna vices*? "Why else does slippery fortune change so much"? 28–9). Thus innocent people sometimes suffer evil: *homines quatimur fortunae salo* ("we humans are buffeted by the sea of fortune," 45). As Magee has pointed out, Boethius represents a world that is at odds with itself, governed by the *conditor orbis* (1) but tyrannized by *fortuna* and *perversi reges* (1.m5. 29, 31, 41).[66] The poem ends with an emotional plea for divinely guided human kingship, which seems futile[67]—confirmed by *Philosophia*, who in the following prose section interprets the plea as an emotional outburst proper to poetry (in *extremo Musae saevientis*, 1.p5.36).

The dualist dilemma presented in 1.m5, two opposing worlds in which divinity, perfection, and the good have little connection with the human condition, is also mentioned in 1.m6.20–3 but revisited in 4.m6. In that poem, *Philosophia* replies to Boethius's stinging indictment of the metaphysical system, not by denying its truth, but by reaffirming the underlying order of it all, the *celsus tonans* (1). Lines 34–48 function as a hymn to God, the *conditor altus*, who operates according to the universal law of love which "is common to everything" (*hic est cunctis communis amor*, 44). Reciprocal love (*alternus amor*, 17) harmonizes opposing forces and phenomena: *ut pugnantia / vivibus cedant umida siccis / iungantque fidem frigora flammis* ("that warring wetness yield to living dryness and the cold join faith with flames," 20–2).

---

66. Magee 2003: 154.
67. 1.m5.46–8 refer to Matt. 6:10. See Magee 2003:153.

Love's harmonizing function is more fully expressed in 2.m8, the last poem of book 2. Love works at both the divine and human levels, holding together the cosmic order (14–15) as well as nations, lovers, and friends (21–7; see also 3.m12.47–8). In two lines, the poet is able to connect the divine and human worlds through love: *si vestros animos amor / quo caelum regitur regat* ("May the love that rules heaven rule your spirits," 29–30). Love is simultaneously the philosophical principle of harmony of Empedocles and the binding social and emotional force for humanity. Without these two aspects of love, both the universe and humanity would be torn apart (16–18). Still, at this point of the *consolatio*, the question remains about how these two different versions of love, one universal and the other particular, the divine and the human, might connect; from the human perspective, love is necessary but not sufficient to prevent tragic events such as Boethius's imprisonment. The separation and commonality between these two registers of love, expressed fully in the poems 2.m8 and 4m.6, is emblematic of a dualist metaphysics that requires both philosophy and poetry to encompass. These poems reveal a particular version of dualism. Unlike typical Platonist dualism, which emphasizes the separation of the immaterial and the material, the perfect and the imperfect, Boethius, through an elegiac sensibility, highlights the two worlds as bound together or related to one another.

A similar opposition and resolution occurs in 5.m3 where Boethius himself articulates an argument against a compatibilist view of providence and free will.[68] From 5.p2.1–5, Boethius, in one form or another, tackles the difficult problem of the opposing truths of free will and determinism. Humans see the issue as a clash of opposites: *quis tanta deus / veris stauit bella duobus, / ... an nulla est Discordia veris* ("What god establishes such a war between two truths ... or is there no discord between truths," 5 m3.2–3; 6). Boethius has reached the point where he can admit that it is the human perspective that is limited and perhaps unable to make the leap of understanding to the connections of the divine and the universal to the human (*sed mens / ... nequit / ... rerum tenues noscere nexus?* ("But is the [human] mind not able to recognize the subtle connections in the universe"? 5.m3.8–10). In a traditional dualist scheme, truths about the divine universe and truths about human life inscrutably exist contrary to each other, for example, (1) God has foreknowledge of every event, and (2) humans have free will to choose in the moment any available action.

---

68. See *cons.* 4.p.6.27–9, where providence is defined as all causes at once of all things within the divine mind (*in ipsa divinae intellegentiae puritate*); in other words, from the synchronic perspective of the divine mind. Fate is a version of providence from the human perspective, which sees reality unfold one cause and one event at a time.

Immediately before this counterargument to the compatibility of freedom and determinism, Boethius at 5.p3.92 argues that if there is no free will, then virtues and vices do not exist; that is, a person does not have responsibility for her actions. Moreover, prayer becomes pointless (101–7), and communion with the divine becomes an impossibility (107–10). In addition, Boethius at lines 73–8 rehearses the criticism of Tiresias's comment on his own prophesizing abilities: *quidquid dicam, aut erit aut non* ("whatever I will say, will happen or will not"; cf. HOR. *sat.* 2.5.59). It would seem that the statement is directed at the human perspective, the receiving of a divine prophecy in a human community: it can be devastatingly difficult to interpret. Or, it can be seen from the divine perspective: whatever happens, *p* or *-p*, God knows it. In addition, at 5.p4.47–54, *Philosophia* argues that small-scale events in the course of human life have no necessity; that is, they can either occur or not occur. Thus, she argues, there is room for human free will. Paradoxically, this would indeed support Tiresias's statement that what he says will either happen or not, be true or not. Boethius is not afraid to use the exemplar of a prophet to argue for the existence of free will and virtue and vice.

Boethius does assume a dualist scheme in which divine thinking and perception are separate from human thinking and perception. In fact, it is this Platonist conception that forms the central problem of the *consolatio*: the relationship between the divine and human worlds. How can Boethius the prisoner, who has lost his wealth, status—and soon his life—recognize and internalize the universal and divine truths about his own particular situation and the broader situation in which his fellow humans find themselves? For to answer this question will allow him (and readers) to cope with his (their) own, human reality. The *consolatio*'s form and content represents a response to this Platonist conundrum, not merely through the creative and argumentative manipulation of ideas such as providence, fate, chance, and free will but according to a literary aesthetics that puts forward poetry, rhetoric, and analytical argument as equal contributors to Boethius's project of internalizing divine thinking.

Boethius rounds out the picture of his modified dualist conception through his idea of (poetic) language as a mediator between the divine and human worlds. All human discourse is imperfect, including philosophical and theological discourse. If it is based on human reasoning, as this discourse is, it will indeed have limits for understanding the divine and humanity's relationship to the divine. In a passage of 4.p6 that attempts to elucidate the distinction between fate and providence, Boethius distinguishes between human reason and true understanding: *Igitur uti est ad intellectum ratiocinatio, ad id quod est id quod gignitur, ad aeternitatem tempus* ("as reasoning is to understanding, as that which becomes is to that which is, as time is to eternity" 4.p6.78–80).

Philosophical discourse is a fully human activity with divine aspirations. For Boethius and Prudentius the same applies to poetry. This reconceptualization of Platonist dualism opens a vital space for poetic discourse on the thorny problems of free will and the ontology of virtues and vices.

13.6. Boethius and Prudentius on Free Will, Virtues, and Vices

The dualist foundation of the Boethius's thought-world also produces in his work a Prudentian conception of the virtues and vices. Because human beings live in the world of good and evil to be freely chosen, virtues and vices are part and parcel of human life but not of the pure goodness of God. At 4.p7.44–5, Boethius emphasizes that a defining feature of virtue is the overcoming of adversity: *ex quo etiam virtus vocatur quod suis viribus nitens non superetur adversis* ("And this is indeed why it is called virtue, because, relying on its own powers, it is not overcome by adversity"). He further describes this adversity in martial terms twice: *sed haec eorum est qui vel in virtute positi contra aspera bellum gerunt, vel a vitiis declinantes virtutis iter arripiunt* ("But this is the case for those who, established in virtue, wage war against adversity, or who, avoiding vices, take the path of virtue," 4.p7.21–3); and *proelium cum omni fortuna animis acre conseritis, ne vos aut tristis opprimat aut iucunda corumpat* ("you engage in a mental battle with every kind of fortune, lest bad fortune oppress you or good fortune corrupt you," 4.p7.47–9). The spiritual adversity that results from fortunes, good or bad, exposes whether a person is virtuous or full of vice.

In the following poem, 4.m7, Boethius gives a series of mythological figures who experienced both good and bad fortunes. Agamemnon, Odysseus, and for most of the poem, Hercules, all struggle to get on fortune's good side. Agamemnon receives a great victory but suffers terrible misfortune: Odysseus also triumphs over his foes, but he does so at great cost; and Hercules performs his labours, but his madness looms. Humans struggle against the self, others, fortune, and the divine. This makes virtue difficult to achieve and internalize. *Philosophia* responds to this state of affairs by arguing at 4.p.7. 17–39 that for the virtuous person all fortunes are good because they provide opportunities for learning and the development of virtue.[69]

---

69. Sweeney 2006: 53–6 discusses the notion of virtue as a struggle against adversity to show that Boethius's spiritual understanding is lacking; i.e., he has not realized that the world's and humans' natural inclination is toward virtue. Sweeney compares this idea of virtue and vice not to the Christian tradition but with Plato's articulation at *rep.* 392, in which virtue is hard and vice easy.

This approach to virtue and vice is readily apparent in the *Psychomachia* of Prudentius. There Prudentius portrays a never-ending struggle to internalize virtue and vanquish vice:

O quotiens animam, **vitiorum peste** *repulsa,*
sensimus incaluisse Deo! quotiens tepefactum
caeleste ingenium post gaudia candida taetro
cessisse stomacho! Fervent **bella horrida**, *fervent*
ossibus inclusa fremit et **discordibus armis**
non simplex natura hominis; nam viscera limo
effigiata premunt animam, contra ille sereno
editus adflatu nigrantis **carcere cordis**
aestuat, et **sordes** *arta* **inter vincla** *recusat.*

How often, when the **plague of sins** has been driven away, we have felt our soul aglow with God! How often, after these pure joys, have we felt our heavenly nature grow cool and yield to foul desire! **Savage war** rages hotly, rages within our bones, and humanity's two-sided nature is in an **uproar of rebellion**. For the flesh that was formed from clay oppresses the spirit, but again the spirit that issues from the pure breath of God is hot within the **prison house of the heart**, and even **in its close bondage** rejects the body's **filth**.[70]

The martial, medical, and Platonist representation of the virtues and vices in language, imagery, and content is canonized by Prudentius. The *consolatio* participates in this tradition. Boethius figures this internal battle in terms of diseased individuals whose faults need to be cut out (*veluti aegros ad medicum ... culpae morbos supplicio resecarent*, 4.p4.150; also, *morbus animorum*, 151; *aegros*, 151), filth (*vitiorumque sordes*, 4.p.4.142), and war (*bellum discors; concordia* (4.m6.18–20); *bellum gerunt* (4.p7.22). Boethius can employ this tradition of description in ways different from Prudentius. For instance, at 4.p4.149–54 *Philosophia* argues that rather than hate the wicked, the good should pity them. This is far from Prudentius's attitude in the *psychomachia*, where hateful, vengeful virtues vanquish vices.

Finally, an approach similar to Prudentius's concerning the relationship between virtues/vices and free will forms a central part of the argument of the *consolatio*. Boethius treats the related problems of Providence versus Fate and

---

70. PRUD. *psych.* 899–907.

God's foreknowledge versus free will in books 4 and 5.[71] He makes the distinction that Fate is the working out of Providence on the human level through events we experience (4.p.6.58–60). In a vivid Neoplatonic simile, Boethius envisages Providence as an axis around which a series of concentric circles turn. The further out a person is, the further from the mind of God she is and therefore subject to the vicissitudes of fate (4.p.6.65–82). That is, as the concentric circles get further away, "free will becomes limited for human souls when they cease to be occupied in contemplating God's mind [the source of Providence], and is reduced still further when, given over to vices."[72]

At 5.m2.2–7, Boethius in another simile of sorts compares Phoebus's imperfect ability to see the future with the flawless foreknowledge of God (*magni conditor orbis*, 7). The following prose section, 5.p3, picks up this comparison to restate the consequences: if free will does not exist, virtues and vices would not exist (5.p3.92–4). The following poem, 5.m3.1–5, expresses the difficulty of what seem to be contradictory truths: how can free will and God's foreknowledge coexist? Boethius introduces the idea of the modes of cognition, in which God's epistemological perspective is separate from that of humans.[73] God's perspective is synchronic, not diachronic as in the case of humans. Without wading through the weeds of his argument, it is clear that virtue and vice are fundamentally human. In fact if one pursues knowingly only vice, then one falls to an ontological status of non-being (4.p2.98–101).

Two passages in the works of Prudentius associate free will with virtue and vice: *ham*. 669–801 and *symm*. 2.471–87. In a large and rich section of the *hamartigenia*, the poet puts forward not a systematic, analytic argument but a poetic, philosophical, and historical case for free will (*argumentum ingens, ham*. 667), the bones of which can be seen in the argument in books 4 and 5 of the *consolatio*. The biblical exempla of Adam and Lot are employed to prove the existence of free will, a topic stimulated by the problem of God's status as exclusively good. Prudentius simply stipulates that God must be completely good, since he gave humans the

---

71. Marenbon 2003: 121–45 treats Boethius's argument in detail. Marenbon views the oppositions of providence vs. fate and God's foreknowledge vs. free will separately but as impinging on each other. He concludes that while Boethius solves the problem of God's foreknowledge vs. free will, he undermines it when he returns to the idea that God is the cause of all events. O'Daly 1991: 28 also sees a failure to solve the problem. For my purposes, the connection between the possibility of engaging in virtue and vice through freely chosen actions furnishes the central motivation for both Prudentius and Boethius.

72. See Marenbon 2003: 123–4.

73. "Modes of cognition" reflects the proposition that knowledge is relative to the knower, in this case God and humans. At 5.p4.75–7, *Philosophia* gives the crucial principle for this idea that knowledge depends on the knower, not the thing known. See Hernández Lobato in this volume on Sidonius, Fulgentius, and Augustine on knowledge.

opportunity to exercise free will after the Fall. A dualist conception is implicit in a brief expression of this idea: *labi hominis, servare Deo est* ("to fall is of man, to save is of God," *ham*. 665). In the world of humans, responsibility for the goodness and badness of actions implies free will. At *ham*. 686–96, Prudentius argues that without free will there would be no virtue (*nec tamen est virtus, ni deteriora refutans / emicat et meliore viam petat indole rectam*. "After all, it is not virtue, unless, by rejecting the worse, it springs forth and seeks the right path through a better nature," *ham*. 695–6). The language of virtue and vice, triggered by the idea of free will, occurs again within the exemplum of Adam (*elige rem vitae; tua virtus temet in aevum / provehat, aeternum damnet tua culpa vicissim*, "choose the way of life; may your virtue bring you to eternity, and your guilt, again, condemn you," *ham*. 705–6) and the exemplum of Lot's wife, whose choice, though not as destructive as Eve's, ruined her alone (*traxerat Eva virum dirae ad consortia culpae: / haec peccans sibi sola perit*, "Eve had drawn her husband into a partnership of cursed guilt: but this woman by her sin brought death on herself," *ham*. 741–2).

In addition, Prudentius highlights the motif of the choice to look back (*respicere*) or not, the choice that Lot made correctly but his wife failed (*ham*. 737, 758, 765, 766, 842). Looking back at the destruction of the city, a symbol of earthly attachments and doing wrong, results in death, whereas not looking back indicates virtue and unity with God and eternal life. Boethius's adaptation of the story of Orpheus in 3.m12 has been called an admonitory exemplum, where Orpheus represents earthly imprisonment through an "attachment to earthly things."[74] This picture has been recently nuanced by scholars who interpret Orpheus's looking back as his (and Boethius's) tendency to return to grief for earthly loss. As Sweeney has noted, the looking back or turning back metaphor also occurs at *cons*. 3.m11.1–5 and *cons*. 3.m12.52–8 and represents looking back in an effort to gain clear vision or see the light. *Cons*. 3.m12.52–8 makes the point that looking back does not accomplish these goals because the things lost are precisely those that must be left behind to progress (*quidquid praecipuum trahit / perdit, dum videt inferos*, "whatever excellence he takes with him, he loses when he looks on those below," *cons*. 3.m12.57–8). As mentioned earlier, at *cons*. 3.m12.52, *vos haec fabula respicit*, Boethius invites the reader to "look back" at the story (*fabula*) of Orpheus who "saw" (*vidit*, 51) his wife die. At 4.p4.106 and 108 Boethius uses forms of *respicere* twice to illustrate that a person can look back with a downward or upward gaze, to see the ground or the stars. Boethius is here tying textual memory and recall in the *fabula* to empirical experience in the world.

---

74. Wetherbee 1974: 78 is quoted by Sweeney 2006: 48. See n. 52.

Acquiring virtue by directing one's sight and soul upward triggers in both authors a Platonist vision in which ascent away from earthly things allows one to rise above fate: for example, in the second major passage, *symm.* 2.471–87, Prudentius, in the midst of revisiting the issue of free will, repudiates fate as something to rise above to achieve virtue. *Spirat enim maiora animus seque altius effert / sideribus transitque vias et nubila fati* ("for the soul breathes better and rises higher than the stars and goes beyond the paths and clouds of fate," *symm.* 2. 480–1).[75] Like Boethius, Prudentius's soul rises from a determinist fate to choosing virtue and knowing God: *quisque putat fato esse locum, sciat omniparentem / nosse Deum nulli vetitum fatalibus astris* ("Whosoever thinks there is room for fate, let him know that no one is prevented by fate in the stars from knowing God, the father of all," *symm.* 2. 477–8). These words come on the heels of Prudentius discussing individuals who are unjustly held in prison. His point is that if fate exists, then no one, the guilty or the innocent, would be responsible for his actions (*symm.* 2.471).

The necessary connection between free will and virtue/vice guides Prudentius's—and Boethius's—moral thinking. Moreover, the scenario parallels the portrayal of Boethius in his cell, a desperate person looking for a way out from his fate. Both writers have a more optimistic view—that human souls are able to overcome fate and reach the divine—than Plato. Boethius and Prudentius engage this problem of dualism through the *fabulae* of Orpheus (not to mention gigantomachy, Odysseus, and Agamemnon) and Lot, respectively. From these stories that reflect the dualist challenge of connecting the human and divine worlds, both authors derive the possibility of salvation through the mediating factor of free will as a function of the choice between virtue and vice. Pure goodness, eternal life, and heaven are possible for the flawed mortal on earth because of free will and the existence of virtues and vices. Both authors express this argument through poetic and philosophical/theological discourse. The merging of these discourses and the re-establishment of poetry's claims to truth produce a dualist poetics that acts as a response to a restrictive Platonist poetics that infused the conditions of poetic production.

13.7. Conclusion: Poetry and the Problem of Language

Scholars have remarked that the *consolatio* ends with a fragmented vision, a struggle to remain committed to virtue without having achieved a transcendent

---

75. Compare the end of the *hamartigenia*, where the Platonist notion of the soul escaping the prison of the body (Prud. *ham.* 851, 927) gives way to a dream sequence in which the soul flies over creation for a near-divine perspective.

vision of the divine.[76] The unity of the dualist worlds of earth and heaven modelled in the poem at 3.m9 seems to have faded away. But the reasons for the difficulty of achieving such a unity are what the *consolatio* is about. The most important reason is that all forms of human discourse are imperfect. At *cons.* 3.p12.63–4, *Philosophia* alludes to the biblical text, Wisdom 8:1, at the end of a complex philosophical argument concerning the power of the highest good, God. Boethius responds that the very words themselves (*haec ipsa ... verba*, 67) of *Philosophia* delight him (*delectant*, 67) much more (*multo magis*, 66) than the sum of her rational arguments (*rationum*, 66). The words that Boethius takes such delight in are the biblical quotations and fictive stories (*fabulae*), like the gigantomachy mentioned in the passage. Words are the focus at the end of 3.p12, where *Philosophia* invokes Plato's authority, saying, *cognatos de quibus loquuntur rebus oportere esse sermones* ("words should be akin to the things spoken about," 111–12). These passages tell readers that the best way to internalize important ideas is through delightful words—note the adverb *sauviter* embedded in the allusion to Wisdom 8:1, but those words must correspond exactly to the concepts they represent. Truth and pleasure (and motivation) intersect at a point where philosophy, the *fabulae* of poetry, and biblical wisdom meet. Boethius's works on logic[77] confirm this conclusion, since he argues that the non-identity of words and things is mediated by asserting distinctions and narrative relationships between them.[78] Because the structure of language does not correspond to the structure of reality (both corporeal and incorporeal), we are left with false natural philosophy and moral depravity, such as the hedonistic pursuit of pleasure—or, in Christian terms, a postlapsarian world. For Boethius, this state of affairs requires humans to have a metalinguistic discussion about the nature of language before applying words to things or concepts.[79] The *consolatio*'s form is an admission of this aspect of the human condition; namely, that philosophical and poetic discourses are bound together in the quest to represent divine and universal truths. They both fall short, but both are necessary for

---

76. Sweeney 2006: 61.

77. Sweeney 2006: 10–13 discusses this idea, which appears in Boethius's commentary on Aristotle's *peri hermeneias*. This is the exceptional instance when I refer to works outside of the *consolatio*. I have focused only on the internal evidence of the *consolatio* in order not to project assumptions from the "more Christian" texts.

78. Hernández Lobato 2012: ch. 6.3.3 and in this volume (284–7) develops the notion of "the poetics of silence" through an examination of Sidonius's *carmen* 9. He argues that by asserting a *recusatio* with no clear resolution, Sidonius furnishes a programmatic statement that posits the making of poetry as a self-defeating enterprise. For late antique poets, the relationship between language and the (divine) world is inscrutable, perhaps even futile.

79. Sweeney 2006: 8–10.

the human attempt to find truth; hence the merging of these discourses in the *consolatio*.

Prudentius appears to have that metalinguistic discussion at *ham.* 201–7 and 272–82.[80] In these passages, he describes Satan's tongue as "split" (*discissa*, 202) with "the art of varied speaking" (*varia ... arte loquendi*, 202) and part of our original sin and thus the source of vice (*hinc natale caput vitiorum*, "from here it is the fountainhead of the vices," 203). The human postlapsarian state has imposed on language an irrevocable association with vice.[81] Thus the linguistic tools that humans employ to refer to things and express ideas are imperfect. Metaphor, simile, and other forms of figuration are at best morally neutral features of language necessary for any type of discourse.[82] We cannot talk our way to the divine, and consequently, both Prudentius and Boethius admit all forms of discourse, including philosophy, are inadequate to the task. This observation catalyzes a poetics that does not see poetry in a (Platonist) hierarchical relationship to prose, dialogue, or philosophical/theological treatise. On the contrary, poetry, like philosophy or theology, may not produce divine truths, but human moral and spiritual truths are a different matter. A recognition of the limits of language allows Boethius and Prudentius to both marshal all the tools of language and construct a morality (i.e., the acquisition of virtue over vice) and internalize an approach to human fortune. In other words, the best that we can do is cure our spiritual ills through the activities of poetry and philosophy.

Read in this way and against the earlier example of Prudentius, the *consolatio* is a response to the question about why a committed Christian like Boethius wouldn't fall back on the revelation of salvation history at his most dire moment. The answer is that he does, but through the connecting of poetic and prosaic forms and sensibilities that represent the whole of human experience as it searches for truth.[83] This poetics, viewed as a response to early Christian Platonist strictures, moves beyond a poetics that is either Christian or secular. Finally, in the Christian poetry of Prudentius, the boundaries between poetic

---

80. Malamud 2011: 104–9.
81. Malamud 2011: 105.
82. Malamud 2011: 109 makes the point that the appearance of Satan coincides with the first sustained simile in the *hamartigenia* and thus portrays the failure of language to represent truth.
83. Poems and prose sections use connective words to continue or conclude the topic under discussion. This is a way for Boethius in the *consolatio* to signal the unity between his poems and prose sections. Examples include *Ita est* at 4.p6.1, *haud aliter* at 1p3.1, *dum* ... at 1.p1.1, *igitur* at 3.p8.1 and 3.p10.1, and an epic locution at 5.p1.1, *dixerat*. See Magee 2003: 148. O'Daly 1991: 35 concludes that tension between poetry and rhetoric still exists in Boethius. But this can also be said for philosophical prose and rhetoric, as Plato in fact does with his distinction between true and false rhetoric in the *Phaedrus*.

and theological discourse become blurred.[84] By calling for the merging of different literary traditions, resuscitating the poetic concept of the *fabula*, and making poetry personal, that is, starting from human thought, emotion, and perception, Prudentius exhibits the beginnings of a fully developed Boethian poetics. And it is with Boethian poetics, indications of which permeate the work of Prudentius, that the *poeta philosophus/theologus* gains a secure foothold in Western literary history.

---

84. Magee 2003: 147 n. 2 says "the *consolatio* will not sustain the naïve dichotomy, prose = 'philosophy', verse = 'literature.'" See also Curley 1987: 356, 359. O'Daly 1991: 34 (following Curley) remarks: "just as poetry is a serious part of the philosophical enterprise, so too the effects of poetry can be paralleled by those induced by prose." Form yields to content and a focus on the audience. Verse and prose are incidental to these priorities.

14

In Praise of the Wax Candle

Augustine the Poet and Late Latin Literature

GILLIAN CLARK

Every created being is like this. It is good, but can be loved well or badly: well when order is safeguarded, badly when order is disturbed. I said this briefly in verses in praise of the wax candle (in laude quadam cerei breuiter uersibus dixi):

Haec tua sunt, bona sunt, quia tu bonus ista creasti.
Nil nostrum est in eis, nisi quod peccamus amantes,
Ordine neglecto, pro te quod conditur abs te.

These things are yours, they are good, because you who are good created them.
Nothing in them is ours, except that we sin in loving,
Order neglected, in place of you what is made by you.

Now if the creator is truthfully loved, that is, if he himself is loved, not something else in his place which is not himself, he cannot be loved badly. (Avg. ciu. 15.22)

14.1. Prologue: Poetry and Ordered Love

Augustine did not list verses "in praise of the wax candle" with his other works in his *Retractationes*.[1] Thus we do not know when he wrote them or what brought them to mind ca. 420 as he worked on book 15 of *City of God*.[2] It is unexpected to find Augustine writing classical hexameters or indeed any poetry, and these three lines prompt wider questions. Why does he seem unaware of the poetry of his own time, even when it is explicitly Christian? What does this tell us about his view of late Latin literature, and why is this brilliant writer of Latin so little discussed in that context? In the closing session

---

1. Thanks to the editors for inviting me to contribute this chapter; to the participants in the Oxford colloquium, especially to Karla Pollmann; to Catherine Conybeare for comments on a draft; and to Carol Harrison and Emma Hornby for an illuminating discussion of music and language. Translations are my own.

2. The verses appear as the first three lines of a poem *de anima* (*Anth. Lat.* ed. Riese 1906: 1.2 no. 489), but editors are rightly reluctant to ascribe to Augustine the complicated lines which follow. The editors of this volume take them as an example of "creative extension by later hands" (Introduction, 4).

of the colloquium which prompted this volume, Jaś Elsner remarked that in the study of late Latin literature there is a huge Augustine-shaped space. This paper suggests that if "literature" means works of high culture and imagination, admired and studied for their style and form and subtle interaction with other such works, Augustine would be pleased by the absence of his writings.[3] He knew that literature in this sense may teach truth and make its readers more aware of the works of God the creator;[4] he saw that the metrical order of poetry is an image of God-given order; but it follows from Augustine's teaching on the right ordering of love that readers will go wrong if they give too much attention to the literary creation of created human beings. He did not wholly reject *litterae*, but he contrasted the works of human ingenuity with *diuina eloquia*, the divine utterances of scripture which spoke to everyone, not only to those with a classical education. He thought that for him as a priest and bishop, the right use of literary skill was to explain these *eloquia* to everyone, in a style which all could understand, so that his hearers were moved to respond with love of God.[5]

14.2. Songs of Praise: The Candle, the "Theatrical Poem," and the Hymns of Ambrose

Only three lines survive from Augustine's verses in praise of a wax candle. Such candles were special, because they gave stronger and steadier light and smelled better than the cheaper domestic alternatives: tallow candles, rush lights, pottery lamps burning African olive oil. Augustine's envisaged audience would recognize *laus cerei* as the "praise of the candle," which is part of the ceremonies at the Paschal Vigil, in the night which leads from Holy Saturday to Easter Sunday. A new fire is kindled, the paschal candle is lit from the fire, and other candles are lit from it as it is carried through the church to be placed by the altar. Then the deacon stands beside the candle to sing a paschal proclamation (*praeconium paschale*), also known as paschal praise (*laus paschalis*). From the seventh century on, this praise was a local variant of the text *Exultet* which is still in use, but in earlier times someone might compose "a praise" (Cross and Livingstone 2005: 593–4, s.v. *Exultet*), and presumably that is what Augustine did (8–9).

Augustine is known to have written verse on two other occasions: a "theatrical poem" at Carthage in the late 370s or early 380s, when he was still a teacher of rhetoric, and a "psalm against Donatists," probably in 393, soon after his

---

3. On "literature" and *litterae*, see Vessey 2012b: 15.
4. Or, without explicitly Christian content, make its readers aware of temporal experience in relation to timeless reality: see Mastrangelo in this volume.
5. Not "communicating doctrine to the masses," *pace* Mastrangelo in this volume, 392.

ordination.⁶ The *theatricum carmen* is lost. It won a competition, but Augustine says only that he was asked what he would pay for a sacrifice to ensure victory and replied that he abhorred such sacrifices (*conf.* 4.2.3). Formal classical style would be appropriate for a performance piece, to win approval from educated members of the audience and to impress others who could recognize the style when they heard it, but many questions remain unanswered. Was the topic prescribed or the metre or both?⁷ Did the author recite the poem, or was it presented by an actor, perhaps to the accompaniment of the cithara, the large stringed instrument used in public performances (Clark 2011: 164–5)? Was it part of a civic ceremony before the entertainment began, or did it appear alongside stage adaptations of Vergil, *pantomimi* dancing show pieces from tragedy, and occasional burlesque (Webb 2008, Schlapbach 2013)? In one of his earliest extant writings (386/7 CE) Augustine commented on theatrical style:

> Poets have been passionate about what people call solecisms and barbarisms, and have preferred to change the names and call them "figures" [*schemata*] and "restructurings" [*metaplasmos*], not to avoid them as obvious faults.⁸ But take these away from poems, and we shall hanker after their sweetest savours. Put many together in one place, and I shall find the whole distasteful: jarring or affected. Apply them to the civilised speech of public life, and who will not tell them to get out and settle in theatres? (*ord.* 2.4.13)

The *theatricum carmen* does not appear in Augustine's *Retractationes*, the chronological list of his writings which starts in 386. In that year he gave up his ambitions for a suitable marriage and a career in the imperial service; he was baptized and intended to live as a servant of God, leading an ascetic life of prayer and study. Such Christian commitment did not necessarily exclude writing poetry (Pollmann 2013). Augustine did not yet know Paulinus of Nola, who was also engaged in transforming his life (Trout 1999, Conybeare 2000),⁹ but he already had an example in the hymns of Ambrose, which he heard in

---

6. An acrostic verse epitaph for the deacon Nabor, killed by Donatists, is ascribed to Augustine (*PL* suppl. 2.356–7), but he does not mention it, and the date and attribution are disputed. Shaw 2011: 624 accepts Augustine's authorship.

7. Consolino, in this volume, discusses the changing relationship between metre and genre: it follows that a *theatricum carmen* was not necessarily composed in Vergilian hexameters.

8. Augustine explained in *doctr. christ.* 2.44–5 that a solecism is a grammatical mistake, such as using *inter* with the ablative, not the accusative, and a barbarism is incorrect pronunciation, such as pronouncing *ignoscĕre* (to forgive) as *ignoscēre*. In *ord.* 2.17.45 he observed that he was himself sometimes accused of solecisms, but Cicero used them deliberately; and that "the speech which saved Rome" (presumably Cicero *in Catilinam*) now sounded barbarous.

9. Paulinus, who came from Bordeaux, was governor of Campania in 381. He returned to Gaul in 383 and was baptized there in 389; he and his wife Therasia began to disengage from their property, and after the death of their baby son, Paulinus was ordained priest (Christmas 394), and they settled at Nola in Campania.

Milan at the time of his baptism (*conf.* 9.6,14–17, esp. 15).[10] Like the Psalms, these hymns moved him deeply. Sung by a Christian congregation, they conveyed truth and prompted right emotion; a few months later, remembered in private, they helped him to recover from the turmoil of grief at his mother's death (ibid. 9.12.32).

Augustine quoted and praised the hymns of Ambrose, but he did not discuss them as poems or reflect on their differences from classical poetry. Like the Psalms, they were an offering of praise to God (Fontaine 1980: 131–44). Even one line could state a fundamental truth: thus the line Augustine quotes most often, *Deus creator omnium*, "God creator of all things," challenges the Manichaeans who held that God did not create the rival power of evil.[11] Ambrose's poetic technique was appropriate for his purpose (Den Boeft 1993, 2007). Instead of classical hexameters, which often require unusual vocabulary and word order and syntax, and instead of varying metres, he used a simple iambic dimeter (acatalectic) with stress accents.[12] Most of these eight-syllable lines are self-contained statements, grouped in four-line stanzas, and in the hymns securely attributed to Ambrose there are no more than eight such stanzas. So the hymns were easy to sing and to remember. *Carmen* means "spell" or "charm" (Harrison 2011) as well as "poem" or "song," and when Ambrose's opponents claimed that he had put a spell on the people, he gladly agreed that *hymnorum meorum carmina*, "the songs/spells of my hymns," had charmed them and made it possible even for the uneducated to preach the doctrine of the Trinity (*epist.* 75A.34).

This is just what Augustine's mother Monnica does in one of the philosophical dialogues he wrote in 386/7 (Conybeare 2006, Clark 2015). The dialogues are concerned with questions which are relevant for everyone: whether there is any certain knowledge (*contra Academicos*), what is the happy life (*de beata uita*), whether there is order in the universe and whether evil is part of that order (*de ordine*). Augustine chose to have as discussants family members who did not have higher education, as well as two students and his friend Alypius, who did. Monnica, like most women, has no formal education. She is presented as an intelligent Christian who has learned from scripture, churchgoing, and prayer; a decade later, in *Confessions* (6.2.2), Augustine described her special respect for

---

10. Another example was offered by Damasus, bishop of Rome 366–84, who composed classical verse inscriptions to commemorate Roman martyrs; see Trout 2016. But Augustine does not mention them; he says very little about his experience in Rome, either in 383/4, before his move to Milan or in 387/8, on his way back to Africa.

11. Williams 2013 suggests that these hymns were like acclamations in expressing support for Ambrose and for his beliefs.

12. See Consolino in this volume on polymetric poems.

Ambrose. Monnica is praised for her clear-headed contributions to debate, but towards the end of *de beata uita* she and other family members fall silent while Augustine gives a long exposition of the liberal arts, exchanging comments only with the educated discussants. Then a juxtaposition of words, "three one God," prompts Monnica to quote a line of a hymn: *foue precantes Trinitas*, "nurture us praying, Trinity" (*beat. uit.* 4.35). This, according to Augustine, sums up a complex discussion. It is the closing line of *Deus creator omnium*.

14.3. Measures: Metre and Order

Ambrose offered Augustine an example of poetry conveying Christian truth, in accessible style and memorable form, to anyone who came to church. Augustine's early dialogues provide a different argument in favour of poetry: it is an image of God-given order, because it is ordered by the rules of metre. Ten years later, in *Confessions*, he gave a specific example:

> I used to compose poetry [*cantabam carmina*, literally "I used to sing songs"], and I was not allowed to put any foot anywhere I wanted. They had to be put differently in different metres, and the same foot could not go in every place in one line. The art by which I composed did not have different rules in different places, but had all of them at once. Yet I did not see that justice, which good and holy men served, has all its rules at once, in a far more excellent and sublime way. It does not vary at all, and yet at various times it does not have all its rules at once, but assigns and instructs what is appropriate. (*conf.* 3.7.14)

In *Confessions*, this analogy answered the Manichaean challenge that the polygamous patriarchs of the Old Testament behaved in ways forbidden in the New Testament. Augustine argued that the patriarchs kept the unvarying rules of sexual morality, namely the avoidance of lust and the use of sexual desire only for lawful procreation; these rules may be differently implemented in different contexts, and the patriarchs served God in a time when God's people were told to increase and multiply.

Augustine contrasted the instability of temporal created things, which are mutable and in movement, with the stability of the eternal. In his dialogue *Order* he explained that poetry is an image of universal order because its movement is metrical: it is ordered by number and by *modus*, a word which can be translated "mode" or "limit."[13] (In English, "numbers," like "measures," continued for centuries to be another name for poetry.) Reason, eager to rise to contemplation

---

13. On Augustine's use of *modus / species / ordo* (mode, form, order) and of *mensura / numerus / pondus* (measure, number, weight, from Wisdom 11:21), see O'Donnell 1992: 2:46–51.

of the divine, began by attending to the first step on the way, namely rationality perceived by sight and hearing (*ord.* 2.14.39).[14] In the case of hearing, there is a difference between the sound of words and what they signify. Augustine gave an example from a classical poem which was so well known that he did not need to identify it:

> So when we hear those lines "why winter suns hasten to dip in ocean, or what delay holds back the tardy nights" [VERG. *georg.* 2.480–1], we praise the metre in one way and the thought in another, and we do not say "it sounds rationally" and "it is said rationally" with the same understanding of "rational."

The ears judge only sound, which is produced by the voice of a living creature (as in tragedy, comedy, chorus, song) or by blowing into an instrument (flutes and the like) or by plucking or striking instruments (cithara, lyre, cymbals). Reason recognized that sounds have little worth unless they are shaped by *dimensio* and *modulatio*, that is, by length and by variation of high and low; she had called these "feet" and "accent" when considering syllables in relation to *grammatica*, the art of language. Reason now arranged long and short feet in ordered sequences and set limits to separable units (*cola*) and to the length of a line.

> [Reason] gave the name of rhythm to that which was not limited by a definite end, but ran on rationally in ordered feet; in Latin, this name could be nothing other than *numerus*. Thus from her poets were born, and when she saw that in them were important matters not only of sounds but also of words and things, she gave them very great honour, and assigned to them power to use any rational falsehood they wanted.[15] And since they had their origin in the first discipline [i.e., grammar], she allowed grammarians to be their judges. (*ord.* 2.14.40).

Reason understood that numbers ruled in all this ordering of rhythm and modulation, and further that numbers are divine and eternal (2.14.41).

This is the rationale for a project Augustine began at the time of his baptism. He believed that the liberal arts train the mind to move beyond particulars to principles and thus to rise to the divine. Inspired by Varro on the liberal arts, he planned to write commentaries on them all (Shanzer 2005). He noted in *Retractationes* (1.11) that the only commentary he completed was *de grammatica*,

---

14. Harrison 2013 discusses hearing, with special reference to Augustine.
15. On poetic licence, see Ware in this volume.

which he then lost. The only commentary to survive was the first part of *de musica*:

> Then, as I mentioned above [*retract.* 1.6], I wrote six books *On Music*, of which the sixth is the best known, because it discusses something worthy of being known: how to reach, from numbers which are corporeal and animated but mutable, the immutable numbers which are already in immutable truth, and thus "the invisible things of God may be seen, understood through the things which were made" [Rom. 1: 20].

Augustine began *de musica* in 387 and finished the first six books about 391, after his return to Africa. Almost twenty years later, in 408/9, Memorius, bishop of Capua, asked for a copy. In explaining why he had started with *de musica* and why he had not completed his plan, Augustine assumed that Memorius understood how numbers order movement and time-bound experience (Harrison 2013: 230):

> In all movement, the power of numbers is most easily considered in vocal sounds [*uoces*]; this consideration strives upwards, as if by steps, to the supreme inwardness of truth, and "in these paths wisdom reveals herself with gladness, and meets with all providence those who love her" [Wisdom 6:17]. So, at the beginning of my retirement [*otium*], when my mind was free from greater and more necessary cares, I chose to practise in those writings you want from me. I wrote six books on rhythm alone, and planned to write perhaps another six on melody [*de melo*], as I hoped to continue in retirement. But after the burden of church concerns was imposed on me, all those delights escaped my hands, so that now it will be difficult even to find the *codex*, since I cannot disregard your wish, which is not a request but an order. If I can send this little work, you will regret not my obedience to you, but your insistent request to me. It is very difficult to understand five of its books unless there is someone who can distinguish the characters of the discussants, and can also in speaking sound the parts of the syllables so that the kinds of rhythms are expressed by them and strike the sense of hearing; especially because in some of them there are included measured intervals of silence, which cannot be perceived at all unless the speaker informs the hearer. (*epist.* 101.3)

As a priest and then a bishop, Augustine did indeed carry the *sarcina episcopalis*, the "bishop's burden" of pastoral work and administration (McLynn 2012). But the last sentence of this quotation, on the difficulty of reading the text aloud, points to other reasons for not finishing *de musica*: both the subject matter and the literary form excluded people whom Augustine wanted to reach.[16]

Augustine was one of those for whom numbers are a language, and like other philosophers, he treated music as audible mathematics (Hochschild 2012: 117–31); performance was for professionals (Clark 2011).[17] Poetry could also be called *musica*, as song inspired by the Muses and ordered by rhythm, but as Augustine said in *de ordine*, poetry depends on sense as well as sound. So he might be expected to think that music is a better expression of eternal numbers, because hearers can focus on ordered sound without needing to understand either a local language or the special vocabulary, grammar and syntax of poetry. But Augustine believed that the words of scripture are *diuina eloquia*, divine utterances, so these words must be the focus of attention.[18] He knew that the Psalms were songs, for their headings call them *psalmi* or *cantici* or both, and he knew that David sang his psalms to the accompaniment of the *psalterium*, a stringed instrument which was still familiar. But instead of taking this as a precedent, Augustine allegorized any references to praising God with musical instruments (e.g., *in psalm.* 32, *enarr.* 2, *serm.* 2:5), and sometimes he allegorized references to singing (ibid. 8). He discussed in *Confessions* (10.33.50) his fear that singing would distract attention from the words of the psalms rather than strengthen the right emotional response to the words.

The psalms are poems, but in the letter to Memorius, Augustine said that he had not written about the *numeri* of the psalms because he did not know them: he knew no Hebrew, not even the alphabet, and translators had rightly sought to convey the sense rather than preserve the rhythms (*ep.* 101.4). Another twenty years later, when completing *De Doctrina* (begun in 396), he still thought this was right:

> We must avoid the risk of subtracting weight from serious divine sayings [*sententiae*] by adding number. The discipline of music, in which number is most fully learned, was not lacking in our prophets, to the point that the learned Jerome mentions the metres [*metra*] used by some of them, that is, in the Hebrew: he did not transfer them, in order to preserve its truth in words. (4.116)

---

16. Augustine observed in an early work (*util. cred.* 7.17) that no one would attempt Terentianus Maurus, the standard treatise on metre, without a teacher.
17. Boethius said explicitly that study of the principles of music was superior to composition and performance; *de institutione musica* 1,34. I owe the reference to Stephen Blackwood.
18. I discussed this further in "Words and Music: Augustine and the Psalms," the third Ptarmigan Lecture in Patristics, Oxford, February 2014.

Jerome discussed metre in the prologue to his translation of the book of Job:

> In the Hebrew, from the start of the volume to the words of Job the writing is prose. Then from Job's words "Perish the day in which I was born, and the night in which it was said 'A man is conceived'" to the place where it is written, before the end of the volume, "Therefore I blame myself and repent in ashes," the verses are hexameters, running in dactyl and spondee, and often, because of the idiom of the language, accepting other feet which are not of the same syllables but are of the same length [literally, "times"]. From time to time the rhythm itself is carried on, sweet and ringing, the numbers freed from the law; prosodists [*metrici*], rather than the ordinary reader, understand this. From the aforesaid verse to the end of the book, the small section which remains is composed of prose. If anyone thinks this incredible, that is, that the Hebrews have metres, and that the Psalter and the Lamentations of Jeremiah and almost all the songs of the scriptures are expressed in the manner of our Flaccus and of the Greek Pindar and Alcaeus and Sappho, let him read Philo, Josephus, Origen and Eusebius of Caesarea, and by their testimony he will prove that I am speaking the truth.

Perhaps it was this observation by Jerome which prompted a question from Memorius about the metre of the psalms. Augustine's reply shows how he gave priority to meaning. He believed that the *numeri* of music and poetry help some people to raise their minds to the eternal numbers, but even before ordination he recognized the need to reach people who were not trained in the liberal arts and whose spoken Latin differed in vocabulary and speech-rhythm from the classical language analysed by *grammatica* and the rhythms analysed by *musica*.

14.4. LITTERAE AND COMMUNICATION: THE "PSALM AGAINST DONATISTS"

Augustine's letter to Memorius contrasts a "liberal education" with the *litterae uere liberales*, the writings which are truly for free people, whereas the corrupt imaginings of poets and the clever debates of philosophers do not bring liberation. It does not follow that Augustine rejected *litterae* always and for everyone, though sometimes he appears to do so. He held that higher education in grammar and rhetoric is not necessary, for even without formal training people can grasp the essentials: scripture provides examples of rhetorical techniques, and these can be used effectively by people who do not know the metalanguage of rhetoric (*doctr. christ.* 2.87–8). He shared Platonist objections to poetry: poets make up things which never happened and give bad moral examples, and the charm of poetry makes people respond to these fictions (Westra 1990, 2007).[19] So he deplored weeping for the fictitious and immoral Dido rather than for the real wretchedness of a soul alienated from God (*conf.* 1.13.22), and he did not try to see deeper meanings in Vergil (Clark 2010). But he also thought that *litterae* can express truth which Christians can welcome (*doctr. christ.* 2.144–7), and in a letter to his friend Evodius, on a problematic passage of scripture (1 Peter 3: 19–20) about Christ freeing spirits who were in the underworld, he hoped that those freed might include poets and orators and philosophers:

> If we said that absolutely everyone who was found there was freed at that time, who would not rejoice if we could show this? Especially because of some who are well known to us by their literary labour [*litterario labore*], whose eloquence and talent we admire; not only poets and orators, who in many passages of their works showed that those false gods of the Gentiles were to be despised and ridiculed, and sometimes even confessed the one true God, although they engaged in superstitious worship with the rest; but also those who said these things not in poetry [*cantando*] or declamation, but in doing philosophy; and many whose *litterae* we do not have, but we have learned in the *litterae* of these authors in what ways their lives were admirable. (*epist.* 164.4, written 414/5)

Litterae can convey truth and moral example, but Augustine's task was not to compose *litterae*: it was to expound the scriptures so that people would understand and respond (Banniard 1992: 65–104). He was ordained priest in 391. He stopped writing philosophical dialogues (Clark 2008): he had tried to make them inclusive, but perhaps he realized that some people find the literary form of dialogue confusing, because it requires them to "separate the speakers" (as he warned Memorius) and to follow argument and counterargument.[20] Augustine's first attempt at exegesis of scripture, *On Genesis against the Manichaeans* (389?), opens in formal classical style, observing that Christians who read his earlier anti-Manichaean works had kindly told him "they would be understood with difficulty or not at all by the less educated, and I should not abandon the general way of speaking [*communem loquendi consuetudinem*] if I thought of expelling these lethal errors from the souls even of the uneducated." The text then continues with deliberate simplicity, but still within the range of classical *sermo humilis*, which is described in a first-century rhetoric treatise as subdued to the "most

---

19. See Mastrangelo in this volume (393–400).
20. Probably changes of speaker were signalled only by a mark in the margin, as in texts of plays. Half a century later, Theodoret, bishop of Cyrrhus, wrote in the prologue to his dialogue *Eranistes* that he had made it easier by putting the name in the margin each time there was a change of speaker.

ordinary custom that belongs to the pure style" (*rhet. ad Her.* 4.11, tr. Burton 2007: 113). But not long after, perhaps in 393, Augustine wrote a consciously un-classical work, the alphabetic *Psalmus contra partem Donati*, "Psalm against the Donatists." Christian innovation rarely extended to non-classical forms; it is of course possible that non-classical poems were not usually copied, and Augustine's survived only because he listed it in *Retractationes*.[21] It is his second known attempt at writing verse.

Donatists (a name given by their opponents) were the majority church in Augustine's diocese of Hippo. They sang their own *psalmi* in church, as well as the psalms of David (Avg. *epist.* 55.18.34); these *psalmi* do not survive, but probably they expressed Donatist beliefs that theirs was the true, pure, catholic church, in succession to those who had not betrayed the faith in time of persecution, and probably they praised the martyrs who had died for those beliefs (Shaw 2011: 466–75). Augustine explained in the *Retractationes* the purpose of his own *psalmus*:

> Wanting the case against the Donatists to come to the knowledge of the very lowest common people, the wholly untrained and uninformed, and to stick in their memory so far as that could be achieved by us, I made a psalm to be sung to them in [the sequence of] Latin letters, but only as far as the letter V. They call this kind "ABC" [*abecedarii*]. I left out the last three [letters], but in their place I added a final, as it were, epilogue, as if Mother Church were addressing them. The *hypopsalma*, which is the response, and the prologue to the case, which is also to be sung, are not in the order of the letters; their order begins after the prologue. I did not want this done as some kind of poem [*aliquo carminis genere*], in case metrical necessity forced me to use some words which are less familiar to the common people. This psalm begins "All who rejoice in peace, judge now the truth," which is the refrain. (*retract.* 1.20)

This careful description, combining bibliographic information and context of writing, also makes a point about the differences between classical poetry and the everyday work songs Augustine mentioned in sermons (Shaw 2011: 466–9). These songs included "ABC" *psalmi*. Augustine observed, discussing a biblical psalm which he knew to be alphabetic, that according to people who knew Hebrew, all the lines in a group of eight began with the same letter. "This is much more carefully done than is the custom for our people making

---

21. Pollmann 2013: 319 notes a few examples of non-classical poetry. One is Commodianus (date uncertain) who used ordinary diction in accentual verse; see Roberts, this volume (373). For Christian alphabetic poems, see Bastiaensen 2007: 267.

in Latin or Punic the psalms they call ABC, for they begin only the first line with the letter they place before it, not all the lines until the group is complete" (*in psalm.* 118, *enarr.* 32.8).²² So the form of the *psalmus* was familiar, and Augustine did not want the metre of "some kind of *carmen*" to make him use unfamiliar words.

A classical *carmen* would have presented Augustine's target audience with problems of vocabulary, grammar and syntax, and metre. Little survives of everyday spoken Latin, but there is enough material to show how it differed from the classical Latin which schoolboys were trained to read and to use in formal speech and writing (Burton 2000: 151–91).²³ The vocabulary of poetry was different again from that of prose, to the point that Varro treated it separately in his work on Latin language (*ling.* 5.1; 6.11).²⁴ There were also differences of rhythm. Rhetoric students learned a range of cadences for ending sentences or sense units; in classical rhetoric these endings (*clausulae*) depended on vowel length, but in later Latin they depended on stress accent. Augustine and some of his contemporaries used both kinds of rhythm, according to context (Oberhelman 1991). Late in life, he commented that the Latin scriptures did not provide *clausulae*, but it would be easy to do so by changing the word order (*doctr.christ.* 4.113–15); interestingly, his translator Roger Green (1995: 250) thinks that in the example Augustine gives, both the original version and the modified version have acceptable endings.²⁵ Classical metre also depended on vowel length, but according to Augustine "African ears" did not distinguish (*non iudicant*) short and long vowels (*doctr. christ.* 4.65). Composing or hearing classical verse required practice. When one Audax sent him a five-line poem requesting a long answer, Augustine observed

> In the fifth and last line there are seven feet: I don't know whether the metre escaped your hearing, or whether you wanted to test that I can still remember how to scan [*diiudicare*] such things. People do perhaps forget when they were once enthusiasts for such things, then made great progress in the writings of the church. (*epist.* 261.5, date uncertain)

The *psalmus contra partem Donati* maximizes the impact of simple language and familiar rhythm. It uses a strong regular beat reinforced by internal rhymes and assonances, especially by the many lines which end in *-áre* or *-ére*. Presumably

---

22. My interpretation of the last sentence differs from that of Shaw 2011: 480. On learned discussion of Psalm 118 by Jerome and Ambrose, see Gualandri in this volume (n. 103).
23. Adams 2013 offers wider discussion of social variation.
24. I owe the reference to Richard Marshall.
25. *Et carnis prouidentiam ne feceritis in concupiscentiis* (Rom. 13:14: "do not provide for the flesh by lusts"), modified to *et carnis prouidentiam ne in concupiscentiis feceritis*.

the singing also reinforced the beat, but we know nothing about the tunes of psalms or other songs, and Augustine did not mention any musical accompaniment. The alphabetic sequence was intended to help memories; the repetitive patterns helped the simple vocabulary and syntax to stick in the mind; lines are self-contained sense units; and the refrain allowed listeners to participate and to voice approval, as they did in acclamations (Shaw 2011: 452–75). Most lines have sixteen syllables, usually achieved by some elision. The rhythm is mostly trochaic (long-short), there is a strong break in the middle of each line, and in each half line there is a strong accent on the penultimate syllable before the break, for example in the refrain:

Vós qui gáudetís de páce // módo uérum iúdicáte.[26]

Here are the opening lines:

Omnes qui gaudetis de pace, modo uerum iudicate.
Foeda est res causam audire et personas accipere
Omnes iniusti non possunt regnum Dei possidere
Vestem alienam conscindas nemo potest tolerare
Quanto magis pacem Christi qui conscindit dignus morte.
Et quis est ista qui fecit quaeramus hoc sine errore.

Abundantia peccatorum solet fratres conturbare.
Propter hoc Dominus noster uoluit nos praemonere
Comparans regnum caelorum reticulo miso in mare
Congregauit multos pisces omne genus hinc et inde
Quos cum traxissent ad litus tunc coeperunt separare.
Bonos in uasa miserunt, reliquos malos in mare.
Quisquis nouit Euangelium recognoscat cum timore.
Videt reticulum Ecclesiam, uidet hoc saeculum mare,
Genus autem mixtum piscis iustus est cum peccatore,
Saeculi finis est litus, tunc est tempus separare.
Qui modo retia ruperunt, multum dilexerunt mare,
Vasa sunt sedes sanctorum, quo non possunt peruenire.
Vos qui gaudetis de pace, modo uerum iudicate.

Bonus auditor fortasse quaerit qui ruperunt rete . . .

---

26. In the *Retractationes*, Augustine gives *omnes*, not *uos*, as the first word. For editions of the *psalmus*, see Hunink 2011: 390 n. 6.

In Praise of the Wax Candle 437

As Augustine said about the psalms of David (*epist.* 101.4), it is not possible in translation to keep both the rhythm and the sense. The translation which follows opts for the sense, in the hope that readers can hear the rhythm in the Latin.

> It's a foul thing to hear a case and favour some.[27]
> The unjust cannot possess God's kingdom.
> Tearing another's clothes is something we can't bear:
> So tearing Christ's peace deserves death.
> Who does this? Let us ask without error.
>
> Abundance of sinners scares the brothers.
> That's why the Lord chose to warn us
> Comparing the kingdom of heaven to a net cast into the sea.
> It brought together many fish, every kind, from here and there,
> And when they dragged it to shore, then they began to separate the fish.
> They put the good ones in containers, and the rest, the bad, in the sea.
> He who knows the Gospel, think of this with fear!
> He sees that the net is the Church, this world is the sea,
> And the mixed kinds of fish are the just man with the sinner.
> The shore is the end of the world: then is the time to separate.
> Those who broke the nets just now greatly loved the sea.
> The containers are the place of the saints, and they cannot go there.
>
> You who rejoice in peace, judge now the truth.
>
> But who broke the nets? the good listener may ask . . .

We have no material for comparison and no way of knowing whether the *psalmus* did stick in the memories of an uneducated audience. Its style is deliberately simple, but its content is not; and though congregations were used to long sermons (Augustine's record is about two and a half hours), it seems long for its purpose. The hymns of Ambrose are short, but the *psalmus* has 297 lines. Augustine's alphabet has twenty letters, from A to V (it includes K but does not distinguish I from J or U from V), each letter introduces a twelve-line stanza, there is a five-line prologue and a thirty-line epilogue, and there are twenty-one repetitions of the refrain. All this would take more than half an hour to sing (Hunink 2011: 400). Considered as poetry, the *psalmus* has had a generally bad

---

27. *Personas accipere*: to be a "respecter of persons," i.e., judge by their status, not by the facts of the case. "God is no respecter of persons" (*non est personarum acceptor Deus*): Deut. 10:17; Acts 10:34.

press (Shaw 2011: 475); the kindest comment is that it is a precursor (or perhaps an early example?) of Romance poetry.[28] This may be the familiar problem of an intellectual trying to write a popular work, or of a prose writer experimenting with verse. Augustine did not try it again, though there was surely a need, for example, to provide more appropriate songs for the vigils he wanted to make less riotous (*ser.* 311.5; Lancel 2002: 156–8).

14.5. Poetry as Evasion: Licentius

Augustine's task was to help people understand and live by the truths revealed in scripture, and this required him to use language they understood, not language constrained by metres they could not hear. But the three lines quoted at the start of this paper show that Augustine could write clearly and simply in classical hexameters, conveying truth in a form which could be used in the liturgy. He knew that the hymns of Ambrose conveyed truth and prompted right emotion, and he thought that poetry was a symbol of universal order. He shared Platonist wariness about the charms of poetic fiction, but he held that *delectatio*, delight, is central to religious feeling (Harrison 2000: 96–7); and Christian poetry did not make things up but praised the wonderful works of the Creator.[29] Augustine would have found time to write poetry if he had thought it a good way to reach people. But he had other priorities, and the dangers he saw are illustrated by a poem which survives in his correspondence (Shanzer 1991). It was written by his former student Licentius, son of his patron Romanianus.

Augustine, dedicating his early dialogue *de ordine* to his friend Zenobius, introduced Licentius as *repente admirabiliter poeticae deditus*, "suddenly and remarkably devoted to poetry" (*ord.* 1.2.5). On his first appearance Licentius is too devoted to poetry to engage in philosophical discussion:

> I was seriously afraid that, in his profound abandonment to the study of poetry, he would be carried far away from philosophy. "I am annoyed," I said "that you pursue these verses of yours, in every kind of metre [*omni metrorum genere*], singing and ululating: they are building a more monstrous wall between you and truth than they are trying to build between

---

28. Bonner 1986: 253–4 cites the classicist William Beare, who saw the *Psalmus* as "a monument of the decay of quantitative verse" but sensibly argued that it is not usefully described as trochaic acatalectic tetrameter in accentual metre; and the historian Pierre Monceaux, who noted the resemblance to later Romance poetry.

29. For Augustine's discussion of words and of delight in words as a way of expounding scripture, see Gualandri in this volume.

your lovers, for they had a breathing space, if only through a crack that developed." At the time, he had started to sing about Pyramus. (1.3.8)

Then Licentius decides that he will after all discuss philosophy. Presumably to show that poetry and philosophy are compatible, Augustine tells him that Zenobius too is concerned about *ordo rerum*, the order of the universe, to the point that he has written a poem (a good poem!), challenging Augustine to respond to his questions; he wants to meet Licentius and was overjoyed on learning that Licentius is *studiosus poeticae*, an enthusiast for poetry (1.7.20). But Licentius is now devoted to philosophy and replies "I have suddenly been made less inclined [*pigrior*] to those metres; something has now shone upon me with a different, a far different light. Philosophy is more lovely." He thanks Christ for this change, and as day breaks (1.8.22) Augustine weeps and prays while Licentius sings under his breath the psalm verse *conuerte nos*: "turn us around, O Lord."

It is a bad sign that Licentius sings the psalm *garrule*, "parrot fashion," like an imitative bird which lacks understanding (Burton 2007: 24). Almost a decade later (394/5), Licentius is still writing poetry, and Augustine and his old friend Alypius (also related to Romanianus) and his new friend Paulinus are all worried about Licentius, because he is still not a committed Christian and they are concerned about his way of life. Augustine's correspondence includes (*epist*. 26) a poem Licentius sent him. It says, at considerable length, that Licentius finds Varro very difficult without Augustine's help, is ready to follow Augustine anywhere, and would like Augustine to send him *de musica*. It reads like an attempt to continue their earlier conversations, full of literary allusions, about the liberal arts as a route to wisdom (Shanzer 1991: 124–33). In his reply Augustine advises Licentius to visit Paulinus at Nola and "learn with what riches of talent he offers to Christ sacrifices of praise" (*epist*. 26.5).[30]

This letter shows that Augustine knew Paulinus was a poet as well as a committed ascetic Christian. Evidence is needed because Augustine does not quote or refer to the poems of Paulinus, either in their surviving correspondence, which admittedly has some gaps (Conybeare 2000: 6), or in other writings. Nor do the letters of Paulinus suggest that he sent Augustine copies of his poems; for example, of the *Natalicia* he composed each year for the festival of Saint Felix, in classical metres but in simple narrative style (Conybeare 2000: 50–3).[31] When Augustine sent Paulinus his dialogue *de libero arbitrio*, he asked in exchange for a work of Paulinus "against the pagans" and for some works of Ambrose

---

30. On Christian poetry as a sacrifice of praise, comparable to liturgy, see Roberts in this volume (382–3).
31. On his polymetric poems, see Consolino in this volume (108–12).

against people who argued that Christ profited from the books of Plato (AVG. *epist.* 31.8; Trout 1999: 203); so unless *contra paganos* was a poem, Paulinus may have thought that Augustine was not interested in poetry. Augustine very rarely quoted anything later than Vergil (Hagendahl 1967: 470–8). His only quotation from a poet of his own time is two lines of Claudian, omitting two half lines, from a panegyric which he assigned to the wrong emperor (*ciu.* 5.26, Clark 2014: 48); he may have found the (mis)quotation but not read the poem.

Augustine was silent about the poetry of Paulinus, but Paulinus was a poet who had given up his worldly career, and Augustine thought he could help Licentius.[32] He wrote to Paulinus (*epist.* 27), and Paulinus wrote to Romanianus (*epist.* 32 in Augustine's correspondence), then turned (32.4) to Licentius and added an elegiac poem to avoid any harshness of tone, because "your letter comes to mind, from which I understood that you are a friend to *musicis modis* [the modes of poetry, discussed above]. I, too, at your age, did not recoil from this study." Augustine did not send a poem and did not comment on the style of the poem Licentius sent. He wrote:

> I was moved by some words in your letters but thought it foolish to discuss them when I am seething with concern for your actions and your whole life. If a verse of yours was perverse because its movement was not in order, if it did not follow its own rules, if it offended the ear of the hearer with unequal measures, you would certainly be embarrassed, and you would not delay or desist until you had put in order, corrected, set right and made equal your verse by learning and practising the art of metre with the most intense zeal and with every effort. But you are not in order; you have perverted yourself; you do not follow the rules of your God, nor are you in harmony with the honorable wishes of your friends, or with your own education, in leading your life; and this, you think, can be put behind you and ignored? As if you matter less to yourself than the sound of your voice, and it matters less that you offend the ears of God with disorderly conduct than if the authority of grammar is angered by your disorderly syllables. You write:
>
> Oh, if new dawn would now with joyful wheels
> Recall past suns in which, with you, we strove
> For liberal study and fair laws of the good
> In midmost Italy and mountains high!
> Harsh cold and silvered frost would not prevent,

---

32. On Paulinus reconciling poetry and theology, see Mastrangelo in this volume (411).

Nor western storms nor raging northern wind,
My anxious following where your footsteps lead.
The only need's for you to give the order.

Woe's me if I don't give the order, if I don't require and command, if I don't ask and plead! But if your ears are closed to my cries, let them be open to your mouth, let them be open to your song. Listen to yourself, you most hard, most monstrous, most deaf! What use to me is a golden tongue and an iron heart? What lamentations, not what songs, would suffice me to bewail your songs, in which I see what soul and what talent I am not allowed to grasp and sacrifice to our God? You wait for me to give the order "be good, be tranquil, be blessed": as if any day's dawning could be more welcome than my enjoying your talent in the Lord, as if either you do not know how I hunger and thirst for you or else do not admit it in this song. Recall the mind with which you wrote this, and say to me now, "The only need's for you to give the order." Here is my order: give yourself to me, if that is all that is needed; give yourself to my Lord, who is the lord of us all, who granted you that talent. What am I but your slave in him, and fellow slave under him?

Once again, this translation aims to convey the sense of the words rather than match the conscious elegance of Augustine's language and the conventional poetic style of Licentius. Here is the Latin:

> *Si uersus tuus momentis inordinatis peruersus esset, si suis legibus non staret, si mensuris imparibus aurem auditoris offenderet, puderet te certe, nec dif feres, nec desisteres donec ordinares, corrigeres, statueres, aequares uersum tuum, discendo et agendo artem metricam acerrimo studio, et labore quolibet: quid cum inordinatus ipse peruerteris, cum legibus Dei tui ipse non stas, neque in agenda uita honestis tuorum uotis et huic ipsi eruditioni tuae concinis, abiiciendum post tergum putas et negligendum? Quasi prae sono linguae tuae sis tibi uilior, et incompositis moribus quod offendis aures Dei leuius sit, quam si incompositis syllabis tuis grammatica succenseret auctoritas. Scribis:*

> *O mihi transactos reuocet si pristina soles*
> *Laetificis aurora rotis, quos libera tecum*
> *Otia tentantes, et candida iura bonorum,*
> *Duximus Italiae medio, montesque per altos!*
> *Non me dura gelu prohiberent frigora cano,*
> *Nec fera tempestas Zephyrum fremitusque Borini,*
> *Quin tua sollicito premerem uestigia passu.*

Hoc opus, ut iubeas tantum.

Me miserum, si ego non iubeo, si non cogo atque impero, si non rogo ac supplico. Sed si aures tuae aduersus meas uoces clausae sunt, ori tuo pateant, pateant carmini tuo; exaudi teipsum, durissime, immanissime, surdissime. Quo mihi linguam auream et cor ferreum? quibus ego non carminibus, sed lamentationibus sufficiam plangere carmina tua, in quibus uideo, quam animam, quod ingenium non mihi liceat apprehendere, et immolare Deo nostro? Exspectas ut ego iubeam, sis bonus, sis quietus, sis beatus; quasi quidquam mihi dierum gratius illucescat, quam ut ingenio tuo fruar in Domino, aut uere tu nescias quam te esuriam et sitiam, aut non hoc ipso id carmine fatearis. Reuoca animum quo ista scripsisti, nunc mihi dic: Hoc opus, ut iubeas tantum. Ecce iussum meum: da mihi te, si hoc opus est tantum; da Domino meo te, qui omnium nostrum dominus est, qui tibi illud donauit ingenium. Nam ego quid sum, nisi seruus tuus per ipsum, et conseruus sub ipso?

Before his quotation from the poem, Augustine makes his point in beautifully balanced classical Latin. Licentius is not using poetry as a way of moving from corporeal numbers to the order of the created universe and to love for its creator. Instead, Licentius loves the corporeal numbers; he would work to put disordered metre right but not to put right his disordered life. Augustine's prose rhythms are classical, he uses wordplay to make contrasts and connections, he builds up lists of verbs; and no doubt he could have named and discussed all these rhetorical techniques. Then he quotes some lines from the poem of Licentius, and after this his style is heightened as he exploits the vocabulary and imagery of the poem and deploys allusions to the classics he and his students had read together. In *de ordine* Licentius quoted Terence as he apologized for refusing to discuss philosophy, and Augustine too quotes Terence (*Ad.* 5.1); he briefly speaks as the worried slave of comedy whose master is in trouble and as the distraught lover of elegy.[33] But he does not offer an exchange of verse, like the poetic exchange of Paulinus and Ausonius (Shanzer 1991: 134–5). That would allow Licentius to continue avoiding the problem by writing yet more lines about his devotion to Augustine or by discussing metre.

Augustine does not offer a poem, but Licentius may allude to his third known attempt at poetry, which includes the contrast between ordered and disordered love. For this attempt there is only the passing reference in *ciu.* 15.22, quoted at the

---

33. The letter thus exemplifies the tension discussed by the editors in the Introduction: shared classical culture is deployed to reject classicizing poetry.

start of this chapter. The context discusses a passage of scripture, "the sons of God saw that the daughters of men were beautiful, and took them as wives" (Genesis 6:2). Augustine interprets this as the mingling of the two cities; he had earlier explained that the heavenly city is the community of all those, angels and humans, who love God, and the earthly city is the community of those, fallen angels and humans, who put themselves before God. Augustine takes the "sons of God" in this problematic passage to be humans who belong to the city of God but love the earthly beauty of women who belong to the earthly city.[34] God created earthly beauty, and it is good; but it is temporal and physical, so if it is loved more than God, that love is disordered. Then, unexpectedly, Augustine restates his point by citing three lines from his praise of the wax candle. He does not restate the argument of his earlier writings that the metrical order of these lines is an image of God-given order.

The three lines are very different from the style of Licentius, for Augustine did not let the metre force him to use unfamiliar language or complicated word order. But it is possible that Licentius alludes to Augustine's poem when he refers to Augustine's part in the Easter ceremonies:

*et cum luciferos praeconia[35] uesper in ortus
distulerit sanctumque super benedixeris ignem,
sis memor ipse mei!*

When evening has deferred proclamation to light-bearing dawn, and you have said a blessing over the holy fire, remember me! (45–7)

That is, "remember me at Easter," the time of baptisms, when candidates kept the Easter vigil as Augustine himself had done at Milan in the days when Licentius was his student. The *praeconium paschale*, the paschal proclamation or paschal praise, would be recited "when evening has deferred proclamation to light-bearing dawn." If there is an allusion to Augustine's poem, it must be an early work, composed before the correspondence of 394/5; composed, if so, before the "bishop's burden" became too heavy for the making of verses, even if the verses helped the church by confronting Donatism or by contributing to the Easter liturgy. There is nothing to show why the "praise of the candle" came to Augustine's mind ca. 420 as he worked on *City of God* 15: perhaps it had been sung at a recent Easter? In 394/5 Augustine said nothing about this connection between Licentius's verses and his own. Instead, he challenged Licentius to act.

---

34. He goes on to discuss the interpretation that the "sons of God" are angels.
35. Shanzer 1991: 119 n. 58 argues for *praeconia* in place of *praecordia*, which is defended by Clarke 1963.

14.6. Conclusion: Poetry and Priorities

Paulinus could show Licentius how poetry can be used as a sacrifice of praise to God (Avg. *epist.* 26.5), and Augustine could use the resources of literary culture to make Licentius realize that his love of poetry was disordered. Poetry has its place. It need not be a distraction: it can be an offering to God. It need not make things up: it can praise the wonderful works of the Creator and tell stories of the saints. Delight in the sweetness of its language and rhythm need not be a danger, for if its content is right, delight will help hearers and readers respond to God; and because this should be its purpose, it should address the widest possible audience.[36] What would Augustine have thought of another poem concerned with wax candles and other *igniculi*, "little fires," first in the house and then in church?[37]

Pinguis quos olei rore madentibus
Lychnis aut facibus pascimus aridis,
Quin et fila fauis scirpea floreis
Presso melle prius conlita fingimus

Viuax flamma uiget, seu caua testula
Sucum linteolo suggerit ebrio
Seu pinus piceam fert alimoniam,
Seu ceram teretem stuppa calens bibit. (Prud. *cath.* 5.13–20)

We pasture them in lamps dripping with the liquid of rich olive oil or on dry torches; we also fashion strands of rushes smeared with flowery honeycomb from which the honey has been pressed. The living flame burns strong, whether the hollow potsherd supplies juice to the drunken strip of linen or the pine brings resinous nourishment or the hot tow drinks the smooth wax.

Pendent mobilibus lumina funibus
Quae subfixa micant per laquearia,
Et de languidulis fota natatibus
Lucem perspicuo flamma iacit uitro

---

36. Christian poetry discussed in other chapters of this volume would move educated readers but would not easily reach others: see, e.g., Kaufmann on Christian cento and other forms of classical intertext, Mastrangelo on Prudentius, Roberts on Lactantius, and Squire on Optatian.

37. O'Daly 2012 offers text, commentary, and a more elegant translation; he does not think (166) there is a specific reference to the Easter vigil. Literary analysis in Clarke 2007.

On swaying ropes hang lights, fixed beneath the coffered ceiling and glittering through it, and the flame nurtured by the slowly swirling liquid throws light through transparent glass. (ibid. 141–4)

Prudentius makes his readers attend to the many materials which nurture these everyday lights: olive oil lamps, torches of dry wood, rushlights held together with beeswax, pottery lamps with linen wicks, pine-resin torches, wax candles with tow wicks, and, in church, the new glass oil holders. He wants his readers to praise the Creator, moving from these little fires to the light given by God. But his lovely lines also make Augustine's point that classical metre can require unfamiliar words in disconcerting word order. In contrast, the surviving three lines on the wax candle could be readily understood when sung, as part of the liturgy, "in a clear voice with appropriate modulation" (*conf.* 10.33.50). Prudentius could move an educated audience; Augustine tried to reach everyone who came; and close contemporaries though they were, there is no evidence that Augustine ever heard of Prudentius.

This paper has suggested reasons for thinking that Augustine would be pleased to find an Augustine-shaped space in the study of late Latin literature. If his readers were to devote time and attention to (for example) the brilliant technique of his letter to Licentius, they would miss his point or, worse, evade it.[38] For many centuries Augustine achieved his aim: he was read for rational meaning rather than rational sound, and his literary skill served his purpose of interpreting scripture so that people would respond to the greatness of God. In the later twentieth century Augustine began to be read as a late antique man, a product of classical education and rhetorical training, who in his own time was not as exceptional or as influential as his later reputation suggests (Marrou 1938, 1949; Brown 1967, with Vessey 1998; O'Donnell 2005). He became a major source for late antique social and intellectual history, especially for the content and methods of education and for its effect on interpretation of texts and on rhetorical technique. But there remains an Augustine-shaped space on the bookshelf of late Latin literature (Vessey 2012a: 253–4).

One reason for this is that anyone might hesitate to discuss Augustine because he wrote so much and because so much has been written about him. There are journals in several languages dedicated to Augustinian studies, the *Revue des Études Augustiniennes* collects the massive annual bibliography, and there are impressive online resources and searchable databases.[39] For classicists

---

38. Like Licentius, they would engage in cultural narcissism: see Elsner, this volume.

39. E.g., www.augustinus.de/, the website of the Zentrum für Augustinus-Forschung at Wurzburg, and www.findingaugustine.org/, a bibliographic collaboration of the Katholieke Universiteit Leuven and Villanova University.

and historians who work on Augustine, there is a further cause for hesitation, in that Augustine's central concerns were philosophical theology and biblical exegesis, and these require different kinds of expertise, both intellectual and practical. Many of those who write about Augustine do so because of their own religious commitment and shape their work, as he did, by prayer as well as by reading and reflection. Some of them live in the way he advocated, as members of the Order of Saint Augustine or of another religious order. No one, classicist or theologian, wants to separate these early Christian texts from their culture, but there is a question how and for what purpose to read them.

Some *litterae* help educated people to turn to God, and some authors of *litterae* are motivated by that concern, not by concern for cultural status or technical skill or relationship to other works of literature. Some authors, though not Christian, voice truths which Christians can welcome. But Augustine's concern was prompting response to the scriptures in which God reveals his will to humanity; he held that the multiple and inconsistent *litterae* of human ingenuity are inferior to the single divinely inspired *scriptura* (*ciu.* 11.1; Vessey 2012b). The techniques of literary criticism can illuminate Augustine's work: exploration of his scriptural imagery and his association of one passage with another (O'Donnell 1992); his own favoured technique of attention to the choice of words and to their implications (Burton 2007); reflection on his interaction with Latin classics (Shanzer 2012) and with other Christian writers (Vessey 2012a, Williams 2012). But from Augustine's perspective, we go wrong if our attention is focused on these created things. He was unquestionably Latin (his Greek was never strong), but he would not have accepted that he was Late or that he wrote Literature. Not Late, because Jesus said "it is not for you to know times and seasons" (Acts 1:7) and because Augustine believed that the rise and decline of empires and cultures depends on the will of God, not on patterns of decadence or on other historical cycles. So he rejected any attempt to determine where we are in relation to the end of time, and any claim that some part of secular culture, in particular classical Roman culture, has a special importance: what matters, in any cultural context, is the commitment of an individual human being to love of God and of neighbour (Clark 2014). Not Literature, because of the range of writing, especially fiction, which is classified as literature, and because of the way it is read and discussed by people who, in Augustine's view, neglect the right order of love.[40]

---

40. Augustine would, e.g., recognize the theme of displacement, absence, and loss identified by Formisano, the gap between words and reality discussed by Hernández Lobato, the concern with written signs and visual images found by Squire in the poems of Optatian. But he would ask how much of this is about human creation, and how many people are excluded from understanding.

Bibliography

Adams, J. (2013) *Social Variation and the Latin Language*. Cambridge, Cambridge University Press.
Adkin, N. (2005) "Some Additions to Maltby's *Lexicon of Ancient Latin Etymologies*." In C. Deroux (ed.), *Studies in Latin Literature and Roman History*, XII. Brussels, Latomus, 74–96.
Adler, J., and U. Ernst (1987) *Text als Figur: Visuelle Poesie von der Antike bis zur Moderne*. Weinheim, VCH.
Agamben, G. (1991) *Language and Death: The Place of Negativity*. Minneapolis, University of Minnesota Press.
Agosti, G. (2009) "Cristianizzazione della poesia greca e dialogo interculturale." *Cristianismo nella storia* 31: 59–81.
Agosti, G. (2012) "Greek Poetry." In S. F. Johnson (ed.) *The Oxford Handbook of Late Antiquity*. Oxford, Oxford University Press, 361–404.
Ahl, F. (1985) *Metaformations: Soundplay and Wordplay in Ovid and Other Classical Poets*. Ithaca, NY, Cornell University Press.
Alici, L., R. Piccolomini, and A. Pieretti (eds.) (2002) *Verità e linguaggio: Agostino nella filosofia del Novecento*, vol. 3. Rome, Città Nuova.
Alvar Ezquerra, A. (2011) "*Technopægnia* latinos." In J. L. Vidal, J. I García Armendáriz, and A. Egea (eds.), 231–62.
Amherdt, D. (2004) *Ausone et Paulin de Nole: Correspondance*. Bern, Peter Lang.
Amherdt, D. (2010) "La *Protrepticus ad nepotem* d'Ausone: Rhétorique et humour, ou Ausone est-il sérieux?" *Mnemosyne* 63: 43–60.
Amsler, M. (1989) *Etymology and Grammatical Discourse in Late Antiquity and the Early Middle Ages*. Amsterdam, Benjamins.
Anderson, W. B. (1936) *Sidonius: Poems, Letters I–II*. Cambridge, MA, Harvard University Press.
Ando, C. (2000) *Imperial Ideology and Provincial Loyalty in the Roman Empire*. Berkeley, University of California Press.
Apollinaire, G. (2004) *Calligrammes: Poems of Peace and War (1913–1916)*. Trans. A. Hyde Greet. Bognor Regis, University Press Group.
Argentieri, L. (2007) "Meleager and Philip as Epigram Collectors." In P. Bing and J. S. Bruss (eds.), 147–64.
Asmis, E. (1992) "Plato on Poetic Creativity." In R. Kraut (ed.), *Cambridge Companion to Plato*. Cambridge, Cambridge University Press.

Auerbach, E. (2003) *Mimesis: The Representation of Reality in Western Literature.* Trans. Willard R. Trask. Princeton, NJ, Princeton University Press.
Augustinus (1954) *Tractatus in Evangelium Iohannis*, ed. R. Willems, Turnhout.
Austin, R. P. (1938) *The Stoichedon Style in Greek Inscriptions.* Oxford, Oxford University Press.
Austin, R. P. (1955) *Vergili Maronis Aeneidos liber quartus.* Oxford, Clarendon Press.
Baehrens, W. A. (1874) *XII Panegyrici Latini.* Leipzig, Teubner.
Baehrens, W. A. (1911) *XII Panegyrici Latini.* Leipzig, Teubner.
Banniard, M. (1992) *Viva voce: Communication écrite et communication orale du IVe au IXe siècle en Occident latin.* Paris, Institut des Études Augustiniennes.
Barasch, M. (1992) *Icon: Studies in the History of an Idea.* New York, New York University Press.
Baratin, M., and F. Desbordes (1982) "Sémiologie et métalinguistique chez saint Augustine." *Langages* 16: 75–89.
Barchiesi, A. (1997) "Otto punti su una mappa dei naufragi." In S. Hinds and D. Fowler (eds.), *Memoria, arte allusiva, intertestualità / Memory, Allusion, Intertextuality* (= *Materiali e Discussioni* 39). Pisa, Istituti Editoriali e Poligrafici Internazionali, 209–26.
Bardill, J. (2012) *Constantine: Divine Emperor of the Christian Golden Age.* Cambridge, Cambridge University Press.
Bardon, H. (1975) [Review of Polara 1973.] *Revue Belge de philologie et d'histoire* 53: 453.
Barkan, L. (2013) *Mute Poetry, Speaking Pictures.* Princeton, Princeton University Press.
Barnes, T. D. (1975) "Publilius Optatianus Porfyrius." *AJP* 96: 173–86.
Barnes, T. D. (1996) "Emperors, Panegyrics, Prefects, Provinces and Palaces (284–317)." *JRA* 9: 532–52.
Barnes, T. D. (2001) "Constantine's Speech to the Assembly of the Saints: Place and Date of Delivery." *Journal of Theological Studies* 52: 26–36.
Barnes, T. D. (2011) *Constantine: Dynasty, Religion, and Power in the Later Roman Empire.* Chichester, Wiley-Blackwell.
Baroin, C. (2010) *Se souvenir à Rome: Formes, représentations et pratiques de la mémoire.* Paris, Belin DL.
Barrett, A. A. (1978) "Knowledge of the Literary Classics in Roman Britain." *Britannia* 9: 309–33.
Bartelink, G. (1979) "Sprachliche und stilistische Bemerkungen in Ambrosius' Schriften." *Wiener Studien* NF 13: 175–202.
Barthes, R. (1974) *S/Z.* Trans. R. Miller. Malden, MA, Blackwell.
Barthes, R. (1977) "The Death of the Author." In R. Barthes (ed.), *Image-Music-Text* (essays selected and trans. S. Heath). London, Fontana, 142–8.
Barthes, R. (1978) *A Lover's Discourse: Fragments.* Trans. R. Howard. New York, Hill and Wang.
Bartsch, S. (1998) "*Ars* and the Man: The Politics of Art in Virgil's *Aeneid*." *CPh* 93: 322–42.
Bassett, S. G. (1991) "The Antiquities in the Hippodrome of Constantinople." *DOP* 45: 87–96.
Bassett, S. G. (2004) *The Urban Image of Late Antique Constantinople.* Cambridge, Cambridge University Press.
Bastiaensen, A. (2007) "Biblical Poetry in Latin Liturgical Texts." In W. Otten and K. Pollmann (eds.), *Poetry and Exegesis in Premodern Latin Christianity: The Encounter between Classical and Christian Strategies of Interpretation.* Leiden, Brill, 265–74.
Baumgartner, A. (1981) *Untersuchungen zur Anthologie des Codex Salmasianus.* Zurich, Universität Zürich.
Bažil, M. (2009) *Centones Christiani: Métamorphoses d'une forme intertextuelle dans la poésie latine chrétienne de l'antiquité tardive.* Paris, Institut d'Études Augustiniennes.

Bécares, V., F. Pordomingo, R. Cortés Tovar, and J. C. Fernández Corte (eds.) (2000) *La intertextualidad en las literaturas griega y latina*. Madrid-Salamanca, Ediciones Clásicas.
Benediktson, D. T. (2000) *Literature and the Visual Arts in Ancient Greece and Rome*. Norman, OK, University of Oklahoma Press.
Benjamin, W. (2002) *The Arcades Project*. Trans. H. Eiland and K. McLaughlin. Cambridge, MA, Harvard University Press.
Benko, S. (1980) "Virgil's Fourth Eclogue in Christian Interpretation." *Aufstieg und Niedergang der Römischen Welt* II.31.1: 646–705.
Bergmann, B. (1996) "The Pregnant Moment: Tragic Wives in the Roman Interior." In N. Kampen (ed.), *Sexuality in Ancient Art*. Cambridge, Cambridge University Press, 199–218.
Bernard, J.-F., P. Bernardi, and D. Esposito (eds.) (2008) *Il reimpiego in architettura: Recupero, trasformazione, uso*. Rome, École française de Rome.
Bernardi Perini, G. (1999–2000) "Virgilio, il Cristo, la Sibilla: Sulla lettura 'messianica' della quarta egloga." *Atti e Memorie dell'Accademia Galileiana di Scienze, Lettere ed Arti in Padova* 102: 115–24.
Bernardi Perini, G. (2001) "I velenosi Assiri, il sorriso impossibile: Note sulla versione greca della quarta egloga di Virgilio e il commento costantiniano." In *Cultura latina cristiana fra terzo e quarto secolo. Atti del Convegno (Mantova, 5–7 novembre 1998)*. Firenze, Olski, 205–24.
Bernt G. (1968) *Das lateinische Epigramm im Übergang von der Spätantike zum frühen Mittelalter*. Münchener Beiträge zur Mediävistik und Renaissance-Forschung 2. Munich, Arbeo-Gesellschaft.
Bertoletti, M., and E. La Rocca (1986) *Rilievi storici capitolini*. Rome, De Luca.
Besançon, A. (2000) *The Forbidden Image: An Intellectual History of Iconoclasm*. Trans. J. M. Todd. Chicago, University of Chicago Press.
Bettetini, M. (1993) *Agostino: Il maestro e la parola*. Milan, Rusconi.
Bettini, M. (1999) *The Portrait of the Lover*. Berkeley, University of California Press.
Bettini, M. (2008) *Voci: Antropologia sonora del mondo antico*. Turin, Einaudi.
Bianchi Bandinelli, R. (1971) *Rome: The Late Empire: Roman Art AD 200–400*. London, Thames and Hudson.
Bing, P., and J. S. Bruss (eds.) (2007) *Brill's Companion to Hellenistic Epigram Down to Philip*. Leiden, Brill.
Black, M. (1970) "The Chi-Rho Sign—Christogram and/or Staurogram?" In W. W. Gasque and R. P. Martin (eds.), *Apostolic History and the Gospel: Biblical and Historical Essays Presented to F. F. Bruce on His Sixtieth Birthday*. Exeter, Paternoster, 319–27.
Blaising, C. (2013) "Are There Conflicting Theologies in the Bible?" In T. L. Wilder and S. B. Cowan (eds.) *In Defense of the Bible: A Comprehensive Apologetic for the Authority of Scripture*. Nashville, B and H Academic, 375–92.
Blanck, H. (1992) *Das Buch in der Antike*. Munich, Beck.
Bleckmann, B. (2015) "Constantine, Rome and the Christians." In J. Wienand (ed.), *Contested Monarchy: Integrating the Roman Empire in the Fourth Century AD*. Oxford, Oxford University Press, 309–29.
Blomgren, S. (1950) "De P. Papinii Statii apud Venantium Fortunatum vestigiis." *Eranos* 48: 57–65.
Bloom, H. (1975) *The Anxiety of Influence: A Theory of Poetry*. Oxford, Oxford University Press.
Bloomer, W. M. (2011) *The School of Rome*. Berkeley, University of California Press.

Bockmann, R. (2013) *Capital Continuous: A Study of Vandal Carthage and Central North Africa from an Archaeological Perspective*. Wiesbaden, Reichert Verlag.
Boeder, M. (1996) *Visa est Vox: Sprache und Bild in der spätantiken Literatur*. Frankfurt, P. Lang.
Bonner, G. (1986) *St Augustine of Hippo: Life and Controversies*. Norwich, Canterbury Press.
Booth, J., and R. Maltby (eds.) (2006) *What's in a Name? The Significance of Proper Names in Classical Latin Literature*. Swansea, Classical Press of Wales.
Booth, W. G. (1983) *The Rhetoric of Fiction*. 2nd edition. Chicago and London, University of Chicago Press.
Borrell Vidal, E. (1991) *Las palabras de Virgilio en Juvenco*. Aurea Saecula 6. Barcelona, University of Barcelona Press. [non vidi]
Bosman, L. (2013) "*Spolia* in the Fourth Century Basilica." In R. McKitterick, J. Osborne, C. Richardson, and J. Story (eds.), *Old Saint Peter's, Rome*. Cambridge, Cambridge University Press, 65–80.
Bouma, J. A. (1968) *Het Epithalamium van Paulinus van Nola*. Amsterdam, van Gorcum.
Bowen, A., and P. Garnsey (2003) *Lactantius: Divine Institutes*. Liverpool, Liverpool University Press.
Bowersock, G., P. Brown, and O. Grabar (eds.) (1999) *Late Antiquity: A Guide to the Postclassical World*. Cambridge, MA, Harvard University Press.
Boyd, B. (1995) "*Non enarrabile textum*: Ecphrastic Trespass and Narrative Ambiguity in the *Aeneid*." *Vergilius* 41: 71–92.
Braginskaya, N. V. (1985) "*Fata libelli*: Das Schicksal der 'Gemälde' des älteren Philostratos." In W. Schuller (ed.), *Antike in der Moderne: Konstanzer althistorische Vorträge und Forschungen*. Konstanz, Universitätsverlag Konstanz, 25–47.
Brandenburg, H. (1979) "Stilprobleme der frühchristlichen Sarkophagkunst Roms im 4. Jahrhundert: Volkskunst, Klassizismus, spätantiker Stil." *MDAI(R)* 86: 439–71.
Bréguet, E. (1969) "Urbi et orbi, un cliché et un theme." In J. Bibauw (ed.), *Hommages à Marcel Renard* I. Brussels, Latomus, 140–52.
Bright, D. (1984) "Theory and Practice in the Vergilian Cento." *Illinois Classical Studies* 9: 79–90.
Brilliant, R., and D. Kinney (eds.) (2011) *Reuse Value: Spolia and Appropriation in Art and Architecture from Constantine to Sherrie Levine*. Aldershot, Ashgate.
Brink, C. O. (1971) *Horace on Poetry: The Ars Poetica*. Cambridge, Cambridge University Press.
Brocca, N. (2003) "A che genere letterario appartiene il *de reditu* di Rutilio Namaziano?" In Consolino, F. E. (ed.), *Forme letterarie nella produzione latina di IV–V secolo, con uno sguardo a Bisanzio*. Rome, Herder.
Brolli, T. (2013) "Writing Commentary on Sidonius' Panegyrics." In J. A. van Waarden and G. Kelly (eds.), *New Approaches to Sidonius Apollinaris*. Leuven, Peeters, 93–110.
Brown, P. (1971) *The World of Late Antiquity, AD 150–750*. London, Thames and Hudson.
Brown, P. (1981) *The Cult of the Saints: Its Rise and Function in Latin Christianity*. Chicago, University of Chicago Press.
Brown, P. (1982) *Society and the Holy in Late Antiquity*. Berkeley, University of California Press.
Brown, P. (1992) *Power and Persuasion in Late Antiquity*. Madison, University of Wisconsin Press.
Brown, P. (2009) *The Cult of the Saints: Its Rise and Function in Latin Christianity*. Chicago, University of Chicago Press. 1st ed., 1981.
Brown, P. (2011) "Back to the Future: Pagans and Christians at the Warburg Institute in 1958." In P. Brown and R. Lizzi Testa (eds.), *Pagans and Christians in the Roman Empire: The*

Breaking of a Dialogue (IVth-VIth Century A.D.); Proceedings of the International Conference at the Monastery of Bose (October 2008). Vienna, LIT Verlag, 17–24.

Brown, P. (2012) *Through the Eye of a Needle: Wealth, the Fall of Rome, and the Making of Christianity in the West, 350–550 AD*. Princeton, NJ, Princeton University Press.

Browning, R. (1982a) "Oratory and Epistolography." In E. J. Kenney and W. V. Clausen (eds.), *The Cambridge History of Classical Literature* II: *Latin Literature*. Cambridge, Cambridge University Press, 755–61.

Browning, R. (1982b) "Poetry." In E. J. Kenney and W. V. Clausen (eds.), *The Cambridge History of Classical Literature* II: *Latin Literature*. Cambridge, Cambridge University Press, 692–722.

Bruhat, M.-O. (1999) "Les *carmina figurata* de Publilius Optatianus Porfyrius: La métamorphose d'un genre et l'invention d'une poésie liturgique impériale sous Constantin." PhD thesis, Université Paris IV (Sorbonne).

Bruhat, M.-O. (2008) "Une poétique du vœu: Inspiration poétique et mystique impérial dans le poème XIX (et quelques autres) d'Optatianus Porfyrius." *Dictynna* 5: 57–108.

Bruhat, M.-O. (2009) "Les poèmes figurés d'Optatianus Porfyrius: Une écriture à contraintes, une écriture de la contrainte." In F. Toulze-Morisset (ed.), *Formes de l'écriture, figures de la pensée dans la culture gréco-romaine*. Lille, Villeneuve d'Ascq, 101–25.

Bruun, P. M. (1963) "Symboles, signes et monogrammes." In H. Zilliacus (ed.), *Sylloge Inscriptionum Christianarum veterum Musei Vaticani*, vol. 2. Helsinki, Helsingfors, 73–166.

Bruun, P. M. (1997) "The Victorious Signs of Constantine: A Reappraisal." *Numismatic Chronicle* 157: 41–59.

Bua, M. T. (1971) "I giuochi alfabetici delle *tavole iliache*." *MemLinc* 8.16: 1–35.

Buisset, D. (2006) "Le poème inexistant, ou Dieu, que le grincement du calame est triste au fond du scriptorium! Essai de lecture du 'poème XXV' d'Optatianus Porfyrius, autrement appelé Porphyre Optatien ou simplement Optatien." *Formules: Revue des littératures à contraintes* 2006: 173–212.

Buonocore, M. (ed.) (1996) *Vedere i classici: L'illustrazione libraria dei testi antichi dall'età romana al tardo medioevo*. Rome, Fratelli Palombi: Rose.

Bureau, B. (2009) "Figures de poètes chez Claudien." In P. Galland-Hallyn and V. Zarini (eds.), *Manifestes littéraires dans la latinité tardive: Poétique et rhétorique*. Paris, Institut d'Études Augustiniennes, 51–70.

Burkitt, K. (2007) "Imperial Reflections: The Post-Colonial Verse-Novel as Post-Epic." In L. Hardwick and C. Gillespie (eds.), *Classics in Post-Colonial Worlds*. Oxford and New York, Oxford University Press, 157–69.

Burton, P. (2000) *The Old Latin Gospels: A Study of Their Texts and Language*. Oxford, Oxford University Press.

Burton, P. (2007) *Language in the Confessions of Augustine*. Oxford, Oxford University Press.

Burzachechi, M. (1955-6) "Sull'uso pre-Constantiniano del monogramma greco di Cristo." *Atti della Pontificia Academia Romana di Archeologia (Rendiconti)* 28.2: 197–211.

Burzachechi, M. (1962) "Oggetti parlanti nelle epigrafi greche." *Epigraphica* 24: 3–54.

Buttrey, T. V. (1983) "The Dates of the Arches of Diocletian and Constantine." *Historia* 2: 375–83.

Butz, P. A. (2010) *The Art of the Hekatompedon Inscription and the Birth of the Stoikhedon Style*. Leiden, Brill.

Calabrese, O. (1992) *Neo-Baroque: A Sign of the Times*. Trans. Charles Lambert. Princeton, NJ, Princeton University Press.

Callu, J.-P. (2009) *Symmaque. Tome V. Discours—Rapports*. Paris, Les Belles Lettres.
Cameron, Alan (1967) "Rutilius Namatianus, St. Augustine, and the Date of the *De Reditu*." *Journal of Roman Studies* 57: 31–9.
Cameron, Alan (1970) *Claudian: Poetry and Propaganda at the Court of Honorius*. Oxford, Oxford University Press.
Cameron, Alan (1977) "Paganism and Literature in Late Fourth Century Rome." In M. Fuhrmann (ed.), *Christianisme et formes litteraires de l'Antiquite tardive en Occident*. Geneva, Fondation Hardt (Entretiens sur l'Antiquité classique XXIII), 1–40.
Cameron, Alan (1980) "Poetae novelli." *HSCP* 84: 127–75.
Cameron, Alan (1992) "Filocalus and Melania." *Classical Philology* 87.2: 140–4.
Cameron, Alan (1995) *Callimachus and His Critics*. Princeton, NJ, Princeton University Press.
Cameron, Alan (2002) "The Funeral of Junius Bassus." *ZPE* 139: 288–92.
Cameron, Alan (2004a) *Greek Mythography in the Roman World*. Oxford, Oxford University Press.
Cameron, Alan (2004b) "Poetry and Literary Culture in Late Antiquity." In S. Swain and M. Edwards (eds.), *Approaching Late Antiquity: The Transformation from Early to Late Empire*. Oxford, Oxford University Press, 327–54.
Cameron, Alan (2011) *The Last Pagans of Rome*. Oxford, Oxford University Press.
Cameron, Averil (1991) *Christianity and the Rhetoric of Empire*. Berkeley, University of California Press.
Cameron, Averil (2014) *Dialoguing in Late Antiquity*. Washington DC, Center for Hellenic Studies.
Cameron, Averil and Hall, S. G. (eds. and trans.) (1999) *Eusebius: Life of Constantine*. Oxford, Clarendon Press.
Camille, M. (1985) "Seeing and Reading: Some Visual Interpretations of Medieval Literacy and Illiteracy." *Art History* 8.1: 26–49.
Canali, L., and F. R. Nocchi (eds.) (2011) *Epigrammata Bobiensia*. Soveria Mannelli, Rubbettino.
Canobbio, A. (2013) "Una preghiera tra serio e faceto: Marziale nel carme 13 di Sidonio Apollinare." *Lexis* 31: 366–90.
Carruthers, M. (1998) *The Craft of Thought: Meditation, Rhetoric, and the Making of Images, AD 400–1200*. New York, Cambridge University Press.
Carson, A. (1992) "Simonides Painter." In R. Hexter and D. Selden (eds.), *Innovations of Antiquity*. New York, Routledge, 51–64.
Cary, P. (2000) *Augustine's Invention of the Inner Self: The Legacy of a Christian Platonist*. Oxford, Oxford University Press.
Cary, P. (2008) *Outward Signs: The Powerlessness of External Things in Augustine's Thought*. Oxford, Oxford University Press.
Castorina, E. (ed., trans., and notes) (1967) *Claudio Rutilio Namaziano: De reditu*. Firenze, Sansoni.
Castrén, P. (1972) "Il calendario dipinto sotto Santa Maria Maggiore. Appendice: I graffiti del vano XVI." *Memorie della Pontifica Accademia Romana di Archeologia* 11: 69–87.
Cavadini, J. C. (1995) "The Sweetness of the Word: Salvation and Rhetoric in Augustine's *De doctrina Christiana*." In D. W. H. Arnold and P. Bright (eds.), *De doctrina Christiana: A Classic of Western Culture*. Notre Dame, IN, University of Notre Dame Press, 164–81.
Cavarzere, A. (ed.) (2003) *Decimo Magno Ausonio, Mosella*. Amsterdam, Hakkert.
Cazzuffi, E. (2014) *Decimi Magni Ausonii Ludus septem sapientum*. Hildesheim/Zurich, Olms.

Chadwick, H. (1981) *Boethius: The Consolations of Music, Logic, Theology, and Philosophy*. Oxford, Oxford University Press.
Charlet, J.-L. (1988) "Aesthetic Trends in Late Latin Poetry (325–410)." *Philologus* 132: 74–85.
Charlet, J.-L. (1991) *Claudien, Oeuvres: Tome 1. Le rapt de Proserpine*. Paris, Les Belles Lettres.
Charlet, J.-L. (1997) "Die Poesie." In Engels and Hofmann (eds.), 495–564.
Charlet, J.-L. (2008) "Tendances esthétiques de la poésie latine tardive (325–470)." *AntTard* 16: 159–67.
Chatterjee, P. (2013) "Vision, Transformation and the Veroli Casket." *Oxford Art Journal* 36: 325–44.
Chazelle, C. M. (1990) "Pictures, Books and the Illiterate: Pope Gregory I's Letters to Serenus of Marseilles." *Word and Image* 6: 138–53.
Chin, C. (2007) "Through the Looking Glass Darkly." In W. E. Klingshirn and L. Safran (eds.), *The Early Christian Book*. Washington D C, Catholic University of America Press, 101–16.
Chinn, C. M. (2007) "Before Your Very Eyes: Pliny *Epistulae* 5.6 and the Ancient Theory of Ekphrasis." *CP* 102: 265–80.
Christian, T. (2015) *Gebildete Steine: Zur Rezeption literarischer Techniken in den Versinschriften seit dem Hellenismus*. Göttingen, Vandenhoeck & Ruprecht.
Christiansen, P. G., and J. L. Sebasta (1985) "Claudian's Phoenix: Themes of Imperium." *AC* 54: 204–24.
Chruzander, C. G. (1897) "De elocutione panegyricorum veterum Gallicanorum quaestiones." PhD thesis, University of Upsala.
Clark, G. (2008) "Can We Talk? Augustine and the Possibility of Dialogue." In S. Goldhill (ed.), *The End of Dialogue in Antiquity*. Cambridge, Cambridge University Press, 117–34.
Clark, G. (2010) "Paradise for Pagans? Augustine on Virgil, Cicero and Plato." In M. Bockmuehl and G. Stroumsa (eds.), *Paradise in Antiquity: Jewish and Christian Views*. Cambridge, Cambridge University Press, 166–78.
Clark, G. (2011) "*Psallite sapienter*: Augustine on Psalmody." In A. Andreopoulos, A. Casiday, and C. Harrison (eds.), *Meditations of the Heart: The Psalms in Early Christian Thought and Practice*. Turnhout, Brepols, 161–80.
Clark, G. (2014) "Fragile Brilliance: Augustine on Decadence and 'Other Antiquity.'" In M. Formisano and T. Fuhrer (eds.), *Decadence or "Other Antiquity"*. Heidelberg, Winter, 35–52.
Clark, G. (2015) *Monica: An Ordinary Saint*. New York, Oxford University Press.
Clarke, A. (1963) "Licentius' *Carmen ad Augustinum* 11.45 seqq. and the Easter Vigil." *Studia Patristica* 8: 171–5 (= *Texte und Untersuchungen* 93, Akademie-Verlag, Berlin).
Clarke, J. (2007) "Theology, Innovation and Poetical Exegesis: The Glass Lamp in Prudentius *Cathimerinon* 5." In W. Otten and K. Pollmann (eds.), *Poetry and Exegesis in Premodern Latin Christianity: The Encounter between Classical and Christian Strategies of Interpretation*. Leiden, Brill, 99–114.
Clarke, J. R. (2007) *Looking at Laughter: Humor, Power and Transgression in Roman Visual Culture, 100 BC–AD 250*. Berkeley, University of California Press.
Clifford, H. (1897) *In Court and Kampong: Being Tales and Sketches of Native Life in the Malay Peninsula*. London, Grant Richards.
Coleman, R. (1977) *Vergil: Eclogues*. Cambridge, Cambridge University Press.
Coleridge, H. N. (1826) *Six Months in the West Indies*. London, John Murray.
Collingwood, R. G. (1930) *The Archaeology of Roman Britain*. London, Methuen.

Colomo, D. (2013) "The *Avis Phoenix* in the Schools of Rhetoric: *P. Mil. Vogl.* I 20 and *P. Lond. Lit.* 193 Revisited." *Segno e testo* 11: 29–78.

Comeau, M. (1930) *La rhétorique de Saint Augustine d'après les Tractatus in Ioannem*. Paris, Boivin.

Commager, S. (1962) *The Odes of Horace: A Critical Study*. New Haven, CT, Yale University Press.

Conant, J. (2012) *Staying Roman: Conquest and Identity in Africa and the Mediterranean, 439–700*. Cambridge, Cambridge University Press.

Condorelli, S. (2008) *Il poeta doctus nel V secolo D. C. Aspetti della poetica di Sidonio Apollinare*. Naples, Loffredo.

Consolino, F. E. (1974) "Codice retorico e manierismo stilistico nella poesia di Sidonio Apollinare." *Annali della Scuola Normale Superiore di Pisa* 4: 423–60.

Consolino, F. E. (1997) "Optaziano Porfirio su Constantino: Il caso del *Carme* 15." In U. Criscuolo and R. Maisano (eds.), *Synodia: Studia humanitatis Antonio Garzya septuagenario ab amicis atque discipulis dicata*. Naples, D'Auria, 181–90.

Consolino, F. E. (2003) "Metri, temi e forme letterarie nella poesia di Ausonio." In F. E. Consolino (ed.), *Forme letterarie nella produzione latina di IV–V secolo*. Rome, Herder, 147–94.

Consolino, F. E. (2009) "Les indications implicites dans l'épithalame d'Ennode pour Maximus (388V = *Carm.* I, 4 H)." In P. Galand-Hallyn and V. Zarini (eds.), *Manifestes littéraires dans la latinité tardive: Poétique et rhétorique*. Actes du Colloque International de Paris, 23–4 March 2007. Paris, Institut d'Études Augustiniennes, 163–84.

Consolino, F. E. (2011) "Recusationes a confronto: Sidonio Apollinare *epist.* IX 13,2 e Venanzio Fortunato *carm.* IX 7." In L. Cristante and S. Ravalico (eds.), *Il calamo della memoria: Riuso di testi e mestiere letterario nella tarda antichità* IV. Trieste, Edizioni Università di Trieste, 101–25.

Consolino, F. E. (2014) "Ennodio e i due epitafi per Cinegia. Qualche riflessione su una *vexata quaestio*." In A. De Vivo and R. Perrelli (eds.), *Il miglior fabbro. Studi offerti a Giovanni Polara*. Amsterdam, Hakkert, 261–71.

Conte, G. B. (1986) *The Rhetoric of Imitation*. Trans. C. Segal. Ithaca, NY, Cornell University Press.

Conte, G. B., and A. Barchiesi (1989) "Imitazione e arte allusiva: Modi e funzioni dell'intertestualità." In G. Cavallo, P. Fedeli, and A. Giardina (eds.), *Lo spazio letterario di Roma anticha*, vol. I: *La produzione del testo*. Rome, Salerno, 81–114.

Conybeare, C. (2000) *Paulinus Noster: Self and Symbols in the Letters of Paulinus of Nola*. Oxford, Oxford University Press.

Conybeare, C. (2006) *The Irrational Augustine*. Oxford, Oxford University Press.

Copeland, R., and P. T. Struck (eds.) (2010) *The Cambridge Companion to Allegory*. Cambridge, Cambridge University Press.

Cosh, S. R., and D. S. Neal (2002–10) *Roman Mosaics of Britain*. 4 vols. London, Society of Antiquities.

Courcelle, P. (1957) "Les exégèses chrétiennes de la quatrième églogue." *Revue des Études Anciennes* 59: 294–319.

Courcelle, P. (1967) *La Consolation de Philosophie dans la tradition litteraire*. Paris, Institut d'Études Augustiniennes.

Courtney, E. (1990) "Greek and Latin Acrostics." *Philologus* 134: 1–13.

Courtney, E. (ed.) (1993) *The Fragmentary Latin Poets*. Oxford, Oxford University Press.

Courtney, E. (ed.) (1995) *Musa Lapidaria: A Selection of Latin Verse Inscriptions*. Atlanta, GA, Scholars Press.
Cox Miller, P. (1998) "Differential Networks: Relics and Other Fragments in Late Antiquity." *Journal of Early Christian Studies* 6: 113–38.
Cox Miller, P. (2009) *The Corporeal Imagination: Signifying the Holy in Late Ancient Christianity*. Philadelphia, University of Pennsylvania Press.
Cózar, R. de (1991) *Poesía e imagen: Formas difíciles de ingenio literario*. Seville, Ediciones El Carro de la Nieve.
Crabbe, A. M. (1981) "Anamnesis and Mythology in the de *consolatio philosophiae*." In L. Obertello (ed.), *Congresso Internazionale di Studi Boeziani* (Pavia, 5–8 October 1980). Rome, Herder.
Cribiore, R. (2001) *Gymnastics of the Mind*. Princeton, NJ, Princeton University Press.
Cross, F., and E. Livingstone (eds.) (2005) *The Oxford Dictionary of the Christian Church*. 2nd edition. Oxford, Oxford University Press.
Cucchiarelli, A. (ed., trans., and notes) (2003) *La veglia di Venere: Pervigilium Veneris*. Milan, Bur.
Cugusi, P. (1996) *Aspetti letterari dei Carmina Latina Epigraphica*. Bologna, Pàtron.
Cullhed, S. (2014) "Proba and Jerome." In M. Formisano and T. Fuhrer (eds.), 199–222.
Cullhed, S. (2015) *Proba the Prophet: The Christian Virgilian Cento of Faltonia Betitia Proba*. Leiden, Brill.
Culpepper Stroup, S. (2013) "Without Patronage: Fetishization, Representation, and the Circulation of Gift-Texts in the Late Roman Republic." In M. L. Sadlow, *The Gift in Antiquity*. West Sussex, Wiley-Blackwell, 107–21.
Cuomo, S. (2000) *Pappus of Alexandria and the Mathematics of Late Antiquity*. Cambridge, Cambridge University Press.
Curley, T. F., III. (1987) "How to Read the *Consolation of Philosophy* as a Work of Literature." *American Journal of Philology* 108: 343–67.
Curran, J. (2012) "Visualizing Christianity in Late Antique Rome." In L. Grig and G. Kelly (eds.), *Two Romes: Rome and Constantinople in Late Antiquity*. Oxford, Oxford University Press, 325–44.
Curtius, E. R. (1953) *European Literature and the Latin Middle Ages*. Trans. W. R. Trask. New York, Pantheon Books.
Curtius, E. R. (1990) *European Literature and the Latin Middle Ages*. English transl. Princeton, NJ, Princeton University Press. Original German edition, Bern, 1948.
Cutino, Michele (2006) "Continuità e innovazione nella poesia latina cristiana del V sec. In Gallia: Il proptrettico alla conversione." *Auctores nostri* 4, 311–50.
Cutler, A. (1974) "The 'Mythological' Bowl in the Treasury of San Marco at Venice." In *Near Eastern Numismatics, Iconography, Epigraphy and History: Studies in Honor of George C. Miles*. Beirut, American University of Beirut, 236–54.
Dachowski, E. (2008) *First among the Abbots: The Career of Abbo of Fleury*. Washington, DC, Catholic University of America Press.
Davenport, C. (2013) "The Governors of Achaia under Diocletian and Constantine." *ZPE* 184: 225–35.
Davis, S. (2000) "Jonah in Early Christian Art: Allegorical Exegesis and the Roman Funerary Context." *Australian Religion Studies Review* 13: 72–83.
Dawson, D. (1992) *Allegorical Readers and Cultural Revision in Ancient Alexandria*. Berkeley, University of California Press.

Deichmann, F. W., and T. Klauser (1966) *Frühchristliche Sarkophage in Bild und Wort*. Beiheft zur Halbjahresschrift Antike Kunst 3. Olten, Urs Graf.
de Jong, I. J. F. (2014) *Narratology and Classics: A Practical Guide*. Oxford, Oxford University Press.
de Lachenal, L. (1995) *Spolia: Uso e reimpiego dell'antico dal III at XIV secolo*. Milan, Longanesi.
Del Chicca F. (1985) "La struttura retorica del panegirico latino tardoimperiale in prosa; teoria e prassi." *Annali della Facoltà di Lettere e Filosofia dell'Università di Cagliari* 6 (43): 86-95.
Delhey, N. (1993) *Apollinaris Sidonius, Carm. 22: Burgus Pontii Leontii*. Berlin and New York, de Gruyter.
De Man, P. (1979) *Allegories of Reading: Figural Language in Rousseau, Nietzsche, Rilke, and Proust*. New Haven, CT, Yale University Press.
De Man, P. (1983) *Blindness and Insight: Essays in the Rhetoric of Contemporary Criticism*. Minneapolis, University of Minnesota Press.
Den Boeft, J. (1979) "Some Etymologies in Augustine's *De civitate Dei* X." *Vigiliae Christianae* 33: 242-59.
Den Boeft, J. (1993) "*Ambrosius lyricus*." In J. Den Boeft and A. Hilhorst (eds.), *Early Christian Poetry: A Collection of Essays*. Leiden, Brill, 77-89.
Den Boeft, J. (2007) "*Cantatur ad delectationem*: Ambrose's Lyric Poetry." In W. Otten and K. Pollmann (eds.), *Poetry and Exegesis in Premodern Latin Christianity: The Encounter between Classical and Christian Strategies of Interpretation*. Leiden, Brill, 81-97.
Dencker, K. P. (2011) *Optische Poesie: Von den prähistorischen Schriftzeichen bis zu den digitalen Experimenten der Gegenwart*. Berlin, de Gruyter.
Derrida, J. (1976) *Of Grammatology*. Trans. G. Chakravorty. Baltimore, Johns Hopkins University Press.
de Trizio, M. S. (2009) *Panegirico di Mamertino per Massimiano e Diocleziano*. Bari, Edipuglia.
Dewar, M. J. (1996) *Claudian: Panegyricus de Sexto Consulatu Honorii Augusti*. Oxford, Oxford University Press.
de Wit, J. (1959) *Die Miniaturen des Vergilius Vaticanus*. Amsterdam, Swets and Zeitlinger.
Dionigi, I. (1988) *Lucrezio: Le parole e le cose*. Bologna, Pàtron.
Dionigi, I. (2005) *Lucrezio: Le parole e le cose*. 2nd edition. Bologna, Pàtron.
Doblhofer, E. (ed.) (1972) *Rutilius Claudius Namatianus: De reditu suo sive iter Gallicum*. 1. *Einleitung, Text, Übersetzung, Wörterverzeichnis*. Heidelberg, Winter.
Doblhofer, E. (ed.) (1977) *Rutilius Claudius Namatianus: De reditu suo sive iter Gallicum*. 2. *Kommentar*. Heidelberg, Winter.
Dodds, E. R. (1965) *Pagan and Christian in an Age of Anxiety*. Cambridge, Cambridge University Press.
Donato, A. (2013) *Boethius' Consolation of Philosophy as a Product of Late Antiquity*. London, Bloomsbury.
Döpp, S. (1995) "Baebianus und Apra. Zu Paulinus Nolanus (?) c. 38" In *Panchaia*. Festschrift für Klaus Thraede, *JAC* Ergänzungsband XXII. Münster, Aschendorf, 66-74.
Doria, C. (1979) "Visual Writing Forms in Antiquity: The *versus intexti*." In R. Kostelanetz (ed.), *Visual Literature Criticism: A New Collection*. Carbondale and Edwardsville, Southern Illinois University Press, 63-92.
Dornseiff, F. (1922) *Das Alphabet in Mystik und Magie*. Leipzig and Berlin, Teubner.
Dörries, H. (1954) *Das Selbstzeugnis Kaiser Konstantins*. Göttingen, Vandenhoeck and Ruprecht.
d'Ors, M. (1977) *El caligrama de Simmias a Apollinaire: Historia y antología de una tradición clásica*. Pamplona, University of Navarra Press.

Dover, K. J. (1978) *Greek Homosexuality.* London, Duckworth.
Dräger, P. (2002) *D. Magnus Ausonius: Mosella, Bissula, Briefwechsel mit Paulinus Nolanus.* Düsseldorf and Zürich, Artemis and Winkler.
Dräger, P. (2011) *Decimus Magnus Ausonius: Sämtliche Werke*: Band 2: *Sämtliche Werke.* Trier, Kliomedia.
Dräger, P. (2012) *Decimus Magnus Ausonius: Sämtliche Werke*: Band 1: *(Auto-) biographische Werke.* Trier, Kliomedia.
Drake, H. A. (1976) *In Praise of Constantine: A Historical Study and New Translation of Eusebius' Tricennial Orations.* Berkeley, University of California Press.
Dronke, P. (1994) *Verse with Prose from Petronius to Dante.* Cambridge, MA, Harvard University Press.
Dubel, S. (1997) "*Ekphrasis* et *enargeia*: La description antique comme parcours." In C. Levy and L. Pernot (eds.), *Dire l'évidence (philosophie et rhétorique antiques).* Paris, L'Harmattan, 249–64.
Dubois, P. (1982) *History, Rhetorical Description and the Epic.* Cambridge, D. S. Brewer.
Düchting, R. (1968) "Sedulius Scottus und P. Optatianus Porfyrius." *MLatJb* 5: 24–8.
Dufallo, B. (2013) *The Captor's Image: Greek Culture and Roman Ekphrasis.* Oxford, Oxford University Press.
Duff, J. W., and A. M. Duff (ed., trans., and notes) (1934) *Minor Latin Poets.* Cambridge, MA, and London, Loeb Classical Library.
Dufraigne, P. (1994) *Adventus Augusti, adventus Christi: Recherche sur l'exploitation idéologique et littéraire d'un ceremonial dans l'antiquité tardive.* Collection des Études Augustiniennes, série antiquité 141. Paris, Institut d'Études Augustiniennes.
Duggan, L. G. (1989) "Was Art Really the 'Book of the Illiterate?'" *Word and Image* 5: 227–51.
Dutsch, D. (1991) "Is Claudian's *De raptu Proserpinae* a Non-political Poem?" *Eos* 79: 217–22.
Eco, U. (1983) *The Name of the Rose.* Trans. W. Weaver. London, Secker and Warburg.
Eco, U. (1984) *Postscript to* The Name of the Rose. Trans. W. Weaver. San Diego, Harcourt Brace Jovanovich.
Eco, U. (1989) *The Open Work.* Trans. A. Cancogni. Cambridge, MA, Harvard University Press.
Eco, U. (1994) *Reflections on the Name of the Rose.* Trans. W. Weaver. 2nd edition. London, Minerva.
Edmunds, L. (1995) "Intertextuality Today." *Lexis* 13: 3–22.
Edmunds, L. (2001) *Intertextuality and the Reading of Roman Poetry.* Baltimore and London, Johns Hopkins University Press.
Edwards, J. S. (2005) "The *Carmina* of Publilius Optatianus Porphyrius and the Creative Process." In C. Deroux (ed.), *Studies in Latin Literature and Roman History*, vol. 12 (= Collections Latomus 287). Brussels, Latomus, 447–66.
Edwards, R. (1976) "Fulgentius and the Collapse of Meaning." *Helios* (n.s.) 3: 17–35.
Ehrling, S. (2011) "*De Inconexis Continuum*: A Study of the Late Antique Wedding Centos." PhD thesis, University of Goteborg.
Eigler, U. (2008) "Urbs und orbis: Rom und sein Reich in der augustischen Literatur." In K. Geus and K. Herrmann (eds.), *Dona sunt pulcherrima: Festschrift für Rudolf Rieks.* Oberhaid, Utopica, 151–66.
Elliott, J. (2013) *Ennius and the Architecture of the* Annales. Cambridge, Cambridge University Press.
Ellis, R. (1904) "Fulgentiana." *Journal of Philology* 29: 61–71.
Elsner, J. (1995) *Art and the Roman Viewer: The Transformation of Art from the Pagan World to Christianity.* Cambridge, Cambridge University Press.

Elsner, J. (1998) *Imperial Rome and Christian Triumph: The Art of the Roman Empire AD 100–450*. Oxford, Oxford University Press.
Elsner, J. (2000) "From the Culture of *Spolia* to the Cult of Relics: The Arch of Constantine and the Genesis of Late Antique Forms." *Papers of the British School at Rome* 68: 149–84.
Elsner, J. (2002a) "Introduction: The Genres of Ekphrasis." *Ramus* 31: 1–18.
Elsner, J. (2002b) "The Birth of Late Antiquity: Riegl and Strzygowski in 1901." *Art History* 25: 358–79.
Elsner, J. (2004) "Late Antique Art: The Problem of the Concept and the Cumulative Aesthetic." In S. Swain and M. Edwards (eds.), *Approaching Late Antiquity: The Transformation from Early to Late Empire*. Oxford, Oxford University Press, 271–309.
Elsner, J. (2006a) "Classicism in Roman Art." In J. Porter (ed.), *Classical Pasts: The Classical Traditions of Greece and Rome*. Princeton, NJ, Princeton University Press, 270–97.
Elsner, J. (2006b) "From Empirical Evidence to the Big Picture: Reflections on Riegl's Concept of *Kunstwollen*." *Critical Inquiry* 32: 741–66.
Elsner, J. (2006c) "Perspectives in art." In N. E. Lenski (ed.), *The Cambridge Companion to the Age of Constantine*. Cambridge, Cambridge University Press, 255–77.
Elsner, J. (2007) *Roman Eyes: Visuality and Subjectivity in Art and Text*. Princeton, NJ, Princeton University Press.
Elsner, J. (2008) "Framing the Objects We Study: Three Boxes from Late Roman Italy." *Journal of the Warburg and Courtauld Institutes* 71: 21–38.
Elsner, J. (2009) "Beyond Compare: Pagan Saint and Christian God in Late Antiquity." *Critical Inquiry* 35: 655–83.
Elsner, J. (2011) "'Pharoah's Army Got Drownded': Some Reflections on Jewish Narrative and Christian Meaning in Late Antiquity." In H. Kessler and D. Nirenberg (eds.), *Judaism and Christian Art*. Philadelphia, University of Pennsylvania Press, 10–44.
Elsner, J. (2013) "*Paideia*: Ancient Concept and Modern Receptions." *International Journal of the Classical Tradition* 20: 136–52.
Engels, L. J., and H. Hofmann (1997) "Literatur und Gesellschaft in der Spätantike: Texte, Kommunikation und Überlieferung." In L. J. Engels and H. Hofmann (eds.), *Spätantike, mit einem Panorama der byzantinischen Literatur: Neues Handbuch der Literaturwissenschaft*, Band 4. Wiesbaden, Aula, 29–99.
Engemann, J. (1997) *Deutung und Bedeutung frühchristlicher Bildwerke*. Darmstadt, Wiss. Buchgesellschaft.
Ernst, U. (1984) "Zahl und Maß in den Figurengedichten der Antike und des Frühmittelalters: Beobachtungen zur Entwicklung tektonischer Bauformen." In A. Zimmermann (ed.), *Mensura: Maß, Zahl, Zahlensymbolik im Mittelalter*. Berlin, de Gruyter, 310–32.
Ernst, U. (1991) Carmen Figuratum: *Geschichte des Figurengedichts von den antiken Ursprüngen bis zum Ausgang des Mittelalters*. Cologne, Böhlau.
Ernst, U. (1992) "Permutation als Prinzip in der Lyrik." *Poetica* 24: 225–69.
Ernst, U. (2002) *Intermedialität im europäischen Kulturzusammenhang: Beiträge zur Theorie und Geschichte der visuellen Lyrik*. Berlin, Erich Schmidt Verlag.
Ernst, U. (ed.) (2012) *Visuelle Poesie: Historische Dokumentation theoretischer Zeugnisse. Band I: Von der Antike bis zum Barock*. Berlin, de Gruyter.
Ernst, U. (ed.) (forthcoming) *Visuelle Poesie: Historische Dokumentation theoretischer Zeugnisse. Band II: Vom Spätbarock bis zur Gegenwart*. Berlin, de Gruyter.
Étienne, R. (1962) *Bordeaux Antique*. Bordeaux, Fédération historique de Bordeaux.

Evenepoel, W. (1993) "The Place of Poetry in Latin Christianity." In J. Den Boeft and A. Hillhorst (eds.), *Early Christian Poetry*. Leiden, Brill, 35–60.
Even-Zohar, I. (1990) *Polysystem Studies* (= *Poetics Today* 11).
Farrell, J., and M. Puttnam (eds.) (2010) *A Companion to Virgil's Aeneid and Its Tradition*. Chichester, Wiley-Blackwell.
Fears, J. Rufus (1977) *Princeps a Diis Electus*. Rome, Papers of the American Academy at Rome.
Fedeli, P. (1989) "I sistemi di produzione e diffusione." In G. Cavallo, P. Fedeli, and A. Giardina (eds.), *Lo spazio letterario di Roma antica*, vol. II: *La circolazione deltesto*. Rome, Salerno, 343–78.
Feeney, D. (2007) *Caesar's Calendar*. Berkeley, University of California Press.
Feldherr, A. (2014) "Viewing Myth and History on the Shield of Aeneas." *Classical Antiquity* 33: 281–318.
Felgentreu, F. (1999) *Claudians* praefationes: *Bedingungen, Beschreibungen und Wirkungen einer poetischen Kleinform*. Stuttgart and Leipzig, Teubner.
Felten, J. (ed.) (1913) *Nicolaus, Progymnasmata*. Leipzig, Teubner.
Fenno, J. (2005) "'A Great Wave against the Stream': Water Imagery in Iliadic Battle Scenes." *American Journal of Philology* 126: 475–504.
Ferrua, A. (1946) "Tavole lusorie scritte." *Epigraphica* 8: 53–73.
Ferrua, A. (1948) "Tavole lusorie scritte (1)." *Epigraphica* 10: 21–58.
Ferrua, A. (1960) *Le pitture della nuova catacomba di Via Latina*. Vatican, Pontificio Istituto di Archeologia Cristiana.
Ferrua, A. (1964) "Nuove *tabulae lusoriae* iscritte." *Epigraphica* 26: 3–44.
Ferrua, A. (2001) *Tavole lusorie epigrafiche*. Vatican, Pontificio Istituto di Archeologia Cristiana.
Filosini, S. (ed. and trans.) (2008) *Paolino di Nola, Carmi 10 e 11*. With an essay by F. E. Consolino. Rome, Herder.
Fink, J., and B. Asamer (1997) *Die römischen Katakomben*. Mainz, von Zabern.
Finney, P. C. (1977) "Antecedents of Byzantine Iconoclasm: Christian Evidence before Constantine." In J. Gutmann (ed.), *The Image and the Word: Confrontations in Judaism, Christianity and Islam*. Missoula, MO, Scholars Press for the American Academy of Religion, 27–47.
Finney, P. C. (1994) *The Invisible God: The Earliest Christians on Art*. Oxford and New York, Oxford University Press.
Fitzgerald, W. (2007) *Martial: The World of Epigram*. Chicago and London, University of Chicago Press.
Flores, E., and G. Polara (1969) "Specimina di analisi applicate a strutture di 'Versspielerei' latina." *Rendiconti dell'Accademia di Archeologia, Lettere e Belle Arti di Napoli* 44: 111–26.
Floridi, L. (2013) "Il realismo dell'arte e il paradosso del retore muto." *Prometheus* 39: 87–106.
Fo, A. (1982) *Studi sulla tecnica poetica di Claudiano*. Catania, Tringale.
Fo, A. (ed.) (1992) *Claudio Rutilio Namaziano: Il ritorno*. Turin, Einaudi.
Follieri, E. (1974) "Tommaso di Damasco e l'antica minuscola libraria greca." *Rendiconti dell'Accademia nazionale dei Lincei (Classe di scienze morali, storiche e filologiche)* 8.29: 145–63.
Fontaine, J. (1975) "Le mélange des genres dans la poésie de Prudence." In *Forma Futuri (Mélanges M. Pellegrino)*. Turin, Bottega d'Erasmo, 755–77.
Fontaine, J. (1976) "Prose et poésie: L'interférence des genres et des styles dans la création littéraire d'Ambroise de Milan." In G. Lazzati (ed.), *Ambrosius Episcopus* I. Milan, Vita e Pensiero, 124–70.

Fontaine, J. (1977) "Unité et diversité du mélange des genres et des tons chez quelques écrivains latins de la fin du IVe siècle: Ausone, Ambrosie, Ammien." In M. Fuhrmann (ed.), *Christianisme et formes litteraires de l'Antiquite tardive en Occident*. Entretiens sur l'Antiquité classique XXIII. Geneva, Fondation Hardt, 425–82.

Fontaine, J. (1980) *Études sur la poésie latine tardive d'Ausone à Prudence*. Paris, Les Belles Lettres.

Fontaine, J. (1981) *Naissance de la poésie dans l'occident chretien: Esquisse d'une histoire de la poesie latine chretienne du IIIe au VIe siècle*. Paris, Institut d'Études Augustiniennes.

Fontaine, J. (1984) "La figure du prince dans la poésie latine chrétienne de Lactance a Prudence." In J. Fontaine, *La poesia tardoantica: Tra retorica, teologia e politica*. Messina, Centro di studi umanistici.

Fontaine, J. (1998a) "Il barocco romano antico. Una corrente estetica perdurante nella letteratura latina." In J. Fontaine, *Letteratura tardoantica: Figure e percorsi*. Brescia, Morcelliniana, 19–41.

Fontaine, J. (1998b) "Postclassicismo, tarda antichità, latino cristiano. L'evoluzione della problematica di una storia della letteratura latina dal III al VI secolo dopo Schanz." In J. Fontaine, *Letteratura tardoantica: Figure e percorsi*. Brescia, Morcelliniana, 43–60.

Fontaine, J. (1998c), "Il cristianesimo è anche antichità classica. Alcune osservazioni sulla cultura e sulla letteratura nel mondo tardoantico." In J. Fontaine (ed.), *Letteratura tardoantica: Figure e percorsi*. Brescia, Morcelliniana, 61–84.

Fontaine, J. (2005) "Education and Learning." In P. Fouracre (ed.), *The New Cambridge Medieval History c. 500–c. 700*, vol. I. Cambridge, Cambridge University Press, 736–45.

Formisano, M. (2003) *Vegezio: Arte della guerra romana*. Milan, Rizzoli.

Formisano, M. (2007) "Toward an Aesthetic Paradigm of Late Antiquity." *AnTard* 15: 277–84.

Formisano, M. (2013) "Grand Finale. Orosius' Historiae adversus paganos or the Subversion of History." In H. Harich-Schwarzbauer and K. Pollmann (eds.), *Der Fall Roms und seine Wiederauferstehungen in Antike und Mittelalter*. Berlin and New York, de Gruyter, 153–76.

Formisano, M. (2014) "Reading Décadence—Reception and the Subaltern Late Antiquity." In M. Formisano and T. Fuhrer (eds.), *Décadence: "Decline and Fall" or "Other Antiquity"?* Heidelberg, Winter, 7–16.

Formisano, M. (2015) "The Desire to Be You. The Discourse of Praise for the Roman Emperor." In P. Antonello and H. Webb (eds.), *Mimesis, Desire and the Novel: René Girard and Literary Criticism*. Michigan, Michigan State University Press, 81–100.

Formisano, M., and T. Fuhrer (eds.) (2014) *Décadence: "Decline and Fall" or "Other Antiquity"*. Heidelberg, Winter.

Formisano, M., and C. Sogno (2010) "*Petite poésie portable*: The Latin *cento* in its Late Antique Context." In M. Horster and C. Reitz (eds.), *Condensing Texts—Condensed Texts*. Stuttgart, Steiner, 375–92.

Foucault, M. (1966) *Les mots et les choses: Une archéologie des sciences humaines*. Paris, Gallimard.

Fowden, G. (2014) *Before and after Muhammad: The First Millennium Refocused*. Princeton, NJ, Princeton University Press.

Fowler, D. (1987) "Vergil on Killing Virgins." In M. Whitby, P. Hardie, and M. Whitby (eds.), *Homo Viator: Classical Essays for John Bramble*. Bristol, Bristol Classical Press and Bolchazy-Carducci, 185–98.

Fowler, D. (1997) "On the Shoulders of Giants: Intertextuality and Classical Studies." *Materiali e discussioni per l'analisi dei testi classici* 39: 13–34.

Fowler, D. (2000a) "Epic in the Middle of the Wood: *Mise en Abime* in the Nisus and Euryalus Episode." In A. Sharrock and H. Morales (eds.), *Intratextuality: Greek and Roman Textual Relations*. Oxford, Oxford University Press, 89–114.
Fowler, D. (2000b) *Roman Constructions: Readings in Postmodern Latin*. Oxford, Oxford University Press.
Franz, M. (1999) *Von Gorgias bis Lukrez: Antike Ästhetik und Poetik als vergleichende Zeichentheorie*. Berlin, Akademie.
Freud, S. (2001) "The Future of an Illusion (1927)." *The Standard Edition of the Complete Psychological Works of Sigmund Freud*, vol. 21. London, The Hogarth Press and The Institute of Psycho-Analysis.
Friedrich, A. (2001) *Das Symposium der "XII sapientes": Kommentar und Verfasserfrage*. Berlin, de Gruyter.
Friedrich, W.-H. (1956) "Episches Unwetter." In H. Erbse (ed.), *Festschrift Bruno Snell*. Munich, Beck, 77–87.
Fuhrmann, M. (1994) *Rom in der Spätantike: Porträt einer Epoche*. Zurich, Artemis and Winkler.
Fuoco, O. (1993) "Tra rivelazione e illusione: La natura nella Mosella di Ausonio." *Bollettino di studi Latini* 23: 329–58.
Galletier, E. (1949–55) *Panégyriques Latins*. 3 vols. Paris, Les Belles Lettres.
Galli, M. (ed.) (2014) I *Vergiliocentones Minores* del Codice Salmasiano, Florence, Le Monnier.
Gamberini, F. (1983) *Stylistic Theory and Practice in Pliny the Younger*. Hildesheim, Weidmann.
Gantz, T. (1993) *Early Greek Myth*, 2 vols. Baltimore, Johns Hopkins University Press.
Ganz, D. (2013) "Individual and Universal Salvation in the *In honorem sanctae crucis*." *Florilegium* 30: 167–89.
García Ruiz, M. P. (2006) *Claudio Mamertino Panegírico (gratiarum actio) al emperador Juliano*. Pamplona, Universidad de Navarra.
García Ruiz M. P. (2013) "Rethinking the Political Role of Pliny's *Panegyricus* in the *Panegyrici Latini*." In Gibson and Rees (eds.), 195–216.
Garipzanov, I. (2015) "The Rise of Graphicacy in Late Antiquity and the Early Middle Ages." *Viator* 46: 1–21.
Garzya, A. (1984) "Retorica e realtà nella poesia tardoantica." In S. Costanza (ed.), *La poesia tardoantica: Tra retorica, teleologia e politica*. Messina, Centro di studi umanistici, 11–49.
Genette, G. (1983) *Narrative Discourse Revisited*. Trans. J. E. Lewin. Ithaca, NY, Cornell University Press.
Genette, G. (1997) *Paratexts: Thresholds of Interpretation*. Trans. J. E. Lewin. Cambridge University Press.
George, J. (1992) *Venantius Fortunatus: A Latin Poet in Merovingian Gaul*. Oxford, Oxford University Press.
George, J. (2004) "Vandal Poets in Their Context." In A. Merrills (ed.), *Vandals, Romans and Berbers*. Aldershot, Ashgate, 133–43.
Gerbrandy, P. (2013) "The Failure of Sidonius' Poetry." In J. A. van Waarden and G. Kelly (eds.), *New Approaches to Sidonius Apollinaris*. Leuven, Peeters, 64–76.
Geyer, A. (1989) *Die Genese narrativer Buchillustration: Der Miniaturenzyklus zur Aeneis im Vergilius Vaticanus*. Frankfurt am Main, V. Klostermann.
Ghilardi, M (2002) "Alle origini del dibattito sulla nascita dell'arte tardoantica. Riflessi nella critica italiana." *Mediterraneo antico* 5: 117–46.
Giardina, A. (1999) "Esplosione di tardoantico." *Studi Storici* 40: 157–180.

Gibson, B. J., and R. D. Rees (eds.) (2013) "Pliny the Younger in Late Antiquity." *Arethusa*, special ed.: 46.2.

Gilbert, G. C. (2001) *The Saints' Three Reasons for Paintings in Churches*. Ithaca, NY, Clandestine Press.

Gillett, A. (2012) "Epic Panegyric and Political Communication in the Fifth-Century West." In G. Kelly and L. Grig (eds.), *Two Romes: From Rome to Constantinople*. Oxford, Oxford University Press, 265–90.

Gioseffi, M. (2004) *Claudiano: Contro Eutropio*. Milan, La Vita Felice.

Girardet, K. M. (2010) *Der Kaiser und sein Gott: Das Christentum im Denken und in der Religionspolitik Konstantins des Grossen*. Berlin, De Gruyter.

Glinsky, M. von (2012) *Simile and Identity in Ovid's Metamorphoses*. Cambridge, Cambridge University Press.

Goldberg, S. M. (2005) *Constructing Literature in the Roman Republic*. Cambridge, Cambridge University Press.

Goldhill, S. D. (1994) "The Naïve and Knowing Eye: Ecphrasis and the Culture of Viewing in the Hellenistic World." In S. D. Goldhill and R. G. Osborne (eds.), *Art and Text in Ancient Greek Culture*. Cambridge, Cambridge University Press, 197–223.

Goldhill, S. (2009) "Introduction." In S. Goldhill (ed.), *The End of Dialogue in Antiquity*. Cambridge, Cambridge University Press: 1–11.

Goldhill, S. (2012) "Forms of Attention: Time and Narrative in Ecphrasis." *CCJ* 58: 88–114.

Goldschmidt, N. (2013) *Shaggy Crowns: Ennius'* Annales *and Virgil's* Aeneid. Oxford, Oxford University Press.

González Iglesias, J. A. (2000) "El intertexto absoluto: Optaciano Porfirio, entre Virgilio y Mallarmé." In V. Bécares, F. Pordomingo, M. Cortés Tovar, and J. C. Fernández Corte (eds.), *Intertextualidad en las Literaturas Griega y Latina*. Madrid, Ediciones Clásicas, 337–66.

Goold, G. P. (1989) *Catullus*. London, Duckworth.

Görler, W. (1969) "Vergilzitate in Ausonius' *Mosella*." *Hermes* 97: 94–114.

Götze, R. (1892) "Quaestiones Eumenianae." PhD thesis, University of Halle.

Gow, A. S. F., and D. L. Page (1968) *The Garland of Philip*. 2 vols. Cambridge, Cambridge University Press.

Grabar, A. (1968) *Christian Iconography: A Study of Its Origins*. Princeton, NJ, Princeton University Press.

Graf, G. (1894) "Akrostichis." In *RE* I.1: 1200–7.

Gransden, K. (1976) *Virgil, Aeneid Book VIII*. Cambridge, Cambridge University Press.

Graver, M. (1993) "*Quaelibet Audendi*. Fortunatus and the Acrostic." *Transactions of the American Philological Association* 123: 219–45.

Green, R. P. H. (1980) "The Correspondence of Ausonius." *L'Antiquité classique* 49: 191–211.

Green, R. P. H. (1989) "Man and Nature in Ausonius' Moselle." *Illinois Classical Studies* 14: 303–15.

Green, R. P. H. (ed.) (1991) *The Works of Ausonius*, edited with introduction and commentary. Oxford, Clarendon Press.

Green, R. P. H (ed. and trans.) (1995) *Augustine De Doctrina Christiana*. Oxford, Oxford University Press.

Green, R. P. H (1999) *Ausoni Opera*. Oxford, Oxford University Press.

Green, R. P. H. (2006) *Latin Epics of the New Testament: Juvencus, Sedulius, Arator*. Oxford, Oxford University Press.

Green, R. P. H. (2010) "Constantine as Patron of Christian Latin Poetry." *Studia Patristica* 46: 65–76.
Grimm, R. (1989) "Poems and/as Pictures: A Quick Look at Two and a Half Millennia of Ongoing Aesthetic Discourse." In R. Grimm and J. Hermand (eds.), *From Ode to Anthem: Problems of Lyric Poetry*. Madison, University of Wisconsin Press, 3–85.
Gruber, J. (ed.) (2013) *D. Magnus Ausonius, "Mosella": Kritische Ausgabe, Übersetzung, Kommentar*. Berlin and Boston, de Gruyter.
Grünewald, T. (1990) *Constantinus Maximus Augustus*. Stuttgart, Franz Steiner Verlag.
Gruzelier, C. E. (1990) "Claudian: Court Poet as Artist." In A. J. Boyle (ed.), *The Imperial Muse: Flavian Epicist to Claudian*. Victoria, Aureal, 299–318.
Gruzelier, C. E. (ed.) (1993) *Claudian: De raptu Proserpinae*. Oxford, Clarendon Press.
Gualandri, I. (1974) "Un papiro milanese, Lattanzio, Claudiano e il mito della fenice." *RAL* 29: 293–311.
Gualandri, I. (1978) [Review of Polara 1971 et al.] *Studi medievali* 18: 178–88.
Gualandri, I. (1979) *Furtiva lectio. Studi su Sidonio Apollinare*. Milan, Cisalpino Goliardica.
Gualandri, I. (1994) "Aspetti dell'ekphrasis in età tardoantica." In *Testo e immagine nell'Alto Medioevo*. Spoleto, Centro italiano di Studi sull'Alto Medioevo, 301–41.
Gualandri, I. (1995) "Prassi esegetica e stile letterario: Alcuni problemi." In C. Moreschini (ed.), *Esegesi, parafrasi e compilazione in eta tardoantica: Atti del Terzo Convegno dell'Associazione di Studi Tardoantichi*. Naples, D'Auria, 147–74.
Guarducci, M. (1965) "Il misterioso 'quadrato magico': L'interpretazione di Jérome Carcopino e documenti nuovi." *ArchClass* 17: 219–70.
Guarducci, M. (1967) "Ancora sul 'quadrato magico'." *ArchClass* 19: 144–5.
Guarducci, M. (1978) "Dal gioco letterale alla crittografia mistica." *ANRW* 2.16.2: 1736–73.
Guichard, L. A. (2006) "Simias' Pattern Poems." In M. A. Harder, R. F. Regtuit, and G. C. Wakker (eds.), *Beyond the Canon*. Leuven, Peeters, 83–103.
Guillaumin, J.-Y. (ed.) (2003) *Martianus Capella, Les noces de Philologie et de Mercure. 7, Livre VII: L'arithmétique*. Paris, Les Belles Lettres.
Guipponi-Gineste, M. F. (2010) *Claudien: Poète du monde à la cour d'Occident*. Paris, De Boccard.
Gurd, S. A. (2012) *Work in Progress: Literary Revision as Social Performance in Ancient Rome*. American Philological Association American Classical Studies 57. New York, Oxford University Press.
Guttilla, G. (1990) "Paolino di Nola: Tre studi II: Wortspiel e nomi propri nelle epistole e nei carmi." In *Polyanthema: Studi di Letteratura cristiana antica offerti a S. Costanza*, = *Studi Tardoantichi* 9: 139–51.
Guttilla, G. (2003) "Filoni pagani e cristiani nell' 'Obitus Baebiani': una nuova lettura del carm. 33 di Paolino di Nola." *Hermes* 131: 90–113.
Guttilla, G. (2004) "Dottrina e retorica cristiana nel carm. 31 di Paolino di Nola." *Augustinianum* 44: 51–90.
Guttilla, G. (2007) "Lingua del miracolo e Wortspiel nei carmi di Paolino di Nola." *Orpheus* (n.s.) 28: 67–99.
Gutzwiller, H. (1942) *Die Neujahrsrede des Konsuls Mamertinus vor dem Kaizer Julian*. Basle, Helbing and Lichtenhahn.
Gutzwiller, K. J. (1997) "The Poetics of Editing in Meleager's Garland." *TAPA* 127: 169–200.
Gutzwiller, K. J. (1998) *Poetic Garlands: Hellenistic Epigrams in Context*. Berkeley, University of California Press.
Gutzwiller, K. J. (2003) "Visual Aesthetics in Meleager and Cavafy." *CML* 23.2: 67–87.

Habinek, T. (2009) "Situating Literacy in Rome." In W. A. Johnson and H. N. Parker (eds.), *Ancient Literacies: The Culture of Reading in Greece and Rome.* Oxford, Oxford University Press, 114–41.

Hagendahl, H. (1967) *Augustine and the Latin Classics.* Studia Graeca et Latina Gothoburgensia 22. 2 vols. Göteborg, Almquist and Wiksell.

Hagstrum, J. (1955) *The Sister Arts: The Tradition of Literary Pictorialism and English Poetry from Dryden to Gray.* Chicago, University of Chicago Press.

Hall, J. B. (1969) *Claudian: De Raptu Proserpinae.* Cambridge, Cambridge University Press.

Hall, J. B. (1985) *Claudi Claudiani Carmina.* Stuttgart, Teubner.

Hamburger, J. (2011) "The Iconicity of Script." *Word and Image* 27: 249–61.

Hamm, U. (2000) "Cyprian, Poet." In S. Döpp and W. Geerlings (eds.), *Dictionary of Early Christian Literature,* English trans. New York, Crossroad. Originally published 1988, Freiburg in Breisgau, Herder.

Hannestad, N. (2001) "The Ruler Image of the Fourth Century: Innovation or Tradition?" In J. R. Brandt and O. Steen (eds.), *Imperial Art as Christian Art—Christian Art as Imperial Art: Expression and Meaning in Art and Architecture from Constantine to Justinian.* Rome, Bardi Editore, 93–107.

Hansen, M. F. (2003) *The Eloquence of Appropriation: Prolegomena to an Understanding of Spolia in Early Christian Rome.* Rome, L'Erma di Bretschneider.

Hardie, P. (1986) *Virgil's Aeneid: Cosmos and Imperium.* Oxford, Oxford University Press.

Hardie, P. (1993) "*Ut pictura poesis?* Horace and the Visual Arts." In N. Rudd (ed.), *Horace 2000, a Celebration: Essays for the Bimillennium.* Ann Arbor, University of Michigan Press.

Hardie, P. (ed.) (1994) *Virgil, Aeneid Book 9.* Cambridge, Cambridge University Press.

Hardie, P. (1997) "Virgil and Tragedy." In Martindale (ed.), 312–26.

Hardie, P. (2002) *Ovid's Poetics of Illusion.* Cambridge, Cambridge University Press.

Hardie, P. (2007) "Polyphony or Babel? Hosidius Geta's *Medea* and the Poetics of the *Cento.*" In S. Swain, S. Harrison, and J. Elsner (eds.), *Severan Culture.* Cambridge, Cambridge University Press, 169–76.

Hardie, P., and Moore, H. (eds.) (2010) *Classical Literary Careers and Their Reception.* Cambridge, Cambridge University Press.

Hardison, O. B.Jr., (intr. and trans.) (1974) "Fulgentius." In A. Preminger, L. Golden, O. B. Hardison Jr., and K. Kerrane (eds.), *Classical and Medieval Literary Criticism: Translations and Interpretations.* New York, Frederick Ungar, 324–40.

Hardwick, L., and C. Stray (eds.) (2008) *A Companion to Classical Receptions.* Oxford, Blackwell.

Harich-Schwarzbauer, H. (2009) "Von Aeneas zu Camilla: Intertextualität im Vergilcento der Faltonia Betitia Proba." In D. van Mal-Maeder, D. Burnier, and L. Núñez (eds.), *Jeux de voix: Enonciation, intertextualité et intentionalité dans la littérature antique.* Bern, Peter Lang, 331–46.

Harries, J. (1994) *Sidonius Apollinaris and the Fall of Rome. AD 407–85.* Oxford, Oxford University Press.

Harrison, C. (2000) *Augustine: Christian Truth and Fractured Humanity.* Oxford, Oxford University Press.

Harrison, C. (2011) "Enchanting the Soul: The Music of the Psalms." In A. Andreopoulos, A. Casiday, and C. Harrison (eds.), *Meditations of the Heart: The Psalms in Early Christian Thought and Practice.* Turnhout, Brepols, 205–23.

Harrison, C. (2013) *The Art of Listening in the Early Church.* Oxford, Oxford University Press.

Harrison, S. J. (2000) *Apuleius: A Latin Sophist.* Oxford, Oxford University Press.

Harrison, S. J. (2001) "Picturing the Future: The Prophetic Ekphrasis from Homer to Vergil." In S. J. Harrison (ed.), *Texts, Ideas and the Classics*. Oxford, Oxford University Press, 70–92.
Harrison, S. J. (2005) "The Poetics of Fiction: Poetic Influence on the Language of Apuleius' *Metamorphoses*." In T. Reinhardt, M. Lapidge, and J. N. Adams (eds.), *Aspects of the Language of Latin Prose: Proceedings of the British Academy* 129. Oxford, Oxford University Press, 273–86.
Harrison, S. J. (2006) "The Primal Voyage and the Ocean of Epos: Two Aspects of Metapoetic Imagery in Catullus, Virgil and Horace." *Dictynna* 4. http://dictynna.revues.org/146.
Harrison, S. J. (2013) *Framing the Ass*. Oxford, Oxford University Press.
Hartel, W. von (1882) *Magni Felicis Ennodii opera omnia*. Recensuit et commentario critico instruxit Guilelmus Hartel. CSEL 6. Vienna, C. Gerold.
Hartel, W. von (1894, 1999) *Sancti Pontii Meropii Paulini Nolani Carmina*. CSEL 30. Vienna, Tempsky. Reprint, Vienna, Österreische Akademie der Wissenschaften.
Haverling, G. (1988) *Studies on Symmachus' Language and Style*. Gothenburg, Acta Universitatis Gothoburgensis.
Hays, G. (1998) "Varia Fulgentiana." *Illinois Classical Studies* 23: 127–37.
Hays, G. (2004) "*Romuleis Libicisque litteris*: Fulgentius and the 'Vandal Renaissance.'" In A. Merrills (ed.) *Vandals, Romans and Berbers*. Aldershot, Ashgate, 101–32.
Hays, G. (intr. and trans.) (2008) "Fabius Planciades Fulgentius." In J. Ziolkowski and M. Putnam (eds.), *The Virgilian Tradition: The First Fifteen Hundred Years*. New Haven, CT, and London, Yale University Press, 660–72.
Heath, J. (2010) "*Nomina Sacra* and the *Sacra Memoria* before the Monastic Age." *Journal of Theological Studies* 61: 516–49.
Heath, J. (2013) *Paul's Visual Piety: The Metamorphosis of the Beholder*. Oxford, Oxford University Press.
Heath, J. (2016) "Sight and Christianity: Early Christian Attitudes to Seeing." In M. J. Squire (ed.), *Sight and the Ancient Senses*. London, Routledge, 228–44.
Heather, P. (2006) *The Fall of the Roman Empire: A New History of Rome and the Barbarians*. Oxford, Oxford University Press.
Heiberg, J. L. (ed.) (1910–15) *Archimedis opera omnia cum commentariis Eutocii*. 3 vols., 2nd edition. Leipzig, Teubner.
Heikel, I. A. (1902) *Eusebius' Werke Band I: Über das Leben Constantins: Constantins Rede an die Heilige Versammlung: Tricennatsrede an Constantin*. Leipzig, Hinrichs.
Helleman, W. (2009) *The Feminine Personification of Wisdom*. Lampeter, Edwin Mellon Press.
Helm, N. W. (1902) "The Carmen Figuratum as Shown in the Works of Publilius Optatianus Porfyrius." *TAPA* 33: 43–9.
Helm, R. (ed.) (1898) *Fabii Planciadis Fulgentii V. C. Opera*. Leipzig, Teubner.
Helm, R. (1956) *Eusebius Werke: Sieber Band: Die Chronik des Hieronymus (Hieronymi Chronicon)*. Berlin, Akademie-Verlag.
Helm, R. (1959) "Publilius Optatianus Porfyrius (= Publilius 29)." *Paulys Realencyclopädie der classischen Altertumswissenschaft* 23.2: 1928–1936.
Henderson, I. (1991) "Quintilian and the Progymnasmata." *Antike und Abendland* 37: 82–99.
Henderson, J. (1996) "Pump Up the Volume: Juvenal, *Satire* 1: 1–21." *PCPhS* 41: 107–31.
Henderson, J. (2007) *The Medieval World of Isidore of Seville: Truth from Words*. Cambridge, Cambridge University Press.
Henderson, J. G. (2013) "A Couple of Things Pliny Can't Help With? *Panegyrici Latini* XI (3)." In Gibson and Rees (eds.), 167–94.

Henig, M. (1997) "The Lullingstone Mosaic: Art, Religion, and Letters in a Fourth-Century Villa." *Mosaic* 24: 4–7.
Henig, M. (2000) "The Secret of the Lullingstone Mosaic." *Kent Archaeological Review* 139: 196–7.
Hernández Lobato, J. (2007a) "Ausonio ante el enigma del número tres: Política y poética en el *Griphus*." In G. Hinojo Andrés and J. C. Fernández Corte (eds.), *Munus quaesitum meritis*. Salamanca, Ediciones Universidad de Salamanca, 455–62.
Hernández Lobato, J. (2007b) "*Murex Sidonius*: Poder y poesía en el *carmen* 13 de Sidonio Apolinar." *Acme* 60 (2): 53–96.
Hernández Lobato, J. (2008) "Nota a Sidonio Apolinar (*Carmen* 13.19)." *Acme* 61 (2), 303–9.
Hernández Lobato, J. (2010a) "Otredad, alterización y apropiación en el discurso cultural del primer Cristianismo. Ambrosio de Milán y la 'reescritura' cristiana del *Tanak*." *Sacris erudiri* 49: 81–126.
Hernández Lobato, J. (2010b) "*Sterilis Camena*. El *carmen* 9 de Sidonio Apolinar o la muerte de la poesía." *Acme* 63.1: 97–133.
Hernández Lobato, J. (2012) Vel Apolline muto: *Estética y poética de la Antigüedad tardía*. Bern, Peter Lang.
Hernández Lobato, J. (2014) *El Humanismo que no fue: Sidonio Apolinar en el Renacimiento*. Bologna, Pàtron.
Hernández Lobato, J. (2016a) "Más allá del pensamiento. El escepticismo epistemológico de Gregorio de Nisa." In C. Lévy and A.-I. Bouton-Touboulic (eds.), *Scepticisme et Religion: Constantes et évolutions, de la philosophie hellénistique à la philosophie médiévale*. Monothéismes et Philosophie 21. Turnhout, Brepols, 157–69.
Hernández Lobato, J. (2016b; in press) "Mystic River: Ausonius' *Mosella* as an Epistemological Revelation." *Ramus* 45.2.
Herzog, R. (1975) *Die Bibelepik der lateinischen Spätantike*. Munich, W. Fink.
Herzog, R. (2002) *Spätantike: Studien zur römischen und lateinisch-christlichen Literatur*. Göttingen: Vandenhoeck and Ruprecht.
Heusch, C. (1997) *Die Achilles-Ethopoiie des Codex Salmasianus*. Paderborn, Schöningh.
Heyworth, S. J., and J. Morwood (2011) *A Commentary on Propertius Book 3*. Oxford, Oxford University Press.
Higgins, D. (1987) *Pattern Poetry: Guide to an Unknown Literature*. Albany, State University of New York Press.
Hilberg, I. (1899–1900) "Ist die Ilias Latina von einem Italicus verfasst oder einem Italicus gewidmet?" *Wiener Studien* 21: 264–305 (and 22: 317–18, "Nachtrag").
Hilton, J. (2001) "Apuleius: Florida." In S. J. Harrison (ed.), *Apuleius: Rhetorical Works*. Oxford, Oxford University Press, 137–76.
Hinds, S (1998) *Allusion and Intertext: Dynamics of Appropriation in Roman Poetry*. Cambridge: Cambridge University Press.
Hinds, S. (2006) "Venus, Varro and the Vates: Toward the Limits of Etymological Interpretation." *Dictynna* 3: 1–64.
Hinds, S. (2012) *Displacing Persephone: Epic between Worlds, Housman Lecture*. London, UCL Department of Greek and Latin.
Hinds, S. (2013) "Claudianism in the *De Raptu Proserpinae*" In T. D. Papanghelis, S. J. Harrison, and S. Frangoulidis (eds.), *Generic Interfaces in Latin Literature*. Berlin, de Gruyter, 169–92.
Hinds, S. (2014) "The Self-Conscious Cento." In M. Formisano and T. Fuhrer (eds.), 171–98.
Hochschild, P. (2012) *Memory in Augustine's Theological Anthropology*. Oxford, Oxford University Press.

Hoogland Verkerk, D. (1999) "Biblical Manuscripts in Rome 400–700 and the Ashburnham Pentateuch." In J. Williams (ed.), 97–120.
Horsfall, N. (2000) *Virgil, Aeneid 7: A Commentary*. Leiden, Brill.
Hose, M. (2007) "Konstantin und die Literatur—oder: Gibt es eine Konstantinische Literatur?" *Gymnasium* 114: 535–58.
Hughes, J. (2014) "Memory and the Roman Viewer: Looking at the Arch of Constantine." In K. Galinsky (ed.), *Memoria Romana: Memory in Rome and Rome in Memory*. Ann Arbor, University of Michigan Press, 103–15.
Hunink, V. J. C. (2001) *Apuleius of Madauros, Florida*. Amsterdam, Gieben.
Hunink, V. J. C. (2011) "Singing Together in Church: Augustine's *Psalm against the Donatists*." In A. Lardinois, J. Blok, and M. van der Poel (eds.), *Sacred Words: Orality, Literacy and Religion*. Leiden, Brill, 389–403.
Hunter, R. (1993) *The Argonautica of Apollonius: Literary Studies*. Cambridge, Cambridge University Press.
Hutchinson, G. (2013) *Greek to Latin: Frameworks and Contexts for Intertextuality*. Oxford, Oxford University Press.
Hwang, A. Y. (2009) *Intrepid Lover of Perfect Grace: The Life and Thought of Prosper of Aquitaine*. Washington, DC, Catholic University of America Press.
Inglebert, H. (2012) "Introduction: Late Antique Conceptions of Late Antiquity." In Scott Johnson (ed.), *The Oxford Handbook of Late Antiquity*. Oxford, Oxford University Press, 1–17.
Isbell, H. (1974) "Decimus Magnus Ausonius: The Poet and His World." In J. W. Binns (ed.), *Latin Literature in the Fourth Century*. London and Boston, Routledge and Kegan Paul, 22–57.
Isetta S. (1980) "Il 'De aue phoenice' attribuito a Lattanzio." *Civiltà classica e cristiana* 1: 385–401.
Jackson, B. D. (1969) "The Theory of Signs in *De doctrina Christiana*." *Revue des Études Augustiniennes* 15: 9–49.
Jackson, B. D. (ed.) (1975) *Augustine, De dialectica*. Dordrecht and Boston, Reidel.
Jacobson H. (1983) *The Exagoge of Ezechiel*. Cambridge, Cambridge University Press.
James, E. (2008) "The Rise and Function of the Concept 'Late Antiquity.'" *Journal of Late Antiquity* 1: 20–30.
James, L. (1996) *Light and Colour in Byzantine Art*. Oxford, Clarendon Press.
James, L. (2004) "Senses and Sensibility in Byzantium." *Art History* 27: 523–37.
James, L. (ed.) (2007) *Art and Text in Byzantine Culture*. Cambridge, Cambridge University Press.
Janan, M. (2009) *Reflections in a Serpent's Eye: Thebes in Ovid's Metamorphoses*. Oxford, Oxford University Press.
Jansen, L. (ed.) (2014) *The Roman Paratext: Frame, Texts, Readers*. Cambridge, Cambridge University Press.
Janson, T. (1964) *Latin Prose Prefaces: Studies in Literary Conventions*. Studia Latina Stockholmiensia 13. Stockholm, Almquist and Wiksell.
Jauss, H. R. (1982) *Toward an Aesthetic of Reception*. Trans. T. Bahti. Minneapolis, University of Minnesota Press.
Jefferson, L. M. (2014) *Christ the Miracle Worker in Early Christian Art*. Minneapolis, Augsburg Fortress.
Jefferson, L. M., and R. M. Jensen (eds.) (2015) *The Art of Empire: Christian Art in Its Imperial Context*. Minneapolis, Fortress Press.
Jensen, R. M. (2000) *Understanding Early Chritian Art*. London, Routledge.
Johnson, R. (1959) "The Poet and the Orator." *CPh* 54: 173–6.

Johnson, S. F. (ed.) (2012) *The Oxford Handbook of Late Antiquity*. Oxford, Oxford University Press.

Jones, C. P. (2014) *Between Pagan and Christian*. Cambridge, MA, Harvard University Press.

Kaesser, C. (2002) "The Body Is Not Painted On: Ekphrasis and Exegesis in Prudentius' *Peristephanon* 9." *Ramus* 31: 158–74.

Kaimowitz, J. (trans.) (2008) *The Odes of Horace*. Baltimore, Johns Hopkins University Press.

Kaiser-Minn, H. (1983) "Die Entwicklung der frühchristlichen Sarkophagplastik bis zum Ende des 4. Jahrhunderts." In D. Stutzinger (ed.), *Spätantike und frühes Christentum*. Ausstellung im Liebieghaus, Museum alter Plastik. Frankfurt am Main, Liebieghaus Museum alter Plastik, 318–38.

Kaldellis, A. (2007) *Hellenism in Byzantium: The Transformation of Greek Identity and the Reception of the Classical Tradition*. Cambridge, Cambridge University Press.

Kallendorf, C. (ed.) (2007) *A Companion to the Classical Tradition*. Oxford, Blackwell.

Karfíková, L., S. Douglass, and J. Zachhuber (eds.) (2007) *Gregory of Nyssa: Contra Eunomium II: An English Version with Supporting Studies*. Leiden, Brill.

Kaschnitz-Weinberg, G (2016) "Review of Alois Riegl, *Die spätrömische Kunstindustrie*, 1927". *Art History* 39: 85–97.

Kaspers, C. (2000) "Hilary of Arles." In S. Döpp and W. Geerlings (eds.), *Dictionary of Early Christian Literature*. English trans. New York, Crossroad, 282–3. Originally published 1988, Freiburg in Breisgau, Herder.

Kaster, R. A. (2005) *Emotion, Restraint, and Community in Ancient Rome*. Classical Culture and Society 1. New York, Oxford University Press.

Kaufmann, F. M. (1995) *Studien zu Sidonius Apollinaris*. Frankfurt am Main, Peter Lang.

Kaufmann, H. (2006a) *Dracontius, Romul. 10 (Medea): Einleitung, Text, Übersetzung, Kommentar*. Heidelberg, Universitätsverlag Winter.

Kaufmann, H. (2006b) "Intertextualität in Dracontius' *Medea* (*Romul.* 10)." *MH* 63: 104–14.

Kay, N. (2001) *Ausonius Epigrams*. London, Duckworth.

Kay, N. (2006) *Epigrams from the Anthologia Latina*. London, Duckworth.

Kehding, O. (1899) "De panegyricis latinis capita quattuor." PhD thesis, University of Marburg.

Keil, H. (1857–70) *Grammatici Latini*. 8 vols. Leipzig, Teubner.

Kelly, G. (2007) "The Sphragis and Closure of the *Res Gestae*." In J. den Boeft, D. den Hengst, H. C. Teitler, and J. W. Drijvers (eds.), *Ammianus after Julian: The Reign of Valentinian and Valens in Books 26–31 of the Res Gestae*. Leiden, Brill, 219–41.

Kelly, G. (2008) *Ammianus Marcellinus: The Allusive Historian*. Cambridge and New York, Cambridge University Press.

Kelly, G. (2013) "Sidonius and Claudian." In J. A. van Waarden and G. Kelly (eds.), *New Approaches to Sidonius Apollinaris*. Leuven, Peeters, 171–91.

Kelly, G. and van Waarden, J. A. (eds.) (forthcoming) *Prolegomena to Sidonius Apollinaris*, Leuven, Peeters.

Kennell, S. A. H. (2000) *Magnus Felix Ennodius: A Gentleman of the Church*. Ann Arbor, University of Michigan Press.

Kenney, E. J. (1984) "The Mosella of the Mosella of Ausonius." *Greece and Rome* 31: 190–202.

Kenney, J. P. (2005) *The Mysticism of Saint Augustine: Rereading the* Confessions. New York, Routledge.

Kessler, H. L. (2000) *Spiritual Seeing: Picturing God's Invisibility in Medieval Art*. Philadelphia, University of Pennsylvania Press.

King, P. (trans. and notes) (1995) *Augustine: Against the Academicians: The Teacher*. Indianapolis, Hackett.

Kinney, D. (1995) "Rape or Restitution of the Past: Interpreting Spolia." In S. C. Scott (ed.), *The Art of Interpreting*. Papers in Art History from the Pennsylvania State University, 9. University Park, Pennsylvania University Press, 53–67.
Kinney, D. (1997) "*Spolia, damnatio* and *renovatio memoriae*." *Memoirs of the American Academy in Rome* 42: 117–48.
Kinney, D. (2012) "Instances of Appropriation in Late Roman and Early Christian Art." *Essays in Medieval Studies* 28: 1–22.
Kirsch, W. (1979) "Strukturwandel im lateinischen Epos des 4.–6. Jhs." *Philologus* 123: 38–53.
Kitzinger, E. (1977) *Byzantine Art in the Making: Main Lines of Stylistic Development in Mediterranean Art, 3rd–7th Century*. Cambridge, MA, Harvard University Press.
Kleiner, D. E. E. (1992) *Roman Sculpture*. New Haven, CT, Yale University Press.
Kleinschmidt, A. L. (2013) *Ich-Entwürfe in spätantiker Dichtung: Ausonius, Paulinus von Nola und Paulinus von Pella*. Heidelberg, Winter.
Kleywegt, A. J. (2005) *Valerius Flaccus, Argonautica, I: A Commentary*. Leiden, Brill.
Klingner, F. (1966) *De Boethii consolatione philosophiae*. Zurich, Weidmann.
Klotz, A. (1911) "Studien zu den *Panegyrici Latini*." *Rheinisches Museum* 66: 513–72.
Kluge, E. (1924) "Studien zu Publilius Optatianus Porfyrius." *Münchener Museum* 4: 323–48.
Kluge, E. (1926) *Publilii Optatiani Porfyrii Carmina*. Leipzig, Teubner.
Knight, G. R. (2005) "Friendship and Erotics in the Late Antique Verse-Epistle: Ausonius to Paulinus Revisited." *RhM* 148.3–4: 361–403.
Knight, G. R. (2006) "Ausonius to Axius Paulus: Metapoetics and the Bissula." *RhM* 149.3–4: 369–85.
Koch, G. (2000) *Frühchristliche Sarkophage*. Munich, Beck.
Koeppel, G. (1986) "Die historischen Reliefs der römischen Kaiserzeit IV: Stadtrömische Denkmäler unbekannter Bauzugehörigkeit aus hadrianischer bis konstantinischer Zeit." *Bonner Jahrbücher* 186: 1–91.
Kramer, J. (1983) *Glossaria bilinguia, in papyris et membranis reperta*. Bonn, Habelt.
Kristensen, T. M. (2013) *Making and Breaking the Gods: Christian Responses to Pagan Sculpture in Late Antiquity*. Aarhus, Aarhus University Press.
Kristeva, J. (1989) *Language—the Unknown: An Initiation into Linguistics*. Trans. A. M. Menke. New York, Columbia University Press.
Kwapisz, J. (2013) *The Greek Figure Poems*. Leuven, Peeters.
Kwapisz, J., D. Petrain, and M. Szymański (eds.) (2013) *The Muse at Play: Riddles and Wordplay in Greek and Latin Poetry*. Berlin, de Gruyter.
Kyriakidis, S. (2007) *Catalogues of Proper Names in Latin Epic Poetry: Lucretius-Virgil-Ovid*. Newcastle, Cambridge Scholars.
La Bua, G. (1999) *L'inno nella letteratura poetica latina*. San Severo, Gerni.
Lamberton, R. (1986) *Homer the Theologian: Neoplatonist Allegorical Reading and the Growth of the Epic Tradition*. Berkeley, University of California Press.
Lancel, S. (2002) *St Augustine*. London, SCM. English translation.
Lancha, J. (1997) *Mosaïque et culture dans l'Occident romain (Ier–IVe s.)*. Rome, L'Erma di Bretschneider.
Langner, M. (2001) *Antike Graffitizeichnungen: Motiv, Gestaltung und Bedeutung*. Wiesbaden, Reichert Verlag.
La Penna, A. (1993) "Il 'lusus' poetico nella tarda antichità: Il caso di Ausonio." In A. Carandini, L. Cracco Ruggini, and A. Carandini (eds.), *Storia di Roma* III.2. Turin, Einaudi, 731–51.
La Penna, A. (1995) "Gli svaghi letterari della nobiltà gallica nella tarda antichità: Il caso di Sidonio Apollinare." *Maia* 47: 3–34.

Lapidge, M. (1977) "The Authorship of the Adonic Verses 'Ad Fidolium' attributed to Columbanus." *StudMed* 18, 2: 249–314.
Laubscher, H. P. (1976) *Arcus Novus und Arcus Claudii: Zwei Triumphbögen an der Via Lata in Rom.* Göttingen, Vandenhoeck and Ruprecht.
Laudani, C (2014) *Nazario: Panegirico in onore di Costantino.* Bari, Cacucci.
Lausberg, H. (1998) *Handbook of Literary Rhetoric: A Foundation for Literary Study.* Trans. M. T. Bliss, A. Jansen, and D. E. Orton. Leiden, Brill.
Leader-Newby, R. (2007) "Inscribed Mosaics in the Roman Empire: Perspectives from East and West." In Z. Newby and R. Leader-Newby (eds.), 179–99.
Leary, T. (2014) *Symphosius—the Aenigmata: An Introduction, Text and Commentary.* London, Bloomsbury.
Lecocq, F. (2011) "Le phénix chez Claudien: La fin d'un mythe. Pour une lecture politique du phénix: Quelques arguments." In F. Garambois-Vasquez (ed.), *Claudien: Mythe, histoire et science.* Saint-Étienne, Université de Saint-Étienne, 113–57.
Lee, B. T. (2005) *Apuleius' Florida: A Commentary.* Berlin and New York, de Gruyter.
Leeb, R. (1992) *Konstantin und Christus: Die Verchristlichung der imperialen Repräsentation unter Konstantin dem Großen als Spiegel seiner Kirchenpolitik und seines Selbstverständnisses als christlicher Kaiser.* Berlin, de Gruyter.
Leone, A. (2013) *The End of the Pagan City: Religion, Economy and Urbanism in Late Antique North Africa.* Oxford, Oxford University Press.
Lerer, S. (1985) *Boethius and Dialogue.* Princeton, NJ, Princeton University Press.
Lessing, G. (1984) *Laocoön: An Essay on the Limits of Painting and Poetry.* Baltimore, Johns Hopkins University Press.
Letrouit, J. (2007) "Pour une approche du *Carmen* XXV de P. Optatianus Porfyrius en terme de dénombrement." *Maia* 49: 73–6.
Levine, A. (2015) "Does the Hinton St Mary Mosaic Depict Christ?" In L. M. Jefferson and R. M Jensen (eds.), 307–49.
Levitan, W. (1985) "Dancing at the End of the Rope: Optatian Porfyry and the Field of Roman Verse." *TAPA* 115: 245–69.
L'Huillier, M.-C. (1992) *L'Empire des Mots: Orateurs Gaulois et Empereurs Romans 3e et 4e Siècles.* Paris, Les Belles Lettres.
Liebeschuetz, W. (2004) "The Birth of Late Antiquity" *Antiquité Tardive* 12: 253–61.
Lissarrague, F. (1992) "*Graphein*: Écrire et dessiner." In C. Bron and E. Kassapoglou (eds.), *L'image en jeu: De l'antiquité à Paul Klee.* Yens-sur-Morges, Cabédita, 189–203.
Liverani, P. (2009) "The Fragment in Late Antiquity: A Functional View." In W. Tronzo (ed.), *The Fragment: An Incomplete History.* Los Angeles, Getty Research Institute, 23–36.
Long, A. A. (2005) "Stoic Linguistics, Plato's *Cratylus*, and Augustine's *De dialectica*." In D. Frede and B. Inwood (eds.), *Language and Learning: Philosophy of Language in the Hellenistic Age.* Cambridge, Cambridge University Press, 37–55.
L'Orange, H. P. (1965) *Art Forms and Civic Life in the Late Roman Empire.* Princeton, NJ, Princeton University Press.
Lovejoy, A. O., and G. Boas (1935) *Primitivism and Related Ideas in Antiquity.* Baltimore, Johns Hopkins University Press.
Lowden, J. (1999) "The Beginnings of Biblical Illustration." In J. Williams (ed.), 9–59.
Loyen, A. (1943) *Sidoine Apollinaire et l'esprit précieux en Gaule aux derniers jours de l'Empire.* Paris, Les Belles Lettres.
Loyen, A. (ed., trans., and notes) (1960) *Sidoine Apollinaire: Poèmes.* Paris, Les Belles Lettres.

Ludlow, M. (2007) *Gregory of Nyssa, Ancient and (Post)Modern*. Oxford, Oxford University Press.
Lühken, M. (2002) *Christianorum Maro et Flaccus: Zur Vergil- und Horazrezeption des Prudentius*. Göttingen, Vandenhoeck and Ruprecht.
Luibheid, C. (trans.) (1987) *Pseudo-Dionysius: The Complete Works*. New York, Paulist Press.
Lunn-Rockliffe, S. (2010) "Commemorating the Usurper Magnus Maximus: Ekphrasis, Poetry, and History in Pacatus' Panegyric of Theodosius." *Journal of Late Antiquity* 3: 316–36.
Luz, C. (2008) "Das Rätsel der griechischen Figurengedichte." *MH* 37: 22–33.
Luz, C. (2010) *Technopaignia: Formspiele in der griechischen Dichtung*. Leiden, Brill.
MacCormack, S. (1976) "Latin Prose Panegyrics: Tradition and Discontinuity in the Later Roman Empire." *REA* 22: 29–77.
MacCormack, S. (1981) *Art and Ceremony in Late Antiquity*. Berkeley, University of California Press.
MacCormack, S. (1998) *The Shadows of Poetry: Vergil in the Mind of Augustine*. Berkeley, University of California Press.
MacIver, C. (2012) *Quintus Smyrnaeus' Posthomerica: Engaging Homer in Late Antiquity*. Leiden, Brill.
Mackail, J. W. (trans.) (1921) "Pervigilium Veneris." In F. W. Cornish, J. P. Postgate, and J. W. Mackail (ed., trans., and notes), *Catullus, Tibullus and Pervigilium Veneris*. London and New York, Loeb Classical Library, 341–66.
Magee, J. (2003) "Boethius's Anapestic Dimeters (a Catalectic), with Regard to Structure and Argument of the *Consolation*." In A. Galonnier (ed.), *Boèce ou la chaîne des savoirs*. Leuven, Peeters.
Maguinness, W. A. (1993) "Locutions and Formulae of the Latin Panegyrists." *Hermathena* 48: 117–38.
Majani, C. (2006) "Fons Aponi in Claudiano, Cassiodoro ed Ennodio: per un'analisi intertestuale." In F. Gasti (ed.), *Atti della terza giornata ennodiana (Pavia 10–11 November 2004)*. Pisa, ETS, 207–18.
Malamud, M. (1989) *A Poetics of Transformation: Prudentius and Classical Mythology*. Ithaca, NY, Cornell University Press.
Malamud, M. (2011) *The Origin of Sin: An English Translation of the* Hamartigenia. Ithaca, NY, Cornell University Press.
Malbon, E. (1990) *The Iconography of the Sarcophagus of Junius Bassus*. Princeton, NJ, Princeton University Press.
Maltby, R. (1991) *A Lexicon of Ancient Latin Etymologies*. Leeds, Francis Cairns.
Maltby, R. (1993) "The Limits of Etymologising." *Aevum Antiquum* 6: 257–75.
Manca, M. (1998) "Un prologo di troppo nel *De aetatibus mundi et hominis* di Fulgenzio." *Quaderni del Dipartimento di Filologia, Linguistica e Tradizione Classica (Università degli Studi di Torino)* 11: 243–6.
Manca, M. (2002) "Una lettura sinottica dei prologhi fulgenziani." *Quaderni del Dipartimento di Filologia, Linguistica e Tradizione Classica (Università degli Studi di Torino)* 16: 319–43.
Manca, M. (ed., trans., and notes) (2003) *Fulgenzio: Le età del mondo e dell'uomo*. Alessandria, Edizioni dell'Orso.
Mango, C. (1963) "Antique Statuary and the Byzantine Beholder." *Dumbarton Oaks Papers* 17: 55–75.
Manieri, A. (1998) *L'immagine poetica nella teoria degli antichi*. Pisa, Istituti editoriali e poligrafici internazionali.

Männlein-Robert, I. (2007) *Stimme, Schrift und Bild: Zum Verhältnis der Künste in der hellenistischen Dichtung*. Heidelberg, Winter.
Marangoni, C. (2007) *Supplementum Etymologicum Latinum* I. Trieste, Edizioni Università di Trieste.
Marenbon, J. (2003) *Boethius*. Oxford, Oxford University Press.
Marías, J. (2000) *The Christian Perspective*. Houston, Halcyon Press.
Markus, R. A. (1972) "Saint Augustine on Signs." In R. A. Markus (ed.), *Augustine, a Collection of Critical Essays*. New York, Anchor Books, 61–91. Reprinted from *Phronesis* 2: 60–83.
Markus, R. A. (1995) "Signs: Communication and Communities in Augustine's De doctrina Christiana." In D. W. H. Arnold and P. Bright (eds.), *De doctrina Christiana, a Classic of Western Culture*. Notre Dame, IN, University of Notre Dame Press, 97–1084.
Markus, R. A. (1997) *Gregory the Great and His World*. Cambridge, Cambridge University Press.
Marrou, H.-I. (1938) *Saint Augustin et la fin de la culture antique*. Paris, de Boccard. 2nd edition with *retractatio*, published 1949.
Marrou, H.-I. (1958) *Saint Augustine et la fin de la culture antique*. Paris, de Boccard.
Marrou, H. I. (1977) *Décadence romaine ou antiquité tardive? IIIe–VIe siècle*. Paris, Éditions du Seuil.
Marrou, H. I. (1982) *A History of Education in Antiquity*. Trans. George Lamb. Madison, University of Wisconsin Press.
Martelli, F. K. A. (2013) *Ovid's Revisions: The Editor as Author*. Cambridge, Cambridge University Press.
Martindale, C. (ed.) (1993) *Redeeming the Text: Latin Poetry and the Hermeneutics of Reception*. Cambridge, Cambridge University Press.
Martindale, C. (ed.) (1997) *The Cambridge Companion to Virgil*. Cambridge, Cambridge University Press.
Mastandrea, P. (1979) *Un neoplatonico latino: Cornelio Labeone*. Leiden, Brill.
Mastrangelo, M. (2008) *The Roman Self in Late Antiquity*. Baltimore, Johns Hopkins University Press.
Mastrangelo, M. (2009) "The Decline of Poetry in the Fourth-Century West." *International Journal for the Classical Tradition* 16: 311–29.
Mastrangelo, M. (2016) "Towards a Poetics of Late Latin Reuse." In S. McGill and J. Pucci (eds.), 25–46.
Mathews, T. (1993) *The Clash of Gods: A Reinterpretation of Early Christian Art*. Princeton, NJ, Princeton University Press.
Mathisen, R. (1991) "Phoebus, Orpheus and Dionysus: Nicknames and the Literary Circle of Sidonius." In R. Mathisen (ed.), *Studies in the History, Literature and Society of Late Antiquity*. Amsterdam, Adolf M. Hakkert Publisher, 29–43.
Mathisen, R. (1993) *Roman Aristocrats in Barbarian Gaul: Strategies for Survival in an Age of Transition*. Austin, University of Texas Press.
Matthews, J. F. (1971) "Gallic Supporters of Theodosius." *Latomus* 30: 1073–99.
Mattiacci, S. (ed.) (1982) *I frammenti dei "poetae Novelli"*. Rome, Edizioni dell'Ateneo.
Mayer, C. P. (1969) *Die Zeichen in der geistigen Entwicklung und in der Theologie des jungen Augustinus*. Würzburg, Augustinus-Verlag.
Mazal, O. (1999) *Geschichte der Buchkultur. Band I: Griechisch-römische Antike*. Graz, Akademische Druck-und-Verlagsanstalt.
Mazzeo, J. A. (1962) "St. Augustine's Rhetoric of Silence." *Journal of the History of Ideas* 23.2: 175–96.
McCartney, E. S. (1919) "Puns and Plays on Proper Names." *Classical Journal* 14/6: 343–58.

McGill, S. (2005) *Virgil Recomposed: The Mythological and Secular Centos in Antiquity*. Oxford, Oxford University Press.
McGill, S. (2007a) "Ausonius' Letter to Hesperius Attached to the *Protrepticus ad nepotem* and Quintilian's *Institutio oratoria* 10.1: 17–19." *CQ* 57: 332–5.
McGill, S. (2007b) "Virgil, Christianity and the *Cento Probae*." In J. H. D. Scourfield (ed.), 173–94.
McGill, S. (2012a) "Latin Poetry." In S. F. Johnson (ed.), *The Oxford Handbook of Late Antiquity*. Oxford, Oxford University Press, 335–60.
McGill, S. (2012b) *Plagiarism in Latin Literature*. Cambridge, Cambridge University Press.
McGill, S. (2014) "Ausonius at Night." *AJP* 135: 123–48.
McGill, S., and J. Pucci (2016) (eds.), *Classics Renewed: Reception and Innovation in the Latin Poetry of Late Antiquity*. Heidelberg, Winter.
McLean, B. H. (2002) *An Introduction to Greek Epigraphy of the Hellenistic and Roman Periods from Alexander the Great down to the Reign of Constantine (323 BC–AD 337)*. Ann Arbor, University of Michigan Press.
McLynn, N. (2012) "Administrator: Augustine in His Diocese." In M. Vessey (ed.), *A Companion to Augustine*. Chichester, Wiley-Blackwell, 310–22.
Mehmel F. (1940) *Virgil und Apollonius Rhodius: Untersuchungen über die Zeitvorstellung in der antiken epischen Erzählung*. Hamburger Arbeiten zur Altertumswissenschaft 1. Hamburg, Hansischer Gildenverlag.
Meijering, R. (1987) *Literary and Rhetorical Theories in Greek Scholia*. Groningen, Egbert Forsten.
Merrills, A. (ed.) (2004) *Vandals, Romans and Berbers*. Aldershot, Ashgate.
Merrills, A., and R. Miles (2010) *The Vandals*. Chichester, Wiley-Blackwell.
Meyer, D. (2005) *Inszeniertes Lesevergnügen: Das inschriftliche Epigramm und seine Rezeption bei Kallimachos*. Stuttgart, Steiner.
Meyer, D. (2007) "The Act of Reading and the Act of Writing in Hellenistic Epigram." In P. Bing and J. S. Bruss (eds.), 187–210.
Meyer, H. (1991) *Antinoos*. Munich, Fink.
Milewska-Waźbińska, B. (2013) "Waste of Time or Artistic Expression? Notes on *Poesis Artificiosa* of the Modern Era." In J. Kwapisz, D. Petrain, and M. Szymański (eds.), 379–99.
Millar, F. (1977) *The Emperor in the Roman World (31 B.C.–A.D. 337)*. Ithaca, NY, Cornell University Press.
Miller, J. F. (1993) "Ovidian Allusion and the Vocabulary of Memory." *MD* 30: 153–64.
Minissale, F. (1975–6) "Il poeta e la nave. Claud. rapt. Pros. I, 1–14." *Helikon* 15–16: 496–99.
Mitchell, W. J. T. (1994) *Picture Theory: Essays on Verbal and Visual Representation*. Chicago, University of Chicago Press.
Mohrmann, C. (1961) "Das Wortspiel in den Augustinischen Sermones." In *Études sur le latin des Chrétiens*, I. Rome, Edizioni di Storia e Letteratura, 323–49. Reprinted from *Mnemosyne* (1936), ser. III, 3, 33–61.
Mohrmann, C. (1976) "Some Remarks on the Language of Boethius's *Consolatio*." In J. J. O'Meara and B. Naumann (eds.), *Latin Script and Letters A.D. 400–900*. Leiden, Brill.
Mondin, L. (ed.) (1995) *Decimo Magno Ausonio, Epistole*. Venice, Il Cardo.
Moravscik, J. M. E., and P. Temko (eds.) (1982) *Plato on Beauty, Wisdom, and the Arts*. London. Rowman and Littlefield.
Morelli, G. (2009) "Lo *Stomachion* di Archimede nelle testimonianze antiche." *Bollettino di storia delle scienze matematiche* 29: 181–206.
Moreschini, C. (2013) *Storia del pensiero cristiano tardo-antico*. Milan, Bompiani.

Moretti, P. F. (2008) "Proba e il cento nuptialis di Ausonio" In P. Moretti, G. Zanetto, and C. Torre (eds.), *Debita dona: Studi in onore di Isabella Gualandri*, Naples, D'Auria, 317–49.

Moretti, P. F. (2009) "L'*utilitas* della formazione scolastica e la prosa delle *Confessiones*." In F. Gasti and M. Neri (eds.), *Agostino a scuola: Letteratura e didattica*. Pisa, Edizioni ETS.

Morford, M. (1992) "*Iubes Esse Liberos*: Pliny's *Panegyricus* and Liberty." *AJPh* 113: 575–93.

Morgan, T. (1998) *Literate Education in the Hellenistic and Roman Worlds*. Cambridge, Cambridge University Press.

Mosshammer, A. (1990) "Disclosing but not Disclosed: Gregory of Nyssa as Deconstructionist." In H. R. Drobner and C. Klock (eds.), *Studien zu Gregor von Nyssa und der christlichen Spätantike*. Leiden, Brill.

Mratschek, S. (2000) "*Codices vestri nos sumus*: Bücherkult und Bücherpreise in der christlichen Spätantike." In A. Haltenhoff and F.-H. Mutschler (eds.), *Hortus litterarum antiquarum: Festschrift fur Hans Armin Gärtner zum 70. Geburtstag*. Heidelberg, Winter, 369–80.

Mratschek, S. (2002) *Der Briefwechsel des Paulinus von Nola: Kommunikation und soziale Kontakte zwischen christlichen Intellektuellen*. Göttingen, Vandenhoeck and Ruprecht.

Mratschek, S. (2015) "A Living Relic for the Vicar of Rome: Strategies of Visualization in a Civil Case." In L. Van Hoof and P. Van Nuffelen (eds.), *Literature and Society in the Fourth Century AD: Performing Paideia, Constructing the Present, Presenting the Self*. Leiden and Boston, Brill, 134–56.

Müller, L. (1877) *Publilii Optatiani Porfyrii Carmina*. Leipzig, Teubner.

Müller-Rettig, B. (1990) *Der Panegyricus des Jahres 310 auf Konstantin den Grossen*. Stuttgart, Franz Steiner.

Nardo, D. (1966-7) "Varianti e tradizione manoscritta in Ausonio." *Atti dell' Istituto Veneto di scienze, lettere, e arti* 125: 321–82.

Nasrallah, L. S. (2010) *Christian Responses to Roman Art and Architecture: The Second-Century Church amid the Spaces of Empire*. Cambridge, Cambridge University Press.

Neher, A. (2004) "The Concept of *Kunstwollen*." *Word and Image* 20: 41–51.

Nesselrath, H-G. (1990) "Lucian's Introductions." In D. A. Russell (ed.), *Antonine Literature*. Oxford, Oxford University Press, 111–40.

Netz, R., and W. Noel (2007) *The Archimedes Codex: How a Medieval Prayer Book Is Revealing the True Genius of Antiquity's Greatest Scientist*. Philadelphia, Da Capo Press.

Newby, Z., and R. Leader-Newby (eds.) (2007) *Art and Inscriptions in the Ancient World*. Cambridge, Cambridge University Press.

Newlands, C. (1988) "*Naturae mirabor opus*: Ausonius' Challenge to Statius in the *Mosella*." *TAPA* 118: 403–19.

Newlands, C. (2011) *Statius: Silvae II*. Cambridge Greek and Latin Classics. Cambridge, Cambridge University Press.

Newman, J. K. (2011) "The Golden Fleece, Imperial Dream." In T. D. Papanghelis and A. Rengakos (eds.), *Brill's Companion to Apollonius Rhodius*. Leiden, Brill, 413–44.

Nicklas, T. (2008) "Das Christentum der Spätantike: Religion von 'Büchern', nicht (nur) von Texten. Zu einem Aspekt der 'Materialität von Kommunikation.'" *TC* 1: 4–8.

Nisbet, R. G. M. (1978) "Virgil's Fourth Eclogue: Easterns and Westerns." *Bulletin of the Institute of Classical Studies* 25: 59–78.

Nisbet, R. G. M., and M. Hubbard (1970) *A Commentary on Horace's Odes Book 1*. Oxford, Oxford University Press.

Nixon, C. E. V. (1983) "Latin Panegyric in the Tetrarchic and Constantinian Period." In B. Croke and A. M. Emmett (eds.), *History and Historians in Late Antiquity*. Sydney, Pergamon Press, 88–99.

Nixon, C. E. V. (1990) "The Use of the Past by the Gallic Panegyrists." In G. Clarke (ed.), *Reading the Past in Late Antiquity*. New South Wales, Australian National University Press, 1–36.

Nixon, C. E. V. (1993) "Constantinus Oriens Imperator: Propaganda and Panegyric: On Reading Panegyric 7 (307)." *Historia* 42: 229–46.

Nixon, C. E. V., and B. Saylor Rodgers (1994) *In Praise of Later Roman Emperors: The Panegyrici Latini*. The Transformation of the Classical Heritage 21. Los Angeles and Oxford, University of California Press.

Norden, E. (1957) *P. Vergilius Maro Aeneis Buch VI*. 4th ed. Stuttgart, Teubner.

Nordenfalk, C. (1970) *Die spätantiken Zierbuchstaben*. Stockholm, Röder.

Nugent, S. G. (1990) "Ausonius' 'Late-Antique' Poetics and 'Post-modern' Literary Theory." *Ramus* 19.1: 26–50.

Nünlist, R. (2009) *The Ancient Critic at Work: Terms and Concepts of Literary Criticism in Greek Scholia*. Cambridge, Cambridge University Press.

Oberhelman, S. (1991) *Rhetoric and Homiletics in Fourth-Century Christian Literature: Prose Rhythm, Oratorical Style, and Preaching in the Works of Ambrose, Jerome and Augustine*. Atlanta, Scholars Press.

O'Daly, G. J. P. (1991) *The Poetry of Boethius*. Chapel Hill, University of North Carolina Press.

O'Daly, G. J. P. (2004) "'Sunt etiam Musis sua ludicra': Vergil in Ausonius." In R. D. Rees (ed.), *Romane memento: Vergil in the Fourth Century*. London, Duckworth, 141–54.

O'Daly, G. J. P. (2012) *Days Linked by Song: Prudentius' Cathemerinon*. Oxford, Oxford University Press.

O'Daly, G. J. P. (2016) "Prudentius: The Self Definition of a Christian Poet." In S. McGill and J. Pucci (eds.), 221–40.

O'Donnell, J. (1992) *Augustine: Confessions*. 3 vols. Oxford, Oxford University Press.

O'Donnell, J. (2005) *Augustine, Sinner and Saint: A New Biography*. London, Profile Books.

O'Hara, J. D. (1996) *True Names: Vergil and the Tradition of Etymological Wordplay*. Ann Arbor, University of Michigan Press.

Okáčová, M. (2006) "The Aural-Visual 'Symbiosis' in the Poetry of Publilius Optatianus Porfyrius (Towards the Disentanglement of the Mystery of Late-Ancient Expansive Grid-Verse)." In J. Nechutová and I. Radová (eds.), *Laetae segetes: Griechische und lateinische Studien an der Masaryk Universität und Universität Wien*. Brno, Masaryk University, 41–50.

Okáčová, M. (2007) "Publilius Optatianus Porfyrius: Characteristic Features of Late Ancient Figurative Poetics." *SPFFBU* 12: 57–71.

Okáčová, M. (2009a) "*Centones*: Recycled Art or the Embodiment of Absolute Intertextuality?" http://www.kakanien.ac.at/beitr/graeca_latina/MOkacova1.pdf.

Okáčová, M. (2009b) "*Ut Imago Poesis*: A Pastiche of Virgil and Ovid in the Cento *Narcissus*." *Graeco-Latina Brunensia* 14: 177–89.

Okáčová, M. (2010) "Mythological Epyllia Written in the Form of Virgilian Centos: A Model Case of Intertextuality." *Graeco-Latina Brunensia* 15: 139–54.

Oliensis, E. (1997) "Sons and Lovers: Sexuality and Gender in Virgil's Poetry" In Martindale (ed.), 294–311.

Olin, M (1992) *Forms of Representation in Alois Riegl's Theory of Art*. University Park, Pennsylvania State University Press.

Onians, J. (1980) "Abstraction and Imagination in Late Antiquity." *Art History* 3: 1–24.

Onians, J. (1999) *Classical Art and the Cultures of Greece and Rome*. New Haven, CT, Yale University Press.

Opelt, I. (1966) "Etymologie." In *Reallexikon für Antike und Christentum* VI: 797–844.

Osborne, M. J. (1973) "The Stoichedon Style in Theory and Practice." *ZPE* 10: 249–70.
Osborne, R., and A. Pappas (2007) "Writing on Archaic Greek Pottery." In Z. Newby and R. Leader-Newby (eds.), 131–55.
Otten, W., and K. Pollman (eds.) (2007) *Poetry and Exegesis in Premodern Latin Christianity*. Leiden, Brill.
Overbeck, B. (2005) "Das Münchner Medallion Constantins der Großen." *Mitteilungen des Österreichischen Numismatischen Gesellschaft* 45: 1–15.
Pabst, A. (1989) *Symmachus: Reden*. Darmstadt, Wissenschaftliche Buchgesellschaft.
Panofsky, E. (1981) "The Concept of Artistic Volition" (1920). *Critical Inquiry* 8: 17–33.
Panofsky, E. (2008) "On the Relationship of Art History and Art Theory: Towards the Possibility of a Fundamental System of Concepts for a Science of Art" (1925). *Critical Inquiry* 35: 43–71.
Panofsky, E. (2012) "On the Problem of Describing and Interpreting Works of the Visual Arts (1932)." *Critical Inquiry* 38: 467–82.
Paolucci, A. (2006) *Il centone Virgiliano Hippodamia dell'Antologia Latina*. Hildesheim, Olms.
Pappas, A. (2013) "The Treachery of Verbal Images: Viewing the Greek *Technopaegnia*." In J. Kwapisz, D. Petrain, and M. Szymański (eds.), 199–224.
Paschoud, F. (1978) "Une relecture poétique de Rutilius Namatianus." *Museum Helveticum* 35: 319–28.
Pasquali, G. (1951) *Stravaganze quarte e supreme*. Venice, N. Pozza.
Pastorino, A. (ed.) (1971) *Opere di Decimo Magno Ausonio*. With introduction, translation, and commentary. Turin, UTET.
Patillon, M. (2008) *Corpus Rhetoricum: Anonyme, Préambule à la rhétorique; Aphthonios, Progymnasmata; Pseudo-Hermogène, Progymnasmata*. Paris, Les Belles Lettres.
Patillon, M., and G. Bolognesi (eds.) (1997) *Aelius Théon: Progymnasmata*. Paris, Les Belles Lettres.
Pavia, C. (1999) *Guida di Roma sotteranea*. Rome, Gangemi Editore.
Pavlovskis, Z. (1967) "From Statius to Ennodius: A Brief History of Prose Prefaces to Poems." *RIL* 101: 535–67.
Pearce, S. (2008) "The Hinton St Mary Mosaic Pavement: Christ or Emperor?" *Britannia* 39: 193–218.
Pease, A. S. (ed.) (1963) *Cicero, De divinatione*. Darmstadt, Wissenschaftliche Buchgesellschaft. Reprint of the original edition 1920–3.
Peiper, R. (1886) *Decimi Magni Ausonii Burdigalensis Opuscula*. Leipzig, Teubner.
Peirano, I. (2012) *The Rhetoric of the Roman Fake: Latin Pseudepigrapha in Context*. Cambridge, Cambridge University Press.
Pelikan, J. (1971) *The Emergence of the Catholic Tradition (100–600)*. Chicago, University of Chicago Press.
Pelttari, A. (2014) *The Space That Remains: Reading Latin Poetry in Late Antiquity*. Ithaca, NY, Cornell University Press.
Pensabene, P. (1999) "Progetto unitario e reimpiego nell' Arco di Costantino." In P. Pensabene and C. Panella (eds.), *Arco di Costantino: Tra archeologia e archeometria*. Rome, L'Erma di Bretschneider, 13–42.
Pensabene, P., and C. Panella (1993–4) "Reimpiego e progettazione architettonica nei monumenti tardo-antichi di Roma." *Atti della Pontificia Accademia Romana di Archeologia. Rendiconti* 66: 111–283.
Pensabene, P., and C. Panella (1999) *Arco di Costantino: Tra archeologia e archeometria*. Rome, L'Erma di Bretschneider.

Pereira Romero, T. (1993) *Silencio y poesía: La obra de Yves Bonnefoy*. Oviedo, Universidad de Oviedo.
Pergola, P., and P. M. Barbini (1997) *Le catacombe romane: Storia e topografia*. Rome, Carocci.
Perkins, P. (1976) "Irenaeus and the Gnostics: Rhetoric and Composition in *Adversus Haereses* Book One." *VC* 30: 193-200.
Perrelli, R. (1992) *I proemi claudianei tra epica ed epidittica*. Catania, Università di Catania.
Petrain, D. (2014) *Homer in Stone: The Tabulae Iliacae in Their Roman Context*. Cambridge, Cambridge University Press.
Petrone, G. (1988) "Nomen/omen: Poetica e funzione dei nomi (Plauto, Seneca, Petronio)." *Materiali e Discussioni* 20-21: 33-70.
Petrovic, A. (2005) "Kunstvolle Stimme der Steine, sprich! Zur Intermedialität der griechischen epideiktischen Epigramme." *A&A* 51: 30-42.
Pichon, R. (1906) "L'origine du recueil des *Panégyrici Latini*." *Revue des études anciennes* 8: 229-49. Also published in Pichon (1906), *Les derniers écrivains profanes, les panégyristes— Ausone—le Querolus—Rutilius Namatianus*. Paris, Ernest Leroux, 270-91. Translated into English in R. D. Rees (ed.) (2012), *Latin Panegyric. Oxford Readings in Classical Studies*. Oxford, Oxford University Press, 55-74.
Pighi, G. B. (1968) "La metrica Latina." In *Enciclopedia classica Sez.* II, vol. VI, II. Turin, Società Editrice Internazionale.
Pipitone, G. (2011) "Tra Optaziano Porfirio e Venanzio Fortunato: Nota intorno alla lettera a Siagrio." *RET* 1: 119-27.
Pipitone, G. (2012a) "Le epistole in prosa premesse al corpus poetico di Optaziano Porfirio." *RET* 2: 1-12.
Pipitone, G. (2012b) *Dalla figura all'interpretazione: Scoli a Optaziano Porfirio: Testo italiano e latino*. Naples, Loffredo Editore.
Pizzolato, L. F. (1987) *Sant'Ambrogio: Commento al Salmo 118*, I-II. Milan, Biblioteca Ambrosiana; Rome, Città Nuova.
Pizzolato, L. F. (2000) "Ambrogio Grammaticus." *Aevum* 74: 207-22.
Platt, V. J., and M. J. Squire (eds.) (forthcoming) *The Frame in Classical Art: A Cultural History*. Cambridge, Cambridge University Press.
Poeschke, J. (ed.) (1996) *Antike Spolien in der Architektur des Mittelalters und der Renaissance*. Munich, Hirmer.
Polara, G. (1971) *Ricerche sulla tradizione manoscritta di Publilio Optaziano Porfirio*. Salerno, Libreria Internazionale Editrice.
Polara, G. (1973) *Publilii Optatiani Porfyrii Carmina*. 2 vols. Turin, Paraviae.
Polara, G. (1974a) "Cinquant'anni di studi su Optaziano (1922-73), I." *Vichiana* (n.s.) 3: 110-24.
Polara, G. (1974b) "Cinquant'anni di studi su Optaziano (1922-73), II." *Vichiana* (n.s.) 3: 282-301.
Polara, G. (1975) "Cinquant'anni di studi su Optaziano (1922-73), III." *Vichiana* (n.s.) 4: 97-115.
Polara, G. (1983) "Ancora un esempio dell'uso di mixtus per il dio christiano." *Orpheus* 4: 113-15.
Polara, G. (1987) "Optaziano Porfirio tra il calligramma antico e il carme figurato di età medioevale." *Invigilata Lucernis* 9: 163-74.
Polara, G. (1987-8) "Le riprese della poesia figurata nella tarda antichità e nell'alto medioevo latino." *Annali della Facoltà di Lettere e Filosofia dell'Università di Napoli* 30: 339-61.
Polara, G. (1989) "I centoni." In G. Cavallo, P. Fedeli, and A. Giardina (eds.), *Lo spazio letterario di Roma antica* III: *La ricezione del testo*. Rome, Salerno, 245-75.
Polara, G. (1991) "Le parole nella pagina: Grafica e contenuti nei carmi figurati latini." *Vetera Christianorum* 28: 291-336.

Polara, G. (1993) "I distici di Ennodio." In G. Catanzaro and F. Santucci (eds.), *La poesia cristiana latina in distici elegiaci*. Assisi, Accademia properziana del Subasio, 217–39.
Polara, G. (1996) "Le parole nella pagina: Grafica e contenuti nei carmi figurati latini." In M. Marin and M. Girardi (eds.), *Retorica ed esegesi biblica: Il rilievo dei contenuti attraverso le forme*. Bari, Edipuglia, 201–45.
Polara, G. (2004a) *Optaziano Porfirio: Carmi*. Turin, Unione Tipografico-Editrice Torinese.
Polara, G. (2004b) "Commenti di lettore e commenti d'autore." In G. Abbamonte, F. C. Bizzarro, and L. Spina (eds.), *L'ultima parola: L'analisi dei testi: Teorie e pratiche nell'antichità greca e latina*. Naples, Arte Tipografica, 273–87.
Pollmann, K. (2004) "Sex and Salvation in the Virgilian *Cento* of the Fourth Century." In R. D. Rees (ed.), *Romane memento: Vergil in the Fourth Century*. London, Duckworth, 79–96.
Pollmann, K. (2009) "Exegesis without End: Forms, Methods, and Functions of Biblical Commentaries." In P. Rousseau (ed.), *A Companion to Late Antiquity*. Oxford, Wiley-Blackwell, 258–69.
Pollmann, K. (2013) "Authority and Arguments in Christian Poetry of Latin Late Antiquity." *Hermes* 141: 309–33.
Porter, J. (2010) *The Origins of Aesthetic Thought in Ancient Greece: Matter, Sensation and Experience*. Cambridge, Cambridge University Press.
Porter, J. (2011) "Against λεπτότης: Rethinking Hellenistic Aesthetics." In A. Erskine, L. Llewellyn-Jones, and S. Winder (eds.), *Creating a Hellenistic World*. Swansea, Classical Press of Wales, 271–312.
Posani, M. R. (1962) "Reminiscenze di poeti latini nella 'Mosella' di Ausonio." *SIFC* 34: 31–69.
Pozzi, G. (1984) *Poesia per gioco: Prontuario di figure artificiose*. Bologna, Mulino.
Pozzi, G. (2002) *La parola dipinta*. 3rd ed. Milan, Adelphi.
Praz, M. (1970) *Mnemosyne: The Parallel between Literature and the Visual Arts*. Princeton, NJ, Princeton University Press.
Prete, S. (1978) *Decimi Magni Ausonii Burdigalensis Opuscula*. Leipzig, Teubner.
Prieto Domínguez, Ó. (2010) *De alieno nostrum. El centón profano en el mundo griego*. Salamanca, Ediciones Universidad de Salamanca.
Prioux, É. (2007) *Regards alexandrins: Histoire et théorie des arts dans l'épigramme hellénistique*. Leuven, Peeters.
Prioux, É. (2008) *Petits musées en vers: Épigramme et discours sur les collections antiques*. Paris, INHA/CTHS.
Prusac, M. (2012) "The Arch of Constantine: Continuity and Commemoration through Reuse" *Acta ad archaeologiam et atrium historiam pertinentia* 25: 127–58.
Pucci, J. (1998) *The Full-Knowing Reader: Allusion and the Power of the Reader in the Western Literary Tradition*. New Haven, CT, Yale University Press.
Purcell, N. (1995) "Literate Games: Roman Urban Society and the Game of *Alea*." *Past and Present* 147: 3–37.
Purcell, N. (2004) "Literate Games: Roman Urban Society and the Game of *Alea*." In R. Osborne (ed.), *Studies in Ancient Greek and Roman Society*. Cambridge, Cambridge University Press, 177–205.
Putnam, M. (1996) *Virgil's Epic Designs: Ekphrasis in the Aeneid*. New Haven, Yale University Press.
Quilligan, M. (1979) *The Language of Allegory: Defining the Genre*. Ithaca, NY, Cornell University Press.
Rabe, H. (ed.) (1913) *Hermogenis Opera*. Leipzig, Teubner.

Rabe, H. (ed.) (1926) *Aphthonius Progymnasmata*. Leipzig, Teubner.
Rabe, H. (ed.) (1928) *Ioannis Sardiani Commentarium in Aphthonii Progymnasmata*. Leipzig, Teubner.
Raby, F. J. E. (1934) *A History of Secular Latin Poetry in the Middle Ages*. 2 vols. Oxford, Clarendon Press.
Raby, F. J. E. (1957) *A History of Secular Latin Poetry in the Middle Ages*. 2 vols., 2nd edition. Oxford, Clarendon Press.
Raquettius (1905) "De auctore carminis *Pervigilium Veneris* inscripti." *Classical Review* 19: 224–5.
Ravenna, G. (1990) *Le nozze di Polemio e Araneola: Sidonio Apollinare*, Carmina XIV–XV. Bologna, Pàtron.
Reed, J. (2007) *Virgil's Gaze*. Princeton, NJ, Princeton University Press.
Rees, R. D. (2004a) "Praising in Prose: Vergil in the Panegyrics." In R. Rees (ed.), *Romane Memento*. London, Duckworth, 33–46.
Rees, R. D. (ed.) (2004b) Romane Memento: *Vergil in the Fourth Century*. London, Duckworth.
Rees, R. D. (2010a) "The Form and Function of Narrative in Panegyric." In D. H. Berry and A. Erskine (eds.), *Form and Function in Roman Oratory*. Cambridge, Cambridge University Press, 105–121
Rees, R. D. (2010b) "Words of Praise in Roman Politics." *Millennium* 2010: 9–28.
Rees, R. D. (2010c) "*Laudes Domini* and the Rhetoric of Praise." *Quaderni Urbinati di Classica Cultura*: 71–84.
Rees, R. D. (2011a) "Afterwords of Praise." In P. Roche (ed.), *Pliny's Praise: The* Panegyricus *in the Roman World*. Cambridge, Cambridge University Press, 175–88.
Rees, R. D. (2011b) "Nailing Down the Poet: Ausonius' *Cupid Crucified*." In P. Millett, S. Oakley, and R. Thompson (eds.), *Ratio et Res Ipsa: Classical Essays Presented by Former Pupils to James Diggle on His Retirement*. Cambridge, Cambridge Philological Society, 135–50.
Rees, R. D. (2012) "Bright Lights, Big City. Rome and the *Panegyrici Latini*." In G. Kelly and L. Grig (eds.), *Two Romes: From Rome to Constantinople*. Oxford, Oxford University Press, 203–22.
Rees, R. D. (2013a) "Pacatus the Poet Doing Plinian Prose." In R. Gibson and R. Rees (eds.), 241–59.
Rees, R. D. (2013b) "The Look of the Late Antique Emperor and the Art of Praise." In H. Lovatt and C. Vout (eds.), *Epic Visions: Visuality in Greek and Latin Epic and Its Reception*. Cambridge, Cambridge University Press, 99–121.
Relihan, J. C. (1984) "Ovid Metamorphoses I.1–4 and Fulgentius' *Mitologiae*." *American Journal of Philology* 105: 87–90.
Relihan, J. C. (1993) *Ancient Menippean Satire*. Baltimore and London, Johns Hopkins University Press.
Rhee, H. (2005) *Early Christian Literature: Christ and Culture in the Second and Third Centuries*. London, Routledge.
Ricci M. L. (1981) *Claudii Claudiani Phoenix (carm. min. 27)*. Bari, Edipuglia.
Riché, P. (1995) *Éducation et culture dans l'Occident barbare. VIe–VIIIe siècle*. Paris, Seuil.
Riedlberger, P. (2010) *Philologischer, historischer und liturgischer Kommentar zum 8. Buch der Johannis des Goripp, nebst kritischer Edition und Übersetzung*. Groningen, Egbert Forsten.
Riegl, A. (1901) *Die spätrömische Kunst-Industrie nach den Funden in Österreich-Ungarn*, Vienna, K. K. Hof- und Staatsdruckerei.
Riegl, A (1985) *Late Roman Art Industry*. Trans. Rolf Winkes. Rome, G. Bretschneider.

Riese, A. (1870) *Anthologia Latina*, vol. II. Leipzig, Teubner.
Riese, A. (1894) *Anthologia Latina*, vol. I. Leipzig, Teubner.
Riffaterre, M. (1980) "Syllepsis." *Critical Inquiry* 6.4: 625–38.
Rijser, D. (2013) "The Poetics of Inclusion in Servius and Sidonius." In J. A. van Waarden and G. Kelly (eds.), *New Approaches to Sidonius Apollinaris*. Leuven, Peeters, 78–92.
Rimell, V. (2006) *Ovid's Lovers: Desire, Difference and the Poetic Imagination*. Cambridge, Cambridge University Press.
Rispoli, G. M. (1984) "φαντασία ed ἐνάργεια negli scolî all'*Iliade*." *Vichiana* 13: 311–39.
Roberts, C. H., and T. C. Skeat (1983) *The Birth of the Codex*. London, British Academy and Oxford University Press.
Roberts, M. (1980) "Prologue to Avitus' *De Spiritalis Historiae Gestis*: Christian Poetry and Poetic License." *Traditio* 36: 399–407.
Roberts, M. (1984) "The *Mosella* of Ausonius. An Interpretation." *TAPA* 114: 343–53.
Roberts, M. (1988) "The Treatment of Narrative in Late Antique Literature." *Philologus* 182: 181–95.
Roberts, M. (1989a) *The Jeweled Style: Poetry and Poetics in Late Antiquity*. Ithaca, NY, Cornell University Press.
Roberts, M. (1989b) "The Use of Myth in Latin Epithalamia from Statius to Venantius Fortunatus." *TAPA* 119: 321–48.
Roberts, M. (2004) "Vergil and the Gospels: The *Evangeliorum libri IV* of Juvencus." In R. Rees (ed.), *Romane memento: Vergil in the Fourth Century*. London, Duckworth, 47–61.
Roberts, M. (2007) "Bringing Up the Rear: Continuity and Change in the Latin Poetry of Late Antiquity." In W. Verbaal, Y. Maes, and J. Papy (eds.), *Latinitas Perennis I: The Continuity of Latin Literature*. Leiden, Brill, 141–67.
Roberts, M. (2009) *The Humblest Sparrow: The Poetry of Venantius Fortunatus*. Ann Arbor, University of Michigan Press.
Roberts, M. (2010) "Late Roman Elegy." In K. Weisman (ed.), *The Oxford Handbook of the Elegy*. Oxford, Oxford University Press.
Roche, P. A. (ed.) (2011) *Pliny's Praise: The* Panegyricus *in the Roman World*. Cambridge, Cambridge University Press.
Rondholz, A. (2012) *The Versatile Needle: Hosidius Geta's Cento "Medea" and Its Tradition*. Berlin, De Gruyter.
Ronning, C. (2007) *Herrscherpanegyrik unter Trajan und Konstantin*. Tübingen, Mohr Siebeck.
Rorty, R. (ed.) (1967) *The Linguistic Turn: Recent Essays in Philosophical Method*. Chicago and London, University of Chicago Press.
Rosa, F. (1997) (ed., trans., and notes) *Fulgenzio: Commento all'Eneide*. Milan, Luni.
Rosati, G. (1983) *Narciso e Pigmalione: Illusione e spettacolo nelle Metamorfosi di Ovidio*. Florence, Sansoni.
Rose, H. J. (1936) *A Handbook of Latin Literature: From the Earliest Times to the Death of St. Augustine*. London, Methuen.
Ross, D. A. (1975) *Backgrounds to Augustan Poetry: Gallus, Elegy and Rome*. Cambridge, Cambridge University Press.
Rossi, A. (2004) *Contexts of War: Manipulation of Genre in Virgilian Battle Narrative*. Ann Arbor, University of Michigan Press.
Rossi, L. (2001) *The Epigrams Ascribed to Theocritus: A Method of Approach*. Leuven, Peeters.
Rühl, M. (2006) "Panegyrik im Quadrat: Optatian und die intermedialen Tendenzen des spätantiken Herrscherbildes." *Millennium* 3: 75–102.
Russell, D. A. (1983) *Greek Declamation*. Cambridge, Cambridge University Press.

Russell, D. A. (1998) "The Panegyrists and Their Teachers." In M. Whitby (ed.), *The Propaganda of Power: The Role of Panegyric in Late Antiquity*. Leiden, Brill, 17–50.
Russell, D. A. (2006) "Rhetoric and Criticism." In A. Laird (ed.), *Oxford Readings in Ancient Literary Criticism*. Oxford, Oxford University Press, 267–83.
Russell, D. A., and N. G. Wilson (1981) *Menander Rhetor*. Oxford, Oxford University Press.
Rutgers, L. V. (2000) *Subterranean Rome: In Search of the Roots of Christianity in the Catacombs of the Eternal City*. Leuven, Peeters.
Salanitro, G. (1997) "Osidio Geta e la poesia centonaria." *ANRW* 2.34.3: 2314–60.
Salanitro, G. (2007) *Alcesta: Cento Vergilianus*. Catania, Bonanno.
Salzman, M. R., and M. Roberts (2011) *The Letters of Symmachus: Book 1*. Writings from the Greco-Roman World 30. Atlanta, Society of Biblical Literature.
Sandnes, K. O. (2011) *The Gospel "According to Homer and Virgil": Cento and Canon*. Leiden, Brill.
Santelia, S. (2005) "Maioriano-Ercole e Sidonio 'supplex famulus': (Sidon. *carm.* 13)." *AFLB* 48: 189–208.
Santelia, S.(ed.) (2009) *Prospero d'Aquitania, Ad coniugem suam*. In appendice: *Liber epigrammatum*. Naples, Loffredo.
Sarris, P. (2011) *Empires of Faith: The Fall of Rome to the Rise of Islam, 500–700*. Oxford, Oxford University Press.
Saussure, F. de (2011) *Course in General Linguistics*. Trans. W. Baskin, ed. P. Meisel and H. Saussy. New York, Columbia University Press.
Saylor Rodgers, B. S. (1980) "Constantine's Pagan Vision." *Byzantion* 50: 259–78.
Sblendorio Cugusi, M. T. (1980) "Un espediente epigrammatico ricorrente nei *Carmina Latina Epigraphica*: L'uso anfibologico del nome proprio. Con cenni alla tradizione letteraria." *Ann. Fac. Mag. Univ. Cagliari* (n.s.) 4: 258–81.
Sblendorio Cugusi, M. T., and P. Cugusi (2007) "Per un nuovo corpus dei *Carmina Latina Epigraphica*. Materiali e discussioni (con un'appendice sull'usus anfibologico degli idionimi a c. di M. T. Sblendorio Cugusi)." *Atti Accademia Nazionale dei Lincei*, Classe di Scienze Morali, Storiche e Filologiche, Memorie, serie IX, vol. XXII, fasc. I.
Scafoglio, G. (1999) "Intertestualità e contaminazione dei generi letterari nella Mosella di Ausonio." *L'Antiquité Classique* 68: 267–74.
Scafoglio, G. (2004) "La *retractatio* della poesia epica nella Mosella di Ausonio." *Wiener Studien* 117: 151–72.
Scanzo, R. (2006) "Leggere l'immagine, vedere la poesia: *Carmina figurata* dall'antichità a Optaziano e Rabano Mauro, al 'New Dada' e oltre." *Maia* 58: 249–94.
Schaff, P., J. G. Pilkington, and J. G. Cunningham (eds. and trans.) (1886) *The Confessions and Letters of St. Augustin*. Buffalo, Christian Literature.
Schanz, M. (1914) *Geschichte der römischen Literatur: Bis zum Gesetzgebungswerk des Kaisers Justinians (Vieter Teil, erster Band: Die römische Literatur von Constantin bis zum Gesetzgebungswerk Justinians; Die Literatur des vierten Jahrhunderts)*. Munich, Beck.
Scheid, J., and J. Svenbro (1996) *The Craft of Zeus: Myths of Weaving and Fabric*. Cambridge, MA, Harvard University Press.
Scheidegger Lämmle, C. (2015) "Einige Pendenzen: Weben und Text in der antiken Literatur." In H. Harich-Schwarzbauer (ed.), *Weben und Gewebe in der Antike: Materialität—Repräsentation—Episteme*. Oxford, Oxbow, 167–208.
Schenkl, C. (1881) "Lectiones Panegyricae." *Wiener Studien* 3: 118–30.
Schenkl, K. (1888) *Poetae christiani minores*. Corpus scriptorum ecclesiasticorum Latinorum, vol. 16. Milan, Hoepli.

Schierl, P. (2009) "*Tu casti rectique tenax*. Gottes- und Kaiserlob in den *Laudes Domini*." In H. Harich-Schwarzbauer and P. Schierl (eds.), *Lateinische Poesie der Spatantike*. Basel, Schwabe, 129–58.

Schindler, C. (2005) "Claudian's Argonautica." In A. Harder and M. Cuypers (eds.), *Beginning from Apollo: Studies in Apollonius Rhodius and the Argonautic Tradition*. Leuven, Peeters, 107–23.

Schindler, C. (2009) *Per carmina laudes: Untersuchungen zur spätantiken Verspanegyrik von Claudian bis Coripp*. Berlin and New York, de Gruyter.

Schipke, R. (2013) *Das Buch in der Spätantik: Herstellung, Form, Ausstattung und Verbreitung in der westlichen Reichshälfte des Imperium Romanum*. Wiesbaden, Reichert Verlag.

Schlapbach, K. (ed.) (2013) *New Perspectives on Late Antique Spectacula*. Studia Patristica 60. Leuven, Peeters.

Schmid, W. (1960) [Review of Speyer 1959.] *Gnomon* 32, 340–60.

Schmid, W. (2010) *Narratology: An Introduction*. Berlin and New York, de Gruyter.

Schmitz, C. (2004) "Das Orpheus-Thema in Claudians 'De raptu Proserpinae.'" In W.-W. Ehlers, F. Felgentreu, S. Wheeler (eds.), *Aetas Claudianea*. Munich, Saur, 38–56.

Scholz, B. (1998) "*Sub oculos subiecto*: Quintilian on Ekphrasis and Enargeia." In V. Robillard and E. Jongeneel (eds.), *Pictures into Words: Theoretical and Descriptive Approaches to Ekphrasis*. Amsterdam, VU University Press, 73–99.

Schottenius, S. (2010) "Typology and the *Cento* of Proba." *QUCC* 95: 43–51.

Scott, S. (2000) *Art and Society in Fourth-Century Britain: Villa Mosaics in Context*. Oxford, Oxford University School of Archaeology.

Scourfield, J. H. D. (ed.) (2007a) *Texts and Culture in Late Antiquity: Inheritance, Authority and Change*. Swansea, Classical Press of Wales.

Scourfield, J. H. D. (2007b) "Textual Inheritances and Textual Relations in Late Antiquity." In J. H. D. Scourfield (ed.), 1–32.

Searle, J. R. (1975) "Indirect Speech Acts." In P. Cole and J. L. Morgan (eds.), *Syntax and Semantics*, vol. 3: *Speech Acts*. New York, Academic Press, 59–82.

Sedlmayr, H. (2001) "The Quintessence of Riegl's Thought" (1929). In R. Woodfield (ed.), *Framing Formalism: Riegl's Work*. Amsterdam, G and B Arts, 11–32.

Seeck, O. (1888) "Studien zur Geschichte Diocletians und Constantins, I. Die Reden des Eumenius." *Neue Jahrbücher für Philologie und Pädagogik* 137: 713–28.

Seeck, O. (1908) "Das Leben des Dichters Porphyrius." *RM* 63: 267–82.

Segal, C. P. (1969) *Landscape in Ovid's Metamorphoses*. Hermes Einzelschriften 23. Wiesbaden, Steiner.

Settis, S. (1986) "Continuità, distanza, conoscenza. Tre usi dell'antico." In S. Settis (ed.), *Memoria dell' antico*. Turin, Einaudi, 375–486.

Shackleton Bailey, D. R. (1982) *Anthologia Latina*. Stuttgart, Teubner.

Shanzer, D. (1991) "*Arcanum Varronis Iter*: Licentius's Verse Epistle to Augustine." *Recherches Augustiniennes* 37: 110–43.

Shanzer, D. (1994) "The Date and Identity of the Centonist Proba." *Recherches Augustiniennes* 27: 74–96.

Shanzer, D. (1998) "The Date and Literary Context of Ausonius's *Mosella*: Valentinian I's Alamannic Campaigns and an Unnamed Office Holder." *Historia* 47: 204–33.

Shanzer, D. (2005) "Augustine's Disciplines: *Silent diutius Musae Varronis*?" In K. Pollmann and M. Vessey (eds.), *Augustine and the Disciplines*. Oxford, Oxford University Press, 69–112.

Shanzer, D. (2009) "Interpreting the Consolation." In J. Marenbon (ed.), *Cambridge Companion to Boethius*. Cambridge, Cambridge University Press, 228–54.

Shanzer, D. (2012) "Augustine and the Latin Classics." In M. Vessey (ed.), *A Companion to Augustine*. Chichester, Wiley-Blackwell, 161–74.
Shaw, B. (2011) *Sacred Violence: African Christians and Sectarian Hatred in the Age of Augustine*. Cambridge, Cambridge University Press.
Sheppard, A. (2014) *The Poetics of Phantasia: Imagination in Ancient Aesthetics*. London, Bloomsbury.
Shorrock, R. (2011) *The Myth of Paganism: Nonnus, Dionysus and the World of Late Antiquity*. London, Bristol Classical Press.
Simonini, L., and F. Gualdoni (eds.) (1978) *Carmi figurati greci e latini*. Pollenza, La nuova foglio.
Sineri, V. (2011) *Il Centone di Proba*. Acireale, Rome, Bonanno Editore.
Sivan, H. (1990) "Redating Ausonius's *Moselle*." *AJP* 111: 383–94.
Sivan, H. (1992) "The Dedicatory Presentation in Late Antiquity: The Example of Ausonius." *Illinois Classical Studies* 17.1: 83–101.
Small, J. P. (2003) *The Parallel Worlds of Classical Art and Text*. Cambridge, Cambridge University Press.
Smolak, K. (1980) "Der Dichter Theon und die Koliamben des Persius." *WS* 14 (93): 175–86.
Smolak, K. (1989) "Publilius Optatianus Porfyrius." In R. Reinhardt (ed.), *Handbuch der lateinischen Literatur der Antike. Fünfter Band: Restauration und Erneuerung—Die lateinische Literatur von 284 bis 374*. Munich, Beck, 237–43, no. 544.
Socas, F. (2011) "Desguace y restauración de la *Anthologia Latina*." In J. L. Vidal, J. I. García Armendáriz, and A. Egea, 17–49.
Sogno, C. (2006) *Q. Aurelius Symmachus: A Political Biography*. Ann Arbor, University of Michigan Press.
Soler, J. (2005) *Écritures du voyage: Héritages et inventions dans la littérature latine tardive*. Paris, Institut d'Études Augustiniennes.
Spallone, M. (1982) "Il Par. Lat. 10318 (Salmasiano): Dal manoscritto alto-medievale ad una raccolta enciclopedica tardo-antica." *Italia Medioevale e Umanistica* 25: 1–72.
Speyer, W. (1959) *Naucellius und sein Kreis: Studien z. d. Epigrammata Bobiensia*. München, Beck, Zetemata 21.
Spier, J. (2007) *Late Antique and Early Medieval Gems*. Wiesbaden, Reichert.
Sprigath, G. K. (2004) "Das Dictum des Simonides: Der Vergleich von Dichtung und Malerei." *Poetica* 36: 243–80.
Squillante, M. (2005) *Il viaggio, la memoria, il ritorno*. Naples, D'Auria.
Squillante, M. (2012) "La voce degli animali tra onomatopea e imitazione." In P. Alberto Farmhouse and D. Paniagua (eds.), *Ways of Approaching Knowledge in Late Antiquity*. Nordhausen, Traugott Bautz, 144–57.
Squire, M. J. (2009) *Image and Text in Graeco-Roman Antiquity*. Cambridge, Cambridge University Press.
Squire, M. J. (2010a) "Making Myron's Cow Moo? Ecphrastic Epigram and the Poetics of Simulation." *AJP* 131: 589–635.
Squire, M. J. (2010b) "Reading a View: Poem and Picture in the *Greek Anthology*." *Ramus* 39: 73–103.
Squire, M. J. (2011) *The Iliad in a Nutshell: Visualizing Epic on the Tabulae Iliacae*. Oxford, Oxford University Press.
Squire, M. J. (2013a) "Ekphrasis at the Forge and the Forging of Ekphrasis: The 'Shield of Achilles' in Graeco-Roman Word and Image." *Word and Image* 29: 157–91.
Squire, M. J. (2013b) "Apparitions Apparent: Ekphrasis and the Parameters of Vision in the Elder Philostratus's *Imagines*." *Helios* 39: 97–140.

Squire, M. J. (2013c) "Invertire l'*ekphrasis*: L'epigramma ellenistico e la traslazione di parola e immagine." *Estetica: Studi e ricerche* 2013: 109–36.

Squire, M. J. (2013d) "Picturing Words and Wording Pictures: False Closure in the Pompeian Casa degli Epigrammi." In F. Grewing, B. Acosta-Hughes and A. Kirichenko (eds.), *The Door Ajar: False Closure in Greek and Roman Literature and Art*. Heidelberg, Winter, 169–201.

Squire, M. J. (2014) "The *Ordo* of Rhetoric and the Rhetoric of Order." In J. Elsner and M. Meyer (eds.), *Art and Rhetoric in Roman Culture*. Cambridge, Cambridge University Press, 353–417.

Squire, M. J. (2015a) "Patterns of Significance: Publilius Optatianus Porfyrius and the Figurations of Meaning." In R. Green and M. Edwards (eds.), *Images and Texts: Papers in Honour of Professor E. W. Handley, CBE, FBA*. London, Institute of Classical Studies, 87–120.

Squire, M. J. (2015b) "Ecphrasis: Visual and Verbal Interactions in Ancient Greek and Latin Literature." *Oxford Handbooks Online*, DOI: 10.1093/oxfordhb/9780199935390.013.58.

Squire, M. J. (forthcoming a) "'How to Read a Roman Portrait'? Optatian Porfyry, Constantine and the *Vultus Augusti*." *Papers of the British School at Rome* 84: 179–240.

Squire, M. J. (forthcoming b) "Optatian and His Lettered Art: A Kaleidoscopic Lens on Late Antiquity." In M. J. Squire and J. Wienand (eds.).

Squire, M. J., and J. Elsner (forthcoming) "Homer and the Ekphrasists: Text and Picture in the Elder Philostratus's *Scamander* (*Imagines* I.1)." In J. Bintliff and K. Rutter (eds.), *The Archaeology of Greece and Rome: Studies in Honour of Anthony Snodgrass*. Edinburgh, Edinburgh University Press, 57–99.

Squire, M. J., and J. Grethlein (2014) "'Counterfeit in Character but Persuasive in Appearance': Reviewing the *Aingima* of the *Tabula Cebetis*." *Classical Philology* 109: 285–324.

Squire, M. J., and C. L. Whitton (forthcoming) "*Machina sacra*: Optatian's Lettered Art of the Christogram." In I. Garipzanov, C. Goodson, and H. Maguire (eds.), *Graphic Signs of Identity, Faith, and Power in Late Antiquity and the Early Middle Ages*. Turnhout, Brepols.

Squire, M. J., and J. Wienand (eds.) (forthcoming) *Morphogrammata/ The Lettered Art of Optatian: Figuring Cultural Transformations in the Age of Constantine*. Paderborn, W. Fink.

Stanton, G. (2004) "The Early Christian Preference for the Codex." In C. Horton (ed.), *The Earliest Gospels: The Origins and Transmission of the Earliest Christian Gospels: The Contribution of the Chester Beatty Gospel Codex P45*. London, Clark, 40–9.

Starr, R. J. (1987) "The Circulation of Literary Texts in the Roman World." *CQ* 37: 213–23.

Stevens, C. E. (1933) *Sidonius Apollinaris and His Age*. Oxford, Oxford University Press.

Stevenson, J. (1978) *The Catacombs: Rediscovered Monuments of Early Christianity*. London, Thames and Hudson.

Stevenson, T. B. (1983) *Miniature Decoration in the Vatican Virgil: A Study in Late Antique Iconography*. Tübingen, Wasmuth.

Stewart H. F., E. K. Rand, and S. J. Tester (eds.) (1918) *Boethius*. Loeb Classical Library. Cambridge, MA, Harvard University Press.

Stewart, S. (1978) *Nonsense: Aspects of Intertextuality in Folklore and Literature*. Baltimore, Johns Hopkins University Press.

Stirling, L. M. (2005) *The Learned Collector: Mythological Statuettes and Classical Taste in Late Antique Gaul*. Ann Arbor, University of Michigan Press.

Stock, B. (1990) *Listening for the Text: On the Uses of the Past*. Baltimore and London, Johns Hopkins University Press.
Stock, B. (1996) *Augustine the Reader*. Cambridge, MA, Harvard University Press.
Stoehr-Monjou, A. (2013a) "Sidonius and Horace: The Art of Memory." In J. A. van Waarden and G. Kelly (eds.), *New Approaches to Sidonius Apollinaris*. Leuven, Peeters, 133–69.
Stoehr-Monjou, A. (2013b) "Une ekphrasis tardive entre traditions poétique et iconographique: Le char de Médée, symbol du Mal (Dracontius, *Romul*. X, 556–69)." *AntAfr* 49: 161–76.
Stover, T. (2013) *Epic and Empire in Vespasianic Rome*. Oxford, Oxford University Press.
Strodel, S. (2002) *Zur Überlieferung und zum Verständnis der hellenistischen Technopaegnien*. Frankfurt am Main, Peter Lang.
Struck, P. T. (2010) "Allegory and Ascent in Neoplatonism." In R. Copeland and P. T. Struck (eds.), *The Cambridge Companion to Allegory*. Cambridge, Cambridge University Press, 57–70.
Sulzberger, M. (1925) "Le symbole de la croix et les monogrammes de Jésus chez les premiers chrétiens." *Byzantion* 2: 337–448.
Suzawa, Y. (2008) *The Genesis of Early Christian Art: Syncretic Juxtaposition in the Roman World*. Oxford, Archaeopress.
Swain, S., and M. Edwards (eds.) (2007) *Approaching Late Antiquity: The Transformation from Early to Late Empire*. Oxford, Oxford University Press.
Sweeney, E. C. (2006) *Logic, Theology, and Poetry in Boethius, Abelard, and Alan of Lille*. New York, Palgrave Macmillan.
Tambling, J. (2010) *Allegory*. London and New York, Routledge.
Taylor, R. (2009) "Death, the Maiden and the Mirror: Ausonius' Water World." *Arethusa* 42: 181–205.
Thilo, G., and H. Hagen (eds.) (1923–7) *Servii grammatici qui feruntur in Vergilii carmina commentarii*. 2nd edition. 3 vols. Leipzig, Teubner.
Thomas, A. (1998) *Christian Celts: Messages and Images*. Stroud, Tempus.
Thomas, R. (1986) "Virgil's *Georgics* and the Art of Reference." *HSPh* 90: 171–98.
Thomas, R. (1999) *Reading Virgil and His Texts: Studies in Intertextuality*. Ann Arbor, University of Michigan Press.
Thomson, H. J. (1949–53) *Prudentius*. 2 vols. Loeb Classical Library. Cambridge, MA, Harvard University Press.
Thraede, K. (1962) "Epos." *RAC* 5: 983–1042.
Thümmel, H. (1978) "Neilos von Ankyra über die Bilder." *Byzantinische Zeitschrift* 71: 10–21.
Tissol, G. (2002) "Ovid and the Exilic Journey of Rutilius Namatianus." *Arethusa* 35: 435–46.
Tizzoni, M. L. (2014) "Dracontius and the Wider World: Cultural and Intellectual Interconnectedness in Late Fifth Century Vandal North Africa." *Networks and Neighbours* 2: 96–117.
Tkacz, C. (2002) *The Key to the Brescia Casket: Typology and the Early Christian Imagination*. Notre Dame, IN, University of Notre Dame Press.
Tommasi Moreschini, C. O. (2007) "Exegesis by Distorting Pagan Myths in Corippus' Epic Poetry." In W. Otten and K. Pollmann (eds.), *Poetry and Exegesis in Premodern Latin Christianity: The Encounter between Classical and Christian Strategies of Interpretation*. Leiden, Brill, 173–97.
Torelli, M. (1992) "Topografia e iconologia: Arco di Portogallo, *Ara Pacis, Ara Providentiae, Templum Solis*." *Ostraka* 1: 105–31.

Torelli, M. (1993a) "Arco di Portogallo." In E. M. Steinby (ed.), *Lexicon Topographicum Urbis Romae* 1. Rome, Edizioni Quasar, 77–9.
Torelli, M. (1993b) "Arcus Novus." In E. M. Steinby, *Lexicon Topographicum Urbis Romae* 1. Rome, Edizioni Quasar, 101–2.
Tougher, S. (2012) "Reading between the Lines: Julian's *First Panegyric* on Constantius II." In N. Baker-Brian and S. Tougher (eds.), *Emperor and Author: The Writings of Julian the Apostate*. Swansea, Classical Press of Wales, 19–34.
Traina, A. (1999) *Forma e suono. Da Plauto a Pascoli*. Bologna, Pàtron.
Trimpi, W. (1973) "The Meaning of Horace's *ut pictura poesis*." *JWI* 36: 1–34.
Tronzo, W. (1986) *The Via Latina Catacomb: Imitation and Discontinuity in Fourth-Century Roman Painting*. University Park, Pennsylvania State University Press.
Trout, D. (1999) *Paulinus of Nola: Life, Letters, and Poems*. Berkeley, University of California Press.
Trout, D. (2010) "Borrowed Verse and Broken Narrative: Agency, Identity, and the (Bethesda) Sarcophagus of Bassa." In J. Elsner and J. Huskinson (eds.), *Life, Death and Representation: Some New Work on Roman Sarcophagi*. Berlin, de Gruyter, 337–58.
Trout, D. (2016) "Poetry on Stone: Epigram and Audience in Rome." In S. McGill and J. Pucci (eds.), 77–96.
Tueller, M. A. (2008) *Look Who's Talking: Innovations in Voice and Identity in Hellenistic Poetry*. Leuven, Peeters.
Turcan-Verkerk, A.-M. (2003) *Un poète latin chrétien redécouvert: Latinius Pacatus Drepanius, panégyriste de Théodose*. Brussels, Latomus.
Uden, J. (2012) "Love Elegies of Late Antiquity." In *A Companion to Roman Love Elegy*, B. K. Gold (ed.). Hoboken, NJ, Wiley-Blackwell.
Unger, D. J., and J. J. Dillon (eds.) (1992) *Against the Heresies: St Irenaeus of Lyons*. Mahwah, NJ, Newman Press.
Usher, M. D. (1998) *Homeric Stitchings: The Homeric Centos of the Empress Eudocia*. Lanham, Rowman and Littlefied.
Valpy, A. J., et al. (1828) *Panegyrici Veteres*. 3 vols. London, Valpy.
Van Dam, R. (2011) *Remembering Constantine at the Milvian Bridge*. Cambridge, Cambridge University Press.
Van den Broek, R. (1972) *The Myth of the Phoenix according to Classical and Early Christian Traditions* (Études préliminaires aux religions orientales dans l'empire romain 24). Leiden, Brill.
Van der Nat, P. G. (1977) "Zu den Vorraussetzungen der christlichen lateinischen Literatur: Die Zeugnisse von Minucius Felix und Laktanz." In *Christianisme et formes littéraires de l'antiquité tardive en occident*. Entretiens sur l'antiquité classique 23. Vandoeuvres, Fondation Hardt, 191–234.
Vandone, G. (2004) *Appunti su una poetica tardoantica: Ennodio, carm. 1, 7–8 = 26–27V*, Pisa, ETS.
van Hoof, L. (2013) "Performing *Paideia*: Greek Culture as an Instrument for Social Promotion in the Fourth Century AD." *Classical Quarterly* 63: 387–406.
Varner, E. (2014) "Maxentius, Constantine, and Hadrian: Images and the Expropriation of Imperial Identity." In S. Birk, T. M. Kristensen, and P. Poulsen (eds.), *Using Images in Late Antiquity*. Oxford, Oxbow, 48–77.
Varone, A. (1979) *Presenze giudaiche e cristiane a Pompei*. Naples, d'Auria.
Vasaly, A. (1993) *Representations: Images of the World in Ciceronian Oratory*. Berkeley, University of California Press.

Vattimo, G. (2005) "L'età dell'interpretazione." In R. Rorty and G. Vattimo, *Il futuro della religione: Solidarieta, carita, ironia*. Milan, Garzanti, 47–57.
Venuti, M. (2009) "Il prologo delle *Mythologiae* di Fulgenzio. Analisi, traduzione, commento." PhD thesis, Università degli studi di Parma.
Venuti, M. (2011) "Allusioni ovidiane nel prologo delle *Mythologiae* di Fulgenzio." In L. Cristante and S. Ravalico (eds.), *Il calamo della memoria IV: Riuso di testi e mestiere letterario nella tarda antichità*. Trieste, Edizioni Università di Trieste, 51–64.
Venuti, M. (2013) "Fulgenzio e Satira." In L. Cristante and T. Mazzoli (eds.), *Il calamo della memoria V: Riuso di testi e mestiere letterario nella tarda antichità*. Trieste, Edizioni Università di Trieste, 187–98.
Vessey, M. (1998) "The Demise of the Christian Writer." *JECS* 6.3: 377–411.
Vessey, M. (2007) "*Quid facit cum Horatio Hieronymus?* Christian Latin Poetry and Scriptural Poetics." In W. Otten and K. Pollman (eds.), 29–48.
Vessey, M. (2012a) "Augustine among the Writers of the Church." In M. Vessey (ed.), *A Companion to Augustine*. Chichester, Wiley-Blackwell, 240–54.
Vessey, M. (2012b) "The History of the Book: Augustine's *City of God* and Post-Roman Cultural Memory." In J. Wetzel (ed.), *Augustine's City of God: A Critical Guide*. Cambridge, Cambridge University Press, 14–32.
Veyne, P. (1968) "Le carré Sator ou beaucoup de bruit pour rien." *Bulletin de l'Association Guillaume Budé: Lettres d'humanité* 27: 427–60.
Vidal, J. L., J. I. García Armendáriz, and A. Egea (eds.) (2011) *Paulo minora: Estudios sobre poesía latina menor y fragmentaria*. Barcelona, Edicions Universitat de Barcelona.
Vinge, L. (1967) *The Narcissus Theme in West European Literature up to the Early Nineteenth Century*. Lund, Gleerup.
Vogel, F. (1885) *Magni Felicis Ennodi opera*. MGH AA 7. Berlin, Weidmann, Repr. anast., Munich 1981.
Vogt, E. (1966) "Das Akrostichon in der griechischen Literatur." *A&A* 13: 80–95.
Von Albrecht, M. (1989) "Proserpina's Tapestry in Claudian's *De Raptu*: Tradition and Design." *Illinois Classical Studies* 14: 383–90.
von Gonzenbach, V. (1961) *Die römischen Mosaiken der Schweitz*. Basel, Birkhäuser.
von Schönborn, C. (1976) *L'Icône de Christ*. Freiburg, Editions Universitaires Fribourg Suisse.
Wagner, P. (1995) *Reading Iconotexts: From Swift to the French Revolution*. London, Reaktion.
Walbank, F. W. (1985) *Studies in Greek and Roman History and Historiography*. Cambridge, Cambridge University Press.
Walcott, D. (1990) *Omeros*. London, Faber and Faber.
Walde, C. (2006) "Muses." In H. Cancik and H. Schneider (eds.), *Brill's New Pauly*. Brill Online (2014), http://referenceworks.brillonline.com/entries/brill-s-new-pauly/muses-e812670.
Walker, J. (2000) *Rhetoric and Poetics in Antiquity*. Oxford, Oxford University Press.
Walla, M. (1969) *Der Vogel Phoenix in der antiken Literatur und der Dichtung des Laktanz* (Dissertation der Universität Wien 29). Vienna, Notring.
Wallraff, M. (2013) *Sonnenkönig der Spätantike: Die Religionspolitik Konstantins des Großen*. Freiburg im Breisgau, Herder.
Walsh, P. G. (ed.) (1975) *The Poems of St. Paulinus of Nola*. Trans. and annotated. Ancient Christian Writers 40. New York, Newman Press.
Ware, C. (2004) "Claudian: The Epic Poet in the Prefaces." In M. Gale (ed.), *Latin Epic and Didactic Poetry*. Swansea, Classical Press of Wales, 181–201.
Ware, C. (2012) *Claudian and the Roman Epic Tradition*. Cambridge, Cambridge University Press.

Ware, C. (2014) "The *Seueritas* of Constantine: Imperial Virtues in *PL* 7(6) and 6(7)." *JLA* 7.1: 86-109.
Ware, C. (2017, forthcoming) "Speaking of Kings and Battle: Vergil as Prose Panegyrist in Late Antiquity." *PVS*.
Warner, J. C. (2005) *The Augustinian Epic: Petrarch to Milton*. Ann Arbor, Michigan University Press.
Webb, R. (2006) "The *Imagines* as a Fictional Text: *Ekphrasis*, *Apatê* and Illusion." In M. Constantini, F. Graziani, and S. Rolet (eds.), *Le défi de l'art: Philostrate, Callistrate et l'image sophistique*. Rennes, Presses Universitaires de Rennes, 113-36.
Webb, R. (2008) *Demons and Dancers: Performance in Late Antiquity*. Cambridge, MA, Harvard University Press.
Webb, R. (2009) *Ekphrasis, Imagination and Persuasion in Ancient Rhetorical Theory and Practice*. Farnham, Ashgate.
Wedeck, H. E. (1960) "The Catalogue in Late and Medieval Latin Poetry." *Medievalia et Humanistica* 13: 3-16.
Weitzmann, K. (1947) *Illustrations in Roll and Codex*. Princeton, NJ, Princeton University Press.
Weitzmann, K. (1959) *Ancient Book Illumination*. Cambridge, MA, Harvard University Press.
Weitzmann, K. (ed.). (1979) *Age of Spirituality: Late Antique and Early Christian Art, Third to Seventh Century*. New York, Metropolitan Museum of Art.
Westra, H. (1990) "Augustine and Poetic Exegesis." In H. A. Meynell (ed.), *Grace, Politics and Desire: Essays on Augustine*. Calgary, University of Calgary Press, 87-100.
Westra, H. J. (2007) "Augustine and Poetic Exegesis." In Otten and Pollman (ed.,), 9-28.
Wetherbee, W. (1972) *Platonism and Poetry in the Middle Ages*. Princeton, NJ, Princeton University Press.
Wetherbee, W. (1974) *Platonism and Poetry in the Twelfth Century: Literary Influence of the School of Chartres*. Princeton, NJ, Princeton University Press.
Wheeler, S. (2007) "More Roman than the Romans of Rome: Virgilian (Self-)Fashioning in Claudian's *Panegyric for the Consuls Olybrius and Probinus*." In J. H. D. Scourfield, 97-133.
Whitbread, L. G. (trans.) (1971) *Fulgentius the Mythographer*. Columbus, Ohio State University Press.
Whitby, M. (2007) "The Bible Hellenized: Nonnus' *Paraphrase* of St John's Bible and 'Eudocia's' Homeric Centos." In J. H. D. Scourfield (ed.), 195-231.
White, H. G. E. (ed., trans., and notes) (1919) *Ausonius*, vol. I. Cambridge, MA, and London, Loeb Classical Library.
White, H. G. E. (ed., trans., and notes) (1921) *Ausonius*, vol. II. Cambridge, MA, and London, Loeb Classical Library.
White, P. (1974) "The Presentation and the Dedication of the *Silvae* and the *Epigrams*." *JRS* 64: 40-61.
White, P. (1993) *Promised Verse: Poets in the Society of Augustan Rome*. Cambridge, MA, and London, Harvard University Press.
Whitmarsh, T. (ed.) (2008) *The Cambridge Companion to the Greek and Roman Novel*. Cambridge, Cambridge University Press.
Wickhoff, F. (1900) *Roman Art: Some of Its Principles and Their Application to Early Christian Painting*. London: Heinemann.
Wienand, J. (2011) "Ein Abschied in Gold: Konstantin und Sol Invictus." In K. Ehling and G. Weber (eds.), *Konstantin der Große: Zwischen Sol und Christus*. Darmstadt, von Zabern, 53-61.
Wienand, J. (2012a) *Der Kaiser als Sieger: Metamorphosen triumphaler Herrschaft unter Constantin I*. Berlin, Akademie Verlag.

Wienand, J. (2012b) "Die Poesie des Bürgerkriegs: Das constantinische *aureum saeculum* in den *carmina* Optatians." In G. Bonamente, N. Lenski, and R. L. Testa (eds.), *Costantino prima e dopo Costantino*. Bari, Edipuglia, 419–44.
Wienand, J. (2012c) "The Making of an Imperial Dynasty: Optatian's *Carmina Figurata* and the Development of the Constantinian *Domus Divina* (317–26 AD)." *Giornale Italiano di Filologia* 3: 225–65.
Wienand, J., and M. J. Squire (2015) "Tagungsbericht: '*Morphogrammata* and the Lettered Art of Optatian.'" *Bollettino di Studi Latini* 45: 708–13.
Williams, J. (ed.) (1999) *Imaging the Early Medieval Bible*. University Park, Pennsylvania State University Press.
Williams, M. S. (2010) "*Sine Numine Nomina*: Ausonius and the Oulipo." In C. Kelly, R. Flower, and M. S. Williams (eds.), *Unclassical Traditions 1. Alternatives to the Classical Past in Late Antiquity*. Cambridge, Cambridge University Press, 90–105.
Williams, M. S. (2012) "Augustine as a Reader of His Christian Contemporaries." In M. Vessey (ed.), *A Companion to Augustine*. Chichester, Wiley-Blackwell, 227–39.
Williams, M. S. (2013) "Hymns as Acclamations: The Case of Ambrose of Milan." *JLA* 6: 108–34.
Williamson, M. (2010) "'The Mirror-Shield of Knowledge': Classicizing the West Indies." In M. Bradley (ed.), *Classics and Imperialism in the British Empire*. Oxford, Oxford University Press, 77–93.
Wills, J. (1996) *Repetition in Latin Poetry: Figures of Allusion*. New York, Oxford University Press.
Winckelmann, J. J. (2006) *History of the Art of Antiquity*. Los Angeles, The Getty Research Institute.
Wind, E. (2009) "On the Systematics of Artistic Problems" (1925). *Art in Translation* 1: 211–57.
Witke, C. (1971) *Numen Litterarum: The Old and the New in Latin Poetry from Constantine to Gregory the Great*. Leiden and Cologne, Brill.
Wittgenstein, L. (1972) *Philosophical Investigations*. Trans. G. E. M. Anscombe. 3rd ed. Oxford, Blackwell.
Wlosok, A. (1982) "Die Anfänge christlicher Poesie lateinischer Sprache: Laktanzens Gedicht über den Vogel Phoenix." In P. Neukam (ed.), *Information aus der Vergangenheit*. Munich, Bayerischer Schulbuch-Verlag, 129–67.
Wlosok, A. (1989) "L. Caecilius Firmianus Lactantius." In Reinhart Herzog (ed.), *Restauration und Erneuerung: Die lateinische Literatur von 284 bis 374 n. Chr.* Handbuch der lateinischen Literatur der Antike 5. Munich, Beck, 375–404.
Wojaczek, G. (1969) *Daphnis: Untersuchungen zur griechischen Bukolik*. Meisenheim an Glan, Hain.
Wojaczek, G. (1988) "Schlüssel und Schlange: Zwei figurale Texte aus Antike und Mittelalter." *Würzburger Jahrbücher für die Altertumswissenschaft* 14: 241–52.
Wolff, É. (2007) *Rutilius Namatianus: Sur son retour*. Paris, Les Belles Lettres.
Wolff, É. (2008) "Vergil and Fulgentius." *Vergilius* 54: 59–69.
Wolff, É. (ed., trans., and notes) (2009) *Fulgence: Virgile dévoilé*. Villeneuve-d'Ascq, Presses Universitaires du Septentrion.
Wolff, É., and P. Dain (ed., trans., and notes) (2013) *Fulgence: Mythologies*. Villeneuve-d'Ascq, Presses Universitaires du Septentrion.
Wollheim, R. (1980) *Art and Its Objects*. 2nd edition. Cambridge, Cambridge University Press.
Wright, D. (1993) *The Vatican Vergil: A Masterpiece of Late Antique Art*. Berkeley, University of California Press.

Zanker, G. (1981) "Enargeia in the Ancient Criticism of Poetry." *Rheinisches Museum* 124: 297–311.
Zicàri, M. (1959) [Review of Speyer 1959.] *ASNP*: 327–34.
Zimmermann, B. (1998) "Die Codexillustration als neuer Kunstzweig: Spiegel einer geänderten Funktion des Buches in der Spätantike." In L. V. Rutgers, P. W. van der Horst, H. W. Havelaar, and L. M. Teugels (eds.), *The Use of Sacred Books in the Ancient World*. Leuven, Peeters, 263–85.
Zimmermann, B. (2001) "'Illustrierte Prachtcodices': Bücherluxus in der Spätantike." In F. Alto Bauer and N. Zimmermann (eds.), *Epochenwandel? Kunst und Kultur zwischen Antike und Mittelalter*. Mainz, von Zabern, 45–56.
Zupi, M. (2007) *Incanto e incantesimo del dire: Logica e/o mistica nella filosofia del linguaggio di Platone (Cratilo e Sofista) e Gregorio di Nissa (Contro Eunomio)*. Rome, Pontificio Ateneo S. Anselmo.

Index Locorum

Accius
  praet.
    24, 328
    27–8, 333
    28, 322
  tragedy fragments
    32, 332
    168, 323
    239, 333
    298, 319, 333
    390, 332
    414, 318
    475, 318
    538, 320
    588, 322
    593, 319, 333
Achilles Tatius, 3.25.5, 384
Acts of the Apostles
  1:7, 446
  10:34, 437n27
Alcesta, 15, 197
de alea (Riese *AL*), 8, 197
Ambrose
  de excessu fratris Satyri, 2.6, 132
  de obitu Valentiniani, 77, 386
  deus creator omnium, 394n12, 427
  epistulae, 75A.34, 427
  explanatio psalmi 118
    19, 144
    19:13, 388n48
  off., 1.50, 396
  prol., 1, 144
Ammianus Marcellinus

14.1.2, 332
14.1.10, 318
14.6.18, 276n100
26.10.15, 348n19
28.4.14, 276n100, 355n46
31.16.9, 349n24, 349n26
Amos, 6:1-2, 136
de anima (Riese *AL*), 424n2
  1.2 no. 489, 4
Anthologia Latina, 181n25, 182, 199. *see also specific authors and titles*
  de anima (Riese), 1.2 no. 489, 4
  Codex Salmasianus, 4, 181, 195–98
    26 Shackleton Bailey, 198
    78–188 Shackleton Bailey, 197n82, 198
    120 Riese (= 109 Shackleton Bailey), 145
    134 Shackleton Bailey, 198
    135 Shackleton Bailey, 198
    136 Shackleton Bailey, 198
    210 Shackleton Bailey, 198
    259 Shackleton Bailey, 198
    286.69 Riese (= 281.69 Shackleton Bailey), 198n87
    286.98 Riese (= 281.98 Shackleton Bailey), 198n87
  Alcesta, 15 Riese, 197
  de alea, 8 Riese, 197
  de ecclesia, 16 Riese, 197
  Europa, 14 Riese (= 132–3 Shackleton Bailey), 197
  Filager, 137–8 Shackleton Bailey, 198
  Hercules and Antaeus, 12 Riese, 197

Anthologia Latina (cont.)
   Hippodamia, 11 Riese, 197
   Narcissus Cento (*see* Narcissus Cento)
   Narcissus epigrams
     26 Shackleton Bailey, 197
     134–6 Shackleton Bailey, 197–98
     210 Shackleton Bailey, 197
     259–60 Shackleton Bailey, 197
   de paneficiis, 7 Riese, 197
   Procne and Philomela, 13 Riese, 197
Anthologia Palatina
   14, 203
   14.15.21–2, 203n98
   14.15.24–7, 203n98
Anthologia Planudea, 241
Antipater (*Anth. Plan.*), 296, 241
Aphthonius, *progymasmata*, 46n64
   12.1, 379n22, 380n25
Apollodorus mythographus, 3.10.3, 352n36
Apollonius Rhodius, *Argonautica*, 361
   1.1–4, 165–66, 354
   1.4, 354
   1.10–11, 354
   1.151–5, 352n36
Apuleius, *florida*, 248
   3, 248
   9, 249
   15, 249
   16, 249
   18, 249
Arnobius, *aduersus nationes*
   1.19, 396n20
   2.19, 396n20
   3.11, 396n20
   4.1–4, 126n12
   4.32–6, 396n20
Augustine
   de beata uita, 4.35, 428
   de ciuitate Dei, 128, 394
     4.11, 129n32
     5.26, 440
     6.5, 395
     7.22, 129n32
     7.24, 129n32
     11.1, 446
     14.26, 132
     15, 424, 443
     15.8–9, 425
     15.22, 4, 424, 442
     15.45–7, 443
     19.10, 394n12
   confessiones, 2, 396
     1.4.4, 302
     1.10.15, 143
     1.13.22, 433
     1.19.30, 143
     2.2.2, 143
     2.7, 397n22
     2.24, 395
     3.7.14, 428
     4.2.3, 426
     4.27, 395
     5.13.23, 133n65
     6.2.2, 427
     6.6.9, 349n23
     8.5.12, 143
     8.12.29, 143
     9.6.14–17, 427
     9.6.15, 427
     9.10.25, 303
     9.12.32, 394n12
     10.33.50, 431, 445
     10.35.52, 394n12
     11.27.35, 394n12
     52.2, 143
   de dialectica, 135
     5, 126n10
     5–6, 133, 133n66
     6, 127
   de doctrina Christiana
     2.1.1, 126
     2.16.26–2.17.27, 394, 395
     2.40.61, 394n13, 395
     2.44–5, 426n8
     2.87–8, 432
     2.144–7, 433
     3.5.9, 126
     4.3.4, 135
     4.5.8, 133n64, 394n13, 395
     4.7.17, 136
     4.14.30, 394n13, 395
     4.21.45–8, 394n13, 395
     4.65, 435
     4.116, 431
   enarrationes in psalmos
     2, 431
     32, *enarr.* 2, *serm.* 2.5, 431
     102.8, 278

118, *enarr.* 32.8, 435
146.11, 288n21
epistulae
   26, 439
   26.5, 382, 382n35, 439, 444
   27, 440
   31.8, 440
   32, 440
   32.4, 440
   55.18.34, 434
   101.3, 430
   101.4, 431, 437
   164.4, 433
   261.5, 435
expositio epist. ad Romanos,
   26.1–3, 165n39
de Genesi contra Manichaeos, 433
de libero arbitrio, 439
de magistro
   11.36, 302n49
   11.38, 303n51
   14.46, 303n51
de musica, 439
de ordine, 428
   1.2.5, 438
   1.3.8, 438–9
   1.7.20, 439
   1.8.22, 439
   2.4.13, 426
   2.14.39, 429
   2.14.40, 429
   2.14.41, 429
   2.16.44, 301n45
   2.17.45, 426n8
psalmus contra partem Donati, 144, 425, 426n6, 432–38
retractationes, 424, 426, 434, 436n26
   1.6, 430
   1.11, 429
   1.20, 144, 434
sermones, 129n35
   2.8, 431
   96.4.4, 132n53
   105.710, 394n14
   114.2, 132n55
   177.3, 132n53
   216.2.2, 132n53
   274.1, 129n37
   282.1.1, 129n38

   295.3.3, 132n54
   311.5, 438
   314.2, 129n39
   315.5, 129n36
   315.7, 129n36
   318.3, 129n39
   341.7.9, 304
tractatus in euangelium Iohannis
   1.8, 125n2
   2, 75
   24.2, 146
   33.11, 140
   37.4, 143
de utilitate credendi, 7.17, 431n16
Aulus Gellius, 17.21.1, 327n25
Ausonius
   Bissula, 100
      17, 237
   Caesares, 23, 237
   cento nuptialis, 8n27, 93, 178–81, 178n8, 179n17, 202, 252n1
      1, 179
      3, 180
      4, 180
      10–11, 256n20
      18, 237
      20, 180
      20–1, 180
      21, 181
      24–5, 180
      25, 180
      26–7, 180
      31–2, 180
      38–40, 180
      41, 180
      42, 180
      43, 180
      44–5, 180
      praef. 4–5, 169
      praef. 10–11, 256n20, 256n23
      praef. 22, 257n27
   Cupido cruciatus, 193n69
      19, 237
   eclogae, 272n86, 272n89
      1–18, 272, 272n85
      3.60–1, 358
      17, 140
      18, 20n61
      19, 272

Ausonius (*cont.*)
  19–25, 272, 272n85
  21, 20n62
  ephemeris totius diei, 100
  epigrammata
    37, 307
    41, 103, 130n42
    42, 101, 103–4, 130n42
    81, 130n42
    106–7, 198
    108, 198
    108–110, 198
    109, 198
    111–12, 198
    111.2, 130n42
  epistulae
    5a.16, 256n20
    5a.18, 256n20
    6, 102, 104–5, 104n8, 105n10
    6.2, 59n94
    6.4, 105n14
    6.35, 105n10
    6.35–6, 105
    7, 105n11
    8, 102, 105, 105n11
    8.31, 105n11
    8.36, 105n11
    9a, 252n1, 261n38
    9b, 130n44, 261n38
    9b.42–50, 130
    9b.44–6, 306n64
    12.35–7, 264n48
    13, 102, 105–6, 105n11, 272n90
    13.2, 106
    13.4, 106
    13.24, 337
    13.59–62, 139n84
    13.67–70, 106
    14, 105–6
    14a, 106
    14a.3–7, 257n27
    14b, 102, 106
    14b.19, 103n6
    14b.24–35, 106
    14b.48–52, 146
    14b.49, 106
    14b.51, 106
    14b.52, 106
    14b.54, 106
  16, 102, 105–7
  16.5, 130n42
  17, 136
  19a, 252n1
  epitaphia
    12, 19n56, 237
    12.1–8, 130
  fasti, 258n29
  gratiarum actio, 313–14, 335–36
    1.4, 336
    1.5, 316
    2.9, 331, 335
    3.13, 320, 327, 328
    4.19–20, 335
    5, 349n20, 356
    6.28, 335
    11.53, 336, 339
    13.59, 335
    13.61, 335
    13.62, 335, 337
    14.65, 335
    15.68, 336
    16.72, 331, 335
    16.74, 335, 337, 337n43
    17.77, 335
    18.79, 336
    18.81, 335
    65, 356n51
    81, 352
  griphus, 252n1
    15, 237
    67, 335
    praef. 3–4, 257n27
  ludus septem sapientum
    1, 274
    1–2, 269
    2–3, 273
    3–4, 269
    4, 273
    4–5, 273
    5, 273
    5–18, 269
    6, 273
    7 274
    7–9, 273
    9, 274
    10, 275n97
    10–12, 274n94
    11–12, 271

13–18, 274
14, 275n97
16, 270n75, 273
17, 275
18, 269, 275
26, 237
praef., 269–75, 269n67,
    271n78, 272n89
Mosella, 2, 15, 21, 207, 210, 213–20,
    222, 226, 229n54, 232, 258, 307,
    307n70, 377
1, 214, 215, 229
2, 229
2–3, 214
5, 215
5–6, 215
12, 223
12–19, 215
13, 233
19–20, 215
43, 214
47, 215
51, 214
53–4, 215
55, 214
85–140, 139
85–149, 19n54
186–8, 216
187, 216
194–5, 216
208, 214n20
220–39, 217
239, 217n28
261, 219
345–7, 217
349–80, 219
374–7, 218
454–8, 337, 339
483, 215
parentalia, 100, 104
5.3–6, 130
10, 237
11.5–8, 130
17, 101, 104
17.1–2, 101
21.8, 338
25.8, 338
praef. B.4, 338
pater ad filium, 257n27

praefationes uariae (Green), 109, 238
1, 237
3, 255n16
3.9–10, 256
3.11–14, 255n19
3.13–14, 255n19
3.15, 259
3.15–16, 256, 256n24
3.17–20, 257
3.21, 260
3.21–2, 260
3.22, 260
4, 272n87
4.1–9, 282n9
professores, 11, 100, 104, 237, 258
6.52–3, 103n6
7.5–8, 130
14.9, 326
19, 102, 104
19.7, 104
21, 102, 104
protrepticus ad Nepotem, 263–68, 264n48
8, 237
41–4, 267
51–5, 267n60
56–65, 267n60
66–95, 267
96–100, 267
praef., 263–66, 266n54
praef. 1–2, 266
praef. 3–4, 263
praef. 5, 264
praef. 6, 264
praef. 7–8, 265
praef. 17–20, 266
technopaegnion, 19n55, 50, 50n76,
    85–86n135, 85n135, 89n145, 143,
    258n29, 269, 271n81
25, 237
praef., 269n67
praef. 10–11, 274n95
Avitus of Vienne
de spiritalis historiae gestis, 397
202.10–12, 397n25
de uirginitate, 275.9–12, 397

Bede, *de arte metrica* (Keil *GL*)
7.1.22.257 = CChr 123A.1.136–7, 112n21
7.258, 27n15

Bernardus Cluniacensis, *de contemptu mundi*, 1.952, 306n61
Besantinus, alter (Palatine Anthology)
   15.25, 38, 41
   15.25.7, 38n47
Boethius
   consolatio philosophiae, 101, 391–93, 400–423, 403n43
     1.m1, 401
     1.m1.1, 409n57
     1.m1.2, 409n57
     1.m1.2–4, 409n57
     1.m2, 401, 406
     1.m3, 401
     1.m3.8, 402
     1.m5.46–8, 413n67
     1.m6.20–3, 413
     1.m7, 402
     1.p1, 406
     1.p1.1, 409n57, 422n83
     1.p1.2, 401
     1.p1.22–5, 391n4
     1.p1.26–41, 5n11
     1.p1.32–3, 401
     1.p1.39–41, 401
     1.p1.40, 406
     1.p1.40–1, 401
     1.p2.1–2, 409n57
     1.p3.1, 422n83
     1.p4.1, 413
     1.p4.18–21, 412
     1.p4.25–7, 413
     1.p4.28–9, 413
     1.p4.45, 413
     1.p4.120–3, 412
     1.p4.149–54, 412
     1.p4.152, 413
     1.p5.36, 413
     2, 414
     2.m8, 414
     2.m8.14–15, 414
     2.m8.16–18, 414
     2.m8.21–7, 414
     2.m8.29–30, 414
     3, 409
     3.m1–3m5, 408n55
     3.m1.5–6, 408
     3.m1.13, 408
     3.m7, 408n55
     3.m9, 408n55
     3.m10, 408n55
     3.m11.1–5, 410n60, 419
     3.m11.9–12, 407
     3.m11.15–16, 406
     3.m12, 408, 408n55, 409n55, 419
     3.m12.1–4, 409n57
     3.m12.7, 409n57
     3.m12.15–17, 409n57
     3.m12.18, 409n57
     3.m12.47–8, 414
     3.m12.49–54, 409n58
     3.m12.51, 419
     3.m12.52, 419
     3.m12.52–8, 419
     3.m12.57–8, 409, 419
     3.p1.1–2, 407n54
     3.p1.1–9, 407
     3.p1.5, 407
     3.p1.5–6, 407
     3.p1.9, 407
     3.p1.13–14, 408
     3.p1.15, 407
     3.p1.16, 407
     3.p8.1, 422n83
     3.p10.1, 422n83
     3.p12, 421
     3.p12.11–12, 421
     3.p12.63–4, 421
     3.p12.66, 421
     3.p12.67, 421
     3.p12.69–70, 408
     4, 418
     4.m6, 413, 414
     4.m6.17, 413
     4.m6.18–20, 417
     4.m6.20–2, 413
     4.m6.34–48, 413
     4.m6.44, 413
     4.m7, 416
     4.p1.1, 407n54
     4.p2.98–101, 418
     4.p4.106, 419
     4.p4.108, 419
     4.p4.142, 417
     4.p4.149–54, 417
     4.p4.150, 417
     4.p4.151, 417
     4.p6, 415

4.p6.1, 422n83
4.p6.6, 407n54
4.p6.27–9, 414n68
4.p6.57, 407n54
4.p6.58–60, 418
4.p6.65–82, 418
4.p6.78–80, 415
4.p7.17–39, 416
4.p7.21–3, 416
4.p7.22, 417
4.p7.44–5, 416
4.p7.47–9, 416
5, 418
5.m2.2–7, 418
5.m2.7, 418
5.m3, 414
5.m3.1–5, 418
5.m3.2–3, 414
5.m3.6, 414
5.m3.8–10, 414
5.p1.1, 422n83
5.p2.1–5, 414
5.p3, 418
5.p3.73–8, 415
5.p3.92, 415
5.p3.92–4, 418
5.p3.101–7, 415
5.p3.107–10, 415
5.p4.47–54, 415
5.p4.75–7, 418n73
5.p6, 402–3, 403n40
5.p6.166–7, 402
5.p6.166–76, 402
5.p6.167, 402
5.p6.169–70, 402
5.p6.170–2, 402
5.p6.171, 402
5.p6.172, 402, 402n39
5.p6.173–4, 402
5.p6.175, 402
5.p6.175–6, 402
de institutione musica, 1.34, 431n17
prosimetra, 100

Callistratus, *Iou.*, 4–8, 350n29
Calpurnius, *eclogae*
   5.10, 334
   5.20, 325
Carmina Latina Epigraphica, 1504, 115

Catullus
   1, 273n91
   1.1, 272, 272n90
   1.1–3, 281
   1.4, 273n91
   3.8, 275n96
   14b.1, 180n17
   14b.1–2, 273
   29.15, 336
   36, 281n7
   61.49, 319, 333
   61.51, 331
   63.39, 322
   64, 152–53, 363n72
   64.2, 362
   64.6, 240
   64.11, 240, 363n72
   64.71, 337
   64.98, 338
   64.130–4, 152
   64.143, 152
   64.165, 337
   64.341, 323
Chromatius of Aquileia, *sermones*, 8.4 (*CCL* 9A.36.83–4), 386
Cicero
   Aratea, 96, 328
   pro Archia
      20, 356n49
      22, 356n49
   Brutus, 62, 349n26
   pro Caecina, 342
   in Catilinam, 426n8
   de diuinatione
      1.44, 328, 333
      2.111, 145
   epistulae ad Atticum, 1.14.3, 271
   de inuentione, 2.51, 324
   pro lege Manilia, 342
      22–3, 366n80
   de natura deorum, 1.16.42, 396n20
   de oratore
      1.70, 349n23
      2.98, 326n25
      2.341, 347n9
      3.67, 326n25
      42, 133n63
      49.163, 132
      65, 140

Cicero (*cont.*)
    65–6, 349n26
    91.72–3, 314
    91.102, 314
  pro Sestio
    56.119, 327n25
    102, 323
  Tusculanae disputationes
    2.8.20, 338
    5.49, 319, 359n60
Claudian
  de bello Getico, 236n4, 360n64
    1–2, 364
    1–3, 361
    1–4, 246
    2, 361
    6, 362
    11–14, 361
    13, 364n77
    14–15, 349n25, 362
    21, 362, 365
    24–5, 362
    27, 362
    27–8, 366
    31–5, 362
    36–7, 364
    37, 363
    38–9, 364
    134–5, 364
    160, 364
    174–93, 363n70
    225–6, 366
    442, 360n64
    571, 366
    604–8, 366
    635, 367
  de bello Gildonico, 246n16
  carmina min.
    25, 123n49
    26, 119
    27.1, 380
    27.1–6, 376
    27.4–6, 389n52
    27.8, 385
    27.17–22, 379
    27.31–5, 377
    27.37–9, 377n13
    27.49–50, 380
    27.50–2, 389n52
    27.50–4, 377
    27.52–5, 381
    27.62–3, 377
    27.76, 385
    27.76–82, 384
    27.80, 385
    27.82, 385
    27.83–8, 377, 385
    27.101, 389n52
    31, 246–47
    41, 108n18
    50, 246
  de consulatu Stilichonis, 360n64
    2.418–19, 385n40
    3, 236n4
  epistula ad Serenam (*carm. min.* 31 Hall), 246–47
  epithalamium dictum Honorio, 123n49, 385n39
    10, 236n4
    87–9, 142n96
  in Eutropium 1 (Hall), 238
  in Eutropium 2 (Hall), 238
    20, 236n4
  fescennini, 100
  in Iacobum (*carm. min.* 50 Hall), 246
  laus Serenae, 360
    160, 360
  panegyricus dictus Honorio cos. III (Hall), 239
    7, 236n4
  panegyricus dictus Honorio cos. IV, 132–6, 368
  panegyricus dictus Honorio cos. VI (Hall), 28, 236n4
  panegyricus dictus Olybrio et Probino coss., 108n18
  panegyricus dictus Mallio Theodoro cos. (Hall), 17, 236n4
  de raptu Proserpinae 1, 238, 247–48, 251
    1.35–6, 226
    1.63–5, 223
    1.64, 226
    1.76, 226
    1.88, 226
    1.93, 226
    1.141–7, 224

Index Locorum   499

1.142–52, 381
1.146, 226
1.153, 381
1.161–6, 381
1.197–201, 224n41
1.246–72, 247
1.248, 224
1.248–65, 224
1.249, 224
1.250, 224
1.251, 224, 225, 226
1.252, 224
1.254, 224
1.257, 225
1.265–7, 247
1.271, 225n43
praef., 239–42
praef. 1–12, 221
de raptu Proserpinae 2, 238, 239, 242–51
2.10, 226
2.21.140–7, 245
2.25.1–4, 246
2.119, 222, 226
2.131–5, 224
2.137, 222
2.207, 226
2.216, 226
2.219, 226
2.220, 226
2.230, 226
2.231, 226
2.234, 226
2.237, 226
2.238, 226
2.246, 226
2.250, 159n28
2.251, 226
2.254–5, 226
2.265, 226
2.277–93, 222
2.284, 223
praef., 242–50
de raptu Proserpinae 3, 238
3.153–6, 225
3.156, 225n43
3.157–8, 225
in Rufinum
1.3, 236n4

1.259, 247
1.282, 360n64
2.5, 236n4
2.501, 332
Claudius Marius Victorius, *alethia*, 377n15
1.237–42, 380n24
Clement of Alexandria, *paed.*,
3.11.59.2, 74n115
Codex Augustaneus 9
Guelferbytanus, 74n115
Folio 5r, 33n35, 34
Codex Latinus, 3225, 48n73
Folio 4^{lr}, 50
Codex Parisinus
7558 IX saec, 113
7806, 74n115
Codex Petropolitanus, Gr. 216, Folio
345v, 72n108
Codex Salmasianus. *see Anthologia Latina*
Colossians, 1:15, 51
Commodianus, *instr.*
6.15, 396n20
8.10–12, 396n20
17.1, 396n20
29.12, 396n20
29.14, 396n20
concilium uasense, 399
Constantine, *epistulae*
2, 84
9, 49n75, 85
10, 48n70
11, 35n39
14, 85
1 Corinthians, 8:10, 396n21
Corippus
Iohannis
8.117–8, 159
8.120–3, 160
8.133–6, 160
praef. 1–15, 165
Iust.
1.7–13, 5n11
1.349–52, 384n37
Corpus Inscriptionum Latinarum VI,
1756b.3, 131
Q. Curtius Rufus, 7.5.29, 357n54
Cyprianus Gallus, *heptateuchos*, 102–3,
114–15. *see also specific books*

Cyprianus Gallus, *heptateuchos*, (*cont.*)
    1098–1103, 142
    Deuteronomy, 152–278, 115, 115n27
    Exodus, 507–42, 115, 115n27
    Numbers, 557–67, 115, 115n27

Deuteronomy
    10:19, 437n27
    21:23, 165n39
    31:30, 115, 115n27
    32.1–43, 115, 115n27
Donatus, *Vita Vergilii*, 1.2.19–25, 346n5
Dosiadas, alter (Palatine Anthology),
    15.26, 38
Dracontius
    de laudibus Dei
        1.241–5, 383
        2.208–44, 383
    Romulea
        8.16–23, 165
        10.562–6, 160–161, 163

de ecclesia (Riese *AL*), 16, 197
Ennius
    annales, 355
        1.1, 320
        1.34, 331
        15.392, 330
        54–5, 354
        285, 338
        380, 319
        446, 318
        446–7, 331
        457–8, 360
        541, 318
    epigrammata, 5.21, 359n58
    fragments, 21, 319, 321
    Medea exul
        208–14, 363n72
        212–213, 354n44
    Quintus Ennius fecit (*Inc.* 53
        Vahlen), 145
    tragedies
        111, 319
        171, 319, 333
        270, 319, 333

Ennodius
    carmina

1.4 = 388 V, 102, 123–24
1.4.1–24, 123
1.4.25–8, 123
1.4.29–52, 123
1.4.53–122, 123
1.7 = 26 V, 102, 121–23, 124
1.7.1–10, 122
1.7.1–32, 121
1.7.11–20, 122
1.7.21–30, 122
1.7.31–2, 122
1.7.33–44, 121, 122
1.7.45–8, 121, 122
1.7.49–68, 122
1.7.69–80, 122
epistulae
    2.6, 398
    5.7 = 219 V, 121
    5.8 = 224 V, 102, 119–20
    5.8.13–14, 119
    7.28 = 361 V, 121
    7.29 = 362 V, 102, 120–21
    7.29.1, 120
    7.29.2–3, 120
    7.29.3–4, 121
    7.29.4, 120
    7.29.5, 121
    7.29.7, 120
    8.21 = 398 V.1–3, 120n41
    8.29 = 406 V, 120n41
    8.29 = 406 V.2, 121
    9.1, 398
    9.9, 398n30
eucharisticum opusc. 5, 398
epigrammata Bobiensia 70, 102, 103n4, 108
Europa (Riese *AL*), 14 (= 132–3 Shackleton
    Bailey *AL*), 197, 198
Eusebius
    chronica
        329, 32, 32n30
        330, 97, 97n166
    historia ecclesiastica, 9.9.10–11, 70n104
    Tricennial Oration, chapters 9–10
        (=Heikel 1902: 217–23), 70n104
    uita Constantini, 14n35
        1.28–32, 70n104
Eutropius, 10.18.3, 349n26
Exodus
    15:1, 115

Index Locorum 501

15:1–17, 115n27
15:1–18, 115
28:17–20, 142
Exultet, 425
Ezechiel, *exagoge*, 265–9, 384, 384n37

Filager (Shackleton Bailey *AL*), 137–8, 198
Fortunatus, *Vita Martini*, 1.176, 389
Fronto
    2.17.2, 347n11
    3.17.2, 314n6, 347
Fulgentius
    de aetatibus mundi et hominis
        129–130.16-1, 293
        129.1-7, 289
        129.10-15, 292
        129.20, 294
    expositio Virgilianae continentiae, 14, 14n36, 165
        83.1-4, 288, 288n19
        83.4-7, 292
        83.6-12, 290
        84.17-19, 290
    mythologiae, 298
        3.3-10, 290
        4-5, 294
        4.14, 294
        6-7.22-4, 295
        7-1, 294
        10-11, 297n37, 302
        10.8 19, 302
        10.11-12, 296
        10.12-13, 296, 297
        10.14, 296
        10.17-18, 297
        11-12.18-2, 301n46, 302
        11.15-18, 295
        12.3-4, 296n33
        12.12, 296n33
        15.1-2, 296n33
        19.18, 297n37, 302
        54.9, 296n33
        74.8-9, 296n33
        78.18-20, 296n33

Genesis
    1:3, 127
    1:6, 127
    1:9, 127

    2:19, 127
    6:2, 443
    16:11, 129n33
    17:19, 129n33
Germanicus, 604, 333
Gregory of Tours, *de cursu stellarum*
    12, 373n3
    14, 115
Gregory the Great, letter to Serenus, 52, 52n80
Guillaume Apollinaire, "Reconnais-toi", 39

heptateuchos. see Cyprianus Gallus, *heptateuchos*
Hercules and Antaeus (Riese *AL*), 12, 197
Hermogenes, *Types of Style*, 2.10.3.89, 347n7
Herodotus, 6.95.1, 352n37
Hesiod
    opera et dies, 232–5, 317
    theogonia
        26–8, 348n17
        27–8, 406n53
Hieronymus. see Jerome
Hilary of Arles, *AL* 487, 102, 115
Hilary of Poitiers, *hymni*
    1, 144n102
    2, 144n102
Hippodamia (Riese *AL*), 11, 197
historia Augusta. see *scriptores historiae Augustae*
Homer
    Iliad
        1.1, 285
        5.85-8, 318
        6.201-2, 352n37
        18.478-608, 190
    Odyssey
        1.1, 285
        9.288-94, 166
        11.206-7, 191
        12.70, 240
        19.107-114, 317
Homeric Hymn to Demeter, 241, 251
Horace
    ars poetica
        38-9, 125n1
        73-4, 346n3
        85, 112n22
        361, 45
        452, 271

Horace (*cont.*)
  carmina
    1.1, 114, 238
    1.3.25–6, 362n68
    1.4.3.7, 320
    1.4.7, 320
    1.9.17, 332, 335
    1.14, 322n20
    1.17.14, 337
    1.17.15, 335
    2.1.12, 333n35
    2.1.22, 321
    2.3, 104–5
    2.3.1–2, 105n10
    2.3.15–16, 104n8
    2.5.7, 337
    2.10.5, 335
    2.15, 365n79
    3.24, 365
    3.24.9–13, 365
    3.24.40–1, 365
    3.24.51–4, 365
    3.30, 114
    3.30.1–2, 307n69
    4.4.41, 331
    4.8.29, 320
    4.9.17–18, 323
    4.9.21, 286n15
  epistulae
    1.1.18, 337
    1.1.28, 352n36
    1.3, 106n16
    1.4.1, 270n75
    1.19.49, 339
    1.20, 259
    2.1.225, 335
    16.53–4, 318
  epodi, 238
    2.1, 114
    7.8, 328
    17.18, 337
  saturae, 270n75
    1.2.90, 352n36
    1.4.72, 334
    1.10.29, 104
    1.10.31–5, 104
    2.2.132, 335, 337
    2.5.59, 415
Hosidius Geta, *Medea* (Riese *AL*), 17, 195, 197

Hrabanus Maurus, *in honorem sanctae crucis*, 27n15
Hyginus, *fabulae*, 22.2, 354n44

Inscriptiones Christianae Vrbis Romae 6.14076, 131n49
Irenaeus, *aduersus haereses*
  1.8.1, 93
  1.9.4, 93
Isaiah, 7:14, 129n33
Isidorus of Seville, *origines*, 1.29, 127n19
Isocrates, *Europe*, 8–10, 345n2

Jerome
  chronica, 324, 326
  epistulae
    20, 136n75
    21.4, 396n21
    21.9, 396
    22.29.7, 396n21
    22.30, 5n13, 18n50
    22.30.4, 396n21
    25, 136n75
    26, 136n75
    30, 136n75
    30.5, 144
    30.13, 135
    34, 136n75
    53, 179n17
    53.7, 95n161
    58.8–11, 399
  Galatians, 3, 396
  in psalm 114.4, 136n75
  in Hieremiam prophetam (*PL* 25.787–9), 136n75
  Job, 432
  de nominibus Hebraicis (*PL* 23.771–858), 136n75
  de situ et nominibus locorum Hebraicorum (*PL* 23.859–928), 136n75
Job, 432
John. *see also* Augustine, *tractatus in euangelium Iohannis*
  1:14, 51
Joshua, 114
Josiah, 129n33
Judges, 114

Julian, *ep.*, 31, 349n26
Justin Maryr, *Apologia*, 1.55, 74n115
Juvenal, *saturae*
    1.10–11, 355n45
    2.38, 174
    8.261, 338
    10.174, 352, 352n39
Juvencus, *libri euangeliorum*, 344, 390n55
    1.25–7, 5n11
    4.568, 156
    4.588–9, 156
    praef. 9–10, 156, 165
3 Kings, 13:2, 129n33

Lactantius
    de aue phoenice, 373–90, 378n19
        1, 376, 380
        1–8, 375
        1–30, 378
        4, 376
        5–8, 380
        8, 376
        21–4, 381
        25, 380
        27–8, 381
        31–58, 378
        34, 377n13
        35–50, 381
        38, 381n31
        39–50, 381
        46, 389
        47–8, 382
        47–50, 377n13
        50, 382
        51–4, 381
        55–6, 381
        57, 381
        63, 381
        79–88, 378, 379
        93, 386n43
        99, 377n13
        107–8, 377n13
        121, 378
        123, 389
        123–50, 378
        124, 379
        125, 379
        130–1, 379
        135–7, 379
        141, 379
        143–6, 377n13
        149, 379
        150, 379
        151, 389
        155–60, 384
        156, 386
        157, 386
        158, 386
        159, 386
        159–60, 386
        161–4, 377, 387
        163, 387n44
        164, 387
        165, 388
        165–70, 377, 388
        166–8, 388
    institutiones diuinae, 382n34
        1.5.8, 394
        1.5.11–14, 394
        1.5.14, 394
        1.9.8–10, 394n11
        1.11.23–5, 394n11
        1.11.30, 394, 394n11
        1.11.36, 394n11
        1.19.5, 394n11
        1.21.44, 394n11
        2.10.12, 394
        2.12.15, 382
        5.1.10, 394
        5.5.1–2, 394
        6.23.37, 387, 387n47
        7.22.1–4, 394
        7.24.7, 174n48
    de mortibus persecutorum,
        44.5, 72n111
    de opificio Dei, 373
Laevius, *pterygium phoenicis*, 38
laus Pisonis, 22–4, 356n49
Leda (Shackleton Bailey *AL*), 129–31, 198
Leo Grammaticus 257, 14n37
Livy
    5.5.2, 318
    6.41.6, 318n14
    24.16.10, 318n14
    38.49.7, 318
    praef., 348n19
Lucan
    1.18, 332

504 Index Locorum

1.53, 337
1.86, 329
1.367, 333
1.647, 318
2.79, 324
3.316, 318, 333
3.474, 337
3.613, 337
3.662, 333
4.76, 318
4.428, 323
4.553, 318, 333
4.559, 325
5.23, 332
5.321, 159
5.357–8, 160
5.363–4, 160
5.628, 332
5.1070, 332
6.192, 330
6.400–1, 363n72
8.526, 318
9.435, 318
9.587, 328
10.132, 318
10.231, 318
10.250, 337
10.429, 325
Lucian
　Dionysus, 250
　Heracles, 250
Lucilius
　101, 331
　1377, 333
Lucretius, *de rerum natura*
　1.55, 320
　1.164, 318
　1.196–7, 91, 145n108
　1.230, 324
　1.275, 323
　1.282, 318
　1.301, 332
　1.945–7, 407n54
　2.49, 317
　2.195, 337
　2.199, 338
　2.328, 338
　2.682–92, 91
　2.682–99, 145n108
　2.976, 331

2.1168, 325
3.1–3, 353
3.189, 332
3.345, 328
3.740, 328
4.213, 322
4.975, 332
4.1083, 322, 327, 333
5.217, 323
5.229, 338
5.251, 323
5.295, 328
5.737–47, 320
5.742, 323
5.747, 338
5.1235, 321
5.1411, 318, 333
5.1427, 318, 333
5.1442, 319
6.155, 338
6.283, 328
6.428, 323
6.548, 332
6.719, 323
6.730, 323
6.1130, 318
Luke
　1:20, 289n22
　23:46, 386n43
Luxorius
　epigram for Hilderic (Riese *AL*), 203
　　(= 194 Shackleton Bailey *AL*), 181n26
　epithalamium Fridi (Shackleton Bailey *AL*)
　　282–370, 197
　　370.61–6, 197

Macrobius, *Saturnalia*, 165–68, 170, 355
　1.17.14, 358n55
　5.1.5, 356n48
　5.3.16, 168
　5.13.17, 166
　5.18.1, 167
　6.1.2, 166
　6.1.6, 167
Manilius
　3.367, 317, 333, 335
　4.581, 339
Martial
　8.76.1, 285n14

11.1.14, 180n17
epistulae
   1.3.3, 259n33
   1.3.4, 259n33
   1.3.9–12, 258
Martianus Capella, 2.125, 123
Matthew, 155
   6:10, 413n67
   16:18–19, 129
Mavortius, *Judgement of Paris* (Riese *AL*), 10, 197
Menander Rhetor, *basilikos logos*, 314, 314n4
   368, 326
   374, 314, 330n27, 340n47
Minucius Felix, *Octauius*, 23.1, 355n47
Modestus, 29.1.11, 327n25

Naevius
   carmina fragment, 14.17, 332
   comedy fragment, 111, 337
Narcissus Cento (Riese *AL*)
   9, 182–204
   9.1, 200n89, 203
   9.2, 185, 188, 193, 194, 195, 200n89, 201
   9.3, 184, 194, 195, 201
   9.4, 184, 186, 187, 191, 195, 201
   9.5, 185, 187, 188, 192, 195, 196, 200n89, 201
   9.6, 189, 190, 192, 199, 200, 200n89, 201
   9.7, 184, 195, 199, 201
   9.8, 187, 200, 201
   9.9, 188, 192, 200, 201
   9.10, 186, 188, 201
   9.11, 183n33, 185, 188, 195, 203
   9.12, 189, 190, 199, 200
   9.13, 183n33, 183n34, 188, 196, 199, 200n89
   9.14, 188, 192, 194, 195
   9.15, 187, 188, 191, 193, 201
   9.15–16, 199, 200
   9.16, 185, 190, 191, 193, 200, 201
Narcissus epigrams (Shackleton Bailey *AL*)
   26, 197
   134–6, 197–98
   210, 197
   259–60, 197
Nemesianus, *cynegetica*, 268, 356n51
Nicaean Creed, 71
Nikolaus, *progymnasmata* (Felten 1913), 46n64

Numbers
   21:17, 115, 115n27
   21:18, 115, 115n27

de obitu Baebiani, 102–3, 113–14, 124
   21–40, 113
   41–60, 113
   61–100, 113
   101–32, 114
Optatian
   carmina, 27
   1–3, 31n26
   1–20, 29n22
   1.1, 31, 85
   1.3–5, 32
   1.7, 35n36
   1.7–8, 33
   1.17, 33n33
   2, 42, 43
   2.11–12, 32
   2.12–18, 29n21
   2.31, 32
   2.ii, 33n33
   3, 33n35, 34, 42, 43, 93n159
   3.12, 33n33
   3.15, 33n33, 84n131
   3.17–18, 84n131
   3.18, 33n33
   3.24, 49n75, 84
   3.28–9, 75, 84n131
   3.30, 48n70
   3.33, 35n36
   3.35, 33n33, 84n131, 85n135
   3.iii, 84n131, 85n135
   3.i–ii, 33n34
   3.iii–iv, 33, 33n33, 33n34
   3.iv, 35n36
   3.v, 33n33
   4, 29n21
   4.1, 53n85, 73n113
   4.2, 35n36
   4.7, 33n33, 73n113
   4.9, 35n36, 84n131
   5, 29n21, 42, 43, 73n113
   5–16, 31n26
   5.2, 53n85
   5.7–8, 33n33
Optatian (*cont.*)
   5.8, 73n113

5.16, 51n77
5.25, 33n33
5.26, 33n33
5.28, 33n33
5.iii, 33n33
6, 42, 43, 86n137, 88n144
6.2, 84n131
6.14, 48n70, 85n135
6.34, 33n33, 53n85
7, 35n38, 42, 43, 86n136
7.5–6, 53n86
7.7, 33n33
7.11, 35n36
7.12, 53n85
7.19, 48n70
7.24, 33n33
7.28, 35n38
7.35, 35n38
8, 42, 43, 51n78, 64, 65, 66, 66n101, 67, 71, 72n111
8.1, 48, 69, 84
8.1–2, 33n33, 49n75
8.2, 53n85, 67
8.4, 68
8.27, 53n85
8.i, 35n36
8.i–ii, 53n85
9, 41, 43
9.6, 85n135
9.13, 35n36, 84n131
9.19, 53n86
9.23, 53n86
9.35–6, 73n113
9.36, 53n86
9.iii, 49n75
9.v, 42n52, 84n131
10, 42, 44
10.9, 33n33
10.10, 51n77
10.18, 49n75, 85n135
10.32, 35n38
10.v, 33n33
11.8, 53n85
12, 41, 41n51, 43, 86n136
12.iii, 33n33
13, 87–88
13.iii, 53n85
14, 42, 43, 51n78, 64, 66, 70n105
14.1–2, 70n105

14.19, 33n33
14.35, 35n38
15, 86–87, 143, 145
15.5, 87
15.6, 33n33
15.9, 87
15.10, 87
15.11, 87
15.11–15, 87n140
15.12–13, 87
15.14–15, 87
15.15, 87
16, 59, 62–64
16.1–2, 64
16.3, 49n75, 62
16.5, 84n131
16.6, 63
16.7, 62
16.8, 62
16.10, 62
16.10–11, 62
16.15, 62
16.21, 62
16.29, 53n85
16.33, 62
16.35, 73n113
16.ii, 51n78
17, 29n21, 29n22
17.1–2, 57
17.8, 84n131
17.8–10, 57, 90n151
17.14–20, 29n21
17.19 (= 18.vi), 35n38
18, 42, 43, 55–58, 73, 86, 86n136, 88n144
18.2, 58
18.11, 35n38
18.17, 56
18.21, 33n33
18.23, 53n85
18.iv, 33n33
19, 41, 43, 51n78, 59, 64, 68, 72–73, 72n111, 73n113, 86, 88n144, 145
19.1, 53, 53n85, 72, 146n112
19.2, 33n33, 73n112, 74
19.4, 35n36, 49n75, 73
19.8, 49n75
19.12, 35, 73

19.13, 73, 73n112, 74n115
19.17, 53n85, 72
19.19, 49n75, 84n131
19.20, 33n33, 48, 48n70
19.25, 84n131
19.26, 73
19.29, 53n85, 72
19.31, 73
19.32, 33n33
19.32–4, 73
19.35, 35, 35n36, 73
20, 31n26, 36, 38, 40n48, 45
20.13, 33n33
20a, 36
20a.9, 35n38
20a12–26, 73n113
20a.22, 32
20b.1–26, 36
20b.4, 84n131
20b.9, 85n135
20b.14–19, 39n48
20b.18, 48n70
21, 41, 43, 50, 86n136
21–8, 29n22
21.4, 49n75, 84, 85n135
21.6, 48n70
21.9, 48n70
21.16, 42n52, 84n131
21.i, 33n33
21.iii, 50
21.i–ii, 40n49, 51
22, 41, 43, 58–59, 71n106, 86n136
22.8, 85n135
22.9, 33n33
22.11, 48, 49n75, 59
22.14, 59n93
22.18, 59n93
22.19, 59n93
22.21, 59n93
22.27, 49n75, 59n93
22.viii, 33n33
22.xiii–xiv, 33n33
23, 43, 59, 60, 86n136
23.3, 60
23.9, 60
23.10, s60
24, 42, 43, 51n78, 59n93, 64, 66n101, 67, 71–72, 71n106, 72n108
24.4, 51n78, 71

24.6, 71n106
24.9, 71n106, 72
24.13, 71n106
24.18, 51n78, 71
24.18–19, 72
24.20, 71n106
24.27, 71n106
24.30, 71n106
24.34, 71n106
24.35, 53n85, 72
25, 86n137, 88–90, 91n155
25.2, 85n135, 89
25.4, 89
25.5, 89
25.9, 89
26, 36, 37, 45
26.1, 36, 38n47
26.2, 48n70
26.5, 35n38
26.7, 36, 48n70
26.18, 48n70
26.19, 36
26.22, 39, 85n135
26.23, 36
27, 36, 37, 45
27.3, 39n48
28, 87
28.1–2, 87
28.3–4, 87
28.5–6, 87
28.7–8, 87
28.9–10, 87
28.9–12, 33n33, 35n38
28.11–12, 87
28.13–14, 87
28.15–16, 87
28.17–18, 87
28.19–20, 87
28.21–2, 87
28.23–4, 87
28.25–6, 87
28.27–8, 87
28.29–30, 87
28.31–2, 87
29–31, 29n22
31, 29n22
31.1, 51n78
31.3, 51n78
31.7, 51n78

508   *Index Locorum*

Optatian (*cont.*)
   31.12, 51n78
 epistula Porf.
   2, 35n39, 85n135
   6, 53n86
Orientius, *commonitorium*,
   114, 374n7
Orosius, *historia*,
   6.9.6, 336
Ovid
 amores, 236
   1.8.10, 174
   1.8.57–8, 91
   1.14.55, 325
   2.6.54, 335, 337
 ars amatoria
   1.462, 321, 333
   2.258, 322
   2.419, 174
   2.481, 174
   3.410, 338
 fasti, 374n6
   2.487, 354n41
   3.471–6, 152, 163
   4.832, 317, 333, 335
   5.558, 317, 333, 335
   6.612, 248n20
 heroides
   5.103, 325
   18.47, 335
 metamorphoses, 368
   1.1–2, 357, 357n53
   1.51, 318
   1.63, 317, 333, 335
   1.87–8, 357, 357n53
   1.94–5, 363n72
   1.102, 365n79
   1.113, 324
   1.129–34, 363n72
   1.141, 363n75
   1.141–50, 366n81
   1.184, 339
   1.218, 333
   1.284, 320, 327, 328
   1.350, 320, 324
   1.379, 325
   1.430, 318
   1.641, 337
   1.780, 331
   2, 161–62, 162n33
   2.150, 161, 162
   2.161–6, 162
   2.173, 332
   2.180, 320, 327, 328
   2.318, 331
   2.409–10, 297n37
   2.642, 323, 335
   2.760, 323
   2.796, 331
   2.827, 325
   3.194, 335, 337
   3.339–510, 184
   3.353–5, 183n35
   3.356–401, 186
   3.372–4, 193
   3.373, 318
   3.389, 193
   3.400, 186
   3.419, 189
   3.422, 189, 192
   3.428–9, 193
   3.463–4, 194
   3.481, 189
   3.483, 318
   3.490, 193
   3.637, 331
   3.646, 322
   4.57, 338
   4.122, 318
   4.122–4, 329
   4.169, 331
   4.232, 336
   4.282, 318
   4.344, 318
   4.348, 318
   4.350, 174
   4.656, 323
   4.776, 318
   5, 220
   5.205, 192, 200n89
   5.268, 320, 324
   5.322, 319, 333
   5.325, 318, 333
   5.359, 324
   6.1–145, 225
   6.151, 319, 333
   6.341, 331
   6.516, 318

6.558, 322
7.36, 318
7.141, 318, 333
7.173, 323
7.205, 332
7.267, 323
7.319–20, 331
7.409, 324
7.540, 331
8.163, 323
8.290, 321
8.304, 352n36
8.573, 337
8.690–1, 328
9.106, 338
9.192, 318
9.199, 322, 323
9.582, 332
9.696, 320, 324
9.744, 321
9.765, 323
10.140, 331
10.243–92, 192
10.248, 189n53
10.255, 189n53
10.275–6, 189n53
10.287, 192, 200n89
10.653, 337
11.77, 337
11.284, 333
11.395, 318
11.516, 318
11.567, 322
11.763, 323, 333, 335
12.76, 325
12.374, 321
13.193, 318
13.289, 200n89
13.731, 338
14.120, 328
14.416, 317, 333, 335
14.430, 338
14.754, 337
14.814, 354n41
15.145, 331
15.195, 328
15.391–407, 374n6
15.632, 323
15.744, 323, 335

tristia
 1.1.1–14, 31
 4.2.42, 338
 4.4.85, 339
 4.7.17, 339

Pacatus Drepanius, *orationes*
 1.1B, 348
 10B, 348
Pacuvius, *tragedies*
 186, 318
 188, 317
 208, 317
 232, 319, 333
 256, 333
 295, 325
 296, 323
 377, 318
 378, 318
 413, 328
Palladius, *de agricultura*, 15, 374n7
de paneficiis (Riese AL), 7, 197
panegyrici Latini, 313–68, 313n1, 313n2, 315n8,
 315n10. *see also specific authors
 and titles*
 1(1) (*see* Pliny the Younger,
  Panegyricus)
 2(12), 314, 336–39
  1.3, 336
  2.1, 336
  3.3, 337
  3.4, 337
  3.5, 319, 320, 325, 328, 337
  4.3, 337
  4.4, 336, 337, 348n16, 349n22
  4.4–5, 339
  4.5, 337, 339, 367
  5.2, 337
  7.4, 337
  8.5, 343
  8.3, 337, 339
  8.4–5, 351n32
  8.5, 339
  9.2, 337
  9.6, 339
  10.2, 337
  11.1, 337
  11.3, 337
  11.4–7, 339

Panegyrici Latini, (cont.)
    13.3, 337
    14.1, 337, 339
    17.2, 336
    18.4, 337
    19.1, 337
    19.2, 337, 339
    20.5, 337
    21.1, 337
    21.4, 337
    23.2, 337
    24.3, 337
    24.5, 338
    25.3, 328, 338
    26.4, 338
    26.5, 338
    29.3, 328, 338
    30.1, 338
    30.2, 338
    32.4, 338
    32.5, 338
    33.2, 336, 338
    33.4, 338, 339
    34.1, 338
    34.3, 338
    34.3–4, 339
    34.4, 338, 339
    35.3, 338
    36.3, 339
    37.3, 338
    37.4, 338
    38.2–4, 339
    38.3, 338
    38.4, 338, 339
    39.1, 336
    40.1, 338, 339
    40.2–4, 339
    41.1, 338
    42.3, 338
    43.4, 339
    44.4, 339
    44.5, 339, 348, 351, 367
    45.2, 339
    47.6, 343, 367
   3(11), 314, 330–32, 344
    3.3, 343
    3.2, 331
    3.3, 332

    4.3, 331
    5.2, 332
    6.4, 331
    8.1, 349n25
    8.1–3, 353
    8.3, 331, 362
    8.104, 349n22
    9.1, 331
    9.2, 331
    9.4, 332
    10.1, 331, 332
    10.2, 331, 335
    11.3, 331n30
    11.4, 331
    12.1, 331n30
    12.3, 331n30
    15.2, 331
    17.1, 331
    17.2, 332, 335
    19.4, 332
    21.5, 332
    23.1, 332
    27.2, 332
    28.5, 331n30, 332, 349n21, 359
    30.1, 332
    31.6, 332
   4(10), 314, 326–30, 340, 344
    3.4, 322, 333
    3.5, 320, 328
    5.6, 330
    7.4, 343
    7.4, 328, 330
    8.4, 328, 338
    11.4, 352
    11.5, 330, 349n22
    12.3, 328
    13.1, 330
    14.2, 328, 330
    14.3, 328
    15.3, 328
    15.5, 349n21
    16.2, 330
    17.2, 328, 330
    17.3, 328
    18.2, 319, 320, 325, 328, 337
    18.6, 328
    19.2, 320, 328
    19.3, 328

22.4, 330
23.4, 328
25.4, 328
25.7, 328
26.4, 325, 328
29.5, 328, 330
30.1, 328
30.3, 334
31.3, 327, 328, 329
32.8, 328
32.9, 329
33.5, 328
33.6, 329
33.7, 329
5(8), 313, 323–24, 340, 341, 348n15
   3.1, 348n19
   6.7, 323
   7.2, 323–24
   9.1.4, 320, 324
   10.2, 324
   11.1, 324
6(7), 313, 322–23, 340
   1–2, 347n14
   1.4, 317
   2.1, 358n55
   5.2, 323
   7.2, 323
   7.5, 351n31
   8.1, 323
   9.2, 323
   10.4, 323
   11.4, 323
   11.5, 323, 333, 335
   15.4, 323
   18.2, 322, 323
   18.4, 323
   18.6, 323
   19.1, 323
   20.2, 323
   21.4, 323
   21.5, 322–23
   21.6, 323
   22, 348n15
7(6), 313, 321–22, 340
   2.5, 322, 327, 333
   4.1, 322
   6, 322
   6.2, 322

   8.2, 350
   8.4, 350
   9.3–4, 322n20
   11, 322
   11.4, 322n20
   12.8, 322
   14.1, 322, 323
   20.7, 322n20
8(4), 313, 320–21, 340
   2.2, 320
   2.3, 320
   3.1, 319, 320
   4.3, 320
   5.2, 320, 327, 328
   6.4, 319, 320, 325, 328, 337
   8.2, 320
   9.1, 320, 324
   10.4, 321
   11.1, 321
   16.4, 321
   18.5, 320, 321
   19.2, 327
9(5), 313, 321, 340, 348n15
   2.4, 321
   4.3, 321
   5.4, 321
   7.3, 321, 355
   9.4, 321
   10.1, 321
   15.2, 321
   17.4, 321, 333
   18.3, 321
   19.2, 321
   21.1, 321
10(2), 313, 317–18, 340
   1.1, 341
   1.3, 315–16, 317, 343, 348n19
   2.1, 317, 333, 335, 351n32
   2.4, 317
   2.5, 350
   3.1, 317
   3.3, 317–18
   3.4, 317
   4.2, 318, 333
   4.3, 318
   5.2, 318
   5.3, 318, 321, 325, 330, 340
   7.4, 318

Panegyrici Latini, (cont.)
    7.5, 318
    9.5, 340
    10.1, 318
    11.3, 317, 330, 352n38
    11.7, 318
    12–13, 340
    12.1, 318
    12.4, 318
    12.5, 318
    12.6, 318
    30.3, 341
    31.1, 358n55
  11(3), 313, 319, 320, 340
    2.3, 319, 320
    3.4, 317, 317n13, 319, 320, 325, 328, 337
    3.6, 319, 333
    4.2, 319
    8.3, 319
    8.4, 351, 368
    14.2, 316, 319, 335, 355
    16.3, 319, 320, 321, 359
    16.4, 319n17
    17.1, 319
    28.5, 356n51
  12(9), 313, 324–26, 340, 341, 356, 368
    1.1, 326, 348
    3.4, 327
    3.5, 327
    4.2, 325
    4.3, 326
    7.1, 327
    7.4, 327
    8.4, 325
    9.4, 325
    9.5, 325, 330
    10.3, 325, 328
    11–13, 324
    11.5, 327
    12.2, 355
    12.3, 357
    12.3–4, 324
    13.4, 325
    13.5, 357
    14.2, 325, 351
    16.2, 358
    17.3, 325
    18.1, 325, 326, 351n34
    21.5, 325
    22.2, 325
    23.4, 325
    24.2, 319, 320, 325, 328, 337
    26.1, 325
    30.3, 326
    42.2, 357
  gratiarum actio (*see* Ausonius, *gratiarum actio*)
  orat (*see* Symmachus, *orationes*)
  panegyricus (*see* Pliny the Younger, *panegyricus*)
Paulinus of Nola
  carmina, 5n11
    7.1, 114
    10, 102, 108–9, 112, 163
    10.1–18, 163
    10.13–14, 374
    10.13–18, 108
    10.19–102, 163
    10.43–5, 411n65
    10.103–331, 163
    11, 102, 109, 112
    11.49–68, 109
    12.1, 131
    17.61–2, 131n47
    20.28–32, 411, 411n64
    21, 102, 108–11, 112, 124
    21.1–36, 109
    21.56–9, 110
    21.100–4, 110
    21.105–271, 109
    21.272–3, 110
    21.272–343, 109
    21.308–9, 131n47
    21.312–21, 131
    21.344–6, 111
    21.344–582, 111
    21.344–858, 109
    22, 113
    23.1–2, 383
    23.9–12, 383
    23.28, 383
    23.70–3, 389n53
    25, 102, 111–12, 114, 374n7
    25.238–41, 111n20
    25.240–1, 131n47
    27, 52n80
    27.511–5, 201n91
    27.514–15, 76

31, 114, 374n7
31.42, 131n47
33, 113
epistulae
  8.3, 114
  16.9, 382, 382n35
  20.6.20–22, 130
  32.6.1–2, 131n47
  38.9.7–10, 131
  49, 74n115
natalicia, 439
Paulinus of Pella,
  eucharistichos, 377n15
Paulinus of Périgueux, *uita Martini*, 389n54
  1–14, 122
  4.245–50, 5n11
Pentadius, *epigrammata* (Shackleton
  Bailey *AL*)
  26, 198
  259, 198
Pentateuch. *see* Cyprianus Gallus,
  heptateuchos; specific books
peruigilium Veneris, 21, 123, 308–9
  429–34, 309
1 Peter, 3:19–20, 433
Petrarch
  eclogae, 10.311–26, 400n36
  Le familiari, 10.4, 392n8
Petronius
  120.72, 331
  Satyricon, 34.10, 103n7
Phaedrus, *fabulae*
  1, 237
  2, 237
  3, 237
  4, 237
  5, 237
Philostratus the Elder, *imagines*,
  44n57, 45n64
Plato
  Ion, 393
  Phaedrus, 422n83
  res publica, 393, 396n20, 405
    10, 411
    392, 403n44, 416n69
    601b, 348n16
Plautus
  Amphitruo
    45, 332

162, 329
193, 331
280.732, 317
643, 320
742, 331
Asinaria
  78, 328
  859, 337
  873, 328
Aulularia
  79, 328
  168, 338
  313, 334
  801, 327
Bacchides, 313, 329
Captiui
  137, 320
  222, 318
Casina, 631, 332
Curculio
  160, 331
  231, 328
  496, 338
Menaechmi
  342, 327
  766, 337
  926, 338
Miles gloriosus
  1.7, 338
  818–20, 318
Mostellaria
  60, 317
  756, 337
  791, 318
  817, 337
Poenulus
  74, 337
  111, 318
  163, 331, 335
  273, 332
  384, 338
  907, 331
  1223, 318
  1323, 331
Persa, 478, 338
Pseudolus
  560, 325
  571, 337
  760, 328

Plautus, (cont.)
  Rudens
    2, 319, 333
    14, 338
    191, 338
    734, 331
  Stichus
    45, 337
    377, 338
  Trinummus, 537, 331
  Truculentus, 256, 328
Pliny the Elder
  historia naturalis, 255
    7.101, 348n17
    praef. 4, 260, 260n35
Pliny the Younger
  epistulae
    3.13.2, 342
    4.18, 326n25
  panegyricus, 313, 342
    2.2, 342n52
    3.5, 349n23
    5.8, 318
    14.5, 322
    15.3, 318
    30.2, 336
    30.4, 318
    38.3, 320
    80.4, 360n62
    81.2, 318
Plutarch, moralia
  de gloria Atheniensium, 346F (=Simon. frg. 190b Bergk), 45n59
  quomodo adulescens poetas audire debeat, 17F, 45n59
poema coniugis ad uxorem, 102–3, 112–13, 124
Polemius Silvius, laterculus (MGH), AA 9.544, 137n79
Porphyry, ad Hor. carmina, 4.9.9, 112n22
Priscianus, partitiones xii uersuum Aeneidos principalium (Keil GL), 3.459–515, 127n16
Proba, cento, 159n27
  3, 346n5
  23, 169
  372–9, 157–159
  384–7, 157–159

Procne and Philomela (Riese AL), 13, 197
Propertius
  3.3.23–4, 241
  4, 374n6
  4.9.1, 117
Prosopography of the Later Roman Empire
  1.139, 268n62
  2.454–6, 120n40
Prosper of Aquitaine, de prouidentia Dei, 374
  95–6, 374
Prudentius
  apotheosis, 238, 404–5
    234–7, 404
    268, 404
    301, 404
    376–80, 404, 404n47
    384–5, 404
    386–93, 405
  cathemerinon
    3.26–30, 5n11
    4, 115
    5.13–20, 444
    5.141–4, 445
    9.8.57–70, 174n48
  contra Symmachum, 238
    1.220, 126
    2.471, 420
    2.471–87, 418, 420
    2.477–8, 420
    2.480–1, 420
  hamartigenia, 238, 422n82
    201–7, 422
    202, 422
    203, 422
    272–82, 422
    665, 419
    667, 418
    669–801, 418
    686–96, 419
    695–6, 419
    705–6, 419
    737, 419
    741–2, 419
    758, 419
    765, 419
    766, 419
    842, 419

851, 420n75
927, 420n75
peristephanon
  5.373-4, 386
  12, 374n7
prologus, 100
  36, 382-83
psychomachia, 238, 403, 417
  899-907, 417n70
Psalms, 427
  1:1, 114
  8:9, 130
  31:1, 114
  49:14, 382
  114.4, 136n75
  118, 135, 435, 435n22
  118 (119), 144
  148, 383
Pseudo-Dionysius the Areopagite, *de mystica theologia*
  1.997b-1000a, 289n21
  1.1000b, 300n44
  3.1033b-c, 301n45
Pseudo-Hermogenes, *progymnasmata* (Rabe 1913), 10.48, 46n64
Publilius Optatianus Porfyrius. see Optatian

Quintilian, *institutio oratoria*
  1.1.26, 91
  1.1.30, 143n98
  1.4.25, 128
  1.5.4, 132n58
  2.5.22, 327n25
  3.7.6, 349n23
  4.2.118, 326n25
  10.1.7, 137n79
  10.1.17-19, 264
  10.4.3, 258n31
  10.4.4, 258n31
  11.3.67, 45
  11.3.153, 314
  12.10.19, 357n54

Revelation, 21:5, 7n21
rhet. ad Her., 4.11, 434
Romans
  1:20, 430

6:6, 165n39
13:14, 435n25
Rutilius Namatianus, *de reditu suo*, 15, 21, 207, 210, 213, 223, 226, 227-33, 229n54, 304, 374n7
  1.1, 232
  1.1-12, 229
  1.3, 229, 305n59
  1.4, 229
  1.13-14, 230
  1.15, 231
  1.18, 231
  1.19, 232
  1.21, 232
  1.27, 232
  1.29, 232
  1.35, 231, 232
  1.37-42, 232
  1.47-72, 231
  1.48, 305n59
  1.57, 231
  1.58, 231
  1.63, 231
  1.65, 231
  1.66, 231
  1.67-8, 233
  1.70, 231, 305n59
  1.77, 231
  1.78, 231
  1.83, 231
  1.91-2, 231
  1.93-4, 231
  1.105-6, 233n59
  1.111, 231
  1.116, 305n59
  1.167, 305n59
  1.169, 305n59
  1.179-81, 232
  1.190, 305
  1.191-2, 305n57
  1.199, 232
  1.200, 305n59
  1.200-1, 232
  1.201, 305
  1.203-4, 305n58
  1.217, 232
  1.226, 305n59, 307n67
  1.231, 305n59, 307n68

Rutilius Namatianus, *de reditu suo*, (cont.)
  1.237, 232
  1.249, 305n59
  1.298, 305n59
  1.309, 305n59
  1.309–10, 306n63
  1.310, 305n59
  1.311–12, 130n46
  1.409, 305, 307n66
  1.409–12, 307n66
  1.410, 307n66
  1.413–14, 307n66, 308n72
  1.415–28, 231
  1.419, 305n59, 308n73
  1.432, 304
  1.434, 305
  1.453, 305n59
  1.467, 305n59
  1.476, 305n59
  1.550, 305n59
  1.559–96, 231
  1.566, 231
  1.569, 232, 305n59
  1.574, 305n59
  1.575, 232
  1.577, 232
  1.579, 232
  2.10, 305n59
  2.40, 305n59
  2.49, 305n59
  2.64, 305n59
  2.283–4, 233
  2.289, 233

scriptores historiae Augustae
  Spartianus, *Geta*
    5.4–5, 134
    5.7–8, 144n104
  Vopiscus, *Prob.*
    4.1, 131n48
    4.4–5, 131n48
Second Council of Toledo (*Toletana Synodus*), 2.1, 399
Sedulius
  carmen paschale, 383
    1.23–6, 383
    4.288, 389
    4.290, 389
  epistulae ad Mac. (*CSEL* 10.171)

    2, 256n20
    7, 256n20
Seneca
  Agamemmnon
    21, 319, 333
    392, 319, 333
    500, 338
    520, 319, 333
  de clementia
    1.5, 318n14
    1.13, 318n14
    2.21, 318n14
    4, 318n14
  epistulae
    33, 327n25
    79.6, 149
  Hercules furens
    357, 325
    693, 328
    928, 328
  Hercules Oetaeus, 1414, 325
  Medea
    301–2, 362n68
    301–64, 363n72
    362–3, 366n81
    373, 323
  Oedipus
    401, 338
    606, 337
    1028, 325
  Phaedra
    57–8, 323
    910, 387n46
    1186, 338
  Thyestes
    581, 338
    676, 317
    822, 317, 333, 335
  Troades, 430–1, 338
Sergius (Keil *GL*)
  4.475, 92n158, 144
  4.475.7, 143n97
Servius
  commentarius in artem Donati, 4.421, 144n101
  Aen.
    1 praef. 165
    4 praef., 165–66, 346n5
Servius auctus, 1.1.5, 356n50

Sidonius Apollinaris
  carmina
    5.279–90, 139
    5.371–2, 284n11
    5.335–8, 138n82
    5.474–7, 138
    7.26–7, 306n65
    7.32–3, 306n65
    7.74–6, 137
    7.79–82, 137
    7.321ff, 138
    7.353–6, 384n37
    8.11–14, 271n83
    9, 284–87, 285n14, 286n15, 296, 297–98, 301, 421n78
    9.2, 281n7, 296
    9.4, 284, 285n14
    9.4–15, 285
    9.5, 130n46, 306n65
    9.9–13, 281n7
    9.10, 287
    9.11, 256n20
    9.14, 256n20
    9.16–317, 285
    9.19–317, 284
    9.94–100, 141n92
    9.318, 284, 286
    9.318–46, 285
    9.329–46, 275n98
    9.340, 287
    9.345–6, 286, 300
    10, 123n49
    11. 17–28, 142
    12, 272n90, 279–83
    12.1, 282
    12.8, 283
    12.9–11, 283
    12.20, 282
    12.22, 282
    13, 102, 116–19, 283–84
    13.1–20, 118, 119n37, 141n92
    13.19, 117n33
    13.21–40, 119n37
    13.25–7, 306n65
    13.35, 284
    13.38–40, 284
    14, 130n46
    15.126–31, 141
    15.127ff, 141n93
    15.141–3, 141
    16.1–5, 5n11
    16.38–9, 289n22
    16.127–8, 130n46, 306n65
    22 epist. 5, 169
    22 epist. 6, 165, 169
    22.136–41, 153–5
    24.10–15, 275n98
  epistulae
    1.11, 280n5, 281
    2, 130n46
    2.2.14, 134
    4.3.7, 139n83
    4.12, 398
    5.17.10, 20n60
    6, 165
    8.11.3 v. 35–36, 130n46
    9.12.1, 398n29
    9.16, 398
    9.16.3.1–20, 122
Silius Italicus, *Punica*
  1.145, 317, 333, 335
  1.232, 331
  1.237, 333
  1.286, 325
  1.296, 338
  1.376, 195, 200n89
  1.515–21, 195
  1.674, 323
  2.23, 333
  2.83, 387n46
  2.92, 325
  2.307, 323
  2.308, 338
  2.315, 338
  2.451, 338
  2.586, 333
  3.275, 323
  3.364, 325
  3.405, 321
  3.437, 320, 327, 328
  3.444, 333
  4.7, 320
  4.149, 328
  4.172, 325
  4.430, 325
  4.593, 337
  5.330, 320, 327
  5.332, 322

Silius Italicus, *Punica*, (cont.)
  5.360, 196, 200n89
  5.433, 317
  5.624, 323
  6.254, 318, 333
  6.446, 337
  7.146, 322
  7.417, 323
  7.421, 338
  7.436, 331
  7.500, 318
  7.665, 333
  8.10, 333
  8.367, 323
  9.93, 338
  10.319, 337
  11.268, 337
  11.518, 320, 327
  12.1, 332
  12.418–19, 325
  12.426, 333
  13.66, 196, 200n89
  13.127, 322
  13.191, 334
  13.550, 338
  13.676, 323
  14.185–6, 338
  14.227, 323
  14.240, 324
  15.576, 322
  16.189, 196, 200n89
  16.269, 174
  17.259, 196, 200n89
Simmias
  axe (Palatine Anthology), 75
    15.22, 38
  egg (Palatine Anthology), 75
    15.27, 38, 40
  wings of Eros (Palatine Anthology)
    15.24, 38
    15.24.1, 38n47
Statius
  Achilleis
    1.117, 323, 335
    1.183, 174
    1.208, 331
    1.251, 320, 324
    1.383, 320, 324
    2.32, 318
    2.111, 323
    2.143–5, 318
  siluae, 169, 237, 241–42
    1.1.52–54, 352n37
    1.2, 173
    1.2.141, 331
    1.2.260, 174
    1.5, 155
    1.5.3, 155
    1.5.33–4, 155
    1.5.36–9, 155
    1.5.34–9, 154
    1.5.60–1, 218
    2.1.110, 328
    2.2, 155, 169
    2.2.85–94, 155
    2.5.1, 318
    3.1, 169
    3.1.126, 334
    4.9.15, 317
    5.1.104, 331
    5.1.137, 333
  praef., 241–42
  Thebaid, 241–42
    1.138, 328
    1.152, 323
    1.179, 325
    1.351, 324
    1.421, 318
    1.449, 338
    2.280, 322, 327, 333
    2.585, 338
    3.218, 325
    3.488, 325
    3.655, 338
    4.6, 328
    4.6–7, 330
    4.91, 318
    4.187, 338
    4.271, 323
    4.705, 323
    5.90, 337
    5.226, 334
    5.254, 331
    5.581, 337
    5.691, 323
    5.715, 333
    6.7, 338
    6.40, 325
    6.123, 338
    6.324, 318

6.382, 324
7.118, 324
7.333, 323
7.565, 318
8.456–65, 318
8.705, 338
9.1, 328
10.119, 324
11.92, 338
11.106, 338
11.610, 338
12.381, 320, 327, 328
12.410, 338
12.634, 318
statuta ecclesiae antiqua, 13.5, 398n31
Symeon Magister 692, 14n37
Symmachus
  epistulae
    1.14, 139–40
    1.31, 264n48
  orationes
    1, 314, 316, 332–33
    1.1B, 350n28
    1.1C, 350n28
    1.2, 332
    1.3, 322, 333, 334
    1.4, 316, 332, 348n16
    1.4–5, 349
    1.5, 317, 333, 335
    1.9, 333
    1.10, 333
    1.13, 319, 333
    1.14, 333
    1.22, 333
    2, 314, 333–34
    2.4, 323, 333–34, 335
    2.8, 333n36, 352n39, 358n55
    2.9, 333–34
    2.10, 334
    2.14, 333–34
    2.21, 318, 333–34, 333n36
    2.26, 333–34
    2.29, 319, 321, 333–34
    2.74D–75A, 350
    3, 314, 334–35
    3.3, 334
    3.5, 335
    3.6, 322, 327, 333, 334
    3.9, 334, 335
    3.11, 317, 333, 335
    3.12, 332, 335
  relationes, 3.3, 126

tabulae Iliacae, 44n57, 47, 74–75, 203
tabulae lusoriae, 92, 92n157
Tacitus
  annales
    6.28, 384
    15.30, 349n25
Terence
  Adelphoe
    5.1, 442
    24, 319
    563, 332
    639, 337
  Andria
    161, 337
    735, 337
  Eunuchus
    42, 269n69
    336, 331
    924, 318
    929, 331, 335
    987, 318
  Heautontimorumenos
    218, 269n69
    572, 337
  Phormio
    34, 319
    44, 338
Terentius, *ad Adelph.*, 1.1.26, 128
Ter. Maur., 2850–1, 112n22
Tertullian
  de cultu feminarum, 3, 336
  de praescr. haer., 38–9, 95n161
  de resurrectione mortuorum, 13.2, 389n52
Theocritus, panpipes (Palatine Anthology), 15.21, 38
Theodoret of Cyrrhus, *Eranistes*, 433n20
Theodosius
  epistulae (Green)
    707.B.1–5, 254
    707.B.4, 257
    707.B.7–11, 255n15
Theon, *progymnasmata* (Patillon and Bolognesi 1997)
    118.7, 45n63
    119, 46n64
Toletana Synodus (Second Council of Toledo), 2.1, 399

Valerius Flaccus, *Argonautica*, 354n43
  1.1, 240n11
  1.1–4, 240
  1.3, 240n11
  1.3–4, 362n68
  1.4, 240n11
  1.45, 320
  1.299, 320, 324
  1.396, 337
  1.462–7, 352n36
  1.505, 325
  1.539, 338
  1.822, 338
  2.104, 331
  2.234, 331
  2.438, 331
  2.519, 320, 327, 328
  3.39, 331
  3.73, 320, 327, 328
  3.400, 324
  4.490, 331
  4.608, 338
  4.711, 338
  5.96, 192n63, 200n89
  5.352, 320, 324
  5.407, 318
  5.445, 338
  6.394, 337
  6.472, 332
  6.510, 331
  6.562, 325
  6.665, 323
  7.312, 322
  7.505, 318, 333
  7.629, 318, 333
  8.90, 323
  8.107, 318, 333
    8.186, 321
Varro, *de lingua Latina*
  5–7, 127n19
  5.1, 435
  5.6, 132
  5.75, 134n68
  6.11, 435
Venantius Fortunatus
  carmina, 137n80
    1.16, 144n102
    3.9.27–32, 383

    3.9.46, 383
    6.1, 173
    6.2.41–8, 173–4
    8.3.263–76, 379
  uita Martini praef., 2.37–40, 5n11
Vergil
  Aeneis, 14, 48, 189, 189n55, 194, 199, 260, 288, 316, 355, 356, 358
    1, 190, 191n60, 200, 358
    1.1, 285n13
    1.33, 319, 320, 325, 328, 337
    1.143, 322
    1.159, 350n27
    1.164, 328
    1.203, 337
    1.223–4, 359
    1.223–4.255, 356n51
    1.224, 317, 319
    1.234, 319, 320
    1.254, 325
    1.254–5, 331
    1.255, 318, 360
    1.259–60, 354n41
    1.287, 318
    1.294–6, 327n26, 358n55
    1.350, 182, 192
    1.352, 183, 192
    1.422, 331
    1.453–95, 189, 199
    1.459, 189
    1.462, 189
    1.464, 182, 189, 201
    1.465, 189
    1.470, 189
    1.475, 325
    1.476, 189
    1.485, 189
    1.488, 189
    1.491–3, 190
    1.495, 182, 189, 190
    1.496, 190
    1.531, 321
    1.543, 327
    1.625, 182, 184
    1.660, 193
    1.663, 320, 324
    1.673, 193
    1.695–755, 185

1.713, 182, 185, 193
1.749, 182, 185
2.57–8, 156
2.64, 156
2.204, 330
2.211–13, 356
2.259, 338
2.272–3, 321
2.301, 317
2.305–7, 326
2.332, 331
2.353, 325
2.557, 332
2.557–8, 339
2.561, 334
2.700, 320, 324
2.725, 331
2.727, 338
2.758, 183, 188
2.779, 332
2.792, 183
2.792–3, 191
3.38, 333
3.39, 331
3.55, 338
3.70, 338
3.144, 323
3.260, 337
3.285, 332
3.374–462, 195
3.389, 183, 183n134, 195
3.389–93, 195n71
3.410, 241
3.422, 318
3.483, 331
3.489, 192
3.490, 182, 192
3.539, 331
3.581, 320, 327, 328
3.622–5, 166
3.629, 183
4.13, 325, 351, 357
4.41, 333, 335, 356n51
4.73, 325
4.266, 322
4.269, 332
4.277, 328
4.284, 320, 324

4.300, 193
4.363, 182, 185
4.365–87, 185
4.462, 329
4.473, 338
4.559, 183, 185
4.562, 185
4.610, 338
4.663–7, 50
4.669, 318
5.15, 323
5.73, 337
5.182, 338
5.199, 331
5.319, 337
5.337, 337
5.436, 338
5.452, 334
5.459, 338
5.505, 320, 327
5.627, 333
5.694, 332
5.810, 332
5.839, 324
5.857, 336
6, 200, 358
6.6, 319
6.14–37, 191
6.17, 155
6.32, 183, 191, 192
6.32–3, 191
6.48, 325
6.53, 320
6.66, 321
6.104, 336
6.107, 324
6.119–20, 248
6.150, 328, 338
6.157–8, 328
6.159, 321
6.640–641, 215n24
6.700, 183
6.700–1, 191
6.726–7, 325
6.792–4, 358
6.798, 332
6.803, 319
6.830, 319

Vergil, (*cont.*)
    6.851, 260, 260n34
    6.853, 260, 327n26
    6.859, 337
    6.861, 182, 187
    6.866, 187
    7.27, 322
    7.74, 338
    7.162, 182, 185
    7.228, 337
    7.251, 182, 185
    7.422, 323
    7.447, 337
    7.473, 182, 187
    7.604, 331
    7.722, 320
    7.807, 323
    7.811, 158
    7.812, 158
    7.813, 158
    8, 190
    8.23, 322
    8.31ff, 325
    8.63, 318
    8.72, 325
    8.81–5, 194
    8.82, 182, 194
    8.87, 323
    8.89, 331
    8.214, 117
    8.220, 332
    8.240, 323
    8.263, 338
    8.270–1, 317
    8.332, 325
    8.476, 336
    8.518–19, 333
    8.538, 325
    8.616, 322
    8.625–731, 190
    8.639–41, 195
    8.676, 323
    8.727, 323, 333, 335
    8.730, 183, 195, 199
    9.32, 323
    9.62, 331
    9.176–81, 186
    9.176–449, 185
    9.182, 186

9.183, 182
9.185, 325
9.314–66, 186
9.336, 182, 186, 187
9.440, 338
9.446, 186
9.449, 260n34
9.514, 337
9.580, 325
9.583, 182, 187
9.586–9, 187
9.685, 183, 187
9.746, 332
9.772, 318
9.812, 328
10.103, 322
10.115, 318
10.141, 318
10.159–60, 327
10.237, 325
10.292, 328
10.303, 182, 188
10.310, 330
10.326, 182, 187
10.522, 318
10.548, 332, 335
10.551, 182, 187
10.552–60, 187
10.592–3, 328
10.652, 174
10.685, 183
11.326, 318
11.347, 336
11.383, 321, 333
11.541, 158
11.544, 158
11.570, 158
11.572, 158
11.601–2, 338
11.651, 322, 323
11.704, 318
11.725, 325
11.890, 328
12.138, 320, 324
12.169–215, 195
12.275, 182, 187, 195
12.294, 328
12.345, 323
12.477–80, 332

12.523–25, 318
12.534, 321
12.559, 328
12.578, 330
12.939, 182, 185, 191
Aeneis (RIB), 2447.9, 48n72
eclogae, 186, 194, 198, 291, 319, 358
    1.52, 182, 194
    2, 193, 194, 201
    2.2, 183
    2.4, 182
    2.4–5, 186
    2.25–7, 193
    2.27, 194
    2.95–6, 286n15
    3.60, 316, 335, 356
    4, 12, 158n24, 159, 174, 334, 363
    4.8, 174
    4.10, 323
    4.18, 158
    4.19, 158
    4.20, 158
    4.21, 323
    4.23, 158
    4.28, 158
    4.34–5, 365
    4.34–6, 363n73
    4.52, 174
    6.34, 320
    6.38, 346n3
    7.3, 323
    7.30, 335, 337
    8.10, 333n35
    10.59, 323
georgica, 194, 198, 291, 339, 358, 363, 367
    1.23, 318
    1.30, 323
    1.40–1, 240
    1.56–7, 380n24
    1.71, 325
    1.85, 338
    1.121–46, 363n73
    1.122, 328
    1.159, 337
    1.201, 318
    1.293, 337
    1.452, 182, 188
    1.461–8, 188
    1.468, 188
    1.508, 357
    2.44, 240
    2.50, 240
    2.76, 322, 327, 333
    2.76–7, 334
    2.135, 328
    2.155–7, 337
    2.177, 331
    2.196, 318
    2.244, 335, 337
    2.283, 327
    2.293, 323
    2.319ff., 320
    2.336, 320
    2.480–1, 429
    2.506, 337
    2.518, 337
    3.199, 323
    3.371, 338
    3.382, 319
    3.408, 333
    3.544, 331
    4, 188, 194
    4.1, 182
    4.13, 323
    4.126, 318
    4.261, 322
    4.372, 318
    4.449, 328
    4.453–527, 248
"Vatican Vergil", 48, 48n73
    Folio 4^{1r}, 50
Vopiscus, *Prob.*
    4.1, 131n48
    4.4–5, 131n48

Wisdom
    6:17, 430
    8:1, 421
    11:21, 428n13

General Index

absence, 1n2
  displacement and, 212–13, 218, 220, 234, 446n40
  of Echo in Ovid's Narcissus narrative, 186
  of meaning, 209
acrostics, 41, 144–45
Aesop, 237
aesthetics
  cumulative, 11
  of centos, 177, 190, 198
  of detail, 11
  of hybridization. *see* hybridization
  of Late Antiquity, 6–16, 207–8, 306, 308, 315, 340–44
  materialist, of Optatian, 29–53, 29n23, 30n30, 30n31, 31n26, 33n33, 33n35, 35n35, 61, 82, 84, 96
  of panegyrics, 340–44
  Platonist, 392–420
  postmodern, and Late Antiquity 19–20
  of reader, 267
  of the fragment, 9
"Alexandrian footnote", 151, 351
Allegories of Reading (de Man), 209–10
allegory, 7, 12, 14
  in Ambrose's works, 144
  in Augustine's works, 431
  Christian view of, 209, 392, 395
  in Claudian's works, 238–39
  displacement and, 207–35
  in Fulgentius's works, 288, 299, 299n41
  in Late Antiquity, 209–10
  poetic license and, 411

reading and, 210, 221, 226
symbols and, 74
allusions, 11–16. *see also* intertextuality; *specific authors, e.g.* Catullus, Ausonius and
  as essential part of content, 153–62
  as formal features, 159–62
  as optional part of content, 155–59
  modes of, 162–64
Ambrose
  allegory in works of, 144
  Augustine and, 426–28, 438–39
  on poetry, 396
Amphitryoniaden, 117
anagrams, 144
Apelles, 33, 33n34
apophatic theology, 7, 288, 289n21, 300, 305
  of Gregory of Nyssa, 20, 279
  of Pseudo-Dionysius the Areopagite, 20
apostrophe, 186, 315, 326, 334
appropriationism of late antique culture, 8
arch of Constantine, 8–10, 95–99, 96n163, 179
Asclepius of Constantinople, 14
Augustine, 424–46
  allegory in works of, 431
  Ambrose and, 426–28, 438–39
  chronology of, 426
  on the futility of language, 302–4
  Licentius and, 438–43
  lost poem of, 425–26, 426n7
  Optatian and, 75
  Paulinus of Nola and, 439–40, 444

General Index

Augustine, *(cont.)*
  on poetry, 394–97, 424–25
  semiotics and, 7, 20, 302–3
  word choice and, 125–29, 131–33, 135–36, 140, 143–44, 146
Ausonius
  allegory and, 213–19, 233
  autobiography and, 267–68
  cataloguing by, 19
  Catullus and, 272–75, 273n91, 274n92, 282n9
  culture and, 256, 265, 267–68, 268n63, 270–71
  on the death of names, 305–8
  displacement and, 213–19, 233
  family of, 263–68
  genre and, 377
  Gratian and, 313–14, 316, 335, 335n37, 339, 341–44
  Hesperius and, 263–68, 264n47, 266n54, 268n63, 268n64
  Horace as inspiration to, 106
  influence of, 124
  on intertextuality, 168–9
  intertextuality and, 179–81, 184, 198, 202
  irony and, 16
  on literary patchwork, 93–95
  ludicity and, 266–67, 271
  Martial and, 255, 258–59
  Pacatus Drepanius and, 254, 269–75, 269n65, 269n67, 270n75, 270n76, 271n81, 272n89, 273n91, 274n93, 274n95, 275n97
  Paulinus of Nola and, 108–9, 124, 252, 271n79, 276
  Pliny the Elder and, 255, 260, 262n35
  on poetic license, 349, 352, 356
  as poet of the Muses, 5n11
  politics and, 261, 267–68, 267n59, 268n62, 276
  polymetry in works of, 100, 103–7, 112
  prefaces in works of, 237–38, 252
  revision process and, 252–77
  self-awareness and, 262–63, 262n40
  Symmachus and, 264n48, 276
  Theodosius and, 254–57, 254n11, 254n13, 255n19, 256n24, 259–63, 260n34, 261n36, 261n37, 262n39

  Vergil and, 8, 260, 260n34
  word choice and, 129–30, 136, 139–40, 143, 146
autobiography
  in Ausonius's works, 267–68
  in Claudian's works, 238, 241–42
Avitus of Vienne, on poetry, 397

banishment. *see* exile
Battle of the Milvian Bridge, 64n99, 70n104, 72n111, 324, 340, 351, 357–58
Bellerophon killing the Chimaera, 14–15, 78–79
Benedict of Nursia, on poetry, 398–99
Boethius, 391–423
  Christian writers and, 391–93
  on free will, 416–20
  poetic license and, 406, 408–11, 419–23
  on poetry, 401–4, 406–11
  polymetry in works of, 100
  on truth, 406–11
  on virtue and vice, 416–20

Calliope, 296–97
captatio beneuolentiae, 252n2, 258–59, 261, 273
carmina cancellatum (gridded poems), of Optatian, 39–43, 54–73
cataloguing, 11, 19, 117, 137–41, 140n89, 360, 377
  negative, 153–55, 169, 284, 287, 297–98
Catullus
  Ausonius and, 272–75, 273n91, 274n92, 282n9
  Sidonius Apollinaris and, 281–82, 281n6, 281n7, 285n14
Ceionius Rufus Volusianus, exile of, 29n22
centos
  aesthetics of, 177, 190, 198
  as form of classicism, 177–82
  Optatian and, 83–84
  pagan culture and, 9, 177–82
  spolia and, 178–81, 188, 195, 200, 203
ceremony
  Christian, 382–83
  ekphrasis, 379–87
chi-rho chrismon
  Constantine and, 64, 67–71

in Optatian's works, 43, 51n78, 64–74, 64n99, 70n105, 72n111, 73n113, 74n115
Christianity/Christian writing, 4–6, 5n11–12, 5n14, 18, 18n50. *see also* Jesus Christ; *specific authors*
  allegory and, 209, 392, 395
  art of, 51–52, 52n80, 77–82
  ceremony and, 382–83
  Edict of Milan and, 61
  iconography and, 16n42
  Incarnation and, 51–52, 52n80, 72
  intertextuality and, 156–59, 163, 169, 174
  language and, 6–7
  miracle narratives and, 387–90
  Narcissus narrative and, 176–77, 181, 184, 194–95, 197, 200–203
  phoenix myth and, 373–74, 382–83, 386–90, 388n48
  Platonist criticism and, 393–400
  poetic license and, 396, 411
  pre-Christian texts and, 12, 14
  scholarship on, 399–400
  silence and, 278, 289, 289n22, 296, 296n34, 299, 303
  song and, 383–84
  as state religion, 1–2, 1n1, 18, 61
  views on poetry and, 393–400
  word choice and, 126–29, 133, 136n75, 144–45
chronology
  of Augustine, 426
  of Claudian's works, 245–47
  of Lactantius's works, 373–74, 373n1, 374n5
  of Optatian's works, 29, 29n22, 73
  of panegyrics, 313, 315–16, 340–43
Cicero
  on poetic license, 349, 349n26
  word choice and, 132–33, 140
classical scholarship, 3–5
classicism
  centos as form of, 177–82
  development of, 7–8
  poetics of, 199–204
Claudian
  allegory in works of, 220–27, 233, 238–39
  autobiography and, 238, 241–42
  chronology of, 245–47
  displacement and, 220–27, 233
  ekphrasis in works of, 224–26, 247–48, 379–81
  Ennodius and, 122
  family in works of, 226–27
  Florentinus and, 245–46, 246n16
  innovation by, 241
  Lactantius and, 379–81, 384–86
  metapoetics in works of, 236–51
  metre and, 375–77
  narrative structure and, 378
  poetic license and, 360–67
  polymetry in works of, 100
  prefaces in works of, 236–51, 252
  prolaliai and, 248–50
  scholarship on, 236–37
  Stilicho and, 238, 245–47
  Vergil and, 363, 365
Claudius Mamertinus, Julian and, 314, 330–32, 341, 341n48, 343
Clement of Alexandria, on Homer, 209
coincidentia oppositorum, 300
Constantine
  arch of, 8–10, 95–99, 96n163, 179
  Battle of the Milvian Bridge and, 64n99, 70n104, 72n111, 324, 340, 351, 357–58
  chi-rho chrismon and, 64, 67–71
  defeat of Licinius by, 70n105
  Edict of Milan and, 61
  Eumenius and, 313, 321, 340
  Nazarius and, 314, 326–30, 326n24, 332, 334, 340–41, 343–44
  Optatian and, 29n22, 31n26, 32, 35n38, 35n39, 43, 50, 53n86, 58, 62, 64, 67–71, 73, 73n112, 74, 74n115, 84, 85n135, 88, 96–98
  panegyrics to, 313–14, 320–24, 326–27, 329, 340–41
  poetic license and, 348–51, 349n22, 356–58, 358n55
Corbridge Lanx, 11–12
Corippus, intertextuality and, 159, 163–65, 172, 175
criticism
  Platonist, 392–420
  silence as result of, 292–93

culture/cultural transition, 17–18
    Ausonius and, 256, 265, 267–68, 268n63, 270–71
    Narcissus narrative and, 176–204
    Optatian and, 27, 51–54, 51n78
    Western tradition and, 1–2, 1n2, 2n4
Cyprianus Gallus, polymetry in works of, 114–15

Dacian campaign, 9, 97–98
dating of works. *see* chronology
de obitu Baebiani, polymetry in, 113–14
displacement
    absence and, 212–13, 218, 220, 234, 446n40
    allegorical reading of, 207–35
    geographic, 218, 223, 233–34
    as metaphor, 221–22
    movement and, 228–33
Donatists, 144, 425, 426n6, 432, 434, 443
Dracontius
    intertextuality and, 160–65, 172
    on song, 383
dynamic signs. *see* semiotics; signs/symbols

Edict of Milan, 61
ekphrasis, 45, 46n64. *see also* visual imagery
    ceremony and, 379–87
    in Claudian's works, 224–26, 247–48
    intertextuality and, 177, 184, 187, 189–91, 199–201
    Optatian and, 45, 46n64
    in panegyrics, 315, 322, 332, 335, 340
elegy, metre and, 374–77
emulation, 9
Ennius
    authority of, 346, 354–56, 359–60
    Cicero and, 356
    Macrobius and, 355
    Mamertinus and, 360
    word choice and, 145
Ennodius
    Christianity and, 121
    Claudian and, 122
    Hilary of Arles and, 119–20
    influences on, 119–20, 123
    innovation by, 123–24
    polymetry in works of, 119–24
epithalamium, 111–2, 123
etymology, word choice and, 127–28, 127n19, 131, 132n56, 133, 135, 143n100

Eumenius, Constantine and, 313, 321, 340
Europa mosaic, Lullingtone, Kent, 48–49
Eusebius
    on Christian art, 52n80
    on Christian symbolism, 70n104
Eusthatius, on intertextuality, 166–67
exile
    of Ceionius Rufius Volusianus, 29n22
    of Optatian, 29n22, 32, 32n30, 49–50
    of Ovid, 29n22
experimentation. *see* innovation/experimentation

fabulae poetarum. *see* poetic license
family
    of Ausonius, 263–68
    in Claudian's works, 226–27
Florentinus, Claudian and, 245–46, 246n16
foreboding, in Narcissus narrative, 187–92
Fortunatus, miracle narratives and, 389
fragmentation
    in Optatian's works, 30, 82–99
    scholarship and, 207–8
    word choice and, 143–46
free will, 416–20
Fronto, on panegyrics, 347
Fulgentius, 14
    allegory in works of, 288, 299, 299n41
    silence and, 288–302, 296n33, 299n41, 305, 308
    Vergil and, 288, 291

gaming tablets (*tabula lusoriae*), 92, 92n157
geographic displacement, 218, 223, 233–34
Gnostics, Irenaeus on, 93
graphic quality of writing, 43–45, 45n59
Gratian, Ausonius and, 105, 313–14, 316, 335, 335n37, 339, 341–44
Gregory of Nyssa
    apophatic theology of, 20, 279
    on Christian art, 51–52, 52n80
Gregory of Tours, Hilary of Arles and, 115
gridded poems (*carmina cancellata*), of Optatian, 39–43, 54–73

Hadrian, 9–10, 97–98
Hercules cup, 12
Hermogenes, on poetic license, 347
Hesperius, Ausonius and, 263–68, 264n47, 266n54, 268n63, 268n64

Hilary of Arles
  Ennodius and, 119–20
  Gregory of Tours and, 115
  on poetry, 398
  polymetry in works of, 115
History of the Art of Antiquity (Winckelmann), 204
Homer
  Clement of Alexandria on, 209
  Vergil and, 200
homoeroticism, Narcissus narrative and, 184–86, 200–201
Horace
  as influence, 114
  as inpiration to Ausonius, 106
  translated mixing languages, 104, 104n8
hybridization, 15–16
  intrasystemic, 15
  intersystemic, 15–6

iconography
  Christian, 16n42
  of the Corbridge Lanx, 12
  of the Veroli casket, 14
idolatry, Christian art as, 52n80
Incarnation, Optatian on, 51–52, 52n80, 72
innovation/experimentation, 14
  Claudian and, 241
  Ennodius and, 123–24
  Mamertinus and, 341
  Nazarius and, 330
  Optatian and, 41, 49–51, 92–95
  Pacatus Drepanius and, 333
  polymetry and, 101
  Prudentius and, 411
  Symmachus and, 333, 341
interpretation
  of objects, 14
  polymetry and, 101
  of signs in Optatian's works, 53–82, 57n92, 73, 73n112
intertextuality, 149–75. *see also* allusions; specific authors, e.g. Catullus, Ausonius and
  allusions and, 153–62
  classical, 152–53
  classical reception and, 170–72
  commentary on, 164–70
  defined, 150–52

ekphrasis and, 177, 184, 187, 189–91, 199–201
  end of, 173–75
  of late Roman literature, 11–16
  modes of, 162–64
  Narcissus narrative and, 176–204
  in panegyrics, 315–44
  polymetry and, 101
  scholarship and, 207–8
interwoven verses (*uersus intexti*), Optatian and, 29n21, 33n35, 35n35, 42–43, 42n52, 50, 59, 66, 69, 70n103, 71, 73n113
Irenaeus
  on Christian art, 52n80
  on the Gnostics, 93
  on literary patchwork, 93, 95
Isocrates, on poetic license, 345

Jerome, 18n50
  Eusebius *Chronicle* and, 32
  on Optatian, 53
  Paulinus of Nola and, 212
Jesus Christ. *see also chi-rho* chrismon; Christianity/Christian writing
  depictions of, 78
  Incarnation and, 51–52, 52n80, 72
  in Optatian's works, 43, 51, 51n78, 62, 64–65, 68–72, 74, 74n115
  in Paulinus of Nola's works, 5n11, 109
  phoenix myth and, 383, 386
  silence of, 288–89, 289n22, 303n51
The Jeweled Style (Roberts), 17, 207–8
Julian
  Claudius Mamertinus and, 314, 330–32, 341, 341n48, 343
  on poetic license, 350, 350n28
Justin Martyr, on Christian art, 52n80
Juvencus, intertextuality and, 155–57

"Kaninchen und Ente" (Wittgenstein), 53–54
knowledge, silence as response to, 290–92
Kulturwollen, 17
Kunstwollen, 17, 19n53, 28

Lactantius
  as Christian writer, 373–74
  chronology of, 373–74, 373n1, 374n5
  Claudian and, 379–81, 384–86
  ekphrasis and, 379–87
  genre of, 374n7, 377–78

Lactantius, (cont.)
  metre and, 374–77
  narrative structure and, 378
  on poetry, 394
  scholarship on, 373–74
language. see also lexis; words/word choice
  chi-rho chrismon in Optatian's works and, 43, 51n78, 64–74, 64n99, 70n105, 72n111, 73n113, 74n115
  etymology and, 127–28, 127n19, 131, 132n56, 133, 135, 143n100
  fragmentation and (see fragmentation)
  juxtaposition of words and, 211
  linguistic turn and, 20, 279, 279n3
  Lucretius' view of, 91
  mixing of (see mixing of languages)
  names and, 129–31
  pagan *versus* Christian, 6–7
  problematization of the notion of, 6–7, 20, 278–9, 302–4, 310
  poetry and, 420–23
  Quintilian's view of, 91
  silence and, 278–310
  sound of, 131–36
  strength of single words and, 125–46
  textual, 216
  visual impact of, 139–43, 146
  wordplay and, 129–31
lexis, 315–44. see also language; words/word choice
licentia poetarum. see poetic license
Licentius
  Augustine and, 438–43
  Paulinus of Nola and, 439–40, 444
Licinius
  Constantine's defeat of, 70n105
  Edict of Milan and, 61
linguistic turn, 20, 279, 279n3
literary patchwork, 92–95
literary *spolia*, 8–10
Lucian, *prolaliai* in works of, 250
Lucretius
  on poetic license, 353–54
  view of language of, 91
ludicity
  in Ausonius's works, 266–67, 271
  in Optatian's works, 50–51, 50n76
  poetic license and, 346

Macrobius
  Ennius and, 355
  on intertextuality, 166–69, 170
  Vergil and, 355–56
"magic square", 47
Majorian, Sidonius Apollinaris and, 116–17, 119, 121, 124, 138–39, 141n92, 281n6, 283
Mamertinus
  Ennius and, 360
  innovation by, 341
  on poetic license, 349, 352–53
  Vergil and, 356, 359–60
Marcus Aurelius, 9, 97–98
Martial
  Ausonius and, 255, 258–59
  polymetry in works of, 100, 119
  prefaces in works of, 237
Martianus Capella
  as influence, 123
  polymetry in works of, 100
materialist aesthetics
  of Optatian, 29–53, 29n23, 30n30, 30n31, 31n26, 33n33, 33n35, 35n35
  parallels with material items and, 46–51
Maus: A Survivor's Tale (Spiegelman), 278
Maximian
  descent from Hercules of, 350
  panegyrics to, 313, 317, 319, 321–22, 322n20, 329
Menander Rhetor, on panegyrics, 314–15, 314n4, 326, 330n27
mesostics, 41, 56, 62, 144–45
metapoetics, in Claudian's works, 236–51
miniatures, 11, 28, 48
miracle narratives, 387–90
misery, silence as response to, 289–90
missorium of Theodosius, 385n38
mixing of languages, 104, 104n8
  in Optatian's works, 43, 59–68, 59n94
movement, displacement and, 228–33
Muses, 5, 5n11, 109
  Calliope and, 296–97
  in Optatian's works, 62, 74
  silence of, 280, 283–87, 309

names
  death of, 304–8, 306–7n66
  meaning of, 129–31

Narcissus narrative
  foreboding in, 187–92
  intertextuality and, 176–204
Nazarius
  Constantine and, 314, 326–30, 326n24, 332, 334, 340–41, 343–44
  innovation by, 330
negation, silence as, 284–87
negative cataloguing, 153–55, 169, 284, 287, 297–98
neologisms, 132, 315, 324, 332–33, 340–43
nostos, 228

Omeros (Walcott), 172, 174
Onians, John, 76–77
Optatian (Publilius Optatianus Porfyrius), 14, 25–99, 143, 145–146, 202–203, 344, 390n55
  Augustine and, 75, 145–146
  centones and, 83–84
  chi-rho chrismon and, 43, 51n78, 64–74, 64n99, 70n105, 72n111, 73n113, 74n115
  Christianity and, 26, 51–54, 51n78, 61
  chronology of, 29, 29n22, 73
  classification of, 28
  Constantine and, 29n22, 31n26, 32, 35n38, 35n39, 43, 50, 53n86, 58, 62, 64, 67–71, 73, 73n112, 74, 74n115, 84, 85n135, 88, 96–98
  criticism of, 25–26, 25n2, 26n6, 26n7, 26n11
  cultural transition and, 27, 51–54, 51n78
  ekphrasis and, 45, 46n64
  exile of, 29n22, 32, 32n30, 49–50
  form of works of, 29, 29n23, 30n30, 30n31, 31–53, 31n26, 33n33, 33n35, 35n35
  fragmentation and, 30, 82–99
  graphic quality of writing and, 43–45
  gridded poems of, 39–43, 54–73
  on the Incarnation, 51–52, 52n80, 72
  influences on, 83, 90–95
  innovation/experimentation and, 41, 49–51, 92–95
  interpretation of, 53–82, 57n92, 73, 73n112
  interwoven verses and, 42–43, 42n52
  Jesus Christ in works of, 43, 51, 51n78, 62, 64–65, 68–72, 74, 74n115
  literary patchwork and, 92–95
  ludicity and, 50–51, 50n76
  materialist aesthetics of, 29–53, 29n23, 30n30, 30n31, 31n26, 33n33, 33n35, 35n35, 61, 82, 84, 96
  metrical play of, 86–92
  Muses in works of, 62, 74
  Ovid as model for, 31–32
  pagan culture and, 26, 51–54, 51n78, 61
  panegyric and, 32–35, 32n30, 33n33, 51, 62
  parallels with material items of works of, 46–51
  picture-poems and, 31, 36–38, 39n48–40n38, 72–74, 95
  progymnasmata and, 45, 46n64
  reappraisal of, 26–27
  semiotics and, 54
  signs/symbols in works of, 29–30, 43, 53–82, 57n92
  spolia and, 30, 95–97
  technopaignia and, 38–41, 38n47, 49
  visual imagery and, 76–82
  word choice and, 146
oratory. *see* panegyrics
Origen, on Christian art, 52n80
Orpheus myth, poetic license in, 408–10, 419–20
Ovid
  exile of, 29n22
  intertextuality and, 152–53, 161–63
  as model for Optatian, 31–32
  Narcissus narrative and, 184, 186, 189–90, 191n61, 192–95, 199–200, 202–3
  Optatian and, 91
  prefaces in works of, 236–37

Pacatus Drepanius
  Ausonius and, 254, 269–75, 269n65, 269n67, 270n75, 270n76, 271n81, 272n89, 273n91, 274n93, 274n95, 275n97
  innovation by, 333
  on poetic license, 348, 351, 367–68
  Theodosius and, 314, 336, 336n42, 339, 341, 343–44
Paeonius, 281n6
Pagan and Christian in an Age of Anxiety (Dodds), 17
pagan culture, 4–6, 5n11–12, 5n14, 18, 18n50
  allegory and, 209

pagan culture, (cont.)
  centos and, 9, 177–82
  language and, 6–7
  Optatian and, 26, 51–54, 51n78, 61
  values of, 9
paideia, 18
palindromes, 46, 144
panegyrics, 4, 6, 313–44
  aesthetics of, 340–44
  chronology of, 313, 315–16, 340–43
  Fronto on, 347
  Menander Rhetor on, 314–15, 314n4, 326, 330n27
  Optatian and, 32–35, 32n30, 33n33, 51, 62
  poetic license in, 315–17, 332, 335, 343, 345–69
  politics and, 345, 347–48
  Publilius Syrus on, 342
  Quintilian on, 314, 327n25
  topos of, 316, 318, 322, 329–30, 332, 334, 336, 339, 341–43
Paulinus of Nola
  Augustine and, 439–40, 444
  Ausonius and, 108–9, 124, 252, 271n79, 276
  Christianity and, 109
  on Christian poetry, 382–83
  as influence, 114
  Jerome and, 212
  Jesus Christ in works of, 5n11, 109
  Licentius and, 439–40, 444
  metre and, 374–75
  poema coniugis ad uxorem and, 112
  poetic license and, 411
  as poet of Christ, 5n11
  polymetry in works of, 108–12
  on song, 382–83
  on visual imagery, 76
  word choice and, 130, 136
Phaedrus, 237
phoenix myth, 373–90
picture-poems
  of Optatian, 31, 36–38, 39n48–40n38, 72–74, 95
  of Simmias, 38, 38n47, 40, 75
Platonist criticism, 392–420
playfulness. *see* ludicity
Pliny the Elder, Ausonius and, 255, 260, 262n35

Pliny the Younger, Trajan and, 313, 342
poema coniugis ad uxorem, polymetry in, 112–13
Poetae Novelli, 103, 103n5
poetic license
  allegory and, 411
  Christian views on, 396
  ludicity and, 346
  in Orpheus myth, 408–10, 419–20
  in panegyrics, 315–17, 332, 335, 343, 345–69
politics. *see also specific rulers, e.g. Constantine*
  Ausonius and, 261, 267–68, 267n59, 268n62, 276
  panegyrics and, 345, 347–48
Porfyrius (Publilius Optatianus Porfyrius): *see* Optatian
Postmodernity and Late Antiquity, 19–20
prefaces
  autobiography in, 241–42
  history of, 236–37
  metapoetics in, 236–51
  prolaliai and, 248–50
  references to revision process in, 252–77
  uses of, 252
Proba, intertextuality and, 157–59, 163–64, 169
progymnasmata, 45, 46n64
Projecta casket, 12, 78, 80
prolaliai, prefaces and, 248–50
propaganda, irony and, 16n44
prosopopoeia, 314–15, 322, 332, 339, 340, 340n47
Prosper of Aquitaine, metre and, 374–75
Prosper of Aquitania, *poema coniugis ad uxorem* and, 112
Prudentius
  innovation by, 411
  poetic license and, 410–11
  on poetry, 382, 403–6
  polymetry in works of, 100
  prefaces in works of, 238
psalms, 383–84
pseudepigrapha, distrust of, 4
Pseudo-Dionysius the Areopagite, apophatic theology of, 20, 279
Publilius Optatianus Porfyrius. *see* Optatian
Publilius Syrus, on panegyrics, 342

Quintilian
    on panegyrics, 314, 327n25
    on poetic license, 349n23
    view of language of, 91
    word choice and, 128

"Rabbit and Duck" (Wittgenstein), 53–54
reading
    aesthetics of reader and, 267
    allegory and, 210, 221, 226
reflection, 216–18
repetition, 229–31
revision process, 252–77
"The Rhetoric of Temporality" (de Man), 209
Riegl, Alois, 17, 19, 19n51, 28
ritual. *see* ceremony
Rutilius Namatianus
    allegory and, 227–34
    on the death of names, 304–8, 306–7n66
    displacement and, 227–34
    repetition in works of, 229–31
    silence and, 304–8, 306–7n66

sarcophagus with biblical imagery, 80, 82
"Sator" palindrome, 46
scholarship
    on Christian poetry, 399–400
    classical, 3–5
    on Claudian, 236–37
    fragmentation and, 207–8
    on genre, 210–11
    intertextuality and, 207–8
    on Lactantius, 373–74
sculptural *spolia*, 8–10, 14
Sedulius
    on Christian poetry, 383
    miracle narratives and, 389
self-awareness
    of Ausonius, 262–63, 262n40
    of Sidonius Apollinaris, 283
semiotics, 7, 20. *see also* signs/symbols
    Optatian and, 54
Sergius, word choice and, 143–45
Servius
    on graphic quality of writing, 44
    on intertextuality, 164–66
    Vergil and, 356
Sidonius Apollinaris

cataloguing by, 19
Catullus and, 281–82, 281n6, 281n7, 285n14
intertextuality and, 153–55, 163–65, 169–73, 175
irony and, 16
Majorian and, 116–17, 119, 121, 124, 138–39, 141n92 281n6, 283
on poetry, 398
polymetry in works of, 116–19
self-awareness of, 283
silence and, 279–89, 284n11, 285n14, 296–98, 300–301, 308
word choice and, 134, 137–39, 141–42
signs/symbols. *see also* semiotics; visual imagery
    allegory and, 74
    chi-rho chrismon, 43, 51n78, 64–74, 64n99, 70n105, 72n111, 73n113, 74n115
    interpretation of, 53–82, 57n92, 73, 73n112
    in Optatian's works, 29–30, 43, 53–82, 57n92, 73, 73n112
silence
    birthplace of words, 293–95
    death of names and, 304–8, 306–7n66
    of Jesus Christ, 288–89, 289n22, 303n51
    of the Muses, 280, 283–87, 309
    as negation, 284–87
    poetics of, 278–310
    as response to the inexpressibility of real knowledge, 290–92
    as response to misery, 289–90
    as result of criticism, 292–93
    as a way to reveal and overcome the limitations of language, 295–304
simile, in panegyrics, 315, 318, 321, 325–26, 329, 332, 334, 340
Simmias, picture-poems of, 38, 38n47, 40, 75
Simonides, on graphic quality of writing, 44–45, 45n59
Six Months in the West Indies (Coleridge), 170–72
song, 383–84
sound
    of language, 131–36
    silence and, 278–310
spaces, reconfiguration of, 212–13, 216–18, 223, 233–34

spolia, 8–10, 14
   centos and, 178–81, 188, 195, 200, 203
   Optatian and, 30, 95–97
Statius
   prefaces in works of, 237
statues. *see* sculptural *spolia*
Stilicho, Claudian and, 238, 245–47
Stoics, word choice and, 133, 135
syllepsis, 211–12
symbols. *see* semiotics; signs/symbols
Symmachorum ivory panel, 11, 13
Symmachus
   Ausonius and, 264n48, 276
   innovation by, 333, 341
   on poetic license, 349
   Valentinian I and, 314, 316, 333
   word choice and, 126, 139–40
synchronicity, 214–15
S/Z (Barthes), 211, 299–300

tabulae Iliacae, 44n57, 47, 74–75, 203
tabulae lusoriae (gaming tablets), 92, 92n157
technopaignia, Optatian and, 49
telestics, 41, 56, 87, 144–45
textual language, 216
Theodosius
   Ausonius and, 254–57, 254n11, 254n13, 255n19, 256n24, 259–63, 260n34, 261n36, 261n37, 262n39
   Pacatus Drepanius and, 314, 336, 336n42, 339, 341, 343–44
   topos/topoi, of panegyrics, 316, 318, 322, 329–30, 332, 334, 336, 339, 341–43
Trajan
   Dacian campaign of, 9–10, 97–98
   Pliny the Younger and, 313, 342

uersus intexti (interwoven verses), Optatian and, 29n21, 33n35, 35n35, 42–43, 42n52, 50, 59, 66, 69, 70n103, 71, 73n113
"Up Country" (Clifford), 170–72

Valentinian I, Symmachus and, 314, 316, 333
the Vandals, 164
   Fulgentius and, 288
   Narcissus narrative and, 176, 181, 181n26, 184–85, 195–97, 202

Venantius Fortunatus
   ekphrasis and, 379
   intertextuality and, 173–75
   on song, 383
Vergil
   Ausonius and, 8, 260, 260n34
   authority of, 346, 354–60
   Claudian and, 363, 365
   Fulgentius and, 288, 291
   Homer and, 200
   Macrobius and, 355–56
   Mamertinus and, 356, 359–60
   Narcissus narrative and, 176–80, 182, 184–203
   Servius and, 356
Veroli casket, 12, 14
Via Latina catacombs, 77–78, 80–81
vice, 416–20
virtue, 416–20
visual imagery, 76–82. *see also ekphrasis*; signs/symbols
visual impact, of word choice, 139–43, 146
vocabulary. *see* language; lexis; words/word choice

The Waste Land (Eliot), 309
Western cultural tradition, 1–2, 1n2, 2n4
Wittgenstein, Ludwig, 53–54, 287, 291
wordplay, 129–31. *see also* words/word choice
words/word choice, 125–46. *see also* language; lexis; wordplay
   cataloguing and, 136–41, 140n89
   etymology and, 127–28, 127n19, 131, 132n56, 133, 135, 143n100
   fragmentation and, 143–46
   as gateway to silence, 295–304
   juxtaposition of words and, 211
   names, meaning of and, 129–31
   neologisms and, 132, 315, 324, 332–33, 340–43
   silence as birthplace of, 293–95
   sound of language and, 131–36
   visual impact of, 139–43, 146
   wordplay and, 129–31

Lightning Source UK Ltd.
Milton Keynes UK
UKHW020004220722
406220UK00003B/24